FROMMER'S

COMPREHENSIVE TRAVEL GUIDE

SCOTLAND '94-'95

by Darwin Porter
Assisted by Danforth Prince

SO-AUL-651

PRENTICE HALL TRAVEL

NEW YORK • LONDON • TORONTO • SYDNEY • TOKYO • SINGAPORE

FROMMER BOOKS

Published by Prentice Hall General Reference
15 Columbus Circle
New York, NY 10023

ISBN 0-671-86799-7
ISSN 1055-5390

Design by Robert Bull Design
Maps by Geografix Inc.

FROMMER'S EDITORIAL STAFF

Editorial Director: Marilyn Wood
Editorial Manager/Senior Editor: Alice Fellows
Senior Editors: Lisa Renaud, Sara Hinsey Raveret
Editors: Charlotte Allstrom, Thomas F. Hirsch, Peter Katucki, Theodore Stavrou
Assistant Editors: Margaret Bowen, Christopher Hollander, Alice Thompson, Ian Wilker
Editorial Assistants: Gretchen Henderson, Douglas Stallings
Managing Editor: Leanne Coupe
Production Supervisor: Dabney Smith

Special Sales

Bulk purchases (10 + copies) of Frommer's Travel Guides are available to corporations at special discounts. The Special Sales Department can produce custom editions to be used as premiums and/or for sales promotion to suit individual needs. Existing editions can be produced with custom cover imprints such as a corporate logo. For more information write to: Special Sales, Prentice Hall Travel, 15 Columbus Circle, New York, NY 10023.

Manufactured in the United States of America

CONTENTS

1 GETTING TO KNOW SCOTLAND 1

1. Geography, History, Politics & People 1
2. Famous Scots 13
3. Art, Architecture, Literature & Music 14
4. Cultural & Social Life 17
5. Sports & Recreation 19
6. Food & Drink 21
7. Recommended Books & Recordings 23

SPECIAL FEATURES
- Did You Know . . . ? 4
- Dateline 5

2 PLANNING A TRIP TO SCOTLAND 27

1. Information, Entry Requirements & Money 27
2. When to Go—Climate, Holidays & Events 31
3. Health, Insurance & Packing 35
4. Tips for the Disabled, Seniors, Singles, Families & Students 36
5. Alternative/Adventure Travel 39
6. Getting There 42
7. Getting Around 50

SPECIAL FEATURES
- What Things Cost in Edinburgh 30
- What Things Cost in Inverness 30
- Scotland Calendar of Events 32
- Edinburgh Calendar of Events 34
- Frommer's Smart Traveler: Airfares 45
- Suggested Itineraries 54
- Fast Facts: Scotland 56

3 THE BORDERS & THE SOUTHWEST 61

1. Jedburgh 63
2. Kelso 64
3. Melrose 68
4. Selkirk 69
5. Innerleithen 70
6. Peebles 71
7. Moffat 73
8. Dumfries 75
9. Castle Douglas 80
10. Kirkcudbright 82
11. Gatehouse-of-Fleet 83
12. Whithorn 85
13. Stranraer 86
14. Portpatrick 87

SPECIAL FEATURE
- What's Special About the Borders & the Southwest 62

4 EDINBURGH 90

1. Orientation 90
2. Getting Around 93
3. Accommodations 97
4. Dining 109
5. Attractions 121
6. Special & Free Events 133
7. Sports & Recreation 134
8. Savvy Shopping 135
9. Evening Entertainment 138
10. Easy Excursions from Edinburgh 142

SPECIAL FEATURES

- *What's Special About Edinburgh 91*
- *Neighborhoods in Brief 92*
- *Fast Facts: Edinburgh 95*
- *Frommer's Smart Traveler: Hotels 99*
- *Frommer's Cool for Kids: Hotels 105*
- *Frommer's Smart Traveler: Restaurants 111*
- *Frommer's Cool for Kids: Restaurants 119*
- *Did You Know . . . ? 124*
- *Frommer's Favorite Edinburgh Experiences 126*
- *Walking Tour: Historic Edinburgh 130*

5 GLASGOW 149

1. Orientation 151
2. Getting Around 154
3. Accommodations 158
4. Dining 167
5. Attractions 176
6. Special & Free Events 186
7. Sports & Recreation 186
8. Savvy Shopping 187
9. Evening Entertainment 188
10. Easy Excursions from Glasgow 192

SPECIAL FEATURES

- *What's Special About Glasgow 150*
- *Neighborhoods in Brief 153*
- *Fast Facts: Glasgow 155*
- *Frommer's Cool for Kids: Hotels 164*
- *Frommer's Smart Traveler: Restaurants 169*
- *Frommer's Cool for Kids: Restaurants 173*
- *Did You Know . . . ? 178*
- *Frommer's Favorite Glasgow Experiences 182*
- *Walking Tour: Historic Glasgow 183*

6 ARGYLL & THE ISLES 201

1. Oban 204
2. Dalmally & Loch Awe 209
3. Inveraray 211
4. The Kintyre Peninsula 214
5. The Isle of Arran 217
6. The Isle of Gigha 221
7. The Isle of Islay 222
8. The Isle of Jura 224

SPECIAL FEATURE

- *What's Special About Argyll & the Isles 202*

7 FIFE & THE CENTRAL HIGHLANDS 225

1. Dunfermline 227
2. Falkland 230
3. The East Neuk 231
4. St. Andrews 235
5. Stirling 240
6. Dunblane 244
7. Doune 245
8. Callander 246
9. Aberfoyle 249
10. Along Loch Lomond 251

SPECIAL FEATURE
● *What's Special About Fife & the Central Highlands 226*

8 TAYSIDE & GRAMPIAN 255

1. Perth 257
2. Crieff 263
3. Comrie 265
4. Aberfeldy 265
5. Dunkeld 266
6. Pitlochry 268
7. Dundee 271
8. Braemar 274
9. Ballater 276
10. Banchory 278
11. Aberdeen 280
12. West Grampian 289

SPECIAL FEATURE
● *What's Special About Tayside & Grampian 256*

9 THE WEST HIGHLANDS 296

1. Around Loch Linnhe & Loch Leven 299
2. Fort William 301
3. Mallaig 305
4. Invergarry 306
5. Aviemore 306
6. Speyside 309
7. Along Loch Ness 313
8. Inverness 316
9. Nairn 323
10. The Black Isle 325
11. Sutherland 329
12. Caithness 332

SPECIAL FEATURE
● *What's Special About the West Highlands 297*

10 THE HEBRIDEAN ISLANDS 336

1. Dornie 337
2. The Kyle of Lochalsh 338
3. The Isle of Skye 341

SPECIAL FEATURE
● *What's Special About the Hebridean Islands 337*

4. Rhum (Also Rum)   346
5. Eigg & Muck   347
6. Coll & Tyree   348
7. Mull   350
8. Iona & Staffa   357
9. The Isle of Colonsay   360
10. Lewis   361
11. Harris   365
12. North & South Uist   367
13. Barra   372

11   THE ORKNEY & SHETLAND ISLANDS   376

1. The Orkney Islands   377
2. Fair Isle   394
3. The Shetland Islands   395

SPECIAL FEATURE
- *What's Special About the Orkney & Shetland Islands 377*

APPENDIX   409

A. Glossary   409
B. Measures & Conversions   410
C. Mileage Chart   411

INDEX   412

LIST OF MAPS

SCOTLAND 2-3

EDINBURGH
Edinburgh
   Accommodations   100-101
Edinburgh Dining   112-113
Edinburgh
   Attractions   122-123
Walking Tour:
   Edinburgh   131

GLASGOW
Glasgow
   Accommodations   160-161
Glasgow Dining   170-171
Glasgow Attractions   180-181
Walking Tour: Historic
   Glasgow   185

REGIONAL & CITY MAPS
The Borders   65
Dumfries & Galloway   77
The Argyll Peninsula   203
The Kingdom of Fife   229
Stirling, Loch Lomond & the
   Trossachs   243
Dundee & Tayside   259
Aberdeen   283
West Grampian &
   Speyside   293
The Far North   327
The Hebridean Islands   339
Orkney & Shetland Islands   379

AN INVITATION TO READERS

In researching this book, we have come across many remarkable establishments, the best of which we have included here. We are sure that many of you will also come across appealing hotels, inns, restaurants, guest houses, shops, and attractions. Please don't keep them to yourself. Share your experiences, especially if you want to comment on places that have been included in this edition that have changed for the worse. You can address your letters to:

Darwin Porter
Frommer's Scotland '94–'95
Prentice Hall Travel
15 Columbus Circle
New York, NY 10023

A DISCLAIMER

Readers are advised that prices fluctuate in the course of time, and travel information changes under the impact of the varied and volatile factors that affect the travel industry. Neither the author nor the publisher can be held responsible for the experiences of readers while traveling. Readers are invited to write to the publisher with ideas, comments, and suggestions for future editions.

SAFETY ADVISORY

Whenever you're traveling in an unfamiliar city or country, stay alert. Be aware of your immediate surroundings. Wear a moneybelt and keep a close eye on your possessions. Be particularly careful with cameras, purses, and wallets—all of which are favorite targets of thieves and pickpockets.

CHAPTER 1

GETTING TO KNOW SCOTLAND

1. GEOGRAPHY, HISTORY, POLITICS & PEOPLE
- **DID YOU KNOW?**
- **DATELINE**
2. FAMOUS SCOTS
3. ART, ARCHITECTURE, LITERATURE & MUSIC
4. CULTURAL & SOCIAL LIFE
5. SPORTS & RECREATION
6. FOOD & DRINK
7. RECOMMENDED BOOKS & RECORDINGS

A small nation ("'Tis a wee country, aye—but a bonny one"), Scotland is only 275 miles long and some 150 miles wide at its broadest point. No one lives more than 40 miles from salt water. But despite its small size, Scotland has extended its influence around the world. And in this land of bagpipes and clans, you'll find some of the grandest scenery in Europe.

Alexander Graham Bell, the inventor, and explorers Mungo Park and David Livingstone came from Scotland. Scotland gave the world such entrepreneurs as Andrew Carnegie, the poet Robert Burns, and the novelist Sir Walter Scott. But, curiously, for a long time its most famous resident has been neither man nor woman—it's the Loch Ness monster!

The border is just a line on a map; you will hardly be aware of crossing out of England into Scotland. But, even though the two countries have been joined constitutionally since 1707, Scotland is very different from England, and is very much its own country. You'll discover lochs and glens, heather-covered moors, twirling kilts and tam o'shanters, pastel-bathed houses and gray stone cottages, mountains, rivers, and streams filled with trout and salmon. Eagles soar and deer run free. Lush meadowlands are filled with sheep, and rocky coves and secret harbors wait to be discovered. You can hear the sound of Gaelic, see a Shetland pony, admire the misty blue hills, and attend a Highland gathering. You'll find quiet contemplation or you can enjoy an activity-filled calendar.

You'll also find one of the biggest welcomes in Europe. But remember one thing. Scotch is a whisky and not the name of the proud people who inhabit the country. They are called Scots, and the adjective is Scottish. Even if you forget and call them Scotch, they'll forgive you. What they won't forgive is calling them English.

1. GEOGRAPHY, HISTORY, POLITICS & PEOPLE

GEOGRAPHY

Scotland is the oldest geological formation of Great Britain, divided physically into three regions: the central Lowlands, where three valleys and the estuaries (firths) of the Clyde, Forth, and Tay rivers make up a fertile belt from the Atlantic Ocean to the North Sea; the southern Uplands, smooth, rolling moorland broken with low crags and threaded with rivers and valleys between the central plain and the English border;

6325
N
John o'Groats
Wick
Thurso
Tongue
A882
A895
Helmsdale
HIGHLAND
A9
Lairg
Ullapool
North West Highlands
A835
Outer Hebrides
Lewis
North Minch
Harris
North Uist
Benbecula
South Uist
Barra
Sea of The Hebrides
Rhum
Eigg
Muck
Coll
Inner Hebrides
Portree
Raasay
Skye
Kyle of Lochalsh
A87
Dornie
A835
Invermoriston
A887
A82
Invergarry
Mallaig
Spean Bridge
A82
A830
Fort William
Onich
Ballachulish
Grampian Mts.
Moray Firth
Strathpeffer
Black Isle
Muir of Ord
Beauly
Inverness
A96
Loch Ness
Monadhliath Mts.
Fort Augustus
Findhern
Forres
Nairn
Lossiemouth
Elgin
Rothes
Dufftown
Grantown-on-Spey
Carrbridge
Aviemore
Kingussie
Newtonmore
A9
Blair Atholl
Pitlochry
A96
A98
Fraserburgh
A952
A92
GRAMPIAN
Aberdeen
A92
Banchory
Ballater
Braemar
Stonehaven
A93
Kirriemuir
Glamis Castle
Montrose

SCOTLAND

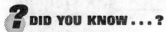

and the granite Highlands, including lochs, glens, and mountains plus the hundreds of islands to the west and north.

Regions in Brief

Edinburgh and the Lothian Region include not only Edinburgh, but West Lothian, most of Midlothian, and East Lothian. The capital of Scotland, Edinburgh, is half medieval and half Georgian. It's at its liveliest at the International Arts Festival every August, but you can visit its castle and walk its "Royal Mile" year-round. Edinburgh is surrounded by some major attractions including the village of Cramond and the ancient town of Linlithgow.

Fife Region East Neuk and St. Andrews (the golf capital of Scotland) are the major attractions here, but this entire region of Eastern Scotland has much to lure you, including Falkland Palace, Culross, Dunfermline Abbey, and the Firth of Forth.

The Borders Witness to a turbulent history, the border between England and Scotland is rich in castle ruins and gothic abbeys. Home of the cashmere sweater and the tweed suit, the Borders proved a rich mine for the fiction of Sir Walter Scott.

Aberdeen and the Grampian Region The old granite-built city of Aberdeen at the mouth of the River Dee is the major center of this history-rich part of northeastern Scotland. Visitors flock here to see Royal Deeside, former retreat of Queen Victoria, and to follow the Whisky Trail.

Glasgow and the Strathclyde Region A renaissance has come to the once grimy and industrial city of Glasgow. The Glasgow Renaissance is real and not just fodder for tourist brochures. The city's Burrell Collection is a major Scottish attraction, and once the visitor has explored Scotland's largest city, other sights in the environs are Loch Lomond and the "Burns Country" around Ayr.

Tayside Carved from the old counties of Perth and Angus, Tayside takes its name from its major river, the Tay, running for 119 miles. One of the loveliest regions of Scotland, it is known for salmon and trout fishing. Major centers include Pitlochry and Dundee. Glamis Castle is one of its ancient monuments.

The Trossachs This is a collective name given to a wild Highland area lying east and northeast of Loch Lomond. Some of the finest scenery in Scotland is found here—loch, mountain, and moor. Read Sir Walter Scott's *Lady of the Lake* or *Rob Roy* for descriptive passages.

Dumfries and Galloway This part of southwestern Scotland is often called the "Lowlands." It incorporates much of the former stamping ground of Robert Burns, and includes such centers as Castle Douglas, Moffat, and Dumfries.

The Argyll Peninsula Once an independent kingdom called Dalriada, this area of western Scotland is centered at Oban. Its major attraction is the Argyll Forest Park, covering some 60,000 acres and offering what is considered the most magnificent scenery in the country.

Arran, Kintyre, and Islay The western coastline of Scotland—one of the most panoramic in Europe—includes the Isle of Arran at the mouth of the Firth of Clyde. This is often called Scotland in miniature, because it takes in such a sweep of scenery, including lochs, glens, moors, and rocky coasts. Kintyre, longest peninsula in

Scotland, stretches for some 60 miles, and the Isle of Islay is the southernmost island of the Inner Hebrides, lying 16 miles west of the Kintyre Peninsula.

Inverness and the Highlands   The capital of the Highlands is Inverness, a royal burgh and seaport, lying on both sides of the Ness River. It is the best base for touring the Highlands, a region of natural grandeur and mystical charm, and is the site of the annual Highland Games.

The Hebridean Islands   The chain of the Inner Hebridean Islands lies just off the west coast of the mainland. The major center here is the Isle of Skye, a mystical island and subject of the Scottish ballad "Over the Sea to Skye." Other islands carry such humorous names as Eigg and Muck. The Outer Hebrides embraces such islands as Lewis (the most northerly), Harris (known for its tweed), North Uist, Benbecula, and South Uist among others.

The Orkney and Shetland Islands   These northern outposts of British civilization are archipelagos consisting of some 200 islands, about 40 of which are inhabited. Rich in Viking heritage, they are far-flung outposts that reward visitors with their scenery and antiquities.

HISTORY

EARLY HISTORY   After the last Ice Age, as long ago as 6000 B.C., the first human beings may have moved into the area of western Scotland known as the Argyll Peninsula. They were followed by Mesolithic people from Ireland, and then by Neolithic Bronze Age and Iron Age tribes originating either in Germany, Iberia, or the coastal areas of the Mediterranean (no one knows for sure). Standing stones, brochs, cromlechs, cairns, and burial chambers attest to this early occupation. Later, a powerful wave of Celtic invaders came from the continent of Europe to the western islands around 3,000 years before the Christian era.

In A.D. 82, working from well-established bases in what is now England, the Roman armies of Agricola pushed into Scotland's southern Uplands and central Lowlands, where marching stations and some permanent encampments were set up. One of the battles waged by Agricola in A.D. 84 (at Mons Graupius) was—considering the number of partici-pants—probably the largest land battle ever waged on British soil. Despite their spectacular bloodletting, the Romans were unsuccessful in subduing what they called Picts, who would storm guerilla-style from forests and glens, dressed in animal skins and, it is reported, painted blue with the juice from the woad plant. The building of Hadrian's Wall effectively marked the northern limits of Roman influence.

By the year A.D. 500 these short dark Picts had been again attacked by the Dalriad Irish, called Scots. These fair-skinned, red- or sandy-haired Celtic newcomers named the land they came to (specifically the Argyll Peninsula of modern Scotland's western shore) Scotia, after their section of Ireland. The newcomers battled with and intermarried with the native Scotians, creating new bloodlines and migratory patterns throughout the country. Druidism, a little-understood mystical form of nature worship whose most visible monuments are runic etchings and prayer circles, flourished. Simultaneously, Britons emigrated from the south, and Norsemen interjected their bloodlines from

DATELINE

- **6000 B.C.** Earliest known res-idents of Scotland establish settle-ments on the Argyll Peninsula.
- **3000 B.C.** Celtic tribes invade, making the use of Gaelic widespread.
- **A.D. 82** Roman armies directed by Agricola push into southern Scotland. Roman victories, however, are short-lived.
- **A.D. 90** Romans abandon hope of conquering Scot-land, retreating to England and the relative safety of Hadrian's Wall.
- **500** Newcomers from Ireland, identi-fied as Scots, in-vade from the west, mingling bloodlines with Norse, Pictish, Celtic, and Teutonic tribes.
- **563** Columba es-tablishes a mission on Iona, accelerat-ing the movement *(continues)*

already established by earlier ecclesiastics to Christianize Scotland.

• **843** Kenneth McAlpin unifies the Picts and the Scots.

• **1005–1034** Malcolm II unites the four major tribes of Scotland into one roughly cohesive unit.

• **1124–1153** David I builds monasteries, consolidates royal power and prestige, and imports clearly defined Norman values.

• **1266** The Hebrides and the coastline of Western Scotland are released from Norse control. The Donald clan consolidates power there into a semiautonomous state within Scotland.

• **1272** Edward I of England embarks on an aggressive campaign to conquer both Wales and Scotland. He is deflected by Robert the Bruce, among others.

• **1314** Victory of Scots over the English armies at Bannockburn leads to the treaty of Arbroath (1320), formally recognizing Scotland's independence from England.

• **1468** The Orkney and Shetland Islands are given to

(continues)

the east, further enriching the genetic melting pot of ancient Scotland. The languages of the era probably included a diverse array of Celtic and Norse dialects with scatterings of low German and Saxon English.

The power of the Scotians, entrenched in western Scotland, was firmly cemented when a missionary named Columba (later canonized) emigrated from Ireland to the Western Islands of Scotland in 563. The rocky Hebridean island of Iona became the base of St. Columba's Christian mission, and he and his followers eventually made widespread Christianity, already introduced to other regions of Scotland by St. Ninian and St. Mungo in Strathclyde and Galloway.

THE MIDDLE AGES By the 9th century the Roman designation *Caledonia* became unpopular, and the name *Scotland* became universally preferred for the foggy and roughshod northern territory. Scots and Picts were united in 843 under the kingship of an early chieftain named Kenneth MacAlpin, but it was the invasionary pressures from England and Scandinavia and the unifying force of Christianity that molded Scotland into a relatively coherent unit. Under the rulership of Malcolm II (1005–1034), the earlier entity created by the union between the Scots and the Picts merged with the British and Angles, who occupied the southwest and southeast of the Scottish mainland. Malcolm's son and heir, Duncan, was eventually killed by Macbeth of Moray, a historic event that fueled the plotlines of one of Shakespeare's most famous plays.

By the 1100s, King David I embarked on one of the most lavish building sprees in Scottish history, erecting many abbeys, including Jedburgh, Kelso, Melrose, and Dryburgh. This extravagance, while providing for modern visitors many photogenic medieval monuments, almost bankrupted his treasury. He imposed relatively sophisticated Norman values onto members of his unpolished court, and at his encouragement, the families of the Norman warriors he had known during his youth immigrated to Scotland, bringing the bloodlines of such ancient names as Fraser, Lamont, Seton, and Lindsay.

During this period, when Europe's feudal system was in full flower, Scotland was almost entirely preoccupied with the territorial battles of clan allegiances and efforts to define its borders with England. A series of politically motivated marriages with English and Norman princesses and the importation into Scotland of English bishops encouraged ever greater cultural assimilation with its southern neighbor.

In 1266, after about a century of Norse control, the foggy and windswept Western Isles and estuaries were returned to Scotland following the Battle of Largs. Despite nominal allegiance to the Scottish monarchs, the inhabitants of this region quickly organized themselves around the Donald (or MacDonald) clan, which for about 100 years became one of the most powerful in Britain. Today, the honorary title of their patriarch, "Lord of the Isles," is still one of the formal titles employed on state occasions by Britain's Prince of Wales.

Late in the 13th century, the ambitious Plantagenet king

of England, Edward I (also known as "Longshanks" and "The Hammer of the Scots"), yearned to rule over an undivided island nation incorporating England, Scotland, and Wales. Many of the heroes of Scottish ballads lived during this period, tenaciously opposing the territorial expansionism of Edward. Their names included Robert the Bruce (Robert I, 1274–1329), who was crowned king of Scotland at Scone in 1306; Sir William Wallace (1270–1305), who drove the English out of Perth and Sterling; and Sir James Douglas ("The Black Douglas," 1286–1330), one of the most successful (and notorious) of the Scots warriors who terrorized the residents of the English borders.

The Victory of Bannockburn in 1314, when the Scots demolished the English armies, was followed by the Declaration of Arbroath and the Treaty of Northampton (1320), which acknowledged Scotland's heady but short-lived independence from England. Despite these political and military conflicts, Scotland continued to evolve culturally as it assimilated linguistic, artistic, religious, and commercial influences from its English neighbor.

In 1468 the Orkneys and Shetlands, Norse to the core, were brought into the Scottish web of power as part of the marriage dowry of the Danish princess, Margaret of Denmark, to the Scottish king James III. This acquisition represents the last successful expansion of Scottish sovereignty, during the period when Scottish power and independence were probably at their zenith.

It was during these years of bitter battles and turmoil that the Scots entered into an alliance with the French, which was to have far-reaching effects. The line of Stuart (or Stewart) kings, so named because the family had become powerful as stewards of the English king, were usually accepted as the lesser of a series of potential evils. Real power, however, lay not with the Stuart kings, but was divided among Scotland's great lords, patriarchs of tribes that eventually evolved into the country's famous clans. Jealous of both their bloodlines and their territories, they could rarely agree on anything other than their common distrust of England. Struggles for power and influence were protracted, bitter, and intensely complicated as religious passions added new dimensions to the era's politics.

THE REFORMATION The passions of the Reformation burst upon the already turbulent Scottish scene of rampant baronial ambition, weak kings, increasingly complicated and dangerous foreign alliances, and the growing resentment against an enormously wealthy Catholic Church.

John Knox was the most articulate and convincing of the several religious leaders who hoped to impose their will upon the Scottish soul. While many of the era's controversies centered on religious doctrines, there was also focus on practical considerations: church administration, funding, and the relationship between church and state. A devoted disciple of the Geneva Protestant John Calvin, and a bitter enemy of both the Catholic and Anglican churches, Knox became famous for the screaming insults he heaped upon ardently Catholic Queen Mary and for his complete and absolute lack of humor. His was a peculiar mixture of piety, conservatism, strict morality, and intellectual inde-

DATELINE

Scotland as part of the marriage dowry of a Danish princess to a Scottish king.

Braveheart

- **late 1400s** The "Auld Alliance" with France, a cynical arrangement based mostly on both countries' mutual distrust of England, is born.
- **1535** At the urging of Henry VIII of England, Parliament officially severs all ties with the Catholic Church, legally sanctioning the Reformation.
- **1561** Queen Mary returns to Scotland from France.
- **1559–1564** John Knox lays out the rough outline of the Scottish Presbyterian Church.
- **1568** Mary is defeated and flees to England.
- **1572** Death of John Knox. His work is continued by Andrew Melville.
- **1587** Execution of Mary, Queen of Scots.
- **1603** Accession to the throne of England of Mary's son, as James I unifies the two countries.
- **1689** Parliament strips the uncompromising Catholic King James II of his title and imports the Protestant William and Mary from Holland to replace him.

(continues)

DATELINE

- **1746** The Battle of Culloden destroys forever any hope of a Stuart revival, and forces the dynasty's Catholic heir, Bonnie Prince Charles, into exile in Paris and Rome.
- **1750–1850** Rapid industrialization of England and Scotland. The Clearances strip many crofters of their farms, creating epic bitterness and forcing new patterns of Scottish migrations.
- **1789** The French Revolution. British monarchists tighten their grip on civil unrest in Scotland.
- **late 19th century** An astonishing success in the sciences propels Scotland into one of the most culturally potent nations on earth, dispersing knowledge and industrial knowhow around the globe.
- **mid-20th century** Decline of traditional industries, especially shipbuilding, painfully redefines the nature of Scottish industry.
- **1970** Discovery of North Sea oil deposits brings new vitality to Scotland.
- **1973** Scotland, as part of Britain, becomes a member of the Common Market.

(continues)

pendence that is still a pronounced feature of the Scottish character.

All of this fitted in neatly with Henry VIII's earlier break (in 1534) with the Catholic Church. Knox quickly filled in Scotland's religious breach by composing a complete code of worship based on rigidly uncompromising Calvinist models. Foremost among the tenets were provisions for a self-governing congregation and pure allegiance to the Word of God as contained within meticulous translations of the Old and New Testaments.

Upon Knox's death (in 1562), his work was continued by the Scots-born, Geneva-trained Andrew Melville, who hated ecclesiastical tyranny even more (if that were possible) than Knox himself. Melville reorganized the Scottish universities and introduced an emphasis on classical studies and the study of the Bible in its original Hebrew and Greek. Under his leadership emerged a clearly defined Scottish Presbyterian Church whose elected leaders were responsible for practical as well as spiritual matters. Cautiously approved by the rulers in London—who probably preferred any form of Protestantism to the Catholicism they were trying hard to eradicate—the organization was ultimately adopted as the Church of Scotland.

Later, the Church of Scotland's almost obsessional insistence on self-government led to endless conflicts with first the Scottish and (after unification) with both the British monarchs and the hierarchies of the Anglican Church.

MARY, QUEEN OF SCOTS, AND JAMES STUART When Mary Stuart ("Queen of Scots") took the throne, she was a Roman Catholic of French upbringing trying to govern an unruly land to which she was a virtual newcomer. After a series of disastrous political and romantic alliances, and endless abortive episodes of often indiscreet intrigue, her life was ended in 1587 in England by the headsman's axe. The order for her execution was issued, reluctantly, by her cousin, Queen Elizabeth I, who considered Mary's presence an incitement both to civil unrest and to the stability of the English throne.

The power of the great lords of Scotland was broken in 1603, when Mary's son, James VI of Scotland, assumed the throne of England as James I, Elizabeth's heir. James succeeded where his doomed mother had failed. First of the Stuarts to occupy the English throne, his coronation effectively united England and Scotland.

Despite the hopes for peace which accompanied the union, religion almost immediately became a prime source of discontent. From their base in England the two Stuart kings attempted during their reigns to promote a church governed by bishops, in opposition to the organization of the Presbyterian Church. So incensed were the Scots that in 1638 they signed the National Covenant, which not only reasserted the principles of the Reformation but questioned the king's right to make laws, a role the "Covenanters" believed should be filled by Parliament. However, the monarch was given a role in their scheme of things, and Scotland's subsequent support of Charles I and his son led to Cromwell's invasion of Scotland, in 1650, when he defeated the Scots decisively at Dunbar. Religious friction continued, however, after the restoration of Charles II to the English throne.

THE JACOBITES In 1689 when Parliament stripped the Catholic king, James II, of his title and imported the Protestant monarchs William and Mary from Holland, the exiled ex-king and then his son James Edward (the Old Pretender) became focal points for Scottish unrest. The Jacobites (the name comes from Jacobus, the Latin form of James) attempted in 1715 to place the Old Pretender on the English throne and restore the Stuart line to power. Though James died in exile, his son Charles Edward (the Young Pretender), better known as "Bonnie Prince Charlie," carried on his father's dream. Known for his charisma, his charm, and with an alcohol-induced instability, he was the central figure of the Jacobite Uprising of 1745.

Though initially promising because of the many Scottish adherents who transcended religious lines to rally to the cause, the rising was completely crushed at the Battle of Culloden, near Inverness, by a numerically superior English army led by the Duke of Cumberland. Many supporters of the Pretender's cause were killed in battle, some were executed, and others fled to the United States and other safe havens. Fearing a rebirth of similar types of Scottish nationalism, the wearing of Highland dress was made illegal until 1782.

The Young Pretender himself was smuggled unglamorously out of Scotland, assisted by a resident of the obscure Hebridean island of South Uist, Flora MacDonald. One of the most visible Scottish heroines of her era, she has ever since provided fodder for the Scottish sense of romance. The Bonnie Prince dissipated himself in Paris and Rome, and the hopes of an independent Scotland were buried forever.

DATELINE

- **1974** Old counties or shires reorganized; many regions are renamed.
- **1979** Scots vote on "devolution" (separation from England): 33% vote yes, 31% vote no, and 36% don't vote at all.
- **1981** Largest oil terminal in Europe launched at Sullom Voe, Shetland Islands.
- **1988** Nationalism revives in Scotland under marching cry of "Scotland in Europe."
- **1992** Scots continue to express dissatisfaction with English rule: polls show one out of two favor independence.

ECONOMIC GROWTH AND THE INDUSTRIAL REVOLUTION During the 18th century, the Scottish economy underwent a radical transformation of growth and diversification. The British government, fearing increased civil unrest, commissioned one of its most capable generals to build a series of roads and bridges throughout the country, presumably to increase military access from London in the event of a revolt.

As trade with British overseas colonies, England, and Europe increased, the great ports of Aberdeen, Glasgow, and Leith (near Edinburgh) flourished. The merchants of Glasgow grew rich on a nearly monopolistic tobacco trade with Virginia and the Carolinas until the outbreak of the American Revolution sent American tobacco elsewhere. Other forms of commerce, however, continued to enrich a battalion of shrewd Scots.

The outbreak of the French Revolution in 1789 engendered so much sympathy in Scotland for the revolutionary cause that a panicked government in London became more autocratic than ever in its attempts to suppress Scottish antimonarchical feelings.

The infamous Clearances (1750–1850) changed forever the demographics of Scotland. Small farmers (crofters) were expelled from their ancestral lands to make way for sheep grazing. Increased industrialization, continued civil unrest, migration into urban centers, and a massive wave of emigration out of Scotland into the United States, Canada, Australia, South Africa, and New Zealand all contributed to a changing national demographic and a dispersal of the Scottish ethic throughout the world.

Meanwhile, rapid progress in the arts, science, and education, and the emergence of a new industrial age meshed neatly with the Scottish genius for thrift, hard work, shrewdness, and conservatism. The 19th century produced vast numbers of prominent Scots who made broad and sweeping progress in all fields of endeavor.

Both the glories and pain of Britain's empire were partially shared by the men, women, and children of Scotland. Many of the Third World's most dedicated missionaries were Scots-born, and many of the inventions that altered the history of the developing world were either invented or installed by Scots genius and industry.

SCOTLAND TODAY Scotland endured bitter privations during the Depression and during the 20th century's two world wars. In the 1960s and 1970s, Scotland found that, like the rest of Britain, its aging industrial plant could not compete with more modern types of commercial competition from abroad.

The most visible decline in Scotland's industrial preeminence occurred in the shipbuilding industries. The vast Glasgow shipyards that once produced some of the world's greatest ocean liners are now bankrupt. The companies that once produced automobiles in Scotland were wiped out during the 1930s. Much of the industrial and commercial control over Scotland begins and ends within the richer and more powerful England, and many commercial enterprises once controlled by Scots have been merged into English or multinational conglomerates.

All is not bleak, however, on the Scottish horizon. The discovery of North Sea oil by British Petroleum in 1970 boosted the Scottish economy considerably and provided jobs for thousands of workers. Oil has continued to play a prominent role in the Scottish economy. In 1981 the largest oil terminal in Europe opened at Sullom Voe in the remote Shetland Islands. Scotland's time-tested crafts (woolen tweeds and knitwear, for example) are thriving, and the market for Scotch whisky has burgeoned around the world. Technical advances in computers and electronics, too, have transformed central Scotland into a manufacturing center for high-tech industries whose future is being eagerly watched by venture capitalists everywhere.

The past two decades have brought political turmoil to Scotland. As part of Britain, it became a member of the European Common Market in 1973, although many Scots opposed entry. In 1974 it underwent a drastic revision of its counties. Many regions were renamed. For example, "Tayside" was carved out of the old counties of Perth and Angus.

Dissatisfaction with English rule dominated the headlines in 1979. The issue was "devolution," or separation from England. The vote was not decisive: 33% in favor of it, 31% against, and 36% deciding to sit this one out. By 1988, and in anticipation of the 1992 economic union, a revival of Scottish nationalism swept the land under the new banner of "Scotland in Europe." This search for a national identity has continued, and polls in 1992 showed that one out of two favor independence from England.

POLITICS

There are two main parties, Conservative and Labour. The Liberals and SDP have joined in an uneasy alliance to form a third party the Social Democratic and Liberal Party, but have not yet made any noticeable impact. The Labour party is very strong in Scotland, particularly around the Central district, taking in Glasgow, where most of the people live. Traditionally, Scots vote left-of-center, and Scottish unions are among the most militant and socialistic in Britain.

Although the government is administered from Westminster in London, Scotland has its own departments in management control and there is a Scottish secretary of state, as well as a substantial parliamentary delegation. Scotland has its own legal system. In spite of the movement toward independence, many Scots still have an allegiance to the Crown that may be colored somewhat by the affection the Scottish people developed for Queen Victoria, who loved Scotland and often stayed at Balmoral Castle. Queen Elizabeth and her family have followed in Victoria's steps, and they are quite frequently a popular part of the Scottish scene.

As in Wales and England, counties, or shires, of Scotland were reorganized and consolidated by an act of Parliament in 1974. Today they are administered as the counties of Western Isles, Highland, Grampian, Strathclyde, Dumfries and Galloway,

Central, Lothian, Tayside, and Fife. The older names, however, are still in common use today.

THE PEOPLE

Scotland is a country of hospitable people, who are descended from an interesting mixture of bloodlines: Celt-Iberian (Pict), Irish Celtic, Roman, Norse, Saxon, Jute, Angle, Norman, and French, with perhaps a few more sources thrown in, what with the seafarers of many nations who have come here through the centuries.

Scotland has a population today of some 5 million people, about 75% of whom live in the Central Lowland area, the fertile strip that stretches from the Firth of Forth to the Firth of Clyde, where most of the industry of the country is found. Outside the big cities of Edinburgh and Glasgow, people live in small towns and on farms, some even in the tiny crofts clinging to steep hillsides in the western Highland county.

To the outsider, Scotland's deepest traditions appear to be based on the clan system of old with all the familiar paraphernalia of tartans and bagpipes that play such a large part in the country's world image. However, this is a romantic memory, and in any case, a good part of the Scots—the Lowlanders, for example—have little or no connection with the clansmen of earlier times.

The religious heritage of Scottish Presbyterianism and the legacy of John Knox are a more prevailing influence. There is still a strain of puritanism that can be seen in Sunday closings and the strict observance of the Sabbath by many people, particularly in rural areas. Tourists and the development of resort areas have begun to have an effect on these customs. The other puritan legacy, a dedication to hard work and enterprise, has made Scotland a desirable place for foreign investors.

Their strength and independent spirit has been carried by the Scots who have spread all over the world, making notable achievements in many fields. Many, however, have stayed home and made their mark from the place where Bronze Age aborigines began the long journey into modern Scotland.

RELIGION

Much of Scotland's history (in fact, even its sense of cohesiveness as a country) has been formed by religious attractions or religious revulsions. Religion and its politics has so deeply affected the Scottish character that it's almost impossible to conceive of a Scottish dialogue where a strong sense of piety and morality doesn't creep in.

From earliest days, religion shaped the character and nation of Scotland. It was the unifying influence of such Catholic missionaries as Columba, Ninian, and Mungo who helped the northern region grasp a sense of its unity through a shared religion. King David I (1124–1153) almost bankrupted Scotland's treasury by building abbeys and convents, and much of the early nationalistic rage Scotland felt against England was engendered when many of those abbeys were raided and sacked during border forays by English bandits. But by the early Middle Ages the perception became strong that Catholicism and its emissaries (most of whom came from Scotland's arch rival, England) meant control over Scottish destiny.

Scottish dissatisfaction with Catholicism found its most vocal spokesman in the fearsome person of John Knox (1513–1572), whose lack of tact would almost

---

IMPRESSIONS

Scotland is renowned as the home of the most ambitious race in the world.
—FREDERIC EDWIN SMITH, RECTORIAL ADDRESS, ABERDEEN, 1928

It is a peculiar element in Scottish humour, as appreciated by Scotchmen, that the harder it is to see, the better it is esteemed. If it is obvious it is of less account. This rests on the intellectuality of the Scotch; having little else to cultivate, they cultivate the intellect. The export of brains came to be their chief item of commerce.
—STEPHEN LEACOCK, HUMOUR, 1935

certainly have cost him his life except for the groundswell of political support his platform uncovered. Ever since his fiery personal blasts against the courtly affectations and intrigues of Mary Queen of Scots, and her Catholic entourage, Scots have always been wary of any form of ecclesiastical control, and especially wary of things "papist." John Knox's genius lay not in his theology, but rather in his vision for the democratic administration of the Presbyterian Church by elected members of each congregation. The tenets (and the austere moral tone) that he and his followers (especially Andrew Melville) popularized lay the foundations of what later became the Church of Scotland.

After the Reformation, as Britain grew more secure in the stability of its mostly Protestant framework, the cultural differences between Anglican England and Presbyterian Scotland became more pronounced and bitter. Ever wary of outside domination (whether it came from Rome or from London) Scots ministers struggled throughout the 17th, 18th, and 19th centuries to resist the "anglicanization" of their national church. Contemporary politicians in London even saw a genuine threat of a Scottish secession from Britain if the Kirk of Scotland was not allowed to choose its own destiny and to vote on its own fiscal and political policies.

Mediation and compromise eventually more or less reconciled the country's ruffled feelings, even if several logical gaps still exist within the religious infrastructure of Britain. Most obvious of these is the pledge of the British monarch to protect the Anglican Church while residing in England, and to protect the Scottish Church while residing in Scotland.

Today, only about 15% of the Scottish population is Catholic, and of those, most can trace their family lineage within the past two centuries to Northern Ireland. The large majority of Scots are Presbyterian, and to a lesser degree, Methodist. (The founder of Methodism, John Wesley, made 22 missionary trips to Scotland throughout his lifetime, but with notably fewer conversions than he inspired in England.) Also in Scotland are scattered pockets of Jews (especially in Glasgow), Jehovah's Witnesses, Baptists, Mormons, and a growing Muslim and Hindu population as Scotland receives waves of immigrants from former parts of the British Empire.

LANGUAGE

During the earliest history of Scotland, its prevailing tongue was a smattering of Norse dialects (brought by foraging Vikings) and—more important—the Celtic language. The first major thrust for the "anglicization" of Scotland came from the English-born Queen Margaret, wife of the 11th-century Scottish King Malcolm III, most of whose subjects were Celts. Margaret's policy of importing English-speaking clergy and her unyielding insistence on English ways and education altered forever the way the Scots expressed themselves.

As the centuries progressed, Gaelic, the original Celtic tongue, diminished in importance—partly because of the deliberate policies of the British government to make English as spoken in the Thames Valley of London the universal and official language of both Britain and, later, the empire. In the 1980s, less than 2% of the Scottish population understood Gaelic in any form. Most of those who do speak it live in the northwestern Highlands and in the Hebridean islands—especially the Island of Skye, where about 60% of the population still use the Gaelic language.

In addition to Gaelic, Scottish English borrowed heavily from Scandinavian, Dutch, and French expressions (thanks partly to the commerce of Scotland with each of those peoples), and during the 1400s and 1500s was considered a literary language of precision and grace. After the removal of the Scottish Court to England in 1603, Scottish English came to be considered a rather awkward dialect of official English.

Scotland never developed the linguistic class divisions that still exist so strongly in England between upper-, middle-, and lower-class speech patterns. Throughout most of its English-speaking history, the hardships of Scotland were suffered in common by a society that was well-knit and had few barriers between the classes. Social snobbery was relatively unknown and the laird and his man conversed as equals.

At the end of the 20th century, the great leveling effects of television and radio have begun to even out some of the more pronounced burrs and lilts of the Scottish tongue. However, the dialect and speech patterns of the Scots are still rich and evocative.

2. FAMOUS SCOTS

James and Robert Adam (1728–1792 and 1730–1794). Two Scottish-born architects whose commissions included some of the most prestigious of their era. Their symmetrical but airy architectural style replaced Palladian Neoclassicism as the preferred choice for country homes and public buildings throughout Britain. Their designs for furniture were later fabricated and popularized by Hepplewhite.

Sir James Matthew Barrie (1860–1937). Scottish-born novelist known for the whimsy and sentimental fantasy of his work. Playwright whose success with more than 20 novels gave birth to the Scottish "kailyard" school of Scottish fiction. He is best remembered for his play *Peter Pan* (1904), originally inspired by dialogues with the young children of family friends in a London park.

Alexander Graham Bell (1847–1922). Edinburgh-born inventor and educator, Bell became a naturalized American citizen in 1882. Beginning his career as a trainer of teachers for the deaf, he used his experiments in electrical and acoustical devices to invent the first telephone.

James Boswell (1740–1795). The most famous and faithful biographer in the history of British letters, he documented both the life and (perhaps more importantly) the times of his mentor, Samuel Johnson, in his *Journal of the Tour to the Hebrides* (1785) and his classic *Life of Samuel Johnson* (1791).

Andrew Carnegie (1835–1919). American industrialist and philanthropist, born Dumfermline, Scotland, immigrated to Allegheny, Pennsylvania, with his parents at age 13. After making a fortune in the Pittsburgh iron and steel industries, he retired and gave away more than $350 million in philanthropic projects, mostly for educational facilities, public libraries, and of course, New York's Carnegie Hall.

Thomas Robert Dewar, 1st Baron Dewar of Homestall (1864–1930). Scottish distiller, raconteur, socialite, and member of Parliament (1900–1906) who—as the London-based agent for his father's small-scale distillery—hugely expanded the British and international market for Scotch whisky.

Sir Alexander Fleming (1881–1955). Scottish-born bacteriologist who shared, with two other scientists, the Nobel Prize in 1945 for the discovery and development, in 1928, of penicillin.

James Hutton (1726–1797). Scottish geologist whose ability to extract sal ammoniac from coal soot helped to fuel the Industrial Revolution. His *Theory of the Earth* (1795) formulated a novel new belief in the patterns of the geologic evolution and led to the modern science of geology.

John Paul Jones (original full name, John Paul) (1747–1792). Scottish-born (in Kirkcudbrightshire) American naval officer, who, after serving with the British merchant marine, immigrated to Virginia (where he added "Jones" to his name). Joining the U.S. navy during the American Revolution, he became one of the new nation's most flamboyant military heroes.

John Knox (1513–1573). Leader of the Scottish reformation, and sworn enemy of such Catholic monarchs as Mary Stuart. His teachings helped shape the democratic form of Scottish government, and set the Scottish Church's austere moral tone for generations to come.

Sir Harry Lauder (Hugh MacLennan) (1870–1950). Scottish music-hall troubadour, considered the finest interpreter of Scottish ballads in modern history. Some of his own compositions have become part of the standard lexicon of Scottish music, and include "Roamin' in the Gloamin'," "Wee Hoose amang the Heather," and "Just a Wee Deoch and Doris."

David Livingstone (1813–1873). Scottish missionary and explorer. Employed in a cotton mill from the age of 10, he was ordained a minister in 1840. He traversed the least-explored regions of Africa, collecting vast amounts of information about the African interior (and discovering both the Zambesi River and Victoria Falls in the process). He eventually mapped a large section of Africa and ended his relationship with Britain's missionary societies, but worked to end the slave trade. Two years before his death, he was rescued from an obscure African village (Ujiji) by Welsh-born journalist and fellow explorer Henry M. Stanley.

Charles Rennie Mackintosh (1862–1928). One of the most famous architects and designers of his day, he gracefully incorporated elements of medieval and Celtic design into buildings and furniture, which richly influenced North America's Arts and Crafts movement. Later in his life, he founded the Glasgow School of Art.

James C. Maxwell (1831–1879). Exposed laws of electrodynamics which laid the groundwork for the eventual development (by other scientists) of TV, radio, X-rays, and ultra-violet light.

Saint Margaret (1043–1093). Granddaughter of Edmund Ironside of England, she married Malcolm III of Scotland. She carried out a reform of the church that minimized the influence of Gaelic monasteries by importing English priests into Scotland. Her anglicization of the Scottish Lowlands and introduction of English was important in making Scotland into a potential English kingdom. She led a life of great piety, and was canonized in 1251.

Robert the Bruce (1274–1329). Crowned Robert I at Scone 1306 in defiance of the English, this legendary hero, with skill and courage, freed Scotland from England. He defeated Edward II of England decisively at the Battle of Bannockburn in 1314; Scotland's independence was formally recognized in the Treaty of Northhampton in 1328. His wise policies as king set Scotland on the way to prosperity.

Adam Smith (1723–1790). Author of what is generally considered one of the most influential books of all time, *Inquiry into the Nature and Causes of the Wealth of Nations* (1776), he is considered the father of the science of political economy. A professor at Glasgow University, he also lectured on theology, jurisprudence, and ethics, and was a friend of everyone from Voltaire to Samuel Johnson.

Thomas Telford (1757–1834). The most famous and prolific Scottish engineer of his day, he designed almost a thousand miles of road in the then wilderness of northern Scotland, and dozens of its canals, bridges, and port facilities. Many of his projects are still in everyday use today.

James Watt (1736–1819). Scottish inventor. Although others had conceived of a steam engine, he perfected its design and his partnership with James Boulton at Birmingham. It was Watt who coined the term "horsepower." The watt, a unit of electrical power, is named in his honor.

3. ART, ARCHITECTURE, LITERATURE & MUSIC

ART & ARCHITECTURE

ART Decorative painting became popular in houses and public buildings in the late 16th and early 17th centuries. Most of this painting was the work of local artisans, who used bright colors to produce designs of fruit and flowers, scenes and quotations from the Bible, and other conventional patterns. Tempera painting on ceilings and paneling can still be seen in such places as Gladstone's Land in Edinburgh and Provost Skene's House in Aberdeen. The tempera painting eventually was replaced by ornamental plasterwork. George Jamesone, who worked as an apprentice to one of the craftsmen in decorative design, was Scotland's first known portrait painter.

A school of portraitists developed in Scotland in the early 18th century, following a rich tradition in England. Allan Ramsay (1718–1784), son of the poet and wigmaker of the same name, was Scotland's first fine artist and is believed to have been an influence on England's Sir Joshua Reynolds. His best work, a picture of his wife, hangs in the National Gallery in Edinburgh. Ramsay eventually moved to London, but his major successor in the field, Sir Henry Raeburn (1756–1823), son of a yarn boiler, did most of his work in Edinburgh. Sir David Wilkie (1785–1841), Scottish genre painter and portraitist, is well represented in the National Gallery of Scotland and in other galleries.

After the end of the 19th century, dominant in the Scottish art world until World War I were landscape painter William MacTaggart and the painters of the Glasgow school.

ARCHITECTURE   Brochs of stone, from about the beginning of the Christian era, were the vertical defense forerunners of Scottish castles. The Norman motte and bailey fortifications came next, and early stone castles had stone curtain walls. In the early Middle Ages, curtain walls and towers were combined, and in many castles, the strong keeps were supplanted by gatehouses. By the 14th century, heavily fortified castles strengthened the power of feudal lords. At Linlithgow, Falkland, and Stirling are castles in the European Renaissance style, a trend royal builders then followed.

Examples of ecclesiastical architecture can be seen through the country, although the Vikings left very little of Celtic church structures intact. The influence of Anglo-Norman colonization can be seen in the ecclesiastical edifices of the 11th and 12th centuries. Parish churches at Dalmeny and Leuchars and the church of David I in Dunfermline are examples of Norman design.

A turn to Gothic style came with the monasteries and cathedrals of the early Middle Ages. In Glasgow, Elgin, and Dunblane, you can see pointed Gothic arches, vaulting, and lancet windows. On St. Giles in Edinburgh is one of the few remaining crown spires used in late Gothic ecclesiastical construction. However, when the barons built churches other than cathedrals, they continued to use a Scottish design with stepped buttresses, crenelated towers, and roofs of stone slab. The ornamentation of churches was removed after the Reformation, but their structural function was retained. In Aberdeen, pre-Reformation woodwork is in existence at King's College and St. Machar's.

Baronial mansions from the late 16th and early 17th centuries show a Scottish architectural influence, with gables, garrets, turrets, towers, and facade adornment. Sir William Bruce (1630–1710) and James Smith (1644–1731) were early architects of note. Bruce's classical style can be seen at Kinross House and the courtyard at the Palace of Holyroodhouse. Smith's preference was Palladian.

The Palladian neoclassical style was further developed by William Adam, father of famous architects Robert Adam (1728–1792) and James Adam (1730–1794). The so-called Adam style of design is known for light, decorative reworking of Greek and Roman classical motifs. Robert Adam's work can be seen at Mellerstain. Handsome examples of the later design of this fine artist can best be seen at Culzean Castle.

The influence of the 19th-century revival of Gothic architecture is evident at Abbotsford, while the baronial style was brought back in the construction of Balmoral Castle. By the end of that century, a more pleasing revival was carried out by Charles Rennie Mackintosh (1868–1928), who used the Scottish vernacular method even in his art nouveau designs, a path also followed by Sir Robert Lorimer in restoring old castles. The restoration idea has caught hold, so that many old houses, manors, and castles are now being given new lease on life instead of being demolished.

Of interest are the dovecotes or pigeon houses seen in many places throughout the country. Their style varies from the tall beehive look to cylinders to rectangular, freestanding boxes, some with stepped roofs, sundials, and even moats and turrets.

LITERATURE

There are few examples of Scottish literature before the latter part of the 14th century, and it was not until the 15th century that alliteration, satire, and fantasy were set down in poetry by such writers as Robert Henryson, William Dunbar, Gavin Douglas, Sir David Lyndsay, and King James I (*The King's Quair*). These poets have been called Scottish Chaucerians, or *makaris,* because they took their ideals of poetic utterance and metrical forms from the English master. The poetry of Dunbar and Henryson in particular influenced modern Scottish renaissance poets.

John Knox (1505–1572) wrote such polemics as *First Blast of the Trumpet*

Against the Monstrous Regiment of Women in his struggle with Mary Queen of Scots. He also authored the *History of the Reformation*. Neither the 16th nor the 17th century showed spectacular literary output in Scotland; what there was was written in English. Writers of note in the early 17th century were poet William Drummond and Sir Thomas Urquhart, who was best known as the translator of Rabelais.

The 18th century saw a spate of lucid and powerful prose writing in English: novelist Tobias Smollett (*Roderick Random* and *Humphrey Clinker*), economist Adam Smith (*The Wealth of Nations*), philosopher David Hume (*Treatise on Human Nature*), and James Boswell, friend and biographer of Dr. Samuel Johnson. It was also in the 18th century that the great Scottish poet, Robert Burns, lived, wrote, and died, leaving a legacy of verse combining the humor and vigor of Scots speech and the lilt of Scottish songs with poetic modes and themes. Burns, Scotland's national bard, known especially for love lyrics and satires, is revered throughout the world. A number of minor poets were also literary lights of the Burns era, among them Allan Ramsay (father of the painter), James Thomson, and James Macpherson.

Ushering in the 19th century was another great Scottish writer, Sir Walter Scott, novelist and poet, known for medieval romanticism (*Ivanhoe*) and perceptive description of character and locales (*The Heart of Midlothian*). The notable historian and essayist Thomas Carlyle was Scotland-born (*Sartor Resartus* and *The French Revolution*). An acclaimed poet, James Hogg, also wrote a prose work, *The Private Memoirs and Confessions of a Justified Sinner*. In the middle of the century, a lion of the literary world was born in Edinburgh: Robert Louis Stevenson (1850–1894), who penned such classics as *Treasure Island, Kidnapped,* and *The Strange Case of Dr. Jekyll and Mr. Hyde,* as well as poems, especially for children.

At the end of the 19th century a school of writing was formed called the Kailyard (or Kaleyard, literally translated as "kitchen garden"). Kailyard writing used Scots dialect and was characterized by descriptions of Scottish life as homey and cozy. The Kailyard idealization of village life was often blasted by other writers who countered it with themes of brutality or tragic melodrama. Stevenson was an early opponent of "Kailyard treacle."

Other notable men of letters who lived and worked in the late Victorian and Edwardian eras are Andrew Lang, poet, essayist, and historian, also known for his collections of fairy tales; John Buchan (*The Thirty-Nine Steps*); and Douglas Brown (*The House with the Green Shutters,* an anti-Kailyard novel). A top figure in this period was Sir James M. Barrie, Scotland's greatest dramatist (*Peter Pan* and *Dear Brutus*), most of whose life was spent in London.

Few people associate that quintessential Londoner, Sherlock Holmes, with Scotland, but the great detective's creator, Sir Arthur Conan Doyle, was born in Edinburgh and studied medicine at the university in that capital city.

Following World War I, the so-called "Scottish Renaissance" moved for a national identity through the use of a synthetic language called Lallans, a name once applied to Lowland Scots but now consisting of a mix of dialects. However, despite these efforts, English remained the language of literature in Scotland, though novelists and poets still often use Scots vernacular.

Some 20th-century writers of note are Edwin Muir, an anti-Renaissance Orkney Islander known for his great metaphysical poetry and his translations of Kafka; James Bridie, playwright and co-founder of the Glasgow Citizens' Theatre; Eric Linklater, Orkney Island-born writer of satirical and comic novels; and the novelist Lewis Grassic Gibbon.

A writer who has won the hearts of readers (and television audiences) around the world, James Herriot (*All Creatures Great and Small*) was born and educated in Scotland; however, he writes about the Yorkshire Dales where he practices veterinary medicine.

MUSIC

The earliest characteristics of Scottish music are found in the folk tradition. Two traditions exist—the Lowland, where the Scottish version of English is spoken, and the Gaelic music of the Highlands and Hebrides. The first Lowland songs and ballads were written down in the Skene Manuscript (now in the National Library of Scotland) around 1615, and in about 1650 numerous published editions of Lowland tunes began to appear. Gaelic songs were not collected until the 19th century, and because the Highland ballads often differed from clan to clan, you may still hear today a version that never has been written down or recorded.

The folk music of the Orkney and Shetland islands has Scandinavian origins. The ancient Norn language was spoken in Orkney until the late 17th century and in Shetland until the mid-18th, but it was allowed to die out, and since folksongs were in that language, tunes have also almost died out.

A feature of Scottish music is the Scotch snap, a form of syncopation consisting of two notes, the second of which is three times as long as the first. The Scotch snap apparently originated in the 18th century and is found in some Scottish authentic tunes as well as in the 18th-century's pseudo-Scottish melodies.

The three national musical instruments of Scotland are the harp, the bagpipe, and the fiddle. The most ancient of these is the harp, of Irish origin. It lost popularity by the 18th century, as the fiddle, flute, and lute took precedence, and some harp music even passed to the bagpipes. Interest in the harp has revived in this century. The fiddle (derived from the early fedyl) edged out two former competitors, the rebec and the croud (the Welsh crwth), for predominance in the bowed-string-instrument category. Today, especially in Strathspey and Shetland, you can hear the fiddle in both solo and concert form.

It may come as a surprise to many to learn that the bagpipe originated in the Near East. It may have been introduced into Britain by the conquering Romans, who found Scotland too tough to tame. The great Highland bagpipe survived the defeat at Culloden, at which time it was outlawed, partly because it was prized as a military instrument, the dread sound of the piper often sending terror through enemy ranks. Later on, piping was encouraged in new Highland regiments, and the Scot became feared throughout the world for his prowess as a soldier and for the brave skirl of the pipes. It is known now chiefly through its use by the pipe bands of Scottish regiments.

The *ceol mor* (great music) of the pipes is the pibroch, a highly developed theme with variations. The art of pibroch is unique to the Highlands. Lighter types of bagpipe music, called *ceol beag* (small music), are marches, dances, and airs. The great Highland bagpipe has two or more pipes sounded by mouth-blown reeds. Wind is fed to the pipes by arm pressure on a skin bag. It is estimated that it takes about seven years to learn to play the great Highland bagpipe well. The Lowland or Border bagpipe, was bellows-blown, but it lost popularity in the 19th century.

Church, court, and concert music also flourished. Before the Reformation most towns of any size had active song schools, mainly under church direction. A major change in church music was brought about by Calvinist reformers who denigrated the organ as a "popish instrument" and destroyed organs everywhere in the 17th century. None of this, however, interfered with the Gaelic "long psalms" of Celtic Scotland in which each line is intoned musically by the leader with the congregation then singing the line.

Choral and orchestral music are widespread today, and universities have healthy music departments. There is a Scottish National Orchestra as well as the BBC Scottish Symphony Orchestra, and a Scottish Opera, plus varied ensembles and musical guilds.

4. CULTURAL & SOCIAL LIFE

HIGHLAND GAMES & GATHERINGS   Highland gatherings or games have their origins in the fairs organized by the tribes or clans for the exchange of goods. At these gatherings there were often trials of strength among the men, and the strongest were selected for the chief's army.

The earliest games were held more than 1,000 years ago. The same tradition is maintained today: throwing hammers, putting rounded stones found in the rivers, tossing tree trunks, running in flat races and up steep hillsides. The playing of bagpipes and the performance of dances have always been part of the gatherings. The "Heavies," a breed of gigantic men, always draw the most attention with their prowess. Of all the events, the most popular—and the most spectacular—is the tossing of the caber (that is, the throwing of a great tree trunk!).

Queen Victoria, who had a deep love for Scotland, popularized the Highland games, which for many decades had been suppressed after the failure of the 1745 rebellion. In 1848 the Queen and her consort, Prince Albert, attended the Braemar Gathering and saw her ghillie, Duncan, win the race up the "hill of Craig Choinnich," as she recorded in her journal.

The most famous gathering nowadays is that at Braemar, held in early September of each year and patronized by the royal family. When that "chief of chiefs" takes the salute, Queen Elizabeth II is fulfilling a role assumed by an ancestor of hers in the 11th century.

Other major games are held at Ballater (Grampian), Aberdeen, Elgin, and Newtonmore.

CLANS, TARTANS & KILTS   The clan tradition of Scotland, dating as it does from the tribal units of the country's earliest Celtic history, was organized into its "modern" form as late as the 11th century, partly in response to the arrival of the Norman threat in England. Power was organized around a series of chieftains, who exacted loyalties from the inhabitants of a particular region in exchange for protection against exterior invasions. Rigidly militaristic and paternalistic—the stuff of which Scottish legend is imbued—the clan tradition is still emphasized today, albeit in a much friendlier fashion than when claymores and crossbows threatened a bloody death or dismemberment for alleged slights on a clan's honor.

The word *clan* derives from the ancient Gaelic word *clann,* meaning "children," and the prefix *Mac* translates as "son of," the same as the prefix O in front of an Irish Gaelic name. Therefore, the Clan MacDonald symbolizes "children of Donald," and Clan MacGregor symbolizes the "children of Gregor."

Chieftains were absolute potentates, with life and death power over members and interlopers, although members of the clan usually viewed their chieftain as a patriarch actively engaged in the perpetuation of the clan's bloodlines, traditions, and honor. The entourage of a chieftain always included bodyguards, musicians (harpers and pipers), a spokesman (known as a "tatler,") and—perhaps most important to latter-day students of clan traditions—a bard. The bard's role was to sing, to exalt the role of the clan and its heroes, to keep a genealogical record of births and deaths, and to compose or recite epic poems relating to the clan's history.

Most of the clans were organized during two distinctly different eras of Scottish history. One of the country's oldest and largest is Clan Donald, whose original organization occurred during the early mists of the Christianization of Scotland, and whose headquarters has traditionally been Scotland's northwestern coast and its western islands. The fragmentation of Clan Donald into subdivisions (which include the Sleat, the Dunyveg, the Clanranald, and the Keppoch clans) happened after the violent battles of succession over control of the clan's destiny in the 1400s. These clan feuds so weakened the once powerful unity of the MacDonalds that a new crop of former vassal tribes within northwest Scotland declared their independence and established new clans of their own. These included the Mackintoshes, the Macleans, the MacNeils, the Mackinnons, and the MacLeods.

Meanwhile, the giant Celtic Earldoms of eastern Scotland disintegrated, and Norman influences from the south became more dominant. Clans whose earliest makeup might have been heavily influenced by Norman bloodlines include Clan Frasier (whose name derives from the French "des fraises," because of the strawberry leaves on the family's coat of arms), de Umfraville, and Rose. Other clans adapted their Celtic names: these include Clan Robertson (Celtic Clan Donnachaidh) and Clan Campbell (Celtic Diarmaid).

Simultaneously, within the border region between England and Scotland, families and clans with differing sets of traditions and symbols held a precarious power over one of the most heavily contested regions of Britain, either enduring or instigating raids upon their territories from both north and south.

A deliberate British policy in the 18th century led to the diminishing of the power of the clans in favor of centralized government. The clans had broken down long before the time that Sir Walter Scott wrote his romantic novels about them, and that Queen Victoria made Scotland socially fashionable thanks to her visits to Balmoral and the Highlands.

Despite the rich traditions of the Lowland and Border clans, it is the traditions of the Highland clans with their costumes, bagpipes, speech patterns, and their grandly tragic struggles that have captured the imagination of the world.

The clans today represent a cultural rather than a political power. The best place to view the clan tradition in its multicolored glory is at any traditional Highland gathering, although other options might include the lone or battalions of bagpipers that seem to show up at everything from weddings, funerals, political rallies, parades, and civic events throughout Scotland.

Garb o' the Gods   Although not every foreign visitor to Scotland is descended from a clan, almost all of them are familiar with plaids and the traditions associated with them. Over the centuries, each clan developed a distinctive pattern to be worn by its members, presumably to better identify its soldiers during the heat of battle. (Although today *tartan* is used interchangeably with *plaid,* the word *tartan* originally referred specifically to a mantle of cloth draped over the back and shoulders.)

The clans developed special dying and weaving techniques whose colors and patterns reflected flair and imagination. The crafts of vegetable dyeing and more sophisticated weaving techniques were raised to both an art and a science and developed as a point of pride for the clan. (Alder bark, when steeped in hot water, produces a black dye; gorse, broom, and knapweed produce different shades of green; cup moss produces purple; dandelion leaves produce magenta; bracken and heather produce yellow; white lichens produce red; and imported indigo produces blue.)

Although they are probably much older, the existence of checkered tartans were first mentioned in an English inventory of 1471. Kilts, of course, enjoy an ancient history and were worn by Roman soldiers as they conquered the known world up to the borders of Scotland. Bonnie Prince Charlie, during his abortive rebellion in 1745, using tartans as a symbol of his army, so threatened his English enemies that they banned the public display of tartans for a brief period after his defeat.

Tartan displays reached their height during the popularization of Scotland by Queen Victoria and her kilt-wearing consort, Albert. The easy availability of wool and the romanticization of the Scottish experience helped to proliferate the region's allure throughout the rest of the English-speaking world.

Today, there are at least 300 clan designs, each subtly different from its neighbor, and each available for sale in the shops and markets of Scotland. If you're not fortunate enough to be of Scottish extraction, Queen Victoria long ago authorized two "Lowland" designs as suitable garb for Sassenachs (Saxons, Englishmen, and more remotely, Americans).

5. SPORTS & RECREATION

GOLF   Scotland gave the world golf, but no one knows just when. As one brochure so colorfully puts it, "Its origins are lost in the mists of antiquity." By the early 1500s it was firmly entrenched. In fact, Mary Queens of Scots is reputed to have played golf. If golfing has a capital, it is St. Andrews, often called "the home of golf." Not only does it have four courses of its own, but nearly a dozen more are within easy reach of the center.

In all, there are some 400 golf courses in Scotland, with 30 courses in Edinburgh. These stretch from the estuary of the Solway Firth at the English border to the Shetland Isles, the northernmost landmass of Britain. Scotland is particularly noted for its links courses, including those at Troon and Turnberry. Links courses were created on ground that provides a link between the land and the sea.

Some of the most important courses include the Old Course at St. Andrews in the east, where a visitor is likely to see the Open Championship being played. For five centuries this golf course has confounded experts by its unpredictable changes and high winds. St. Andrews is also the home of the Royal and Ancient, established in 1754 and the headquarters of golf ever since. It dictates the rules and regulations of this worldwide sport. Around the corner from the Royal and Ancient, on Albany Place, is Tom Auchterlonie's famous shop, where the Auchterlonie family has produced golf clubs for generations.

The Gleneagles Hotel is a mecca for golfers. The setting is the only five-star hotel in Scotland. American golfers at Gleneagles find the turf of its greens more like those they are familiar with Stateside.

The Turnberry Hotel Golf Course, on the west coast of Scotland, exists in the shadow of the famed Edwardian Hotel, now splendidly restored. In addition to the Ailsa Course, the most famous, there are half a dozen championship links courses in the general vicinity. These include Royal Troon, which was laid out along the beachfront, and the Prestwick Golf Course, which has been the scene of 24 Opens. Turnberry, incidentally, was the creation of Mackenzie Ross, considered the greatest of Scottish golf architects. After the war, he created two magnificent golf courses from what had been an airfield.

Less known to Americans, Royal Dornoch in remote Sutherland in the northwest of Scotland, some 60 miles beyond Inverness, has one of the greatest courses. One American golf magazine rated it as among the six finest golf courses in the world. Golf, according to records, was played on this course as early as 1616. It is known for its 14th hole, "Foxy," a 450-yard double "dog-leg."

Charges can vary widely. The larger courses have caddies who charge a fixed fee for their services. Tipping is left up to you. At the clubhouse on most courses you can rent equipment, or else you can do so at pro shops at hotels. Many clubs prohibit the use of caddy cars. Sometimes, especially in summer, the major clubs have catering facilities for food and drink.

FISHING   Many anglers consider Scotland a paradise, citing its fast-flowing rivers, the availability of Atlantic salmon ("the king of all gamefish"), and some of the most beautiful scenery in Europe, along with the marvelous hospitality extended by its innkeepers. Permits for fishing (often arranged by your hotel) can be expensive. For one of the grand beats on the River Tay, a week's permit could run into hundreds of pounds. However, there are many lesser-known rivers where a club ticket costs only pounds a day.

The Tweed and the Tay are just two of the famous Scottish salmon rivers. In Perthshire, the Tay is the broadest and longest river in the country. The Dee, with all its royal associations, is the famous salmon-fishing river of Aberdeenshire. The royal family fishes this river. The queen herself has been seen casting from these banks. Other anglers prefer to fish the Spey, staying at one of the inns along the Malt-Whisky Trail. Certain well-heeled fishermen travel every year to Scotland to fish in the lochs and rivers of the Outer Hebrides.

In general the season for salmon fishing in Scotland runs from the latter part of February until sometime in late October. But these dates vary from region to region.

HEALTH & FITNESS FACILITIES   A wide range of health and fitness facilities is offered at a number of hotels in England and Scotland, together with sporting amenities, such as golf, riding, and fishing at some places. Included in the hotels' offerings are saunas, solariums, gymnasiums, whirlpools, steam cabinets, massage facilities, slimming and beauty treatments, jogging tracks, squash and tennis courts, and indoor or outdoor heated swimming pools. Health farms and hydros are also available, with a selection of therapies and treatments, such as Swedish, gyratory, and underwater massages, deep-cleansing facials, hair removal by waxing, manicure, and pedicure.

6. FOOD & DRINK

FOOD

MEALS AND DINING CUSTOMS The Scots eat early. Dinner in some places, especially the more economical guesthouses, is served only between 7 and 8pm (no exceptions for latecomers). In major hotels you can often order dinner until 9pm, but rarely later. Lunch is traditionally served from 12:30 to 2pm.

Some guest houses, B&Bs, or small hotels offer a "high tea" at around 6 or 6:30pm. This meal, found only in Scotland and northern England, consists of tea, bread, butter, jam, and cakes, as well as a cooked dish, say, haddock and chips, a gammon steak (that's ham), or perhaps cottage pie. Some places also serve a normal dinner later, but I guarantee you won't have room for it if you made the most of your "tea."

Many Scots who dine out always head for the nearest hotel. Scotland appears to have few independent restaurants—that is, those operating outside hotels—except in such large cities as Edinburgh and Glasgow.

Many smaller, independently run restaurants in villages and towns offer a tea-room menu, catering mainly to summer tourists. Cafés and coffee bars abound in the towns; many serve acceptable fare, especially baked goods. Others manage to get by offering the typical and monotonous plate of fish and chips along with overcooked peas, invariably frozen.

CUISINE For years the cuisine was the domain of oats and fish. Scots still use oats and not just for the traditional morning porridge that many people find the best in the world. They do many things with oats, including rolling herring in it and frying it. Oatcake, a crunchy, biscuit-like roundel, has always been a great staple in Scotland.

However, regardless of their world reputation, Scots do not survive on a basic diet of oatmeal. Now Scotland has a well-stocked larder with imports from all over the world, but everything seems to taste better when its made from local produce.

The beginning dinner course—called a "starter" in Britain—is usually a bowl of soup, a welcome form of nourishment in a misty climate. The barley—Rabbie's "barley bree"—that doesn't make it to the whisky distillery may end up in Scotch broth, flavored with neck of mutton. The other national soup is cock-a-leekie, made by boiling fowl along with leeks. Traditionally prunes were added to sweeten the mixture, especially if the leeks were bitter. Scotland has a number of interesting variations on the typical stock in the soup kettle. For example, one soup is made with young nettles along with sausages, sour cream, and spinach. Another is called cullen skink, a fish soup made with finnan haddock, onion, milk, potato, and other ingredients. Sometimes a soup may be familiar—for example, crab soup—but in Scotland it will appear on the menu under the label of *partan bree*.

The so-called national dish of Scotland is haggis, which is often accompanied by the national drink, malt whisky. One wit once described this dish as a "castrated bagpipe." It is said that few Scots ever eat this dish, although they present it to tourists as their "national dish." Regardless of what you might be told facetiously, haggis is not a bird. Therefore you should turn down invitations—usually offered in pubs—to go on a midnight haggis hunt. Cooked in a sheep's paunch (nowadays more likely a plastic bag), it is made with bits and pieces of the lung, liver, and heart of a sheep mixed with suet and spices, along with onions and oatmeal. Haggis is most often served with neeps (turnips) and tatties (potatoes). It is sometimes served with

IMPRESSIONS

Oats—a grain which is generally given to horses, but in Scotland supports the people.
—SAMUEL JOHNSON, *A DICTIONARY OF THE ENGLISH LANGUAGE*, 1755

"clapshot," a Scottish version of a dish known south of the border as "bubble and squeak."

One of Scotland's best-known exports is pedigree Aberdeen Angus beef. In fact, the famous "ye olde" roast beef of England often came from Scotland. To earn much needed currency, the frugal Scots had to ship their beef to England, reserving the blood for themselves, which they turned into black pudding. Game plays an important part in the Scottish diet, perhaps less so than in years gone by. Still, there is much game in the north and west, including woodcock, red deer, grouse, and capercaillie. Rabbit and hare have always been well known in the crofter's kitchen.

Scottish lamb is known for its tender, tasty meat. A true connoisseur can taste the difference in lamb by its grazing grounds. These range from the coarse pastureland and seaweed of the Shetlands to the heather-clad hills of the mainland. Many Scots seem to prefer lamb roasted simply without fancy sauces, but they also use the meat in a number of hot pots and casseroles, along with stews and mutton pies. These are elegant dishes. Then there is also "mince and tatties," which means mashed potatoes cooked with ground meat.

Chicken appears frequently on the Scottish table. An old Scottish dish, a roasting chicken, is called "stoved howtowdie." With rounds of spinach and poached eggs and bacon added as a garnish, it's called "howtowdie wi' drappit eggs."

Fish is a mainstay of the diet, and well it should be in this land of seas, rivers, and lochs (lakes). Many Scots eat fish for breakfast, including whitefish, haddock, herring, and the pink-fleshed brown trout. A popular dish is finnan haddie (haddock), which is said to have originated in Findon, south of Aberdeen. It is often poached lightly in milk or cream. The modest herring is transformed into the elegant kipper, sometimes called the Loch Fyne kipper, because the best are said to come from there. Another well-known dish is Arbroath smokies, which are made from fresh haddock that is then smoked. Scotland's game fish is salmon. When it is turned into smoked Scottish salmon, it is exported to grace the tables of the world. Scotland has such great salmon rivers as the Tay, Esk, Tweed, Islay, and Spey.

Dundee marmalade, made originally with oranges from Seville, is now a mandatory accompaniment with toast at many of the breakfast tables of Britain. Dundee, in fact, was the site of the world's first marmalade factory. The city is also known for its famed Dundee cake, a light fruit cake. Desserts, using local ingredients, often become imaginative concoctions such as plum and Drambuie mousse.

The Scots are among the good bakers of Europe. Many small tea rooms still prefer to bake their own scones, buttery shortbread, and fruity breads. The heather honey is justly celebrated, and jams make use of Scotland's abundant harvest of soft fruit. Raspberries, for example, are said to be among the finest in the world.

You will most definitely want to try some of the excellent cheeses produced in Scotland. The mild or mature cheddars are perhaps the best known. A famous hard cheese, Dunlop, comes from the Orkney Islands as well as Arran and Islay. One of the best-known cheeses from the Highlands is called Caboc, a creamy rich cheese, formed into cork shapes and rolled in pinhead oatmeal. Many varieties of cottage cheese are flavored with herbs, chives, or garlic.

DRINK

"It is the only liquor fit for a gentleman to drink in the morning if he can have the good fortune to come by it . . . or after dinner either." Thus wrote Sir Walter Scott of the drink of his country—scotch whisky. Of course if you're there, or for that matter almost anywhere in Britain or Europe, you don't have to identify it as scotch whisky when you order. That's what you'll get if you simply order whisky. In fact, in some parts of Scotland, England, and Wales, they look at you oddly if you order "scotch" as you probably do in the United States.

The true difference in the scotch whiskies you may have become accustomed to seeing on bars or shelves of liquor stores in the United States is whether they are blends or single-malt whiskies. Many connoisseurs prefer single malts, whose tastes depend on their points of origin: Highlands, Lowlands, Islay, or Campbeltown on Kintyre. These are usually seen as "sipping whiskies," not to be mixed with water (well, maybe soda) and not to be served with ice. Many have come to be used as an after-dinner drink, served in a snifter like cognac.

The blended scotches came into being both because the single malts were for a long time too harsh for delicate palates and because they were expensive and time consuming to produce. A shortcut came into being in which the clear and almost tasteless alcohol produced in the traditional way could be mixed with such ingredients as American corn, Finnish barley, Glasgow city tapwater, and caramel coloring, with a certain percentage of malt whiskies that flavors the entire bottle. Whichever you prefer, both the single malts and the blends must be made within the borders of Scotland and then aged for at least three years before they can legally be called scotch whisky.

Two after-dinner drinks are scotch-based liqueurs—Drambuie and Glayva. The recipe for Drambuie, better known to Americans than Glayva, is supposed to have been given to its first producers, the Mackinnons of Strath on the Isle of Skye, by an impecunious guest, Bonnie Prince Charlie. The name of the drink is derived from the Gaelic *an dram buidheach,* meaning a dram that satisfies.

The making of Scottish beer—the ales drunk by the common folk in earlier days—almost died out when palates became more adapted to scotch whisky and when a malt tax was levied in the 18th century, to be followed in the 19th century by beer duty. The brewing industry has made a comeback in the last quarter century, and Scottish beer, or "scotch ale," is being produced. Real ale is beer made from malted barley, hop flowers, yeast, and water, with a "fining" process (use of an extract from the swim bladders of certain fish) to complete the brewing. Ales are fermented in casks in a series of steps, and a product is now being turned out by Scotland's breweries. Scottish ale, either dark or light, is malty and full of flavor.

Scottish wine? The average visitor may be unaware that such a product exists. In a land of whipping winds and falling rain, there is not only a Scottish wine, but it's usually drunk in half-pint mugs instead of tulip-shaped glasses. Of course, growing wine grapes in this hostile soil is not possible, so the canny Scots make a golden liquid from trees and from Highland wildflowers instead. Clans have jealously guarded their wine-making secrets for centuries.

One of the best wines is a crisp and dry brew, Silver Birch, always chilled and best served with wild salmon from Scottish rivers or just sipped at a wine bar. Queen Victoria drank it because she'd heard that it prevented baldness. Made from the same silver birch trees, Sparkling Silver Birch is a brut bubbly. A country wine, Elderflower, is a medium-sweet white wine, often consumed with desserts, although some diners prefer it with Scottish lamb. Bramble wine (sometimes called Blaeberry) is "bloody red" and made from blackberries. Try it with Scottish venison or an Angus steak. The tayberry, a cross between a blackberry and a raspberry, produces a rather strong medium dry wine of that name. A medium dry white wine is made from gooseberries.

The clever wine producers of Scotland even bottle a citrus wine made from oranges and lemons grown in Scottish greenhouses. Many devotees drink "Crabbies," a green ginger wine said to date back to the time of the second Jacobite Rebellion of 1745. The brew is powerful and tart, a spicy elixir.

---

7. RECOMMENDED BOOKS & RECORDINGS

BOOKS

TRAVEL   Since the middle ages, English writers have been fascinated by the idiosyncrasies of their northern neighbors. Without contest, the most influential (and perhaps the most curmudgeonly) of these was Samuel Johnson, whose usually negative impressions were recorded by Scottish-born James Boswell in *James Boswell's Journal of a Tour to the Hebrides with Samuel Johnson* (1773, reprinted by Littlefield, Adams in 1978). In the same vein is Donald E. Hayden's *Wordsworth's Travels in Scotland* (University of Oklahoma Press, 1988), and—of particular interest to North Americans—James Bennett Nolan's *Benjamin Franklin in Scotland and Ireland 1759-1771* (University of Pennsylvania Press, 1938).

ART *Scottish Art 1460-1990,* by Duncan Macmillan (Trafalgar Square, 1992), is an expensive book ($90) so many devotees will prefer to check it out of a library. But it is perhaps the definitive statement on Scottish paintings and includes some 350 plates, mostly in color, which explains its high price tag. Written by an art historian and curator at the University of Edinburgh, it depicts Scottish art—"filled with vibrancy and originality"—from the royal miniatures of James IV's court to romantic landscapes to today's generation, devoted to explosive experimentation.

BIOGRAPHY *Burns: A Biography of Robert Burns,* by James MacKay (Mainstream, 1993), is one of the best works devoted to Scotland's national poet (1759-1796), in that it relies often on primary source materials and not previously published information. The life of Burns is portrayed against the historical framework of 18th-century Scotland. A Burns scholar, MacKay defends the author of *Tam O'Shanter* and *Auld Lang Syne* against previously published charges that he was a drunkard and a rake.

Today's most famous Scot is revealed in a biography, *Sean Connery: From 007 to Hollywood Icon,* by Andrew Yule (Fine, 1992), who traces the legendary actor's rise from humble origins in Edinburgh to later success "escaping bondage" in such films as *Rising Sun.* Like all true Scotsmen, Connery is said to have a fascinated interest in golf (playing it) and money (not spending it). Scottish-American readers may find the early years of growing up in Edinburgh during the Depression the most interesting.

Curriculum Vitae, an autobiography of Muriel Spark (Houghton Mifflin Company, 1993), is a book in which this gifted writer sets the record straight about her first 39 years, up to 1957 and the publication of her novel *The Comforters.* The best parts are about her life as a child in Edinburgh. She tells how at age 5 she was sent to Gillespie's, an Edinburgh day school. There she became a pupil of Miss Christina Kay, who in time would appear as the immortal Miss Jean Brodie in Ms. Spark's later fiction.

FICTION *Morning Tide,* by Neil Gunn (republished by Walker, 1993), was actually written in the 1930s, and helps explain why Gunn (1891-1973) is considered perhaps the master of modern Scottish fiction. It is a straightforward account of a boy's coming of age in a small fishing village in Scotland in the last years of Victoria's reign.

MUSIC & LORE The myth and lore of Scotland has always been best expressed in its oral and musical traditions. David D. Buchan's *The Ballad and the Folk* (Routledge and Kegan Paul, 1972) and John Pinkerton's *Select Scottish Ballads* (an edited 1982 reprint by AMS Publishers of a 1783 original), both of which offer poetic and charming insights into a still-thriving art form. You might also consult Roger Fiske's *Scotland in Music* (Cambridge University Press, 1983). Also useful is George B. Douglas and Richard Dorson's *Scottish Fairy and Folk Tales* (a 1977 reprint by Ayer & Co. of a 1901 classic).

HUMOR Scottish humor, whose innuendo was always credited for making life on the heath and highlands more bearable, can be better understood through Julie MacDonald's *Scottish Proverbs* (edited by John and Jean Zug, and published in 1987 by Penfield), and W. B. Burnett's *Scotland Laughing* (Albyn Press, 1955). Broader in its scope and self-satire is Malcolm Lawson-Paul's *Clan Chowder (the MacTanistry Papers Embellished)* (Debrett, 1982), a compilation of the kinds of jokes and lampoons that spread with Scottish emigrations throughout the British Empire.

HISTORY Good historical overviews of Scotland, beginning with its earliest prehistory, is Michael Jenner's *Scotland Through the Ages* (Viking Penguin, 1990), Rosalind Mitchison's *A History of Scotland* (Methuen, 1970), and W. Croft Dickinson and George S. Pryde's *A New History of Scotland* (Nelson, 1961). Also insightful, perhaps because of its authorship by a famous Scots novelist, is Alistair

Maclean's *Alistair Maclean Introduces Scotland* (edited by Alastair Dunnett, McGraw Hill, 1972).

Dealing in detail with the famous personalities of the 16th century is Alison Plowden's *Elizabeth Tudor and Mary Stewart: Two Queens in One Isle* (B & N Imports, 1984). Antonia Fraser's *Mary, Queen of Scots* (Dell, 1984) is a highly readable biography. Also by Antonia Fraser is a short, very subjective, and exceedingly charming anthology, *Scottish Love Poems: A Personal Anthology* (Peter Bedrik Books, 1989).

Other historical eras are analyzed by Iain Moncreiffe in *The Highland Clans* (Potter, 1968), and by Richard B. Sher and Jeffrey R. Smitten in *Scotland and America in the Age of Enlightenment* (Princeton University Press, 1990). Also interesting is David Daiches's *A Hotbed of Genius: The Scottish Enlightenment 1730–1790* (Columbia University Press 1987), and Henry Hamilton's *The Industrial Revolution in Scotland* (Littlefield, Adams, 1966). For U.S. citizens of Scots descent, a richly evocative book, much applauded in the American South, is Duane Gilbert Meyers *The Highland Scots of North Carolina* (University of North Carolina Press, 1987).

James Kerr's *Fiction Against History: Scott as Storyteller* (Cambridge University Press 1989) explores the fiction as well as the sense of historical destiny of Scotland's "national troubador," Sir Walter Scott. In her book, *Burns and Tradition* (University of Illinois Press, 1984) Mary Ellen Brown explores the values of Robert Burns and the influence upon him of Scotland's lore and history.

The more recent Scottish experience, particularly the events engendered by the flow of black gold from the North Sea, is carefully described in T. M. Lewis's and J. H. McNicoll's *North Sea Oil and Scotland's Economic Prospects* (Crown Helm Publications, 1978). In the same vein is Charlotte Lythe's and Madhavi Mamjudar's *The Renaissance of the Scottish Economy* (G. Allen & Unwin, Co., 1982). Appropriate for anyone interested in European history just before, during, and after World War II is T. Christopher Smout's *A History of the Scottish People 1930–1950* (Yale University Press 1986).

CLANS & THEIR SYMBOLS   Finally, on a purely decorative and symbolic level, but with rich interest for anyone tracing genealogical roots, is Robert Bain's *The Clans and Tartans of Scotland*, enlarged and re-edited by Margaret MacDougall, with heraldic advice supplied by P. E. Stewart-Blacker and with dozens of illustrations (Fontana-Collins, 1985). Somewhat shorter and more succinct is *Tartans,* edited and published by the Belvedere Editions of Rizzoli International, 1989.

RECORDINGS

CLASSICAL MUSIC   In the elegant courts of such culture-conscious monarchs as Mary Stuart, music was imported from both England and France. The madrigals and choral compositions of the Scottish 16th century can be found in a collection of songs by the Scottish Early Music Consortium, *Mary's Music* (Chandos CHAN 9332). During the same era, a Scottish-born composer, Robert Carver (1490–1546), created a remarkable body of polyphonic vocal music whose allure has grown increasingly fashionable among British music buffs in the 1990s. Carver's music can be appreciated on *Scottish Renaissance Polyphony Vols. 1 & 2,* as performed by the Scottish choral group Capella Nova (Tavener ASV CDGAU 124).

TRADITIONAL SCOTTISH CHORAL, HARP & PIPE MUSIC   For an excellent introduction to the glories of Gaelic song, try the Glasgow Gaelic Musical Association's album *Gaelic Galore* (Lismore, LCOM 9037), or the Glasgow Phoenix Choir's album *With Voices Rising* (Lismor LCOM 9024).

Alison Kinnaird has been honored as Scotland's finest harpist. Teaming her efforts with female vocalist Christine Primrose, their subtle interpretations of traditional songs are available on *The Quiet Tradition* (Temple COMD 2041). The stirring performances of Hamish Moore, frequently named as one of Scotland's finest pipers, can be appreciated on *Cauld Wind Pipes* (Dunkeld DUN/C 003) and on a companion recording called *Open Ended* (Dunkeld DUN/C 006). A different piper known either as Pibroch or Piobaireachd (depending on whether you endorse the English or Gaelic spelling of his name) can be heard on a recording entitled *The Classical Music of the Great Highland Bagpipe* (Lismore LCOM 9016). To simplify matters for neophytes, one of the finest collections of bagpipe music in recent history assembles the most stirring songs by Scotland's greatest musicians onto one recording, *The Pipes and Drums of Scotland* (Lismore LCOM 9001).

SCOTTISH FOLK MUSIC   Probably the most visible of the Scottish folk groups is the Corries, whose spirited (and sometimes passionate) music was popular even before its foremost composer, Roy Williamson, composed "Flower of Scotland." Probably the best insight into both their poetry and patriotism is available in *The Complete Corries* (EM MCLICF6032), or *The Best of the Corries* (Pick MC PWKMC4054P).

Runrig are probably the most popular band in Scotland today. Known during their early days for the authenticity and flair of their Gaelic recordings, Runrig have lately adopted a more contemporary sound that combines rock and folk music. Examples of both their early and recent music include *Play Gaelic* (CM LPNA105) and *Big Wheel* (EMI LP CH121858).

The style of Capercaillie is perhaps more earthily rooted to conservative Scottish traditions. To date, significant recordings include *Crosswinds* (CM CD GUD1077), *Blood Is Strong* (CM LP GPN1001), and *Sidewalk* (CM MCC51F1094).

Dick Gaughan, a folk artist from the old school, and often compared to Woody Guthrie, is a committed and outspoken socialist whose songs are genuinely stirring, red-blooded, and devoted to the self-sufficiency of a proud and independent Scotland. Two representative recordings include *Call It Freedom* (CM LP LM030), and *Dick Gaughan Live in Edinburgh* (CM MC MMC041).

Of special interest are Jean Redpath's recordings (considered the most authoritative and evocative ever recorded) of the songs of Robert Burns. Unless supplies are sold out (a real possibility, considering both the academic and popular appeal of these recordings), look for Jean Redpath's *Songs of Robert Burns Volumes 1-7* (CM MCTRAX 17).

Many other Scottish traditionalists play sometimes inspired versions of time-tested North British melodies, sometimes in Gaelic. A handful of the more reliable favorites include David MacLean, Billy Connolly, Andy Stewart, Kenneth McKellan, the Alexander Brothers, a group known as the Shorts and Dykehead, and—perhaps most famous and influential of all (credited with keeping Scottish spirits aloft during and just after World War II)—the singing sensation of Harry Lauder.

CHAPTER 2

PLANNING A TRIP TO SCOTLAND

1. **INFORMATION, ENTRY REQUIREMENTS & MONEY**
- **WHAT THINGS COST IN EDINBURGH**
- **WHAT THINGS COST IN INVERNESS**
2. **WHEN TO GO—CLIMATE, HOLIDAYS & EVENTS**
- **SCOTLAND CALENDAR OF EVENTS**
- **EDINBURGH CALENDAR OF EVENTS**
3. **HEALTH, INSURANCE & PACKING**
4. **TIPS FOR THE DISABLED, SENIORS, SINGLES, FAMILIES & STUDENTS**
5. **ALTERNATIVE/ADVENTURE TRAVEL**
6. **GETTING THERE**
- **FROMMER'S SMART TRAVELER: AIRFARES**
7. **GETTING AROUND**
- **SUGGESTED ITINERARIES**
- **FAST FACTS: SCOTLAND**

This chapter is devoted to the where, when, and how of your trip—the advance-planning issues required to get it together and take to the road.

After deciding where to go, most people have two fundamental questions: What will it cost? and How do I get there? This chapter will answer both these questions and also resolve other important issues such as when to go, what pretrip preparations are needed, where to obtain more information about the destination, and many more.

1. INFORMATION, ENTRY REQUIREMENTS & MONEY

SOURCES OF INFORMATION

There are more than 170 tourist information centers in Scotland. All are well signposted in their cities or towns, and some are closed in winter.

To write for information about Scotland, the address is the **Scottish Tourist Board,** 23 Ravelston Terrace, Edinburgh, Scotland EH4 3EU.

IN NORTH AMERICA Before you go, you can also obtain information from the following **British Tourist Offices** in the United States: 2580 Cumberland Pkwy., Atlanta, GA 30339-3909 (tel. 404/432-9635); 875 North Michigan Ave., Suite 1510, Chicago, IL 60611-1977 (tel. 312/787-0490); Cedar Maple Plaza, 2305 Cedar Springs Rd., Suite 210, Dallas, TX 75201 (tel. 214/720-4040); World Trade Center, 350 South Figueroa St., Suite 450, Los Angeles, CA 90071 (tel. 213/628-3525); and 40 West 57th St., New York, NY 10019 (tel. 212/581-4700).

In Canada, information is available at 111 Avenue Rd., Suite 450, Toronto, ON M5R 3J8 (tel. 416/925-6326).

IN THE U.K. Detailed information is further available in London from the Scottish Tourist Board, 19 Cockspur St., SW1Y 5BL (tel. 071/930-8661). In Scotland, most major cities and towns have tourist offices (see "Essentials" under individual towns).

OTHER SOURCES For general information, always check **newspapers and magazines.** To find the latest articles published about Scotland, go to your library and ask for the *Reader's Guide to Periodical Literature* and look up Scotland or the city of interest.

The **U.S. State Department** also publishes background bulletins. Contact the Superintendent of Documents, U.S. Government Printing Office, Washington, DC 20402 (tel. 202/783-3238).

A good **travel agent** can also provide information, but make sure the agent is a member of the American Society of Travel Agents (ASTA) so that you can complain to the ASTA Consumer Affairs Department, 1101 King St., Alexandria, VA 22314, if you receive poor service.

ENTRY REQUIREMENTS

DOCUMENTS All U.S. citizens, Canadians, Australians, New Zealanders, and South Africans must have a passport with at least 2 months' remaining validity. No visa is required. The Immigration office will also want proof of your intention to return to your point of origin (usually a round-trip ticket) and visible means of support while you're in Britain. If you are planning to fly from, say, the U.S. to the U.K. and then go to a country that requires a visa (India, for example), it's wise to secure that visa before your arrival in Britain.

CUSTOMS Visitors from overseas entering Britain may bring in 200 cigarettes and 1 quart of liquor. If you come from the European Community (EC, or Common Market) area, you're allowed 300 cigarettes and 1 quart of liquor, provided that you bought and paid tax in another EC country. If you buy your allowance on a ship or plane, you may import only 200 cigarettes and 1 liter of liquor. There is no limit on money, film, or other items for your own use, except that all drugs other than medical supplies are illegal. Commercial goods such as video films and nonpersonal items will require posting a bond and will take a number of hours to clear Customs. Importing live birds or animals is forbidden and they will be destroyed.

U.S. citizens returning home who have been away for 48 hours or more are allowed to bring back, once every 30 days, $400 worth of merchandise duty-free. You'll be charged a flat rate of 10% duty on the next $1,000 worth of purchases. Be sure to have your receipts handy. On gifts, the duty-free limit is $50.

MONEY

CURRENCY/CASH The currency of Britain is the **pound sterling (£),** made up of 100 **pence (p).** Scotland issues its own pound notes, but English and Scottish money is interchangeable. Pence come in 1p, 2p, 5p, 10p, and 50p coins. Notes are issued in £1, £5, £10, and £50 denominations.

CURRENCY EXCHANGE For the best exchange rate, go to a bank, not to a hotel or shop. Traveler's checks (for which you'll receive a better rate than cash) can be changed at the airport and some travel agencies, such as American Express and Thomas Cook. Note the rates; it can sometimes pay to shop around.

Many hotels in Scotland will simply not accept a dollar-denominated check, and if they do, they'll certainly charge for the conversion. In some cases they'll accept countersigned traveler's checks, or a credit card.

If you're prepaying a deposit on hotel reservations, it's cheaper and easier to pay with a check drawn upon a British bank. This can be arranged by a large commercial bank or by a currency specialist like **Ruesch International,** 1350 Eye St. N.W., Washington, DC 20005 (tel. 202/408-1200, or toll free 800/424-2923). To place an order, call them and tell them the type and amount of the sterling-denominated check

THE POUND & THE DOLLAR

At this writing $1 equals approximately 66p (or £1 = $1.50), and this was the rate of exchange used to calculate the dollar values given in this guide. This rate fluctuates from time to time and may not be the same when you travel to Scotland. Therefore the following table should be used only as a guide:

U.K.£	U.S.$	U.K.£	U.S.$
.05	.08	15	22.50
.10	.15	20	30.00
.25	.38	25	37.50
.50	.75	30	45.00
.75	1.15	35	52.50
1	1.50	40	60.00
2	3.00	45	67.50
3	4.50	50	75.00
4	6.00	55	82.50
5	7.50	60	90.00
6	9.00	65	97.50
7	10.50	70	105.00
8	12.00	75	112.50
9	13.50	100	150.00
10	15.00	125	187.50

you need. Ruesch will quote a U.S. dollar equivalent, adding a $2 fee per check as their service fee. After receiving your dollar-denominated personal check for the agreed-upon amount, Ruesch will mail you a sterling-denominated bank draft, drawn at a British bank and payable to whatever party you specified, for the agreed-upon amount. Ruesch will also convert checks in foreign currency into U.S. dollars, provide foreign currencies in cash from over 120 countries, and sell traveler's checks payable in either dollars or any of six other currencies, including pounds sterling. In addition to its Washington, D.C., office, Ruesch maintains offices in New York, Los Angeles, Chicago, Atlanta, and Boston, although the Washington, D.C., office can supply, through phone orders, any of the bank draft and traveler's check services mentioned above. Ruesch will mail brochures and information packets upon request.

Traveler's checks are the safest way to carry cash while traveling. Most banks will give you a better exchange rate for traveler's checks than for cash. If you can, purchase them in pound denominations. The following are the major issuers of traveler's checks:

American Express (tel. toll free 800/221-7282 in the U.S. and Canada) charges a 1% commission. Checks are free to members of the American Automobile Association.

Barclay's Bank/Bank of America (tel. toll free 800/221-2426 in the U.S. and Canada). Through Barclay's subsidiary, Interpayment Services, Visa traveler's checks are sold, which are denominated in either U.S. dollars or British pounds.

Citicorp (tel. toll free 800/645-6566 in the U.S. and Canada) issues checks in U.S. dollars, pounds, or German marks.

MasterCard International/Thomas Cook International (tel. toll free 800/223-9920 in the U.S., or 212/974-5695, collect, from the rest of the world).

Each of these agencies will refund your checks if they are lost or stolen, upon sufficient documentation or their serial numbers. When purchasing checks, ask about refund hotlines; American Express and Bank of America have the greatest number of offices around the world.

CREDIT CARDS Credit cards are useful in Scotland, although you should be warned that many of the low-cost establishments, especially B&B houses, do not accept them. **Visa** is the most widely used card, along with **Eurocard** (the same as **MasterCard**). **American Express** is often accepted, mostly in the middle- and upper-bracket category. **Diners Club** is the least accepted of the "big four."

Credit cards can save your life when you're abroad. With American Express and Visa, for example, not only can you charge purchases in shops and restaurants that take the card, but you can also withdraw sterling from bank cash machines at many locations in Scotland. Check with your credit-card company before leaving home.

If you make a purchase with a credit card, remember that credit-card companies compute the rate on the date the charge is posted, not on the date you actually made the transaction.

WHAT THINGS COST IN EDINBURGH	U.S. $
Taxi from the airport to the city center	18.00
Local telephone call	.20
Double room at the Caledonian Hotel (deluxe)	274.00
Double room at the Sibbet House (moderate)	90.00
Double room at the A Haven (budget)	54.00
Continental breakfast in a hotel	6.00
Lunch for one at the Indian Cavalry Club (moderate)	12.50
Lunch for one at Henderson's (budget)	10.00
Dinner for one, without wine, at Pompadour (deluxe)	85.00
Dinner for one, without wine, at Cosmo (moderate)	36.00
Dinner for one, without wine, at the Alp-Horn (budget)	20.00
Pint of beer	3.25
Coca-Cola	1.25
Cup of coffee	1.25
Roll of ASA 100 color film, 36 exposures	7.50
Admission to Edinburgh Castle	4.20
Movie ticket	6.50
Theater ticket at King's Theatre	8.60–32.00

WHAT THINGS COST IN INVERNESS	U.S. $
Average taxi ride in the city center	8.00
Local telephone call	.20
Double room at the Culloden House (deluxe)	285.00
Double room at the Kingsmill (moderate)	165.00
Double room at the Ballifeary (budget)	81.00
Continental breakfast in a hotel	5.75
Lunch for one at Brookes Wine Bar (moderate)	15.00
Lunch for one at the Pancake Palace (budget)	10.00
Dinner for one, without wine, at the Culloden House (deluxe)	50.00
Dinner for one, without wine, at the Stakis Steakhouse (moderate)	26.00
Dinner for one, without wine, at Dickens International Restaurant (budget)	18.00
Pint of beer	3.00
Coca-Cola	1.10
Cup of coffee	1.10

	US$
Roll of ASA 100 color film, 36 exposures	6.60
Admission to Culloden Battlefield	2.30
Movie ticket	6.00
Theater ticket to Eden Court Theatre	12.00

2. WHEN TO GO — CLIMATE, HOLIDAYS & EVENTS

CLIMATE

Weather is of vital concern in Scotland. It can seriously affect your travel plans. For **weather forecasts** covering the whole of Scotland, call 031/246-8021 in Edinburgh or 041/246-8021 in Glasgow. For weather reports in the Edinburgh area, call 031/246-8091, and in Glasgow and environs, 041/246-8091.

The Lowlands of Scotland usually have a moderate year-round temperature. In spring, the average temperature is 53°F, rising to about 65° average in summer. By the time the crisp autumn has arrived, the temperatures have dropped to spring levels. In winter the average temperature is 43°F. Temperatures in the north of Scotland are lower, especially in winter, and you should dress accordingly. It rains a lot in Scotland, but perhaps not as much as age-old myths would have it: The rainfall in Edinburgh is exactly the same as that in London. Always take your raincoat with you.

Edinburgh's Average Daytime Temperature and Days of Rain

	Jan	Feb	Mar	Apr	May	June	July	Aug	Sept	Oct	Nov	Dec
Temp. (°F)	38	38	41	45	50	56	58	58	55	50	42	40
Days of Rain	12	11	11	12	12	10	10	13	11	12	13	13

Glasgow and Central Scotland's Average Daytime Temperature and Days of Rain

	Jan	Feb	Mar	Apr	May	June	July	Aug	Sept	Oct	Nov	Dec
Temp. (°F)	37	37	40	44	51	58	62	59	55	49	41	39
Days of Rain	11	13	14	13	14	15	16	15	12	14	13	13

HOLIDAYS

The following holidays are celebrated in Scotland: New Year's (Jan 1–2), Good Friday and Easter Monday, May Day (May 1), spring bank holiday, the first Monday in August, Christmas Day (Dec 25), and Boxing Day (Dec 26).

SCOTLAND
CALENDAR OF EVENTS

JANUARY

☐ **Burns Night** celebrations take place on the 24th at Ayr (near his birthplace), and also at his favorite towns of Dumfries and Edinburgh. Naturally, there are many toasts with scotch and the eating of the haggis, whose arrival is announced by a bagpipe. For more information, call 0292/284196 in Ayr, 031/5571700 in Edinburgh, or 0387/53862 in Dumfries.

☐ **Up Helly Aa.** The most northerly town in Great Britain, Lerwick, in the Shetland Islands, still clings to tradition by staging an ancient Norse fire festival on the last Tuesday in January. Its aim is to encourage the return of the sun after the pitch-dark days of winter. Its highlight is the burning of a replica of a Norse longboat. For more information, call 0595/3434 in Lerwick.

FEBRUARY

☐ **Aberdeen Angus Cattle Show,** staged early in the north at Perth, draws the finest cattle raised in Scotland. Sales are lively. For more information, call 0738/38353 in Perth.

MARCH

☐ **Whuppity Scourie.** In Lanark, in the Strathclyde district, residents get so tired of winter that they stage this traditional ceremony to chase it away. On the first day of the month. For more information, call 0555/61661 in Lanark.

☐ **Annual Drama Festival** takes place the last week in the month of Tobermory, on the Isle of Mull. This cultural event draws some of Britain's finest theatrical talent. For more information, call 0688/2020 in Tobermory.

APRIL

☐ **Hamilton Flat Races** are run at Hamilton, near Glasgow, in the Strathclyde district. For more information, call 041/2044400 in Glasgow.

☐ **The Kate Kennedy Procession and Pageant** is a historic university pageant staged annually in the university city of St. Andrews in eastern Scotland. For more information, call 0334/72021 in St. Andrews.

MAY

☐ **Scottish Motorcycle Trials** are run for 6 days at the beginning of the month, drawing aficionados from all over Europe. The venue is Fort William (phone 0397/703781 in Fort William for more information.

☐ **Ayr Music Festival** is the major cultural event on the Ayr calendar, attracting an array of classical talent from all over Scotland. Phone 0292/284196 in Ayr for more information.

☐ **Pitlochry Theatre Festival**—Scotland's "theater in the hills"—launches its season in mid-month, lasting to October, at Pitlochry. Call 0796/472215 for more information.

JUNE

✪ *SELKIRK COMMON RIDING* *This is the most elaborate and impressive display of horsemanship in Scotland, celebrating Selkirk's losses in the 1560 Battle of Flodden—only one Selkirk soldier returned alive from the battle to warn the town before dropping dead in the marketplace. Some*

400 horses and riders parade through the streets. A young unmarried male of the town is crowned as the cornet, representing the soldier who sounded the alarm.
   Where: *Selkirk.* ***When:*** *The second Friday following the first Monday in June.* ***How:*** *Call 0750/20054 in Selkirk for more information.*

☐ **Guid Nychtburris** is an age-old festival taking place in Dumfries at mid-month. It's an event similar to, but less impressive festival than, the Selkirk Common Riding (see above).

☐ **Lanimer Day** is celebrated in Lanark on whichever Thursday falls between June 6 and 12. It's a week of festivities, with a ritual procession around the town's boundaries, the election of a Lanimer Queen and a Cornet King, and a parade with floats, along with Highland dances and bagpipe playing. Call 0555/61661 for more information.

☐ **Beltane Day** is celebrated in Peebles on the third week in June, with festivities beginning on the Wednesday before midsummer day (June 22). A town "Cornet" rides around to see that the boundaries are safe from the "invading" English, a young girl is elected Festival Queen, and her court is filled with courtiers, swordbearers, guards, and attendants. Children of the town dress in costumes for parade floats through the streets. Call 0721/20138 in Peebles for more information.

JULY

☐ **Promenade Concerts** are presented at Kelvin Hall by the Scottish National Orchestra, weekly throughout the rest of the summer, in Glasgow. Phone 041/2044400 in Glasgow for more information.

☐ **Folk Festival,** one of the best and the best attended, occurs the second week of the month in Glasgow. Some of the finest Scottish folk music can be heard here. Phone 041/2044400 in Glasgow for more information.

AUGUST

☐ **Lammas Fair** is a medieval market on the second Monday and Tuesday of the month at St. Andrews in eastern Scotland. Phone 0334/72021 in St. Andrews for more information.

☐ **World Pipe Band Championships** are staged around mid-month in Glasgow. Phone 041/2044400 in Glasgow for more information.

☐ **Highland Games and Gatherings** are presented at various venues throughout the country, including Aberfeldy, Perth, Crieff, Ballater, Oban, and Portree on the Isle of Skye. More details are available from the Scottish Tourist Board (see "Sources of Information" in "Information, Entry Requirements & Money," above).

SEPTEMBER

☐ **Ben Nevis Mountain Race** takes place on the first Saturday at Fort William in the Highlands. Phone 0397/703781 in Fort William for more information.

○ *HIGHLAND GAMES AND GATHERINGS   The Queen and many members of the royal family often show up for this annual event, with its massed bands, piping and dancing competitions, and performances of great strength by a tribe of gigantic men.*
   Where: *Braemar.* ***When:*** *The first Saturday in September.* ***How:*** *Write or call the tourist office in Braemar, The Mews, Mar Road, Braemar, Aberdeenshire, AB35 5YP (tel. 03397/41600), about tickets and actual dates.*

OCTOBER

☐ **Highland Autumn Cattle Show** takes place at Oban, in western Scotland, at mid-month. Phone 0631/63122 in Oban for more information.

NOVEMBER

☐ **Christmas Shopping Festival** occurs from the third week in Aberdeen for those who want to shop early for Christmas. Phone 0224/632727 in Aberdeen for more information.

☐ **International St. Andrews Day Dinner**—only Scottish specialties, of course—is presented on the last day of the month. Phone 0334/72021 in St. Andrews for more details.

DECEMBER

☐ **Flambeaux Procession** is a torchlight parade on New Year's Eve in Comrie, Tayside. There is no office to write for information, other than the Scottish Tourist Board (see "Information, Entry Requirements & Money," above).

EDINBURGH
CALENDAR OF EVENTS

MARCH

☐ **Edinburgh Folk Festival** A feast of Scottish folk tunes is presented at various venues at the end of the month. For more information, call 031/5571700.

APRIL

☐ **Exhibitions at the Royal Scottish Academy** Changing exhibitions of international interest are offered here mid-month. It's an annual event. For more information, call 031/5571700.

JUNE

☐ **Royal Highland Show,** devoted to agriculture and commerce, is staged at Ingliston Showground on the outskirts of Edinburgh at mid-month.

AUGUST

✪ *EDINBURGH FESTIVAL   This, the best-known festival in Scotland, is held for 3 weeks in late summer (more about this in the chapter on Scotland's capital). Called an "arts bonanza," it draws major talent from around the world. More than a thousand shows are presented, and a million tickets are sold. Book, jazz, and film festivals are also staged at this time, but nothing tops the Military Tattoo against the backdrop of spotlit Edinburgh Castle.*

Where: At various venues in Edinburgh. When: For 3 weeks in August (dates vary). How: For information about tickets and the various events presented every year, write the Festival Society, 21 Market St., Edinburgh, Scotland EH7 5AB (tel. 031/226-4001).

☐ **Winter Antiques Fair,** the third week in the month, draws dealers and buyers from all over Europe and America. For more information, call 031/5571700.

3. HEALTH, INSURANCE & PACKING

HEALTH PREPARATIONS You will encounter few health problems traveling in Scotland. The tap water is safe to drink, the milk is pasteurized, and health services are good. Occasionally the change in diet may cause some minor diarrhea so you may want to take some antidiarrhea medicine along.

Carry all your vital medicine in your carry-on luggage and bring enough prescribed medications to sustain you during your stay. Bring along copies of your prescriptions that are written in the generic—not brand-name—form. If you need a doctor, your hotel can recommend one or you can contact your embassy or consulate.

If you suffer from a chronic illness, talk to your doctor before taking the trip. For such conditions as epilepsy, diabetes, or a heart condition, wear a **Medic Alert Identification Tag.** The tag not only will alert any doctor to your condition but also provides the number of Medic Alert's 24-hour hotline so that a foreign doctor can obtain medical records for you. For a lifetime membership, the cost is $35, $45, or $60. Contact the Medic Alert Foundation, P.O. Box 1009, Turlock, CA 95381-1009 (tel. 800/432-5378).

FINDING A DOCTOR If you need a doctor, your hotel can recommend one or you can contact your embassy or consulate. Before you leave home, you can obtain a list of doctors in Scotland from the **International Association for Medical Assistance to Travelers (IAMAT).** Contact IAMAT in the United States at 417 Center St., Lewiston, NY 14092 (tel. 716/754-4883); in Canada, at 40 Regal Rd., Guelph, ON N1K 1B5 (tel. 519/836-0102); or in Europe, at 57 Voirets, 1212 Grand-Lancy-Geneva, Switzerland.

INSURANCE Before purchasing any additional insurance, check your homeowner's, automobile, and medical insurance policies as well as the insurance provided by credit-card companies and auto and travel clubs. You may have adequate off-premises theft coverage; your credit-card company may even provide flight cancellation coverage if the ticket is charged to the card. Remember, Medicare only covers U.S. citizens traveling in Mexico and Canada.

Also note that to submit any claim you must always have thorough documentation, including all receipts, police reports, medical records, and the like.

If you are prepaying for your vacation or are taking a charter or any other flight that has cancellation penalties, look into cancellation insurance.

The following companies will provide further information:

Travel Guard International, 1145 Clark Street, Stevens Point, WI 54481 (tel. toll free 800/826-1300), which, at a cost of $52, offers a comprehensive 7-day policy that covers basically everything: emergency assistance, accidental death, trip cancellation and interruption, medical coverage abroad, and lost luggage. There are restrictions, however, which you should understand before you accept the coverage.

Access America, 6600 West Broad St., Richmond, VA 23230 (tel. 804/285-3300 or toll free 800/284-8300), offers a comprehensive travel insurance and assistance package, including medical expenses, on-the-spot hospital payı medical transportation, baggage insurance, trip cancellation/interruption insuı and collision-damage insurance for a car rental. Their 24-hour hotline connects you to multilingual coordinators who can offer advice and help on medical, legal, and travel problems. Packages begin at $27.

Healthcare Abroad (MEDEX) This company offers coverage for between 10 and 90 days at $3 per day; this policy includes accident and sickness coverage to the tune of $100,000. Medical evacuation is also included, along with a $25,000 accidental death and dismemberment compensation. Provisions for trip cancellation and lost or stolen luggage can also be written into this policy at a nominal cost. They can be contacted at Wallach and Co., 107 W. Federal St., P.O. Box 480, Middleburg, VA 22117-0480 (tel. 703/687-3166 or toll free 800/237-6615).

Mutual of Omaha (Tele-Trip) This company offers insurance packages priced at from $113 for a three-week trip. Included in the packages are travel-assistance services, and financial protection against trip cancellation, trip interruption, flight and baggage delays, accident-related medical costs, accidental death and dismemberment, and medical evacuation coverages. Application for insurance can be taken over the phone for major credit card holders at toll free 800/228-9792. Their address is Mutual of Omaha Plaza, Omaha, NE 68175.

Travelers Insurance Company, Travel Insurance Division, One Tower Square, 10 NB, Hartford, CT 06183-5040 (toll free 800/243-3174). Travel accident and illness coverage starts at $10 for 6–10 days; $500 worth of coverage for lost, damaged, or delayed baggage costs $20 for 6–10 days; and trip cancellation costs $5.50 for $100 worth of coverage. Written approval is necessary for cancellation coverage above $10,000.

INSURANCE FOR U.K. TRAVELERS Most big travel agents offer their own insurance, and will probably try to sell you their package when you book a holiday. Think before you sign. Britain's Consumers' Association recommends that you insist on seeing the policy and reading the fine print before buying travel insurance.

You should also shop around for better deals. Try **Columbus Travel Insurance Ltd.** (tel. 071/375-0011) or, for students, **Campus Travel** (tel. 071/730-3402). If you're unsure about who can give you the best deal, contact the **Association of British Insurers,** 51 Gresham St., London EC2V 7HQ (tel. 071/600-3333).

WHAT TO PACK Always pack as light as possible. Sometimes it's hard to get a porter or a baggage cart in rail and air terminals. Also, airlines are increasingly strict about luggage, both carry-on and checked items. Checked luggage should not total more than 62 inches (width plus length plus height), or weigh more than 70 pounds. Carry-on luggage shouldn't be more than 45 inches (width plus length plus height) and must fit under your seat or in the bin above.

The most essential items in your Scottish wardrobe are a good raincoat, an umbrella, and a sweater or jersey. A hat and warm scarf will also help keep you comfortable.

Note also that Scottish people tend to dress up rather than down, and that they dress very well indeed, particularly at theaters and concerts. Nobody will bar you for arriving in sports clothes, but you may feel awkward, so include at least one smart suit or dress in your luggage. Better-class restaurants usually demand that men wear ties and bar shorts or jogging clothing.

Take at least one outfit for chilly weather and one outfit for warm weather. Even in the summer, you may suddenly experience cool weather. Always take two pairs of walking shoes in case you get your shoes soaked and need that extra pair.

4. TIPS FOR THE DISABLED, SENIORS, SINGLES, FAMILIES & STUDENTS

FOR THE DISABLED   In the U.S. Before you go, there are many agencies that can provide advance planning information. For example, contact the **MossRehab,**

1200 West Tabor Rd., Philadelphia PA 19141 (tel. 215/456-9600). They have names and addresses of accessible hotels, restaurants, and attractions, often based on firsthand reports of travelers who have been there.

You can also obtain a copy of *Air Transportation of Handicapped Persons,* published by the U.S. Department of Transportation. It's free if you write to Free Advisory Circular No. AC12032, Distribution Unit, U.S. Department of Transportation, Publications Division, M-4332, Washington, DC 20590.

You may also want to consider joining a tour of disabled visitors. Names and addresses of such tour operators can be obtained by contacting the **Society for the Advancement of Travel for the Handicapped,** 347 Fifth Avenue, New York, NY 10016 (tel. 212/447-7284). Yearly membership dues are $45 for adults or $25 for senior citizens and students. Send a self-addressed, stamped envelope.

The Federation of the Handicapped, 211 West 14th St., New York, NY 10011 (tel. 212/727-4200), also operates tours for members, who pay a yearly fee of $45 for adults or $25 for senior citizens and students.

For the blind, the best information source is the **American Foundation for the Blind,** 15 West 16th St., New York, NY 10011 (tel. 212/620-2000, or toll free 800/232-5463).

In the U.K. RADAR (the Royal Association for Disability and Rehabilitation) publishes two annual holiday guides for the disabled: "Holidays and Travel Abroad" (£3.50 in the U.K., £5 in Europe, £7 in other destinations) and "Holidays in the British Isles" (£5 in the U.K., £8 in Europe, £11 in other destinations). RADAR also provides a number of holiday fact sheets on such subjects as sports and outdoor holidays, insurance, financial arrangements, and accommodations with nursing care for groups or for the elderly. There is a nominal charge for all these publications, which are available by calling 071/637-5400 or by writing RADAR, 25 Mortimer St., London W1N 8AB.

Another good resource is the **Holiday Care Service,** 2, Old Bank Chambers, Station Road, Horley, Surrey RH6 9HW (tel. 0293/774-535; fax 0293/784-647), a national association that advises on vacations for the elderly and the disabled, and also provides competitive travel insurance designed for people with pre-existing medical conditions. Their Holiday Care Awards recognize those in the tourism industry who provide excellent service for people with disabilities.

Accessible hotels and accommodations inspected by the Holiday Care Service throughout the U.K. will now be offering special discounted rates to bookings made through the Holiday Care office. For inquiries and reservations, call their Reservation Helpline at 0891/515-494 (calls are 36p per minute in off-peak hours and 48p per minute at peak times).

If you're flying, the airline and ground staff will help you on and off planes, and reserve seats for you with sufficient leg room, but it is essential to arrange for this assistance *in advance* by contacting your airline. The **Air Transport Users' Committee,** 2/F, Kingsway House, 103 Kingsway, London WC2B 6QX, publishes a free pamphlet called "Care in the Air," which is full of good information. You can also call the information desk at RADAR (tel. 071/637-5400) with questions.

FOR SENIORS Many senior discounts are available, but more than some may require membership in a particular association.

For information before you go, obtain a copy of *Travel Tips for Older Americans* (publication no. 8970, cost $1) from the Superintendent of Documents, U.S. Government Printing Office, Washington, DC 20402 (tel. 202/783-5238). Another booklet—this one is free—*101 Tips for the Mature Traveler* is available from Grand Circle Travel, 347 Congress St., Suite 3A, Boston, MA 02210 (tel. 617/350-7500, or toll free 800/221-2610); this travel agency also offers escorted tours and cruises for seniors.

SAGA International Holidays, 222 Berkeley St., Boston, MA 02116 (tel. toll free 800/343-0273), runs all-inclusive tours for seniors, preferably for those 60 years or older. Insurance is included in the net price of their tours.

In the United States, the best organization to join is the **AARP (American**

Association of Retired Persons). Members are offered discounts on car rentals, hotels, and airfares. The association group travel is provided by the AARP Travel Experience from American Express. Tours may be purchased through any American Express office or travel agent or by calling toll free 800/927-AARP. Cruises may be purchased only by telephone (tel. toll free 800/745-4567). Flights to the various destinations are handled by either of these toll-free numbers as part of land arrangements or cruise bookings. For more information, contact AARP at 601 E St. NW, Washington, DC 20049 (tel. 202/434-2277).

Information is also available from the **National Council of Senior Citizens,** 1331 F St., NW, Washington, DC 20004 (tel. 202/347-8800). A nonprofit organization, the council charges $12 per person/couple for which you receive a monthly newsletter, part of which is devoted to travel tips. Discounts on hotel and auto rentals are provided.

Elderhostel, P.O. Box 1959, Wakefield, MA 01880-5959 (tel. 617/426-7788), offers an array of university-based summer educational programs for senior citizens throughout the world, including England and Scotland. Most courses last around 3 weeks and are remarkable values, considering that airfare, accommodations in student dormitories or modest inns, all meals, and tuition are included. Courses include field trips, involve no homework, are ungraded, and emphasize liberal arts. Participants must be over 60, but each may take a companion who is at least 50. Meals consist of solid, no-frills fare typical of educational institutions worldwide. The program provides a safe and congenial environment for older single women, who make up some 67% of the enrollment.

Mature Outlook, 6001 North Clark St., Chicago, IL 60660 (tel. toll free 800/336-6330), is a travel club for people over 50 years of age, and it's operated by Sears Roebuck & Co. Annual membership is available for $9.95, and the outfit issues a bimonthly newsletter featuring discounts at hotels.

FOR SINGLE TRAVELERS Unfortunately for the 85 million single Americans, the travel industry is geared to duos. Singles often wind up paying the penalty. It pays to travel with someone, and one company that resolves this problem is **Travel Companion,** which matches single travelers with like-minded companions. It's headed by Jens Jurgen, who charges between $36 and $66 for a 6-month listing in his well-publicized records. People seeking travel companions fill out forms stating their preferences and needs and receive a mini-listing of potential travel partners. Companions of the same or opposite sex can be requested. A bimonthly newsletter averaging 34 large pages also gives numerous money-saving travel tips of special interest to solo travelers. A sample copy is available for $4. For an application and more information, contact Jens Jurgen at Travel Companion, P.O. Box P-833, Amityville, NY 11701 (tel. 516/454-0880).

Singleworld, 401 Theodore Fremd Ave., Rye, NY 10580 (tel. 914/967-3334 or toll free 800/223-6490), is a travel agency that operates tours for singles. Two basic types of tours are available: youth-oriented tours for people in their 20s or 30s and jaunts for "all ages." Annual dues are $25.

FOR FAMILIES Advance planning is the key to a successful overseas family vacation. If you have very small children, you should discuss your vacation plans with your family doctor.

On airlines, a special menu for children must be requested at least 24 hours in advance, but if baby food is required, bring your own and ask a flight attendant to warm it to the right temperature. Take along a "security blanket" for your child—a pacifier, a favorite toy or book—or, for older children, something to make them feel at home in different surroundings, like a baseball cap, a favorite T-shirt, or some good-luck charm. Draw up guidelines on bedtime, eating, keeping tidy, being in the sun, even shopping and spending—they'll make the vacation more enjoyable.

Make advance arrangements for cribs, bottle warmers, and car seats if you're driving anywhere (in Scotland, small children aren't allowed to ride in the front seat). Ask the hotel if it stocks baby food, and, if not, take some with you and plan to buy the rest in local supermarkets.

Babysitters can be found for you at most hotels, but you should always insist, if possible, that you secure a babysitter with at least a rudimentary knowledge of English. With the influx of foreign workers in Scottish hotels, you can no longer be certain that all members on the staff speak English.

Family Travel Times is published ten times a year by TWYCH, Travel With Your Children, and includes a weekly call-in service for subscribers. Subscriptions cost $55 a year and can be ordered by writing to TWYCH, 45 West 18th St., 7th Floor, New York, NY 10011 (tel. 212/206-0688). TWYCH also publishes two nitty-gritty information guides, *Skiing with Children* and *Cruising with Children,* which sell for $29 and $22, respectively, and are discounted to subscribers to the newsletter. An information packet describing TWYCH's publications including a recent sample issue is available by sending $3.50 to the above address.

FOR STUDENTS   Council Travel, a subsidiary of the Council on International Educational Exchange (CIEE), is America's largest student, youth, and budget travel group, with more than 60 offices worldwide.

Council Travel has offices throughout the United States, including the main office at 205 East 42nd St., New York, NY 10017 (tel. 212/661-1414). Call toll free 800/GET AN ID to find the location nearest you. International Student Identity Cards (ISIC) are available to all bona fide students from any Council Travel office for $15 and entitle the holder to generous travel and other discounts. In Britain the card costs £5 and is available from the CIEE office at 28A Poland St., London WIV13DB (tel. 071/437-7767 or 287-3337).

Discounted international and domestic air tickets are available with special prices for student and youth travelers. Eurotrain rail passes, YHA passes, weekend packages, overland safaris, and hostel/hotel accommodations are all bookable from Council Travel.

Council Travel also sells a number of publications for young people considering travel abroad. Publications include *Work, Study, Travel Abroad: The Whole World Handbook; Volunteer: The Comprehensive Guide to Voluntary Service in the U.S. and Abroad;* and *The Teenager's Guide to Study, Travel, and Adventure Abroad.*

IYHF (International Youth Hostel Federation) was designed to provide bare-bones overnight accommodations for serious budget-conscious travelers. For information, contact American Youth Hostels (AYH)/Hostelling International, 733 15th St., NW, Suite 840, Washington, DC 20005 (tel. 202/783-6161). Membership costs $25 annually except for those under 18, who pay $10, and those over 54, who pay $15.

5. ALTERNATIVE/ADVENTURE TRAVEL

With the advent of the 1990s, a demand has emerged for specialized travel experiences. There is also an increased demand for organizations that can provide like-minded companions to share in such travel plans.

Caveat: Under no circumstances is the inclusion of an organization in this guide to be interpreted as a guarantee either of its creditworthiness or its competency. Information about the organizations coming up is presented only as a preliminary preview so you can follow up with your own investigation.

EDUCATIONAL/STUDY TRAVEL   The philanthropic nonprofit **People to People International,** 501 East Armour Blvd., Kansas City, MO 64109 (tel. 816/531-4701), organizes collegiate and high school ambassador programs, where participants spend a month in Europe studying for credit.

There is also a department to facilitate visits by North American professionals to their counterparts in countries around the world. This usually occurs in a convention setting, requires 2 to 3 weeks' time away and might include doctors, lawyers, farmers, or those in other specialized careers. Privileges include travel opportunities, newsletters, and a magazine. Annual fees are $25 for families, $15 for individuals, and $10 for students.

HOMESTAYS A nonprofit organization called **Friendship Force,** 575 South Tower, 1 CNN Center, Atlanta, GA 30303 (tel. 404/522-9490), exists for the purpose of fostering and encouraging friendship among peoples around the world. Visits usually occur once a year. Because of group bookings, airfare to the host country is usually less than for individual APEX tickets. Each participant must spend 2 weeks in the host country (primarily in Europe, but also throughout the world); one full week must be spent in the home of a family as a guest. Most volunteers spend the second week traveling in the host country. No particular study regime or work program is expected of participants, but only a decorum and interest level that speaks well of America and its residents.

Servas, Suite 407, 11 John St., New York, NY 10038 (tel. 212/267-0252), whose name translates as "to serve" in Esperanto, is a nonprofit, nongovernmental, international, interfaith network of travelers and hosts whose goal is to build world peace, goodwill, and understanding. Servas travelers stay without charge in a privately owned home for visits lasting a maximum of 2 days. A day visit or a shared meal is also possible. Visitors pay a $55 annual membership fee and are interviewed for suitability by one of more than 200 Servas interviewers throughout the country. They then receive a Servas directory listing the names and addresses of Servas hosts. Hosts eager to meet other members of Servas live throughout the world, including all the countries of Europe.

A number of hosts operating under a code of conduct set up by the **British Tourist Authority** provide an ideal way to find out about the British way of life. For information on this program, BTA publishes a booklet listing dozens of agencies and services offering help in finding the place where you might like to stay for a happy British holiday. If possible, interested persons should call in person at the British Travel Centre, 12 Regent St. Piccadilly Circus, in London. In the U.S., write to any of the Tourist Authority offices listed in "Sources of Information" above.

HOME EXCHANGES Home exchanges can be fun and save money. **Intervac U.S.** is part of the largest worldwide home exchange network. It publishes three catalogues a year, containing more than 8,800 homes in more than 36 countries. Members contact each other directly. The $62 cost, plus postage, includes the company's three catalogs plus the inclusion of your own listing in whichever catalog you select. If you want to publish a photograph of your home, it costs $11 extra. Hospitality and youth exchanges are also available. Contact the organization at P.O. Box 590594, San Francisco, CA 94119 (tel. 415/435-3497, or toll free 800/756-HOME).

The Invented City publishes home listings in February, May, and November of each year, listing more than 200 homes in England alone. For a $50 fee, they will list your home with your preferred time for an exchange, your occupation, and hobbies. Contact them at 41 Sutter St., Suite 1090, San Francisco, CA 94104 (tel. 415/673-0347, or toll free 800/788-CITY.)

Vacation Exchange Club, P.O. Box 650, Key West, FL 33041 (tel. 305/294-3720, or toll-free 800/638-3841), will send you four directories a year—in one of which you are listed—for $60.

TRACING YOUR ANCESTRAL ROOTS If you have a name beginning with "Mac" (which simply means son), or one of the other Scottish names, you may have descended from a clan, a group of kinsmen claiming a common ancestry. Clans and clan societies have their own museums throughout Scotland, and local tourist offices will have details about where to locate them. In bookstores throughout Scotland, you can purchase clan histories and maps.

In Edinburgh and Glasgow, genealogical firms specialize in tracing Highland family histories. Write to **New Register House,** 3 West Register St., Edinburgh EH1 3YT, for a full list of their search fees and the extent of their records before going there yourself. Scottish ancestor hunters come here bitten by the genealogy bug, and facilities get crowded in summer. The house has on record details of every birth, marriage, and death in Scotland since 1855. There are also old parish registers, the earliest dating from 1553, which list baptisms, marriage banns, and burials, but these older records are far from complete. It also has census returns for every decade from 1841 to 1891 and such data records as the foreign marriages of Scots, adopted children's registers, and war registers.

ADVENTURE/WILDERNESS TRAVEL   Whether by bicycle or on foot, the following organizations offer tours for the athletic who want to explore "the wilds," or at least country roads, before they disappear forever.

The goal of **Outward Bound**, 384 Field Point Rd., Greenwich, CT 06830 (tel. 203/661-0797, or toll free 800/243-8520 outside Connecticut), is to help people "go beyond their self-imposed limits, to use the wilderness as a metaphor for personal growth and self-discovery." Training sessions last from 3 days to 3 months. The location of these courses is usually in a wilderness setting near the sea or high in the mountains. Outward Bound maintains 50 different schools and centers throughout the world, at least six of which are in western Europe.

Wilderness Travel, Inc., 801 Allston Way, Berkeley, CA 94710 (tel. 510/548-0420, or toll free 800/368-2794 outside California), is one of the largest tour operators in California specializing in mountain and bicycle tours of Europe, offering at least 16 outdoors-oriented trips, including mountain-climbing tours of Wales and Scotland. Call or write for more information.

Scottish Bicycle Tours are arranged by Peter Costello Tours, P.O. Box 23490-PR, Baltimore, MD 21203 (tel. 301/783-1229), lasting 6 to 9 days. The southeast of Scotland (the Borders) and the southwest (Dumfries & Galloway) are explored on these tours, which cost $900 for 6 days or $1,250 for 9 days, including most food. Bikes cost extra.

English Lakeland Ramblers, 18 Stuyvesant Oval, 1A, New York, NY 10019 (tel. 212/505-1020, or toll free 800/724-8801 outside New York), although basically concerned with England's lakeland, also offers a walking tour of Scotland's Highlands and islands. The Isle of Skye has the most dramatic landscape. An eight-day itinerary costs $1,595, including 5 scenic guided walks, 7 nights of lodging, 8 breakfasts, lunches, and 7 dinners, along with sightseeing visits and admission fees.

FARMHOUSE HOLIDAYS   One unusual way to learn to understand the agricultural roots of Scotland is to overnight on a Scottish farm. **Scottish Farmhouse Holidays,** 10 Drumtenant, Ladybank, Fife KY7 7UG (tel. 0337/830451; fax 0337/831301), will find you an appropriate croft. The company was established in 1982 by Scots-born Jane Buchanan, who describes herself as a farmer's daughter, a farmer's wife, a businesswoman steeped in both agriculture and tourism, and a former exchange student with 4H programs in Michigan and Utah.

Only family-managed working farms are selected for the program, most within easy driving distance of at least a handful of historic sites. Many (but not all) of the farmhouses are at least a century old, and many have been in the same family for several generations. Rates for bed and breakfast in bathless rooms are £13–£14 ($19.50–$21), while rates for dinner, bed, and breakfast run £18–£24 ($27–$36), depending on the establishment. Rooms with private shower and toilet are available for a supplement of £5 ($7.50) per person. Occupants of single rooms usually pay a supplement of £5 ($7.50) as well. If you're interested, the most reliable way to make a booking is to call the number given above. A free brochure is available.

EDUCATIONAL/STUDY TRAVEL   **NRCSA (National Registration Center for Study Abroad)** This organization will register you at your school of choice in Great Britain; in Scotland it is the University of Edinburgh. They will also arrange for room and board and make your airline reservations—all for no extra fee. Their catalog is $3; ask for a free copy of their newsletter. NRCSA can be contacted at 823 N. Second St., Milwaukee, WI 53203 (tel. 414/278-0631).

UNIVAC (University/Vacations)   This organization offers liberal arts programs at Edinburgh, Oxford, and Cambridge. Courses usually last 7 to 12 days and combine lectures, excursions, and guided walking tours; there's no pressure to prepare papers or take final exams. All adults over 18 can attend and there are no formal academic requirements. You live at the colleges and eat either in an elaborate dining hall or the more intimate fellows' dining rooms. For information, contact UNIVAC, the International Building, 9602 N.W. 13th St., Miami, FL 33171 (tel. 305/591-1736, or toll-free 800/792-0100). In Great Britain, headquarters are at 8 Beaufort Place, Cambridge CB5 8AG; in summer, Brasenose College, Oxford OXI 4AJ, England.

6. GETTING THERE

BY PLANE

While the facts and figures below are as accurate as research can make them, the fast-moving economics of the airline industry, particularly since deregulation, make them all very tentative. Always check for the very latest flight and fare information, as well as new European routes that might suddenly have opened just before your trip.

The best strategy before buying your ticket involves shopping around, and remaining as flexible about flight dates as possible. Keep calling the airlines or your travel agent because often, as the departure date nears, airlines will discount seats if a flight's not fully booked.

Other general rules to keep in mind are that fares are usually lower during the week (Monday through Thursday noon) and that there are also seasonal fare differences (peak, shoulder, and basic). Transatlantic peak season is summer, basic season is winter, and shoulder season is in between. Travel during Christmas and Easter weeks is usually more expensive than in the weeks just before or after those holidays.

In any season, airlines offer regular first-class, business, and economy seating. Most airlines also offer discounted fares, such as the Advance Purchase Excursion (APEX), which carry some restrictions (some severe). These usually include the need for an early purchase, a minimum stay abroad, and cancellation or alteration penalties.

The Major Airlines

British Airways (tel. toll free 800/247-9297 in the U.S. and 081/897-4000 in London) the national carrier of Britain, with equipment and service that has been judged as some of the best, operates the greatest number of flights into all parts of the country, including Scotland, and provides en route the added bonus of an advance preview of British manners, methods, and style. Beneficiary of a 1991 expenditure of $17 million (part of which was spent to upgrade the ground facilities most used by North American travelers), the airline is the only non-U.S. carrier with its own terminal at New York's JFK.

Three nonstop flights per week go directly from New York to Scotland's busiest airport, Abbotsinch, outside Glasgow, a 90-minute car or bus ride from Edinburgh. Glasgow-bound flights depart every Tuesday, Thursday, and Saturday at 6:15pm from JFK and arrive at 6am the following morning. BA serves at least 20 North American cities with nonstop flights at least once a day into London's most convenient airport, Heathrow. From Heathrow, BA offers 18 nonstop flights daily from both Edinburgh and Abbotsinch, Glasgow. Some Scotland-bound passengers opt for flights into Manchester, a city in the Midlands of England that is closer to the Highlands and Islands of Scotland than London. BA offers frequent flights into Manchester, many nonstop, from various parts of the U.S.

British Airways telephone representatives in North America can give price and schedule information, and make reservations for flights, hotels, car rentals, and tours within the U.K. Ask about the **British Airways Super Shuttle Saver** fares, which can save you up to 50% on travel to certain key British cities. Trips must be reserved and ticketed 2 weeks in advance, and you can fly only during off-peak times. This usually (but not always) is restricted to anytime on weekends, or weekdays between 10am and 3:30pm, and any night flight after 7pm. Other cost-conscious options include a 14-day round-trip APEX that must be reserved and paid for 14 days in advance, and travel completed within 3 months of departure.

American Airlines (tel. toll free 800/433-7300) is the U.S. carrier with the most routes into London. There is a daily nonstop to Glasgow from Chicago, as well as four daily nonstops from New York's JFK to Heathrow, and American offers between one and two flights a day from Chicago's O'Hare airport to Manchester, England, depending on the season, and one daily flight from JFK to Manchester daily. American also offers at least one daily nonstop to London from Chicago, Dallas/Fort Worth, Los Angeles, Boston, Philadelphia, and Miami.

Hot on the heels of American is its strongest U.S. competitor, **Delta** (tel. toll free 800/241-4141). Well financed and much expanded since the 1980s, Delta's routes include daily nonstop flights to London's Gatwick airport from its headquarters in Atlanta, as well as flights from Cincinnati, Detroit, and Miami.

United Airlines (tel. toll free 800/241-6522) offers daily nonstop service to Glasgow from Dulles airport in Washington, D.C. It also flies to London's Heathrow from New York's JFK, San Francisco, Washington, D.C., Los Angeles, and New Jersey's Newark airport.

Despite the sale to American Airlines in the late 1980s of its best and most traveled routes into London, **TWA** (tel. toll-free 800/221-2000) is still a visible presence on the transatlantic routes, offering daily nonstop service to Gatwick airport from St. Louis, Baltimore, and Philadelphia.

Northwest Airlines (tel. toll-free 800/225-2525) operates nonstop flights between Boston and Glasgow daily in summer; somewhat less frequently in winter. It also offers daily nonstop flights from Minneapolis to Gatwick and from Boston to Gatwick. Thanks to Northwest's recent partnership with the national airline of Holland, KLM, Northwest also offers easy connections through Amsterdam to Britain and most of the other countries of Europe.

Long considered a no-frills alternative to western Europe's larger airlines, **Virgin Atlantic Airways** (tel. toll-free 800/862-8621) now offers services, amenities, and, in many cases, prices comparable to those of most of the world's major carriers. Owned by the same entrepreneurs who established Virgin Atlantic Records and some of London's more unusual nightclubs, the airline flies to London's Gatwick from Boston, Orlando, and Miami, and to London's Heathrow from Los Angeles, Newark, and JFK. Depending on point of origin, flights leave between four to seven times a week.

For travelers departing from Canada, **Air Canada** (tel. toll free 800/776-3000) flies to London's Heathrow from both Toronto and Montréal nonstop daily, and has three to seven flights a week, depending on the season, between Toronto and Manchester. There are also nonstop flights from both Calgary and Edmonton three to seven times a week, depending on the season. From Vancouver, daily flights either transfer through Edmonton or fly directly—about once a week—to London nonstop. Once at Heathrow, flights to several Scottish cities such as Glasgow and Edinburgh can be arranged. This add-on to your itinerary can be arranged when the initial flight is booked in Canada.

Best-for-the-Budget Fares

APEX Generally, your cheapest option on a regular airline is to book an APEX fare, hopefully taking advantage of any price war being waged over the Atlantic at the time of your booking. By planning your trip carefully, and defining your dates several weeks in advance, you might save yourself hundreds of dollars. At press time, for example, British Airways offered an "instant purchase" APEX ticket from New York to either London or Glasgow, with the usual requirement of a 21-day advance purchase waived (note that during the lifetime of this edition, BA might reimpose its 21-day advance purchase requirement). As part of a sales promotion that tends to repeat itself at regular intervals, tickets could be booked up until the day prior to departure. They required a stay abroad of at least one Saturday night and at most 31 days. The round-trip high-season fare for this "instant purchase" was $559. In low season, the same APEX ticket, required a 21-day advance purchase, a minimum stay of 7 nights, and a maximum stay of 45 days. The round-trip price of $379, of course, was subject to change, although last-minute sales promotions might make it even lower, depending on market conditions.

As at virtually every other airline, the issuance of any ticket required the payment of a $21 surcharge for airport services. Depending on the ticket, changes in itineraries and flight dates are either not allowed or are possible only upon payment of an additional fee.

For purposes of contrast only, it's useful to note that the "straight economy fare" between New York and London or Glasgow applicable throughout the year, was quoted at $1,326 round-trip. Although this particular economy-class ticket carried absolutely no restrictions of any kind, the added cost is probably not worth the extra convenience and freedom.

SPECIAL PROMOTIONAL FARES British Airways is always introducing promotional fares designed to make travel to Britain more affordable than ever. These fares usually carry restrictions such as a stay abroad of between 6 and 30 days, and unavailability of travel during certain peak holiday periods.

The Late Saver Fare is another possible option. It offers deeply discounted tickets that become available only 48 hours prior to a Britain-bound flight from any of British Airways' North American departure points.

These fares are cited only to give you an idea of what is likely to be available. Even though they may be discontinued, rest assured that others will quickly come along to take their place.

DISCOUNTS Senior citizens (anyone over 60) are sometimes granted discounts of 10% on selected published fares whose details vary with the season and according to market conditions. Senior citizens, in some cases, qualify for less stringent restrictions on APEX cancellation policies.

BA also offers youth fares to ages 12 to 24 for round-trip transatlantic tickets whose return can be scheduled for up to a full year from the date of departure. Reservations for youth fares can be accepted only 72 hours or less prior to departure. Youth fares, when available, also apply to one-way tickets.

Note that both senior citizen's fares and youth fares might be undercut at any time with more attractive offers to the general public that are part of recurring sales promotions. As always, it's best to communicate with a reservations agent for the whole story about the many available options.

Other Good-Value Choices

BUCKET SHOPS In the 1960s, mainstream airlines in Britain gave this insulting name to resellers of unsold tickets consigned to them by major transatlantic carriers; it might be more polite to refer to them as "consolidators." They act as clearinghouses for blocks of tickets usually discounted 20% to 35% below the full fare. Terms of payment can vary—anything between last-minute and 45 days prior to departure. Tickets can be purchased through regular travel agents, who mark up the ticket 8% to 10% or more, thereby greatly reducing your discount.

A survey of flyers who use consolidators voiced only one major complaint: use of such a ticket doesn't qualify you for an advance seat assignment, and you are therefore likely to be assigned a "poor seat" at the last minute. The survey revealed that most passengers estimated their savings at around $200 per ticket; nearly a third reported savings of up to $300 off the regular price. But—and here's the hitch—many who booked consolidator tickets reported no savings at all because the airline had matched the consolidator fare by announcing a promotional fare. The situation is a bit tricky and calls for some careful investigation on your part.

Bucket shops abound from coast to coast. Look also for their ads in your local newspaper's travel section—they're usually very small and a single column in width. Since dealing with unknown bucket shops might be a little risky, it's wise to call the Better Business Bureau in your area to see if complaints have been filed against the company from which you plan to purchase a fare. Here are some recommendations:

TFI Tours International, 34 West 32nd St., 12th Floor, New York, NY 10001

FROMMER'S SMART TRAVELER: AIRFARES

1. Take off-peak flights. That means not only autumn to spring departures, but Monday through Thursday for those midweek discounts.
2. Avoid any last-minute change of plans (if you can help it)—that way you'll also avoid penalties airlines impose for changes in itineraries.
3. Keep checking the airlines and their fares. Timing is everything. A recent spot-check of one airline revealed that in just 7 days it had discounted a New York–London fare by $195.
4. Shop all airlines that fly to your destination.
5. Always ask for the lowest fare, not just a discount fare.
6. Ask about frequent-flyer programs to gain bonus miles.
7. Check "bucket shops" for last-minute discount fares that are even cheaper than the advertised slashed fares.
8. Ask about air/land packages. Land arrangements are often cheaper when booked with an air ticket.
9. Check "standby" fares offered by Virgin Atlantic Airways.
10. Fly free or at a heavy discount as a "courier."

(tel. 212/736-1140 in New York State, or toll free 800/825-3834 elsewhere in the United States).

25 West Tours, 2490 Coral Way, Miami, FL 33145 (tel. 305/856-0810) in Miami; toll free 800/423-6954 in Florida, or 800/225-2582 elsewhere in the United States).

Sunline Express Holidays, Inc., 607 Market St., San Francisco, CA 94105 (tel. 415/541-7800, or toll free 800/786-5463).

Travel Management International, 18 Prescott St., Suite 4, Cambridge, MA 02138 (tel. toll free 800/245-3672), offers a wide variety of discount fares, including youth fares. Often, its contract fares are lower than those offered by some rebators (see below).

CHARTER FLIGHTS Strictly speaking, a charter flight is an aircraft reserved months in advance for a one-time-only transit to some predetermined point. Before paying for a charter, check the restrictions on your ticket or contract. You may be asked to purchase a tour package and pay far in advance. You'll pay a stiff penalty (or forfeit the ticket entirely) if you cancel. Charters are sometimes canceled when the plane doesn't fill up. In some cases, the charter-ticket seller will offer you an insurance policy for legitimate cancellation (hospital confinement or death in the family, for example). There is no way to predict whether a proposed flight will cost less on a charter or from a bucket shop. You have to investigate at the time of your trip.

One of the biggest charter operators is **Travac,** 989 Sixth Ave., New York, NY 10018 (tel. 212/563-3303, or toll free 800/TRAV-800). Other Travac offices include 6151 W. Century Blvd., Los Angeles, CA 90045 (tel. 310/670-9692); 166 Geary St., San Francisco, CA 94108 (tel. 415/392-4610); and 2601 Jefferson St., Orlando, FL 32803 (tel. 407/896-0014). The **Council on International Educational Exchange (Council Travel),** 205 E. 42nd St., New York, NY 10017 (tel. 212/661-0311, or toll free 800/800-8222) also arranges charters.

REBATORS To confuse the situation even more, rebators also compete in the low-cost air-travel market. These outfits pass along to the passenger part of their commission, although many of them assess a fee for their services. Most rebators offer discounts that range from 10% to 25% (but this could vary from place to place), plus a $25 handling charge. They are not the same as travel agents, although they sometimes offer similar services, including discounted land arrangements and car rentals.

Some rebators include **Travel Avenue,** 180 North Des Plaines, Chicago, IL

60661 (tel. 312/876-1116, or toll free 800/333-3335); **The Smart Traveller,** 3111 SW 27th Ave., Miami, FL 33133 (tel. 305/448-3338, or toll free 800/448-3338); and **Pennsylvania Travel,** 15 Maple Ave., Paoli, PA 19301 (tel. 215/251-9944, or toll free 800/331-0947).

STANDBYS A favorite of spontaneous travelers with no scheduled demands on their time, standby fares leave your departure to the whim of fortune in the hope that a last-minute seat will become available. Most airlines don't offer standbys. However, **Virgin Atlantic Airways** (tel. toll free 800/862-8621) features both a day-of-departure and a day-prior-to-departure standby fare to London from JFK, Newark, Orlando, Miami, and Boston, but only between mid-October and late March.

GOING AS A COURIER This cost-cutting technique may not be for everybody. You travel as a passenger and courier, and for this service you'll secure a greatly discounted airfare.

You're allowed one piece of carry-on luggage only; your baggage allowance is used by the courier firm to transport its cargo (which, by the way, is perfectly legal—often documents). As a courier, you don't actually handle the merchandise you're "transporting" to Europe—you just carry a manifest to present to Customs. Upon arrival, an employee of the courier service will reclaim the company's cargo. (Incidentally, you fly alone, so don't plan to travel with anybody.)

Most courier services operate from Los Angeles or New York, but some operate out of other cities, such as Chicago or Miami. Courier services are often listed in the *Yellow Pages* or in advertisements in travel sections or newspapers.

Try **Now Voyager,** 74 Varick St., Suite 307, New York, NY 10013 (tel. 212/431-1616, 24-hours). Now Voyager works with six daily flights to London, one of which allows couriers a stay of up to 30 days and transport of a modest amount of personal luggage. Now Voyager also offers flights to other destinations, including many to London. Also try **Halbert Express,** 147-05 176th St., Jamaica, NY 11434 (tel. 718/656-8189 from 10am to 3pm daily), one of Now Voyager's clients.

The **International Association of Air Travel Couriers,** P.O. Box 1349, Lake Worth, FL 33460 (tel. 407/582-8320), for an annual membership of $35, will send you six issues of its newsletter, *Shoestring Traveler,* and about half a dozen issues of *Air Courier Bulletin,* a directory of air courier bargains around the world. Other advantages of membership are that photo identification cards are issued, and the organization acts as a troubleshooter if a courier runs into difficulties.

BY TRAIN

From England, two main rail lines link to Scotland. The most popular route is from King's Cross Station in London to Edinburgh, going by way of Newcastle and Durham. Trains cross from England into Scotland at Berwick upon Tweed. This line is the fastest way of reaching the Scottish capital other than flying. Fifteen trains a day leave London for Edinburgh from 8am to 6pm. Night service is more limited, and sleepers must be reserved. Three of these trains go on to Aberdeen.

If you're going on to the Western Highlands and Islands, Edinburgh makes a good gateway, with better train connections to those areas than Glasgow. The fastest train is the *Flying Scotsman,* a limited-stop express train reaching Edinburgh 4 hours after its departure from London.

West-coast rail links Euston Station in London to Glasgow, by way of Rugby, Crewe, Preston, and Carlisle, with nearly a train per hour during the day. Most of these trains take about 5 hours to reach Glasgow. You can also take the *Highland Chieftain,* going direct to Stirling and Aviemore, terminating in Inverness, the capital of the Highlands. There is overnight sleeper service from Euston Station to Glasgow, Perth, Stirling, Aviemore, Fort William, and Inverness. It's possible to book a family compartment.

Scotland is also served by other trains from England, including regular service from such cities as Birmingham, Liverpool, Manchester, Southampton, and Bristol. If you're in Penzance (Cornwall), you can reach either Glasgow or Edinburgh directly by train without having to return to London.

BY BUS

Long-distance buses (called coaches) are the least expensive means of reaching Scotland from England. Some 20 coach companies run services, mainly from London to either Edinburgh or Glasgow. The major operators are National Express, Scottish Omnibuses, Western SMT, Stagecoach, and Eastern Scottish. It takes 8 to 8½ hours to reach either Edinburgh or Glasgow from London.

It is estimated that coach fares are about one-third of the rail charges for comparable trips into Scotland. Most coaches depart from Victoria Coach Station in London. If you're visiting from June through August, it's wise to make seat reservations at least 3 days in advance (4 or 5 days in advance if possible). The timetables for the various coaches are available from **Coach Travel Centre,** 13 Regent St., London SW1Y 4LR (tel. 071/7300202). Travel centers and travel agents also have details. Most travel agents in London sell coach seats and can make reservations for you.

BY CAR

If you're driving north to Scotland from England, it's fastest to take the M1 north from London. You can reach the M1 by driving to the ring road from any point in the British capital. Southeast of Leeds you'll need to connect with the A1 (not a motorway), which you take north to Scotch Corner. There the M1 resumes, ending south of Newcastle upon Tyne. From there you can take the A696, which becomes the A68 for its final run north into Edinburgh.

If you're in the west of England, you can go north along the M5, which begins at Exeter (Devon). Eventually this will merge with the M6. Continue north on the M6 until you reach a point north of Carlisle. From Carlisle you cross into Scotland near Gretna Green. Continue north along the A74 via Moffat. The A74 will eventually connect with a motorway, the M74, which heads toward Glasgow. If your goal is Edinburgh, not Glasgow, various roads will take you east to the Scottish capital, including a motorway (M8) that goes part of the way, as do the A702, A70, and A71 (all these routes are well signposted).

BY SHIP

Cunard Line, 555 Fifth Avenue, New York, NY 10017 (tel. 212/880-7500, or toll free 800/221-4770), boasts as its flagship the *Queen Elizabeth 2,* quite accurately billed as "the most advanced ship of the age." It is the only ocean liner providing regular transatlantic service—26 sailings a year between July and December—docking at such cities as New York, Baltimore, and Fort Lauderdale before sailing to the European ports of Cherbourg, France, and Southampton, England. Built along the Clyde River near Glasgow in the late 1960s, the QE2 has been modernized. On board, you'll find four swimming pools, a sauna, nightclubs, a balconied theater, a cinema, chic boutiques (including the world's first seagoing branch of Harrods), five restaurants, paddle-tennis courts, and a children's playroom staffed with English nannies.

The lifestyle during this leisurely voyage includes the QE2 Spa at Sea; a computer learning center; seminars by trained professionals on astrology, cooking, art, fitness, and health; and a Festival of Life series that introduces you to such personalities as James Michener, Carly Simon, Dick Cavett, and Ben Kingsley.

Fares are extremely complicated, based on cabin standard and location and the season of sailing. In thrift/superthrift season—roughly defined as late autumn—sailings usually cost a minimum of $2,170 in transatlantic class and around $3,515 in first class. Prices go steeply uphill from there, eventually reaching a maximum of $10,930 for a suite in high season. The most modest fare starts at $1,295 and is confirmed on a space-available basis three weeks prior to sailing. These prices are per person, based on double occupancy. All passengers pay a $155 port tax, regardless of the class of cabin. Many different packages are promoted, most of which add on relatively inexpensive airfare from your home city to the port of departure, plus a return to your home city from London on British Airways.

From Southampton, you can make rail connections north to Scotland.

PACKAGE TOURS

FOR GOLFERS Many visitors consider golf and its whisky as Scotland's most enviable attributes. But while the whisky is usually readily available, access for nonmembers to the country's maze of golf courses is not. Scotland contains more than 400 golf courses, but until recently the only way many North Americans could swing a few irons on a Scottish green was to register at a hotel with its own golf course and play as one of the side benefits of his or her sojourn. Access to Scotland's legendary golf courses was usually impossible, despite repeated attempts by individual golfers to batter down the nearly impenetrable barriers of a "members only" system.

All that changed in 1988, however, with the establishment of a New York–based company, **Golf International,** 275 Madison Ave., New York, NY 10016 (tel. 212/986-9176, or toll free 800/833-1389). The company maintains a branch office in St. Andrew's, the ivy-clad *sanctum sanctorum* of the golfing world, and caters to golfers of moderate to advanced abilities with carefully choreographed packages. Against hitherto impossible odds, the company will guarantee their clients' starting times at 40 or so of the most sought-after golf courses of Scotland, including the previously mentioned St. Andrews, as well as Carnoustie, Royal Troon, Prestwick, and Gullane. Potential clients, in self-organized groups of anywhere from 2 to 12, proffer a "wish list" of the courses they'd like to play. Starting times are prearranged (sometimes rigidly) with an ease that an individual traveler or even a conventional travel agent would find impossible.

Packages can be arranged for anywhere from 5 to 14 days (the average package is about 7 days) and can include as much or as little golf, at as many different courses, as a client might want. Weekly prices, with hotels, breakfasts, car rentals, greens fees, and the services of a greeter and helpmate at the airport upon arrival, range from $1,800 to $2,750 per person. Discounted airfares to Scotland can also be arranged. For more information, talk to one of Golf International's sales agents at the toll-free number listed above.

GENERAL TOURS Europe's largest tour operator is Britain's national airline, **British Airways** (tel. toll free 800/AIRWAYS for details).

BA has a full spectrum of what they call "designer holidays," constructed for radically differing kinds of clients. Offerings include carefully structured, tightly scheduled motorcoach tours for clients who feel they need the greatest amount of channeling and guidance. Equally popular are tours designed for independent souls needing no more than discounted vouchers for a car rental and prereserved rooms at specific types of hotels. Depending on your tastes and your pocketbook, BA can arrange vouchers for discounted accommodations in everything from simple inns to the finest baronial mansions of Scotland and can also provide you with a cost-conscious rented car so you can drive yourself over the mountains and through the glens without interference from guides and fellow travelers.

Tours can be as straightforward as a 1-day jaunt from London to Scotland for a round of golf (with a return to London in time for cocktails), or a 3- or 5-day escorted tour through the gardens and manor houses of Royal Deeside. Also available are 1- and 2-week motorcoach tours of the Highlands and islands, with perhaps a detour to visit a local exhibition of Highland Games.

RAILWAY TOURS Ever since Scots-born James Watt invented the steam engine, much of the lore of Scotland involves the entrepreneurial and engineering challenges sparked by the construction and maintenance of its railway lines. Today historians and nostalgia buffs appreciate the complicated network of steel that crisscrosses Scotland's dramatic terrain.

In keeping with these traditions of the steam age, **Abercrombie & Kent,** 1520 Kensington Rd., Oak Brook, IL 60521 (tel. toll free 800/323-7308), offers what have been called the most glamorous railway tours in Europe. On a solidly elegant train known as the *Royal Scotsman,* the experience has been compared to a movable version of a five-star hotel with an equivalent restaurant, an amply stocked bar car, and an expert group of well-informed lecturers and guides.

Abercrombie & Kent is the only U.S. sales agent for this train, and bases much of its European reputation upon it. Known for its carriage-trade adventure tours to such places as China, the Antarctica, or Vietnam, and the Great Rift Valley of Africa, Abercrombie is a respected tour operator whose equivalent rail tours in France and Switzerland are cited by many organizations as being especially appropriate for disabled, elderly, or infirm passengers.

The train incorporates only eight passenger cars (each built in the old-fashioned tradition of 1940s style and comfort, one of the most sophisticated restaurants in Scotland, and a big-windowed bar and observation car with a veranda trailing along at the back. Accommodations are snug but elegant, with wood paneling, private bathrooms, conventional (not bunk-style) beds, climate control, full-length wardrobes, and many of the accessories you'd find on an elegant private yacht.

Tours usually begin and end at Edinburgh's Waverley Station, include a guide and an animated university-class lecturer, and completely eliminate the hassles and inconveniences of baggage transfers through the entire 6-day tour. Itineraries include overnight stopovers at quiet railway sidings along the way and a wide array of landscapes such as the regions around Glasgow, Fort William, Mallaig, Perth or Pitlochry, Inverness and the historic battlefield of Culloden Moor, Keith and the Hebridean island of Skye, Aberdeen, and Dundee and Royal Deeside. Included in the cost are motorcoach excursions and tours of castles, manor houses, gardens, and historic sites of Scotland, many of which are not open to the general public.

The all-inclusive price for the 5-night/6-day tour is $5,700 per person.

SEA CRUISES No area of Scotland is ever far from a loch, an estuary, or the wide open sea, a fact that has greatly affected the country's history. One of the best ways to visit its far-flung islands is by ship, a means of transport offering a luxury and convenience difficult to duplicate any other way.

One company especially geared for this kind of travel is **Hebridean Island Cruises,** Acorn Park, Skipton, North Yorkshire, BD23 2UE. Tel. 0756/701-338, or toll-free 800/659-2648 from the U.S. and Canada. Established in 1989, and the only cruise operators to sail solely in British waters, the company operates a single ship, the *Hebridean Princess,* a shallow-draft, much refitted and retooled remake (in 1990) of an older vessel. Equipped with 29 staterooms and a crew of 38, it can carry up to 48 passengers in cozy circumstances to some of the most remote and inaccessible regions of Scotland. The ship is equipped with beach landing craft especially useful during explorations of the fragile ecosystems and bird life of the more remote islands.

The company offers eight different itineraries that focus either on nature and ecology or on the castles, gardens, and archeology of Scotland. Tours usually depart from the port of Oban, and cruise through the Inner and Outer Hebrides and the Orkneys, stopping in places such as Saint Kilda's, the most remote and westerly of the islands, known for its bird life and tundra. Tours are offered only between March and October, and cost from £400 ($600) per person, double occupancy, for a simple inside cabin during a three-day cruise, to £7,100 ($10,650) per person, double occupancy, for a stateroom with a private balcony during a 14-day cruise. All meals and shore excursions are included in the price, but liquor tabs at the well-stocked bar, wine at dinner, and gratuities are extra.

Another, better-known company, offering more luxurious tours through the islands and lochs of Scotland is **Cunard** (tel. toll free 800/221-4770), whose top-of-the-line yacht *Vistafjord* offers some of the most upscale accommodations within Cunard's 13-vessel inventory. *Vistafjord* sails every June from Southampton, England, in a circuitous route that encompasses many of the ports of Ireland and Scotland. Stops are usually scheduled for Le Havre (France), Guernsey (the Channel Islands), Cobh, Waterford, and Dublin (Ireland), Inveraray, Stornoway, and Kirkwall

(Scotland), Copenhagen, and Kiel, near Hamburg. Per-person prices, double occupancy, for the entire two-week circuit begin at around $5,000. Free air transport from most of the eastern seaboard of North America is included, with modest supplements for transfers from such other places as California.

7. GETTING AROUND

BY PLANE

British Airways U.K. Airpass allows travel in a continuous loop to between 3 and 12 cities on BA's domestic routes. Passengers must end their journey at the same point they began. If such a ticket is booked (say, London to Manchester to Glasgow to Aberdeen to the Shetland Islands, with an eventual return to London), each segment of any itinerary will cost (subject to change) £49 ($73.50). This is considerably less (as much as 50% less) than if each segment were booked individually. The pass is available for travel to about a dozen of the most visited cities and regions of Britain. It must be booked and paid for at least 7 days before departure from the United States, and all sectors of the itinerary must be booked simultaneously. Some changes are permitted in flight dates (but not in the cities visited) after the ticket is issued. Check with BA for full details and restrictions (tel. toll free 800/247-9297).

BY TRAIN

The *Flying Scotsman* takes 4 hours to make the 393-mile journey from London to Edinburgh. Because of either connecting trains or direct service, Scotland can be reached by rail from any train station in England or Wales. Sleeping cars operate between London, Bristol, and Plymouth to all major Scottish cities, including Edinburgh, Inverness, and Perth.

For information on rail travel in Scotland, call or write Manager of Public Affairs, ScotRail, 58 Port Dundas Rd., Glasgow G4 0HG, Scotland (tel. 041/332-9811).

The cost of rail travel here can be quite low, particularly if U.S. travelers take advantage of certain cost-saving travel plans, some of which can only be purchased in North America, before leaving for Scotland. You should be warned that your Eurailpass is not valid on trains in Great Britain.

BRITRAIL PASS This pass permits unlimited rail travel in England, Scotland, and Wales on all British rail routes (it is not valid on ships between the U.K. and the Continent, the Channel Islands, or Ireland). An 8-day gold (first-class) pass costs $299; a silver (economy-class) pass, $219; a 15-day pass costs $489 and $339, respectively; a 22-day pass costs $645 and $425; and a 1-month pass, $775 and $495. Kids 5 to 15 pay half fare, and under-5s are free.

Youth passes (for ages 16 to 25), all silver, are $179 for 8 days, $269 for 15 days. If you choose to go first class, you pay full adult fare.

BritRail also offers a **Senior Citizen gold pass** to people 60 and over. For 8 days, it's $279 in first class, $199 in second; for 15 days, $455 in first class, $305 in second; for 22 days, $599 in first class, $379 in second; and for 1 month, $725 in first class, $445 in second.

Note: Prices for BritRail passes are higher for Canadian travelers because of the different conversion rate for Canadian dollars.

BritRail passes cannot be obtained in Britain, but should be secured before leaving North America either through a travel agent or by writing or visiting BritRail Travel International, 1500 Broadway, New York, NY 10036. Canadians can write to P.O. Box 8910, 250 Eglinton Ave., Toronto, Ontario M4P 3EI. BritRail passes do not have to be predated. Validate your pass at any British Rail station when you start your first rail journey.

BRITRAIL FLEXIPASS The Flexipass lets you travel anywhere on British Rail, but it's available for 8 days or for 15 days only. The 8-day Flexipass can be used for any 4 nonconsecutive days out of 8 and costs $249 in first class, $189 in economy. Seniors pay $229 in first class or $169 in second class, and youths 16 to 25 pay $155 to travel economy class. The 15-day Flexipass can be used for any 8 nonconsecutive days of travel out of 15 and costs $389 in first class, $269 in economy. A senior pass is $365 in first class, $245 in second class; the youth economy class is $219.

Flexipass must also be purchased from either your travel agent or from BritRail Travel International in the U.S. and Canada (see addresses above).

TRAVELPASS FOR SCOTLAND If you plan to tour throughout the U.K., one of the previously described BritRail passes might be appropriate for your needs. If you plan to focus intensively on Scotland, however, a BritRail pass might not be adequate. Recognizing the inadequacy of BritRail passes for intensive tours of Scotland, the Scottish Tourist Authorities developed the **Freedom of Scotland Travel Pass.** Designed for the serious Scottish enthusiast, it offers unlimited transportation on trains, buses, and most ferryboats throughout Scotland. It includes access to obscure bus routes to almost-forgotten hamlets, and free rides on ferries operated by Scotland's two major companies, Caledonian MacBrayne and P&O Lines. Their ferries connect to the Western Islands, the islands of the Clyde, and the historic Orkney Islands.

The travelpass covers all the Scottish rail network and is usable from Carlisle on the western border of England and Scotland and from Berwick-on-Tweed on the eastern Scottish border. In addition, if one has to fly into London and wants to go straight to Scotland from there, a reduced rate for round-trip fare is available between London and Edinburgh or Glasgow for travelpass holders.

The Freedom of Scotland Travelpass is available for 8 days for $145, 15 days for $205, and 22 days for $209. When the traveler validates the pass at the beginning of the first journey, he or she will receive a complete pack of rail, bus, and ferry schedules and a "Countdown Card" for discounts at participating shops, sightseeing attractions, and restaurants. For more information, contact **Scots-American Travel Advisors,** 26 Rugen Dr., Harrington Park, NJ 07640 (tel. 201/768-5505, or toll free 800/247-7268). Information is also available from the Manager of Public Affairs, British Rail-Scottish Region, ScotRail House, 58 Port Dundas Rd., Glasgow G4 0HG, Scotland (tel. 041/332-9811).

BY BUS

No doubt about it, the cheapest means of transport for the budget traveler to Scotland from London is the bus or coach. It is also the least expensive means of travel within Scotland.

All major towns have a **local bus service.** Every tourist information center throughout the country will provide details about half-day or full-day bus excursions to scenic highlights. If you want to explore a particular area, you can often avail yourself of an economical bus pass. If you're planning to travel extensively in Scotland, see the Travelpass for Scotland, already described in "By Train," above.

Many adventurous travelers like to explore the country on one of the **postal buses,** which carry not only mail but a limited number of passengers to rural areas. Ask at any local post office for details. A general timetable is available at the head post office in Edinburgh.

The **Scottish Citylink Coaches** are a good bet. They link the major cities (Glasgow and Edinburgh) with the two most popular tourist centers, Inverness and Aviemore. Travel is fast, the prices low. For example, it takes only 3 hours to reach Aviemore from Edinburgh. Inverness is just 3½ hours from Edinburgh. There is also a direct Scottish Citylink overnight coach making the run from London to Aviemore and Inverness at reasonable fares.

Coaches offer many other popular runs, including links between Glasgow and Fort William, Inverness and Ullapool, and Glasgow and Oban. For more detailed information, get in touch with Highland Scottish, Seafield Road, Inverness (tel. 0463/237575); or Scottish Citylink, Buchanan Street Bus Station, Glasgow (tel. 041/332-9191), and St. Andrew Square Bus Station, Edinburgh (tel. 031/557-5717).

BY CAR

Scotland has many excellent roads, often "dual carriageways," as well as fast trunk roads linking the Lowlands to the Highlands. In more remote areas, especially the islands of western Scotland, single-lane roads exist. Here, caution in driving is most important. Passing places are provided.

However, many of the roads are unfenced, and livestock can be a serious problem when you're driving either day or night. Drive slowly when you're passing through areas filled with sheep.

CAR RENTALS   In brief, it's best to shop around, compare prices, and have a clear idea of your automotive needs before you reserve a car. All companies give the best rates to clients who reserve at least 2 business days in advance and who agree to return the car to its point of origin. It is also an advantage to keep the car for at least 1 week, as opposed to 3 or 4 days. Be warned that all car rentals in the U.K. are slapped with a 17.5% government tax known as VAT.

To rent a car in Scotland, your passport and your own driver's license must be presented along with your deposit. No special British or international license is needed.

Partly because of the huge number of visitors to the United Kingdom, the car-rental market is among the most competitive in Europe. Several recent arrivals on the car-rental scene promise lower rates. Most companies require an advance reservation at least 2 (and sometimes 3) business days for the most favorable rate, and some require that drivers be at least 21 (in some cases, 23) years of age.

Of the big three, **Budget** (tel. toll free 800/527-0700) offers some of the cheapest cars, including a small but peppy Ford Fiesta, barely big enough to fit two people with their luggage inside. With unlimited mileage, it rents for £98 ($147) per week, plus tax of 17.5%, plus a well-spent £8 ($12) per day for collision-damage insurance. Be fully warned, however, that even with the purchase of this insurance, you'll still be liable for up to £100 ($150) in costs in the event of an accident.

You might also compare prices with **Hertz** (tel. toll free 800/654-3001) whose similar car—also with unlimited mileage—costs £119 ($178.50) per week. Tax of 17.5% is extra, although if you ask, Hertz offers plans whereby insurance, taxes, and safeguards against currency exchange fluctuations are factored into the rates. (Depending on your needs and private insurance, this may or may not save you money. It sometimes pays to break the package offers into their different components to see if they're really cheaper.) Hertz's collision insurance, if priced separately from their packages, usually costs from £7 ($10.50) extra per day, and covers all but the first £50 ($75) of damage in the event of an accident. Some of the cheapest deals at Hertz are available through British Airways' reservations network. Renters who fly BA transatlantic and reserve a car simultaneously with their ticket reservations, thanks to BA's volume buying, can get a Hertz car with a daily rental reduced to between $13 and $54 a day, depending on the vehicle, plus tax and insurance, with unlimited mileage included.

Budget, Hertz, and their major competitor, **Avis** (tel. toll free 800/331-2112) also offer a wide range of midsize cars, including the very popular Ford Sierra.

Cautious and thrifty renters have increasingly taken notice of **EuroDollar Rent-a-Car** (tel. toll free 800/800-6000) and Alamo (tel. toll free 800/522-9696), whose rates in Britain (including Scotland) tend to be competitive with their better-known colleagues. In some instances, EuroDollar rents a pint-size Vauxhall Nova for rates similar to those charged by Budget (see above), but requires an advance payment about a week ahead.

Also worthwhile (and sometimes even cheaper) are the services of a car-rental reservations network based in Florida. **I.T.S. of Broward County,** 3332 N.E. 33rd St., Fort Lauderdale, FL 33308 (tel. toll free 800/521-0643, 800/227-8990, or 800/248-4350), represents two of Britain's largest car-rental companies, Kenning and Town & Country. I.T.S. usually offers prices ranging up to 40% lower than those available at most car-rental kiosks. Prepayment is not required, although a printed confirmation will be faxed or mailed to anyone who reserves a car in advance. Cars can be arranged for pickup at any of the major airports of the U.K. (including

Glasgow, Aberdeen, and Edinburgh), include unlimited mileage, and carry the possibility of buying optional but all-inclusive collision insurance priced around £6–£9 ($9–$13.50) per day, depending on the value of the car.

At press time, a week's rental of a Rover Mini or Fiat Panda costs £64.50 ($96.80) plus tax; and a similar rental of a midsize Ford Sierra costs £125 ($187.50), plus tax. Be warned, however, that pickups at certain off-the-beaten-path places might require a phone call upon your arrival before an I.T.S. representative arrives to carry you to what might be an out-of-the-way (and sometimes unlikely) location. If you can maintain your sense of humor, you might save enough money on the car rental to make the inconvenience worthwhile.

CAR INSURANCE   With the rise in inflation and a staggering increase in the cost of car repairs, insurance premiums are on the rise worldwide, many benefits have been decreased, and it's more important than ever to purchase additional insurance to avoid financial liability in the event of an accident.

In other words, it pays to ask questions—lots of them—before renting a car. You can purchase a collision-damage waiver at each of the major car-rental companies for around £8 ($12) a day. Without it, you might be responsible for up to the full cost of the eventual repairs of the vehicle. Considering the unfamiliar practice of driving on the left, different road rules, and roads that tend to be narrow and sometimes congested, I consider purchase of an optional collision-damage waiver almost essential. Additional personal accident insurance (which covers unforeseen medical costs in the event of an accident) costs around £1.75 ($2.60) a day.

Check to see if you are covered by the credit card you use, thus avoiding the added cost of coverage if possible. This can make a big difference in your bottom-line costs.

GASOLINE   There are plenty of gas (petrol) stations in the environs of Glasgow and Edinburgh. However, in remote areas they are often few and far between, and many are closed on Sunday. If you're planning a lot of Sunday driving in remote parts, always make sure that your tank is full on Saturday.

DRIVING RULES & REQUIREMENTS   In Scotland you drive on the left and pass on the right. Road signs are clear and the international symbols unmistakable.

To drive a car in Scotland, U.S. visitors need a passport and driver's license (no special British license is needed). The wise driver will secure a copy of the *British Highway Code*, available from almost any stationers or news agent.

A *Word of Warning:* Pedestrian crossings are marked by striped lines (zebra striping) on the road and flashing orange curbside lights. Drivers *must* stop and yield the right of way if a pedestrian has stepped out into the zebra zone to cross the street. Wearing seat belts is mandatory in the British Isles.

ROAD MAPS   The best road map, especially if you're trying to locate some obscure village in Scotland or Wales, is **The Ordnance Survey Motor Atlas of Great Britain,** revised annually and published by Temple Press. It's available at most bookstores in Scotland. If you're in London and plan to head north to Scotland, go to W. & G. Foyle Ltd., 113-119 Charing Cross Rd., London, W.C.2 (tel. 071/439-8501).

In addition, the Scottish Tourist Board publishes its own road map, **Touring Map of Scotland,** available at most bookstores. Other excellent maps include **Michelin's Map of Scotland** (no. 401) and **Michelin's Map of Great Britain** (no. 986). Before you leave America, you can purchase these maps at the British Travel Bookshop, 551 Fifth Ave., 7th Floor, New York, NY 10176 (tel. 212/490-6688).

BREAKDOWNS   Membership in one of the two major auto clubs can be helpful: the **Automobile Association (AA)** at Fanum House, Basingstoke Hampshire RG21 2EA (tel. 0256/20123), or the **Royal Automobile Club (RAC),** Spectrum, Bond Street (P.O. Box 700), Bristol, Avon BS99 1RB (tel. 0272/232340). You can secure membership in one of these clubs through the car-rental agent. Upon joining, you'll be given a key to the roadside emergency telephone boxes.

HITCHHIKING   Hitchhiking is legal. However, getting into a car with any stranger anywhere in the world can be extremely dangerous, especially for solo travelers. This guide does *not* recommend hitchhiking anywhere in the world today. If you do hitchhike, always exercise caution. In Great Britain, it's illegal to hitchhike on motorways. The cleaner and tidier you look, the better your chances for getting a ride. Have a board with your destination written on it to hold up for drivers to see.

BY FERRY

You can use a variety of special excursion fares to reach Scotland's islands. They are available from Caledonian MacBrayne for the Clyde and the Western Isles or from P&O Ferries, serving Orkney and Shetland. Caledonian MacBrayne, operating 30 ferries in all, sails to 23 Hebridean and all Clyde islands. The fares, times of departure, and other requirements are in a special book, **Getting Around the Highlands and Islands,** published by the Highlands and Island Development Board. It details all the data you'll need for road, rail, sea, and air timetables to the Highlands and islands. Renewed annually, it is available throughout Scotland.

There are reasonably priced fares for vehicles and passengers on certain multiroute journeys using Hebridean and Clyde ferry services. The most popular service is the short crossing between Kyle of Lochalsh and Kyleakin on the Island of Skye. Longer passages go to the Outer Hebrides, including Lewis and Harris. For some of the longer journeys you can rent two- or four-berth cabins. You can also avail yourself of a number of options, including Hebridean Drive-Away Tours (packaged tours for motorists). Many bargain tickets are offered, including Excursion Return, Family, Island Hopscotch, Car-Rover, and Earlybird Savers. Car Rover tickets, valid for 8 or 15 days for the Firth of Clyde and the Western Islands, are available from British Rail and Sealink offices. Short day trips are available on the Firth of Clyde.

More details can be supplied by **Caledonian MacBrayne,** The Ferry Terminal, Gourock PA19 1QP, Renfrewshire (tel. 0475/33755).

P&O Ferries operates the services to the Orkney and Shetland Islands. Information is available from Orkney & Shetland Services, Jamieson's Quay, Aberdeen AB9 8DL (tel. 0224/572615).

SUGGESTED ITINERARIES

IF YOU HAVE 1 WEEK

Day 1: From England, enter Scotland through the southeast known as "the Borders." At Newcastle upon Tyne (England), take the A696 in the direction of Otterburn. It becomes the A68 and will lead you right into Jedburgh and then via the A6091 into Melrose, the heart of the Border Country with its ancient abbeys. From Melrose, take the A6091 west in the direction of Galashiels. The road runs into the A7 north. At Galashiels, turn west onto the A72 in the direction of Peebles for an overnight stopover.

Day 2: You'll wake up at Peebles in the Tweed Valley, with its associations with Sir Walter Scott, the novelist, whose home can be visited at nearby Abbotsford. From Peebles it's a short drive along a secondary road, the A703, and then the main A702 leading into Edinburgh, which many critics consider one of the most beautiful cities of Europe.

Days 3 and 4: Spend this time—too little, actually—exploring the attractions of the Old and New Towns and walk along the Royal Mile after visiting Edinburgh Castle.

Day 5: Cross the Forth Bridge, taking the southern coastal road along the firth, and head east to the ancient Kingdom of Fife. Follow the coastal road to visit the fishing villages of East Neuk, eventually reaching the capital of golf, St. Andrews, at a point 49 miles from Edinburgh. Overnight in St. Andrews.

Day 6: To save time, you can take the A91 west to return to Edinburgh. In the vicinity of Loch Leven and its historic castle, this becomes an express highway, returning to Edinburgh across the Forth Bridge. From Edinburgh, depart the city on the express highway, the M9, going to Stirling, 37 miles away. You'll be within sight of that city's famous castle within the hour. Overnight in Stirling.

Day 7: Head for the Trossachs, one of the most beautiful scenic areas of Scotland. The A84 goes west in that direction, but eventually you must cut onto the A821, a little northwest of Callander. The Trossachs have been called "Scotland in miniature," and include Loch Katrine and the famous Loch Lomond. Sometimes this is called "Rob Roy Country" or "Lady of the Lake Country" because Sir Walter Scott used the area as a setting for his novels. You can either stay overnight at a country hotel somewhere in the Trossachs or continue west to Loch Lomond.

IF YOU HAVE 2 WEEKS

Days 1–7: Spend the first week as outlined above.

Day 8: The next day, leave the Trossachs or Loch Lomond. Go along the western shore of Loch Lomond, connecting with the A83, which will take you to Inveraray, a small holiday resort, seat of the dukes of Argyll at Inveraray Castle. Overnight there.

Day 9: From Inveraray, you can head north along the A819 to Dalmally, which lies along the A85. Continue east from Dalmally until you reach the junction with the A82. There you can head north, going through Glencoe, site of the famous 1692 massacre. If you stay on the A82, you'll reach Fort William for the night.

Days 10 and 11: After a night in Fort William, continue north along the A82 until you reach the junction at Invergarry. There you can turn west along the A87, taking you on the "road to the isles." At Kyle of Lochalsh, frequent ferries sail back and forth to Skye, the most visited of Scottish islands. Since you'll spend a good part of the day getting there, allow Day 11 for exploring the island.

Days 12 and 13: Head back to Invergarry after a visit to Skye. Instead of turning south again to Fort William, head north to Inverness, a distance of 41 miles. The A82 will take you along the western bank of Loch Ness where, as you drive along, you can try to spot the monster rearing its head from the water. You'll arrive in the late afternoon in Inverness, capital of the Highlands, where you can overnight. While still based at Inverness, spend Day 13 exploring the Culloden Battlefield and other attractions in the environs.

Day 14: Head south again to Glasgow and try to see as many of that city's many attractions as time allows—at least the Burrell Collection.

IF YOU HAVE 3 WEEKS

Days 1–14: Spend your first 2 weeks as outlined above.

Day 15: Allow another full day to take in more of the attractions of Glasgow.

Day 16: From Glasgow, take the A77 southwest in the direction of Ayr where you can overnight in Robert Burns Country, with a side visit to see the Burns attractions at nearby Alloway.

Day 17: Leave Ayr and continue a circuitous route north along the coast to Oban, a bustling port and one of Scotland's leading coastal resorts, lying about 85 miles northwest of Glasgow.

Days 18 and 19: From Oban, take a ferry to the Isle of Mull. Try for an early departure so you'll have the rest of the day to explore Mull at your leisure. While still based in Mull, save Day 19 for exploring the neighboring islands of Iona— resting place of 48 Scottish kings, plus Fingal's Cave on the Isle of Staffa, which inspired Mendelssohn to write the *Fingal's Cave Overture.*

Day 20: Return to Oban and head south to the Kintyre Peninsula, the longest peninsula in Scotland, stretching for some 60 miles. Enjoy the scenery along the way and overnight in Campbeltown, a fishing port at the southern tip.

Day 21: Head north again from Campbeltown to West Tarbet, where you can take a Caledonian MacBrayne Steamer to the Isle of Islay, the southernmost island of the Inner Hebrides, lying 16 miles west of Kintyre Peninsula. Spend the rest of the day exploring the island.

A THEMED ITINERARY — THE TRAIL OF ROBERT BURNS

Day 1: In one very busy day in the county town and royal burgh of Dumfries, in the Scottish Lowlands, you can see sights famously associated with the national poet of Scotland. He died at Burns House, on Burns Street, which is now a museum of memorabilia. On the banks of the River Nith you can visit a converted 18th-century watermill that has been turned into the Robert Burns Centre with various exhibitions, some audiovisual, connected with the bard.

Later you can go to the Burns Mausoleum, the family tomb in St. Michael's Churchyard. The Dumfries Museum and Camera Obscura, at the intersection of Church Street and Rotchell Road, also has many Burns relics. Finally, to cap your day and to visit a much needed refueling stop, have a pint at Globe Inn, where Burns drank with his friends. His favorite chair is still there, but you can't sit in it.

Day 2: From Dumfries, continue northwest along the A76, which becomes A70 as it winds west into Ayr, a good center for touring Burns Country. Around Ayr you can see the 13th-century Auld Brig o' Ayr, the poet's "poor narrow footpath of a street," and can also visit a Burns museum, now housed in the Tam o'Shanter Inn on Ayr High Street (this was an alehouse in Rabbie's day). The Auld Kirk of Ayr dates from 1654, and in it Burns was baptized. For your refueling, visit the local pub, Rabbie's Bar, on Burns Statue Square. Overnight in Ayr.

Day 3: While still based in Ayr, true fans of the Scottish bard will continue their exploration of Burns Country for another day. In Tarbolton village, 7½ miles northeast of Ayr, stands the Bachelors' Club on Sandgate, a 17th-century house where in 1780 Burns and his friends founded a literary and debating society.

In the afternoon you can go to Alloway, 2 miles south of Ayr where Burns was born on January 25, 1759, in a gardener's cottage. There a 200-year-old inn, the Burns Monument Hotel, looks out onto the Doon River and the bridge, Brig o'Doon, immortalized in *Tam o'Shanter*. You can also visit the Burns Monument and Gardens, the Burns' Cottage and Museum, and the Land o'Burns Centre.

FAST FACTS SCOTLAND

American Express   In Edinburgh there is an American Express office at 139 Princes St. (tel. 031/225-7881). There's another American Express office in Glasgow at 115 Hope St. (tel. 041/226-3077).

Babysitters   If you're traveling with small children, your best bet is to ask your hotel to recommend someone as a babysitter. Expect to pay the cost of travel to and from your hotel.

Business Hours   Most **banks** are open Monday through Thursday from 9:30am to 12:30pm and 1:30 to 3:30pm. Friday hours are often 9:30am to 1:30pm. Basic **bar and pub hours** are Monday through Saturday from 11am to 11pm, but this can vary widely; Sunday hours are usually 12:30 to 2:30pm and 6:30 to 11pm, but some pubs are closed Sunday. **Office hours** are Monday through Friday from 9am to 5pm; the lunch break lasts an hour, but most places stay open all day. **Post offices** and sub post offices are centrally situated and are open Monday through Friday from 9am to 5pm and on Saturday from 9am to noon. **Stores** are generally open Monday through Saturday from 9am to 5:30 or 6pm. Most stores close early on a Tuesday or Wednesday afternoon.

Camera/Film   All types of film are available, especially in Glasgow, Inverness, and Edinburgh. Processing takes about 24 hours, and many places will do it almost while you wait. There are few restrictions on the use of your camera, except when notices are posted, as in churches, theaters, and certain museums. If in doubt, ask.

Climate   See "When to Go," above.

Crime   See "Safety," below.

Currency   See "Information, Entry Requirements, and Money," above.

Customs   See "Customs" under "Entry Requirements" in "Information, Entry Requirements, and Money."

Dentists   You can find one listed in the yellow pages of the telephone book or you can ask at your hotel. Appointments are usually necessary, but if you are in pain a dentist will generally fit you in.

Doctors   Hotels have their own list of local practitioners. If not, dial "0" (zero) and ask the operator for the local police, who will give you the name, address, and phone number of a doctor in your area. Emergency treatment is free, but if you're admitted to a hospital, referred to an outpatient clinic, or treated for an already existing condition, you will be required to pay. You will also pay if you visit a doctor in his or her office or if the doctor makes a "house call" to your hotel.

Documents   See "Information, Entry Requirements, and Money."

Driving Rules   See "Getting Around," in this chapter.

Drug Laws   Britain is becoming increasingly severe in enforcing antidrug laws. Persons arrested for possession of even tiny quantities of marijuana have been deported, forced to pay stiff fines, or sentenced to jail for 2 to 7 years. Possession of "white powder" drugs such as heroin or cocaine carries even more stringent penalties.

Drugstores   In Britain they're called "chemist" shops. Every police station in the country has a list of emergency chemists. Dial "0" (zero) and ask the operator for the local police. Emergency drugs are normally available at most hospitals, but you'll be examined to see that the drugs you request are really necessary.

Electricity   The electricity is 240 volts AC (50 Hz). Some international hotels are specially wired to allow North Americans to plug in their appliances, but you'll usually need a transformer plus an adapter for your electric razor, hairdryer, or soft contact lens sterilizer. Ask at the electrical department of a large hardware store for the size converter you'll need.

Embassies and Consulates   The **United States Consulate** is in Edinburgh at 3 Regent Terrace (tel. 031/5568315), open Monday through Friday from 10am to noon and 1 to 4pm. The **Australian Consulate** is at 80 Hanover Street, Edinburgh (tel. 031/2266271), and is open Monday through Friday from 10am to 4pm. Some nationals have to use London to conduct their business: They should go to the **Canadian High Commission,** MacDonald House, 1 Grosvenor Square, W.1 (tel. 071/629-9492); the **New Zealand High Commission** at New Zealand House, 80 Haymarket at Pall Mall, London S.W.1 (tel. 071/930-8422), open Monday through Friday from 10am to noon and 2 to 4pm; or the **Irish Embassy,** 17 Grosvenor Square, London S.W.1 (tel. 071/235-2171), open Monday through Friday from 9:30am to 5pm.

Emergencies   For **police, fire, or ambulance,** dial **999.** Give your name, address, and phone number, and state the nature of the emergency. Misuse of the 999 service will result in a heavy fine (cardiac arrest, yes; dented fender, no).

Etiquette   In short, be normal and be quiet. The Scots do not like hearing other people's conversations. In pubs, you are not expected to buy a round unless someone has bought you a drink; don't talk religion or politics.

Hairdressers   Ask at your hotel. Hairdressing services are available in most department stores, and for men, at the main railway stations in Edinburgh and Glasgow.

Hitchhiking   See "Getting Around" "By Car" above.

Holidays   See "When to Go" above.

Information   See "Information, Entry Requirements, and Money" above.

Laundry/Dry Cleaning   Most stores and most hotels need 2 days to do the job. Edinburgh and most provincial towns have laundrettes where you can wash and dry your own clothes, but there are no facilities for ironing. Many laundrettes also have dry-cleaning machines. One-day dry-cleaning service is available.

Legal Aid   Your consulate or high commission (see above) will give you advice if you run into trouble. They can advise you of your rights and even provide a list of attorneys (for which you'll have to pay if services are used), but they cannot interfere on your behalf in the legal process of Great Britain. For questions about American citizens who are arrested abroad, including ways of getting money to them, telephone the Citizens Emergency Center of the Office of Special Consulate Services in Washington, D.C. (tel. 202/647-5225). Other nationals can go to their nearest consulate or embassy.

Libraries   Every town has a public library, and as a visitor you can use the reference sections. Lending, however, is restricted to local citizens.

Liquor Laws   The legal drinking age is 18. Children under 16 aren't allowed in pubs, except in certain rooms, and then only when accompanied by a parent or guardian. Don't drink and drive—penalties are stiff. Basically, you can get a drink from 11am to 11pm, but this can vary widely, depending on the discretion of the local tavern owner. Not all pubs are open on Sunday; those that are generally stay open from 12:30 to 2:30pm and 6:30 to 11pm. Hotel residents can usually purchase alcoholic drinks outside regular hours.

Lost Property   Report the loss to the police first, and they will advise you where to apply for its return. Taxi drivers are required to hand lost property to the nearest police station. For lost passports, credit cards, or money, report the loss and circumstances immediately to the nearest police station. For lost passports, you should then contact your consulate or high commission (see "Embassies and Consulates," above). For lost credit cards or traveler's checks, report immediately to the issuing bank or company.

Luggage Storage   You may want to make excursions throughout Scotland taking only your essentials along. It's possible to store suitcases at most railway stations, but you must be prepared to allow luggage to be searched for security reasons, and be warned: If you object, you could be viewed with suspicion.

Mail   Have your mail addressed "Poste Restante" at any of the big towns, or give your hotel address. When claiming personal mail, always carry identification. To send an airmail letter to North America costs 39p (60¢) and postcards require a 33p (50¢) stamp. British mail boxes are painted red and carry a royal coat-of-arms as a signature. A letter generally takes about 7 to 10 days to arrive in the U.S. All post offices will accept parcels for mailing providing they are properly and securely wrapped.

Maps   See "Road Maps" in "Getting Around: By Car," above.

Newspapers and Magazines   Each major Scottish city publishes its own newspaper. News is often dominated by local events of little interest to visitors; however, these papers are a good source of information about local happenings and presentations, often cultural. All newsstands carry the major London papers as well. In summer, you can generally pick up a copy of the *International Herald Tribune,* published in Paris, along with the European editions of *USA Today, Time,* and *Newsweek* to bring you up to date on world affairs.

Passports   See "Information, Entry Requirements, and Money," above.

Pets   It is illegal to bring pets into Britain from any other country, except with veterinary documents, and even then they are subject to a quarantine of 6 months. Hotels have their own rules, but generally do not allow dogs in restaurants or public rooms, and often not in bedrooms either.

Police   The best source of help and advice in emergencies is the police (for non-life-threatening situations, dial "0" [zero] and ask for the police, or 999 for emergencies). If the local police can't assist, they will have the address of a person who can. Losses, theft, and other crimes should be reported immediately to the police.

Radio/TV   There are 24-hour radio channels operating throughout the United Kingdom. TV starts around 6am with breakfast TV and educational programs. Lighter entertainment begins around 4 or 5pm, after the children's programs, and continues until around midnight. There are now four television channels—two commercial and two BBC without commercials.

Religious Services   Times of services are posted outside the various places of worship. Scotland is in the main a Protestant nation, but in the larger cities all major faiths are represented. Nearly all the churches in Scotland are hospitable to visitors.

Rest Rooms   These are usually found at signs saying PUBLIC TOILETS. They are clean, often have an attendant, and may be used with confidence. Hotels can be used, but they discourage nonresidents. Garages (filling stations) do not always have facilities for the use of customers. There's no need to tip, except to a hotel attendant.

Safety   Although crime is not a serious problem for the average visitor to Scotland, many areas in and around Glasgow are dangerous, with dozens of muggings reported weekly. Caution should always be taken. Never leave your car unlocked and always protect your valuables. Be aware of your immediate surroundings. Wear a moneybelt and hold on to your camera or purse. It's your responsibility to be aware and be alert even in the most heavily touristed areas.

Shoe Repairs   Many of the large department stores of Britain have "Shoe Bars" where repairs are done while you wait.

Smoking   Banned at an increasing number of places, many bed-and-breakfast houses accept only nonsmokers as guests. Trains have "smokers," and in most buses smoking is allowed in a specially designated section. Some restaurants restrict smoking, as do certain theaters and other public places.

Taxes   There is no local sales tax. However, Great Britain imposes a standard Value-Added Tax (called VAT, for short) of 17½%. Most Common Market countries already have a tax similar to VAT. In Britain, hotel rates and meals in restaurants are taxed 17½%; the extra VAT charge will show up on your bill unless otherwise stated. This VAT is in addition to the service charge; should the service charge be 15%, you will in effect be paying 32½% higher than the prices quoted. The service charges, if included as part of the bill, are also taxable!

As part of an energy-saving scheme, the British government has also added a special 25% tax on gasoline ("petrol").

Telephone, Telex, and Fax   Consult "Directory Enquiries" ("Information") to aid you; dial 192, give the operator the town where you want the number, the subscriber's name, and then the address.

If you're calling from a **pay phone,** the machine will accept all British coins except 1p. A local call costs 10p (20¢). Phone books contain detailed instructions about how to make a call in the British Isles. You can also dial the operator for assistance. There are special phone booths used only by phone-card holders. The phone cards are sold at post offices and at the tourist board in denominations of £1, £2, £10, and £20. You put your card into the phone box and make your call. The card is valid until all its units have been used.

Telexes are mostly restricted to business premises and hotels. If your hotel has a **Telex,** they will send it for you. You may need to arrange the receipt of an expected message in advance. British Telecom sends **telegrams and telemessages.** Depending on your location in Scotland, you dial either 190 or 100 on your phone and ask for the telegram-telemessage service. Telemessages are used for sending messages within the U.K. An overseas telegram is used to reach non-British destinations. If your message is more than 50 words, consider a Mailgram; you must know the zip code, however. Each of the three will usually be delivered the following day, unless a bank holiday intervenes.

Time   Britain is based on Greenwich mean time (GMT), with British summer time (BST, or GMT + 1 hour) used roughly from April to October. When it's noon in Edinburgh or Glasgow it's 7am in New York, 6am in Chicago, 5am in Denver, and 4am in Los Angeles.

Tipping   For **cab drivers,** add about 10% to 15% to the fare as shown on the meter. However, if the driver personally unloads or loads your luggage, add 25p (45¢) per bag.

As to **hotel staff,** porters get 75p ($1.10) per bag. In top-ranking hotels the concierge will often submit a separate bill, showing charges for newspapers and the like; if he or she has been particularly helpful, tip extra.

Hotels often add a service charge of 10% to 15% to bills. In smaller B&Bs, the tip is not likely to be included. Therefore, tip for special services, such as the waiter who serves you breakfast. If several people have served you in a B&B, many guests ask that 10% to 15% be added to the bill and divided among the staff.

In both **restaurants and nightclubs,** a 15% service charge is added to the bill. To that, add another 3% to 5%, depending on the quality of the service. Waiters in deluxe restaurants and nightclubs are accustomed to the extra 5%, which means you'll end up tipping 20%. If that seems excessive, you must remember that the initial service charge reflected in the fixed price is distributed among all the help. Sommeliers (wine stewards) get about £1 ($1.50) per bottle of wine served. Tipping in pubs is not common, although in cocktail bars the waiter or barmaid usually gets about 75p ($1.10) per round of drinks.

For other services, barbers and hairdressers expect 10% to 15%. Tour guides expect £2 ($3), although it's not mandatory. Petrol station attendants are rarely tipped. Theater ushers also don't expect tips, but won't turn one down either.

Tourist Offices   See "Information, Entry Requirements, and Money," in this chapter, and also specific cities and towns in the chapters that follow.

Visas   See "Information, Entry Requirements, and Money," in this chapter.

Water   Tap water is considered safe to drink throughout Scotland.

Weather   Robert Louis Stevenson said it all: "The weather is raw and boisterous in the winter, shifty and ungenial in summer, and downright meteorological purgatory in spring." If you're planning a motor trip for the day, always check the weather forecasts in the local newspapers or listen to the early-morning radio and TV broadcasts. Call 0898/881921 for weather and road conditions about mainland Scotland.

Yellow Pages   Throughout Scotland, local phone books contain yellow pages at the back of the book. If you can't find what you're looking for, you may not be looking under the proper English equivalent. For example, instead of drugstore, try "Chemist" or "Pharmacist."

CHAPTER 3

THE BORDERS & THE SOUTHWEST

- **WHAT'S SPECIAL ABOUT THE BORDERS & THE SOUTHWEST**
1. **JEDBURGH**
2. **KELSO**
3. **MELROSE**
4. **SELKIRK**
5. **INNERLEITHEN**
6. **PEEBLES**
7. **MOFFAT**
8. **DUMFRIES**
9. **CASTLE DOUGLAS**
10. **KIRKCUDBRIGHT**
11. **GATEHOUSE-OF-FLEET**
12. **WHITHORN**
13. **STRANRAER**
14. **PORTPATRICK**

Romantic castle ruins and Gothic skeletons of abbeys in the ballad-rich Borders stand as reminders of the interminable battles that once raged between England and the proud Scots. For a long time the so-called Border Country was a no-man's land, a land of plunder and destruction.

The border country is also the land of Sir Walter Scott, master of romantic adventure, who died in 1832.

Southeastern Scotland contains the remains of four great abbeys built by David I in the mid-12th century: Dryburgh (where Scott was buried), Melrose, Jedburgh, and Kelso.

The Borders are also the home of the cashmere sweater and the tweed suit. Many mills can be visited in the Borders, and you can often find good shopping buys. Nearby mills will accept visitors at certain times of the year (hours likely to vary greatly). Ask, if available, at the local tourist office for a **"Borders Woollen Trail"** brochure, which will explain how you can visit the mills, the museums, and the mill shops. You can see and follow the process of weaving cloth from start to finish.

You can either enter Scotland through the southeast, the Border country, or through Dumfries and Galloway. Southwestern Scotland, part of the famous "Lowlands," is often overlooked by motorists rushing north from the Lake District of England. But this Burns country is filled with rewarding targets, a land of unspoiled countryside, fishing harbors, artists' colonies of color-washed houses, and romantically ruined abbeys and castles dating from the days of the border wars.

It's a fine country for touring, and most of its hotels are of the small, Scottish provincial variety—that usually means a warm welcome from a smiling staff and good traditional Scottish cookery with local produce.

SEEING THE BORDERS & THE SOUTHWEST
GETTING THERE

If you're driving between London and Edinburgh, following a route through the northeast of England, you'll traverse the Borders region, perhaps entering through the Cheviot Hills south of Jedburgh. Trains from London's King's Cross Station (tel. 071/2782477 in London for schedules) run through here to Waverley Station in Edinburgh. Trains enter Scotland at Berwick upon Tweed. From Berwick, a network of local buses runs between the villages and towns.

Dumfries and Galloway don't have a major airport, so the nearest airport is Glasgow Airport, about 75 miles north of Dumfries. Bus travel isn't recommended for reaching the region, but once you are there you'll find it a usually reliable means of transport for getting around. Many of the smaller towns have no rail connections.

☑

WHAT'S SPECIAL ABOUT
THE BORDERS & THE SOUTHWEST

Great Towns/Villages

- ☐ Dumfries, an exceedingly ancient city, the best base for exploring Galloway.
- ☐ Kelso, a historic Borders town, which Sir Walter Scott found "the most beautiful."
- ☐ Kirkcudbright, ancient burgh and intriguing old town, where artists often fill its color-washed houses.
- ☐ Melrose, site of ruined Melrose Abbey and Scott's home at Abbotsford.
- ☐ Peebles, a royal burgh and county town in the Valley of the Tweed, with gardens and castles nearby.
- ☐ Stranraer, largest town in Wigtownshire and the terminal of the 35-mile ferry crossing to Northern Ireland.

Ancient Monuments

- ☐ Jedburgh Abbey, founded by King David in 1147, one of Scotland's finest abbeys.
- ☐ Dryburgh Abbey, now in Gothic ruins, burial place of Sir Walter Scott.
- ☐ Sweetheart Abbey, outside Dumfries, the ruins of a Cistercian abbey founded in 1273, with memories of riches and romance.

Historic Homes and Castles

- ☐ Floors Castle, outside Kelso, designed in 1721 by William Adam and home of the present Duke of Roxburghe.

- ☐ Abbotsford, home of Sir Walter Scott from 1812 until his death, with much memorabilia collected by the novelist.
- ☐ Traquair House, outside Innerleithen, one of the oldest inhabited and most romantic homes of Scotland.
- ☐ Drumlanrig Castle, Thornhill, from the 17th century, a pink castle filled with treasures and paintings (Leonardo to Rembrandt).

Parks and Gardens

- ☐ Threave Garden, outside Castle Douglas, National Trust for Scotland gardens built around a baronial mansion.
- ☐ Dawyck Botanic Garden, outside Peebles, run by the Royal Botanic Garden of Edinburgh.

Literary Shrines

- ☐ Burns Mausoleum, St. Michael's Churchyard, Dumfries, is where Scotland's national poet is buried, in the same town where he composed "Auld Lang Syne."

Three rail lines pass through the region from London's Euston Station (tel. 071/3879400 in London for schedules) en route to Glasgow. Dumfries is the best center if you're traveling by rail. You can also use Stranraer on the west coast. A car is ideal. The principal express highway through the area is the Carlisle–Glasgow route, the A74, cutting north and south.

SUGGESTED ITINERARY

Day 1: From England, make Jedburgh your entry into Scotland and arrive in time to see its abbey and Mary Queen of Scots House. Overnight there.

Day 2: From Jedburgh, continue northeast to Kelso to see its abbey and Floors Castle. If time remains, visit Mellerstein in the environs. Overnight in Kelso.

Day 3: Head for Melrose via Dryburgh, where you can visit Dryburgh Abbey and later see the famous "Scott's View" over the Tweed. Overnight in Melrose after seeing its abbey and motor museum and visiting Abbotsford, Scott's former home on the outskirts.

Day 4: Pass through Innerleithen and pay a visit to Traquair House before proceeding to travel on to Peebles for the night. At Peebles, visit Neidpath Castle and Dawyck Botanic Garden.

Day 5: From Peebles continue south to Moffat for lunch, and overnight in Dumfries.

Day 6: Explore the environs of Dumfries; see Threave Castle and Threave Garden. Overnight in Castle Douglas.

Day 7: Continue southwest to Kirkcudbright, see the town, and enjoy lunch there. In the afternoon do some exploring at Gatehouse-of-Fleet and head for Newton Stewart. From there, drive south to Wigtown, but return to Newton Stewart for the night.

Day 8: Continue west to Stranraer for an overnight stopover, and see Glenluce Abbey along the way. If time remains, pay a late afternoon visit to Portpatrick, where you can also find accommodations for the night if you don't want to stay in Stranraer.

1. JEDBURGH

325 miles N of London, 48 miles SE of Edinburgh

GETTING THERE By Train There is no direct rail link to Jedburgh. The nearest rail station is at Berwick upon Tweed (tel. 0289/306771 in Berwick for rail information, tickets, or schedules). From Berwick you can journey to Jedburgh by bus; call the Tourist Information Office, tel. 0289/330077, for bus schedules.

By Bus Daily buses from Edinburgh arrive at Jedburgh. A bus leaving Edinburgh at 8:50am will arrive at Jedburgh at 10:55am. In Edinburgh, call 031/557-5717 for information.

By Car At Corbridge (England), continue north into Scotland along the A68, using Jedburgh as your gateway town into the Borders.

ESSENTIALS The **tourist office** is at Murray's Green (tel. 0835/63435). The **telephone area code** for Jedburgh is 0835.

Designated a royal burgh by William the Lion in 1165, the little town of Jedburgh, divided by the River Jed, developed around Jedburgh Abbey on a Roman road called Dere Street. Today the market town gives little hint of the turbulence of its early history, brought about by its position in the beleaguered border area.

WHAT TO SEE & DO

JEDBURGH ABBEY, Abbey Place. Tel. 031/244-3101 in Edinburgh for information.

This famous ruined abbey, founded by King David in 1138, is one of the finest in Scotland. Inside is a small museum, containing fragments of medieval works. There is also a Visitors Centre, showing a film of the history of the area. It's in the town center near the police station.

Admission: £2 ($3) adults, £1 ($1.50) children.

Open: Apr–Sept, Mon–Sat 9:30am–6pm or dusk, Sun 2–6pm; Oct–Mar, Mon–Sat 9:30am–4pm.

MARY QUEEN OF SCOTS HOUSE, Queen St. Tel. 0835/63331.

Here she stayed for 6 weeks and almost died after a tiring ride visiting her beloved Bothwell at Hermitage Castle in 1566. The house, in the center off High Street, contains articles dealing with her life (a watch, a communion service, her death mask), paintings, and engravings. She later wrote, "Would that I had died at Jedworth," a reference to her stay in this house. Ancient pear trees still stand on the grounds, a reminder of the days when Jedburgh was famous for its fruit. "Jethard pears" were hawked in the streets of London.

Admission: £1.10 ($1.70) adults, 55p (80¢) children.

Open: Mar–Oct, Mon–Sat 10am–5pm, Sun 1–5pm. **Closed:** Nov–Feb.

CASTLE GAOL, Castlegate. Tel. 0835/63254.

This museum stands today on the site of Jedburgh Castle. When it was opened in 1825 it was considered a "modern reform jail." Now it serves the community as a museum of social history.

Admission: 80p ($1.20) adults, 40p (60¢) children.

Open: Easter–Sept., Mon–Sat 10am–5pm, Sun 1–5pm. **Closed:** Oct–Easter.

WHERE TO STAY

FERNIEHIRST MILL LODGE, Hwy. A68, Jedburgh, Roxburghshire TD8 6PQ. Tel. 0835/63279. 11 rms (8 with bath). TEL **Directions:** Take the A68 2½ miles south of Jedburgh; if notified, car sent to meet clients.

$ Rates (including Scottish breakfast): £21 ($31.50) per person in rooms with or without private bath. MC, V. **Parking:** Free.

This is a modern guest house with a wing containing comfortable but functional bedrooms with pinewood paneling, a lounge, and a breakfast/dining room. A fixed-price dinner is offered for £12.50 ($18.80). Horseback riding (experienced riders only, please) might be a welcome break from motor touring, and costs about £7 ($10.50) per hour. Riding packages are available, but only for equestrians willing to stay for a full week.

JEDFOREST COUNTRY HOUSE HOTEL, Camptown, Jedburgh, Roxburghshire TD8 6PJ. Tel. 08354/274. 12 rms (4 with bath). TV **Directions:** Take the A68 4 miles south of Jedburgh.

$ Rates (including Scottish breakfast): £28 ($42) single without bath, £34 ($51) single with bath; £48 ($72) double without bath, £52 ($78) double with bath. MC, V. **Parking:** Free.

In an idyllic setting, this hotel stands in 30 acres of wooded valley alongside the River Jed. The main house, with steep gables and high ceilings, is 125 years old and contains eight well-furnished rooms. An annex contains four contemporary rooms. All rooms have such amenities as electric blankets, trouser presses, hairdryers, and tea- or coffee-making equipment. The hotel also has a lounge bar with an open coal fireplace where you can order drinks and sample the bar menu or the home-cooked dinner menu. There's also a public bar where you can play pool and darts.

WHERE TO DINE

THE CARTERS' RESTAURANT, Abbey Place. Tel. 0835/63414.

Cuisine: SCOTTISH/CONTINENTAL.

$ Prices: Appetizers £2.10–£3.50 ($3.20–$5.30); main courses £5.50–£11 ($8.30–$16.50); bar lunches from £3.95 ($5.90). AE, MC, V.

Open: Lunch daily noon–2pm; dinner daily 6–9pm.

This pub with a downstairs dining room built of old abbey stones is in a building with a long history—it was a local grammar school from 1779, before finding its present role. This is the favorite gathering place for locals who know that its owner, Michael Wares, serves good food and drink. Soups, bar snacks, and coffee are served daily in the lounge bar. Try filet mignon, stir-fry chicken, and lamb chops Tyrolean.

2. KELSO

44 miles SE of Edinburgh, 68 miles NW of Newcastle upon Tyne, 12 miles E of Melrose

GETTING THERE By Train The nearest rail connection is Berwick upon Tweed, from which you can take a bus to Kelso.

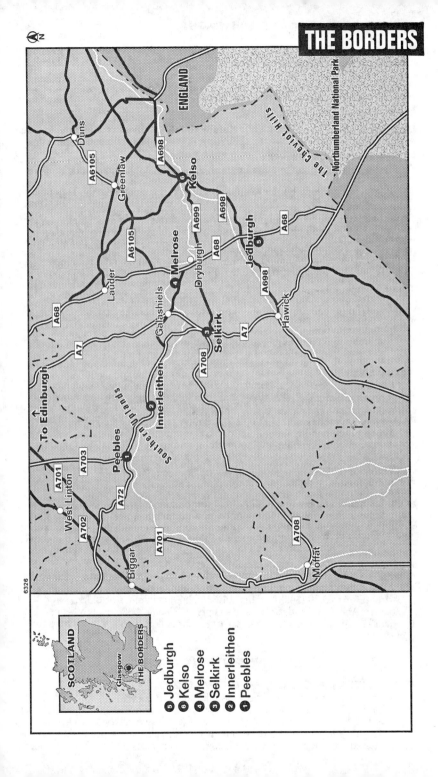

THE BORDERS

N

ENGLAND

Northumberland National Park

The Cheviot Hills

Duns

A6105

Greenlaw

A6105

Lauder

A68

A7

To Edinburgh ←

Southern Uplands

Peebles ❶

A703

A701

A72

West Linton

A702

A701

Biggar

Kelso ❻

A698

A699

A698

Melrose ❹

Dryburgh

A68

A698

Jedburgh ❺

A68

A698

Galashiels

Selkirk ❸

A7

Hawick

Innerleithen ❷

A708

A708

Moffat

6326

SCOTLAND

Glasgow

THE BORDERS

❺ Jedburgh
❻ Kelso
❹ Melrose
❸ Selkirk
❷ Innerleithen
❶ Peebles

By Bus   From Edinburgh, board the bus to Galashiels, with connecting service on to Kelso. In Edinburgh, phone National Express at 031/4528777 for schedules and more information.

By Car   If you're driving from Jedburgh (see above), follow the A698 northeast to Kelso.

ESSENTIALS   The summer-only **Kelso Tourist Office** is at Turret House, Abbey Court (tel. 0573/223464). Call for information about bus schedules from Berwick upon Tweed. The **telephone area code** is 0573.

Another typical historic border town, Kelso lies at the point where the Teviot meets the Tweed. Sir Walter Scott called it "the most beautiful, if not the most romantic, village in Scotland." A settlement that grew up around a river ford, important as the first such crossing place west of Berwick, developed into a town around Kelso Abbey, established in 1128. In 1614, when Robert Ker was created first Earl of Roxburghe, the town became a "burgh of barony."

During the abortive rising of 1715, James Stuart, "the Old Pretender" was proclaimed king as James VIII of Scotland and James III of England in the town marketplace.

Kelso today is a flourishing market town, the center of an agricultural district boasting farming and stock raising, and one of the best centers for touring the Borders.

WHAT TO SEE & DO

KELSO ABBEY.

Once a great ecclesiastical center, Kelso Abbey has lain in ruins since late in the 16th century when it suffered its last and most devastating attack and was declared officially defunct. The lands and remaining buildings were given to the Earl of Roxburghe. It was the oldest (1128) and probably the largest of the Border abbeys, as well as one of the richest, under the Scottish clergy. In 1919 the Duke of Roxburghe gave the abbey to the nation.

Admission: Free.

Open: Apr–Sept, Mon–Sat 9:30am–7pm, Sun 2–7pm; Oct–Mar, Mon–Sat 9:30am–4pm, Sun 2–4pm.

FLOORS CASTLE, on the A697, just north of Kelso. Tel. 0573/23333.

Kelso is the home of the present Duke of Roxburghe, who lives here at Floors Castle, designed in 1721 by William Adam and remodeled in the mid-19th century by William Playfair. Part of the castle, which is open to the public, contains superb French and English furniture, porcelain, tapestries, and paintings by such artists as Gainsborough, Reynolds, and Canaletto. There are a licensed restaurant, coffee shop, and gift shop as well as a walled garden and garden center. The castle was a major location for the Tarzan film *Greystoke*.

Admission: £3.20 ($4.80) adults, £1.60 ($2.40) children 8 or older.

Open: Apr–June and Sept, Sun–Thurs 10:30am–4:45pm; July–Aug, daily 10:30am–4:45pm. Closed Oct–Mar. **Directions:** Follow the signs north from Kelso center.

NEARBY HISTORIC HOMES

MELLERSTAIN, in Gordon. Tel. 0573/410225.

The seat of the earls of Haddington, Mellerstain is most often visited on a day trip from Edinburgh, 37 miles away. One of Scotland's famous Adam mansions, it lies near Bordon, 9 miles northeast of Melrose and 7 miles northwest of Kelso.

Mellerstain enjoys associations with Lady Grisell Baillie, a Scottish heroine whose courage saved her father's life. Lord Haddington is her descendant. William Adam built two wings of the house in 1725, and the main building was designed by his more famous son, Robert, some 40 years later. You will see the interior, with its decorations and ceilings designed by Robert Adam, and the impressive library as well as paintings by old masters and antique furniture. Later, from the garden terrace you can look south to the lake, with the Cheviot Hills in the distance, a panoramic view. Afternoon tea is served, and souvenir gifts are on sale.

Admission: £3 ($4.50) adults, £1.50 ($2.30) children.

Open: May–Sept, Sun–Fri 12:30–4:30pm. **Closed:** Oct–Apr. **Directions:** From Edinburgh, follow the A68 to Earlston, then follow the signs to Mellerstain for another 5 miles. From Kelso, head northwest along the A6089 until you see the signposted turn to the left.

WHERE TO STAY & DINE

EDNAM HOUSE HOTEL, Bridge St., Kelso, Roxburghshire TD5 7HT. Tel. 0573/224168. Fax 0573/226319. 32 rms (all with bath). TV TEL

$ Rates (including Scottish breakfast): £42 ($63) single; £60–£84 ($90–$126) double. MC, V. **Parking:** Free.

The Ednam House Hotel is a conversion of a Georgian house into a hotel often referred to as "that lovely place beside the river." The hotel, lying on the fringe of Kelso, has a good atmosphere, and the bedrooms are well kept, some with river views. Built in 1761, the hotel was purchased from the duke of Roxburghe in 1928, and is one of the finest examples of Georgian architecture in the Borders. A few of the bedrooms are spacious and airy, although late arrivals might be given the more cramped quarters. For those wanting to chance it with the highly unreliable Scottish sun, there is a terrace. A fixed-price dinner costs £16.50 ($24.80).

SUNLAWS HOUSE HOTEL, Hwy. A698, Helton, Kelso, Roxburghshire TD5 8JZ. Tel. 0573/450331. Fax 0573/450611. 22 rms (all with bath), 1 suite. TV TEL **Directions:** Take the A698 3 miles southwest of Kelso.

$ Rates (including Scottish breakfast): £85 ($127.50) single; £128 ($192) double; £135 ($202.50) four-poster room; £155 ($232.50) suite. AE, DC, MC, V. **Parking:** Free.

The manorial walls of this late 19th-century castle rise on 200 acres of woodland, lawns, and gardens. It was built as the family home of the Roxburghe family, who valued its location on the trout-filled Teviot River. In 1982 it was converted, with the blessing of the duke and duchess, into a country hotel. Sunlaws maintains 6 bedrooms in the old stable block and another 16 units in the main house. Amid a subdued but elegant decor, the hotel has four low-burning fireplaces even in summer.

Many guests come for shooting and fishing; others to watch the wildlife, especially deer. A glassed-in conservatory offers clusters of wicker chairs for enjoying drinks or tea when the weather is fine. A tennis court and croquet lawn are on the grounds.

EN ROUTE TO MELROSE VIA DRYBURGH

From Kelso, it's only a short drive on the A699 to **Dryburgh,** where Sir Walter Scott is buried at **Dryburgh Abbey.** From Edinburgh take the A68 to Jedburgh and turn on the B6404 at St. Boswells. These Gothic ruins are surrounded by gnarled yew trees and cedars of Lebanon, said to have been planted there by knights returning from the Crusades. Admission is £2 ($3) for adults, £1 ($1.50) for children under 16. It is open April through September, Monday to Saturday from 9:30am to 6pm and on Sunday from 1:30 to 6pm. From October through March, hours are Monday to Saturday from 9:30am to 4pm and Sunday from 1:30 to 4pm. Near Dryburgh is **"Scott's View,"** over the Tweed to his beloved Eildon Hills, considered one of the most beautiful views in the region. You can see this view by going north from Dryburgh along the B6356 (it's signposted).

The adjoining town is **St. Boswells.** This old village, 40 miles southeast of Edinburgh, stands on the Selkirk-Kelso road, near Dryburgh Abbey. It lies 4 miles east of Melrose and 14 miles west of Kelso.

3. MELROSE

37 miles SE of Edinburgh, 70 miles NW of Newcastle upon Tyne

GETTING THERE By Train The nearest rail connection is Berwick upon Tweed, to which Melrose is linked by bus; call the Tourist Information Office, tel. 0289/330733, for bus schedules.

By Bus From Edinburgh, board the bus to Galashiels, with connecting service to Melrose. In Edinburgh, phone National Express at 031/4528777 for more information.

By Car From Edinburgh, Melrose can be reached by going southeast along the A7, signposted Galashiels. From Kelso, take the A699 west to St. Boswells, and at the junction with A6091 head northwest.

ESSENTIALS A summer-only **tourist office** is open at Priorwood Gardens, near the abbey (tel. 089682/2555). The **telephone area code** is 089682 for 4-figure numbers, 0896 for 6-figure numbers.

Melrose enjoys many associations with Sir Walter Scott, who was instrumental in getting repairs made to the ruins of Melrose Abbey in the early 19th century. In the shadow of the Eildon hills, the town developed around the abbey, in the way towns did in the Middle Ages. In summer, visitors congest the attractive little town, finding it a good center for exploring the border area.

WHAT TO SEE & DO

MELROSE ABBEY, Abbey St. Tel. 089682/2562.
   The beautiful ruins are all that's left of the ecclesiastical community established by Cistercian monks in 1136. The pure Gothic lines of the ruins were made famous by Sir Walter Scott, whose appreciation of the site led to repairs of the decayed remains and made them a popular goal for travelers. The heart of Robert the Bruce was supposed to have been interred in the abbey, although the location is unknown. Look for the beautiful carvings and the tombs of other famous Scotsmen buried in the chancel. In Scott's *The Lay of the Last Minstrel*, the abbey's east window received rhapsodic treatment, and in *The Abbott and the Monastery,* Melrose appears as "Kennaquhair."
   Admission: £1.70 ($2.60) adults, 90p ($1.40) children.
   Open: Apr–Sept, Mon–Sat 9:30am–6:30pm, Sun 2–6:30pm; Oct–Mar, Mon–Sat 9:30am–4:30pm, Sun 2–4:30pm.

A NEARBY ATTRACTION

ABBOTSFORD, Hwy. B6360, Melrose. Tel. 0896/2043.
   This was the home that Sir Walter Scott built and lived in from 1812 until he died. It contains many relics, including one hall filled with spoils the famous author collected from the battlefield at Waterloo. Other exhibits include his clothes and his death mask. Especially interesting is his study, with his writing desk and chair. In 1935 two secret drawers were found in the desk. One of them contained 57 letters, part of the correspondence between Sir Walter and his wife-to-be.
   Admission: £2.50 ($3.80) adults, £1.25 ($1.90) children.
   Open: Apr–Oct, Mon–Sat 10am–5pm, Sun 2–5pm. **Closed:** Nov–Mar. **Directions:** Head just off the A7, south of the junction with the A72, onto the B6360, some 2½ miles southeast of Galashiels.

WHERE TO STAY & DINE

BURT'S HOTEL, Market Sq., Melrose, Roxburghshire TD6 9PN. Tel. 089682/2285. Fax 089682/2870. 21 rms (all with bath or shower). TV TEL

$ Rates (including Scottish breakfast): £39 ($58.50) single; £68 ($102) double. AE, DC, MC, V. **Parking:** Free.

In the center of town, within walking distance of the abbey, this family-run inn offers a taste of small-town Scottish flavor. It was built in 1722 between the main square and a garden, which today sends the aroma of summer greenery into the restaurant. The decor is modern, using pastels for a light, airy feeling. Rooms are restful with a relaxing ambience, and contain radios, hairdryers, and tea- or coffee-making equipment.

There is an attractive bar, offering inexpensive, tasty lunches, with Windsor chairs and a coal-burning fireplace. Bar lunches and suppers range from £5 ($7.50) to £6 ($9). You can also take a table d'hôte lunch in the hotel restaurant for £13.75 ($20.60) and a table d'hôte dinner for £18.50 ($27.80). You can also order à la carte.

4. SELKIRK

40 miles SE of Edinburgh, 73 miles SE of Glasgow

GETTING THERE By Train Take the train to Berwick upon Tweed, the nearest rail connection. Proceed the rest of the way by bus; call the Tourist Information Office, tel. 0289/330733, for bus schedules.

By Bus Buses running between Newcastle upon Tyne and Edinburgh make stops at Selkirk. Most visitors arrive by bus from Edinburgh (tel. 031/4528777 for ticket information and data about departures).

By Car From Edinburgh, head southeast along the A7 to Galashiels, then cut southwest along the B6360. From Melrose, take the B6360 southwest to Selkirk.

ESSENTIALS A summer-only **tourist office** is at Halliwell's House (tel. 0750/20054). The **telephone area code** is 0750.

In the heart of Sir Walter Scott country, this royal burgh and county town can make an ideal center for exploring some of the historic homes in the Borders. It is noted for its tweed industry, and many mills can be visited on day trips. Check with the tourist office (see above) at the time of your visit. Selkirk was the birthplace of the African explorer Mungo Park. Both explorer and novelist are honored with statues.

WHAT TO SEE & DO NEARBY

BOWHILL, Hwy. A708 west of Selkirk. Tel. 0750/20732.

IN THEIR FOOTSTEPS

Sir Walter Scott [1771–1832] This novelist and poet was a master of romantic adventure in a panoramic setting, as exemplified by such works as *Ivanhoe, Rob Roy, Kenilworth,* and *The Bride of Lammermoor.* Troubled by finances and ill health much of his life, he spent his latter years writing to clear his enormous debts.

• **Birthplace:** Born into an old Border family at Edinburgh on August 15, 1771, Scott became permanently lame after an attack of fever in infancy.

• **Residences:** Scott lived at Abbotsford from 1812 until he died, and the home with much memorabilia is open to the public (it lies 2½ miles southeast of Galashiels in the Borders).

• **Favorite Haunts:** Scott's View, near Abbotsford—his beloved lookout point over the River Tweed toward the Eildon Hills, a spot where he found inspiration.

• **Resting Place:** Dryburgh Abbey.

This 18th- and 19th-century Border home of the Scotts, the dukes of Buccleuch, contains a rare art collection, French furniture, porcelain, silverware, and mementos of Sir Walter Scott, Queen Victoria, and the Duke of Monmouth. It also has paintings by Canaletto, Claude, Raeburn, Gainsborough, and Reynolds. There is an Adventure Woodland play area, a Victorian kitchen, an audiovisual presentation, a gift shop, and a tea room/restaurant. Sotheby's Works of Art courses are offered here.

Admission: £3 ($4.50) adults, £1 ($1.50) children.

Open: July only, daily 1–4:30pm. **Closed:** Aug–June. **Directions:** Take the A708 Moffat road 3 miles west of Selkirk.

WHERE TO STAY & DINE

HEATHERLIE HOUSE HOTEL, Heatherlie Park, Selkirk, Selkirkshire TD7 5AL. Tel. 0750/21200. 7 rms (6 with bath). TV

$ Rates (including Scottish breakfast): £19.50 ($29.30) single without bath, £25.50 ($38.30) single with bath; £46 ($69) double with bath. MC, V. **Parking:** Free.

An imposing stone and slate Victorian mansion with steep gables and Victorian turrets, this hotel was built a century ago by a local mill owner. Set in 2 acres of wooded lands, the hotel is west from the center along the Green, only a short walk from the town of Selkirk and local woolen mills. The bedrooms are spotlessly maintained and comfortably furnished.

A coal-burning fireplace adds warmth to the lounge where reasonably priced bar meals are available daily from noon to 9:30pm, and the high-ceilinged dining room is open for dinners in the evening from 5:30 to 9pm. A table d'hôte dinner costs £10 ($15).

---

5. INNERLEITHEN

16 miles W of Melrose, 25 miles S of Edinburgh

GETTING THERE By Train Take the train to Berwick upon Tweed, where you can make bus connections to Innerleithen; call the Tourist Information Office, tel. 0289/330733, for bus schedules.

By Bus From Edinburgh, the Lowland Scottish bus (no. 62) runs here daily.

By Car Take the A7 southeast from Edinburgh, then continue southwest along the B709.

ESSENTIALS The tourist office at Peebles (see below) has data on the area. The **telephone area code** is 0896.

Most visitors know Innerleithen's chief sight, Traquair House, better than they do the town itself. Innerleithen is a modest little mill town east of Peebles. The unmarred beauty of the River Tweed valley as seen from the town's surrounding hillsides remains constant. Ballantyne cashmeres are manufactured here.

WHAT TO SEE & DO

TRAQUAIR HOUSE, along the A72, 16 miles west of Melrose. Tel. 0896/830323.

This place is perhaps the oldest-inhabited and most romantic house in Scotland. Dating back to the 10th century, it is rich in associations with Mary Queen of Scots and, later on, with the Jacobite risings. Its treasures include glass, embroideries, silver, manuscripts, and paintings. Of particular interest is a brewhouse equipped as it was two centuries ago and still used regularly. The great house is lived in by the Stuarts of Traquair. There are craft workshops to be seen on the grounds, as well as a maze and woodland walks.

Admission: £3.50 ($5.30) adults, £1.50 ($2.30) children.

Open: May–June and Sept, daily 1:30–5:30pm; July–Aug, daily 10:30am–5:30pm. **Closed:** Oct–Apr.

WHERE TO STAY & DINE

TRAQUAIR ARMS HOTEL, Innerleithen, Peeblesshire EH44 6PD. Tel. 0896/830229. Fax 0896/830260. 10 rms (all with bath). TV
$ Rates (including Scottish breakfast): £35 ($52.50) single; £54 ($81) double. DC, MC. **Parking:** Free.

This small border-town hostelry was built as a coaching inn around 1780 and has later Victorian additions. Open fires await you in the bar lounge and fresh flowers in the dining room enhance the pleasant surroundings. The hotel also offers comfortably furnished bedrooms with tea/coffee-making facilities and views over the valley. It's within a 5-minute walk of the River Tweed, and salmon and trout fishing can be arranged for guests.

You can relax and enjoy dinner from a table d'hôte menu, which is changed daily, costing £13.50 ($20.30) to £16 ($24). Vegetarian and special diets can be arranged. All dishes are freshly prepared on the premises by the chef/proprietor and his staff. The hotel was a finalist in the "Best Pub Food in Britain" contest in 1993.

AN EXCURSION TO LAUDER

One of the most imposing country houses of Scotland, ✪ **Thirlestane Castle** on the A68 at Lauder in Berwickshire (tel. 05782/430), overlooks Leader Water, about half a mile from town, 10 miles north of Melrose, 28 miles south of Edinburgh on the A68. The castle has been in the ownership of the Lauderdale family since 1218. A T-shaped building, the castle has a keep from around the end of the 16th century. The structure was much altered after Queen Victoria took the throne to begin her long reign. The interior rooms are known for their ornamental plaster ceilings, considered the finest in the country from the Restoration period. In the old nurseries there's a Historic Toy Collection, and "Border Country Life" exhibitions have been installed on the grounds, depicting life in the Borders from prehistoric times until the present. This family home and grounds are open on Easter Sunday and Monday; during May, June, and September on Wednesday, Thursday, and Sunday; and in July and August on Sunday through Friday. The grounds are open from noon to 6pm; the castle and exhibitions, from 2 to 5pm. Admission to the castle, toy collection, and exhibitions is £3 ($4.50) for adults, £2.50 ($3.80) for children, and £7 ($10.50) for a family ticket.

6. PEEBLES

23 miles S of Edinburgh, 53 miles SE of Glasgow, 20 miles W of Melrose

GETTING THERE By Train Trains arrive in Berwick upon Tweed, where bus connections can be made to Peebles.

By Bus Buses between Newcastle upon Tyne and Edinburgh also service Peebles. Most visitors arrive from Edinburgh (phone 031/5575717 there for information about tickets and schedules).

By Car Take the A703 south from Edinburgh.

ESSENTIALS The April-to-November **Peebles Tourist Information Centre** is at Chamber Institute, High Street (tel. 720138). The **telephone area code** is 0721.

This royal burgh and county town is a market center in the Valley of the Tweed. Scottish kings used to come here when they went to hunt in Ettrick Forest. The town is noted for its large woolen mills.

Peebles is also known as a "writer's town." Sir John Buchan (Baron Tweedsmuir), Scottish author and statesman who died in 1940 and is remembered chiefly for writing the adventure story *Prester John* in 1910, lived here. He was also the author of *The Thirty-Nine Steps* (1915), the first of a highly successful series of secret-service thrillers and later a Hitchcock film. In 1935 he was appointed governor-general of Canada. Robert Louis Stevenson once lived at Peebles, and drew upon the surrounding countryside in his novel *Kidnapped*, published in 1886.

WHAT TO SEE & DO

NEIDPATH CASTLE, Tweeddale, on the A72, 1 mile west of Peebles. Tel. 0721/720333.

Located on the north bank of the Tweed, this is an early 14th-century L-shaped tower house. A rock-cut well and a pit prison are inside the 11-foot-thick walls. The castle was besieged by Cromwellian forces in 1650, and soon after the Civil War it was upgraded for 17th-century living. However, by late in the 18th century it had become abandoned by its owner and lived in by tenants. Artifacts found in the castle can be seen, including a tartan display.

Admission: £1.50 ($2.30) adults, 75p ($1.10) children.

Open: Mar 28–Sept, Mon–Sat 11am–5pm, Sun 1–5pm; Oct, Tues only 11am–4pm. **Closed:** Nov–Mar 27.

KAILZIE GARDENS, Kailzie on the B7062, 2½ miles southeast of Peebles. Tel. 0721/7200017.

The 17 acres of formal walled garden, dating from 1812, include a rose garden, woodland, and burnside walks. Restored during the last 20 years, it provides a stunning array of plants from early spring to late autumn, and has a collection of waterfowl and owls. There is an art gallery, a shop, and a restaurant.

Admission: £2 ($3) adults, £1.80 ($2.70) children.

Open: Easter to the end of Oct, daily 11am–5:30pm.

DAWYCK BOTANIC GARDEN, on the B712, 8 miles southwest of Peebles. Tel. 07216/254.

This botanic garden, run by the Royal Botanic Garden in Edinburgh, has a large variety of conifers, some exceeding 100 feet in height, as well as many species of flowering shrubs. There is also a fine display of early spring bulbs, plus pleasant woodwalks rich in wildlife interest.

Admission: £1 ($1.50) adults, 50p (80¢) children.

Open: Mar 15–Oct 22, daily 10am–6pm. **Bus:** Local bus marked "Biggar."

WHERE TO STAY

CRINGLETIE HOUSE HOTEL, Eddleston, Peebles, Peebleshire EH45 8PL. Tel. 0721/730233. Fax 0721/730244. 13 rms (all with bath). TV TEL

$ Rates (including Scottish breakfast): £60 ($90) single; £86 ($129) double. MC, V. **Parking:** Free. **Closed:** Early Jan to mid-Mar.

This imposing country hotel, with towers and turrets, stands on 28 acres of private grounds on the A703, 3 miles north of Peebles. It's like a small French château, built of red sandstone. Your hosts, Mr. and Mrs. Stanley Maguire, receive you in their baronial mansion. The hotel rents spacious and comfortable bedrooms. The public rooms are rich in character and style, as befits a Victorian mansion. There is an elevator as well.

Mrs. Maguire is in charge of the hotel's restaurant. In elegant surroundings, you are given a limited but well-selected choice of dishes, and attentive service. In season the vegetables come fresh from Mrs. Maguire's garden. She has her own style of cooking, and her special dishes include a delectable smoked-haddock mousse. A Sunday luncheon costs £14 ($21), and a four-course dinner, served from 7:30 to 8:30pm, goes for £23.50 ($35.30). Lunch is à la carte Monday through Saturday, costing £5 ($7.50) and up. You should be punctual, because of the short serving hours (the food is freshly cooked), and you'll need a reservation.

THE TONTINE, 39 High St., Peebles, Peebleshire EH45 8AJ. Tel. 0721/ 720892. Fax 0721/729732. 35 rms (all with bath). TV TEL.

$ Rates (including Scottish breakfast): £65 ($97.50) single; £80–£90 ($120–$135) double. AE, DC, MC, V. **Parking:** Free.

The Tontine was originally constructed in 1807 by a group of hunters, who sold shares in its ownership to their friends. Several decades ago it was transformed into a private hotel. Flower boxes adorn its stone lintels and a stone lion guards the fountain in its forecourt. Inside, a cozy and rustic bar, the Tweeddale Shoot Bar, evokes a much older shooting club from the 16th century. The Adam-style dining room is considered one of the architectural gems of Peebles, containing tall fan-topped windows, Scottish antiques, and a minstrel's gallery. The bedrooms are in an angular modern wing built in back of its 19th-century core. Units are equipped with radios and coffee makers. The most expensive rooms have a view of the river.

WHERE TO DINE

THE HORSE SHOE INN, Eddleston. Tel. 0721/730225.
   Cuisine: SCOTTISH. **Reservations:** Not needed.
$ Prices: Appetizers £1.20–£4.95 ($1.80–$7.40); main courses £4.95–£6.55 ($7.40–$9.80). AE, DC, MC, V.
   Open: Lunch Mon–Sat 11:30am–2pm, Sun 12:30–2:30pm; dinner Mon–Sat 5:30–10pm, Sun 6:30–10pm.

In the center of the village of Eddleston, 4½ miles north of Peebles, this country-comfortable place is one of the best in the region for top-quality beef and steaks. Salmon dishes have also made this place popular. Appetizers include everything from the chef's own pâté with oat cakes to smoked Shetland salmon with brown bread. House favorites include steak-and-stout pie, Meldon game pie, and vegetable moussaka. Lunch and dinner are usually served in the bar. On Friday and Saturday nights and on Sunday at lunch, the bar is supplemented with a more formal dining room. Prices in this section rise to £2 ($3) to £7 ($10.50) for appetizers, with main courses costing from £7 ($10.50) to £12 ($18).

---

7. MOFFAT

61 miles S of Edinburgh, 22 miles NE of Dumfries, 60 miles SE of Glasgow

GETTING THERE By Train The nearest railway station is in Lockerbie, 15 miles south of Moffat. Lockerbie's railway station, however, is small and quiet, and access to Lockerbie sometimes requires a change of train in Dumfries. Therefore, passengers from Edinburgh or Glasgow often get off the train at Dumfries, and then transfer to a bus.

By Bus National Express runs buses from Dumfries to Moffat four or five times a day, depositing them on the town's High Street after a 30-minute ride. The same company also runs buses from Lockerbie to Moffat, which visit four times a day. Call 0387/53496 in Dumfries for more information.

By Car   From Dumfries, head northeast along the A701; from Edinburgh, head south along the A701.

ESSENTIALS   A summer-only **tourist information center** is at Churchgate (tel. 0683/20620). The **telephone area code** is 0683.

An Annandale town, Moffat thrives as a center of a sheep-farming area, symbolized by a statue of a ram on the wide High Street. It has been a holiday resort since mid-17th century, because of the curative properties of its water. It was here that Robert Burns composed the drinking song "O Willie Brew'd a Peck o' Maut." Today people visit this town on the banks of the Annan River for its good fishing and golf.

North of Moffat is spectacular hill scenery. Five miles northwest is a huge, sheer-sided 500-foot-deep hollow in the hills called the **Devil's Beef Tub,** where border cattle thieves, called *reivers*, hid cattle lifted in their raids.

Northeast along Moffat Water, past White Coomb, which stands 2,696 feet high, is the **Grey Mare's Tail,** a 200-foot hanging waterfall formed by the Tail Burn dropping from Loch Skene. It is under the National Trust for Scotland.

WHERE TO STAY & DINE

ANNANDALE ARMS, High St., Moffat, Dumfriesshire DG10 9HF. Tel. 0683/20013. Fax 0683/21395. 17 rms (11 with bath). TV TEL
$ Rates (including Scottish breakfast): £26 ($39) single without bath; £40 ($60) single with bath; £40 ($60) double without bath; £58 ($87) double with bath. MC, V. **Parking:** Free.

The Annandale Hotel has been a coaching inn since the 18th century, housing travelers who crossed through the Border Country en route to Edinburgh. However, the inn has been modernized and the rooms, including the public ones, are immaculately kept. The proprietors have built a good reputation for their cuisine, which includes Scottish specialties. The last dinner is served at 9pm, at a cost of £12 ($18) and up. It's in the center of town, but provides ample car parking on its own grounds.

AUCHEN CASTLE HOTEL, Beattock, Dumfriesshire DG10 9SH. Tel. 06833/407. Fax 06833/667. 24 rms (all with bath). TV TEL **Directions:** Take the A74, 2 miles north of Moffat.
$ Rates (including continental breakfast): £47.50 ($71.30) single; £52–£70 ($78–$105) double. MC, V. **Parking:** Free.

Near the village of Beattock, the most luxurious accommodations in the area are found at the Auchen Castle Hotel, a Victorian mock-castle, really a charming country house built on the site of Auchen Castle, with terraced gardens, a trout-filled loch, and vistas from its windows. The bedrooms are often spacious and invariably comfortable. Fourteen of the hotel's 24 rooms are in the main house (known as the castle), whereas the remaining 10 are in the Cedar Lodge, an annex built on the grounds in the late 1970s.

The lofty dining room overlooks ornamental grounds that flower in late spring. Simple dishes such as Scottish roast beef are appetizingly prepared. The well-appointed tables and efficient staff complement the atmosphere. Lunch (bar lunches only) is daily from noon to 2pm and dinner from 7 to 9pm; a dinner goes for £16.70 ($25.10).

BEECHWOOD HOTEL, Harthope Place, Moffat, Dumfriesshire DG10 9RS. Tel. 0683/20210. Fax 0683/20889. 7 rms (all with bath). TV TEL
$ Rates (including Scottish breakfast): £46.90 ($70.40) single; £66.90 ($100.40) double. AE, MC, V. **Parking:** Free.

The Beechwood Hotel was originally built as the 19th-century headquarters of "Miss Thompson's Private Adventure Boarding Establishment and School for Young Ladies." Today it is a charming country hotel and restaurant. It lies behind a dark facade of chiseled stone at the end of a narrow rural lane at the north end of town between the local church and school.

A "tea lawn," smooth as a putting green, is the site for outdoor refreshments on sunny days. Each of the bedrooms has a certain amount of homespun charm. If you just want to stop in for a meal (and you'll be welcome if you phone in advance), lunch is daily from noon to 1:30pm; dinner, from 7:30 to 9pm. A fixed-price dinner costs £18 ($27).

MOFFAT HOUSE HOTEL, High St., Moffat, Dumfriesshire DG10 9HL. Tel. 0683/20039. Fax 0683/21288. 20 rms (all with bath). TV TEL
$ Rates (including Scottish breakfast): £45 ($67.50) single; £68 ($102) double. Half board £51.50–£62.50 ($77.30–$93.80) per person. AE, DC, MC, V. **Parking:** Free.

The Moffat House Hotel is considered one of the town's most architecturally noteworthy buildings—it was constructed in 1751 by John Adam. It sits in a garden in the center of town behind a chiseled facade of red and black stone, with a pair of symmetrical wings stretching out on either side. Ancient trees shelter its rear. Each of the modernized bedrooms contains comfortable and functional furniture.

The hotel offers some of the best food in town, especially at night when the chef prepares an international menu. Bar suppers are served Monday through Thursday from 6 to 9pm and on Friday through Sunday from 5 to 9:30pm. However, dinner in the regular restaurant, costing from £15 ($22.50), is served from 7 to 8:45pm only, and is likely to feature a bill of fare including a haunch of venison, mallard duck in cherry sauce, and fresh salmon.

---

8. DUMFRIES

80 miles SW of Edinburgh, 79 miles SE of Glasgow, 34 miles NW of Carlisle

GETTING THERE   By Train   Seven trains per day make the run from Glasgow's Central Station, taking 1¾ hours. A one-way ticket is £11 ($16.50) but only £12.50 ($18.80) round-trip. For 24-hour information about departures, call 041/2042844 in Glasgow.

By Bus   Western Scottish Buses depart from both Glasgow's Buchanan Street Station and Anderston Station; a one-way fare is £6.50 ($9.80). Buses also run down from Edinburgh's St. Andrew's Square, a one-way ticket costing £5 ($7.50). For complete bus information into Dumfries, call the bus station information center there (tel. 0387/53496).

By Car   From Edinburgh, take the A701 to Moffat, then continue southwest to Dumfries. From Glasgow, take the M74, which becomes the A74 before it approaches Moffat. At Moffat, continue southwest along the A701.

ESSENTIALS   The **tourist information office** is at Whitesands (tel. 0387/53862). The **telephone area code** is 0387.

A county town and royal burgh, this Scottish Lowland center enjoys associations with Robert Burns and James Barrie. In a sense it rivals Ayr as a mecca for Burns admirers. He lived in Dumfries from 1791 until his death in 1796. Here he wrote some of his best-known songs, including "Auld Lang Syne" and "Ye Banks and Braes of Bonnie Doon." A statue of Burns stands on High Street. Barrie was a pupil at the Academy, and he later wrote that he got the idea for *Peter Pan* from his games in the nearby garden.

At the Whitesands, four bridges span the Nith. The earliest of these was built by Devorgilla Balliol, widow of John Balliol. Their son, John Balliol was Scotland's "vassal king," after Edward I of England, "Hammer of the Scots," had established himself as Scotland's overlord. The bridge originally had nine arches, but now has six and is still in constant use as a footbridge.

The wide esplanade was once the scene of horse and hiring fairs and now is a fine place to park your car and explore the town.

WHAT TO SEE & DO

In **St. Michael's Churchyard,** a burial place for at least 900 years, stands the **Burns Mausoleum.** The poet is buried there along with his wife, Jean Armour, as well as five of their children. Burns died in 1796, but his remains weren't moved to the tomb until 1815. In the 18th-century Church of St. Michael you can still see the pew used by the Burns family.

St. Michael's Church on St. Michael's Street is the original parish church of Dumfries and its founding is of great antiquity. The site was probably sacred before the advent of Christianity. It appears that a Christian church has stood there for more than 1,300 years. The earliest written records date from the reign of William the Lion (1165–1214). The church and the churchyard are interesting to visit because of all its connections with Scottish history, continuing through World War II.

The **Mid Steeple** on High Street was built in 1707 as municipal buildings, courthouse, and prison. The old Scots "ell" measure of 37 inches is carved on the front of the building. A table of distances on the building includes the mileage to Huntingdon, England, which in the 18th century was the destination for Scottish cattle drovers driving their beasts south for the markets of London.

DUMFRIES MUSEUM, Church St. Tel. 0387/53374.

The largest museum in southwestern Scotland, the Dumfries Museum is in a converted 18th-century windmill on top of Corbelly Hill. The **Camera Obscura,** on the upper floor of the museum, provides panoramic views of the town and surrounding countryside.

Admission: Museum, free; Camera Obscura, 70p ($1.10) adults, 35p (50¢) children.

Open: Museum, Apr–Sept, Mon–Sat 10am–1pm and 2–5pm, Sun 2–5pm; Oct–Mar, Tues–Sat 10am–1pm and 2–5pm. Camera Obscura, Apr–Sept, Mon–Sat 10am–1pm and 2–5pm, Sun 2–5pm. **Closed:** Oct–Mar. **Directions:** Cross the river at St. Michael's Bridge Road and turn right onto Church Street.

BURNS HOUSE, Burns St. Tel. 0387/55297.

Scotland's national poet died in this house off St. Michael's Street. The simple, unpretentious stone structure contains personal relics and mementos of the poet.

Admission: 70p ($1.10) adults, 35p (50¢) children.

Open: Apr–Sept, Mon–Sat 10am–1pm and 2–5pm, Sun 2–5pm; Oct–Mar, Tues–Sat 10am–1pm and 2–5pm.

OLD BRIDGE HOUSE, Mill Rd. at Devorgilla's Bridge. Tel. 0387/56904.

This building dates from 1662, and has been restored and furnished in a style typical of its era. Devorgilla's Bridge itself was constructed in the 15th century.

Admission: Free.

Open: Apr–Sept, Mon–Sat 10am–1pm; Sun 2–5pm. **Closed:** Oct–Mar. **Directions:** From Whitesands, cross the river at Devorgilla's Bridge.

ROBERT BURNS CENTRE, Mill Rd. Tel. 0387/64808.

On the banks of the River Nith you'll find this converted 18th-century watermill. Facilities include an exhibition on the poet, a café, and an audiovisual theater showing films about Burns and the town of Dumfries.

Admission: Exhibition, free; audiovisual theater, 70p ($1.10) adults, 35p (50¢) children.

Open: Apr–Sept, Mon–Sat 10am–8pm, Sun 2–5pm; Oct–Mar, Tues–Sat 10am–

DUMFRIES & GALLOWAY

Milleur Point
Loch Ryan
Stranraer
Portpatrick
Cairnryan
Barrhill
Carsphairn
Galloway Forest Park
Newton Stewart
Glenluce
Luce Bay
Port William
Moll of Galloway
Wigtown
Whithorn
Wigtown Bay
Burrow Head
Gatehouse of Fleet
New Galloway
Loch Ken
Castle Douglas
Kirkcudbright
Dalbeattie
Dumfries
Thornhill
Moffat
Lockerbie
Annan
Solway Firth

701
709
74
75
76
702
710
711
712
713
714
715
716
746
747
77
78
6327

① Moffat
② Dumfries
③ Castle Douglas
④ Kirkcudbright
⑤ Gatehouse-of-Fleet
⑥ Whithorn
⑦ Stranraer
⑧ Portpatrick

SCOTLAND
Edinburgh

1pm and 2–5pm. **Directions:** From Whitesands, cross the river at Devorgilla's Bridge.

NEARBY ATTRACTIONS

Based in Dumfries, you can set out on treks in all directions. South on the 710 leads to the village of New Abbey, dominated by the red sandstone ruins of ☼ **Sweetheart Abbey,** the Cistercian abbey founded in 1273 by Devorgilla Balliol. When her husband, John Balliol the Elder, died, she became one of the richest women in Europe. Most of Galloway, as well as estates and castles in England and land in Normandy, belonged to her. Devorgilla founded Balliol College, Oxford, in her husband's memory. She kept his embalmed heart in a silver and ivory casket by her side for 21 years until her death in 1289 at the age of 80, when she and the casket were buried beside Balliol in front of the abbey altar. The abbey gained the name of "Dulce Cor," Latin for "sweet heart," a term that has become a part of the English language.

Built into a wall of a cottage in the village is a rough piece of sculpture showing three women rowing a boat—an allusion to the bringing of sandstone across the Nith to build the abbey.

Directly south from New Abbey on the A710 to Southerness are the **Abigland Gardens** at Kirkbean (tel. 038788/283), 15 miles southwest of Dumfries. This is where John Paul Jones, "father" of the American Navy, was born. You can visit the woodland with its water gardens arranged around a secluded bay, walking in the pathways where the great admiral once worked as a boy. The gardens are open May through September, Tuesday to Sunday from 2 to 6pm, charging adults £2 ($3); children pay 50p (80¢). There's a tea room.

Alternatively, you can head south from Dumfries for 8 miles on the B725 to **Caerlaverock Castle,** near the mouth of the River Nith, 2 miles south from Glencaple. Once the seat of the Maxwell family, this impressive ruined fortress dates back to the 1270s. The castle is triangular with round towers. The interior was reconstructed in the 17th century as a Renaissance mansion, with fine carving. The castle is open April through September, Monday to Saturday from 9:30am to 6:30pm and on Sunday from 2 to 6:30pm; October through March, Monday to Saturday from 9:30am to 4:30pm and on Sunday from 2 to 4:30pm. Admission is £1.20 ($1.80) for adults, 60p (90¢) for children. A Western Scottish bus (#721) goes from Dumfries to Caerlaverock Castle at the rate of 5 per day, but not on Sunday.

Near the castle is the **Caerlaverock National Nature Reserve** between the River Nith and Lochar Water. It's a noted winter haunt of wildfowl, including barnacle geese.

After leaving the castle, continue east along the A725 to the village of **Ruthwell,** about 10 miles southeast of Dumfries. There, at the early 19th-century Ruthwell Church, you'll see one of the most outstanding crosses of the Dark Ages. Standing 18 feet high, the cross is believed to date from the 8th century. Engraved with carvings, it bears the earliest-known specimen of written English (a Christian poem in Runic characters).

North from Dumfries via the A76 is **Ellisland Farm** (tel. 038774/426), where from 1788 to 1791 Robert Burns made his last attempt at farming. The present occupants of the house will show you through the Burns Room. At this farm Burns wrote "Tam o'Shanter." Admission is free, but visitors are asked to call for an appointment.

Continuing north, still on the A76, you reach **Thornhill,** a country resort—familiar to Burns—overlooking the River Nith. From here it's possible to branch out for excursions in many directions.

The main target is ☼ **Drumlanrig Castle,** Thornhill DG3 4AQ (tel. 0848/30248), the seat of the dukes of Buccleuch and Queensberry, built between 1679 and 1689. It lies 3 miles north of Thornhill, off the A76 and 16 miles southwest of the A74 at Elvanfoot. This pink castle contains some outstanding paintings, including a famous Rembrandt, a Leonardo da Vinci, and a Holbein, and relics related to Bonnie Prince Charlie. The castle stands in a parkland ringed by wild hills, and there's even an "Adventure Woodland Playground." The gardens are gradually being restored to their

1720 magnificence. There's a working crafts center in the old stable yard, with independent craft workers in a variety of skills. Meals are served in the old kitchen hung with gleaming copper. The castle and park are open May through August, Monday to Saturday from 11am to 5pm, and on Sunday from 1 to 5pm. The castle closes on Thursday, although the park remains open. Admission is £4 ($6) for adults and £2.50 ($3.80) for children.

WHERE TO STAY

CAIRNDALE HOTEL AND LEISURE CLUB, 132–136 English St., Dumfries, Dumfrieshire DG1 2DF. Tel. 0387/54111, or toll free in the U.S. 800/INTER 50. Fax 0387/50555. 76 rms (all with bath), 3 suites. TV TEL
$ Rates (including Scottish breakfast): £45–£65 ($67.50–$97.50) single; £75–£85 ($112.50–$127.50) double; from £99 ($148.50) suite. AE, DC, MC, V. **Parking:** Free.

The Cairndale Hotel is a fine and substantial choice. Its bedrooms have been attractively decorated, with special care paid to modern amenities. All contain clock-radio alarms, hairdryers, and hot-beverage facilities. Executive rooms and suites also contain queen-size beds, minibars, trouser presses, and whirlpool baths, and the public lounges are handsomely decorated.

You have a choice of two bars, and guests quickly decide which one they'll make their "local." Dinner, served until 9pm, is generally quite good, including roast sirloin of Galloway beef, Arbroath smokies, mealed herring with Arran sauce, or perhaps Ecclefechan flan with Drambuie cream. A three-course table d'hôte lunch goes for £8.50 ($12.80) and a four-course dinner costs £14.95 ($22.40). In addition, a Continental Café Bar overlooks the hotel's heated indoor swimming pool, and The Forum offers light snacks and refreshments daily. A carvery restaurant, Sawney Bean's Bar and Grill, serves tasty bar snacks, lunches, and dinners as well. Regular entertainment May through October includes a dinner dance on Saturday and a popular Cairndale Ceilidh and "Taste of Scotland" dinner every Sunday night with a piper, accordionist, drummer, soloist, and Highland dancer. The hotel is owned and managed by the Wallace family, who also run their own butcher business. A Leisure Center includes a swimming pool, sauna, steam room, spa bath, solarium, health and beauty salon, gym, and bar and grill.

STATION HOTEL, 49 Lovers Walk, Dumfries, Dumfriesshire DG1 1LT. Tel. 0387/54316. Fax 0387/50388. 32 rms (all with bath). TV TEL
$ Rates (including Scottish breakfast): £65 ($97.50) single; £75–£80 ($112.50–$120) double. AE, DC, MC, V. **Parking:** Free.

The Station Hotel is among the most traditional of Dumfries, a few steps from the gingerbread-fringed train station. Built of hewn sandstone at the turn of the century, its design of heavy timbers, polished paneling, soaring ceilings, and open fireplaces reminds visitors of alpine hotels in Switzerland. However, the welcome and dinner menu at the Dining Room are purely Scottish (see "Where to Dine," below). Before dinner, drinks can be enjoyed in the lounge bar, followed by dinner in a high-ceilinged room framed on one side with bay windows overlooking century-old trees and the station. The modernized bedrooms are accessible via long corridors of old-fashioned design. Each contains a tea maker, comfortable bed, and electric trouser press.

WHERE TO DINE

BRUNO'S, 3 Balmoral Rd. Tel. 0387/55757.
   Cuisine: ITALIAN. **Reservations:** Required Sat–Sun.
$ Prices: Appetizers £1.50–£7.50 ($2.30–$11.30); main courses £7.95–£15 ($11.90–$22.50); three-course fixed-price dinner £14.50 ($21.80); £5.95 ($8.90) pasta supper menu. MC, V.
   Open: Dinner only, Wed–Mon 6:30–10pm.

It may seem ironic to recommend an Italian restaurant in the heart of Rabbie Burns territory, in the town center across from Balmoral Hotel, but Bruno's serves some of the best food in town. It is most unassuming, but that's part of its charm. The chef's repertoire is familiar: First-rate minestrone, homemade pastas, saltimbocca alla romana and pollo alla diavolo, but it's done with a certain flair. The veal is particularly tender, and the tomato sauce well spiced and blended. Bruno's serves only dinner and a special three-course menu is very popular with customers.

THE DINING ROOM/SOMEWHERE ELSE BISTRO, in the Station Hotel, Lovers Walk. Tel. 0387/54316.
 Cuisine: SCOTTISH/INTERNATIONAL. **Reservations:** Recommended.
$ Prices: Dining Room, appetizers £1.50–£5.80 ($2.30–$8.70); main courses £7.30–£15 ($11–$22.50); fixed-price dinner £14.50 ($21.80). Bistro, appetizers £1.25–£3.50 ($1.90–$5.30); main courses £6–£10 ($9–$15); fixed-price carvery lunch (two courses) £6.50 ($9.80). AE, DC, MC, V.
 Open: Dining Room, dinner only, daily 7–9pm (last order). Bistro, lunch daily noon–2pm; dinner daily 5–10pm.

The Dining Room of what was once the grand hotel of Dumfries still lives up to high standards, within a room whose dimensions and detailing evokes the Edwardian age. From its big windows you'll have a view of the ornate Victorian gingerbread of the nearby train station. The table d'hôte dinner includes a satisfying array of such dishes as chicken "whisky sour," and local trout in a sauce of smoked salmon and mushrooms.

Lunches and less formal evening meals are served in the cellar-level Bistro, which has an entrance of its own around the back of the hotel. There, simple but savory dishes include grilled sausages and steaks, selections of traditional roasts, fish dishes, and such lighthearted bistro food as salads and vegetarian dishes. Everywhere, you'll get an idea of the social life that pervades this closely knit town.

BURNS'S FAVORITE "HOWFF"

GLOBE INN, 56 High St. Tel. 0387/52335.
 Cuisine: SCOTTISH. **Reservations:** Not needed.
$ Prices: Appetizers 85p–£1.50 ($1.30–$2.30); main courses £1.75–£3.50 ($2.60–$5.30); bar lunch from £4 ($6). No credit cards.
 Open: Mon–Fri 11am–11pm; Sat 11am–midnight; Sun 12:30–11pm.

This was a favorite haunt of Burns, who used an old Scottish expression, *howff*, meaning a small, cozy room, to describe his local. He not only imbibed here, but had a child with the barmaid, Anna Park. The pub, in business since 1610, is reached down a narrow flagstone-paved passageway off High Street opposite the Marks & Spencer Department Store. You can go here for lunch, drinks, or to play a nightly game of dominoes. A little museum is devoted to Burns, and on window panes upstairs you can see verses he scratched with a diamond. In this convivial atmosphere, you can order cooked bar lunches. The menu includes such items as kipper's pâté, haggis, mealed herring, and Globe steak pie. Food is served only Monday through Saturday at lunchtime, lasting from noon to 3pm. No food is served at night or on Sunday.

---

9. CASTLE DOUGLAS

16 miles SW of Dumfries, 98 miles SW of Edinburgh, 49 miles SE of Ayr

GETTING THERE By Train The nearest railway station is in Dumfries, and everyone in Castle Douglas makes good use of it. Trains arrive in Dumfries from all over Britain, especially from Glasgow. Call 0387/55115 in Dumfries for information.

By Bus There are buses from Dumfries to Castle Douglas every hour throughout the day and early evening; travel time is about 30 minutes. The buses are maintained by the Great Western Bus Co. Call 0387/53496 in Dumfries for more information.

By Car From Dumfries, head southwest along the A75.

ESSENTIALS A summer-only **tourist information center** is at Markethill (tel. 0556/2611). The **telephone area code** is 0556.

An old cattle- and sheep-market town, Castle Douglas, at the northern tip of Carlingwark Loch, makes a good touring center for Galloway. On one of the islets in the loch is an ancient lake dwelling known as a "crannog."

WHAT TO SEE & DO

Unique in the country, **Orchardton Tower,** off the A711, 5½ miles southeast of Castle Douglas, is an example of a round tower house. It was constructed around 1450 by John Cairns, and if you ask the custodian, who lives at the cottage nearby, you can see inside. This is the only round tower in Scotland (they were usually built in Ireland). Later on, the site was purchased by a member of the Maxwell family. The adventures of one family member, Sir Robert Maxwell of Orchardton, a fervent Jacobite who was captured in the Battle of Culloden, figured in Sir Walter Scott's novel *Guy Mannering*. Admission is free.

The **Mote of Urr,** off the B794, 5 miles northeast of Castle Douglas, is a circular mound enclosed by a deep trench. Students of history will know that this is an example of the motte-and-bailey–type defense popular in Norman days.

THREAVE CASTLE, 1½ miles west of Castle Douglas on an islet in the River Dee.
The favorite excursion is to Threave Castle, the ruined 14th-century stronghold of the Black Douglases. The four-story tower was built between 1639 and 1690 by Archibald the Grim, Lord of Galloway. In 1455 Threave Castle was the last Douglas stronghold to surrender to James II, who employed "Mons Meg" (the famous cannon now in Edinburgh Castle) in its subjection. Over the doorway projects the "gallows knob" from which the Douglases hanged their enemies. The castle was captured by the Covenanters in 1640 and dismantled.

Owned by the National Trust, the site must be reached by a half-mile walk through farmlands, and then by small boat across the Dee. A ferry charge of £1 ($1.50) for adults and 50p (80¢) for children is the only alternative to that long walk. Last sailing to the castle is at 6pm. For information, get in touch with 20 Brandon St., Edinburgh (tel. 031/2443087).

Admission: Free.
Open: Apr–Sept, Mon–Sat 9:30am–6:30pm, Sun 2–6:30pm. **Closed:** Oct–Mar.

THREAVE GARDEN, off the A75. Tel. 0556/2575.
A mile southeast of the castle, the gardens are built around Threave House, a Scottish baronial mansion. It is under the protection of the National Trust for Scotland, which uses it as a school for gardening and a wildfowl refuge. The garden is at its best in April when the daffodils bloom, and in June when rhodendrons and the rock garden are in flower. There is a visitor center and a restaurant.

Admission: £2.80 ($4.20) adults, £1.40 ($2.10) children.
Open: Garden, daily 9am–sunset; visitor center, daily 9am–5:30pm. **Directions:** Take the A75 half a mile west of Castle Douglas.

WHERE TO STAY & DINE

DOUGLAS ARMS, King St., Castle Douglas, Kirkcudbrightshire DG7 1DB. Tel. 0556/2231. Fax 0556/4000. 25 rms (16 with bath). TV TEL
$ Rates (including Scottish breakfast): £24 ($36) single without bath; £29.50 ($44.30) single with bath; £44 ($66) double without bath; £52 ($78) double with bath. MC, V. **Parking:** Free.
The Douglas Arms is a 200-year-old coaching inn, but it has been turned into a modernized hotel, right in the center of town. Behind a rather stark, two-story facade, the public rooms are bright and cheerful, giving you a toasty feeling on a cold night. Bedrooms have color-coordinated schemes. Dinner is served until 9pm, and of course,

trout and salmon are featured along with good beef and lamb. An à la carte dinner begins at £13 ($19.50).

KING'S ARMS, St. Andrew's St., Castle Douglas, Kirkcudbrightshire DG7 1EL. Tel. 0556/2626. Fax 0556/2097. 10 rms (8 with bath).

$ Rates (including Scottish breakfast): £18 ($27) single without bath, £22 ($33) single with bath; £36 ($54) double without bath, £40 ($60) double with bath. AE, DC, MC, V. **Parking:** Free.

Ⓢ Open all year, this longtime inn provides good accommodations ranging from rooms for single travelers to families. Each bedroom is well furnished and comfortable, and eight are equipped with TVs and phones. A sun patio for tea or coffee, perhaps a "sundowner" of malt whisky, is also provided. Guests can enjoy bar snacks during the day and fixed-price or à la carte menus in the dining room at night. The cuisine is essentially British, with a natural emphasis on Scotland. The range of food offered is extensive, featuring local produce when possible, including Solway salmon and succulent Galloway beef. Prices range from £3.50 ($5.30) for bar snacks to £16 ($24) and up for dinner. There is also a reasonably priced selection of wines available in one of three bars. The helpful staff will direct you to various activities in the area, including a nine-hole golf course within a 45-minute drive.

---

10. KIRKCUDBRIGHT

108 miles SW of Edinburgh, 28 miles SW of Dumfries, 50 miles E of Stranraer, 10 miles SW of Castle Douglas

GETTING THERE **By Train** Go to Dumfries (see above), then proceed by bus the rest of the way.

By Bus Kirkcudbright lies on the same bus route that serves Castle Douglas from Dumfries, with departures during the day about once per hour. For bus information in Dumfries, call 0387/53496.

By Car From Castle Douglas (see above), continue along the A75 southwest until you come to the junction with the A711, which you take into Kirkcudbright.

ESSENTIALS An Easter to October **tourist information office** is at Harbour Square (tel. 30494). The **telephone area code** is 0557.

Ｓtewartry's most ancient burgh, Kirkcudbright (pronounced "Kir-*coo*-bree") lies at the head of Kirkcudbright Bay on the Dee estuary. This intriguing old town's color-washed houses are inhabited, in part, by artists. There is a lively group of weavers, potters, and painters who live and work in the 18th-century streets and lanes.

WHAT TO SEE & DO

In the old town graveyard are memorials to Covenanters and to Billy Marshall, the tinker king who died in 1792 at the age of 120, reportedly having fathered four children after the age of 100.

McLellan's Castle, built in 1582 for the town's provost, Sir Thomas McLellan, dominates the center of town. This castellated mansion has been a ruin since 1752. Lying off High Street, it is open April through September, Monday to Saturday from 9:30am to 6pm and on Sunday from 2 to 6pm; off-season, to 4pm. Admission is £1 ($1.50) for adults and 50p (80¢) for children.

The **Tolbooth,** a large building, dates back to the 16th and 17th centuries, and in front of it is a **Mercat Cross** of 1610. The Tolbooth is a memorial to John Paul Jones (1747–1792), the gardener's son from Kirkbean who became a slave trader, a privateer, and in due course, the father of the American Navy. For a time before his emigration he was imprisoned for murder in the Tolbooth.

Art exhibitions are regularly sponsored at **Broughton House,** High Street (tel. 0557/30437), a 17th-century mansion that once belonged to E. A. Hornel, the artist. The house contains a large reference library with a Burns collection, along with pictures by Hornel and other artists, plus antiques and other works of art. You can stroll through its beautiful garden. Broughton House is open from Easter to mid-October, Wednesday to Monday from 11am to 1pm and 2 to 5pm; in winter, by prior arrangement only. Admission is £1.50 ($2.30) for adults, 50p (80¢) for children.

In addition, the **Stewartry Museum**, St. Mary Street, in Kirkcudbright (tel. 0557/31643), contains a fascinating collection of antiquities, depicting the history and culture of Galloway. In March and April it is open Monday to Saturday from 11am to 4pm; May through June, Monday to Saturday from 11am to 5pm; July through August, Monday to Saturday from 11am to 7:30pm and on Sunday from 2 to 5pm; September, Monday to Saturday from 11am to 5pm; October, Monday to Saturday from 11am to 4pm; and November through February, Saturday only, 11am to 4pm. Admission is £1 ($1.50) for adults and free for children.

WHERE TO STAY

SELKIRK ARMS, Old High St., Kirkcudbright, Kirkcudbrightshire DG6 4JG. Tel. 0557/30402. Fax 0557/31639. 15 rms (all with bath/shower). TV TEL

$ Rates (including Scottish breakfast): £42 ($63) single; £69 ($103.50) double. AE, DC, MC, V. **Parking:** Free.

The Selkirk Arms, where Robert Burns stayed when he composed the celebrated "Selkirk Grace," has an inviting atmosphere and a helpful staff. Bedrooms have been recently refurbished, and all have tea/coffee makers. The restaurant offers a wide range of fresh local produce; bar lunches and suppers are also available. The lounge bar features an array of malt whiskies. The hotel has ample parking and a spacious garden in the rear. The neighborhood evokes memories of John Paul Jones. Little art galleries display the works of local painters.

WHERE TO DINE

AULD ALLIANCE RESTAURANT, 5 Castle St. Tel. 0557/30569.
Cuisine: SCOTTISH/FRENCH. **Reservations:** Essential.
$ Prices: Appetizers £2.60–£5.20 ($3.90–$7.80); main dishes £7.50–£15 ($11.30–$22.50). No credit cards.
Open: Dinner only, daily 6:30–9pm (last booking). **Closed:** Halloween–Easter.

⑤ One of the most appealing restaurants in the region is this family-owned and -operated restaurant whose owners are almost obsessed with the freshness of the fish they serve. Located in a 19th-century building whose walls were built with stones from the ruins of Kirkcudbright Castle, a minute's walk from the town's harborfront, the restaurant is the domain of Alistair Crawford, who prepares a savory cuisine served by his wife, Anne, and their sons, Andrew and Alistair, Jr. The restaurant takes full advantage of the legendary freshness and flavor of salmon—likely to have been caught several hours before their preparation—in the Kirkcudbright estuary and its tributary, the River Dee.

A special house dish is "queenies," or queen-size scallops that usually inhabit deeper waters than the great scallop. They may be yellow, orange, pink, red, purple, or brown in color. Other choices include a pâté of chicken livers flavored with wild Scottish garlic, and a dessert crêpe layered with fresh Scottish raspberries and freshly made ice cream, drizzled in chocolate sauce, and dusted with cinnamon.

11. GATEHOUSE-OF-FLEET

113 miles SW of Edinburgh, 33 miles SW of Dumfries, 42 miles E of Stranraer

GETTING THERE By Train Go first to Dumfries (see above), then continue the rest of the way by bus.

By Bus Four buses a day arrive in Gatehouse-of-Fleet from Dumfries. The trip, although short, takes 90 minutes because the bus stops frequently along the way. For information about schedules, call 0387/53496 in Dumfries.

By Car   From Castle Douglas (see above), continue west along the A75.

ESSENTIALS   A summer-only **tourist information center** operates from the Town Car Park (tel. 0557/814212). The **telephone area code** is 0557.

This sleepy former cotton town on the Water of Fleet was the Kippletringan in Sir Walter Scott's *Guy Mannering*. Burns composed "Scots Wha Hae wi' Wallace Bled" on the moors nearby and wrote it down in the Murray Arms Hotel there.

The town's name probably dates from 1642 when the English government opened the first military road through Galloway to assist the passage of troops to Ireland. In 1661 Richard Murray of Cally was authorized by Parliament to widen the bridge and to erect beside it an inn which was to serve as a tollhouse, with the innkeeper responsible for the maintenance of a 12-mile stretch of road. This is believed to have been the original house on the "gait," or road, which later became known as the "gait house of Fleet," and by 1790 it was being written in its present form and spelling. This ancient "gait house" is now part of the Murray Arms Hotel, used as a coffee room, and is probably the oldest building still in existence in the town.

WHAT TO SEE & DO

West of Gatehouse, on the road to Creetown, is the well-preserved 15th-century **tower of the McCullochs,** with its sinister "murder hole" over the entrance passage. Through this trapdoor, boiling pitch was poured onto attackers.

Cardoness Castle was originally the seat of the McCulloch family, one of whom, Sir Godfrey McCulloch, was the last person in Scotland to be executed by the "Maiden," the Scots version of the guillotine, at Edinburgh in 1697. The location is off the A75, a mile southwest of Gatehouse-of-Fleet. It is open from April to the end of September, Monday to Saturday from 9:30am to 6:30pm and on Sunday from 2 to 6:30pm; the remainder of the year, closing time is 4pm. Admission is £1 ($1.50) for adults, 50p (80¢) for children.

WHERE TO STAY & DINE

CALLY PALACE HOTEL, along the A75, Gatehouse-of-Fleet, Kirkcud-brightshire DG7 2DL. Tel. 0557/814342. Fax 0557/814522. 55 rms (all with bath). TV TEL
$ Rates (including Scottish breakfast): £45 ($67.50) single; £85 ($127.50) double. MC, V. **Parking:** Free.
The Cally Palace Hotel is a large 18th-century mansion standing in 100 acres of gardens and wooded parkland, 1½ miles south by the A75. Especially popular with more mature travelers, it is an oasis of peace and quiet—most comfortable, more suited for someone who wishes to spend a few days in Galloway than for the fleeting overnight motorist. The public lounges are overscale with some fine period pieces. Amenities include an indoor Leisure Centre, a bar, table tennis, and pool, in addition to tennis, putting, croquet, sauna, game fishing, loch boating, and dancing at certain times of the year. Some of the bedrooms have balconies opening onto the grounds. Rooms come in widely varying styles and sizes, but all have hot-beverage facilities. A dinner-dance is held on Saturday night.

MURRAY ARMS, Ann St., Gatehouse-of-Fleet, Kirkcudbrightshire DG7 2HY. Tel. 0557/814207. Fax 0557/814370. 13 rms (all with bath). TV TEL
$ Rates (including Scottish breakfast): £39.50 ($59.30) single; £79 ($118.50) double. AE, DC, MC, V. **Parking:** Free.
The Murray Arms is a long, low, white-painted building that was a posting inn in the 18th century, its coffeehouse dating back to 1642. Burns wrote his stirring song "Scots Wha' Ha'e" while staying at the inn, the occasion still commemorated by the Burns Room with its Leitch pictures. The inn has been considerably updated and

modernized by the laird of the Cally Estate, and that is as it should be, since it was James Murray of Cally who made the Murray Arms into a coaching inn so long ago. Now it's back in the same family after a long departure. Standing by an old clock tower, the inn has long been known for its food and hospitality.

In addition to two bars, the house has a sun lounge and two other lounges. You can stop in for a complete dinner in its attractively decorated restaurant opening onto the garden. From 7:30 to 9pm daily, you can order a table d'hôte meal for £17.50 ($26.30). Specialties include Galloway beef and fresh Solway Firth salmon. The Lunky Hole Restaurant is open daily from noon to 9:45pm and serves a wide variety of hot and cold food.

12. WHITHORN

10 miles S of Wigtown, 152 miles SW of Edinburgh,
72 miles SW of Dumfries, 34 miles SE of Stranraer

GETTING THERE **By Train** The nearest railway stations are Dumfries (see above) and Stranraer (see below). Trains seem equally frequent to both of these because, although Dumfries is larger, Stranraer is a strategic departure point for ferries to Ireland. Dumfries and Stranraer lie 75 minutes' and 60 minutes' drive, respectively, from Whithorn.

By Bus The Great Western Bus Company operates two buses a day to Whithorn from both Stranraer and Dumfries. These buses stop at many different places along the way, making the trip somewhat tedious. From London and Glasgow, National Express's City Link Division runs buses to Whithorn about once a day.

By Car From Newton Stewart, continue south along the A714 until you come to the junction with the A746, which you take south to Whithorn.

ESSENTIALS The nearest **tourist office** is in Newton Stewart. The **telephone area code** is 0988.

Whithorn is a modern town with a small museum containing ancient crosses and tombstones, including the 5th-century **Latinus Stone,** the earliest Christian memorial in Scotland.

WHAT TO SEE & DO

Whithorn Priory (tel. 09885/500508), 45–47 George St., was founded at Whithorn in A.D. 397 by St. Ninian, the son of a local chieftain. He built what was probably the first Christian church in Scotland, "Candida Casa" or "White House." In the 12th century, Fergus, Lord of Galloway, built a priory. The church and monastery were destroyed in the 16th century. Excavations in the ruins have revealed fragments of wall covered in pale plaster believed to be from Ninian's Candida Casa. The ruins are entered through the Pend, a 17th-century arch on which are carved the Royal Arms of Scotland. The site is open from April 6 through October, daily from 10:30am to 5pm. Admission is £2.50 ($3.80) adults, £1.25 ($1.90) children.

A moorland walk to the west coast 2½ miles away leads to **St. Ninian's Cave** in Port Castle Bay, used by the missionary as a retreat.

The **Isle of Whithorn,** 3 miles southeast of the town, is where St. Ninian landed about A.D. 395 on his return from studying in Rome, to bring Christianity to Scotland. The ruins of a plain 13th-century chapel are here, but no signs of any earlier church. On the point of the promontory are the remains of an Iron Age fort and a late 17th-century tower.

WHERE TO STAY & DINE

CASTLEWIGG HOTEL, along the A746, Whithorn, Wigtownshire DG8 8DL. Tel. 0988/500213. 7 rms (3 with bath). TV TEL

$ Rates (including Scottish breakfast): £19 ($28.50) single without bath; £22–£25

($33–$37.50) single with bath; £38 ($57) double without bath; £44–£50 ($66–$75) double with bath. No credit cards. **Parking:** Free.

ⓢ Two miles north of Whithorn beside the A746, this small country hotel enjoys sweeping views to the north and east. More than 200 years old, it was originally built as the dower house of Castle Wigg, which today lies in ruins less than half a mile away. Guests may enjoy the residents' lounge with its bar service and color TV, the spacious dining room, and the lounge bar. Dinners begin at £12 ($18) for three courses. They are served in a bar/pub or else a slightly more formal restaurant. The hotel specializes in hunting and fishing expeditions to the surrounding fields, forests, and streams.

13. STRANRAER

132 miles SW of Edinburgh, 75 miles W of Dumfries, 51 miles SW of Ayr

GETTING THERE   By Train   Monday through Saturday four trains per day run from Glasgow to Stranraer, and seven trains on Sunday. The one-way fare is £16 ($24). In Glasgow, call 041/2042844 24 hours a day for information about schedules.

By Bus   Bus no. 502 departs Newton Stewart for Stranraer seven times per day (trip time: 30 minutes).

By Car   From Dumfries (see above), continue west along the A75.

By Ferry   Sealink Ferries (tel. 0776/2262 in Stranraer) go back and forth between Stranraer and Larne, Northern Ireland. Seven ferries depart daily Monday through Saturday, and five on Sunday. Trip time is 2 hours, 20 minutes. The one-way fare is £18 ($27) for adults and £8 ($12) for children. Weather conditions can interfere with ferry departures.

ESSENTIALS   A summer-only **tourist information center** is at 1 Bridge St. (tel. 0776/2595). The **telephone area code** is 0776.

The largest town in Wigtownshire, Stranraer is the terminal of the 35-mile ferry crossing from Larne, Northern Ireland. An early chapel, built by a member of the Adair family near the 16th-century **Castle of St. John** in the heart of town, gave the settlement its original name of Chapel, later changed to Chapel of Stranrawer and then shortened to Stranraer. The name is supposed to have referred to the row or "raw" of original houses on the "strand" or burn, now largely buried beneath the town's streets. The Castle of St. John became the town jail and in the late 17th century held Covenanters during Graham of Claverhouse's campaigns of religious persecution.

WHAT TO SEE & DO

To the east of Stranraer are the **Castle Kennedy Gardens** (tel. 0776/2024), a late 19th-century Scots baronial mansion. In the grounds are the White and Black lochs and the ruins of Castle Kennedy, built during the reign of James IV but burned down in 1716. The gardens contain one of the finest pinetums in Scotland. In the right season you can wander among blossoming rhododendrons, azaleas, and magnolias. The castle is not open to the public, but the gardens are, from Easter through September, daily from 10am to 5pm. Admission is £2 ($3) for adults and £1 ($1.50) for children.

WHERE TO STAY

CRAIGNELDER HOTEL, Cairn Ryan Rd., Stranraer, Wigtownshire DG9 8HA. Tel. 0776/3281. 13 rms (all with bath). TV TEL

$ Rates (including Scottish breakfast): £30 ($45) single; £50 ($75) double. MC, V.
Parking: Free.

This comfortably weatherproof hotel was built before World War I near the wharves that service the ferryboat to Ireland. Cream-colored and angular, the hotel is functionally but attractively decorated, and has been severely modernized during its lifetime. Bedrooms are comfortable, with window curtains, hot-beverage facilities, and contemporary furniture. On the premises are two different bars, a restaurant, and a clientele that seems to be constantly waiting for a ferryboat to carry them home to Ireland. A fixed-price dinner costs £10.50 ($15.80).

NORTH WEST CASTLE HOTEL, Royal Crescent, Stranraer, Wigtown-shire DG9 8EH. Tel. 0776/4413. Fax 0776/2646. 64 rms (all with bath), 7 suites. TV TEL **Directions:** Walk 3 minutes north of the ferryboat terminal.

$ Rates (including Scottish breakfast): £49 ($73.50) single; £70 ($105) double; £82 ($123) suite. No credit cards. **Parking:** Free.

This is the largest and most prominent hotel in Stranraer. Its oldest part was built in 1820 by Capt. Sir John Ross, R.N., the Arctic explorer. (The hotel owners will give you a brochure that relates the exploits and disappointments of this local hero.) The original building has been altered and expanded with a modern flat-roofed addition that contains most of the comfortably modern bedrooms. The lounges are cozy, the dining room is impressive. Fresh local ingredients are used in the in-house restaurant, where continental food with Scottish overtones is served. The bars in the hotel's cellar are well stocked, but I prefer the Ross Lounge, with its views of the harbor. Further amenities include a garden, a sauna, a solarium, a curling rink, a games room, an indoor swimming pool, and dancing to a live band most Saturday nights in winter.

WHERE TO DINE

L'APÉRITIF RESTAURANT, London Rd. Tel. 0776/2991.
Cuisine: ITALIAN/INTERNATIONAL. **Reservations:** Recommended.
$ Prices: Appetizers £1.60–£3 ($2.40–$4.50); main courses £4.50–£7.70 ($6.80–$11.60); pizzas £4–£6 ($6–$9). No credit cards.
Open: Lunch Mon–Sat noon–2pm; dinner Mon–Sat 5:30–9:30pm.

This place, directly east of town, has some of the best and most reasonably priced food at the port. Operated by Italians, it has two lounges, one containing a pub popular with the locals. In the evening you also have the choice of ordering continental meals on an à la carte menu upstairs. Homemade soups, fresh salads, pastas, and hot dishes are offered at lunch. You can also get pizza here.

14. PORTPATRICK

141 miles SW of Edinburgh, 60 miles SW of Ayr,
8 miles SW of Stranraer, 80 miles W of Dumfries

GETTING THERE   By Train   Go to Stranraer (see above) by train, then take a bus to Portpatrick.

By Bus   Bus no. 64 from Stranraer makes frequent runs throughout the day between Stranraer and Portpatrick.

By Car   From Stranraer, take the A77 southwest.

ESSENTIALS   The nearest tourist information office is in Stranraer (see above). The **telephone area code** is 077681.

Until 1849 steamers sailed the 21 miles from Donaghdee in Northern Ireland to Portpatrick, which became a honeymoon haven "Gretna Green" for the Irish.

Couples would land on Saturday, have the banns called on Sunday, and marry on Monday. When the harbor became silted up, Portpatrick was replaced by Stranraer as a port. Commanding a clifftop to the south are the ruins of Dunskey Castle, a grim keep built in 1510 by John Adair.

WHAT TO SEE & DO

Ten miles south of Portpatrick is the little hamlet of **Port Logan.** In the vicinity is **Logan House** (not open to the public), the seat of the McDouall family, which could trace their ancestry so far back that it was claimed they were as "old as the sun itself." This family laid out the gardens at Logan.

    Logan Botanic Garden, an annex of the Royal Botanic Garden, Edinburgh, contains a wide range of plants from the warm temperate regions of the world. Cordylines, palms, tree ferns, and flowering shrubs grow well in the mild climate of southwestern Scotland. The garden is open from March 15 through October, daily from 10am to 6pm. Admission is £1.50 ($2.30) for adults and 50p (80¢) for children. There is a pleasant refreshment room at the entrance. The site is 14 miles south of Stranraer off the B7065. For information, telephone 077686/231.

    The ancient church site of **Kirkmadrine** lies in the parish of Stoneykirk, south of Portpatrick. The site now has a modern church, but there is an old graveyard and early inscribed stones and crosses, including three of the earliest Christian monuments in Britain, showing the chi-rho symbol and inscriptions dating from the 5th or early 6th century.

WHERE TO STAY

KNOCKINAAM LODGE HOTEL, along the A77, Portpatrick, Portpatrickshire DG9 9AD. Tel. 077681/471. Fax 077681/435. 10 rms (all with bath). TV TEL

$ Rates (including half board): £80–£118 ($120–$177) single; £160–£200 ($240–$300) double. AE, DC, MC, V. **Parking:** Free. **Closed:** Jan 4 to mid-Mar.

    Instead of going to the larger town, Stranraer, you might prefer to stay at the Knockinaam Lodge Hotel, 3¼ miles southeast off the A77, built as a Victorian holiday house in 1869 and enlarged in 1901. It stands on a little terraced bay right at the foot of a deep and thickly wooded glen, surrounded on three sides by cliffs, looking out to sea and the distant Irish coast. In the heat of World War II, Sir Winston Churchill chose the lodge for a secret meeting with General Eisenhower. The prime minister enjoyed a long hot bath (in a tub that's still here) while smoking a cigar. Knockinaam is run in the best country-house tradition by the resident owners. There is a garden with lawns running down to a private sandy beach.

    Dining/Entertainment: The lodge serves the best food in the area. All ingredients used in the kitchen are fresh. You can dine in the restaurant overlooking the sea as it breaks over the rocks at the end of the garden, enjoying tender Galloway beef, lobsters, scallops, and other local dishes, accompanied by home-grown vegetables. Both à la carte and table d'hôte meals are cooked to order. Service is polite and efficient. Lunch, daily from noon to 1:30pm, is offered for £23 ($34.50); a fixed-price dinner, from 7:30 to 9pm, costs £30 ($45).

    Services: 24-hour room service, laundry, babysitting.

    Facilities: Sea fishing, helipad, croquet.

FERNHILL HOTEL, Heugh Rd., Portpatrick, Wigtownshire DG9 8TD. Tel. 077681/220. Fax 077681/596. 21 rms (20 with bath). TV TEL **Directions:** On the approach to Portpatrick, turn right at the War Memorial.

$ Rates (including Scottish breakfast): £40 ($60) single without bath, £50–£65 ($75–$97.50) single with bath; £70–£90 ($105–$135) double with bath. AE, DC, MC, V. **Parking:** Free.

A widely acclaimed accommodation, this gray stone 1872 building stands on its own grounds above the village, looking down at the harbor. It is a 5-minute walk from the first tee of the clifftop Dunskey Golf Course. Bedrooms are decorated with color-coordinated style and flair. The most desirable accommodations are the six executive rooms opening onto the sea; three have patio doors leading to private balconies. The windows are double glazed, and amenities often include tea makers, trouser presses, and hairdryers. The Cocktail Bar with its lounge and the Victorian Conservatory have a panoramic view over the town and sea. The excellent cuisine, using Scottish produce whenever available, is one of the reasons for staying here. Meals begin at £15 ($22.50).

WHERE TO DINE

OLD MILL HOUSE, High St. Tel. 077681/358.
   Cuisine: SCOTTISH. **Reservations:** Recommended.
$ Prices: Appetizers £1.40–£3 ($2.10–$4.50); main courses £3–£12 ($4.50–$18). MC.
   Open: Lunch daily 11am–2:30pm; dinner daily 6–10:30pm. **Closed:** Jan–Mar.
A white-walled building with an open-air swimming pool, this restaurant is set into a garden beside a running stream at the edge of town, the first building you see as you enter Portpatrick from Stranraer. In the 18th century it was a mill. It offers good food and a big-windowed view of a forested ravine. Most guests gravitate toward the cozy pub, with a wood fire. Specialties include fresh salmon, sirloin steak, and sole meunière. The restaurant also rents two bedrooms, all with bath, plus one suite. These rooms are doubles, costing £52 ($78), the suite rising to £30 ($45) per person for up to four occupants, including a Scottish breakfast.

CHAPTER 4

EDINBURGH

1. ORIENTATION
- **WHAT'S SPECIAL ABOUT EDINBURGH**
- **NEIGHBORHOODS IN BRIEF**

2. GETTING AROUND
- **FAST FACTS: EDINBURGH**

3. ACCOMMODATIONS
- **FROMMER'S SMART TRAVELER: HOTELS**
- **FROMMER'S COOL FOR KIDS: HOTELS**

4. DINING
- **FROMMER'S SMART TRAVELER: RESTAURANTS**
- **FROMMER'S COOL FOR KIDS: RESTAURANTS**

5. ATTRACTIONS
- **DID YOU KNOW . . . ?**
- **FROMMER'S FAVORITE EDINBURGH EXPERIENCES**
- **WALKING TOUR: HISTORIC EDINBURGH**

6. SPECIAL & FREE EVENTS

7. SPORTS & RECREATION

8. SAVVY SHOPPING

9. EVENING ENTERTAINMENT

10. EASY EXCURSIONS FROM EDINBURGH

Edinburgh has been called one of the fairest cities in Europe, "the Athens of the North," and it's the gateway to central Scotland. You cannot only explore the capital city but use it as a base for excursions to the beautiful Trossachs (Scotland's Lake District), the silver waters of Loch Lomond, and the Kingdom of Fife on the opposite shore of the Firth of Forth.

Edinburgh is a city filled with historical and literary associations—John Knox, Mary Queen of Scots, Robert Louis Stevenson, Sir Arthur Conan Doyle (creator of Sherlock Holmes), David Hume, Alexander Graham Bell, Sir Walter Scott, and Bonnie Prince Charlie are all part of its past.

Edinburgh has become famous as the scene of an ever-growing international festival, with its action-packed list of cultural events. But that shouldn't be your only reason for visiting the ancient seat of Scottish royalty. Its treasures are available all year. In fact, when the festival-hoppers have gone home, the pace is more relaxed, prices are lower, and the people themselves, under less pressure as hosts, return to their traditional hospitable nature.

1. ORIENTATION

ARRIVING

BY PLANE Edinburgh is about an hour's flying time from London, 393 miles to the South. **Edinburgh Airport** lies 10 miles northwest of the center, receiving flights only from within the British Isles and the rest of Europe. It's connected by frequent 30-minute bus rides to midtown. A double-decker Airlink bus makes the trip between the airport and the city center, letting you off near Waverley Bridge, centrally located between the Old Town and New Town; the one-way fare is £3 ($4.50). It's also possible to take a taxi in the city for £12 ($18) or more, depending on traffic conditions. Telephone 031/3331000 for flight information.

BY TRAIN InterCity trains link London with Edinburgh and are fast and efficient, providing both restaurant and bar service as well as air conditioning.Trains from London's King's Cross Station arrive in Edinburgh at **Waverley Station** (tel. 031/5562451) at the east end of Princes Street (tel. 071/2782477 in London for rail information about departures and tickets). Trains depart London every hour or so, taking 4 to 5½ hours. An overnight sleeper—for

WHAT'S SPECIAL ABOUT EDINBURGH

Museums
- ☐ National Gallery of Scotland, although small as national galleries go, has a well-chosen collection of European masters.
- ☐ Scottish National Gallery of Modern Art displays the genius of many of the 20th century's greatest artists, from Henry Moore to Picasso.

Parks and Gardens
- ☐ Royal Botanic Garden, everything from the giant water lilies of Amazonia to desert succulents.

Architectural Highlights
- ☐ The Royal Mile, a collection of medieval buildings and narrow alleys, between the Palace of Holyroodhouse and Edinburgh Castle.
- ☐ New Town, a Georgian town across the valley, with Princes Street its major boulevard, and the north side of Charlotte Square designed by Robert Adam.

Cool for Kids
- ☐ Edinburgh Zoo, Scotland's largest animal collection, set in 80 acres of parkland.

Castles and Palaces
- ☐ Edinburgh Castle, the city's most ancient structure, where you can visit the State Apartments, former stamping ground of Mary Queen of Scots.
- ☐ Palace of Holyroodhouse, built more than 300 years ago for the royalty of Scotland, now occupied by Queen Elizabeth when she's in town.

Special Events/Festivals
- ☐ Edinburgh Festival, one of northern Europe's major cultural extravaganzas in late summer, attracting some of the world's finest artists in all fields.

which reservations are required—also runs between London and Edinburgh. Taxis and buses are found right outside the station once you've arrived in Edinburgh.

BY BUS The least expensive way to go from London to Edinburgh is by bus, but it's a long (8 hours) journey. Nevertheless, it'll get you there for only about £28 ($42) one way or £35 ($52.50) round-trip. Scottish CityLink coaches depart from London's Victoria Coach Station, delivering you to Edinburgh's **St. Andrew's Square Bus Station,** St. Andrew Square (tel. 031/5575717 in Edinburgh for more data).

BY CAR Edinburgh lies 46 miles east of Glasgow and 105 miles north of Newcastle upon Tyne in England. There is no express motorway linking London and Edinburgh. The M1 from London takes you part of the way north. But you'll have to come into Edinburgh along secondary roads, including the A68 or the A7 from the southeast, the A1 from the east, or the A702 from the north. The A71 or the A8 comes in from the west, the A8 connecting with the M8 just west of Edinburgh. An "M" in the road designation stands for a motorway or express highway. The A90 comes down from the north over the Forth Road Bridge.

TOURIST INFORMATION

To take care of tourist lodging all year and to answer questions about sightseeing, the **Edinburgh & Scotland Information Centre,** Waverley Shopping Centre, 3 Princes St. (tel. 051/5571700), lists small hotels, guest houses, and private homes (see "Where to Stay," in this chapter, for more details). The information center also sells bus tours, theater tickets, and souvenirs of Edinburgh. There's also an Information and Accommodation desk at Edinburgh Airport (tel. 031/3332167), open according to the frequency of incoming flights.

CITY LAYOUT

Edinburgh is divided into an **Old Town** and a **New Town.** Chances are, you will find lodgings in the New Town and visit the Old Town only for dining, drinking, shopping, or sightseeing.

The New Town, with its world-famous **Princes Street,** came about in the 18th century in the "Golden Age of Edinburgh." Everybody from Robert Burns to James Boswell visited Edinburgh in that era. The first building went up in New Town in 1767, and by the end of the century classical squares, streets, and town houses had been added. Princes Street runs for about a mile, following a straight pattern. It is known for its shopping and also its beauty, as it opens onto the Princes Street Gardens with stunning views of the Old Town.

North of Princes Street, and running parallel to it, is the second great street of New Town, **George Street.** It begins at Charlotte Square and runs east to St. Andrew Square. Directly north of George Street is another impressive thoroughfare, **Queen Street,** opening onto Queen Street Gardens on its north side.

In Edinburgh, you also hear a lot about **Rose Street,** directly north of Princes Street. It has more pubs per square block than any other place in Scotland, and is also filled with shops and restaurants.

Everyone, seemingly, has heard of **"The Royal Mile,"** which is the main street of the Old Town. Actually it is not one street, but four, consisting of Castlehill, Lawnmarket, High Street, and Canongate. Beginning at Edinburgh Castle, it runs all the way to the Palace of Holyroodhouse. A famous street which lies to the south of the castle (you have to descend to it) is **Grassmarket,** where convicted criminals were once hung on the dreaded gallows that stood there.

Of course Edinburgh consists of a lot more squares, terraces, crescents, gardens, and streets than those mentioned. Discovering its hidden lanes and branching out to some of its interesting satellite communities is one of the reasons for coming here.

FINDING AN ADDRESS Street numbering can be confusing. Edinburgh's streets often follow no pattern whatsoever, and both their naming and house numbering seem to have been perpetrated by a group of xenophobes with an equal grudge against postal carriers and foreigners.

Edinburgh is checkered with innumerable squares, terraces, "circuses," "wynds," and "closes," which jut into or cross or overlap or interrupt whatever street you're trying to follow, usually without the slightest warning.

House numbers run in odds, evens, clockwise, or counterclockwise as the wind blows. That is, when they exist at all—and frequently they don't. Many establishments in Edinburgh (and throughout Scotland) do not use street numbers. This is even truer when you leave Edinburgh and go to a provincial town. Even though a road might run for a mile, some buildings on the street will be numbered; others next door will say only "King's Road" or whatever, giving no number, even though their neighbor next door uses a number. This is just one aspect that makes traveling around Scotland a bit maddening. Of course, you can always ask for a location to be pinpointed, and locals are generally glad to assist a bewildered foreigner.

Get a detailed map of Edinburgh before setting out. If you're seeking an address, try to get the cross street ("near the corner of," etc.) instead of settling just for the street name with or without a number.

NEIGHBORHOODS IN BRIEF

The Old Town This is where Edinburgh began. Its "backbone," as mentioned, is the Royal Mile, a medieval thoroughfare stretching for about a mile from Edinburgh Castle running downhill to the Palace of Holyroodhouse. It is composed of four interconnected streets, including Castlehill nearest the castle, plus Lawnmarket and High Street. Canongate, the fourth section of the Royal Mile, was once a separate burgh. This is "perhaps the largest, longest, and finest street for buildings and number of inhabitants in the world," or so wrote English author Daniel Defoe.

The New Town Lying below Old Town, New Town burst into full bloom between 1766 and 1840, one of the largest Georgian developments in the world. It takes in most of the northern half of the heart of the city, covering some 790 acres. With about 25,000 citizens living within its boundaries, it is known as the largest "conservation area" in all of Britain. It is made up of a network of squares, streets, terraces, and "circuses," which reach Haymarket in the west to Abbeyhill toward the east. New Town also goes from Canonmills on the northern perimeter down to Princes Street along the southern tier. Its main artery is Princes Street.

Marchmont   Lying about a mile south of High Street, the suburb of Marchmont borders a public park, the Meadows. It was constructed in the main between 1869 and 1914 as a massive building program to make new housing for people who could no longer afford to live in New Town.

Bruntsfield   This suburb lies to the west on the other side of Bruntsfield Links. Now a residential district of moderate-income families, it was the ground on which James IV once gathered the Scottish army, which he then marched to its defeat at Flodden in 1513. Plague victims were once brought here for burial, but now suburban gardens have grown over those graves. Many low-cost B&B houses are found in this area.

Churchill   Churchill is known as "holy corner" because of the wide array of Scottish churches inside its borders at the junctions of Colinton Road, Chamberlain Road, and Bruntsfield Road. These churches are primarily for local worshippers and are not of any great artistic worth. Many famous Scots have lived in this district, including Jane Welsh Carlyle. George Meikle Kemp, the architect who created the Scott Monument in Princes Street, was also a former resident.

Leith   The Port of Leith lies only a few miles north of Princes Street, and is the city's major harbor opening onto the Firth of Forth. It is today going through a gentrification program, and many visitors come here to patronize its restaurants and pubs, which specialize in seafood. The Port of Leith isn't what it used to be in terms of maritime might, and its glory days existed back when stevedores unloaded cargoes by hand—not the giant containers used today. Leith was once a bitter rival of Edinburgh, but now, as one local resident put it, "We're just another bloody part of Auld Reekie."

Newhaven   The adjacent fishing village to Leith, Newhaven was once known as "Our Lady's Port of Grace." This former little fishing harbor with its bustling fishmarket was greatly altered in the 1960s. Many of its "bow-tows" (a nickname for closely knit, clannish residents) were uprooted, like the Leithers, in a major gentrification program. Many of the old houses of the fisherfolk have been restored, and the fishwife no longer goes from door to door hawking fish from her basket (known as a *creel*). She'd gut and filet the fish right on your doorstep if you asked her. Founded in the late 1400s, Newhaven centered around its harbor, now mostly filled with pleasure craft instead of fishing boats.

2. GETTING AROUND

BY PUBLIC TRANSPORTATION

Buses   will probably be your chief method of transport in the Scottish capital. The fare you pay depends on the distance you ride. The minimum fare is 32p (48¢) for three stages or less, and the maximum fare is £1.70 ($2.60) for 44 or more stages. (A stage is not a stop; it's a distance of about half a mile with a number of stops.) Children ages 5 to 15 pay from 32p (48¢) to 80p ($1.20), and children 4 and under ride free.

Discount Passes   There are several types of bus passes for extended tourist visits to their city. The **Edinburgh Free Ticket** allows 1 day of unlimited travel on city buses for £1.75 ($2.60) for adults and £1.20 ($1.80) for children. Another form of extended ticket is a **TouristCard,** allowing unlimited travel on all city buses for a time period of between 2 and 13 days, plus special discounts at certain restaurants and for tours of selected historical sites. A 2-day TouristCard costs £4.40 ($6.60) for adults and £3.20 ($4.80) for children; a 13-day TouristCard goes for £17.60 ($26.40) for adults and £12.55 ($18.80) for children.

For daily commuters or for diehard Scottish enthusiasts, a **RidaCard** season ticket allows unlimited travel on all buses at £8 ($12) for adults for 1 week and £26 ($39) for 4 weeks. Travel must begin on Sunday. Prices for children are £5 ($7.50) for 1 week, £16 ($24) for 4 weeks.

These tickets and further information may be obtained at the **Waverley Bridge Transport Office,** Waverley Bridge in Edinburgh (tel. 031/5544494), or the **Lothian Region Transport Office,** 14 Queen Street (tel. 031/2204111).

BY TAXI

As a last resort, try hailing a cab or waiting at a taxi stand. Meters begin at 90p ($1.60). Taxi ranks are found at Hanover Street, North St. Andrew Street, Waverley Station, Haymarket Station, and Lauriston Place. Fares are displayed in the front of the taxi, and charges are posted, including extra charges for night drivers or destinations outside the city limits. You can also call a taxi: Try **City Cabs** (tel. 2281211) or **Central Radio Taxis** (tel. 2292468).

BY CAR

RENTALS Car rentals are relatively expensive, and driving in Edinburgh is a tricky business, even for native motorists. It's a warren of one-way streets, with parking spots at a premium. However, you will find a car most convenient if you'd like to tour in the countryside. Most companies will accept your U.S. driver's license, provided you have held it for more than a year and are over 21.

Many companies grant discounts to clients who reserve in advance (see "Car Rentals," under "Getting Around" "By Car" in Chapter 2, for toll-free numbers and a preview of rates). It is better to reserve cars before you arrive in Edinburgh. Most of the major car-rental companies such as Avis and Hertz maintain offices at the Edinburgh Airport should you want to rent a car on the spot. Call **Avis** (tel. 031/3331866), **Hertz** (tel. 031/3331019), or **Eurodollar** (tel. 031/3332588).

Rates begin at £28 ($42) per day (although this could vary greatly from place to place), or £135 ($202.50) per week, with unlimited mileage.

PARKING It's expensive and difficult to find. Metered parking is available. You'll need the right change and also to watch out for traffic wardens who issue tickets. Some zones are marked PERMIT HOLDERS ONLY. Don't park there unless you have a permit as a local resident—your vehicle will be towed if you do. A yellow line along the curb indicates "No Parking."

Major parking lots (car parks) are found at Castle Terrace, a large multistory car park convenient for Edinburgh Castle and the west end of Princes Street; at Lothian Road, a surface car park near the west end of Princes Street; at St. John Hill, a surface car park convenient for the Royal Mile, the west end of Princes Street, and Waverley Station; and at St. James Centre (entrance from York Place), a multistory car park close to the east end of Princes Street.

BY BICYCLE

You can rent bikes by the day or by the week from a number of outfits. Nevertheless, bicycling is not a good idea for most visitors, because the city is constructed on a series of high ridges and terraces.

You may, however, want to rent a bike for exploring the flatter countryside. Try **Central Car Hire,** 13 Lochrin Place (tel. 2286333), off Home Street in Tollcross, near the Cameo Cinema. Depending on the type of bike, charges range from £5 ($7.50) to £12 ($18) per day. A deposit of £20 ($30) to £40 ($60) is imposed. The shop is open Monday to Saturday from 10am to 5:30pm, and May through September only, also on Sunday from 10am to noon and 5 to 7pm.

ON FOOT

This is the best way to explore Edinburgh, but be careful. Many Americans have accidents because they look the wrong way when crossing a street. Remember, cars drive on the left. Always look both ways before stepping off a curb.

Because of its narrow lanes, "wynds," and closes, the Old Town can only be explored in any depth on foot. Edinburgh is fairly convenient for the visitor who likes to walk, as most of the attractions are along the Royal Mile, along Princes Street, or in one of the major streets of the New Town.

 EDINBURGH

American Express   The office in Edinburgh is at 139 Princes Street (tel. 225-7881), five blocks from Waverly Station, open Monday through Friday from 9am to 5pm and on Saturday from 9am to noon.

Area Code   The telephone area code is 031.

Baby-sitters   Contact **Guardian Babysitting, 28** Strathalmond Park (tel. 3392288), or make arrangements through your hotel.

Business Hours   In Edinburgh, **banks** are usually open Monday through Thursday from 9:30am to 12:30pm and 1:30 to 3:30pm, on Friday from 9:30am to 1:30pm. **Shops** are generally open Monday through Saturday from 10am to either 5:30 or 6pm; on Thursday stores are open until 8pm. **Offices,** in the main, are open Monday through Friday from 9am to 5pm.

Car Rentals   See "Getting Around" "By Car," in this chapter.

Climate   See "When to Go," in Chapter 2.

Crime   See "Safety," below.

Currency   See "Information, Entry Requirements & Money," in Chapter 2.

Currency Exchange   There is a Bureau de Change of the Clydesdale Bank at 5 Waverley Bridge and at Waverley Market.

Dentist   For a dental problem, go to the **Dental Surgery School,** 31 Chambers Street (tel. 2259511), open Monday through Saturday from 9 to 10:15am and 2 to 3:15pm.

Doctor   In a medical emergency, you can seek help from the **Edinburgh Royal Infirmary,** 1 Lauriston Place (tel. 2292477).

Drugstores   There are no 24-hour drugstores (called "chemists" or "pharmacies") in Edinburgh. The major drugstore is **Boots,** 48 Shandwick Place (tel. 2256757), which is open Monday through Friday from 9am to 9pm.

Embassies and Consulates   The place to go for emergency problems such as lost passports is the **American Consulate,** 3 Regent Terrace (tel. 5568315). The **Australian Consulate** is at 80 Hanover Street (tel. 2266271). Citizens of such countries as Canada, New Zealand, South Africa, or Ireland should apply to their various embassies in London.

Emergencies   Call **999** in an emergency to summon police, an ambulance, or firefighters.

Eyeglasses   Your best bet is **Boots Opticians,** 101–103 Princes St. (tel. 2256397), open Monday through Saturday from 9am to 5:30pm. On Thursday, the shop stays open until 7:30pm. Eyeglasses can either be repaired or replaced here.

Hairdressers/Barbers   The best place to go is **Roots Hair Design,** 8A Stafford St. (tel. 2255555), which accepts both women and men.

Holidays   See "When to Go," in Chapter 2.

Hospital   The best is the **Royal Infirmary,** 1 Lauriston Pl. (tel. 2292477). It's also the most convenient.

Hotlines   For a rape crisis center, call 5569437.

Information   See "Tourist Information," under "Orientation," in this chapter.

Laundry/Dry Cleaning   If you're looking for a launderette, go to **Bruntsfield Launderette,** 108 Bruntsfield Pl. (tel. 2292669), open Monday through Friday from 9am to 5pm and on Saturday from 9am to 4pm. For your dry-cleaning needs, check out **Pullars & Sons,** 23 Frederick St. (tel. 2258095), open Monday through Friday from 8:30am to 5:30pm and on Saturday from 8:30am to 5pm.

Libraries The largest library in Edinburgh, and the most central, is Edinburgh's **Central Library,** at George IV Bridge (tel. 2255584). Its Edinburgh Room contains information on the life in Edinburgh of such famous Scots as Stevenson and Sir Walter Scott himself. Collections are devoted to genealogy, music, and fine art, along with a large collection of prints and an audio library.

Lost Property If you've lost property (or had it stolen), go to Police Headquarters on Fettes Avenue (tel. 3313131).

Luggage/Storage/Lockers You can store luggage at **Waverley Station** at Waverley Bridge (tel. 5562451), which is open daily from 6:10am to 11pm.

Newspapers/Magazines Published since 1817, *The Scotsman* is considered Britain's quality daily newspaper. Along with national and international news, it is strong on the arts. Among magazines, the field is not outstanding, except for the *Edinburgh Review,* published quarterly by the University Press. It is mainly a cultural journal. London papers are sold at most newsstands, along with the *International Herald Tribune, USA Today,* and the European editions of *Time* and *Newsweek.*

Photographic Needs All your photographic needs can be met at **Edinburgh Cameras,** 55 Lothian Road (tel. 2294416), which is open Monday through Saturday from 9am to 5:30pm.

Police See "Emergencies," above.

Post Office The Edinburgh Branch Post Office, 2–4 Waterloo Pl. (tel. 5508232), is open Monday through Thursday from 9am to 5:30pm, on Friday from 9:30am to 5:30pm, and on Saturday from 9am to 12:30pm.

Radio The national network is BBC Radio Scotland (FM 92.4–94.7 MW, 810kHz/370m) dominated by news and talk shows. The local commercial station is Radio Forth (FM 97.3 MW, 1548kHz).

Religious Services If you're Catholic, you can attend **St. Mary's Metropolitan Cathedral,** Broughton Street (tel. 5563339). The Scottish Episcopal Church is represented at **St. Mary's Cathedral,** Palmerston Place (tel. 2256293). Baptists can worship at **Bristo Church,** Buckingham Terrace (tel. 3323682), and the Hebrew congregation meets at the **Synagogue** at 4 Salisbury Road (tel. 6673144). There is also a Methodist church, **Central Halls,** at Tollcross (tel. 2297937). Of course there are many **Church of Scotland** (Presbyterian) churches.

Rest Rooms These are found at rail stations, terminals, restaurants, hotels, pubs, and department stores. Edinburgh also has a system of public toilets, often marked WC (water closet), found at various strategic corners and squares throughout the city, but likely to be closed late in the evening.

Safety Edinburgh is generally safer than Glasgow, and is in fact one of the safest capitals of Europe for a visitor to stroll about—either day or night. But that doesn't mean that crimes, especially muggings, don't exist. They do, largely because of Edinburgh's shockingly large drug problem.

As in any unfamiliar city, it's wise to stay alert and be aware of your immediate surroundings, because every society has its share of criminals. Wear a moneybelt, keep your wallet in an inside pocket, and don't sling your camera or purse over your shoulder, particularly at night or in crowded places. This will minimize the possibility of becoming the victim of a crime. Keep your valuables in a safety-deposit box at your hotel.

Shoe Repairs A chain operation, **Mister Minit,** 22 Frederick St. (tel. 2266741), only a few blocks from the east end of Princes Street, is open Monday through Friday from 8am to 5:30pm and on Saturday from 8am to 5pm.

Taxes A 17½% Value-Added Tax (known as VAT) is added to all goods and services in Edinburgh, as elsewhere in Britain. There are no special city taxes.

Taxis See "Getting Around," in this chapter.

Telegram, Telex, and Fax In Edinburgh, to send a Telex anywhere in the world 24 hours a day, call 4927111. Telegrams and faxes can be sent at the Hope Street Post Office (tel. 2266823).

Television BBC Scotland and Scottish Television (STV) are Glasgow-based television stations which reach Edinburgh with their daily roundup of news, features, comedy, and drama, plus documentaries.

Transit Information Contact the **Waverley Bridge Transport Office,** Waverley Bridge (tel. 5544494), or the **Lothian Region Transport Office,** 14 Queen St. (tel. 2265087).

Weather For full details of Edinburgh weather forecasts (also, the surrounding region) and road conditions, call 0898/881921. This number also provides data about weather information for Lothian, the Borders, Tayside and Fife, Glasgow and western Scotland, the Grampian Region, and the Highlands.

3. ACCOMMODATIONS

Edinburgh offers a full range of accommodations at different price levels throughout the year. However, during the 3-week period of the festival, the establishments fill up with international visitors, so it's prudent to reserve in advance.

To take care of tourist lodging all year, the **Edinburgh & Scotland Information Centre,** Waverley Shopping Centre, 3 Princes St. (tel. 031/5571700), compiles a well-investigated and lengthy list of small hotels, guest houses, and private homes that provide B&B for as little as £13 ($19.50) per person. You can write in advance, but allow about 4 weeks' notice, especially during the summer and during the festival weeks.

A £3 ($4.50) booking fee and a 10% deposit are charged. There's also an information and accommodation desk at Edinburgh Airport, open according to the frequency of incoming flights.

Opening hours are as follows: January through March and November and December, Monday to Saturday from 9am to 6pm; April and October, Monday to Saturday from 9am to 6pm, Sunday from 11am to 6pm; May through June and September, Monday to Saturday from 9am to 7pm, Sunday from 11am to 7pm; July and August, Monday to Saturday from 9am to 8pm, Sunday from 11am to 8pm.

In this guide, the designation "Very Expensive" is for double rooms priced at £165 ($247.50) to £250 ($375) a night. "Expensive" is for rooms ranging from £110 ($165) to £155 ($232.50) a night. "Moderate" places charge £60 ($90) to £110 ($165) for double rooms. Anything under £60 ($90) for a double room is rated "Inexpensive." Often this category will dip as low as £36 ($54) for two people per night, including breakfast.

IN THE CENTER
VERY EXPENSIVE

BALMORAL HOTEL, Princes St. Edinburgh, Lothian EH2 2EQ. Tel. 031/556-2414, or toll free 800/225-5843 in the U.S. Fax 031/557-3747. 167 rms (all with bath), 22 suites. A/C MINIBAR TV TEL **Bus:** 4, 15, or 44.

$ Rates: £115 ($172.50) single; £165 ($247.50) double. Suites £250–£600 ($375–$900). Scottish breakfast £13.50 ($20.30) extra. AE, DC, MC, V. **Parking:** £10 ($15).

After a series of unfortunate ownerships during the 1980s, when its massive premises were sometimes in limbo between investment groups, this legendary hotel reopened in 1991 after an expenditure of $35 million under a new name, the Balmoral. It was originally opened in 1902 as the largest, grandest, and most impressive hotel in the north of Britain. With a location almost directly above the Waverley Railway Station and built of soft-beige stone, it features a soaring clock tower that many residents of Edinburgh consider one of the landmarks of their city. Bedrooms are comfortable, distinguished, conservative, and rather large, a graceful reminder of Edwardian sprawl with a contemporary twist. The hotel is under the management of the Forte chain.

Dining/Entertainment: The hotel's most elegant eatery, the Grill Room, is separately recommended in "Dining." More convivial is an informal brasserie, Bridges, which is open every day from 7am to 11pm for platters, salads, and drinks. Tea is served in the high-ceilinged Palm Court every afternoon, and whisky is available at any of the hotel's several bar areas. (Foremost among these is N.B.'s, a Scottish pub whose entrance opens directly onto Princes Street.)

Services: 24-hour room service, laundry, valet, concierge.

Facilities: A large and well-equipped health club with Jacuzzi, sauna, exercise equipment, and a pool; direct access to the city's largest railway station; hairdresser, and shops selling cakes, cashmere, crystal, and flowers.

CALEDONIAN HOTEL, Princes St., Edinburgh, Lothian EH1 2AB. Tel. 031/2252433. Fax 031/2256632. 216 rms (all with bath), 23 suites. MINIBAR TV TEL **Bus:** 4, 15, or 44.

$ Rates: £95–£145 ($142.50–$217.50) single; £165–£250 ($247.50–$375) double; from £275 ($412.50) suite. Continental breakfast £10.50 ($15.80) extra. AE, DC, MC, V.

Originally built in 1903, this is Edinburgh's most visible and legendary hotel, with commanding views over Edinburgh Castle and the Princes Street gardens. The material that was used to construct it, Dumfriesshire stone, a form of deep-red sandstone, was used only in three other buildings in town, a fact of which the hotel is justifiably proud. Completely renovated in 1991, the hotel remains one of the city's landmarks, with pastel-colored public rooms reminiscent of an age of Edwardian splendor. Bedrooms are conservatively comfortable, each with video movies and a solid dignity.

Dining/Entertainment: The hotel contains two bars, a traditionally inspired pub, Platform 1, where live entertainment is presented on most evenings, and Carriages Bar, set adjacent to Carriages Restaurant. More formal meals are served in the Pompadour Restaurant (see "Dining," below). A traditional British tea is featured throughout the late afternoon in the hotel's high-ceilinged lounge.

Services: 24-hour room service, babysitting, laundry, valet.

Facilities: Garden, hairdresser, Scottish shop.

HOWARD HOTEL, 32–36 Great King St., Edinburgh, Lothian EH3 6QH. Tel. 031/5573500. Fax 031/5576515. 14 rms (all with bath), 2 suites. TV TEL **Bus:** 13, 23, 27, or C5.

$ Rates (including Scottish breakfast): £110 ($165) single; £180 ($270) double; £55 ($82.50) suite. AE, DC, MC, V. **Parking:** Free.

Three Georgian terrace houses have been combined into a comfortable resting place at one of the finest hotels in Edinburgh. The decor is both traditional and modern. The rooms have hot-beverage facilities and radios, among other amenities.

Dining/Entertainment: After relaxing in the lounge, you might want to patronize an elegant restaurant in the basement, known as No. 36. Specialties include smoked Scottish salmon and pan-fried Scottish sirloin. Lunches are à la carte and rather light, priced at about £8 ($12) each, whereas a three-course table d'hôte dinner goes for £24.95 ($37.40). In the basement is a cocktail lounge, and drinks are also served in the lounge.

Services: 24-hour room service, babysitting, laundry, valet.

Facilities: Club-style lounges.

EXPENSIVE

CARLTON HIGHLAND HOTEL, 19 North Bridge, Edinburgh, Lothian EH1 1SD. Tel. 031/5567277. Fax 031/5562691. 207 rms (all with bath), 6 suites. MINIBAR TV TEL **Bus:** 4, 15, or 44

FROMMER'S SMART TRAVELER: HOTELS

VALUE-CONSCIOUS TRAVELERS SHOULD
TAKE ADVANTAGE OF THE FOLLOWING:

1. Reductions in rates for rooms with private bath. Usually a room with a shower is cheaper than a room with a private bath, or even cheaper is a room with a basin only.
2. You'll often pay at least 30% less than individual "rack" rates (off-the-street independent bookings) if you book a package tour (or book land arrangements with your air ticket).
3. Sometimes on-the-spot bargaining can bring down the cost of a hotel room. There might be a businessperson's or schoolteacher's discount.
4. There may be reductions at some hotels if you pay cash instead of with a credit card.
5. Some hotels may offer long-term discounts if you're planning to spend more than 1 week in a place.

QUESTIONS TO ASK IF YOU'RE ON A BUDGET

1. Is there a garage? What's the charge?
2. Is there a surcharge on either local or long-distance calls? In some places, it might be an astonishing 40%. Make your calls at the nearest post office.
3. Does the hotel include service in the rates quoted, or will a service charge be added on at the end of your stay?
4. Is the 17½% Value-Added Tax (VAT) included, or will it be added on later?
5. Is breakfast (continental or Scottish) included in the rates?

$ Rates (including Scottish breakfast): £92–£104 ($138–$156) single; £138 ($207) double; from £260 ($390) suite. AE, DC, MC, V. **Parking:** Free.
The Carlton Highland Hotel was originally built as one of Edinburgh's leading department stores. But in 1984 a team of entrepreneurs converted it into a plush hotel. Its Victorian turrets, Flemish-style gables, and severe gray stonework rise imposingly from a street corner on the Royal Mile, a few paces from Waverley Station. The interior was converted into a bright and airy milieu of hardwood paneling, pastel colors, and modern conveniences. Each bedroom has a kind of Scandinavian simplicity and comfort, with such amenities as a coffee maker, hairdryer, and trouser press.
   Dining/Entertainment: A pianist entertains guests in the lounge, and the hotel also has a nightclub, Minus One, with disco action. The hotel's restaurant, Quills, is designed like a private 19th century library. Meals begin at £15 ($22.50). A buffet is offered at the Carlton Court Carvery.
   Services: 24-hour room service, babysitting, laundry/valet, hairdresser.
   Facilities: Exercise room with a swimming pool, whirlpool, sauna, two squash courts, and an aerobics studio.

GEORGE INTER-CONTINENTAL, 19–21 George St., Edinburgh, Lothian EH2 2PB. Tel. 031/2251251. Fax 031/2265644. 195 rms (all with bath), 10 suites. MINIBAR TV TEL **Bus:** 4, 15, or 44.
$ Rates: £125–£135 ($187.50–$202.50) single; £145–£155 ($217.50–$232.50) double; from £250 ($375) suite. Continental breakfast £9.50 ($14.30) extra. AE, DC, MC, V. **Parking:** Free.
The George Hotel is concentrated quality. A member of the Inter-Continental Hotel group, the George is only short blocks from Princes Street, in the midst of a number of boutiques and bus, rail, and air terminals. All the bedrooms have been refurnished and redecorated, and offer radios and hot-beverage facilities. The public rooms have retained the style, elegance, and old-fashioned comfort of a country house.

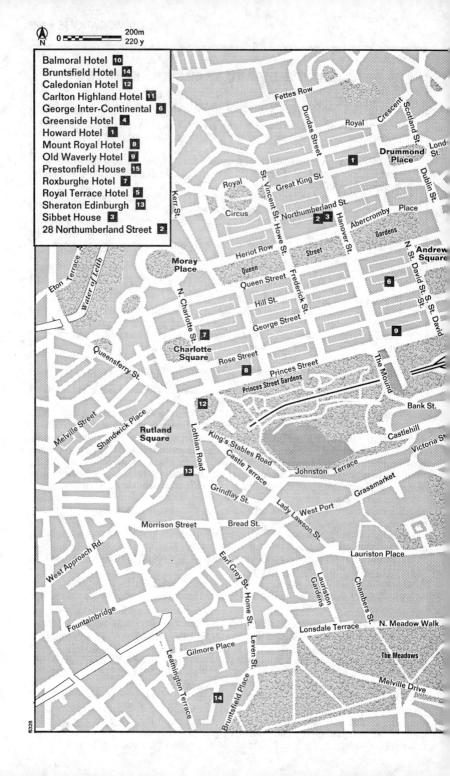

Balmoral Hotel **10**
Bruntsfield Hotel **14**
Caledonian Hotel **12**
Carlton Highland Hotel **11**
George Inter-Continental **6**
Greenside Hotel **4**
Howard Hotel **1**
Mount Royal Hotel **8**
Old Waverly Hotel **9**
Prestonfield House **15**
Roxburghe Hotel **7**
Royal Terrace Hotel **5**
Sheraton Edinburgh **13**
Sibbet House **3**
28 Northumberland Street **2**

Annandale St.

Brunswick Road

Elm Row

East London St.

Union Street

Mongomery Street

Mongomery Street

Broughton Street

Union Place

Hillside

Crescent

London Road

Albany Street

4

Royal Terrace

5

York Place

Elder St.

Leith Street

Calton Hill

Regent Gardens

Regent Terrace

Waterloo Place

Regent Road

Abbey Hill

10

Calton Road

North Bridge

11

Bridge

Market St.

Jeffrey Street

Canongate

High St.

High Street

St. Mary's St.

Holyrood Road

South Bridge

The Queen's Drive

Cowgate

Chambers St.

Drummond St.

Pleasance

Holyrood Park

N Bridge

College St.

Bristo Place

Potterrow

Nicolson St.

West Richmond

St. Leonard's St.

The Queen's Drive

George Square

Buccleuch Street

Crosscauseway

Clerk St.

Middle Meadow Walk

Buccleuch Place

Meadow Lane

Dalkeith Road

The Meadows

Melville Drive

S. Clerk St.

15

East Preston St.

Dining/Entertainment: The Carvers Table offers a selection of prime Scottish beef, roast lamb, or roast pork. Le Chambertin, the hotel's exclusive French restaurant, is open Monday through Saturday (see "Dining," below). The bar has a clublike atmosphere.

Services: 24-hour room service, babysitting, laundry/valet.

Facilities: Public lounge linking reception with the new wing.

MOUNT ROYAL HOTEL, 53 Princes St., Edinburgh, Lothian EH2 2DG. Tel. 031/2257161. Fax 031/2204671. 154 rms (all with bath). TV TEL Bus: 2, 4, 15, 21, or 44.

$ Rates (including continental breakfast): £89 ($133.50) single; £109–£119 ($163.50–$178.50) double. AE, DC, MC, V. **Parking:** Free on street.

The Mount Royal Hotel is right in the middle of the famed thoroughfare, complete with its major shops. A modern world emerges as you climb the spiral staircase or take an elevator to the second floor, with its reception rooms and lounges, and floor-to-ceiling windows opening onto views of the Old Town. In reality, Mount Royal is a remake of an old hotel, from the 1860s, providing streamlined bedrooms with a view. The emphasis is utilitarian—not on frills—although the comfort is genuine.

Dining/Entertainment: The main dining room serves reasonably priced lunches and dinners, offering both a carving table and à la carte menus. Lunch costs about £6 ($9); dinner, £14 ($21). The lounge on the second floor, with floor-to-ceiling windows offering views over the Scott Memorial and Princes Street, provides a wide range of savory and sweet snacks and beverages throughout the day.

Services: Room service, laundry/valet, babysitting.

OLD WAVERLEY HOTEL, 43 Princes St., Edinburgh, Lothian EH2 2BY. Tel. 031/5564648. Fax 031/5576316. 66 rms (all with bath). TV TEL Bus: 4, 15, or 44.

$ Rates (including Scottish breakfast): £76 ($114) single; £122 ($183) double. AE, DC, MC, V. **Parking:** £4 ($6) for 8 hours.

The Old Waverley Hotel has turn-of-the-century origins, but it can be an ideal stopover for those desiring a central establishment, which has been refurbished to provide modern amenities, with personnel giving efficient service. The lounges on the second floor have been given that contemporary look. Some of the rooms look onto Princes Street and, at night, the floodlit castle. The hotel has a good restaurant serving à la carte and table d'hôte meals.

The restaurant is a carvery-style affair, the charges depending on how many courses you take. Lunches cost from £4.50 ($6.80) to £6.50 ($9.80), with dinners going for £11.75 ($17.60) to £13.50 ($20.30).

ROXBURGHE HOTEL, 38 Charlotte Sq., Edinburgh, Lothian EH2 4HG. Tel. 031/2253921. Fax 031/2202518. 75 rms (all with bath), 2 suites. A/C TV TEL **Bus:** 3, 21, 26, 31, or 85.

$ Rates (including Scottish breakfast): £75–£85 ($112.50–$127.50) single; £110–£120 ($165–$180) double; £160 ($240) suite. AE, DC, MC, V. **Parking:** £6 ($9).

The Roxburghe Hotel is an Adam building of dove-gray stone, a stately four-story town house opening directly onto a tree-filled square. The hotel is central, a short walk from Princes Street. The atmosphere is traditional, as reflected in the drawing room, with its ornate ceiling and woodwork, and tall arched windows opening toward the park, and antique furnishings. All the bedrooms, reached by elevator, have clock radios, trouser presses, and tea and coffee makers, plus sewing kits, shower caps, and foam baths, as well as baskets of fruit. The units, each renovated in 1993, are handsomely traditional, a favorite scheme being Adam-style paneling.

Dining/Entertainment: A place to congregate for drinks is the Consort Bar, with its festive decor. A dining room serves not only good meals, such as steaks and game, but gives diners a view of the square. The Melrose Room Buttery serves light refreshments.

Facilities: Residents' lounge.

ROYAL TERRACE HOTEL, 18 Royal Terrace, Edinburgh, Lothian EH7 5AQ. Tel. 031/5573222. Fax 031/5575334. 97 rms (all with bath), 4 suites. TV TEL **Bus:** 4, 15, or 44.

$ Rates: £98–£110 ($147–$165) single; £135–£150 ($202.50–$225) double; from £185 ($277.50) suite. Continental breakfast £6.50 ($9.80) extra. AE, DC, MC, V. **Parking:** 20p (30¢) per hour on street Mon–Sat 8:30am–5:30pm; free otherwise.

The Royal Terrace Hotel has been called "the country-house hotel in the city." Offering luxurious double bedrooms, it was formed from three four-story Georgian town houses, rising on an elegant crescent, about a 10-minute stroll from Waverley Station. Rooms have a host of amenities, including hairdryers and in-house movies. Each has a marble bathroom, and some contain whirlpool baths. The restoration, while providing the most up-to-date comfort, retained much of the period styling, with oil paintings, antiques, open Adam fireplaces, carpets, and Viennese crystal chandeliers; some have four-poster beds.

Dining/Entertainment: Both international and Scottish dishes are served in the Peacock Restaurant, preceded by a before-dinner drink in the well-stocked Peacock Bar, which has more than 21 brands of the finest malt whiskies.

Services: Room service, babysitting, laundry/valet.

Facilities: Elegant Victorian conservatory; Leisure Club with indoor pool, Jacuzzi, sauna, massage room, steam room, and solarium.

SHERATON EDINBURGH, 1 Festival Sq., Edinburgh, Lothian EH3 9SR. Tel. 031/2299131, or toll free 800/325-3535 in the U.S. and Canada. Fax 031/2284510. 263 rms (all with bath), 16 suites A/C MINIBAR TV TEL **Bus:** 4, 15, or 44.

$ Rates: £95 ($142.50) single; £125 ($187.50) double; from £240 ($360) suite. Continental breakfast £10 ($15) extra. AE, DC, MC, V. **Parking:** Free.

Town leaders still praise the development of a former railway siding, only a short walk from Princes Street, into one of the most glamorous hotel and office complexes in Scotland. The hotel is elegantly appointed, with soaring public rooms. Designers drew upon local loyalties by choosing appropriate tones of thistle and mauve for much of the carpeting. This, coupled with a central location and a well-chosen staff, makes this the most appealing modern hotel in the capital.

The spacious, well-upholstered rooms offer double glazing on the windows, and easy contact with a team of concierges. The prices of accommodations are reasonable, considering the quality of the hotel. More glamorous and more expensive suites are also available.

Dining/Entertainment: A plushly modern cocktail bar is a favorite rendezvous for dozens of local residents, while the main restaurant, with its views over the fountain on Festival Square, presents well-prepared main courses and a lavish Sunday buffet. In 1993, the hotel opened two restaurants: The Terrace, with views of the castle, a brasserie-style restaurant with a conservatory atmosphere where chefs prepare specialties just for you, plus The Grill Room, small and intimate with traditional warm wood paneling, providing the best of Scottish produce.

Services: 24-hour room service, babysitting, laundry/valet.

Facilities: A leisure center offers a swimming pool, whirlpool, sauna, and fully equipped gym.

MODERATE

SIBBET HOUSE, 26 Northumberland St., Edinburgh, Lothian EH3 6LS Tel. 031/5561078. Fax 031/5579445. 3 rms (all with bath) TV TEL. **Bus:** 13, 23, or 27.

$ Rates (including Scottish breakfast): £50–£55 ($75–$82.50) single; £60–£65 ($90–$97.50) double. MC, V.

Set on a residential terrace within a 10-minute walk of Princes Street, this is a sandstone-fronted Georgian house originally built in 1809. Today, it's the cheerful domain of James Sibbet and his French-born wife Aurora, who do everything they can to distinguish their family home from "just another hotel." If asked, James (proud of his Lowland Scottish origins) will play the bagpipes. There's a garden in front, a drawing room/salon where, if requested, drinks can be served, and an ambience that never wavers from its homelike presentation. Bedrooms are comfortable and well upholstered, and the neighborhood offers an abundance of restaurants for evening meals.

28 NORTHUMBERLAND STREET, 28 Northumberland St., Edinburgh, Lothian EH3 6LS. Tel. 031/5578036. Fax 031/5583453. 5 rms (3 with bath) TV TEL. **Bus:** 13, 23, or 27.

$ Rates (including Scottish breakfast): £30 ($45) single; £60 ($90) double. MC, V.

This house, set adjacent to the previously recommended Sibbet House, was built during the same era, with many of the same architectural premises as its neighbor. Owned and managed by Ian and Eirlys Smith, it offers cozy and comfortable bedrooms outfitted like those in a private home, a large dining room for the ample breakfasts that the Smiths prepare every morning for their guests. The house lies within a 10-minute walk north of Princes Street. Although only three of the building's rentable bedrooms contain private bathrooms, the other two have exclusive use of separate bathrooms that lie just across one of the upstairs hallways.

INEXPENSIVE

A HAVEN, 180 Ferry Rd., Edinburgh, Midlothian EH6 4NS. Tel. 031/5546559. 11 rms (6 with bath). TV TEL **Bus:** 1, 6, 7, 11, 14, 25, or 69.

$ Rates (including Scottish breakfast): £20 ($30) single without bath, £25 ($37.50) single with bath; £36–£40 ($54–$60) double without bath, £45–£59 ($67.50–$88.50) double with bath. MC, V. **Parking:** Free.

This is a semidetached gray stone four-story Victorian house, within a 15-minute walk or a 5-minute bus ride north of the rail station. Rooms are substantially furnished with traditional pieces. Moira and Ronnie Murdock extend a Scottish welcome in this family-type place. They have a licensed bar but serve only breakfast. Located in an Edinburgh district of character, the establishment has many antiques and skylights.

GREENSIDE HOTEL, 9 Royal Terrace, Edinburgh, Midlothian EH7 5AB. Tel. 031/5570022. 12 rms (7 with bath). **Bus:** 4, 15, or 44.

$ Rates (including Scottish breakfast): £26.50 ($39.80) single without bath, £33.50 ($50.30) single with bath; £49 ($73.50) double without bath, £55 ($82.50) double with bath. No credit cards.

A substantial Georgian house, the Greenside is furnished with a number of antique pieces to give it the right spirit. There are singles, doubles, twins, and three family rooms, all centrally heated and all with hot and cold water. There is a color TV set in the lounge, where coffee and tea are available all day. Most guests approve of the full breakfast included in the rates.

WEST OF THE CENTER
EXPENSIVE

HILTON NATIONAL, Bells Mills, 69 Belford Rd., Edinburgh, Lothian EH4 3DG. Tel. 031/3322545. Fax 031/3323805. 143 rms (all with bath), 1 suite. TV TEL **Bus:** 13, 26, 31, 85, or 86.

$ Rates: £98–£113 ($147–$169.50) single; £130–£145 ($195–$217.50) double; £195 ($292.50) suite. Scottish breakfast £10.50 ($15.80) extra. AE, DC, MC, V. **Parking:** Free.

The Hilton National is a contemporary accommodation set beside the Water of Leith outside the historic district of Edinburgh, 1 mile west of the center. Public rooms are generous in space, and the hotel offers well-furnished bedrooms, each with a clock radio. Some of the rooms—called Plaza Rooms—are the most elegant of all.

Dining/Entertainment: A section of the hotel was a grain mill in Victoria's day, and that old commitment is still honored by the naming of the Granary Bar, which has a certain elegantly rustic quality. Late arrivals will find dinner served until 10pm in the Pavilion Restaurant.

Services: 24-hour room service, laundry/valet.

Facilities: Business Centre reception.

MODERATE

BARNTON THISTLE HOTEL, 562 Queensferry Rd., Edinburgh, Lothian EH4 6AS. Tel. 031/3391144. Fax 031/3395521. 50 rms (all with bath). TV TEL **Bus:** 18, 40, 41, or 82.

$ Rates: £75 ($112.50) single; £85 ($127.50) double. Scottish breakfast £8.75 ($13.10) extra. AE, DC, MC, V. **Parking:** Free.

The Barnton Thistle Hotel stands at a crossroads between Edinburgh and the airport. A Victorian architectural curiosity, it has a balconied tower rising in the center. However, the bedrooms are up-to-date. This long-established hotel has its devotees, largely a commercial clientele, but it's suitable for visitors as well, especially in summer. There are generous public areas, including two bars. Fifty well furnished and maintained bedrooms are rented, with trouser presses and hot beverage facilities.

The hotel's restaurant serves international foods. Room service, laundry, babysitting, and a sauna are offered.

ELLERSLY COUNTRY HOUSE HOTEL, 4 Ellersly Rd., Edinburgh, Lothian EH12 6HZ. Tel. 031/3376888. Fax 031/3132543. 54 rms (all with bath). TV TEL **Directions:** Take the A8 2½ miles west of the city center.

$ Rates: £80 ($120) single; £99 ($148.50) double. Scottish breakfast £8.50 ($12.80) extra. AE, DC, MC, V. **Parking:** Free.

Standing in secluded gardens, this Edwardian country house is about a 5-minute ride from the center. Staying here has been said to offer the "privacy of a home," in a dignified residential section near the Murrayfield rugby grounds. It's one of the best of the moderately priced hotels of Edinburgh, renting well-equipped bedrooms. Accommodations are either in the main house or an annex. After a refurbishment program, the hotel is better than ever. Service is first class.

The hotel possesses a well-stocked wine cellar and offers good-tasting meals, with dinner going for £22.50 ($33.80). Room service and laundry/valet are offered.

 FROMMER'S COOL FOR KIDS: HOTELS

Thrums Hotel (see page 107) This hotel takes its name from J. M. Barrie's fictional designation of his hometown of Kirriemuir. Barrie is known to children as the author of *Peter Pan*. Kids are made especially welcome here and are housed in family rooms with their parents.

Teviotdale House (see page 108) Some enthusiastic visitors rate this place the best B&B in Edinburgh. Three rooms are large enough for families up to four members. Great value.

Nova Hotel (see page 107) This hotel features five spacious family rooms, each designed for total comfort. It's in a quiet secluded cul-de-sac.

HOLIDAY INN GARDEN COURT HOTEL, 107 Queensferry Rd., Edinburgh, Lothian EH4 3HL. Tel. 031/3323442. Fax 031/3323408. 118 rms (all with baths). TV TEL **Bus:** 18, 40, 41, or 82.
$ Rates (including Scottish breakfast): £69.50–£84.50 ($104.30–$126.80) single or double. AE, DC, MC, V. **Parking:** Free.

A favorite of business travelers, this six-story hotel was originally built in 1965, beside the road leading to the airport and the Forth Bridge Road. It was taken over by Holiday Inn in 1991 and improved and upgraded into a clean, efficiently managed hotel with contemporary furnishings and a capable staff. The comfortably unpretentious bedrooms contain trouser presses and radios, and sometimes offer views out over the Firth of Forth and the city's cathedral.

Dining/Entertainment: The hotel's bistro-style restaurant offers a three-course dinner for £14.75 ($22.10), and less formal lunches in a bar setting for around £5 ($7.50) each.

THE LODGE HOTEL, 6 Hampton Terrace, Edinburgh, Lothian, EH12 5JD. Tel. 031/3373682. Fax 031/3131700. 12 rms (all with bath). TV **Bus:** 12, 26, or 31.
$ Rates (including Scottish breakfast): £40–£45 ($60–$67.50) single; £55–£80 ($82.50–$120) double. MC, V. **Parking:** Free.

Set within a quarter-mile of the Haymarket district, this pleasant and comfortable guest house was originally built in 1825 as the manse for the nearby Presbyterian Church. Sheltered by solid stone walls, the hotel contains cozy bedrooms filled with homey touches, and boasts a small but well-kept walled garden in back, and a carpark in front. George and Linda Jarron will prepare evening meals for guests, priced at £13.50 ($20.30) each, and offer directions about nearby bus routes to the attractions of Edinburgh.

INEXPENSIVE

DUNSTANE HOUSE HOTEL, 4 West Coates, Edinburgh, Lothian EH12 5JQ. Tel. 031/3375320. 15 rms (all with shower, 4 with toilet). TV **Bus:** 26, 31, or 69.
$ Rates (including Scottish breakfast): £33.50 ($50.30) single with shower but no toilet; £62 ($93) double with shower but no toilet; £35 ($52.50) single with shower and toilet; £70 ($105) double with shower and toilet. AE, DC, MC, V.

⑤ Originally built around 1850 as the home of a wealthy merchant, this stone-sided house sits behind a pleasant garden, a 10-minute walk from Princess Street. The owner, Helen Hunter, maintains the place in well-scrubbed condition, with respectful awareness of the building's architectural importance. Only about four of the bedrooms have private toilets; the others lie off the public hallways, which are interconnected via a labyrinth of narrow staircases.

SOUTH OF THE CENTER
MODERATE

BRAID HILLS HOTEL, 134 Braid Rd., Edinburgh, Lothian EH10 6JD. Tel. 031/4478888. Fax 031/4528477. 68 rms (all with bath), 1 suite. TV TEL **Bus:** 11 or 15.
$ Rates (including Scottish breakfast): £79 ($118.50) single; £89–£99 ($133.50–$148.50) double; £149 ($223.50) suite. AE, DC, MC, V. **Parking:** Free.

The Braid Hills Hotel is a stone house with turrets and gables in the Edwardian style; however, it dates from Victoria's reign in the 1880s. It's one of the best of the country-house–type hotels right outside Edinburgh, opening onto views of the city. The location of this long-established hotel is about 15 minutes from Princes Street. It offers well-furnished rooms, each with a trouser press.

The restaurant features Scottish and continental cuisine, with both table d'hôte and à la carte menus.

BRUNTSFIELD HOTEL, 69–74 Bruntsfield Place, Edinburgh, Lothian

EH10 4HH. Tel. 031/2291393. Fax 031/2295634. 50 rms (all with bath). TV TEL **Bus:** 11, 15, 16, 17, or 23.
$ Rates (including Scottish breakfast): £71–£85 ($106.50–$127.50) single; £85–£110 ($127.50–$165) double. AE, DC, MC, V. **Parking:** Free.

The Bruntsfield's neo-Gothic facade overlooks an expanse of city park. Like the other 19th-century buildings lining this residential street, it is built of evenly spaced rows of honey-colored stones. Inside, the hotel is neat and stylish, with a formal milieu of French-inspired armchairs and pastel shades of peach and blue. Just across the street are the trees and putting greens of what may be the world's oldest golf course, the Bruntsfield Links. The bedrooms are comfortably renovated, each with a radio, trouser press, hairdryer, tea and coffee maker, and in-house movies. There's an attractive restaurant on the premises, the Potting Shed, along with a bar. Dinners cost £18 ($27).

DONMAREE HOTEL, 21 Mayfield Gardens, Edinburgh, Lothian EH9 2BX. Tel. 031/6673641. Fax 031/6679130. 17 rms (all with bath). TV TEL **Bus:** 42 or 46.
$ Rates (including Scottish breakfast): £50 ($75) single; £70–£80 ($105–$120) double. AE, DC, MC, V. **Parking:** Free.

The Donmaree Hotel, only 15 minutes from Princes Street, is a formally elegant Victorian villa ringed with hedges and rose borders along with a small but impeccably manicured lawn. It's on a busy street with other Victorian homes that rent out rooms, but they aren't as good as the Donmaree. Dating from 1869, the hotel has been extensively refurbished to its Victorian best. It offers beautifully furnished bedrooms, all with hot-beverage facilities. It is an individual hotel with much to recommend it, not the least of which is its highly rated restaurant, the Donmaree.

NOVA HOTEL, 5 Bruntsfield Crescent, Edinburgh, Lothian EH10 4EZ. Tel. 031/4476437. Fax 031/4528126. 10 rms (all with bath or shower). TV TEL **Bus:** 42 or 46.
$ Rates: £30–£35 ($45–$52.50) single; £60–£70 ($90–$105) double; £65 ($97.50) family room for up to three. MC, V. **Parking:** Free.

The Nova Hotel is in a quiet cul-de-sac near the city center, with a view over Bruntsfield Links in front and the Pentland Hills to the back. Visitors are welcomed to its large, well-appointed bedrooms, all with hairdryers, trouser presses, hot-beverage facilities, and full central heating. On the ground floor, guests enjoy the cocktail bar, and the public bar also provides an inviting atmosphere.

PRESTONFIELD HOUSE, Priestfield Road, Edinburgh, Lothian. EH16 5UT. Tel. 031/6683346. Fax 031/6683976. 5 rms (2 with bath). TV TEL **Bus:** 21 or 33.
$ Rates (including Scottish breakfast): £70 ($105) single without bath, £75 ($112.50) single with bath; £80 ($120) double without bath, £105 ($157.50) double with bath. AE, DC, MC, V. **Parking:** Free.

Rising in Jacobean splendor above 26 acres of forest, field, and garden, this establishment is more celebrated as a restaurant than as a hotel (see "Dining," below). Some visitors, however, appreciate its historic calm, its sense of decorum, its venerable 17th-century architecture, and the peacocks and Highland cattle that strut or stroll decoratively across the grounds. Accommodations are dignified and elegant, decorated in a Scottish country-house theme. In most cases, they don't contain private bathrooms, but adequate facilities are located off the hallways.

THRUMS PRIVATE HOTEL, 14–15 Minto St., Edinburgh, Midlothian EH9 1RQ. Tel. 031/6675545. 15 rms (14 with bath). TV TEL **Bus:** 3, 7, 8, 31, or 37.
$ Rates (including Scottish breakfast): £35 ($52.50) single without bath, £45 ($67.50) single with bath; £65–£70 ($97.50–$105) double with bath; £85 ($127.50) family rooms. No credit cards. **Parking:** Free.

The Thrums takes the fictional name of J. M. Barrie's designation of his hometown of Kirriemuir. This choice hotel's well-decorated and furnished bedrooms are situated in two buildings and all have radios, tea/coffee makers, electric blankets, and hairdryers. Family rooms are also offered, and a peaceful garden is at guests' disposal. A small bar is available to residents. The hotel operates an à la carte restaurant for lunches and dinners, where a three-course meal costs £6–£15 ($9–$22.50). Good fresh produce is used in the preparation of all meals. A children's menu is available.

INEXPENSIVE

TEVIOTDALE HOUSE, 53 Grange Loan, Edinburgh, Lothian EH9 2ER. Tel. 031/6674376. Fax 031/6674376. 7 rms (all with bath). TV TEL **Bus:** 42.

$ **Rates** (including Scottish breakfast): £22–£42 ($33–$63) single; £46–£60 ($69–$90) double. AE, MC, V. **Parking:** Free.

Some visitors rate this Victorian town house, on a main bus route leading to the heart of the city, as the finest B&B accommodation in Edinburgh. Jane E. Coville's attention to detail has earned her an enviable reputation. All the bedrooms have hot and cold running water, hairdryers, and restful beds. The house is completely nonsmoking.

The home-cooked breakfast may be the highlight of your dining for the day, and may include smoked salmon, kippers, and home-baked bread and scones. The house lies about 10 minutes from Princes Street, Waverley Station, and Edinburgh Castle.

NORTH OF THE CENTER

MODERATE

COMMODORE HOTEL, West Marine Drive, Cramond Foreshore, Edinburgh, Lothian EH4 5EP. Tel. 031/3361700. Fax 031/3364934. 51 rms (all with bath). TV TEL **Bus:** 8A or 14.

$ **Rates** (including continental breakfast): £55 ($82.50) single; £69.50 ($104.30) double. Scottish breakfast £6.75 ($10.10) extra. AE, DC, MC, V. **Parking:** Free.

The Commodore Hotel was originally built in the 1960s and has nearly doubled in size since then. It sits on the banks of the Forth River, near the Forth River Bridge, which handles traffic from the main autoroute, the M8; it's a 15-minute drive northwest of Princes Street. The hotel occupies grounds between the river and a parkland, and each of its well-furnished bedrooms has big windows overlooking either the park or the river. Each unit has a hairdryer and trouser press. This hotel is a member of a chain, Friendly Hotels, which is firmly entrenched in Scotland as a leader of moderately priced hotels. Golfers appreciate the nearby access to a local course known as Silver Knowes.

CASTLE & COUNTRY HOUSE HOTELS

To fulfill your fantasy, you might want to spend your first night in Scotland in a real castle or a baronial country house surrounded by gardens and spacious grounds.

AT BONNYRIGG

DALHOUSIE CASTLE, Bonnyrigg, Edinburgh, Lothian EH19 3JB. Tel. 0875/20153. Fax 0875/20153. 25 rms (all with bath), 2 suites. TV TEL

$ **Rates** (including Scottish breakfast): £82 ($123) single; £130 ($195) double; £160–£200 ($240–$300) suite. AE, DC, MC, V. **Parking:** Free.

Dalhousie Castle dates back to the 13th century, and over its long history it has entertained such illustrious guests as Edward I, Henry IV, Oliver Cromwell, Sir Walter Scott, and Queen Victoria. Today it's the family seat of the Ramsays of Dalhousie, who have converted it into a luxurious hotel, yet retained some of its finest architectural features. It lies off the A7 Carlisle–Edinburgh road, just outside the village of Bonnyrigg, 8 miles southeast of Edinburgh. A turreted and fortified house, with ramparted terraces and battlements, it offers such delights as a dungeon restaurant, which offers many local Scottish dishes. The rooms all have plenty of space for sitting and relaxing. Two suites have four-poster beds. For true palatial living, you might want to take one of the two-room suites with double or twin beds. The castle overlooks the banks of South Esk, from which came the red sandstone to build it. The hotel can arrange salmon and trout fishing, horseback riding, and shooting.

AT NORTH MIDDLETON

BORTHWICK CASTLE, North Middleton, Gorebridge, Midlothian EH23 4QY. Tel. 0875/20514. Fax 0875/21702. 10 rms (all with bath). TEL
$ Rates (including Scottish breakfast): £80–£150 ($120–$225) single; £95–£165 ($142.50–$247.50) double. AE, DC, MC, V. **Parking:** Free.

Set in a pastoral valley about 12 miles south of Edinburgh, three-quarters of a mile south of the hamlet of North Middleton, just off the A7 motorway, this is the ancestral home of Lord Borthwick. This noble twin-towered keep, built in 1430, is the finest example of its kind in Britain today. It was here that the ill-fated Mary Queen of Scots sought refuge with her third husband, the Earl of Bothwell, in 1567. In 1650 the castle was besieged by the armies of Oliver Cromwell, and the damage inflicted by their cannon fire can still be seen. Inside, the building's centerpiece is the Great Hall, which boasts a minstrels' gallery, a hooded fireplace, a 40-foot vaulted ceiling in the Gothic style, a collection of medieval armor, and an alcove bar with a reassuringly complete collection of single malt whiskies. A four-course fixed-price dinner is available at £30 ($45) per person.

All bedchambers are centrally heated. The most expensive long ago sheltered the historic figures mentioned above. Four contain four-poster bedrooms, and each has a scattering of antiques and chintz fabrics. Borthwick Castle is known for the excellence of its cuisine, its personal service, its authentic medieval ambience, and the recreation of a gracious lifestyle of an earlier era.

4. DINING

The Scots are hearty eaters—and you may like the sizes of their portions as well as the quality of their fare, with choices from river, sea, and loch. You can dine on a cock-a-leekie soup, fresh Tay salmon, haggis, neeps, tatties, and whisky, Aberdeen Angus filet steak, potted hough, poacher's soup, and good old stovies and rumbledethumps. If none of the above tempts you, you'll find that French cuisine has made an inroad at many of the first-class hotels.

An "Expensive" restaurant can charge £18 ($27) to £25 ($37.50) for dinner for one, excluding wine and tips. "Moderate" restaurants charge £15 ($22.50) to £18 ($27) per person for dinner, and anything £15 ($22.50) or under is considered "Inexpensive."

IN THE CENTER
NEW TOWN
Expensive

L'AUBERGE, 56 St. Mary's St. Tel. 5565888.
Cuisine: FRENCH. **Reservations:** Required. **Bus:** 1, 6, 34, or 35.
$ Prices: Appetizers £4.50–£10 ($6.80–$15); main courses £13–£17 ($19.50–$25.50); fixed-price meals £13 ($19.50) at lunch, £19.85 ($29.80) at dinner. AE, DC, MC, V.
Open: Lunch daily 12:15–2pm; dinner daily 7–9:30pm.

L'Auberge, just off the Royal Mile, between Cowgate and Canongate, is ranked among the top three or four restaurants in Edinburgh. As its name suggests, the cuisine is French, backed up by a carefully chosen wine list. Service is perhaps the most polished in the Scottish capital. Game and fish are specialties, and each dish—whether from the moors, loch, or sea—is individually prepared. Some of the main dishes taste as if you've been transported to the Périgord region of France. The menu changes frequently but has been known to offer confit of duck in a Madeira wine sauce with mushrooms, Scottish salmon in a Provençal vinaigrette sauce, and grilled shark with butter sauce, or perhaps filet or pork with fennel and anchovies.

POMPADOUR ROOM, in the Caledonian Hotel, Princes St. Tel. 2252433.
Cuisine: SCOTTISH/FRENCH. **Reservations:** Required. **Bus:** 4, 15, or 44.
$ Prices: Appetizers £6.50–£12 ($9.80–$18); main courses £19–£22 ($28.50–$33); fixed-price lunch with a half bottle of wine £27 ($40.50); fixed-price dinner without wine £35 ($52.50). AE, DC, MC, V.
Open: Lunch Mon–Fri 12:30–2pm; dinner daily 7:30–10:30pm.

The Pompadour Restaurant is one of the finest in Edinburgh, on the mezzanine floor of the famous hotel, serving fine Scottish and French cuisine. The restaurant has been refurbished, with gray wall panels interspersed with panels of floral-patterned silk. The chef blends cuisine moderne with traditional menus in this intimate, luxurious place. A special daily lunch menu reflects the best produce available from the markets that day, and Scottish salmon, venison, and other game are often included in a meal. The à la carte menu also features fresh produce from both local and French markets—items such as goose liver with wild mushrooms, filet of lamb with spinach and rosemary, and charlotte of marinated salmon filled with seafood. There is a no-smoking area. Jackets and ties are requested for men, and reservations are required.

Moderate

ALP HORN RESTAURANT, 167 Rose St. Tel. 2254787.
Cuisine: SWISS/FRENCH. **Reservations:** Recommended. **Bus:** 31 or 33.
$ Prices: Appetizers £2.10–£7.60 ($3.20–$11.40); main courses £6.50–£10.85 ($9.80–$16.30). MC, V.
Open: Lunch Mon–Sat noon–2pm; dinner Mon–Sat 6:30–10pm.
The Alp Horn Restaurant, in an antique stone building on a street long famous for its pubs, provides a meal that's like a vacation in Switzerland. The wooden door opens to reveal an interior accented with checked gingham curtains, potted plants, and simple wooden tables and chairs, everything in the Swiss chalet style. As you'd expect, the menu offers air-dried meats (Grisons style), several fondues, venison in season, and a version of Rösti, the famous potato dish of Switzerland. Fresh Scottish fish is also served. All this might be capped off with a slice of Apfel Strudel.

COSMO RISTORANTE, 58A North Castle St. Tel. 2266743.
Cuisine: ITALIAN. **Reservations:** Required. **Bus:** 31 or 33.
$ Prices: Appetizers £5–£8 ($7.50–$12); main courses £9–£13 ($13.50–$19.50). AE, MC, V.
Open: Lunch Tues–Fri noon–2:15pm; dinner Tues–Sat 7–10:15pm.
Cosmo Ristorante is one of the most heavily patronized Italian restaurants in the Scottish capital. Courtesy, efficiency, and good cookery are featured here. In season you can ask for mussels as an appetizer. Soups and pastas are always reliable. Remember that the cost as well as the portion of your pasta is doubled if you order it as a main course. I've found the veal dishes the best cooked and a good value, although you may be attracted to the seafood. Saltimbocca is a specialty, and the kitchen is known for its light-handed Italian-inspired preparations of Italian fish. The cassata siciliana is well made and not unbearably sweet.

THE DRAGON'S CASTLE, 21 Castle St. Tel. 2257327.
Cuisine: CHINESE. **Reservations:** Recommended Sat–Sun. **Bus:** 2, 3, 4, 11, 12, 16, 17, 22, 31, 33, 36, 41, 44, or 69.
$ Prices: Appetizers £1.40–£4 ($2.10–$6); main courses £5.30–£14.50 ($8–

FROMMER'S SMART TRAVELER: RESTAURANTS

1. Enjoy lunch at some of Edinburgh's first-class restaurants that offer a fixed-price luncheon at such reasonable prices that the kitchen actually loses money.
2. Select fixed-price luncheons or dinners when offered; it's at least a 30% savings off the à la carte menu.
3. Look for daily specials on the à la carte menu. They're invariably fresh, and often cheaper than regular à la carte listings.
4. Drink the house wine—it's a fraction of the price of bottled wine.
5. Watch the booze: Wine and liquor are expensive in Edinburgh.

$21.80); fixed-price three-course meals £4.50 ($6.80) at lunch, £13 ($19.50) at dinner. AE, MC, V.

Open: Mon–Thurs noon–11:30pm, Fri–Sat noon–11:45pm, Sun 12:30–11pm.

The Dragon's Castle is the oldest-established Chinese restaurant in Edinburgh. Its success has been attributed to the fact that it opened in an auspicious year—the Year of the Dragon in the Chinese zodiac calendar. Cantonese and Pekinese cuisine is served, as well as seafood and a selection of European dishes. Menus list a choice of fixed-price meals, for two to six people. Prices for main dishes ordered individually are reasonable. Three-course business lunches are offered during the week from noon to 2pm, costing only £4.20 ($6.30).

INDIAN CAVALRY CLUB, 3 Atholl Place. Tel. 2283282.

Cuisine: INDIAN. **Reservations:** Required. **Bus:** 3, 21, 23, or 26.

$ Prices: Appetizers £1.45–£5 ($2.20–$7.50); main courses £6–£10 ($9–$15); five-course table d'hôte dinner £16 ($24); two-course buffet lunch £6.95 ($10.40). AE, DC, MC, V.

Open: Lunch daily noon–2pm; dinner daily 5:30–11:30pm.

This place surfaces near the top of the list of the many Edinburgh dining rooms that specialize in Indian food. Vegetarians flock here, and all guests can enjoy the elegant atmosphere that evokes the British heyday in India, when Queen Victoria was known as Empress of India. Along with the classic and tandoori food items from India many dishes are based on recipes from Nepal or Burma.

MARTINS, 70 Rose St., North Lane. Tel. 2253106.

Cuisine: BRITISH. **Reservations:** Required. **Bus:** 31 or 33.

$ Prices: Appetizers £3.90–£8.40 ($5.90–$12.60); main courses £14–£14.95 ($21–$22.40); fixed-price two-course lunch £10.30 ($15.50). MC, V.

Open: Lunch Tues–Fri noon–2pm; dinner Tues–Thurs 7–10pm, Fri–Sat 7–10:30pm.

This is a chic and gastronomically sophisticated restaurant run by Martin and Gay Irons, its tuned-in owners. Their fixed-price lunch is one of the best dining values of Edinburgh. The decor emphasizes clear natural lighting by day and focused spotlights at night, each aimed at a series of contemporary prints by Scottish artists. A pinewood bar is found in the corner. Food selections are limited but choice, offering about four appetizers and four main courses every day. Everything is fresh and made on the spot, including the bread. All ingredients are Scottish. Fresh fish offerings might, for example, include pan-fried turbot with a coulis of tomato and herbs, or haunch of venison served pink with a sauce made with wild Scottish mushrooms. They have about 130 different wines in the cellar.

THE OYSTER BAR, 17 W. Register St. Tel. 5564124.

Cuisine: SEAFOOD/GAME. **Reservations:** Recommended year-round, but essential during the festival. **Bus:** 42 or 44.

Alp Horn Restaurant **8**
Baked Potato Shop **13**
Circles Coffee House **12**
Cosmo Ristorante **1**
Dragon's Castle **6**
Grill Room **5**
Helios Fountain **18**
Henderson's Salad Table **2**
Indian Cavalry Club **10**
Jackson's Restaurant **14**
Kalpna **20**
Kelly's **19**
L'Auberge **16**
Le Chambertin **3**
Martins **7**
Mr. Boni's Ice Cream Parlour **21**
Oyster Bar **4**
Pancake Place **15**
Pierre Victoire **17**
Pompadour Room **9**
Prestonfield House **23**
Szechuan House **22**
Witchery by the Castle **11**

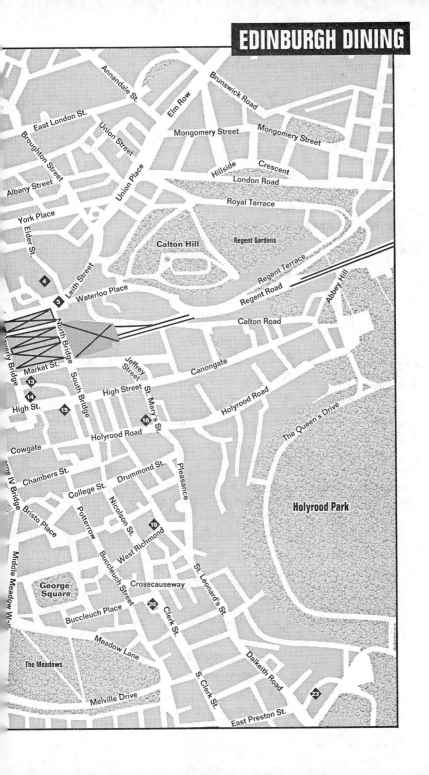

$ Prices: Appetizers £3–£8 ($4.50–$12); main courses £10–£22 ($15–$33); three-course Sun brunch £15 ($22.50). MC, V.

Open: Lunch Mon–Sat noon–2pm; dinner daily 7–10:30pm; brunch Sun 12:30–2:30pm.

✪ Its physical plant is one of the most elegant and dramatic in Edinburgh, thanks to its richly ornate Victorian bar and its soaring windows inset with stained-glass depictions of 19th-century Scotsmen in full Highland dress. It is also the most sought-after of the several different dining areas in the historic Café Royal, one of the largest and busiest dining emporiums in Edinburgh. This intimate and quiet corner specializes, as its name implies, in seafood, plus game dishes. You might like the salmon with mussels, shrimp with Camembert and white wine, or the steak in a black-butter sauce. You can also select oak-smoked haddock poached in cream and topped with spinach.

The Oyster Bar is also the best place to go for a Sunday brunch.

VERANDAH TANDOORI, 17 Dairy Rd. Tel. 3375828.
   Cuisine: NORTH INDIAN. **Reservations:** Required. **Bus:** 3, 4, 43, 44, or 66.
$ Prices: Appetizers £2.25–£4.25 ($3.40–$6.40); main courses £5–£15 ($7.50–$22.50); fixed-price lunch or dinner £33 ($49.50) for 2. AE, DC, MC, V.
   Open: Lunch daily noon–2:30pm; dinner daily 5–11:45pm.

Verandah Tandoori, near the Haymarket depot, offers better-than-average food from northern India and Bangladesh. A much-awarded restaurant, it deserves its good reputation. Vegetarians, of course, flock here, and you can select from a wide range of classic and tandoori food items made with excellent, fresh ingredients.

Inexpensive

SZECHUAN HOUSE, 12-14 Leamington Terrace. Tel. 2294655.
   Cuisine: SZECHUAN. **Bus:** 9, 10, or 27.
$ Prices: Appetizers £1.75–£9.90 ($2.60–$14.90); main courses £5.25–£10 ($7.90–$15). MC, V.
   Open: Dinner only, Tues–Sun daily 5:30pm–midnight.

⑤ You don't come here for elegant trappings, but you get zesty, savory platters of poultry and fish, especially chicken, duck, and prawns. You might begin with either "bang-bang" chicken or fishhead soup, and follow with diced chicken with chili or fried squid family style. Vegetarians can also dine happily. The cookery is classic and authentic, as the chef, Chao Gang Liu, comes from Szechuan province.

WHIGHAM'S WINE CELLARS, 13 Hope St. Tel. 2258674.
   Cuisine: SCOTTISH. **Reservations:** Required. **Bus:** 2, 4, or 34.
$ Prices: Appetizers £1.70–£4.95 ($2.60–$7.40); main courses £3.95–£6.75 ($5.90–$10.10). V.
   Open: Lunch Mon–Sat noon–2:30pm; dinner Mon–Sat 6pm–midnight.

Whigham's Wine Cellars lie in a basement in the heart of Edinburgh's financial center. Before the premises became a fashionable wine-cellar restaurant, wine was actually bottled here. Whigham's has been in business since the mid-18th century, and it used to ship wines to the American colonies. Walk across its mellowed, old stone floors until you find an intimate alcove. A range of continental wines is offered. Each day, you can make your selection from an assortment of appetizers and plats du jour. Their smoked fish (not just salmon) is exceptional. Marine fresh oysters come from Lock Fyne, and smoked venison occasionally appears on the menu.

OLD TOWN

Moderate

JACKSON'S RESTAURANT, 209 High St., Royal Mile. Tel. 2251793.
   Cuisine: SCOTTISH. **Reservations:** Required. **Bus:** 35.
$ Prices: Appetizers £5–£8 ($7.50–$12); main courses £12.50–£16 ($18.80–$24). AE, DC, MC, V.
   Open: Lunch Mon–Fri noon–2pm; dinner daily 6:30–10:30pm.

Serving a cuisine described as "Scottish with a French flair," this bustling and popular restaurant is in the austere but cozy stone cellar of a 300-year-old building originally built by entrepreneurs named the Jackson Brothers. Your apéritif might be one of any of almost 40 kinds of Highland malts, or perhaps a glass of Scottish wine, before you select from a "Taste of Scotland" menu featuring local ingredients. The charming staff might help you translate such items as "beasties of the glen" (a poetic designation for haggis with a whisky-cream sauce), noisettes of venison served in a blackberry, red currant, and port wine sauce, and "kilted salmon pan-fried in a green ginger and whisky sauce."

PIERRE VICTOIRE, 10 Victoria St. Tel. 2251721.
   Cuisine: FRENCH. **Reservations:** Required. **Bus:** 1, 6, 34, or 35.
$ **Prices:** Appetizers £2.50–£3.80 ($3.80–$5.70); main courses £5.80–£7.80 ($8.70–$11.70); fixed-price lunch £4.90 ($7.40). MC, V.
   Open: Lunch Mon–Sat 11am–3pm; dinner Mon–Sat 5:30–11pm. Open Sun (same hours) during Edinburgh Festival.

This was the original model for a series of franchise copies, each named Pierre Victoire, which have sprouted up in recent years in three or four other areas of Edinburgh. Many residents still prefer the original to the newer versions. It's an ideal stopover if you're antique shopping and climbing Victoria Street. It's also one of the most popular evening gathering places as it keeps long hours. Wine specials "direct from France" are posted on the blackboard. In a bistro setting with crowded tables, you can order grilled mussels in garlic with Pernod butter, salmon with ginger, or roast pheasant with Cassis. Pierre le Vicky, the owner and chef de cuisine, is well known locally, so advance reservations are needed. Vegetarians are also welcome.

WITCHERY BY THE CASTLE, Castlehill, Royal Mile. Tel. 2255613.
   Cuisine: SCOTTISH. **Reservations:** Advised. **Bus:** 1, 34, or 35.
$ **Prices:** Appetizers £2.95–£9.95 ($4.40–$14.90); main courses £16–£20 ($24–$30); two-course lunch £10.40 ($15.60). AE, DC, MC, V.
   Open: Lunch daily noon–3pm; dinner daily 6–11pm.
This place bills itself as the "oldest most haunted" restaurant in town. The building has been linked with witchcraft since the period between 1470 and 1722 when more than 1,000 people were burned alive on Castlehill. One of the victims is alleged to haunt the Witchery. She is known as Old Mother Long Nose, once a practitioner of herbal medicine, and a model of her sits by the entrance. James Thomson, the owner, uses his creative flair as a chef to make the restaurant a member of the "Taste of Scotland" program for good Scottish food and hospitality. Menus change seasonally and might include Skye prawns or Tay salmon. Angus steak is a specialty. Vegetarian dishes are also offered, and desserts are homemade. Some 170 wines and 40 malt whiskies are available.

SOUTH OF THE CENTER
MODERATE

KELLY'S, 46 West Richmond St. Tel. 6683847.
   Cuisine: MODERN BRITISH/MODERN FRENCH. **Reservations:** Recommended. **Bus:** 11, 12, or 14.
$ **Prices:** Fixed-price dinner (three courses) £19.50 ($29.30). AE, DC, MC, V.
   Open: Dinner only, Tues–Sat 6:45–9:30pm (last order). **Closed:** October.

Catering to a dinner-only crowd of barristers, artists, financiers, and employees of the nearby university, this stylish restaurant sports a peach-colored decor whose accessories are vaguely reminiscent of a sophisticated restaurant in California. Within a 20-minute walk south of the center in a residential neighborhood, the place offers an intimate setting lined with flowers, bleached pine furniture, watercolors, and unusual ceramics. Meals are prepared by Jacquie Kelly and her husband Jeff, who manages the dining room as well as the art gallery (Kelly's) located next door. Focusing on fresh ingredients and vaguely inspired by the culinary techniques of Paul Bocuse, the menu includes such dishes as galantine of duck with Cumberland sauce; a parcel of turbot with a seafood mousse, a timbale of leeks and lemons, and a dill-flavored beurre blanc sauce; filet of brill in pepper sauce; and a platter containing both loin of lamb and breast of pigeon bound together with port-flavored cranberries. Dessert might be a simple but succulent lemon tart with *crème anglaise*. A sophisticated but fairly priced wine list is available.

LEITH

In the northern regions of Edinburgh, Leith is the old port town, opening onto the Firth of Forth. Once it was a city in its own right until it was slowly absorbed into Edinburgh. After decades of decay, parts of it are gradually being restored into modernized "flats," along with a collection of restaurants, wine bars, and pubs.

EXPENSIVE

THE VINTNERS ROOM, The Vaults, 87 Giles St., Leith. Tel. 5548423.
Cuisine: FRENCH/SCOTTISH. **Reservations:** Recommended. **Bus:** 7 or 10.
$ Prices: Appetizers £3.50–£6.50 ($5.30–$9.80); main courses £12–£16 ($18–$24). Fixed-price lunches (in wine bar only), £8–£10.75 ($12–$16.10) AE, MC, V.
Open: Lunch Mon–Sat noon–2:30pm; dinner Mon–Sat 7–10:30pm. **Closed:** Two weeks at Christmastime.

Many Edinburghers consider a trek out to the 19th-century port of Leith well worth the effort because of the ambience created by The Vintner's Room. The stone-fronted building that contains it was originally built around 1650 as a warehouse for the barrels of wine and port that came in from Europe's mainland. Near the entrance, beneath a venerable ceiling of oaken beams, a wine bar serves platters and drinks beside a large stone fireplace, with glasses of wine priced at from £1.50 ($2.30) each. Most diners, however, head for the small but elegant dining room, where most of the illumination comes from flickering candles. There, elaborate Italianate plasterwork decorates a room that functioned 300 years ago as the site of wine auctions. Owners Tim and Sue Cummings, who manage the kitchens and front rooms, respectively, prepare a sophisticated cuisine that might include seafood salad with mango mayonnaise, a terrine of smoked salmon and rabbit, loin of pork with mustard sauce, and filet of turbot with essence of crabmeat, all of it finished off with a two-chocolate mousse served with a bitter chocolate sauce. The wine list, perhaps out of respect for the premises' original function, is appropriately elaborate.

MODERATE

DENZLER'S 121, 121 Constitution St., Leith. Tel. 5543268.
Cuisine: SCOTTISH. **Reservations:** Recommended. **Bus:** 16.
$ Prices: Appetizers £2.40–£5.75 ($3.60–$8.60); main courses £9.10–£10.85 ($13.70–$16.30). AE, DC, MC, V.
Open: Lunch Tues–Fri noon–2pm; dinner Tues–Sat 6:30–10pm.

Just beyond Leith Walk, this restaurant took over the former North of Scotland Bank building. Today, many consider it the finest dining choice in Leith. Although a Swiss restaurant, the decor has contemporary Scottish pictures. Guests meet in the cocktail bar for drinks, perhaps studying the wine list that includes Swiss Fendant and Dole wines, as well as those from such faraway places as Chile and Argentina. Nothing is more typically Swiss than the appetizers, Bundnerpattli, wafer-thin slices of air-dried Swiss beef and ham from the Grisons. The most typical main course is emincée de veau Zurichoise, slices of veal with mushrooms in a cream sauce served with Spätzli. Of course, it wouldn't be a Swiss restaurant without fondue.

INEXPENSIVE

SHORE BAR AND RESTAURANT, 3 The Shore, Leith. Tel. 5535080.
Cuisine: SEAFOOD/GAME. **Reservations:** Required. **Bus:** 16.
$ Prices: Appetizers £1.80–£5 ($2.70–$7.50); main courses £5.50–£11.50 ($8.30–$17.30). MC, V.
Open: Lunch daily noon–2:30pm; dinner daily 6:30–10:15pm.

The only indication that you've arrived at this waterfront restaurant is a sign that says

WINE AND SPIRIT MERCHANTS painted in gilt letters on the big-windowed facade. Formerly a run-down pub, it had been converted into this cozily intimate rendezvous for Edinburghers wanting to get away from it all. The blue and white dining room has a blackboard menu that changes twice daily. Lunch and dinner are served every day and might include Stilton-and-leek soup, salmon with a sorrel hollandaise, whole baked brill, beef with apricots, and spicy king prawns.

SKIPPER'S BISTRO, 1A Dock Place, Leith. Tel. 5541018.
   Cuisine: SEAFOOD. **Reservations:** Required. **Bus:** 16.
$ Prices: Appetizers £1.60–£5.90 ($2.40–$8.90); main courses £7.80–£9.80 ($11.70–$14.70); fixed-price 2-course menu £14.50 ($21.80); fixed-price 3-course menu £17.50 ($26.30). AE, MC, V.
   Open: Lunch Mon–Sat 12:30–2pm; dinner Mon–Sat 7:30–10pm.
One of the foremost restaurants in Edinburgh's port area, off Commercial Street near a canal, this former pub was skillfully "gentrified" by Allan and Jen Corbett with well-polished brass, the antique chairs, and the marble-top bars. Coffee rounds off the flavor of the meals, which might include a marinade of kipper, trout au gratin, scallops thermidor, and a mousseline of seafood.

WATERFRONT WINE BAR, 1C Dock Place, Leith. Tel. 5547427.
   Cuisine: SEAFOOD. **Bus:** 16.
$ Prices: Appetizers £1.80–£4.80 ($2.70–$7.20); main courses £5.50–£9.50 ($8.30–$14.30). No credit cards.
   Open: Lunch Mon–Fri noon–2:30pm, Sat noon–3pm; dinner Mon–Thurs 6–9:30pm, Fri–Sat 6–10pm.
This is a pleasant place whose brick and stone walls are adorned with old prints, maps, photographs, and other nautical memorabilia. A large vine acts like a pergola, letting dappled sunlight play across the tables. During the summer, you can be seated at a table on a floating raft. Wine lovers enjoy vintage wine by the glass and a large selection by the bottle. An array of daily specials is listed on the blackboard. Beer begins at £1.70 ($2.60).

PRESTONFIELD

EXPENSIVE

PRESTONFIELD HOUSE, Priestfield Rd., Edinburgh, Lothian. EH16 5UT. Tel. 6683346.
   Cuisine: BRITISH. **Reservations:** Necessary. **Bus:** 21, 33.
$ Prices: Appetizers £4.60–£9.90 ($6.90–$14.90); main courses £13.20–£17.95 ($19.80–$26.90). Table d'hôte lunch £17 ($25.50); table d'hôte dinner £22 ($33).
   Open: Lunch daily 12:30–2pm; dinner daily 7–8:30pm.
Hidden away amid 23 acres of privately owned parkland and gardens, 3 miles south of Edinburgh's center, this is one of the most elegant restaurants in town, a venue for graceful celebrations for local residents who reserve for birthday dinners many months in advance. Some kind of manor house has stood on the site since 1355, although the graceful Dutch-style rooflines of the Jacobean building you'll see today date from 1687. Highland cattle and peacocks add to the ornamentation of the grounds. Inside, is an enviable collection of antiques.

   Menu items include grilled smoked salmon served with braised leeks and gazpacho sauce, marinated smoked pigeon with an avocado and raspberry salad, filet of halibut with Provençal nut butter, baked fillet of lamb in phyllo pastry with tomatoes and wild mushrooms, and venison and oyster pie with spring vegetables. Men are requested to wear jackets and ties.

   The establishment contains five rentable bedrooms, described more fully in "Accommodations."

SPECIALTY DINING

VEGETARIAN

HELIOS FOUNTAIN, 7 Grassmarket. Tel. 2297884.

Cuisine: VEGETARIAN. **Bus:** 2 or 12.
$ Prices: Appetizers £1.10–£1.95 ($1.70–$2.90); main courses £1.25–£2.50 ($1.90–$3.80). MC, V.
Open: Mon–Sat 10am–6pm; during the festival, daily 10am–8pm.

The food at this Old Town restaurant, one of the best vegetarian spots in Edinburgh, is prepared from mostly organically or biodynamically grown produce, and the menu is carefully selected and produced daily. Full tables testify to the quality of the place. While sitting on cushioned stools and benches, enjoying herb tea, you can select one of the good-tasting soups (ever had parsnip?), later enjoying a potato-and-eggplant curry or a quiche (perhaps pepper and broccoli) made with "free-range" eggs. Casseroles are especially notable, including pimiento and chestnut.

HENDERSON'S SALAD TABLE, 94 Hanover St. Tel. 2252131.

Cuisine: VEGETARIAN. **Bus:** 23 or 27.
$ Prices: Appetizers 80p–£1.10 ($1.20–$1.70); main courses £2.60–£3 ($3.90–$4.50). AE, DC, MC, V.
Open: Mon–Sat 8am–11pm.

This is a Shangri-La for health-food lovers, as well as those who want an array of nutritious salads. It's self-service, and you can pick and choose eggs, carrots, grapes, nuts, yogurt, cheese, potatoes, cabbage, watercress—you name it. Hot dishes such as peppers stuffed with rice and pimiento are served on request. Among homemade desserts you may choose a fresh-fruit salad or a cake with double whipped cream and chocolate sauce. Henderson's is furnished with pinewood tables (often shared) and chairs. The wine cellar provides a choice of 30 wines, most of which may be had by the glass. A variety of music, ranging from classical to jazz to folk, is played live every evening. The adjoining Bistro Bar serves meals with table service from noon to 5pm daily.

KALPNA, 2-3 St. Patrick Sq. Tel. 6679890.

Cuisine: INDIAN. **Reservations:** Required Fri–Sat. **Bus:** 5, 11, 13, or 51.
$ Prices: Appetizers £2–£3.50 ($3–$5.30); main courses £3.25–£8.50 ($4.90–$12.80); fixed-price menus £7–£8.50 ($10.50–$12.80); all-you-can-eat Indian buffet £12.50 ($18.80). MC, V.
Open: Lunch Mon–Fri noon–2pm; dinner Mon–Sat 5:30–11pm.

Kalpna is a southern Indian vegetarian restaurant, remarkably reasonable in price considering the quality of its ingredients. Its name is translated as "imagination," and that is reflected in the often subtle flavors. However, the food can also be sharply spiced and beautifully colored when it reaches your plate. Try such specialties as daal tarka (yellow lentils cooked in the traditional style) or ringna bhajee (eggplant cooked with tomatoes spiced with fenugreek leaves and asafoetida). Khoya Kaju is based on the chef's own recipe, using cashew nuts, khoya (reduced cream), sultanas, pistachio, nutmeg, and fresh coriander leaves. Lassi (a yogurt drink) is the preferred beverage, or Kingfisher beer.

FAST FOOD

THE BAKED POTATO SHOP, 56 Cockburn St. Tel. 2257572.

Cuisine: VEGETARIAN WHOLE-FOOD TAKE-AWAY. **Reservations:** Not accepted. **Bus:** 5.
$ Prices: Food items 40p–£2.45 (60¢–$3.70). No credit cards.
Open: Mar–Oct, Sun–Thurs 9am–11pm, Fri–Sat 9am–1am; Nov–Feb, daily 9am–9pm.

This is arguably the least expensive restaurant in a very glamorous neighborhood, and it attracts mobs of office workers every day, most of whom carry their food away for consumption on one of the dozens of outdoor seating areas scattered in the vicinity of the Royal Mile and High Street. Place your order at the countertop and it will be served in ecology-conscious recycled cardboard containers by the T-shirt and apron-clad staff. Only free-range eggs, whole foods, and vegetarian cheeses are used. Food items include more than 20 different kinds of salads, large and

FROMMER'S COOL FOR KIDS: RESTAURANTS

Mr. Boni's Ice Cream Parlour Every kid comes away loving Mr. Boni, who makes the best homemade ice cream in Edinburgh, plus sandwiches, jumbo hot dogs, and beefburgers with french fries. Mr. Boni's is located at 4 Lochrin Bridge (tel. 2295319).

The Pancake Place (see page 119) Pancakes in all their many different varieties are served to delight, although many kids prefer the baked potatoes stuffed with various fillings or one of the tasty hamburgers.

Henderson's Salad Table (see page 118) The leading vegetarian restaurant of Edinburgh has an array of nutritious salads, followed by some of the most delectable homemade desserts in the city.

Witchery by the Castle (see page 115) Kids delight in being taken to this Royal Mile restaurant that claims to be the "oldest and most haunted" restaurant in Old Town. The homemade desserts are sumptuous too.

flaky baked potatoes (dug from the soil of nearby East Lothian) stuffed with your choice of half a dozen hot fillings, India-inspired curried dumplings known as bhajias, and such other dishes as mushroom risotto, chili, and cauliflower in cheese sauce. New Age nostalgia buffs can even sample the establishment's version of vegetarian haggis. There's a small table, seating no more than six diners.

CIRCLES COFFEE HOUSE, 324-326 Lawnmarket. Tel. 2259505.
  Cuisine: SCOTTISH. **Bus:** 1 or 6.
  $ Prices: Appetizers 95p ($1.40); main courses £2.50–£4.50 ($3.80–$6.80). No credit cards.
  Open: Daily 10am–5:30pm; during the festival, daily 9:30am–11pm. **Closed:** Jan.
Circles, housed in a stone structure dating from the 18th century, lies along the Royal Mile about 300 feet from Edinburgh Castle. Here at the self-service counter you can select homemade soup, quiche, lasagne, and salads priced per portion. Follow this by freshly made trifle, cheesecake, shortbread, or a selection of home-baked pastries. It's licensed, so you can drop in for a drink as well as a coffee.

THE PANCAKE PLACE, 130 High St., Royal Mile. Tel. 2251972.
  Cuisine: PANCAKES. **Bus:** 1, 6, 34, or 35.
  $ Prices: Appetizers 85p–£1.80 ($1.20–$2.70); main courses £1.99–£3.50 ($3–$5.30). No credit cards.
  Open: Daily 8am–9pm.
Part of a franchise chain, the Pancake Place features pancakes in all varieties as well as stuffed baked potatoes, hamburgers, and vegetarian selections. An average meal may consist of filled pancakes, an appetizer or homemade soup, and dessert.

HOTEL DINING

DONMAREE HOTEL RESTAURANT, 21 Mayfield Gardens. Tel. 6673641.
  Cuisine: BRITISH. **Reservations:** Recommended. **Bus:** 42 or 46.
  $ Prices: Appetizers £3.30–£5.50 ($5–$8.30); main courses £9.20–£12.50 ($13.80–$18.80); table d'hôte lunch £17.50 ($26.30) AE, DC, MC, V.
  Open: Lunch daily 12:30–2pm; dinner daily 6:30–10pm.
The previously recommended Donmaree Hotel (see "Accommodations," above) also offers a well-respected restaurant, with good food and service. It's in a residential

neighborhood behind a gray stone facade, 15 minutes from Princes Street. It has been beautifully decorated in the spirit of its Victorian origins under the direction of Mr. and Mrs. Galt. The chef might offer a pot-roasted pheasant, rack of lamb marinated in honey and red wine, or roast duckling with an orange and Curaçao sauce.

GRILL ROOM, in the Balmoral Hotel, 1 Princes Street. Tel. 5562414.
   Cuisine: SCOTTISH/CONTINENTAL. **Reservations:** Recommended.
$ Prices: Appetizers £6–£14 ($9–$21); main courses £15–£21 ($22.50–$31.50). AE, DC, MC, V.
   Open: Lunch daily noon–2:30pm; dinner daily 7–10:30pm.

⭐ This is the premier restaurant within one of the most impressive hotel renovations Edinburgh has seen in recent memory. Established in 1991 during the $35-million renovation of the Balmoral Hotel, the Grill Room is an intimate, crimson-colored enclave one floor below the reception area of the hotel. Walls are studded with Scottish memorabilia in patterns just informal enough to be sporting, and just formal enough to be very, very elegant. You'll sit in comfortably upholstered ivory-colored armchairs as a staff pampers you with attentive service. Menu specialties include spinach salad wilted in hot vinaigrette with bacon; turbot from the North Sea flavored with rosemary; seven kinds of grilled steak; smoked seabass with saffron-basil dressing and ratatouille; zucchini flowers filled with crabmeat mousse; three kinds of fish, mousseline sauce, and squid-ink pasta; and a rosette of Scottish salmon with whisky, Pernod and dill sauce. One of the many desserts to tempt you might include raspberry bavarois fenced in chocolate with a brandy basket filled with seasonal berries.

LE CHAMBERTIN, in the George Inter-Continental, 21 George St. Tel. 2251251.
   Cuisine: FRENCH. **Reservations:** Required. **Bus:** 4, 15, or 44.
$ Prices: Appetizers £4.75–£12.50 ($7.10–$18.80); main courses £13.50–£22 ($20.30–$33). AE, DC, MC, V.
   Open: Lunch Mon–Fri 12:30–2:30pm; dinner Mon–Sat 7:30–10pm.
In the evening, guests can select from a wide choice of wines, including special bottles from the Chambertin district of France. The à la carte menu is well balanced and features many traditional dishes and, subject to availability, lobster, mussels, oysters, and venison. You might begin with marinated or smoked Scottish salmon, or wild hare sautéed with juniper berries and served in a nest of buttered noodles. Roast breast of quail with wild mushrooms in a creamy chive sauce is another specialty. Dover sole can be grilled or served meunière, or else diners can enjoy filet of beef sautéed with rosemary on a bed of wild mushrooms. Several specialties from the grill, include chateaubriand for two persons.

PICNIC SUPPLIES & WHERE TO EAT THEM

If the weather is right, Edinburgh makes an ideal venue for a picnic, as the city is filled with gardens and parks, notably the spacious **Holyrood Park,** in back of the Palace of Holyroodhouse. Here you can enjoy not only a view but some dramatic landscaping, including a loch and rocky crags. Others prefer to go to **Arthur's Seat** and the **Salisbury Crags** nearby for the best view of "Auld Reekie" and the Firth of Forth. You can also go to the centrally located **Princes Street Gardens,** which divide the Old Town from the New Town. There are dozens of wooden benches where you can enjoy your picnic, but remember not to litter.

For your supplies, you can go to the **Waverley Market** on Princes Street, where separate stalls serve a variety of food, everything from whole-meal scones to a Cornish pasty. Purchase something to drink with the makings of your picnic, and the day is yours. The market is open daily from 9:30am to 5:30pm.

There's also a prepared-food supermarket in the basement of the **Marks & Spencer** department store, 53 Princes St., offering an array of freshly made sandwiches, cakes, fruits, pasta salads, and regular salads. It's open Monday through Saturday from 9am to 6pm.

5. ATTRACTIONS

SUGGESTED ITINERARIES

IF YOU HAVE 1 DAY   The choice is fairly obvious. Visit Edinburgh Castle as soon as it opens in the morning, then walk the Royal Mile to the Palace of Holyroodhouse, former abode of Mary Queen of Scots. Look out over the city from the vantage point of Arthur's Seat, and stroll through Princes Street Gardens, capping your day with a walk along the major shopping thoroughfare, Princes Street. To be really authentic, order a typically Scottish dinner of haggis in the evening, washed down with a wee dram of scotch.

IF YOU HAVE 2 DAYS   Spend your first day as above. On your second day, in the morning head for Old Town again, but this time take a good part of the day to explore its narrow streets, "wynds," and closes, and visiting John Knox House, the High Kirk of St. Giles, Lady Stair's House, and other small museums. After lunch, climb the Scott Monument for a good view of Old Town and the Princes Street Gardens. Spend the rest of the afternoon exploring the National Gallery of Scotland.

IF YOU HAVE 3 DAYS   Spend the first 2 days as suggested above. Occupy Day 3 becoming acquainted with the major attractions of New Town, including the Royal Museum of Scotland, the National Portrait Gallery, Georgian House, and the Royal Botanic Garden.

IF YOU HAVE 5 DAYS   Spend Days 1 to 3 as suggested above. On the fourth day take a trip west to Stirling Castle and see some of the dramatic scenery of the Trossachs. On the fifth day, you'll feel like a native (few foreign visitors stay in Edinburgh more than 3 days). This will afford you the chance to see many of the city's minor but interesting attractions, including the Scottish United Services Museum, Camera Obscura, the Scotch Whisky Heritage Centre, and Dean Village. If time remains, cap your day with a call on the Edinburgh Zoo.

THE TOP ATTRACTIONS
THE ROYAL MILE

The Royal Mile stretches from Edinburgh Castle all the way to the Palace of Holyroodhouse. Walking along, you'll see some of the most interesting old structures in Edinburgh, with their turrets, gables, and towering chimneys. Take bus no. 1, 6, 23, 27, 30, 34, or 36 to reach it.

Inside the **High Kirk of St. Giles** on High Street (tel. 2259442), one outstanding feature is its Thistle Chapel, designed by Sir Robert Lorimer, housing beautiful stalls and notable heraldic stained-glass windows. The church is open Monday through Saturday from 9am to 5pm and on Sunday from 1 to 5pm. Of course, you are welcome to join in the cathedral's services on Sunday conducted at various times from 7am to 9pm. A group of cathedral guides is available at all times to conduct guided tours. John Knox, the leader of the Reformation in Scotland, was minister of St. Giles from 1560 to 1572. Admission is free, except for the 50p (75¢) charge to visit Thistle Chapel.

Lady Stair's House lies in a close of the same name off Lawnmarket (tel. 2252425, ext. 6593). It was built in 1622 by a prominent merchant burgess and takes its name from a former owner, Elizabeth, the dowager Countess of Stair. Today it's a treasurehouse of portraits, relics, and manuscripts relating to three of Scotland's greatest men of letters—Robert Burns, Sir Walter Scott, and Robert Louis Stevenson. It's open Monday through Saturday from 10am to 5pm (until 6pm from June to September). Admission is free.

The **Museum of Childhood**, 42 High Street (tel. 2252424, ext. 6646), stands

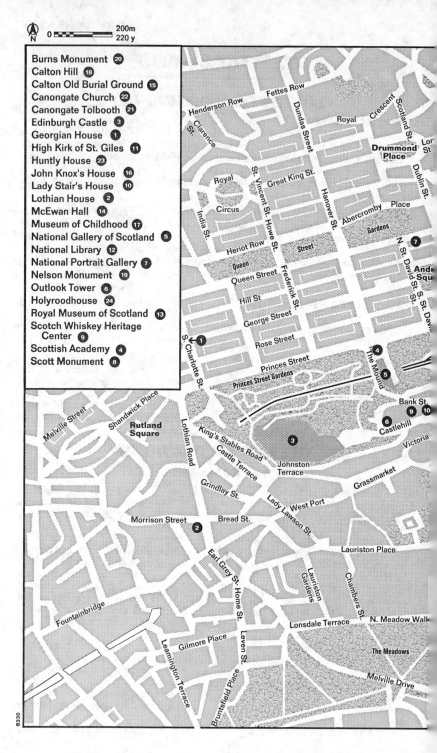

0   200m
N   0   220 y

Burns Monument **20**
Calton Hill **18**
Calton Old Burial Ground **15**
Canongate Church **22**
Canongate Tolbooth **21**
Edinburgh Castle **3**
Georgian House **1**
High Kirk of St. Giles **11**
Huntly House **23**
John Knox's House **16**
Lady Stair's House **10**
Lothian House **2**
McEwan Hall **14**
Museum of Childhood **17**
National Gallery of Scotland **5**
National Library **12**
National Portrait Gallery **7**
Nelson Monument **19**
Outlook Tower **6**
Holyroodhouse **24**
Royal Museum of Scotland **13**
Scotch Whiskey Heritage
   Center **9**
Scottish Academy **4**
Scott Monument **8**

Annandale St.

Brunswick Road

East London St.

Elm Row

Union Street

Mongomery Street

Mongomery Street

Broughton Street

Union Place

Hillside   Crescent

London Road

bany Street

Royal Terrace

York Place

Elder St.

18

Regent Gardens

Calton Hill

Leith Street

19

Regent Terrace

Waterloo Place

15

Regent Road

Abbey Hill

North Bridge

20

Calton Road

24

Market St.

South Bridge

Jeffrey Street

21 **22**

16

Canongate

23

High Street

St. Mary's St.

17

Holyrood Road

Holyrood Road

The Queen's Drive

11 †

owgate

Holyrood Road

2

Holyrood Park

Chambers St.

13

College St.

Drummond St.

Pleasance

Bristo Place

Potterow

Nicolson St.

West Richmond

14

Buccleuch Street

St. Leonard's St.

George Square

Buccleuch Place

Clark St.

Meadow Lane

The Meadows

Melville Drive

S. Clerk St.

Dalkeith Road

East Preston St.

⁇ DID YOU KNOW . . . ?

- Monuments to native son Sir Walter Scott abound in Edinburgh, but he wrote surprisingly little about the city of his birth.
- In 1842 the city had 200 brothels, the best on Rose Street. Business peaked at the annual reunion of the General Assembly of the Church of Scotland.
- Burke and Hare were the original "body-snatchers," robbing fresh graves to sell bodies to surgeons for anatomical dissection.
- It was at the Palace of Holyroodhouse that Mary Queen of Scots, while pregnant, witnessed the butchery of her Italian favorite, David Rizzio.
- A Lincoln Monument, built in 1893, honors the Scottish-American soldiers who died in America's Civil War.

just opposite John Knox's House, the first museum in the world devoted solely to the history of childhood. Contents of its three floors range from antique toys to games to exhibits on health, education, and costumes. Because of the youthful clientele it naturally attracts, it ranks as the "noisiest museum in the world." It is open June through September, Monday to Saturday from 10am to 6pm (to 5pm the rest of the year), and also from 2 to 5pm on Sunday during the Edinburgh Festival. Admission is free.

Farther down the street at 43–45 High Street is **John Knox's House** (tel. 5569579), with a history going back to the late 15th century. Even if you're not interested in the reformer who founded the Scottish Presbyterian Church, you may want to visit his house, as it is characteristic of the "lands" that used to flank the Royal Mile. All of them are gone now, except Knox's house, with its timbered gallery. Inside, you'll see the tempera ceiling in the Oak Room, along with exhibitions of Knox memorabilia. The house may be visited Monday through Saturday from 10am to 4:30pm for £1.25 ($1.90) for adults, £75 ($1.10) for children.

Continue along Canongate toward the Palace of Holyroodhouse. At 163 Canongate stands one of the handsomest buildings along the Royal Mile. The **Canongate Tolbooth** was constructed in 1591 and was once the courthouse, prison, and center of municipal affairs for the burgh of Canongate.

Across the street at 142 Canongate is **Huntly House** (tel. 2252424, ext. 4143), an example of a restored 16th-century mansion. Now it is Edinburgh's principal museum of local history. You can stroll through period rooms and reconstructions Monday through Saturday from 10am to 5pm (until 6pm from June to September). During the festival it's also open on Sunday from 2 to 5pm. Admission is free.

At 354 Castlehill, Royal Mile (tel. 2200441), the **Scotch Whisky Heritage Center** is privately funded by a conglomeration of Scotland's biggest whisky distillers. It highlights the economic effect of whisky on both Scotland and the world and illuminates the centuries-old traditions associated with whisky making, showing the exact science and art form of distilling. There is a 7-minute audiovisual show, and an electric car ride moves past 13 theatrical sets showing historic moments in the whisky industry. Prebooked groups of 8 persons or more, for a supplemental £10 ($15), can experience a tutored whisky tasting where four different malts are offered. Otherwise, admission is £3.20 ($4.80) for adults, £2 ($3) for senior citizens, £1.75 ($2.60) for children ages 5 to 17. Open year-round from 10am to 5pm.

EDINBURGH CASTLE, Castlehill. Tel. 2279846.

✪ It is believed that the ancient city grew up on the seat of the dead volcano, Castle Rock. Early history is vague, although it is known that in the 11th century Malcolm III (Canmore) and his Saxon queen, later venerated as St. Margaret, founded a castle on this spot. The only fragment left of their original castle, in fact the oldest structure in Edinburgh, is St. Margaret's Chapel, built in the Norman style, the oblong structure dating principally from the 12th century.

Inside the castle you can visit the State Apartments, particularly Queen Mary's Bedroom, where Mary Queen of Scots gave birth to James VI of Scotland (later James I of England). Scottish Parliaments used to convene in the Great Hall. The highlight is the Crown Chamber, which houses the Honours of Scotland (Scottish Crown Jewels), used at the coronation of James VI, along with the scepter and the sword of state of

Scotland. The French Prisons were put to use in the 18th century, and these great storerooms housed hundreds of Napoleonic soldiers during the early 19th century. Many of them made wall carvings that you can see today.

Admission: £4 ($6) adults, £1 ($1.50) children under 16.
Open: Apr–Sept, Mon–Sat 9:30am–5:15pm, Sun 11am–5:05pm; Oct–Mar, Mon–Sat 9:30am–4:15pm, Sun 12:30–3:35pm. **Bus:** 1 or 6.

PALACE OF HOLYROODHOUSE, Canongate eastern end of the Royal Mile. Tel. 5561096.

This palace was built adjacent to an Augustinian abbey established by David I in the 12th century. The nave, now in ruins, remains today. James IV founded the palace nearby in the early part of the 16th century, but only the north tower is left. Much of what you see today was ordered built by Charles II.

In the old wing the most dramatic incident in the history of Holyroodhouse occurred when Mary Queen of Scots was in residence. Her Italian secretary, David Rizzio, was murdered (with 56 stab wounds) in the audience chamber by Mary's husband, Lord Darnley, and his accomplices. A plaque marks the spot where he died on March 9, 1566. One of the more curious exhibits is a piece of needlework by Mary, depicting a cat-and-mouse scene (her cousin, Elizabeth I, is the cat!).

The palace suffered long periods of neglect, although it basked in glory at the ball in the mid-18th century thrown by Bonnie Prince Charlie. The present Queen and Prince Philip live at Holyroodhouse whenever they visit Edinburgh. When they're not in residence, the palace is open to visitors.

Admission: £3 ($4.50) adults, £1.50 ($2.30) children under 16.
Open: Mon–Sat 9:30am–5:15pm, Sun 10:30am–4:40pm. **Closed:** Last 2 weeks in May and 3 weeks in late June and early July (dates vary). **Bus:** 1 or 6.

OTHER TOP ATTRACTIONS

SCOTT MONUMENT, in the East Princes Street Gardens. Tel. 2252424, ext. 6678.

The Gothic-inspired Scott Monument is the most famous landmark of Edinburgh, completed in the mid-19th century. Sir Walter Scott's heroes are carved as small figures in the monument, and you can climb to the top. West Princes Street Gardens has the first ever Floral Clock, which was constructed in 1904.

Admission: 75p ($1.10).
Open: Apr–Sept, Mon–Sat 9am–6pm; Oct–Mar, Mon–Sat 9am–3pm. **Bus:** 1 or 6.

NATIONAL GALLERY OF SCOTLAND, 2 The Mound. Tel. 5568921.

This museum is located in the center of Princes Street Gardens. The gallery is small as national galleries go, but the collection was chosen with great care and has been expanded considerably by bequests, gifts, and loans.

Recent major acquisitions include Giulio Romano's *Vièrge à la Legende*. Other Italian paintings are Verrocchio's *Ruskin Madonna,* Andrea del Sarto's *Portrait of a Man,* Domenichino's *Adoration of the Shepherds,* and Tiepolo's acclaimed *Finding of Moses.*

The Duke of Sutherland lent the museum some paintings, including two Raphaels, *Holy Family with a Palm Tree* and the *Bridgewater Madonna;* Titian's two Diana canvases, and his Venus rising from the sea; and the *Seven Sacraments,* a work of the great 17th-century Frenchman Nicolas Poussin.

The Spanish masters are represented in El Greco's *Savior* and the mysterious *Fabula,* Velázquez's *Old Woman Cooking Eggs,* an early work by that great master, and *Immaculate Conception* by Zurbarán, his friend and contemporary.

The northern schools are represented by an early Netherlandish masterpiece historically linked to Edinburgh, Hugo van der Goes's *Trinity Altarpiece,* on loan from the Queen. The Flemish school emerges notably in Rubens's *The Feast of Herod* and *The Reconciliation of Jacob and Esau.* The Dutch excel with Rembrandt's *Woman in Bed,* superb landscapes by Cuyp, Ruisdael and Hobbema, and one of the gallery's most prized acquisitions, *Interior of St. Bavo's Church,*

Haarlem, by Pieter Saenredam, his largest and arguably finest painting, bought in 1982.

The most valuable gift to the gallery since its foundation, the Maitland Collection, includes one of Cézanne's *Mont St-Victoire* series, as well as works by Degas, van Gogh, Renoir, Gauguin, and Seurat, among others. A rare early Monet, *Shipping Scene—Night Effects,* was bought in 1980. In the same year, for the first time in living memory, a stunning landscape, *Niagara Falls, from the American Side,* by the 19th-century American painter Frederic Church, went on show.

You can also see excellent examples of English painting: Gainsborough's *The Hon. Mrs. Graham* and Constable's *Dedham Vale,* along with works by Turner, Reynolds, and Hogarth. Naturally, the work of Scottish painters is prominent. In the new wing, opened in 1978, Henry Raeburn is at his best in the whimsical *The Rev. Robert Walker Skating on Duddingston Loch.*

Admission: Free.

Open: Mon–Sat 10am–5pm, Sun 2–5pm (during the festival, Mon–Sat 10am–6pm, Sun 11am–6pm). **Bus:** 3, 21, or 26.

MORE ATTRACTIONS

CAMERA OBSCURA, Castlehill. Tel. 2263709.

It's at the top of the Outlook Tower and offers a magnificent view of the surrounding city. Trained guides point out the landmarks and talk about Edinburgh's fascinating history. In addition, there are several entertaining exhibitions, all with an optical theme, and a well-stocked shop selling books, crafts, and compact discs.

Admission: £2.90 ($4.40) adults, £1.50 ($2.30) children.

Open: Nov–Mar, daily 10am–5pm; Apr–Oct, daily 9:30am–6pm. **Bus:** 1 or 6.

ROYAL OBSERVATORY VISITOR CENTRE, Blackford Hill. Tel. 6688405.

This place shows the works of the Scottish National Observatory at home and

---

FROMMER'S FAVORITE EDINBURGH EXPERIENCES

Contemplating Edinburgh from Arthur's Seat At 823 feet (reached from a climb up Holyrood Park) you'll visit the Highlands in miniature. The view from here has been called "magical," praised by such literary figures as Dorothy Wordsworth. Scots congregate here to await the solstice.

Visiting Dean Village About 100 feet below the level of the rest of the city, a few minutes from the West End, Dean Village is an 800-year-old grain milling town on the Water of Leith. Go here to soak up local color—never better in summer than from its woodland walk along the river. Exotic denizens of nearby Stockbridge village amuse with their zany makeup and dress.

Shopping Along Princes Street This is the main street of Edinburgh—for locals, the equivalent of New York's Fifth Avenue. Flower-filled gardens stretch along the street's whole south side. When not admiring the flowers, you can window-shop and make selections from the country's finest merchandise on the north side—everything from kilts to Scottish crystal.

A Pint in an Edinburgh Pub The city is famous for its pubs. Sampling a pint of McEwan's real ale or Tennent's lager is a chance to soak up the special atmosphere of Edinburgh, following an age-old tradition set by such figures as Robert Louis Stevenson and Arthur Conan Doyle when they were Edinburgh University students in the 1870s.

abroad, featuring the finest images of astronomical objects, Scotland's largest telescope, and a display of antique instruments. There is also a panoramic view of the city from the balcony. An exhibit, *The Universe*, uses photographs, videos, computers, and models to take you on a cosmic whirlwind tour from the beginning of time to the farthest depths of space in a couple of hours. The astronomy shop is well stocked. The location is in a public park on the south side of Edinburgh.

Admission: £1.50 ($2.30) adults, 75p ($1.10) children ages 5–16.
Open: Apr–Sept, daily noon–5pm; Oct–Mar 1–5pm. **Bus:** 40 or 41.

MUSEUMS

ROYAL MUSEUM OF SCOTLAND, Queen St., or Chambers St. Tel. 2257534.

Two long-established museums, the Royal Scottish Museum and the National Museum of Antiquities, were combined in 1985 to form a single institution, although they are still in separate buildings. Displays at both museums range through the decorative arts, ethnography, natural history, geology, archeology, technology, and science.

The Chambers Street building near the Royal Mile, begun in 1861, is a fine example of Victorian architecture and houses international collections in the arts and sciences. The Findlay Building, on Queen Street, opened in 1890, contains collections of Scottish artifacts from prehistoric times to the present.

Admission: Free, except for some temporary exhibitions.
Open: Mon–Sat 10am–5pm, Sun noon–5pm. **Directions:** Walk south from Waverley Station for 10 minutes to reach the Chambers Street branch or take bus no. 1 or 6; walk north from Waverley Station for 10 minutes, or 5 minutes from the bus station, to get to the Queen Street branch.

SCOTTISH NATIONAL GALLERY OF MODERN ART, Belford Rd. Tel. 5568921.

In 1984 Scotland's national collection of 20th-century art moved into an art gallery converted from a former school building dated 1828. It is set in 12 acres of grounds just a 15-minute walk from the west end of Princes Street. The collection is international in scope and quality in spite of its modest size.

Major sculptures sited outside the building include pieces by Henry Moore and Barbara Hepworth. Inside, the collection ranges from a fauve Derain and cubist Braque and Picasso to recent works by Paolozzi. There is a strong representation of English and Scottish art. Highlights of the collection include works by Vuillard, Matisse, Miró, Magritte, Léger, Jawlensky, Kirchner, Kokoschka, Dix, Ernst, Ben Nicholson, Nevelson, Pollock, Beuys, Balthus, Hanson, De Andrea, Lichtenstein, Kitaj, and Hockney. Prints and drawings can be studied in the Print Room. The licensed café sells light refreshments and salads.

Admission: Free.
Open: Mon–Sat 10am–5pm, Sun 2–5pm. **Bus:** No. 13 stops right by the gallery, but is infrequent; nos. 18, 20, and 41 pass along Queensferry Road, a 5-minute walk up Queensferry Terrace and Belford Road from the gallery.

SCOTTISH NATIONAL PORTRAIT GALLERY, 1 Queen St. Tel. 2257534.

Housed in a red stone Victorian Gothic building by Rowand Anderson, this portrait gallery gives you a chance to see what the famous people of Scottish history looked like. The portraits, several by Ramsay and Raeburn, include everybody from Mary Queen of Scots to James VI and I, from Sir Walter Scott to Robert Burns, from Flora Macdonald to Ramsay Macdonald.

Admission: Free.
Open: Mon–Sat 10am–5pm, Sun 2–5pm. **Bus:** 18, 20, or 41.

SCOTTISH UNITED SERVICES MUSEUM, Edinburgh Castle, Castlehill. Tel. 2257534.

Your entrance ticket to the Edinburgh Castle includes entry to the galleries of this national museum dealing with the history of the navy, army, and air force at all periods. It is considered unique and comprehensive, the longest-established collections of British armed forces historical material in the United Kingdom. The Scottish regiments of the British Army figure strongly, and new displays in the North Museum block deal with the story of the Scottish soldier. The history of the Royal Navy and Royal Air Force in their Scottish contexts is interpreted in galleries opposite the Scottish Crown Jewels.

Admission: Free with ticket to Edinburgh Castle.

Open: Apr–Sept, Mon–Sat 9:30am–5:50pm, Sun 11am–5:50pm; Oct–Mar, Mon–Sat 9:30am–5:05pm, Sun 12:30–4:20pm. **Bus:** 1 or 6.

GARDENS

ROYAL BOTANIC GARDEN, Inverleith Row. Tel. 5527171.

Gardeners and nature lovers in general will be attracted to the garden. Main areas of interest in the garden are the Exhibition Plant Houses, Inverleith House, Exhibition Hall, Alpine House, the Demonstration Garden, annual and herbaceous borders (summer only), the copse, the Woodland Garden, Wild Garden, Arboretum, Peat Garden, Rock Garden, Heath Garden, and the Pond.

The range of Exhibition Plant Houses includes displays of the fern forests of the southern hemisphere, the giant water lilies of Amazonia, and desert succulents of arid areas. It is open all year daily from 9am to 1 hour before sunset.

Admission: Voluntary donation.

Open: May–Aug, daily 10am–8pm; Sept–Oct and Mar–Apr, daily 10am–6pm; Nov–Feb, daily 10am–4pm.

CASTLES

CRAIGMILLAR CASTLE, Craigmillar Castle Rd. Tel. 6614445.

In the southeastern sector of Edinburgh, this castle is one of the city's most interesting sights, but perhaps because of its obscure location, one of the most overlooked. The location is out the A68, about 3½ miles south of the heart of the city. The 14th-century keep that once stood proudly here is now in ruins, but is impressive nevertheless. In the early 1400s this keep was enclosed by a "curtain wall" that saw much bloodshed. Inside, the apartments were built primarily in the 16th and 17th centuries. Mary Queen of Scots often spent time here.

Admission: £1.20 ($1.80) adults, 60p (90¢) children.

Open: Mon–Sat 9:30am–6:30pm, Sun 2–6:30pm. **Bus:** 42 there, 46 return.

LAURISTON CASTLE, Cramond Rd. S. Tel. 3362060.

This fine country mansion standing in extensive grounds overlooking the Firth of Forth lies on the outskirts of Edinburgh about 3¼ miles northwest of Princes Street. The 16th-century tower house has extensive 19th-century additions and well-preserved Edwardian interiors. The last inhabitant, William Reid, was the proprietor of Morison & Co., a prestigious firm of cabinetmakers and house furnishers. A keen collector of furniture and antiques, he purchased Lauriston upon his retirement in 1902, to provide an appropriate setting for his extensive collections.

Visits are by guided tour only, each tour lasting approximately 45 minutes and the last one beginning 40 minutes before closing time.

Admission: £2 ($3) adults, £1 ($1.50) children.

Open: April–Oct, Sat–Thurs 11am–1pm and 2–5pm; Oct–Mar, Sat–Sun 2–4pm.

Directions: Take the A90 toward Forth Road Bridge and turn right at the Quality Street junction (look for signs pointing to Lauriston Castle); then proceed down Cramond Road South. **Bus:** Lothian Region No. 41 from the Mound or George Street.

CALTON HILL

This hill is often credited with giving Edinburgh a look somewhat like that of Athens. It's a hill of monuments, and when some of them were created they were called "instant ruins" by critics of the day. The landmark Calton Hill lies off Regent Road at the eastern sector of Edinburgh. Rising 350 feet, the hill is visited not only by those wishing to see its monuments but also by those wanting to enjoy the panoramic views of the Firth of Forth and the city spread beneath it. The Parthenon was reproduced in part on this location in 1824. The intention of the builders was to honor the brave Scottish dead, killed in the Napoleonic wars. However, the city fathers ran out of money and the monument—often referred to as "Scotland's shame"—was never finished. The Nelson Monument, containing relics of the hero of Trafalgar, dates from 1815 and rises more than 100 feet above the hill. A time ball at the top falls at 1 o'clock every day. The monument (tel. 5562716) is open April through September on Monday from 1 to 6pm; Tuesday to Saturday from 10am to 6pm. From October through March, Monday to Saturday, hours are 10am to 3pm. Admission is 60p (90¢). Take buses 26, 85, or 86.

DEAN VILLAGE

Most visitors who want to see all the major sights of Edinburgh head here to view one of the most photographed and characteristic sights in the city. Set in a valley about 100 feet below the level of the rest of Edinburgh, the village is filled with nostalgic charm. A few minutes from the West End, it's located at the end of Bell's Brae, off Queensferry Street, on the Water of Leith. The settlement dates from the 12th century, and the fame of Dean Village grew as a result of its being a grain-milling center. You can enjoy a celebrated view by looking downstream under the high arches of Dean Bridge, designed by Telford in 1833. It's customary to walk along the water in the direction of St. Bernard's Well.

SPECIAL-INTEREST SIGHTSEEING
FOR THE ARCHITECTURE ENTHUSIAST

At some point the Old Town became too small. The burghers decided to build a whole new town across the valley, so the marsh was drained and eventually turned into public gardens. Princes Street is the most striking boulevard. Architecturally, the most interesting district of the New Town is the north side of Charlotte Square, designed by Robert Adam. It was young architect James Craig who shaped much of the Georgian style of the New Town, with its crescents and squares.

At 7 Charlotte Square, a part of the northern facade, is the restored building known simply as the **Georgian House** (tel. 2252160). It's a prime example of Scottish architecture and interior design in the zenith of the New Town. Originally the home of John Lamont XVII, known as "the last of the patriarchs and the first of the moderns," the house was refurbished and reopened to the public by Scotland's National Trust. The furniture in this Robert Adam house is mainly Hepplewhite, Chippendale, and Sheraton, all dating from the 18th century. In a ground-floor bedroom is a sturdy old four-poster with an original 18th-century canopy. The dining-room table is set for a dinner on fine Wedgwood china, and the kitchen is stocked with gleaming copper pots and pans. The house is open April through October, Monday to Saturday from 10am to 4:30pm and on Sunday from 2 to 4:30pm. Admission is £2.80 ($4.20) for adults, £1.40 ($2.10) for children.

As an Old Town complement to the New Town Georgian House, the National Trust for Scotland opened in a 1620 tenement in the Royal Mile, **Gladstone's Land,** 477B Lawnmarket (tel. 2265856), an upstairs apartment of four rooms furnished as it might have been in the 17th century. On the ground floor, reconstructed shop booths display replicas of goods of the period. It is open April through October, Monday to Saturday from 10am to 5pm and on Sunday from 2 to 5pm. Last admission is 30 minutes before closing. The admission charge is £2.40 ($3.60) for adults, £1.20 ($1.80) for children.

FOR THE LITERARY ENTHUSIAST

Many sites have special appeal for literary fans, including **Lady Stair's House** (see "The Royal Mile" in "The Top Attractions") with its memorabilia of such Scottish writers as the national poet, Robert Burns, along with Sir Walter Scott and Robert Louis Stevenson.

There's a monument to Scott at the Princes Street Gardens. Along the Royal Mile you can visit Deacon Brodie's Tavern (see below), which was named for the Edinburgher who was the inspiration for Robert Louis Stevenson's *The Strange Case of Dr. Jekyll and Mr. Hyde,* although Stevenson set his story in foggy London town, not Edinburgh.

Stevenson was born at 8 Howard Place in 1850. This Georgian terrace house, dating from 1820, is now a private home and cannot be visited inside, although nothing prevents you from stopping and taking a picture of its interior.

FOR VISITING AMERICANS

Below Waterloo Place, on the flatter slope of Calton Hill (see above), visitors can walk through the **Old Calton Cemetery,** dating from the 1700s. Many famous Scots were buried here, often with elaborate tombs honoring their memory—notably the Robert Adam–designed tomb for the philosopher David Hume.

For Americans, however, the curiosity here is the **Lincoln Monument,** which Edinburghers erected in 1893. It was dedicated to the thousands of American soldiers of Scottish descent who lost their lives in America's Civil War.

COOL FOR KIDS

Other than the Old Town with its castles and palaces, two attractions always thrill children—the Museum of Childhood (see "The Royal Mile" in "The Top Attractions," above), and the Edinburgh Zoo (see below).

EDINBURGH ZOO, 134 Corstorphine Rd. Tel. 3349171.

Just 10 minutes from Edinburgh's city center, the zoo is Scotland's largest animal collection, set in 80 acres of scenic hillside parkland offering unrivaled views from the Pentlands to the Firth of Forth. The zoo contains more than 1,500 animals, including many endangered species—snow leopards, white rhinos, pygmy hippos, and many more. Famous for its penguins, the zoo has the largest colony in Europe, with four different species, plus the world's largest penguin enclosure. A penguin parade is held daily at 2pm April through September only.

Admission: £4.80 ($7.20) adults, £2.50 ($3.80) children; £13 ($19.50) family ticket.

Open: Apr–Sept, daily 9am–6pm; Oct–Mar, daily 9am–4:30pm. Opens at 9:30am Sun year-round. **Bus:** 2, 26, 69, 85, or 86 from Princes Street.

WALKING TOUR — HISTORIC EDINBURGH

Start: Edinburgh Castle.
Finish: Princes Street Gardens.
Time: 3 hours.
Best Times: Any sunny day.
Worst Time: Morning and early-evening rush hours.

Begin by walking up to:

1. **Edinburgh Castle,** where you can visit, among other attractions, St. Margaret's Chapel and see Mons Meg, a 15th-century artillery piece. The castle well is 110 feet deep and has been in use since 1313 . . . at least.

The Royal Mile (the generic name of four different streets) starts from the Castle Esplanade at Castlehill. Walk along Castlehill. The house at the top of Castle Wynd is known as the Cannonball House because of the ball embedded in the gable on its west side. At the Church of Tolbooth St. John's, services are celebrated in Gaelic.

The street now becomes Lawnmarket, once the center for linen sellers. Farther on, stop at:

2. **Gladstone's Land,** 447B Lawnmarket, an example of a 17th-century tene-

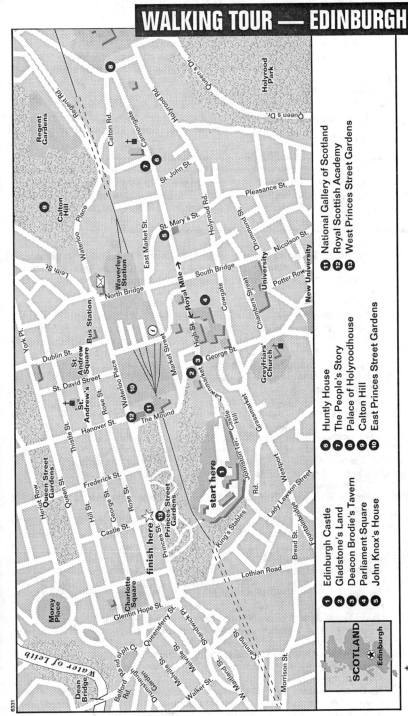

WALKING TOUR — EDINBURGH

SCOTLAND
Edinburgh ★

1. Edinburgh Castle
2. Gladstone's Land
3. Deacon Brodie's Tavern
4. Parliament Square
5. John Knox's House
6. Huntly House
7. The People's Story
8. Palace of Holyroodhouse
9. Calton Hill
10. East Princes Street Gardens
11. National Gallery of Scotland
12. Royal Scottish Academy
13. West Princes Street Gardens

Church ✝   Post Office ⊠   Information ⓘ

ment building. The six-story building was completed in 1620. A reconstructed shop booth displays replicas of 17th-century goods.

Next you come to Brodie's Close, the 18th-century home of the notorious Deacon Brodie, a respectable councillor by day and a thief by night. He was hanged in 1788. The mechanism used for the "drop" had previously been improved by Brodie himself—for use on others!

Lawnmarket ends at the intersection of Bank Street and George IV Bridge, and you can see the brass strips on the road in the southeast corner of the busy junction marking the site of the scaffold where public hangings were continued until 1864.

REFUELING STOP   The most famous pub along the Royal Mile is: **3. Deacon Brodie's Tavern,** 435 Lawnmarket. It honors Deacon Brodie, the inspiration for Robert Louis Stevenson's *The Strange Case of Dr. Jekyll and Mr. Hyde.* Snacks such as cottage pie and scotch eggs are served, or you can drop in only for a drink.

The Royal Mile continues, as High Street, with:

4. **Parliament Square,** on the right. In the square is Parliament House, built in 1632, along with Parliament Hall, a fine Gothic hall with an open timber roof. The building is now the Courts of Justice, and it is sometimes possible to attend sessions by using door 11.

Farther on is:

5. **John Knox's House,** 43–45 High St., associated with James Mossman, goldsmith to Mary Queen of Scots, as well as John Knox, who was Scotland's religious reformer. Linked with the John Knox House, the Netherbow Theatre and Café marks the halfway point of the Royal Mile. Almost opposite is the Museum of Childhood, really intended more for adults than for children. Still farther on is Chessells Court, once an excise office (robbing it was Deacon Brodie's last crime).

Next comes the City Museum in:

6. **Huntly House,** 142 Canongate, a restored 16th-century mansion that was the home of the first Marquess of Huntly in 1636. You can visit its displays of Edinburgh silver and glass, Scottish pottery, and other relics. Opposite is:

7. **The People's Story,** 163 Canongate, Tolbooth, a museum in the Canongate Tolbooth, with an exhibition illustrating the story of the ordinary people of Edinburgh from the late 18th century to the present day.

Continue walking up the Royal Mile until you reach the:

8. **Palace of Holyroodhouse,** at the end, the former abode of Mary Queen of Scots but today used by Queen Elizabeth II whenever she's in Edinburgh.

After a visit, walk back up Canongate and High Street along the Royal Mile to Canongate Church, then take Tolbooth Wynd to the footpath leading to Regent Road and Princes Street. When you reach Regent Road, turn left and continue along Waterloo Place with:

9. **Calton Hill** on the right. On top of the hill are the Nelson Monument, the City Observatory, and the unfinished "Parthenon," intended to be a memorial to the dead of the Napoleonic wars. On this street is the General Post Office and the Philatelic Bureau, and, opposite, the Register House, where most of Scotland's historic and legal records since the 13th century are stored.

Walk by the Waverley Railway Station to the left, and then you'll be in the:

10. **East Princes Street Gardens,** with the Scott Monument, a 200-foot spire forming a canopy over the statue of Sir Walter Scott and his dog.

Next on the left is the:

11. **National Gallery of Scotland,** 2 The Mound, called "the most enjoyable small gallery in Europe." It has any number of masterpieces, ranging from Raphael to Turner, as well as the world's finest collection of Scottish masterpieces. Also on the Mound is the:

12. **Royal Scottish Academy,** widely acknowledged as one of the foremost exhibitions of contemporary art in Scotland.
    Next you reach:
13. **West Princes Street Gardens** and the famous Floral Clock, believed to be the oldest in the world, built in 1903. A cuckoo announces each quarter hour and the flowers often portray some current local event. Also in the gardens is the American War Memorial, erected by Americans of Scottish descent and sympathies, and the Churches of St. John and St. Cuthbert, the former having a brass-rubbing center in its church hall.

ORGANIZED TOURS

If you want a quick introduction to the principal attractions in and around Edinburgh, then consider one or more of the tours offered by the **Lothian Region Transport,** 14 Queen St. (tel. 5544494). You won't find a cheaper way to hit the highlights, and later you can go back on your own if you want a deeper experience. The coaches (buses) leave from Waverley Bridge, near the Scott Monument. The tours start in April and run through late October. A curtailed winter program is also offered.

You can see most of the major sights of Edinburgh, including the Royal Mile, Holyrood Castle, Princes Street, and Edinburgh Castle by double-deck motorcoach for £4 ($6) for adults and £1.50 ($2.30) for children. This ticket is valid all day on any LRT Edinburgh Classic Tour bus, which allows passengers to get on and off at any of the 15 stops along its routes. Buses depart from the Waverley Railway Station every day beginning at 9:10am, and depart every 15 minutes in summer, and about every 30 minutes in winter, then embark on a touristic circuit of Edinburgh which—if you remain on the bus without ever getting off—will take about 2 hours. Guided commentary is offered along the way. Most participants find it easy to pick up the thread of their visit as their tour progresses, despite the frequency of their exits and entrances into one or another of the vehicles.

LRT also operates half-day and full-day motorcoach excursions throughout the various regions of Scotland. White-sided buses identified by their black trim depart from the Waverley station for visits to such places as Loch Lomond, Loch Katrine, Culzean Castle and the Trossachs, St. Andrews, the Isle of Arran, and selected sights in Braemar and Deeside. Their prices, depending on the distance they travel from Edinburgh and their duration, range from £6.50 ($9.80) to £21 ($31.50) per person, and, in some cases, include lunch. Itineraries vary with the day of the week, although of particular interest is the Friday-afternoon Murder and Mystery Tour that focuses on historical and bizarre tales of crime and deceit connected with Old Edinburgh. Departing every Friday at 7pm, it includes a basket supper, requires advance reservations, and costs £8 ($12) per person.

Tickets for any of these tours can be bought at LRT offices at Waverley Bridge, or at 14 Queen St., or at the tourist information center in Waverley market. Advance reservations are a good idea for the half-day and full-day tours. For more information, call 031/2204111 24 hours a day.

6. SPECIAL & FREE EVENTS

The highlight of Edinburgh's year—some would say the only time when the real Edinburgh emerges—comes in the last weeks of August during the **Edinburgh International Festival.** Since 1947 the festival has attracted artists and companies of the highest international standard in all fields of the arts, including music, opera, dance, theater, exhibition, poetry, and prose, and "Auld Reekie" takes on a cosmopolitan air.

During the period of the festival, one of the most exciting spectacles is the Military Tattoo on the floodlit esplanade in front of Edinburgh Castle, high on its rock above the city. Vast audiences watch the precision marching of Scottish regiments and military units from all parts of the world, and of course the stirring skirl of the bagpipes and the swirl of the kilt.

Less predictable in quality but greater in quantity is the **Edinburgh Festival Fringe,** an opportunity for anybody—whether an individual, a group of friends, or a whole company of performers—to put on their own show wherever they can find an empty stage or street corner. Late-night reviews, outrageous and irreverent contemporary drama, university theater presentations, maybe even a full-length opera—Edinburgh gives them all free rein. As if that weren't enough, Edinburgh has a **Film Festival,** a **Jazz Festival,** a **Television Festival,** and a **Book Festival** (every second year) at the same time.

Ticket prices vary from £1 ($1.75) up to about £21 ($36.75) a seat, but if you move fast enough, there aren't many events that you can't see for £2.50 ($4.40).

Information can be obtained at **Edinburgh International Festival,** 21 Market St., Edinburgh EH1 1BW (tel. 031/2264001).

Other sources of information include **Edinburgh Festival Fringe,** 180 High St., Edinburgh EH1 1BW (tel. 031/2265257); **Edinburgh Book Festival,** 25A S.W. Thistle Street Lane, EH2 1EW (tel. 031/2251915); **Edinburgh Film Festival,** 88 Lothian Rd., Edinburgh EH3 9BZ (tel. 031/2284051); and **Edinburgh Military Tattoo,** 22 Market St., Edinburgh EHL 1QB (tel. 031/2251188).

7. SPORTS & RECREATION

SPECTATOR SPORTS

HORSE RACING Place your bets at the **Musselburgh Racecourse,** Musselburgh Park (tel. 6652185), which lies about 4 miles east of Edinburgh. In summer, races are on a flat circular track, while in winter, the more elaborate "National Hunt" format challenges horses and riders to a series of jumps and obstacle courses of great technical difficulty.

RUGBY One of the more physical of British sports is played at **Murrayfield Stadium,** Murrayfield (tel. 3372346), home of the National Rugby Team of Scotland, which lies about a mile west of Edinburgh center. Attracting one of the most loyal of entourages, the sport is played between September and April, usually on Saturday. Some of the most passionate matches are those among teams from the five-nation bloc comprising Scotland, Wales, England, Ireland, and France. These matches are presented only between January and March, when most sports enthusiasts in Scotland seem to talk about very little else. Entrance to the stadium, depending on the seat and the game, ranges in price from £11 ($16.50) to £20 ($30).

SOCCER You might quickly get swept up in the zeal of Edinburghers for their local soccer (referred to as "football") clubs. Both teams, when not battling with one another, challenge other teams from throughout Europe. The home of the Edinburgh Hearts (more formally known as the Heart of Midlothian Football Club) is at **Tynecastle Park,** Gorgie Road (tel. 3376132); the home of the Hibs (short for the Hibernians) is at **Easter Road Park,** Easter Road (tel. 6612159). The traditional playing times are Saturday afternoons, when games are likely to be televised in pubs throughout Scotland.

PARTICIPATORY SPORTS

GOLF The finest golf courses in Scotland tend to be uncompromisingly reserved for members only. One reasonably well-maintained public golf course that welcomes nonresidents is the **Carrick Knowe Golf Course,** Balgreen Road (tel. 3371096), and the **Port Royal Golf Course,** Ingliston (tel. 3334377). Both are especially busy on weekends, so an advance phone call and a scheduled arrival for a weekday are usually the best insurance for an agreed-upon starting time.

ICE SKATING The **Murrayfield Ice Rink,** Riversdale Crescent (tel. 3376933), offers a rink, along with skate rentals, in wintertime. Phone in advance to avoid arriving during practice by the local ice hockey teams.

SAILING Visit the Firth of Forth firsthand by renting a sailboat. For information, contact the **Port Edgar Sailing Centre,** Port Edgar, South Queensferry (tel. 3313330). Located about 9 miles west of the city center, between Easter and mid-October it offers instruction in small-craft sailing, canoeing, and powerboating, as well as half-day rentals.

SKIING Even the highest peaks of Scotland aren't cold enough to permit year-round skiing, so if you yearn to practice your slalom during your stay in Edinburgh, you'll have to improvise. One possible solution is the **Hillend Ski Centre,** Hillend Park, Biggar Road (tel. 4454433), the largest "dry ski" center in Europe. Located 5 miles south of Edinburgh, it has three different slopes covered with gray-colored nylon bristles whose texture emulates approximately the feel of freshly fallen snow. One of the slopes is about 1,200 feet, allowing dry-ski enthusiasts to career down one of the highest hills this side of St. Moritz. Open daily (except Christmas and New Year's) from 9:30am to 10pm, it can be reached by bus no. 4 from Princes Street. A chair lift, costing £1.45 ($2.20) for adults and 95p ($1.40) for children, leads to a lofty perch where there's a panoramic view unfolding. You can see the whole of the city of Edinburgh and across the River Forth to the Hills of Fife.

SQUASH The **Craiglockhart Sports Centre,** 177 Colinton Rd. (tel. 4430101), offers several squash courts, and you can rent equipment if you need it. Somewhat more expensive are the squash courts at **Marco's Leisure Centre,** 51 Grove St. (tel. 2282141). Nonmembers can't reserve courts, but if you show up to use the gym there and a court becomes available, you'll probably be allowed to use it.

SWIMMING There are several small, Victorian-era swimming pools scattered around Edinburgh, but the undisputed leader of them all is the modern Olympic-size **Royal Commonwealth Pool,** 21 Dalkeith Rd. (tel. 6677211). In a low-slung concrete building on the outskirts of town, it opened in 1970 in time for the world-famous Commonwealth Games, which were hosted that year in Edinburgh. Access to the pool costs £1.40 ($2.10), while access to the (sexually segregated) saunas costs £5 ($7.50). Take bus no. 3, 7, 21, or 33. It's open Monday through Saturday from 9am to 9:30pm and on Sunday from 10am to 4pm. Call before you go to avoid arriving during specially scheduled tournaments.

TENNIS Several tennis courts are within an easy commute of the center. These include the **Craiglockhart Sports Centre,** 177 Colinton Rd. (tel. 4430101). Advance reservations are necessary, and of course, your plans will quickly go awry if it starts to rain. (You'll also find badminton courts and a gym.) More convenient (and sometimes more crowded) are a handful of concrete-surfaced public tennis courts behind George Square, on the north side of the public park known as the Meadows.

8. SAVVY SHOPPING

Shopping hours for most shops are from 9am to 5:30pm. Many remain open Thursday until 8pm. On Wednesday many Edinburgh shops close in the afternoon, although the bigger stores along Princes Street are open all day. Nearly all stores are closed Sunday.

The best buys are in tartans and woolens, along with bone china and Scottish crystal. New Town's Princes Street is the main shopping artery. George Street and Old Town's Royal Mile are also major shopping arteries.

BOOKS

JAMES THIN, 57 George St. Tel. 5566743.
This has been the leading bookseller in Edinburgh since 1848. Tastes and reading

customs have changed over those many decades, but James Thin keeps abreast of those changes. The store has all sorts of titles about Edinburgh life, and is well endowed with both light and heavy reading matter. There's a quiet tea room upstairs.

WATERSTONES, 13–14 Princes St. Tel. 5563034.
This bookstore is giving the legendary James Thin serious competition. It has a wide range of stock in nearly all fields of publishing. There's a branch office at 83 George St. (tel. 2253436).

BRASS

TOP BRASS, 77 Dundas St. Tel. 5574293.
Most of the one-of-a-kind items sold here originated within a 100-mile radius of Edinburgh, although lately inventory has even poured in from as far away as France and Germany. Co-owners Nick Carter and Tom O'Donnell scout the Highlands and northern England for the best brassware of the 18th to the early 20th century. This is not only the most desirable brass shop in Edinburgh, but one of the most comprehensive in Scotland. The owners offer brass bed frames and headboards, fire fenders, light fixtures, and chandeliers, with occasional pieces of unusual hardware. Larger items can be packaged and shipped.

BRASS RUBBINGS

SCOTTISH STONE & BRASS RUBBING CENTRE, Trinity Apse, Chalmers Close, near the Royal Mile. Tel. 5564364.
For beautiful wall hangings, you can make your own brass rubbings or buy them ready-made. You can visit the center's collection of replicas molded from ancient Pictish stones, rare Scottish brasses, and medieval church brasses. No experience is needed to make a rubbing. The center will show you how and supply materials.

CLOTHING

MILLSHOP, 134C Princes St. Tel. 2252319.
One of about 30 such shops through the United Kingdom, it sells knitwear, skirts, giftware, and travel rugs. You can purchase some good Scottish woolens here. Most of the merchandise is made in Britain.

CRYSTAL

EDINBURGH CRYSTAL, Eastfield, Penicuik. Tel. 0968/675128.
The Edinburgh crystal factory lies about 10 miles south of Edinburgh, just off the A701 to Peebles, devoted entirely to handmade crystal glassware. Tours of the factory, during which you can watch the glassmakers at work, are available Monday to Friday from 9am to 3:30pm. The Visitor Centre is the starting point for the tour and is the location of the factory shop where the world's largest collection of Edinburgh crystal is on view and on sale. Here, too, are the inexpensively priced factory seconds. The Centre also has a woolen mill and a coffee shop specializing in home baking. Open Monday through Saturday from 9am to 5pm and on Sunday from 11am to 5pm. **Bus:** 62, 64, 65, 81, or 87.

DEPARTMENT STORES

DEBENHAM'S, 109–112 Princes St. Tel. 2251320.
This, along with Jenners (see below), competes for the honor of the best department store in Edinburgh. Its modernized Victorian shell stocks a wide array of Scottish and international merchandise in a marble-covered department-store format.

JENNERS, 48 Princes St. Tel. 2252442.
Everyone in Edinburgh has probably been to Jenners at least once. Its Neo-Gothic facade, opposite the Sir Walter Scott Monument, couldn't be more prominent. Its array of Scottish and international merchandise qualifies it as one of the best-stocked department stores in town.

DOLLS

DOLLS HOSPITAL [GERALDINE'S OF EDINBURGH], 35A Dundas St. Tel. 5564295.

A purveyor of innocence and nostalgia on a grand scale, this is the only shop of its kind in Edinburgh. Entirely lined with glass-fronted display cases, it operates as a basement showroom for Edinburgh's only doll factory, with more than 100 richly costumed dolls on exhibit. Each of the heirloom-quality dolls requires about 10 full days' labor to create, and each reflects what connoisseurs consider the climax of the doll-maker's art, the Victorian and Edwardian ages. Each has a hand-painted porcelain head and sometimes elaborate coiffure made from modacrylic fibers. Dolls range in price from £50 ($75) to £400 ($600). Also available are all-mohair, fully jointed teddy bears, any of which would make a memorable souvenir for your favorite child.

JEWELRY

ROBERT ANTHONY, 108B Rose St. Tel. 2264550.

Considered one of the best jewelry stores in Edinburgh, it sells new, antique, and secondhand jewelry, as well as gold chains, diamonds, and fine gemstones. Of enduring popularity, however, are the collections of gold bangles and pendants available immediately in 9-karat gold. (If you prefer 18-karat gold, it can be crafted for you in about a week.) Representative memorials to your Highland fling might be a depiction, in gold, of Scottish pipers and/or dancers, thistles, and tiny replicas of both Edinburgh Castle and its famous cannon, Mons Meg. Prices for these begin at around £23 ($34.50) each.

KNITWEAR

THE SHETLAND CONNECTION, 491 Lawnmarket. Tel. 2253525.

The owner of this shop, Moira-Ann Leask, promotes the knitting skills of the Shetland knitter, and her shop is packed with sweaters, hats, and gloves in colorful Fair Island designs. She also offers hand-knitted mohair, Aran, and Icelandic sweaters. Her oldest knitter is 86 years old. Items range from fine ply cobweb shawls to chunky ski sweaters. Each one is handcrafted by skilled knitters in top-quality wool. A large range of Celtic jewelry and gifts makes this shop a top-priority visit.

MALLS

WAVERLEY MARKET SHOPPING CENTER, next to Waverley Station, Princes Street. Tel. 5573759.

There is something for everyone here, all under one roof in the center of Edinburgh. You can browse through some 80 shops on three levels selling fashion, accessories, gifts, books, jewelry, beauty products, and a wide selection of Scottish arts and crafts. A Food Court has tempting snacks, and top-quality produce is for sale in the Food Hall. Unique handmade items can be purchased in the craft center.

MUSIC

VIRGIN RETAIL MUSIC, 131 Princes St. Tel. 2254583.

One of the biggest selections of records, CDs, and tapes in Scotland is found here. The shop displays special strength and insights into both traditional and Scottish music. The staff is knowledgeable and charming, and also eager to imbue their love of Scottish music to interested visitors.

SCOTTISH WARES

CLAN TARTAN CENTRE, 70–74 Bangor Rd., Leith. Tel. 5535100.

Long recognized for its wide displays of tartans, this is one of the leading specialists in Edinburgh, regardless of which clan you claim as your own. If you want help in identifying a particular tartan, the staff at this shop will assist you.

JOHN MORRISON LTD., 461 Lawnmarket. Tel. 2258149.

This is a marvelous place for tartans. Orders can be mailed throughout the world if you can't take delivery of your Highland dress. Women can order an authentic hand-tailored kilt or a semi-kilt or a kilt skirt. The store also provides evening sashes and stoles to match a skirt. The store specializes in kilts for men, a heavy hand-woven worsted in your favorite tartan. To go with it, there are doublets and jackets. That's followed up with accessories, a jabot and cuffs along with kilt hose and a tie.

JAMES PRINGLE WOOLEN MILL, 70–74 Bangor Rd., Leith. Tel. 5535161.

Whether you have a clan to your name or would like to borrow one, this is the place to go. The mill produces a large variety of top-quality wool items, including a range of Scottish knitwear—cashmere sweaters, tartan and tweed ties, travel rugs, tweed hats, tam-o'-shanters. In addition, the mill has the only Clan Tartan Centre in Scotland, where more than 2,500 sets and trade designs are accessible through their research facilities offered for your use. A free audiovisual presentation shows the history and development of the tartan. You can visit free, as well as taking advantage of free taxi service to the mill from anywhere in Edinburgh (ask at your hotel). Open Monday through Saturday from 9am to 5:30pm, and also on Sunday from 10am to 5:30pm from April through December.

TARTAN GIFT SHOPS, 54 High St. Tel. 5583187.

If you've ever suspected that you might be Scottish, this establishment will show you a chart indicating the place of origin (within Scotland) of your family name. You'll then be faced with a bewildering array of hunt and dress tartans for your personal use. The high-quality wool is sold by the yard as well as in the form of kilts for both men and women. There's also a line of lambswool and cashmere sweaters, and all the accessories to round out your perfect image as a Scot. The shop lies in a stone-fronted building close to John Knox's house.

WHISKY

THE SCOTCH MALT WHISKY SOCIETY, The Vaults, 87 Giles St., Leith. Tel. 5543452.

For that wee dram, this is the place. It is Edinburgh's leading specialist shop for single malt Scotch whisky aficionados. It also sells a wide range of single malts. Many of its bottles have been called "unique." Since the whisky has not been chill filtered, the brew retains its cask character.

9. EVENING ENTERTAINMENT

The city offers an array of theater, opera, dance, ballet, and other nighttime diversions as well, especially in its pubs, where you can often hear traditional Scottish music for the price of your brew. Discos, although not plentiful, do exist.

Ask for a free copy of **What's On in Edinburgh** at the Tourist Information Office at Waverley Market. Pocket size and easy to carry, this pamphlet is published monthly, and it lists all the major happenings around town, ranging from theater to art exhibitions, from sports events to films. You might also buy a copy of a magazine, **The List,** published biweekly. It's also available at the Tourist Information Office, costing £1 ($1.50). It has more detailed information than What's On, and its staff also reviews events in Edinburgh.

THE PERFORMING ARTS

KING'S THEATRE, 2 Leven St. Tel. 2291201.

This is the premier theater of Edinburgh, offering a wide repertoire of classical entertainment, including ballet and opera. West End productions from London are also presented at this 1,600-seat Victorian theater.

Admission: Tickets, £4–£16 ($6–$24).

PLAYHOUSE THEATRE, 18–22 Greenside Place. Tel. 5572950.

The largest theater in Edinburgh, this 3,100-seat playhouse was originally built in 1929 at the height of the vaudevillian age. Inspired by London's Palladium, it retains the gold and scarlet trappings of its construction and a hint of the greasepaint of long-ago stars. The Edinburgh home of both the Scottish Ballet and the Scottish Opera, its most popular performances are presented every Saturday. In addition to the more formal venues, the establishment presents rock concerts, operettas, musical comedies, experimental theater, and a wide array of musical acts from England, North America, and Europe. In summer, many performances of the Edinburgh Festival are presented on the premises. The box office, which has its own access to Greenside Place, is open Monday through Saturday from 10am to 6pm.

Admission: Tickets, £5–£25 ($7.50–$37.50).

THE QUEEN'S HALL, Clerk St. Tel. 6682019.

Queen's Hall is home to the Scottish Chamber Orchestra and a major venue for the Edinburgh International Festival. It also plays host to a full range of concerts, from classical to rock music, including a Friday-night jazz club. The box office and restaurant are open daily from 10am to 5pm.

Admission: Tickets, £5–£18 ($7.50–$27).

USHER HALL, Lothian Rd. near Princes St. Tel. 2288616.

Originally built of buff-colored sandstone in 1914, with a design inspired by the Royal Albert Hall in London, this is the home of the Royal Scottish Orchestra, and Edinburgh's chief venue for orchestral and choral music, presented on Friday nights between October and April. Lesser musical ensembles are scheduled throughout the week. Less frequent are presentations of such musical events as Gilbert and Sullivan operettas by Edinburgh's D'Oyly Carte Opera company. In summertime, the space is rented to the organizers of the Edinburgh Festival. The box office is open Monday through Saturday from 10am to 5pm.

Admission: Tickets, £5–£18 ($7.50–$27).

THEATERS

THE NETHERBOW ARTS CENTRE, 43 High St. Tel. 5569579.

Performances at this theater have been called "informal," but productions are often experimental and delightful. It's new Scottish theater at its best. Ask about lunchtime performances as well if you're not too busy sightseeing during the day.

Admission: Tickets, £2.50–£5 ($3.80–$7.50).

Open: Box office, Mon–Sat 10am–6pm.

ROYAL LYCEUM THEATRE, Grindlay St. Tel. 2299697.

The resident company here enjoys an enviable reputation for its presentations, which may range from Shakespeare to new Scottish playwrights. The theater is in a beautiful Victorian building dating from 1883 that contains a restaurant, four bars, and facilities for the disabled. The box office is open Monday through Saturday from 10am to 8pm.

Admission: Tickets, £4–£12 ($6–$18).

THE MAJOR CONCERT & PERFORMANCE HALLS

King's Theatre, 2 Leven St. (tel. 2291201).
Playhouse Theatre, 18–22 Greenside Pl. (tel. 5572950).
The Queen's Hall, Clerk Street (tel. 6682019).
Royal Lyceum Theatre, Grindlay Street (tel. 2299697).
Traverse Theatre, Cambridge Street (tel. 2281404).
Usher Hall, Lothian Road (tel. 2288616).

TRAVERSE THEATRE, Cambridge St. Tel. 2281404.
Traverse is one of the few theaters in Britain funded solely to present new plays by British writers and first translations into English of international works. In a new location, it now offers two theaters under one roof: Traverse 1 with a seating capacity of 250, and Traverse 2 with a smaller capacity of 100. On the premises a bar and café open at 10am serving theater patrons throughout the day.
Admission: Tickets, £3.50–£7 ($5.30–$10.50).

THE CLUB & MUSIC SCENE
DANCE CLUBS

BUSTER BROWNS, 25–27 Market St. Tel. 2264224.
Edinburgh's most consistently popular nightclub (with a clientele usually between ages 18 and 35) occupies the premises of what was originally built as the city's fruit and vegetable market in 1812. Later, it served as the Scottish headquarters of British Rail because of its location: Appropriately, it hangs suspended over the railway tracks behind the city's main station. Voted Scotland's best disco in 1991, it is affectionately referred to as "Buster's" by almost everyone in town. It is open Friday through Sunday from 10:30pm to 3:30am (when the bar closes). Music shuts down at 5am. Drinks being at £1.40 ($2.10); beer, £1.70 ($2.60) a pint.
Admission: £3 ($4.50) Fri and Sun, £4 ($6) Sat.

CENTURY 2000, 31 Lothian Rd. Tel. 2297670.
This is considered the largest disco in Edinburgh. It's also one of the most popular. The under-25 crowd flocks here in droves. But it's only open two nights a week, as disco devotees of Edinburgh seem to find other diversions on weeknights.
Admission: £3 ($4.50) 10pm–midnight; £5 ($7.50) midnight–4pm.
Open: Fri–Sat 10pm–4am.

FOLK MUSIC & CEILIDHS

Folk music is presented in many clubs and pubs in Edinburgh, but these strolling players tend to be somewhat erratic or irregular in appearances. It's best to read notices in pubs and talk to the tourist office to see where the ceilidh will be on the night of your visit.
In addition to various pubs that sometimes feature folk music, the **Edinburgh Folk Club,** Osborne Hotel, York Place (tel. 3394083), offers folk music every Wednesday at 8:15pm.
Some hotels regularly feature traditional Scottish music evenings. You might check with the **Carlton Highland Hotel** on North Bridge (tel. 5567277) or the **George Hotel** on George Street (tel. 2251251) to see if any program is featured at the time of your visit to Edinburgh. **Jamie's Scottish Evening** is often presented at the King James Hotel on Leith Street (tel. 5560111).

ROCK & JAZZ

THE MALT SHOVEL, 11–15 Cockburn St. Tel. 2256843.
Every night, it dispenses lots of real ales and single-malt whiskies to a neighborhood clientele, but every Tuesday its live bands draw in a bigger-than-average crowd. Live jazz and traditional Scottish music are featured. Both are open daily from noon to 11:30pm (last orders). Live music is presented only on Tuesday from 9 to 11:15pm. A pint of ale runs £1.60 ($2.40).
Admission: Free.

THE BAR SCENE
PUBS

BLACK BULL, 12 Grassmarket. Tel. 2256636.
Because of this establishment's location on a shop-lined street below the Royal

Mile, it is often overlooked by visitors. You can take a shortcut on foot from Edinburgh Castle by descending a steep flight of stone steps, but most pub crawlers enjoy window-shopping along the city streets. The pub is decorated like a scarlet version of a Victorian railway car, and an ascending series of platforms leading up to the carved bar. Of course, the head of a black bull is one of the pub's focal points. The place jumps at night to the recorded music of whatever group is hot at the time. The pub is open Monday through Saturday from 11am to 12:45am and on Sunday from 12:30pm to 11pm. Lager costs £1.50 ($2.30) per pint.

CAFÉ ROYAL CIRCLE BAR, 17 W. Register St. Tel. 5561884.

This is the most famous pub of Edinburgh and a long-enduring favorite. One part of this pub is now occupied by the superb but rather expensive Oyster Bar of the Café Royal. However, life in the Circle Bar continues at its old pace. The opulent trappings of the Victorian era are still to be seen here. Go up to the serving counter, which stands like an island in a sea of drinkers, and place your order. Hours are 11am to 11pm Monday through Thursday, 11am to midnight on Friday and Saturday, and 7pm to midnight on Sunday. Beer begins at £1.70 ($2.60).

DEACON BRODIE'S TAVERN, 435 Lawnmarket. Tel. 2256531.

Established in 1806, this is the neighborhood pub along the Royal Mile. It perpetuates the memory of Deacon Brodie, good citizen by day, robber by night. The tavern and wine cellars contain a cocktail and lounge bar. It offers a traditional pub setting and lots of atmosphere, making it popular with visitors and locals alike. The tavern is open daily from 11am to 11pm. Light meals cost from £4.50 ($6.80); beer £1.50 ($2.30).

GUILDFORD ARMS, 1–5 W. Register St. Tel. 5564312.

The Guildford Arms got a facelift back to the "mauve era" of the 1890s, although a pub has stood on this spot for 200 years. This Victorian-Italianesque corner pub, still harboring its oldtime memories, has one of the most intriguing decors of any pub in Edinburgh. It has seven arched windows with etched glass, plus an ornate ceiling, and is large, bustling, and at times a bit rough—but it's got plenty of character. Upstairs is a fish-and-chips emporium run by the same company, where a platter of greasy goodies from the sea costs from £4 ($6). Place your order at the upstairs bar. At festival time, jazz is presented here nightly. It's open Monday through Wednesday from 11am to 11pm, Thursday through Saturday from 11am to midnight, and on Sunday from 12:30am to 11pm. Bar snacks run 32p (50¢) to 80p ($1.20); beer costs £1.38 ($2.10) to £1.70 ($2.60).

KENILWORTH, 152–154 Rose St. Tel. 2258100.

This intriguing bar was named after the novel by Sir Walter Scott. Originally built as a private home, it was sold to a brewery in 1904, when it was lavishly decorated and turned into a popular pub in the Edwardian style. In 1981 its owners initiated a piece-by-piece renovation of each detail of the elaborately crafted interior. The blue and white wall tiles, coupled with the rows of stained-glass windows, a massive wooden bar, and a coal-burning fireplace, make for an alluring bar that attracts members of the performing arts. Hours are 11am to 11pm daily. Drinks cost from £1.50 ($2.30) per shot; ales begin at £1.38 ($2.10).

GAY BARS & CLUBS

BLUE OYSTER CLUB, 96A Rose Street Lane North. Tel. 2266458.

One of the most popular gay clubs in Edinburgh is right in the center of town, off the Royal Mile, lying on this famed street of restaurants and pubs. As in most gay clubs, the action begins here late at night. A wide range of music is presented. Beer costs from £1.70 ($2.60) a pint, and hours are Thursday from 10:30pm to 4am, Friday from 11pm to 4am, and Saturday from 10:30pm to 6am.

LAUGHING DUCK, 24 Howe St. Tel. 2256711.

Although a handful of other gay bars have come and gone, and continue to trickle in a bit of biz, at press time this one was the most consistently reliable. In a very large once-private duplex apartment within a 7-minute walk north of Princes Street, it attracts a very mixed crowd of gay men, as well as a scattering of women. Music videos play, and the music goes on and on. Every Tuesday night the scene is devoted to karaoke performances by members of the audience. Every other Wednesday is "Lady Samantha's Night," when gay women take over. (Every alternate Wednesday gay Bingo parties are held upstairs.)

On Friday and Saturday nights what is ordinarily just a pub becomes a gay disco (from 10pm to 2am) on the street level. The rest of the week, it's a pub. It's open Monday through Wednesday from noon to 1am, Thursday through Saturday from noon to 1:30am, and on Sunday from 6:30pm to 1am. Pints of lager run £1.30 ($2) to £1.70 ($2.60); drinks start at £1.60 ($2.40).

FILMS

The leading cinema houses include **Filmhouse,** Lothian Road (tel. 2282688). Film fans claim this house is the best cinema venue in Edinburgh. It offers many foreign-language films, specializing in quality productions that are often offbeat and not commercial but are diverting and diverse. You can also see films at **ABC,** also on Lothian Road (tel. 2293030). **Dominion** is another leading cinema, on Newbattle Terrace (tel. 4472660). If you don't like what's playing at any of the above, try the **Odeon Cinemas,** Clerk Street (tel. 0426/915468). Prices start at £3. ($4.50).

10. EASY EXCURSIONS FROM EDINBURGH

LINLITHGOW

In this royal burgh, a county town in West Lothian, 18 miles west of Edinburgh, Mary Queen of Scots was born. The roofless Linlithgow Palace, site of her birth in 1542, can still be viewed here today, even if it is but a shell of its former self. Buses and trains arrive daily from Edinburgh. The ride takes only 20 to 25 minutes.

WHAT TO SEE & DO

LINLITHGOW PALACE, south shore of Linlithgow Loch, Linlithgow. Tel. 031/2443101.

The birthplace of Mary Queen of Scots, as mentioned above, this was once a favorite residence of Scottish kings. The queen's suite was in the north quarter, but this was rebuilt for the homecoming of James VI (James I of Great Britain) in 1620. The palace was burned in 1746. The Great Hall is on the first floor, and a small display shows some of the more interesting architectural relics. The palace is half a mile from Linlithgow Station.

Admission: £1.50 ($2.30) adults, 80p ($1.20) children.

Open: Apr–Sept, Mon–Sat 9:30am–6pm, Sun 2–6pm; Oct–Mar, Mon–Sat 9:30am–4pm, Sun 2–4pm.

ST. MICHAEL'S PARISH CHURCH, within the precincts of Linlithgow Palace. Tel. 0506/842195.

South of the palace stands the medieval kirk of St. Michael the Archangel, considered one of the best examples of a medieval parish church.

Admission: Free.

Open: June–Sept, daily 10am–noon and 2–4pm; Oct–May, Mon–Fri 10am–noon and 2–4pm.

HOPETOUN HOUSE, 2 miles from Forth Road Bridge near South Queensferry off the A904. Tel. 031/3312451.

Set in the midst of beautifully landscaped grounds laid out along the lines of Versailles, Hopetoun House lies near the Forth Road Bridge at South Queensferry, off the A904, 10 miles from Edinburgh. This is Scotland's greatest

Adam mansion, and a fine example of 18th-century architecture. It is the seat of the Marquess of Linlithgow, whose grandfather and father were respectively the governor-general of Australia and the viceroy of India. You can wander through splendid reception rooms filled with 18th-century furniture, paintings, statuary, and other works of art. From a rooftop viewing platform you look out over a panoramic view of the Firth of Forth. Or you can take the nature trail, explore the deer parks, investigate the Stables Museum, or stroll through the formal gardens, all on the grounds. Near the Ballroom Suite, refreshments are available.

Admission: £3.30 ($5) adults, £1.60 ($2.40).

Open: Easter weekend and May–Sept, daily 11am–5pm. **Closed:** Oct–Apr.

WHERE TO DINE

CHAMPANY, Champany Corner. Tel. 050683/4532.

Cuisine: SCOTTISH. **Reservations:** Required. **Directions:** Take the A904, 2 miles northeast of Linlithgow to the junction with the A803.

$ Prices: Appetizers £3.50–£8.50 ($5.30–$12.80); main courses £12.50–£19.50 ($18.80–$29.30); fixed-price lunch £18.50 ($27.80). AE, DC, MC, V.

Open: Dining room, lunch Tues–Sat 12:30–2pm; dinner Tues–Sat 7–10pm. Chophouse, lunch daily 12:30–2pm; dinner daily 7–10pm. **Closed:** Dec 24–Jan 12.

Set in a converted farmhouse, you'll find the best steaks in Britain here. The owner, Clive Davidson, is an expert on beef, and he insists that his steaks be 1¼ inches thick, and his meat is hung for at least 4 weeks, which adds greatly to its flavor. He also prepares an assortment of oysters, salmon, and lobsters that are kept in a pool on the premises. Next door to the main dining room is a chophouse that has less expensive cuts. You can choose your own cut and watch it being grilled. There is also a raw bar. Meals in the chophouse begin at £12 ($18).

DALKEITH

A small town in Midlothian, Dalkeith was a baronial burgh when the Douglas clan held sway. Today the town center is modern, but there are also several historic buildings. On the A68 near the busy A7, Dalkeith lies between the South Esk and North Esk rivers, 7 miles southeast of Edinburgh.

WHAT TO SEE & DO

DALKEITH PARK, east end of Dalkeith High St., Dalkeith. Tel. 031/ 6635684.

This is the site of **Dalkeith Palace,** rebuilt and redesigned by Sir John Vanbrugh, circa 1700. George IV, Victoria, and Edward VII stayed in the former palace during visits to Edinburgh.

Instead of visiting a palace, visitors flock here today to explore the woodland and riverside walks in and around the extensive grounds of the palace. Luring guests are natural trails and an adventure woodland play area, a tunnel walk, and an Adam bridge. A ranger service offers regular guided walks.

Admission: £1 ($1.50) for adult and child ticket.

Open: Apr–Oct, daily 11am–6pm; Nov, Sat–Sun 11am–dusk. **Directions:** Take the A68 to Dalkeith, 7 miles south of Edinburgh, and follow the signs off High Street.

WHERE TO STAY

COUNTY HOTEL AND RESTAURANT, 152 High St., Dalkeith, Midlothian EH22 1AY. Tel. 031/6633495. Fax 031/6630208. 20 rms (all with bath). TV TEL

$ Rates (including Scottish breakfast): £38 ($57) single; £55 ($82.50) double; £60 ($90) family rooms. No credit cards. **Parking:** Free.

This hostelry is run by Philip Coppola and sons, a tradition going back 30 years. All rooms have radios and hot-drink equipment, among other amenities. The County

Restaurant serves meals all day, and the hotel also has a bar and an elevator to all floors.

WHERE TO DINE

GEORGE'S PIZZA AND SPAGHETTI HOUSE AND CAVALIERE RESTAURANT, 124–126 High St. Tel. 031/6634492.
Cuisine: ITALIAN. **Reservations:** Not needed.
$ Prices: Appetizers £1.40–£3.65 ($2.10–$5.50); main courses £4–£9.50 ($6–$14.30). MC, V.
Open: Lunch daily 12:30–2:30pm; dinner daily 5pm–1am.

George's serves the best food and has perhaps the longest name in town. Many people drop in to enjoy pizza, which comes in several varieties, along with a bottle of wine. The pastas, including the creamy lasagne, are generally excellent, and you can also order more substantial fare, including some of the best of Scottish beef, served in the classic grilled T-bone way, or given a continental flair and offered with a perfectly balanced brandy sauce. Fresh fish, including mussels, are served in savory sauces. The atmosphere is that of a typical Italian trattoria.

HADDINGTON

Created as a royal burgh by David I, this small town of East Lothian lies on the Tyne River, about 17 miles east of Edinburgh, a 30-minute drive. In the 15th century it was Scotland's largest town, but its fortunes declined thereafter. Today it is one of the best-preserved historic towns of Scotland. A Haddington bus runs down from Edinburgh.

The standard of innkeeping has considerably improved since the 18th century: In 1742, Dr. Alexander Carlyle, in his autobiography, noted that even though "the second tavern in Haddington now supplied knives, forks, and spoons for their table, they had but one glass on the table, which went round with the bottle."

WHAT TO SEE & DO

On the right bank of the river, in the industrial suburb of Giffordgate, Scottish reformer John Knox was believed to have been born in 1505. Much to the chagrin of the Catholic Mary Queen of Scots, he rose from these dire origins to found the Scottish Presbyterian church.

St. Mary's Church, Sidegate (tel. 062082/5111), built in the 14th century along the river, in red and gray sandstone, contains the tomb of Jane Welsh, who was born in the town. She married historian Thomas Carlyle. John Knox once worshiped here.

The **Jane Welsh Carlyle Museum,** Lodge Street (tel. 062082/3738), is the former home of this woman who was an influential thinker in her own right. Her home, with its drawing room, garden rooms, and Regency gardens, is open April through September, Wednesday to Saturday from 2 to 5pm. Admission is £1 ($1.50) for adults and accompanying children are admitted free.

You can visit **St. Mary's Pleasance,** Sidegate, which are the gardens of Haddington House. They have been brought back to life in the style of the 1600s. In season you can wander among the sunken gardens, enjoying the roses and herbs.

WHERE TO STAY

THE GEORGE, 91 High St., Haddington, East Lothian EH41 3ET. Tel. 062082/3372. 13 rms (5 with bath). TV TEL
$ Rates (including Scottish breakfast): £26 ($39) single without bath, £29 ($43.50) single with bath; £36 ($54) double without bath, £40 ($60) double with bath. AE, DC. **Parking:** Free.

This is the finest inn in town, with comfortably appointed rooms. It's been going since the 18th century from its location at the end of High Street. It first opened as The Old Post House. Daniel Defoe, author of *Robinson Crusoe,* called it: "The best Inn I have seen in Scotland, and inferior to none I have seen on the London Road." Other famous figures who patronized the place included the 18th-century author Thomas

Carlyle, along with the Hanoverian General Sir John Cope and Prime Minister A. J. Balfour. The food is a medley of Scottish and continental dishes, and service is polite and efficient. Lunch begins at £4.95 ($7.40) while a dinner goes for £10 ($15) and up.

WHERE TO DINE

BROWNS HOTEL, 1 West Rd., Haddington, East Lothian EH41 3RD. Tel. 062082/2254.
   Cuisine: BRITISH/FRENCH. **Reservations:** Recommended.
$ **Prices:** Table d'hôte dinner £23.50 ($35.30); lunch Sun £16.80 ($25.20). AE, MC, V.
   Open: Lunch Sun noon–2pm; dinner Mon–Sat 7:30–9pm.

⊕ On the main road into Haddington off the A1 from Edinburgh, Browns is the domain of Colin Brown, the most accomplished chef in the area. The menu is based on seasonal produce and the inspiration of Mr. Brown. The cookery shows both British and French influences, and the place is full of character—it's a small, special restaurant.

Located at the edge of town, the hotel also rents five attractively furnished bedrooms, all of which contain a private bath or shower. Charges for B&B range from £59.50 ($89.30) daily in a single to £78 ($117) in a double.

DUNBAR

In East Lothian, southeast of North Berwick and 28 miles east of Edinburgh, Dunbar, another royal burgh, is a popular seaside resort at the foot of the Lammermuir Hills. The River Tyne reaches the North Sea nearby, and it was here that Cromwell landed his invasion forces, heading for Edinburgh. Direct trains run through from Edinburgh.

WHAT TO SEE & DO

On a rock above the harbor are the remains of **Dunbar Castle,** Victoria Harbour, built on the side of an earlier castle that dated from 856. Today the kittiwakes live where once "Black Agnes," the Countess of Dunbar, held off the English in 1339. Mary Queen of Scots fled there with Darnley in 1566, immediately after the murder of her secretary, Rizzio. The Battle of Dunbar was fought in 1650 between Cromwell's army and the Scots. The Scots, led by David Leslie, fought valiantly but lost. Nearly 3,000 were killed in one day. The ruins are open all the time.

About 6½ miles west of Dunbar sits **Hailes Castle,** just off the A1 and also reached by a little road running from East Linton to Haddington. On the bank of the River Tyne, this castle was not a fortress for military action but rather a fortified mansion home and is considered one of the outstanding examples of 13th-century masonry construction. Mary Queen of Scots slept here in 1545 when she was being escorted to Dunbar from Edinburgh by the Earl of Bothwell. At Hailes, you can see a vaulted bakehouse in the cellar of a 15th-century structure, plus a chapel. You can go through a little gate in the north wall of the castle and stroll along a grassy promenade along the Tyne. The castle is an open site.

If you take a walk up the hill from the main gate of Hailes Castle, on the south wall you'll come to **Traprain Law,** where an ancient hill fort stood in the Iron Age, although there's not much to see there now except the view of the castle below. It is believed that the hill was once occupied by the Votadini, a tribe allied to the Romans.

WHERE TO STAY & DINE

BATTLEBLENT HOTEL, Edinburgh Rd., West Barns, Dunbar, East Lothian EH42 1TS. Tel. 0368/62234. Fax 0368/62234. 7 rms (all with bath or shower). TV TEL
$ **Rates** (including Scottish breakfast): £27.50–£29.50 ($41.30–$44.30) single; £53.50–£56.50 ($80.30–$84.80) double. AE, DC, MC, V. **Parking:** Free.
A mile outside Dunbar, the Battleblent lies on the A1 London–Edinburgh road 26 miles from Edinburgh near the A1087 roundabout. The castlelike hotel is set on a hill surrounded by 3 acres of its grounds overlooking Balhaven Bay on the Firth of Forth.

The bedrooms are large, high-ceilinged, and comfortable, with hot-beverage facilities and radio alarms, among other amenities.

Good food is served in the dining room daily from 6:30 to 11pm. Tender Scottish sirloin steaks from the grill are a specialty, and fresh vegetables, some from the hotel's garden, are used when possible. Inexpensive bar lunches are available from noon to 2pm. Locals and visitors socialize in the Tudor Lounge Bar or dance and dine in the Function Club Bar.

NORTH BERWICK

This royal burgh, created in the 14th century, was once an important Scottish port. In East Lothian, 24 miles east from Edinburgh, it is today a holiday resort popular with the Scots and an increasing number of foreigners. Visitors are drawn to its golf courses, beach sands, and harbor life on the Firth of Forth. You can climb the rocky shoreline or enjoy the heated outdoor swimming pool in July and August.

North Berwick lies on a direct rail line from Edinburgh (trip time: 30 minutes). There is also bus service to North Berwick from Edinburgh, taking 1¼ hours.

WHAT TO SEE & DO

At the **information centre,** Quality Street (tel. 0620/2197), you can pick up data on how to take boat trips to the offshore islands, including **Bass Rock,** a breeding ground inhabited by about 10,000 gannets. The volcanic island is 1 mile in circumference. It's possible to see the rock from the harbor. The viewing is even better at **Berwick Law,** a volcanic lookout point.

Some 2 miles east of North Berwick on the A198 stand the ruins of the 14th-century diked and rose-colored **Tantallon Castle** (tel. 031/2443101). This was the ancient stronghold of the Douglases from its construction in the 14th century until its defeat by Cromwell's forces in 1650. Overlooking the Firth of Forth, the castle ruins still are formidable, with a square, five-story central tower and a dovecote, plus the shell of its east tower, a D-shaped structure with a wall from the central tower. Tantallon Castle can be visited April through September, Monday to Saturday from 9:30am to 6pm and on Sunday from 2 to 6pm; October through March, Monday, Tuesday, and Saturday from 9:30am to 4pm, Wednesday and Thursday from noon to 4pm, Sunday from 2 to 4pm. Admission is £1.50 ($2.30) adults, 80p ($1.20) children.

WHERE TO STAY

THE MARINE, 18 Cromwell Rd., North Berwick, East Lothian EH39 4LZ. Tel. 0620/2406, or toll-free in U.S. 800/225-5843. Fax 0620/4480. 78 rms (all with bath), 5 suites. TV TEL

$ Rates (including Scottish breakfast): £65–£85 ($97.50–$127.50) single; £85–£110 ($127.50–$165) double; from £140 ($210) suite. AE, DC, MC, V. **Parking:** Free.

This is a fine, turreted Victorian Hotel, commanding stunning views across the West Links Course, some of whose putting greens come close to the hotel's foundations. The location is only a 30-minute drive from Edinburgh Castle, an ideal base for either touring or golfing.

The Marine is a home away from home for Nicklaus, Trevino, Player, and most of the USA Ryder Cup Team during the Open, and lies in an area with almost 20 golf courses nearby. Inside, there's the aura of an elegant country house. The hotel has recently undergone refurbishment, and all the bedrooms have private baths, color TVs, tea- and coffee-making equipment, and trouser presses. The bar is lined with antique golfing photos. Additional facilities include saunas, squash, snooker, putting, tennis, gardens, and children's playgrounds.

The cuisine is international, with many Scottish specialties. Dinners cost from £15.95 ($23.90) to £17.95.

WHERE TO DINE

CASTLE'S RESTAURANT, 35 High St. Tel. 0620/3434.

Cuisine: SCOTTISH. **Reservations:** Recommended.
$ Prices: Appetizers £1.95–£4.95 ($2.90–$7.40); main courses £6.25–£12.95 ($9.40–$19.40). AE, MC, V.
Open: Lunch Mon–Fri noon–2pm, Sat–Sun noon–3pm; dinner nightly 7–10pm.
Contained within two rooms of one of North Berwick's older houses, midway along the town's main thoroughfare, this comfortable restaurant serves pleasing portions of food made almost exclusively with Scottish ingredients. Established in the early 1990s by Ralph Ellsdale and Andrew Thom, former restaurant managers of the Edinburgh Sheraton Hotel, it serves filet steaks of Angus beef, wild duckling with cherries, pheasant, salmon with dill, langoustines, and stuffed eggplant. The setting is cozy, with ample use of cotton and linen.

GULLANE

Lying 19 miles east of Edinburgh in East Lothian, Gullane, with a population of around 2,000 people, is really a pocket of posh. Not only does it have one of the great country hotels of Scotland (see "Where to Stay," below), but it's also home to a small restaurant (see "Where to Dine," below) that some food critics have suggested is "the best in Scotland."

WHERE TO STAY

GREYWALLS HOTEL, Muirfield, Duncur Rd., Gullane, East Lothian EH31 2EF. Tel. 0620/842144. Fax 0620/842241. 23 rms (all with bath). TV TEL
$ Rates (including Scottish breakfast): £90 ($135) single; £150 ($225) double. AE, DC, MC, V. **Parking:** Free.

About 5 miles from North Berwick (follow the signs from the A198), an excellent place to stay is Greywalls Hotel. An Edwardian country house, designed as a private home by the renowned architect of his day, Sir Edwin Lutyens, it was visited from time to time by King Edward VII, who admired the views across the Firth of Forth and south to the Lammermuir Hills. The gardens were laid out by Gertrude Jekyll, who often worked with architect Lutyens in supplying a complete Edwardian home package. Today Greywalls is the property of Giles and Ros Weaver who have combined the atmosphere of a home with the amenities of a delightful country-house hotel. In the paneled library, guests relax on comfortable sofas before a blazing log fire (in cool weather). The garden room is done in bamboo furnishings. There is also a small bar. The bedrooms vary in size: Some smaller ones are simply decorated and others, more spacious, are furnished with period pieces.

Dining/Entertainment: The food served in the elegant dining room reflects culinary expertise. Light French-style dishes are made almost as appealing to the eye as to the palate. Specialties include fresh seafood. Other tasty main courses might be venison, breast of pheasant, smoked duck, or local beef. Meals cost £17 ($25.50) to £33 ($49.50). Men are required to wear jackets and ties in the dining room, which is open daily from 12:30 to 2pm and 7:30 to 9:30pm. Greywalls is open from April to the end of October.

Services: 24-hour room service, laundry, babysitting.
Facilities: Hard tennis court, croquet lawn, 10 golf courses within 5 miles.

WHERE TO DINE

LA POTINIÈRE, Main St., Gullane. Tel. 0620/843214.
Cuisine: FRENCH. **Reservations:** Required.
$ Prices: Fixed-price four-course lunch £16.75 ($25.10) Mon–Tues and Thurs–Sat; £17.50 ($26.30) Sun; fixed-price five-course dinner Fri–Sat £26 ($39). AE, DC, MC, V.
Open: Lunch Sun–Tues and Thurs–Sat at 1pm; dinner Fri–Sat at 8pm. **Closed:** June 1–7 and Oct.

La Potinière is a small and pretty restaurant beautifully run by David and Hilary Brown. The excellent food produced by Hilary, using local ingredients so far as possible, is complemented by a fine choice of wines from the cellar supervised by David. The first course is usually a light and subtly flavored soup, followed by a fish dish, perhaps a mousseline, or by one of Hilary's creations. The main courses, from steak to turkey to lamb, are all done with flair. Cheese and dessert wind up the meal. A special dinner is served on Friday and Saturday only, starting promptly at 8pm; reservations for this five-course gourmet's delight should be made well in advance. No smoking is permitted in the dining room.

DIRLETON

Another popular excursion from Edinburgh is to this little town that vies for the title of "prettiest village in Scotland." The town plan, drafted in the early 16th century, is essentially unchanged today. Dirleton has two greens shaped like triangles, with a pub opposite Dirleton Castle, placed at right angles to a group of cottages. Dirleton is a preservation village and as such is subject to careful control of any development. It's on the Edinburgh–North Berwick road (the A198). North Berwick (see above) is 5 miles to the east and Edinburgh 19 miles to the west.

WHAT TO SEE & DO

DIRLETON CASTLE, Dirleton, East Lothian. Tel. 062085/330.

A rose-tinted 13th-century castle with surrounding gardens, once the seat of the wealthy Anglo-Norman de Vaux family, Dirleton Castle looks like a fairytale fortification, with its towers, arched entries, and an oak ramp similar to the drawbridge that used to protect it. The prison, bakehouse, and storehouses of the castle are carved from bedrock. Ruins of the great hall and kitchen can be seen, as well as what's left of the lord's chamber where the de Vaux family lived. You can see windows and window seats, a wall with a toilet and drains, and other household features. The 16th-century main gate has a hole through which boiling tar or water could be poured to discourage unwanted visitors.

The castle's country garden and a bowling green are still in use, with masses of flowering plants rioting in the gardens and bowlers sometimes seen on the green. A 17th-century dovecote with 1,100 nests stands at the east end of the garden. A small gate at the west end leads onto one of the village greens.

Admission: £1.70 ($2.60) adults, 90p ($1.40) children.

Open: Apr–Sept, Mon–Sat 9:30am–6pm, Sun 2–6pm; Oct–Mar, Mon–Sat 9:30am–4pm, Sun 2–4pm.

WHERE TO STAY & DINE

THE OPEN ARMS, Dirleton, East Lothian EH39 5BG. Tel. 062085/241.
7 rms (all with bath). TV TEL
$ Rates (including Scottish breakfast): £60–£80 ($90–$120) single; £110–£120 ($165–$180) double. MC, V. **Parking:** Free.

The Open Arms will receive you in keeping with the promise of its name. This old stone hostelry has been transformed into a handsome hotel and restaurant, serving the finest food in the area. Off the A198 overlooking the castle ruins, the hotel is owned by Arthur Neil, who has built up an enormous local reputation for serving Scottish dishes. Try, for example, cranachan (a concoction of oatmeal, heavy cream, and brambles). Cold Scottish salmon served encased in pastry is one of the inn's specialties. Another specialty of 40 years' standing is a stew of fresh mussels and onions. On one recent occasion, the luncheon menu featured a first for me—smoked mackerel with gooseberry-cream sauce. You might begin with a real "Taste of Scotland" specialty, lentil broth with oatmeal, about which, the Scots say, you can "stand up your spoon in it." The people who serve are informed and skillful. Dinners begin at £22 ($33). Lunch is served daily from 12:30 to 2:15pm and dinner nightly from 7 to 10pm.

The Open Arms will also receive you as an overnight guest. However, it's small, only seven bedrooms, each with private bath, color TV, phone, and joy of joys, room service available at no extra cost. Log fires crackle and blaze, and it must surely be a golfer's paradise, as it's surrounded by eight courses.

CHAPTER 5

GLASGOW

- **WHAT'S SPECIAL ABOUT GLASGOW**
- **1. ORIENTATION**
- **NEIGHBORHOODS IN BRIEF**
- **2. GETTING AROUND**
- **FAST FACTS: GLASGOW**
- **3. ACCOMMODATIONS**
- **FROMMER'S COOL FOR KIDS: HOTELS**
- **4. DINING**
- **FROMMER'S SMART TRAVELER: RESTAURANTS**
- **FROMMER'S COOL FOR KIDS: RESTAURANTS**
- **5. ATTRACTIONS**
- **DID YOU KNOW . . . ?**
- **FROMMER'S FAVORITE GLASGOW EXPERIENCES**
- **WALKING TOUR: HISTORIC GLASGOW**
- **6. SPECIAL & FREE EVENTS**
- **7. SPORTS & RECREATION**
- **8. SAVVY SHOPPING**
- **9. EVENING ENTERTAINMENT**
- **10. EASY EXCURSIONS FROM GLASGOW**

Glasgow lies only 40 miles west of Edinburgh, but forms an amazing contrast. Glasgow today is rich in sightseeing attractions of its own, including some of the most important art in Britain. It's also a showcase for some of the greatest Victorian architecture in the country, a style appreciated far more today than in previous decades.

Scotland's largest city, its commercial capital, and Britain's third-largest city, Glasgow has long been famous for its shipbuilding, ironworks, and steelworks. Home to half of Scotland's population, it stands on the banks of the River Clyde. It is the birthplace of the *Queen Mary,* the *Queen Elizabeth,* and many other ocean-going liners. But Glasgow is no longer the smoking industrial city that used to be blighted by the Gorbals, one of the worst slums in Europe. Urban-development schemes have brought about a great change, although, as tourist officials concede, bad reputations are long in dying.

The city is emerging as a tourist and major sightseeing destination, a move aided in part by the decision to locate the Scottish Exhibition and Conference Centre here. Local officials have long talked of a "renaissance." Industrial grime is being sandblasted away, obsolete housing has been replaced in section after section, overcrowding in the city center has been reduced, and more open space and less traffic congestion mean cleaner air.

The Victorian splendor of the city has reemerged. John Betjeman and other critics have hailed Glasgow as "the greatest surviving example of a Victorian city." The planners of the 19th century thought on a grand scale in designing the terraces and villas west and south of the center.

Glasgow's origins are very ancient, making Edinburgh, for all its wealth of history, seem comparatively young. The village that became the city grew up beside a ford 20 miles from the mouth of the River Clyde, and was once a medieval ecclesiastical center. Prosperity began in the 17th century and continued through the 18th, when its merchants set out to dominate the trade of the western seas. The Clyde was widened and deepened, and the city's expansion engulfed the smaller medieval towns of Ardrie, Renfrew, Rutherglen, and Paisley.

Glasgow is a good center for touring Loch Lomond, Loch Katrine, and the resorts along the Ayrshire coast, an hour away by frequent train service (see "Easy

WHAT'S SPECIAL ABOUT GLASGOW

s/Villages

- cotland's largest city and ial capital, "the greatest ample of a Victorian city."
- Ayr, most popular resort on Scotland's west coast, a good center for the Burns Country.
- Troon, a summer bathing resort and sports mecca, with several golf links.
- Prestwick, the oldest recorded baronial burgh in Scotland, site of Prestwick Airport.

Beaches

- Troon's 2 miles of sandy beaches, looking out upon the Firth of Clyde to the Isle of Arran.
- Ayr, a holiday resort with 2½ miles of sand beaches attracting thousands of bathers in summer.

Historic Castles

- Culzean Castle, Maybole, Eisenhower's Scottish retreat, a masterpiece of Robert Adam architecture.

Museums

- Burrell Collection, a wealthy shipowner's art gift to the city, more than 8,000 items from the ancient world to the modern.

- Hunterian Art Gallery, with an array of world masterpieces, including works by everybody from Rembrandt to Whistler.
- Art Gallery and Museum at Kelvingrove, home of Britain's finest civic collection of British and European paintings.

Religious Shrines

- The Cathedral of St. Kentigern, mainland Scotland's only complete medieval cathedral, dating from the 12th and 13th centuries.

Parks and Gardens

- Botanic Gardens, Great Western Road, famed for its plant collections, especially its begonias and orchids.

Architectural Highlights

- The buildings of Charles Rennie Mackintosh, distinguished innovator in art and architecture.

Literary Shrine

- Burns Cottage and Museum, Alloway, with much of the poet's original furnishings, including the bed in which he was born.

Excursions," below). From Glasgow you can also explore the heart of Burns Country, the Stirling area, Culzean Castle, and the Trossachs. On Glasgow's doorstep is the scenic estuary of the Firth of Clyde, down which you can cruise on a paddle-steamer. The Firth of Clyde is one of the loveliest waterways in the world, with its long sea lochs, islands, and hills.

Greenock is an important industrial and shipbuilding town on the Clyde estuary a few miles west of the center of Glasgow, where in 1736 James Watt, inventor of the steam engine, was born. A huge Cross of Lorraine on Lyle Hill above the town commemorates Free French sailors who died in the Battle of the Atlantic during World War II.

Past Greenock, sea lochs strike into the Strathclyde hills—**Gareloch, Loch Long, and Loch Goil**—with Holy Loch pointing more to the west. This was once a holiday region, but that changed with the onset of World War II. Holy Loch now has its Polaris base, and British atomic subs are stationed in these waters. There are new seaports on Loch Long and the Gareloch. Loch Long *is* long, but its name derives from the Gaelic word meaning "a ship," and means the "loch of the ships." Long before the Clyde was world famous for shipbuilding, the galleys of the old chieftains sheltered in these waters. Vikings hauled their boats overland from Loch Long to raid the country around Loch Lomond.

Gourock, 3 miles west of Greenock, is a resort and yachting center. On the cliff side of Gourock is **"Granny Kempock,"** a 6-foot-high stone of gray schist that was probably significant in prehistoric times. In past centuries it was used by fishermen for rites to ensure fair weather. Couples planning marriage used to circle Granny to get her blessing and to ensure fertility in their marriage.

From Gourock, car-ferries take travelers to **Dunoon** on the Cowal Peninsula. You can also visit **Rothesay** and the **Isle of Bute,** where the Glaswegians themselves go for fun in the sun.

In what was once an industrial wasteland between Hamilton and Motherwell, the Strathclyde Regional Council has created the 1,600-acre **Strathclyde Regional Park,** with a 2-mile loch, the site of many water sports including competition sailing. There is also a bird sanctuary and a nature reserve, along with the Hamilton Mausoleum.

All these attractions are part of Strathclyde, Scotland's biggest unit of local government, taking in some 5,348 square miles. The name is ancient; Irish chroniclers wrote of the kingdom of Stratha Cluatha (Valley of the River Clyde) some 1,500 years ago. Strathclyde was known to the Romans, who called its people Damnonii. The old capital, Dumbarton, was selected because its high rock provided a natural fortress in the days when local people had to defend themselves against enemy tribes. Picts and Scots from the north attacked with frequency, Northumbrian Anglo-Saxons came up from the south to do damage, and Vikings descended from the far-northern climes. The region finally fell to the Scots of Dalriada in the 10th century.

The fortunes of Strathclyde changed dramatically in the 18th century when the Clyde estuary became the gateway to the New World. Glasgow merchants grew rich on tobacco and then on cotton. It was the fastest-growing region in Britain in the days of the Industrial Revolution. Factories turned out textiles; then came heavy engineering, shipbuilding, and chemicals. Glasgow's fame grew and grew until it became known as "the Second City of the Empire."

The Clyde begins at its source in the high uplands of Lanarkshire. It runs along for 50 miles before flowing through Glasgow.

1. ORIENTATION

ARRIVING

BY PLANE The **Glasgow Airport** is at Abbotsinch (tel. 041/8484440) 10 miles west of the city via the M8 motorway. You can use the regular Glasgow city-link bus service to get to the city center. Take bus no. 500 or 501 to reach the Buchanan Street Bus Station in the center of Glasgow. The ride takes about 20 minutes and costs £2 ($3). A taxi to the city center costs about £10 ($15). You can also go from the airport to Edinburgh by bus, the trip taking 1¾ hours and costing £5 ($7.50) per ticket.

British Airways runs almost hourly "shuttle" service from London's Heathrow Airport to Glasgow Monday through Friday. The first flight departs London at 7:15am, the last one leaving at 8:15pm; service is reduced on weekends, depending on volume. For flight schedules and fares, call British Airways at 66 Gordon St. in Glasgow (tel. 041/3329666).

British Airways planes from Boston or New York now fly direct to Glasgow Airport (see "Getting There" in Chapter 2).

BY TRAIN For British Rail the headquarters in Glasgow is at the **Central Station** and **Queen Street Station** (tel. 041/2042844 for information). For sleeper reservations by credit card, call 041/2212305. The Queen Street Station serves the north and east of Scotland. Trains arrive from Edinburgh at the rate of one every 30 minutes during the day; a one-way ticket between the two cities costs £5.50 ($8.30). You'll also be able to visit such Highland destinations as Inverness and Fort William from this station. Central Station serves southern Scotland, England, and Wales.

Trains arrive from London Euston and Kings Cross stations (tel. 071/3877070) in London for schedules) frequently throughout the day (trip time: approximately 5½ hours). The first train departs Euston at 6:25am and the last train runs out of Euston at 11:45pm. Try to avoid Sunday travel, however; frequency of trains is considerably reduced and the trip takes 7 hours then, maybe longer, because of more stopovers en route.

Luggage storage is possible at both of these stations (see "Fast Facts: Glasgow," below).

Hotels do not cluster around these stations as they do in most European cities.

BY BUS The **Buchanan Street Bus Station** (tel. 041/3329191) lies two blocks north of Queen Station on North Hanover Street. Scottish Citylink (tel. 041/3329191) runs daily coaches from London's Victoria Coach Station to Buchanan frequently throughout the day. Buses from London take from 7½ to 8½ hours to reach Glasgow, depending on the number of stops en route. Scottish Citylink also has frequent bus service to and from Edinburgh, a one-way ticket costing only £3.70 ($5.60).

The other bus station in Glasgow, **Anderston Station** (tel. 041/2487432), a few blocks beyond Central Station on Argyle Street, is used mainly for intra-city and suburban bus trips.

BY CAR From England in the south, Glasgow is reached by the M74, a continuation of the M8 that goes right into the city, making an S-curve. Call your hotel and find out what exit you take. The M8, another express motorway, links Glasgow and Edinburgh.

Other major routes into the city are the A77 northeast from Prestwick and Ayr, and the A8 from the west (this becomes the M8 around the port of Glasgow). The A82 comes in from the northwest (the Highlands) on the north bank of the Clyde. The A80 also goes into the city (this route is the southwestern section of the M80 and M9 from Stirling).

Glasgow lies 40 miles west of Edinburgh, 221 miles north of Manchester, and 388 miles north of London.

CITY LAYOUT

Monumental Glasgow—that is, the "Victorian City" and "Merchant City," along with the Central Station—lies on the north bank of the River Clyde, which runs through the metropolis. The ancient center of Glasgow has as its core the great Glasgow Cathedral, a perfect example of pre-Reformation Gothic architecture which, in part, dates back to the 12th century. Behind it lies the Necropolis, burial ground of many Victorian merchants. Across the square is Provand's Lordship, the oldest house in the city (built in 1471). Down High Street can be found the Tolbooth Steeple (1626) at Glasgow Cross, while nearer the River Clyde is Glasgow Green, Britain's first public park (1662).

From Ingram Street, South Frederick Street will take you to George Square, with its many statues, including one dedicated to Sir Walter Scott. This is the center of modern Glasgow.

Over the centuries the city headed west, first to Merchant City, a compact area of imposing buildings. This is the location of the National Trust for Scotland's shop and visitor center at Hutcheson's Hall. The broad pedestrian thoroughfares of Buchanan Street, Argyle Street, and Sauchiehall Street are the heart of the shopping district.

Glasgow's West End is just a short taxi journey from the city center. It is easily accessible from any part of the city and close to the M8 motorway (inner ring road) and the Clydeside Expressway. An extensive network of local bus routes serves the West End. The Glasgow underground (subway) operates a circular service; by boarding at any station on the system passengers can reach the four stations serving the district—Kelvinbridge, Hillhead (the most central), Kelvin Hall, and Partick.

The West End is the finest example in Britain of a great Victorian city. The terraces of the Park Conversation Area rise to afford excellent views of the West End. Across Kelvingrove Park is the Art Gallery and Museum. Nearby, the tower of Glasgow

University dominates Gilmorehill. Beyond is the Hunterian Art Gallery, home to a famous collection of Whistlers. Just a few strides away is Byres Road, a street of bars and shops, along with restaurants. To the north is the Botanic Gardens.

A little more than 3 miles southwest of the city center lies the Pollok Country Park and Pollok Estate. An extensive network of bus routes passes close by the park area, which is also served by two suburban rail stations. An electric bus service is in operation from the Country Park Gates on Pollokshaws Road to Pollok House and the Burrell Collection Gallery. The Burrell Collection is housed in the heavily wooded Pollok Country Park, Scotland's top tourist attraction and the focal point of any visit to the South Side. Nearby is the 18th-century Pollok House.

Extensive parklands and greenery characterize the southern environs of the city. In addition to the Pollok Country Park and Estate, there is Haggs Castle Golf Club, home of the Glasgow Open, and Bellahouston Park, scene of the historic papal visit in 1983. En route to the Burrell Collection, you cross by the 148-acre Queens Park, honoring Mary Queen of Scots, where panoramic views of the city are possible from the hilltop. Near Maxwell Park is the Haggs Castle Museum in a 400-year-old building.

FINDING AN ADDRESS   Street numbering is often confusing. Glasgow was built in various sections and districts over the years, and massive sections have been torn down—some for slum clearance, others to make way for new highways. Therefore, following a consistent street plan can be tough, as squares or terraces can suddenly interrupt a route you're tracing.

House numbers can run in odds or evens, clockwise or counterclockwise, and sometimes Glaswegians don't even use numbers at all. Therefore don't be surprised to see "Blackfriars Street" given as an address without a number. Get a detailed map of Glasgow before setting out. Since the numbering is confusing, always find the nearest cross street, then look for your location from there. If it's a hotel or restaurant, the sign for the establishment is likely to be more prominent than the number anyway.

NEIGHBORHOODS IN BRIEF

Old Glasgow   This is where St. Mungo arrived in 543 and built his little church in what is now the northeastern part of the city. At the top of High Street stands Glasgow Cathedral. One of Britain's largest Victorian cemeteries is in this section; after leaving the cathedral, turn left and then left once more. The Necropolis is entered by crossing over the Bridge of Sighs. Old Glasgow's major terminus is High Street Station near the former site of the University of Glasgow. Its largest "green lung" is Glasgow Green, opening onto the River Clyde. This has been a public park since 1662.

Along the River Clyde   Glasgow is no longer as dependent on the Clyde as it was once when it was said: "The Clyde made Glasgow; Glasgow made the Clyde." Visitors take the Clyde Walkway stretching from King Albert Bridge, at the western end of Glasgow Green, for 2 miles downstream to Stohcross. Stohcross is now the site of the Scottish Exhibition and Conference Centre. The river is crossed by several bridges, one named for Queen Victoria, another for her consort, Albert.

The Merchant City   Leaving High Street, Glasgow spread west in the 18th century, largely because of profits made from sugar, cotton, and tobacco in trade with the Americas. This area extends mainly from Trongate and Argyle Street in the south to George Street in the north. Its major terminus is Queen Street Station, and its major shopping venue is Argyle Arcade. It is also the site of City Hall and Strathclyde University.

Glasgow Center   Continuing its western progression, the city center of Glasgow is now dominated by the Central Station on Hope Street. This is the major shopping district of Glasgow, including such venues as the Princes Square Shopping Mall. The Stock Exchange is also in this section, as is the Anderston Bus Station (near the Central Station).

The West End   Lying beyond Charing Cross in the west end is the University of Glasgow and several of the city's major galleries and museums, some of which are in Kelvingrove Park.

2. GETTING AROUND

BY PUBLIC TRANSPORTATION

BY BUS Glasgow is serviced by two principal bus companies, the Kelvin Central (with blue-and-yellow buses) and the Strathclyde Transport (in stark orange). Some of Kelvin Central's buses are of the old London variety (painted red). Service is frequent throughout the day, but after 11pm night service is greatly curtailed. The two major bus stations are the Buchanan Street Bus Station, North Hanover Street (tel. 041/3329191), two blocks north of Queen Station, and the Anderston Station, Argyle Street (tel. 041/2487432), lying near the Central Station. Fares are 50p (75¢), but you must have the exact change.

BY SUBWAY Called "Clockwork Orange" by Glaswegians, a 15-stop underground services the city. The nickname comes from the vivid orange of its trains. Most Underground trains operate from these stops every 5 minutes, with longer intervals between trains on Sunday and at night. Service is Monday through Saturday from 6:30am to 10pm and on Sunday from 11am to 6pm. Fares are 50p (75¢). However, you can go to the Travel Centre at St. Enoch's Square (tel. 041/2264826), two blocks from the Central Station, any time Monday through Saturday from 9:30am to 5:30pm. There you can purchase an Underground pass, valid for unlimited travel on the system for 1 day for £1.75 ($2.60); a weekly pass sells for £4.50 ($6.80).

BY TAXI

With some 1,400 taxis in its fleet, a private taxi is another means of getting about, although the most expensive. Fares are displayed on a meter next to the driver. For service, phone **TOA Taxis** (tel. 3327070). Taxis are the same excellent ones as found in Edinburgh or London. When a taxi is available on the street, a TAXI sign on the roof is lit a bright yellow. Most taxi trips within the city cost £2.50 ($3.80) to £3.50 ($5.30), with an extra 10p (20¢) assessed for each additional passenger. A 15p (20¢) surcharge is imposed from midnight to 6am. Tip at least 10% of the fare shown on the meter.

BY CAR

RENTALS Driving around Glasgow is a tricky business, even for native motorists. It's a warren of one-way streets, and parking spots are at a premium. You had best depend on public transportation.

However, you will find a car most convenient for touring this part of Scotland. Car rentals are relatively expensive. Most companies will accept your U.S. driver's license, provided you're more than 21 years old and have held the permit for more than a year. Many companies grant discounts to clients who reserve in advance (see "Getting Around" "By Car" in Chapter 2 for toll-free numbers and a general preview of rates). It's better to reserve a car before you arrive in Glasgow.

The **Automobile Association** maintains a 24-hour toll-free phone number that can be called if your car breaks down anywhere in Britain; toll free 0800/887766. For general information about AA services within Glasgow, call 041/204-0911.

A roughly equivalent organization, the **Royal Automobile Club,** also has a toll-free 24-hour breakdown service; toll-free 0800/828282. For general information about RAC services within Glasgow, call 041/248-4444.

Note that if you've rented a car within Britain, each of the car-rental companies there offer their own in-house road service facilities you can call if your rented vehicle breaks down. Ask the rental agent for this number; it's usually prominently listed as part of the rental contract.

Avis Rent-a-Car is at 161 North St. (tel. 041/2212827), **Budget Rent-a-Car** at 101 Waterloo St. (tel. 041/8770501), and **Europcar** at 556 Pollockshaw Rd. (tel. 041/4235661).

Typical rates average £20 ($30) to £30 ($45) per day, although this could vary greatly from place to place, usually on the higher side.

PARKING   It's expensive and difficult to find. Metered parking is available, but you'll need the right change—20p (30¢) coins. You must also watch out for zealous traffic wardens who issue tickets. Some zones are marked PERMIT HOLDERS ONLY. Don't park there unless you have a permit as a local resident—your vehicle will be towed if you do. A yellow line along the curb indicates "No Parking."

Multistory car parks (parking lots), open 24 hours a day, are found at Anderston Cross, Cambridge Street, George Street, Mitchell Street, Oswald Street, and Waterloo Streets.

BY BICYCLE

You can rent bikes by the day or by the week from a number of outfits. Bicycling is quite possible in much of Glasgow, particularly the flatter areas of the city. You can also use a bike for exploring the surrounding countryside.

For what the Scots call "cycle hire," go to the **Raleigh Cycle Center,** two branches on the periphery of Glasgow: one at 1417 Dumbarton Rd., Scottstoun (tel. 041/9581055), and another at 193 Clarkston Rd., Cathcart (tel. 041/6372439). Cycles and mountain bikes are rented here, and tour suggestions are freely shared. Charges begin at £5 ($7.50) per day and go up, with a deposit usually beginning at £25 ($37.50).

ON FOOT

This is the best way to explore Glasgow, but be careful. Many Americans have accidents because they look the wrong way when crossing a street. Remember, cars drive on the left. Always look both ways before stepping off a curb.

The center of Glasgow is laid out on a grid system, which makes map reading relatively easy. You can get around to many of the major attractions in the center by foot, since distances are not great. However, many of the major attractions, such as the Burrell Collection, are in the environs, and for those you'll need to rely on public transportation, of course.

FAST FACTS: GLASGOW

American Express   The office in Glasgow is at 115 Hope St. (tel. 2263077), open Monday and Wednesday through Friday from 9am to 5pm, on Tuesday from 9:30am to 5pm, and on Saturday from 9am to noon.

Area Code   The telephone area code is 031.

Babysitters   Make arrangements through your hotel, as far in advance as possible. In some of the B&Bs, local proprietors will sometimes look after small children.

Bookstores   One of the best-stocked stores is the long-established **William Porteous & Co. Ltd.,** 9 Royal Exchange Pl. (tel. 2218623). It specializes in Scottish books, maps, and guidebooks, and has a wide range of reading material. It's open Monday through Friday from 8:30am to 5:15pm and on Saturday from 8:30am to 5pm.

Founded in the mid-18th century, **John Smith & Son,** 57 St. Vincent St. (tel. 2217472), is a thoroughly Scottish bookshop, called "part of Scotland's cultural history." A wide range of books of all types are available Monday through Wednesday and Friday from 9am to 5:30pm, on Tuesday from 9am to 9:30pm, and on Saturday from 9am to 5:15pm.

Business Hours   Most **offices** are open Monday through Friday from 9am to either 5 or 5:30pm. Most **banks** are open Monday through Wednesday and on Friday from 9:30am to 4:45pm and on Thursday from 9:30am to 5:30pm. **Shops** are generally open Monday through Saturday from 10am to either 5:30 or 6pm. Some stores, usually smaller ones, close for lunch from 1 to 2pm. On Thursday stores remain open until 7pm.

Car Rentals   See "Getting Around," in this chapter.

Climate   See "When to Go," in Chapter 2.

Crime   See "Safety," below.

Currency   See "Information, Entry Requirements & Money," in Chapter 2.

Currency Exchange   The tourist office (see above) will exchange most major foreign currencies, as will the American Express office (see above). City-center banks operate *bureaux de change,* and nearly all banks will cash traveler's checks if you have the proper identification. **Thomas Cook** at the Glasgow Airport (tel. 8402299) operates a Bureau de Change service daily, including Sunday, from 7am to 11pm in summer. In the off-season, hours are Monday through Saturday from 8am to 8pm and on Sunday from 8am to 6pm. It also operates a larger branch at 15 Gordon St. (tel. 2219431), open Monday through Saturday from 9am to 4:30pm.

Dentist   The best bet for temporary visitors is to visit one of the finest dental schools in Britain. Treatment is available to anyone with an emergency (a dental emergency is defined as someone in pain or with dental difficulties). Services are free, and the best part is the ability to receive almost immediate treatment. Treatment is conducted by students in training, always with professional supervision. Present yourself and your pain to the **Glasgow Dental Hospital and School** at 378 Sauchiehall St. (tel. 041/3327020). The emergency service for pain relief currently operates Monday to Friday, 9am to 10:30am and 2 to 3:30pm. Sunday service is from 10:30am to noon. Charges are made for Sunday Emergency Services (run by private practitioners at commercial prices). Charges for Monday to Friday Emergency Service are dependent on the nature of the emergency and whether the Scottish Home and Health Department "Guidelines on Exemption from Charges" apply.

Doctor   The major hospital is the **Royal Infirmary,** 82–84 Castle St. (tel. 5523535).

Drugstores   The best is **Scots,** 200 Sauchiehall St. (tel. 3321925), open Monday through Wednesday from 9:30am to 5:30pm, on Thursday from 8:45am to 7pm, and on Friday and Saturday from 8:45am to 6pm.

Embassies and Consulates   **Australia** and the **United States** have consulates in Edinburgh (see "Fast Facts: Edinburgh," in Chapter 4). Citizens of such countries as **Canada, New Zealand, South Africa,** or **Ireland** should apply to their various embassies in London.

Emergencies   Call **999** in an emergency to summon the police, an ambulance, or firefighters.

Eyeglasses   One of the most respected opticians in Scotland is **Dolland & Aitchison,** originally established in 1837, which can usually replace broken eyeglasses in about an hour. They maintain a branch at 133 Wellington St. (tel. 2485402) and an even busier branch (which goes under the name of Eyeland Express) at 3 Union St. (tel. 2044394). The Union Street branch specializes in contact lenses as well as in eyeglasses.

There is also a limited number of frames and a resident optometrist at the 200 Sauchiehall St. branch of **Boots Chemists** (tel. 3321925).

Hairdressers/Barbers   The best place to go in all of Glasgow is **Taylor Ferguson,** 106 Bath St. (tel. 3320397), award-winning stylists. They are open Monday through Wednesday from 9am to 6pm, on Thursday and Friday from 9am to 7:15pm, and on Saturday from 9am to 4pm. Always call for an appointment.

Holidays   See "When to Go," in Chapter 2.

Hospitals   See "Doctor," above.

Hotlines   The police emergency number, **999,** is the major "hotline" in Glasgow. Women in crisis may want to call the **Women's Centre** (tel. 2211177). Gay men can call the **Gay Switchboard** (tel. 2218372) daily from 7 to 10pm, and there's also a **Lesbian Line** (tel. 2484596), open Monday only from 7 to 10pm. Call the **Rape Crisis Centre** at 2218448.

Information   See "Tourist Information" below.

Laundry/Dry Cleaning   Try the **Park Laundrette** at 14 Park Rd., which is open Monday through Friday from 8:30am to 8pm, and on Saturday and Sunday from 9am to 6:30pm.

Library   The Central Library in Glasgow—the city's largest and best stocked—is on North Street at Kent Road (tel. 2217030). Considered one of the largest libraries in Europe, it's a massive 19th-century pile dedicated to the academic pursuit of all kinds of research. Newspapers and books, as well as miles of microfilm, are available.

Liquor Laws   Most pubs are open Monday through Saturday from 11am to midnight and on Sunday from 12:30 to 2:30pm and 6:30 to 11pm.

Lost Property   The Lost Property Department is at Angus House, Anderston Centre (tel. 2042626).

Luggage Storage/Lockers   There are two Left Luggage Offices in Glasgow, including the main one at the Central Station (tel. 3354362), open Monday through Friday from 6:30am to 11pm and on Saturday and Sunday from 7:30am to 11pm. The other office is at the Queen Street Station (tel. 3353256), open Monday through Saturday from 7am to 10pm and on Sunday from 10am to 6pm.

Newspapers/Magazines   Published since 1783, the *Glasgow Herald* is the major newspaper. In addition to its coverage of national, international, and financial news, foreign visitors often read it for its sports and cultural listings. It also informs you on the latest films being shown in Glasgow. The *Evening Times,* another newspaper, covers mainly local news. The major tabloid is the *Daily Record,* most widely read in Scotland. All the major London newspapers are also on sale. *Scottish Field* and *Scots Magazine* are monthly publications, dealing with many topics of interest to visitors to Scotland. The *International Herald Tribune* and *USA Today* are also for sale in many places, along with European editions of *Time* and *Newsweek.*

Photographic Needs   Many family-run film-supply stores lie scattered throughout Glasgow, but one of the city's most visible emporiums of film and virtually everything else is **Boots Chemists,** 494 Sauchiehall St. (tel. 3326729) or at 200 Sauchiehall St. (tel. 3321925) at the corner of Cambridge Street. Perhaps the most centrally located of all the Boots branches is among the 50 stores of the new Saint Enoch Centre, Argyle Street at St. Enoch Square (tel. 2487387).

Police   In an emergency, call 999.

Post Office   The main branch is at 2–5 George Square (tel. 2264260). If you want your mail sent general delivery, mark it "Poste Restante" and send it to this branch, using the postal code of G2 1AA. Hours are Monday through Friday from 9am to 5:30pm and on Saturday from 9am to 12:30pm.

Radio   BBC Radio Scotland (FM 92.5–94.6 MW, 810kHz/370m) is a national network featuring both the latest news and lots of talk shows. The local station, emphasizing local events, is Radio Clyde (FM 102.5 MW, 1152kHz/261m).

Religious Services   Most churches conduct services at 11am on Sunday, including the Church of Scotland, **St. George's Tron Church,** 165 Buchanan St. (tel. 2212141); **Catholic Church,** 196 Clyde St. (tel. 2265898), and the **Episcopal Church** of Scotland, 5 St. Vincent Pl. (tel. 2215720). The **Jewish Orthodox Synagogue** is at Garnethill, 29 Garnet St. (tel. 3324151).

Rest Rooms   These are found at rail stations, bus stations, air terminals, restaurants, hotels, pubs, and department stores. Glasgow also has a system of public toilets, often marked WC (for water closet) found at various strategic corners and squares throughout the city, but likely to be closed late in the evening.

Safety   Glasgow is the most dangerous city in Scotland, but relatively safe when compared to other cities of its size in Europe. Muggings do occur, and often they are related to Glasgow's rather large drug problem. The famed "razor gangs" of Calton, Bridgeton, and the Gorbals are no longer around to earn the city a reputation for violence, but you still must be alert and aware of your immediate surroundings. Wear a moneybelt, and don't sling your camera or purse over your shoulder, particularly at night or in crowded places. Wear the strap diagonally across your body. This will minimize the possibility of your becoming the victim of a crime. Keep your valuables in a safety-deposit box at your hotel.

Shoe Repairs   Go to the basement of **Fraser's Department Store,** Buchanan Street (tel. 2213880), which is the Glasgow version of Harrods Department Store in London.

Taxes   A 17½% Value-Added Tax (known as VAT) is added to the cost of all goods and services in Glasgow, as elsewhere in Britain. Otherwise, there are no special city taxes.

Taxis   See "Getting Around," in this chapter.

Telegram, Telex, and Fax   Phone 071/4927111 to send a telex anywhere in the world. The service is available 24 hours a day. Faxes and telegrams can be sent at the post office (see above) during regular business hours.

Television   BBC Scotland and Scottish Television (STV) are the two major stations based at Glasgow. Throughout the day they offer programs of Scottish news and features, although both their programs are the same as those carried over the national BBC networks.

Tourist Information   The **Greater Glasgow Tourist Board,** 35–39 St. Vincent Pl. (tel. 041/2044400), is the most helpful office in the country.

Transit Information   For 24-hour passenger inquiries regarding rail travel in Scotland, call 2042844. The Buchanan Street Bus Station is reached at 3329191, and the Anderston Station at 2487432. For flight schedules at Glasgow Airport at Abbotsinch, call 8484440.

Weather   For the latest weather information, call the Glasgow Weather Centre (tel. 2483451). Although the center of Glasgow lies closer to the Arctic Circle than does the Kremlin in Moscow, the climate in Glasgow is much milder because of the warming effect of the Atlantic's Gulf Stream. Temperatures rarely drop below zero in winter, and summers are cool with the mercury usually in the middle 60s (°F). Glasgow experiences about 40 inches of rainfall per year. May through September are considered the ideal times to visit. At midsummer, the sun rises at 5:30pm and you can still read in the daylight as late as 9:30pm.

3. ACCOMMODATIONS

Glasgow offers a full range of accommodations at different price levels throughout the year. Because of the city's growing popularity as a tourist destination, it often experiences a shortage of beds in summer, especially late July and August. Therefore, many discreet travelers planning a visit to Glasgow at that time make reservations at least 2 months in advance.

The designation, "Very Expensive," indicates double rooms ranging in price from £110 ($165) to £155 ($232.50). "Expensive" is used for double rooms costing from £99 ($148.50) to £110 ($165). "Moderate" double rooms drop considerably in price, ranging from a low of £62.50 ($93.80) to a high of £91 ($136.50); and, finally, anything under £60 ($90) is considered "inexpensive" for a double room, at least by the standards of Glasgow. *Note:* Weekend discounts may considerably alter the price scales mentioned above. See individual hotel tariffs for weekend bargains.

CENTRAL GLASGOW
VERY EXPENSIVE

GLASGOW HILTON INTERNATIONAL, 1 William St., Glasgow G3 8HT.
   Tel. 041/2045555, or toll-free 800/445-8667 in the U.S. or Canada. Fax 041/2045004. 315 rms (all with bath), 4 suites. A/C MINIBAR TV TEL **Bus:** 62 or 64.

$ Rates: £115–£125 ($172.50–$187.50) single or double. Suites from £250 ($375) each. Weekend discounts available, depending on bookings. Scottish breakfast £12.50 ($18.80) extra. AE, DC, MC, V. **Parking:** £8 ($12).

Opened late in 1992, this is the only five-star hotel in Glasgow. It's housed in the tallest building (20 floors) in all of Scotland. Set in the heart of the West End's business district, near the northern end of Argyll Street and near exit 18 (Charing Cross) of the M8 motorway, it rises in dignified modernity within a sheathing of light brown stone. Bedrooms, plush and conservative, are popular both with upscale vacationers and business travelers, and offer some of the finest views of Glasgow anywhere, stretching over the city as far as the legendary dockyards of the Clyde. The three uppermost floors are devoted to executive rooms, which benefit from the complimentary bar and enhanced facilities of a semi-private club room. Throughout the hotel, the staff, youthful and well-trained, are alert, helpful, and uniformed.

Dining/Entertainment: The hotel's most upscale restaurant, Cameron's, is separately recommended in the "Dining" section. Almost as appealing is Menskey's, some of whose inspiration came from a New York deli, offering all-day dining every day of the week. Fixed-price meals cost from £9.95 ($14.90) at lunch, and from £12.95 ($19.40) at dinner. No one ever goes thirsty at the Hilton: Two bars pouring two-fisted libations include the Scotch Bar, which inventories more than 200 kinds of single malts and blends, served within a room outfitted like an upscale Scottish hunting lodge. Raffles, deriving its theme from the legendary hotel in Singapore, celebrates the role of Scotland during the building of the British Empire and serves the best gin martini in town.

Services: 24-hour room service, laundry, babysitting, a sophisticated concierge.
Facilities: The Leisure Club, which aficionados claim is one of the best-equipped health clubs in Glasgow, contains an indoor swimming pool, Jacuzzis, and saunas. There are also two amply stocked gift shops, and a hairdresser for men and women.

GLASGOW MARRIOTT, 500 Argyle St., Glasgow G3 8RR. Tel. 041/ 2265577. Fax 041/2217676. 298 rms (all with bath), 6 suites. TV TEL **Underground:** St. Enoch.
$ Rates: £110–£125 ($165–$187.50) single; £110–£135 ($165–$202.50) double. Breakfast £10.25 ($15.40) extra. AE, DC, MC, V. **Parking:** Free.
One of the leading hotels in the city is the Marriott. Its soaring profile adds a vivid accent to the Glasgow City skyline from its perch at the Anderston exit of the M8. Its bedrooms are among the finest in the city, with all modern amenities, private baths, and free in-house movies. After work, dozens of local residents unwind in the popular bars, where open fireplaces compete with fountains and plants for visual supremacy.

Dining/Entertainment: A trio of restaurants offers you a wide choice of dining to suit any occasion. These include the Café Rendezvous, serving international and British food; L'Academie, a French à la carte restaurant; and the Terrace, informal à la carte service.

Services: 24-hour room service, laundry service, babysitting, courtesy coach.
Facilities: Squash courts, spacious well-equipped gym, health and beauty salon, hairdresser, whirlpool, sauna, large indoor pool.

EXPENSIVE

COPTHORNE HOTEL, George Sq. Glasgow, GD2 1DS. Tel. 041/ 3326711. Fax 041/3324264. 135 rms (all with bath), 5 suites. TV TEL
$ Rates: Fri–Sun (including Scottish breakfast): £52 ($78) single; £76 ($114) double or suite. Mon–Thurs £92 ($138) single; £104 ($156) double; £130 ($195) suite. Scottish breakfast £9.25 ($13.90) extra. AE, DC, MC, V. **Parking:** £5 ($7.50).
The Copthorne Hotel is a landmark hotel near the Queen Street Station, where trains depart for the north of Scotland. Its high-ceilinged design was originally constructed as the North British Hotel, until foreign investors renovated it into a more luxurious format. When the public rooms of the hotel were renovated, the designers searched for antiques and glistening marble panels. Each of the rooms offers in-house movies, plush carpeting, and an upgraded decor.

The hotel's role in history was played when Winston Churchill met here in Room 21 with Harry Hopkins, FDR's envoy, in 1941, a pivotal meeting that is credited with securing Hopkins's support for the Lend-Lease Bill, a commitment that eventually helped usher the U.S. into an active participation in the European theater of World War II.

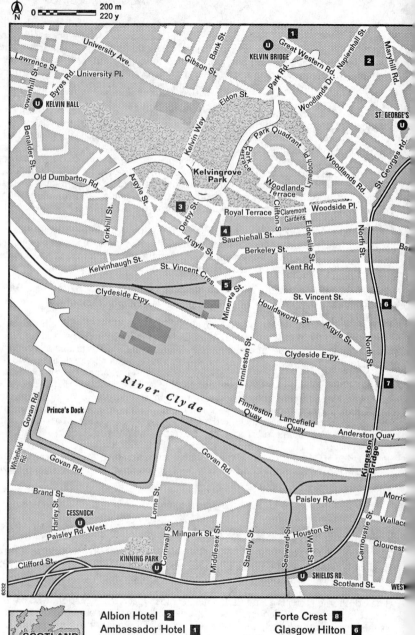

SCOTLAND
Glasgow

Albion Hotel **2**
Ambassador Hotel **1**
Argyll Hotel **4**
Babbity Bowster **12**
Central Hotel **10**
Copthorne Hotel **11**

Forte Crest **8**
Glasgow Hilton **6**
Glasgow Marriott **10**
Hospitality Inn **9**
Kelvin Park Lorne Hotel **3**
Kirkland House **5**

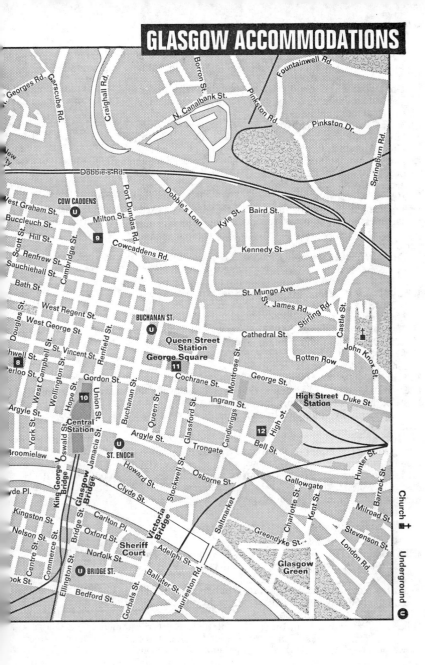

Dining/Entertainment: The more formal dining room is called Windows on the Square, while La Mirage Café and Bar is one of the most alluring spots in Glasgow for a drink or a light meal.

Services: 24-hour room service, laundry/valet, babysitting.

Facilities: Business center; gym nearby.

FORTE CREST, 23 Bothwell St., Glasgow, G2 7EN. Tel. 041/2482656. Fax. 041/2218986. 254 rms (all with bath), 3 suites. A/C MINIBAR TV TEL **Underground:** Central Station.

$ Rates: Fri–Sat £59.50 ($89.30) single or double; Sun–Thurs £99 ($148.50) single or double; £170–£210 ($255–$315) suite. Scottish breakfast £9.95 ($14.90) extra. AE, DC, MC, V. **Parking:** £6 ($9).

The Forte Crest is a modern four-star hotel in the heart of the city. It has well-appointed bedrooms and suites, all with hot-beverage facilities, hairdryers, trouser presses, private baths, and electronic door-locking systems. During the week it's filled mainly with commercial travelers, but on weekends it's likely to be patronized by vacationers.

Dining/Entertainment: The hotel has two restaurants and two bars catering to many tastes.

HOSPITALITY INN, 36 Cambridge St., Glasgow G2 3HN. Tel. 041/ 3323311. Fax 041/3324050. 297 rms (all with bath) A/C MINIBAR TV TEL **Underground:** Cowcaddens. **Bus:** 23.

$ Rates: Mon–Thurs £85 ($127.50) single; £110 ($165) double or suite; Fri–Sun £52.50 ($78.80) single; £64.50 ($96.80) double or suite. Scottish breakfast £9.95 ($14.90) extra. AE, DC, MC, V. **Parking:** Free.

Located in the commercial heart of Glasgow, a 5-minute walk north of the Central Station, this eight-story high-rise hotel was built in the early 1980s and ever since has been considered one of the best in the moderately priced category. Each conservatively styled bedroom is suitable for one to two people, and contains a radio and a wake-up alarm. In an unusual but not unheard-of situation, suites and double rooms cost the same.

On the premises is a paneled, brick-accented cocktail lounge, an airy and spacious dining room (The Prince of Wales), and a garden-inspired coffee shop offering one of the best lunchtime values in Glasgow. Designed as a carvery-style lunch costing £9.75 ($14.60), it features a self-service array of salads, each laid out on a bed of ice. Dinner costs £15.25 ($22.90). The bar remains open every night for residents until 1am, and room service is available all night long.

MODERATE

✓ CENTRAL HOTEL, 99 Gordon St., Glasgow G1 3SF. Tel. 041/2219680. Fax 041/2263948. 219 rms (all with bath). TV TEL **Underground:** Central Station.

$ Rates (including continental breakfast): Fri–Sun (including Scottish breakfast), £35 ($52.50) single, £70 ($105) double. Mon–Thurs £55 ($82.50) single, £69.50 ($104.30) double. Scottish breakfast £9 ($13.50) extra. **Parking:** £5.50 ($8.30).

When it officially opened in 1883, the Central Hotel was the grandest hotel Glasgow had seen. Near the rail station, it was the landmark of the city's most famous street. Now revamped and restored to its former glory, it is owned by Friendly Hotels, who specialize in offering excellent rooms at affordable prices. Today the Central is the unquestioned leader in its price bracket.

The massive baronial wooden staircase leading from the lobby to the upper floors was painstakingly stripped and refinished as part of the continuing restoration of this historic building. Sandblasting of the facade revealed elaborate Victorian cornices and pilasters, heretofore concealed. The hotel's finest hour might have been the transmission, shortly after World War II, of the first TV broadcast on a private line extending from London to a bedroom on the fourth floor of this hotel.

Each bedchamber is comfortable and is priced according to size and plumbing. The bar with its old panels has a good selection of Highland malts, and the Entresol Restaurant serves freshly prepared Scottish food.

INEXPENSIVE

BABBITY BOWSTER, 16–18 Blackfriars St., Glasgow G1 1PE. Tel. 041/5525055. Fax 041/5525215. 6 rms (all with bath). **Underground:** Buchanan Street. **Bus:** 18, 61, or 62.

$ Rates: £36 ($54) single; £56 ($84) double. Breakfast 75p–£4.50 ($1.10–$6.80) extra. AE, MC, V. **Parking:** Free.

Babbity Bowster, in the heart of Glasgow in an area known locally as Merchant City, is a small but delightful hotel that doubles as an art gallery. Named for an ancient Scottish fertility dance, the hotel is in a Robert Adam building once used as a fruit and flower shop. The work of Glaswegian artists is displayed in the upstairs restaurant, and pictures in the frequently changed exhibits are for sale.

The restaurant has a reputation for good food, attracting students and teachers from Strathclyde University up the road. The menu changes daily. Traditional Scottish ales, Murphy's stout from Cork, and whisky are served, and musical events are also presented in the café-bar on some Sunday evenings.

KIRKLAND HOUSE, 42 St. Vincent Crescent, Glasgow G3 8NG. Tel. 041/2483458. 8 rms (all with bath). TV **Underground:** Partick.

$ Rates (including continental breakfast): £30 ($45) single; £55 ($82.50) double. No credit cards. **Parking:** Free.

Ⓢ Situated on a lovely, quiet street, Kirkland House offers pleasant rooms, each with hot- and cold-water basin and tea/coffee maker. This hotel is about a 10-minute walk from the art museum, university, and the Scottish Exhibition Centre. Kirkland is an early Victorian crescent house, and it is maintained to a high standard. The hotel is centrally heated, and you get a warm welcome from the owners, Carole and Ewing Divers. Ewing is a keen admirer of American swing band music and has a superb collection of 78-RPM gramophone records, old photographs, and pictures on show. Guests are welcome to listen to recordings of Harry James, Benny Goodman, and many others of the Great Swing Era.

THE WEST END
VERY EXPENSIVE

ONE DEVONSHIRE GARDENS, 1–3 Devonshire Gardens, Glasgow G12 OUX. Tel. 041/3392001. Fax 041/3371663. 27 rms (all with bath), 2 suites. TV TEL **Underground:** Partick.

$ Rates (including continental breakfast): £125 ($187.50) single; £155 ($232.50) double; £180 ($270) suite. AE, DC, MC, V. **Parking:** Free.

★ In 1880, house no. 1 was built as an upper-crust private home, but by the early 1980s it had degenerated into a seedy rooming house. In 1986 a professional designer bought it and embarked on a major restoration, making it more elegant than it was in its heyday. Behind its sandstone facade he added such Georgian touches as cove moldings patterned into laurel and urn motifs, along with floral-patterned chintz, comfortable seating arrangements, and a scattering of antiques, all against a backdrop of deep-blue walls. At the sound of the doorbell, a pair of chambermaids clad in Edwardian costumes with frilly aprons and dust bonnets appear at attention to welcome you. Each of the eight upstairs bedrooms, individually designed, is impeccably furnished in the best of period taste and offers double bed, private bath, and lots of luxurious accessories. The success of the first venture led to the acquisition of nos. 2 and 3, bringing the room count to 27. The newer rooms have the same facilities and are priced the same. The location is in the Hyndland district, just west of the center, in a neighborhood of stone Victorian houses.

Dining/Entertainment: See "Dining," below.

Services: 24-hour room service, laundry service/valet.
Facilities: Patio garden.

EXPENSIVE

STAKIS GROSVENOR HOTEL, 1–10 Grosvenor Terrace, Great Western Road, Glasgow G12 0TA. Tel. 041/3398811. Fax 041/3340710. 90 rms (all with bath), 3 suites. TV TEL **Underground:** Hillhead. **Bus:** 20, 51, or 66.

$ Rates: Fri–Sun (including Scottish breakfast): £51 ($76.50) single, £74 ($111) double; Mon–Thurs £89 ($133.50) single, £99 ($148.50) double. Scottish breakfast £8.50 ($12.80) extra. Suites £114–£150 ($171–$225). AE, DC, MC, V. **Parking:** Free.

When a team of engineers used a revolutionary technique of impregnating the decaying sandstone of this hotel's neoclassical facade with a combination of fiberglass and concrete, the city offered them an architectural award. It was at this time that the Greek-owned Stakis company almost completely gutted the interior, reconstructing it in a casino-style sweep of crystal chandeliers and brassy accents. Today the hotel is considered one of the most comfortable in town, offering well-furnished bedrooms.

Dining/Entertainment: The hotel maintains a piano bar within its only restaurant, The West End, where a color scheme of green and blue accents well-prepared fixed-price lunches and dinners that cost £8.50 ($12.80) and £15 ($22.50), respectively, every day of the week. One floor above the lobby level is an upstairs sitting room with bar service.

Services: 24-hour room service, laundry/valet, babysitting.
Facilities: Ample parking ground.

MODERATE

JURYS POND HOTEL, 2–4 Shelley Rd., Glasgow G12 0XP. Tel. 041/3348161. Fax 041/3343846. 133 rms (all with bath). TV TEL **Underground:** Hillhead.

$ Rates: Mon–Thurs £62.50 ($93.80) single or double; Fri–Sun £41 ($61.50) single; £49.90 ($74.90) double. Scottish breakfast £7.50 ($11.30) extra. AE, DC, MC, V. **Parking:** Free.

A good bet for a comfortable room in a pleasant setting is this modern hotel at the edge of town reached along the A82, 3 miles east of the city center. It's set in a green area beside a duck-filled pond, which is partially screened by trees from the hotel. Part of the benefits include the use of the glass-walled indoor pool, exercise machines, and saunas. Each of the functional and sunny bedrooms has a VCR. The hotel maintains a re-creation of a French bistro, Reed's, where set menus cost £7.95 ($11.90) at

---

 FROMMER'S COOL FOR KIDS: HOTELS

Hospitality Inn *(see page 162)* In the heart of the city, this eight-story hotel offers roomy bedrooms suitable to tuck children in. Kids like the self-service carvery-style lunch, one of the best dining values in Glasgow.

Jurys Pond Hotel *(see page 164)* At the edge of town, this hotel has spacious green spaces around a duck-filled pond. Kids can enjoy an indoor pool.

Albion Hotel *(see page 165)* This Victorian crescent house not only offers well-furnished family rooms but is opposite a park, west of the city center.

Glasgow Marriott *(see page 159)* Large and bustling in the city center, this hotel has a children's playroom, gym, and a coffee shop that serves meals kids like from 11am to 10:30pm.

lunchtime and £15 ($22.50) at dinnertime. One of the hotel's bars is set in a glassed-in balcony above the swimming pool.

KELVIN PARK LORNE HOTEL, 923 Sauchiehall St., Glasgow G3 7TE. Tel. 041/3344891. Fax 041/3371659. 99 rms (all with bath). TV TEL **Underground:** Kelvin Hall. **Bus:** 46, 57, or 64.

$ Rates (including Scottish breakfast): Fri–Sun £40 ($60) single; £50 ($75) double. Mon–Thurs, £70 ($105) single or double. Scottish breakfast £8 ($12) extra. AE, DC, MC, V. **Parking:** Free.

Set in the heart of the residential West End, this is a comfortable and discreet hotel whose public rooms are accessorized in the style of the famous turn-of-the-century Scottish designer, Charles Rennie Mackintosh. Though the hotel was built 40 years ago, after the designer's death, its bar (Newbery's, honoring Fra Newbery, Mackintosh's mentor) and restaurant (Butler's) are both designed according to Mackintosh's theories.

The hotel's bedrooms were completely renovated in 1991, resulting in a neutrally modern kind of contemporary comfort.

Dining/Entertainment: Butler's offers a fixed-price menu at £8.95 ($13.40) at lunchtime and £15 ($22.50) in the evening. Otherwise, à la carte meals cost around £22 ($33) each. Typical dishes include duckling in orange sauce, salmon braised in Madeira, a selection of vegetarian dishes, and herb-flavored lamb.

Services: 24-hour room service, laundry, babysitting.

TOWN HOUSE HOTEL, 54 West George St., Glasgow G2 1NG. Tel. 041/3323320. Fax 041/3329756. 33 rms (all with bath), 2 suites. MINIBAR TV TEL **Bus:** 41, 52, or 57.

$ Rates (including Scottish breakfast): Sun–Thurs £80 ($120) single; £91 ($136.50) double. Fri–Sat £50 ($75) single; £60 ($90) double. AE, DC, MC, V. **Parking:** Free.

Grandiose and imposing, the building that contains this hotel was built in 1907 of red sandstone as the headquarters for a then-prominent organization for men, The Glasgow Liberal Club. Shortly thereafter, it was bought by the Royal Scottish Academy of Music and Drama, which used it for reading rooms and lecture halls until the early 1980s. In 1990, it reopened after restoration as "a country-house hotel in the middle of town." As you ascend the steps to your room, notice the bas-reliefs honoring European composers.

Each of the bedrooms is high-ceilinged and large with individual decorations and formal touches. There's a restaurant on the premises, The Music Room, serving fixed-price lunches and dinners every day for £19 ($28.50) each, beneath an ornately frescoed ceiling showing cherubs at play.

WICKETS HOTEL, 52–54 Fortrose St., Glasgow G11 5LP. Tel. 041/ 3349334. Fax 041/3349334. 10 rms (all with bath). TV TEL **Underground:** Partick. **Bus:** 5A, 62, or 64.

$ Rates (including Scottish breakfast): £54.95–£84 ($82.40–$126) single; £64.95–£94 ($97.40–$141) double; £99 ($148.50) family room. AE, DC, MC, V. **Parking:** Free.

Better known for its dining and drinking facilities than for its handful of comfortable bedrooms, the Wickets is an undiscovered gem lying in Glasgow's West End, opposite one of the city's largest cricket grounds (the West of Scotland Cricket Club). Each of the rooms has tea-making facilities and a brightly cheerful decor.

The Conservatory Restaurant is the glamour spot of the hotel, offering both regional and continental fare amid old photographs of local cricket teams. Fixed-price meals are served throughout the day and evening, and cost £9.95 ($14.90) to £13.95 ($20.90) each. Adjacent to the restaurant is an open-air beer garden—one of the few in Glasgow. A few steps away, Randall's Wine bar sells wine by the glass in a sophisticated art deco setting filled with Erté fashion prints. The bar food is excellent.

INEXPENSIVE

ALBION HOTEL, 405 N. Woodside Rd., Glasgow G20 6NN. Tel. 041/

3398620. Fax 041/3348159. 17 rms (all with shower). TV TEL **Underground:** Kelvinbridge.

$ Rates (including Scottish breakfast): £30–£35 ($45–$52.50) single; £45–£50 ($67.50–$75) double; £55 ($82.50) family room. AE, DC, MC, V. **Parking:** Free.
This recently refurbished 1860s structure is set on a Victorian crescent opposite a park, west of the city center. Robert and Irene McQuade rent well-furnished bedrooms, all with toilets, sinks, radio, and beverage-making facilities. Its location in the West End makes it convenient for the city center, art galleries, museums, and many local restaurants and brasseries.

AMBASSADOR HOTEL, 7 Kelvin Dr., Glasgow G20 8Q1. Tel. 041/ 9461018. Fax 041/9455377. 14 rms (all with bath). TV TEL **Underground:** Hillhead.

$ Rates (including Scottish breakfast): £35 ($52.50) single; £50 ($75) double; £55 ($82.50) family room. MC, V. **Parking:** Free.
Across from the BBC Studios and the Botanic Garden, this is a small, privately run hotel in a Victorian town house that is considered one of the better B&Bs in Glasgow. Singles and doubles are rented, along with some family rooms, each comfortably furnished and well decorated, and each with a private bath. Amenities include trouser press, hairdryer, tea/coffee maker, radio alarm, and central heating. The hotel is well situated for exploring the West End. Several art galleries and many good local restaurants or brasseries are nearby. Dinner is served nightly from 7 to 9pm.

ARGYLL HOTEL, 973 Sauchiehall St., Glasgow G3 7TQ. Tel. 041/ 3373313. Fax 041/3373283. 32 rms (all with bath). TV TEL **Underground:** St. George's Cross.

$ Rates (including Scottish breakfast): £46 ($69) single; £56 ($84) double. MC, V. **Parking:** Free.
This hotel is small but special, a privately owned Georgian building near many of the major points of interest in Glasgow, including Glasgow University, the Museum and Art Gallery, the Kelvin Hall International Sports Arena, and the Scottish Exhibition Centre. Although completely modernized, it shows a healthy respect for tradition. The hotel overlooks Kelvingrove Park. Bedrooms are comfortable and convenient, each with such amenities as a tea/coffee maker, hairdryer, and digital radio. Room service is available, as are dry cleaning and laundry. On the premises Scoffs Restaurant serves three meals a day, and a special feature is its garden dining. Both international and Scottish specialties are offered.

KIRKLEE HOTEL, 11 Kensington Gate, Glasgow G12 9LG. Tel. 041/ 3345555. Fax 041/3393828. 9 rms (all with bath). TV TEL **Underground:** Hillhead. **Bus:** 11, 20, 57, or 66.

$ Rates (including Scottish breakfast): £45 ($67.50) single; £59 ($88.50) double. MC, V. **Parking:** Free on the nearby streets.

Its red-brick walls were originally built in 1903 by a shipping magnate. Today it's graced with a rose-packed front garden that has won several awards from the Glasgow garden club. Behind the richly ornate stained-glass door you'll find sedately comfortable bedrooms, each of which contains a tea/coffee maker, a trouser press, and hairdryer. Mr. and Mrs. Peter Steven opted long ago to eliminate their dining room, so breakfast is served in each resident's room. The establishment is near the university, the Botanic Gardens, and the city's major art galleries.

PLACES TO STAY NEARBY

GLEDDOCH HOUSE HOTEL, Langbank, Renfrewshire PA14 6YE. Tel. 047554/711. Fax 047554/201. 31 rms (all with bath), 2 suites. TV TEL **Directions:** 15 miles west of Glasgow (see below).

$ Rates (including Scottish breakfast): £90 ($135) single; £130 ($195) double; £170 ($255) suite. AE, DC, MC, V. **Parking:** Free.

The former residence of Sir James Lithgow, the Gleddoch House Hotel was converted in 1974 to a deluxe hotel set on large grounds, including farmlands, riding stables, an 18-hole golf course, and gardens. The rooms are named for birds—Golden Eagle, Mallard, Osprey—and have good baths, plus radios, hairdryers, trouser presses, and hot-beverage facilities. The paneled hallway is bright with a roaring fire, and there's a cozy bar. The residents' sitting room is upstairs.

Breakfast is a leisurely, help-yourself affair. At lunch, you can order smoked trout and salmon mousse, clear Highland game broth, and perhaps a traditional warm pudding. A fixed-price lunch costs £15 ($22.50) and up. In the evening, you can dine from an à la carte menu, although I recommend the fixed-price dinner for £29.50 ($44.30). The four courses change daily, and might include home-cured salmon, Scottish lamb, duck, or beef, and one of the tempting hot or cold desserts. Many guests prefer to have lunch in the Golf Club House. There are a sauna and a plunge pool, as well as horseback riding.

To get there, drive west along the A8/M8 from Glasgow and the Erskine Bridge toward Greenock and Gourock. Turn left at the sign for Langbank on the B789, going left again under the railway bridge and then steeply up the hill to the hotel entrance on the right.

KIRKTON HOUSE, Cardross, Dunbartonshire G82 5EZ. Tel. 0389/ 841951. Fax 0389/841868. 6 rms (all with bath). TV TEL 18 miles W of Glasgow; 14 miles W of Glasgow Airport.

$ Rates (including Scottish breakfast): £29.50–£34.50 ($44.30–$51.80) per person. Half board £49–£52 ($73.50–$78) per person. MC, V. **Parking:** Free.

This 160-year-old converted farmhouse, with stable and paddock, opens onto views of the River Clyde. It is only about 35 minutes by car from Glasgow and about a 20- to 35-minute drive from the airport. Many American visitors, arriving in Glasgow for the first time, and unfamiliar with driving on the left, base here for the first night before attempting to drive into the congested city. Old world charm and modern amenities are combined. Bedrooms are comfortably furnished and spacious, and two units are on the ground floor. The others are suitable as a double or family room, with such amenities as hairdryer, radio alarm clocks, and tea- and coffee-making equipment. An extensive breakfast menu is prepared to order, and the dinner menu is changed daily. Children are especially welcome, and laundry, ironing, and babysitting can be arranged. The farm is also a base for exploring Loch Lomond and the Trossachs.

4. DINING

Those days are long gone when a meal out in Glasgow meant mutton pie and chips. Some of the best of Scottish food—including Highland lamb, moor grouse, salmon trout, and Aberdeen Angus steaks—is now offered, along with continental dishes and a rising number of foreign restaurants, especially Indian and Chinese. Of course, Glasgow is filled with the usual fish-and-chips shops and burger joints as well.

Many restaurants close on Sunday, and most are shut by 2:30pm, reopening again for dinner around 6pm.

Restaurants rated "expensive" charge from £25 ($37.50) to £30 ($45) per person for a meal, meaning an appetizer, main course, and dessert, including VAT. Wine and service are extra. Restaurants deemed "moderate" ask from £15 ($22.50) to £25 ($37.50) for a meal. Any meal under £15 ($22.50) is considered "inexpensive," at least by the standards of Glasgow. The prices indicated above are for dinners. Cheap bar lunches or pub grub cut down luncheon costs considerably.

CENTRAL GLASGOW

EXPENSIVE

THE BUTTERY, 652 Argyle St. Tel. 041/2218188.
Cuisine: SCOTTISH. **Reservations:** Recommended. **Underground:** St. Enoch's.

$ Prices: Appetizers £3–£6.50 ($4.50–$9.80); main courses £11–£14 ($16.50–$21); bar platters at the Oyster Bar £4–£6 ($6–$9) each. AE, DC, MC, V.

Open: Lunch Mon–Fri noon–2:30pm; dinner Mon–Sat 7–10:30pm; bar Mon–Sat noon–2:30 and 6–11pm.

This is the perfect huntsman's restaurant, with oaken panels, racks of wine bottles, and an air of baronial splendor. The bar in the anteroom used to be the pulpit of a church. The waitresses wear high-necked costumes of which Queen Victoria would have approved. Menu items include smoked trout, rare roast beef, terrine of Scottish seafood, and several sophisticated preparations of venison—two of these include roebuck in a madeira sauce with skirlie (a traditional Scottish combination of oats, bacon, and onions fried in bacon fat), and filet of venison with apples, pears, and brown lentils in a nutmeg sauce. The Buttery's less formal restaurant, the Belfry, lies in the cellar, and is recommended separately (see below).

ROGANO, 11 Exchange Pl. Tel. 041/2484055.
Cuisine: SCOTTISH/INTERNATIONAL. **Reservations:** Advisable but not necessary. **Underground:** Buchanan Street.
$ Prices: Appetizers £4.50–£9 ($6.80–$13.50); main courses £10–£27.50 ($15–$41.30); fixed-price lunch £15 ($22.50). AE, DC, MC, V.
Open: Restaurant, lunch Mon–Sat noon–2:30pm; dinner Mon–Sat 7–10:30pm; Sun 6–10pm. Café, Mon–Thurs noon–11pm, Fri–Sat noon–midnight, Sun 6–10pm.

Rogano has one of the most perfectly preserved art deco interiors in Scotland. Its decor dates from 1934, when Messrs. Rogers and Anderson combined their talents and names to create an ambience that has hosted virtually every star of the British film industry since the invention of the talkies. The bartender has been employed for decades. You can enjoy dinner in an ambience of lapis lazuli clocks, etched mirrors, spinning ceiling fans, cozy semicircular banquettes, and potted palms. The array of menu items, changing every two months, is likely to emphasize seafood. There are at least six varieties of temptingly rich desserts. A less expensive menu is offered downstairs in the Café Rogano, where meals begin at £12 ($18).

MODERATE

THE BELFRY, 652 Argyle St. Tel. 041/2210630.
Cuisine: SCOTTISH. **Reservations:** Recommended. **Underground:** St. Enoch's.
$ Prices: Appetizers £2–£4 ($3–$6); main courses £6–£9 ($9–$13.50). AE, DC, MC, V.
Open: Lunch Mon–Fri noon–2:30pm; dinner Mon–Thurs 6–10pm, Fri–Sat 6–11pm.

Each element of the decor of this place, on the basement level of the Buttery (see above), came from a church in northern England: pews, pulpits, and stained glass that create a cozy ambience. It's probably the only pub in Glasgow that affords a contemplation of Christ in Majesty while its patrons enjoy a pint of ale. The cramped and partially exposed kitchen produces daily specials such as poached salmon in a lemon mayonnaise, smoked mackerel pâté, and chicken-and-broccoli pie. Meals can be accompanied by a vintage from the wine list.

CRANNOG SEAFOOD, 28 Cheapside St. Tel. 041/2211727.
Cuisine: SEAFOOD/FRENCH. **Reservations:** Recommended. **Underground:** Anderston Station.
$ Prices: Appetizers £2.50–£5.50 ($3.80–$8.30); main courses £6.50–£12 ($9.80–$18); fixed-price lunch £8.50 ($12.80). MC, V.
Open: Lunch Tues–Sat noon–2:30pm; dinner Tues–Thurs 6–9:30pm; dinner Fri–Sat 6–10:30pm.

After achieving success with the Crannog Seafood Restaurant in Fort William in 1989, Finlay Finlayson opened this restaurant in Glasgow and its success was immediate. The catch from Finlayson's own fishing boat is served by the kitchen. The daily

FROMMER'S SMART TRAVELER: RESTAURANTS

1. Enjoy lunch at some of Glasgow's first-class restaurants that offer a fixed-price luncheon at reasonable prices.
2. Select fixed-price luncheons or dinners, at least a 30% savings off the à la carte menu.
3. Look for daily specials on the à la carte menu. They're invariably fresh, and often cheaper than regular à la carte listings.
4. Drink the house wine—it's a fraction of the price of bottled wine.
5. Watch the booze: Wine and liquor are expensive in Glasgow.

changing lunch menu is one of the city's best dining values, although you can return in the evening to enjoy more elaborate fare. Langoustines are a specialty, and Finlayson also serves some courses from his own smokehouse such as smoked salmon or smoked mussels with aïoli. Almost anything looks good, be it trout, oysters, or herring. Pan-fried haddock is invariably featured, as are seafood lasagne and fish pie.

HO WONG RESTAURANT, 82 York St. Tel. 041/2213550.
Cuisine: CHINESE. **Reservations:** Required. **Underground:** Central Station.
$ **Prices:** Appetizers £2.50–£6 ($3.80–$9); main courses £8–£11 ($12–$16.50); three-course lunch £6.90 ($10.40). AE, DC, MC, V.
Open: Lunch Mon–Sat noon–2pm; dinner Mon–Sat 5:30pm–midnight, Sun 6pm–midnight.

Two blocks from the Central Station, Ho Wong is one of the finest Chinese restaurants in the city. Jimmy Ho and David Wong, inspired by the Hong Kong kitchen, opened this "remote outpost" of their Oriental cuisine in faraway Glasgow. The cookery is enjoyable, the service obliging. You can pause for a drink in the front, perusing the menu, before you are shown to your table in the rear. Sweet-and-sour dishes, such as king prawns, lead the popularity charts. As a novelty, some dishes are labeled "bird's nest dishes," others "sizzling" dishes. There are at least eight duck dishes on the menu, along with four types of fresh lobster.

OCTOBER CAFÉ, The Rooftop, Princes Square. Tel. 041/2210303.
Cuisine: INTERNATIONAL. **Reservations:** Recommended. **Underground:** St. Enoch's.
$ **Prices:** Appetizers £2.50–£4 ($3.80–$6); main courses £6.50–£10 ($9.80–$15). MC, V.
Open: Restaurant, lunch Mon–Sat noon–2:30pm; dinner Mon–Sat 6–11pm. Café, Mon–Sat noon–11pm.

At the top of the Princes Square shopping district, this bar and restaurant offers a widely diversified cuisine, which reflects culinary influences worldwide. Try a wide array of dishes—everything from Perthshire game terrine with beetroot and tarragon dressing to mussels with white wine, flavored with herbs and garlic. Chicken might be stuffed with cream cheese and broccoli, or else you might order teriyaki beef with wasabi. For dessert, try either crème brulée or chocolate terrine with an espresso sauce. If you prefer, you can also order from the café menu, including such dishes as smoked salmon roulade or baked Camembert in phyllo pastry. Most plates in the café cost from £2.95 ($4.40) to £4.75 ($7.10).

INEXPENSIVE

THE CARVERY, in the Forte Crest Hotel, Bothwell St. Tel. 041/2482656.
Cuisine: BRITISH. **Reservations:** Not needed. **Underground:** Central Station.

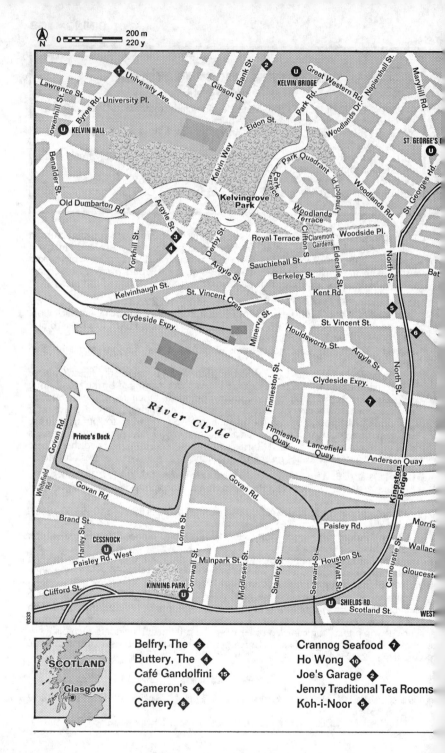

0 ⊨⊨⊨⊨⊨ 200 m
220 y

Lawrence St.
University Ave.
University Pl.
Byres Rd.
Bank St.
Gibson St.
U Joe's Garage ❷
U KELVIN BRIDGE
Great Western Rd.
Park Rd.
Napiershall St.
Maryhill Rd.

Gowanhill St.
U KELVIN HALL
Benalder St.
Eldon St.
Woodlands Dr.
Woodlands Rd.
St. Georges Rd.
ST. GEORGE'S

Old Dumbarton Rd.
Kelvin Way
Park Terrace
Park Quadrant
Lynedoch St.
Woodlands Terrace
Woodside Pl.
North St.

Yorkhill St.
Argyle St.
Derby St.
3
4
Royal Terrace
Clifton St.
Claremont Gardens
Elderslie St.
Bat

Kelvingrove Park

Sauchiehall St.
Berkeley St.
Kent Rd.

Kelvinhaugh St.
St. Vincent Cres.
Minerva St.
St. Vincent St.
5
6

Clydeside Expy.
Houldsworth St.
Argyle St.
North St.

Finnieston St.
Clydeside Expy.
7

River Clyde

Govan Rd.
Prince's Dock
Finnieston Quay
Lancefield Quay
Anderson Quay

Whitefield Rd.
Govan Rd.
Govan Rd.
Paisley Rd.
Kingston Bridge
Morris

Brand St.
Harley St.
U CESSNOCK
Paisley Rd. West
Lorne St.
Cornwall St.
Milnpark St.
Middlesex St.
Stanley St.
Seaward St.
Houston St.
Watt St.
Carnoustie St.
Wallace
Gloucest

Clifford St.
U KINNING PARK
U SHIELDS RD.
Scotland St.
WEST

SCOTLAND
Glasgow

Belfry, The ❸
Buttery, The ❹
Café Gandolfini ⓯
Cameron's ❻
Carvery ❽

Crannog Seafood ❼
Ho Wong ❿
Joe's Garage ❷
Jenny Traditional Tea Rooms
Koh-i-Noor ❺

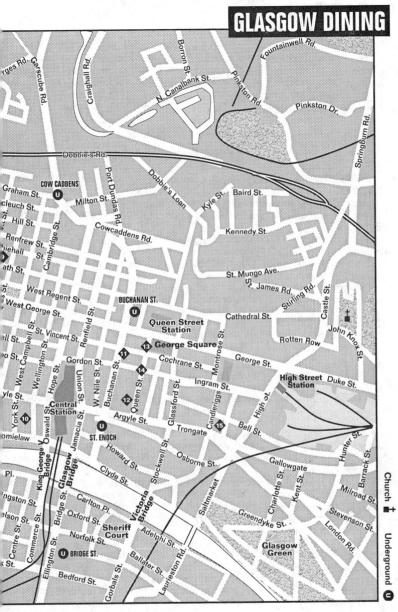

e Mirage Café-Bar ⑬

ctober Café ⑫

ogano ⑭

biquitous Chip ❶

Villow Tea Room ❾

Church ✝ Underground Ⓤ

$ Prices: Buffet £14 ($21). AE, DC, MC, V.
Open: Lunch daily noon–2pm; dinner Mon–Sat 5:30–10pm, Sun 6:30–10pm.

The price of a meal at the Carvery is low considering what you get. In an ambience of brick-lined walls, napery-covered tables, and pinpoint lighting, you can select from one of Glasgow's most amply stocked buffets. The buffet is spread on an altarlike centerpiece, laden with dishes both hot and cold. It's augmented with carved roasts and joints produced by uniformed chefs.

THE WEST END

EXPENSIVE

ONE DEVONSHIRE GARDENS, 1 Devonshire Gardens. Tel. 041/ 3392001.
Cuisine: BRITISH. **Reservations:** Required. **Underground:** Partick.
$ Prices: Three-course lunch £19 ($28.50); four-course dinner £35 ($52.50). AE, DC, MC, V.
Open: Lunch Sun–Fri noon–2pm; dinner daily 7–11pm.

The high-ceilinged restaurant of One Devonshire Gardens, recommended as a hotel (see "Accommodations," above), has become one of Glasgow's most charming and unusual dining rooms since its inception in 1986. You dine amid flowery Victorian-inspired wallpaper, with servers dressed in frilly aprons and muslin mob caps. You go first to the drawing room, elegantly decorated, where drinks are served as you peruse the menu. A fixed-price menu at both sessions offers an ample choice, and quality ingredients are handled with care and finesse in the kitchen. Perhaps you'll begin with a curried-parsnip soup, then follow with terrine of brill and trout, going on to rack of Borders lamb.

MODERATE

UBIQUITOUS CHIP, 12 Ashton Lane, off Byres Rd. Tel. 041/3345007.
Cuisine: SCOTTISH. **Reservations:** Recommended. **Underground:** Hillhead. **Bus:** 11, 20, 57, or 66.
$ Prices: Appetizers £2.95–£9.45 ($4.40–$14.20); main courses £9.95–£14.95 ($14.90–$22.40); bar meals average £5 ($7.50) each. AE, DC, MC, V.
Open: Restaurant, lunch Mon–Sat noon–2:30pm; dinner daily 5:30–11pm. Bar, daily noon–10pm.

This well-known traditional restaurant lies within the roughly textured stone walls of stables that were built originally for the elegant nearby houses. Its interior contains a glass-covered courtyard, and masses of climbing vines that entwine themselves along the rafters of the ceiling. Upstairs is a pub, where informal platters are served simultaneously with pints of lager and whiskies.

Despite the implications of this establishment's name, its menu does *not* include fish and chips. Specialties fuel the brain as well as the stomach, and might include a western Highland seafood salad, a vegetarian strudel with yellow-pepper sauce, young grouse served blood-red with a bread sauce, and filet of Loch Lomond salmon with a cucumber-dill sauce. Other dishes include marinated haunch of venison from the forests of Inverness with rowanberry jelly, and "Ayr-landed cod on a bed of clapshot." Bar meals, consumed upstairs, are cheaper than those in the restaurant, and might include such dishes as chicken, leek, and white wine casserole or finnan haddies with bacon.

INEXPENSIVE

KOH-I-NOOR, 235 North St., Charing Cross. Tel. 041/2211555.
Cuisine: INDIAN. **Reservations:** Recommended. **Underground:** Charing Cross. **Bus:** 50 or 51.
$ Prices: Appetizers £2–£6.25 ($3–$9.40); main courses £5.50–£9.50 ($8.30–

$14.30); three-course business lunch from £5 ($7.50); Sun buffet £15 ($22.50) for two; Mon–Fri buffet from £10 ($15). AE, DC, MC, V.

Open: Sun–Thurs noon–midnight, Fri–Sat noon–1am.

This is one of the city's leading Indian restaurants, and it's most reasonable in price. The family that runs it comes from the Punjab, and naturally such Punjabi specialties as paratha and bhuna lamb are recommended. In this large spacious restaurant, guests enjoy many fish, chicken, beef, and prawn dishes, most of which are cooked with spicy curries. The Sunday Indian buffet is a Glasgow event and one of the great food values of the city; the Indian buffet weekdays is another treat. You can also order a three-course business lunch.

A NEARBY PLACE TO DINE

55 B.C., 128 Drymen Rd., Bearsden. Tel. 041/9427272.

Cuisine: INTERNATIONAL/SCOTTISH. **Reservations:** Recommended for restaurant; not necessary for the bar. **Directions:** From Glasgow's center, take the Clydesdale Expressway to Anniesland and from there follow the signs to Bearsden. **Bus:** 18.

Prices: In bar, platters £4.25–£4.50 ($6.40–$6.80); in restaurant, appetizers £2.50–£4.25 ($3.80–$6.40); main courses £6.75–£9.95 ($10.10–$14.90). MC, V.

Open: In bar, lunch daily noon–3pm, dinner daily 5–6:30pm. In restaurant, lunch Mon–Sat noon–2pm, dinner Mon–Sat 7–10pm.

Named in honor of the year the ancient Romans invaded Britain (a date that is, at least in theory, memorized by schoolchildren throughout the country), this restaurant is boisterous, convivial, and fun. Set within a 15-minute drive north of Glasgow's center, in the suburb of Bearsden, it offers a large, and usually crowded, bar area near the entrance, and a quieter and much smaller restaurant in back. Meals in the bar might include a sandwich of the day, a soup of the day, or a combination of the two, lasagne, chili, or any of several different salads. Preferred drinks include pints of lager, priced at from £1.60 ($2.40) each, or frothy drinks you might have expected in the Caribbean (piña coladas, margaritas, etc.)

The restaurant in back offers more elaborate fare, including breast of duck on a bed of pineapple and pink peppercorns, marinated chicken served with Japanese spices on a bed of stir-fried vegetables, or filet of pigeon in a thyme and honey sauce. Despite the allure of this establishment's food, many of its clients come just for the sense of companionship and the crowd.

 FROMMER'S COOL FOR KIDS: RESTAURANTS

Joe's Garage *(see page 174)* When your child doesn't take to haggis and neeps, head here for such familiar fare as burgers, pizzas, and Tex-Mex dishes.

Willow Tea Room *(see page 175)* Time was, when it was a big treat for a Glaswegian child to be taken here for delectable pastries and ice-cream dishes. It still is.

Le Mirage Café Bar *(see page 175)* A good luncheon stopover, in the center of Glasgow, this is a kid pleaser, with its tasty chili, lasagne, and well-stuffed sandwiches.

Café Gandolfi *(see page 174)* At this popular Scottish venue, kids always find something to order from the menu, perhaps a soup-and-salad lunch, followed by one of the homemade ice creams, reportedly the best in the city. A 10-year-old Chicago boy, eating at the table next to mine, endorsed the daily special: cheese gougère stuffed with mushrooms and ham.

SPECIALTY DINING

BREAKFAST

Joe's Garage (see "Fast Food," below) serves American breakfasts with pancakes and maple syrup on Sunday. It has a good family atmosphere.

Café Gandolfi (see "A Local Favorite," below) is an ideal choice for breakfast if you can wait until 9am when it opens Monday through Saturday. The croissants are the most popular item to order, although many Glaswegians prefer the Scottish fruit scones.

The **Jenny Traditional Tea Rooms** (see "Tea Rooms," below) is an excellent choice for breakfast, Monday through Saturday beginning at 7:45pm. Breakfast is served until 11am when the lunch crowd takes over. You can breakfast on warm croissants with jam, or else order what Scots call the "traditional fry-up," that is, fried eggs, bacon, "the works" for £4.45 ($6.70).

FAST FOOD

JOE'S GARAGE, 52 Bank St. Tel. 041/3395407.

Cuisine: INTERNATIONAL. **Reservations:** Recommended. **Underground:** Kelvin Bridge. **Bus:** 54.

$ Prices: Appetizers £2.95–£4 ($4.40–$6); main courses £5.50–£10 ($8.30–$15); pint of lager £1.95 ($2.90). AE, DC, MC, V.

Open: Lunch Mon–Fri noon–3pm; dinner Mon–Fri 5pm–midnight, Sat–Sun noon–midnight.

Lively, irreverent, and hip, it welcomes anyone interested in either a drink, a meal, or a convivial need to mingle. Amusingly decorated in a style best described as new-world kitsch, it contains old gas pumps, battered license plates from a surprising array of U.S. states, and a proudly unfurled Confederate American flag. Menu items include burgers, pizzas, steaks, Scottish lamb chops, and such Tex-Mex specialties as nachos.

A LOCAL FAVORITE

CAFÉ GANDOLFI, 64 Albion Street. Tel. 041/5526813.

Cuisine: SCOTTISH/FRENCH. **Reservations:** Not taken. **Underground:** St. Enoch's.

$ Prices: Appetizers £1.85–£3.80 ($2.80–$5.70); main courses £6–£7.50 ($9–$11.30). No credit cards.

Open: Mon–Sat 9am–11:30pm.

Many a student at the University of Glasgow will take you here citing this popular café in Merchant City as their favorite "caff." The remake of a Victorian pub, it has rustic wooden floors and designer furniture. You may sometimes have to wait for a table in this bustling atmosphere. Guests sit on wood benches and stools. At lunch you should look for any blackboard specials. Vegetarians will also find solace here; otherwise, if you don't fill up on soups and salads, try their smoked venison with gratin dauphinois or else smoked pheasant with an onion tartlet. Baked fish with potatoes is invariably featured.

VEGETARIAN

More and More, **Café Gandolfi** (see "A Local Favorite," above) is placing menu emphasis on vegetarian dishes. The vegetarian can always come in here at any time—breakfast, lunch, or dinner—and find something good to eat, and service throughout the day.

The **October Café** (see recommendation above) also serves vegetarian meals.

TEA ROOMS

THE JENNY TRADITIONAL TEA ROOM, 18 Royal Exchange Square. Tel. 041/2044988.

Cuisine: SCOTTISH. **Reservations:** Not needed. **Underground:** Queen Street Station.

$ Prices: Appetizers £1–£3.50 ($1.50–$5.30); main courses £2–£4.25 ($3–$6.40); afternoon tea £4.75 ($7.10). AE, DC, V.

Open: Mon–Sat 7:45am–6:45pm; Sun 11am–5:45pm.

A re-creation of a Victorian tea room, "The Jenny" is an ideal place for a pick-me-up at any time during the day. Many arrive for breakfast, although the place is at its most popular for the set afternoon tea. Waitresses in floral print dresses add to the charm. If you're visiting for lunch, try such dishes as one of the meat pies (steak and mushroom, or turkey and corn). On a sideboard near at hand, you can help yourself to some homemade baked goodies for the set afternoon tea.

WILLOW TEA ROOM, 217 Sauchiehall St. Tel. 041/3320521.

Cuisine: INTERNATIONAL. **Reservations:** Recommended.

$ Prices: Appetizers £1–£3.50 ($1.50–$5.30); main courses £2–£4 ($3–$6); afternoon tea with pastry £3.50 ($5.30). No credit cards.

Open: Mon–Sat 9:30am–4:30pm.

One of the best places for tea, light lunches, and snacks, this famed place is on the major shopping artery of the city. All the sensation when it opened in 1904 for its design by Charles Rennie Mackintosh, the Willow Tea Room has been restored to its original condition. On the ground floor is a well-known jeweler, M. M. Henderson Ltd. The "room de luxe" is found in the heart of the architecturally interesting old building, and it's elegantly furnished with tables and chairs made to the Mackintosh design. It's fashionable to drop in here for afternoon tea any time of day. You can also order such dishes as homemade soup, chili, and lasagne.

HOTEL DINING

CAMERON'S, In the Glasgow Hilton International, 1 William St. Tel. 041/2045555.

Cuisine: MODERN BRITISH. **Reservations:** Recommended. **Bus:** 62 or 64.

$ Prices: Appetizers £4.50–£12 ($6.80–$18); main courses £10–£18 ($15–$27). Table d'hôte menus £16.50–£19.50 ($24.80–$29.30) at lunch; £35 ($52.50) at dinner. AE, DC, MC, V.

Open: Lunch daily noon–2:30pm; dinner daily 7–11pm.

This is the most glamorous restaurant within the newest and most visible hotel in Glasgow. Set adjacent to the reception area, it contains four different sections, each outfitted like the interior of a baronial hunting lodge in the wilds of Highland Scotland. Amid scarlet walls and the accessories of an upscale Edwardian-era "sporting life," you can enjoy such specialties as fresh local asparagus with seasonal leaves and herb butter sauce; terrine of four kinds of Perthshire game (pheasant, grouse, venison, and pigeon); a trio of salmon (tartare, gravlax, and smoked); suprême of Tay salmon with spaghetti of vegetables, dill, and white wine and butter sauce; baked suprême of turbot with potato scales and a tomato, saffron, and mixed pepper sauce; and lusty, well-flavored portions of grilled Aberdeen Angus steaks (both filets and sirloins). Dessert might be a gratin of fresh fruit with a Grand Marnier sabayon and passion fruit sorbet. Since its opening in 1992, an array of Glasgow's most prominent music, sports, and political stars have enjoyed this restaurant, with the promise of many more to come.

LE MIRAGE CAFÉ-BAR, in the Copthorne Hotel, George Square. Tel. 041/3326711.

Cuisine: SCOTTISH/INTERNATIONAL. **Reservations:** Not required. **Underground:** Buchanan Street.

$ Prices: Appetizers £1.50–£3 ($2.30–$4.50); main courses £4–£7 ($6–$10.50). AE, DC, MC, V.

Open: Meals Mon–Sat noon–12:30am; Sun 12:30–2pm; drinks Mon–Sat 11am–11pm; Sun 12:30–11pm.

The ground-floor café of Le Mirage contains Italian architectural elements: a comfortable wooden bar from Venice, a Florentine gazebo crafted from mahogany and stained glass; and a quartet of Venetian lions from what used to be the legs of an antique couch. The bar and café, which adjoin a more expensive restaurant, are in the same building where a historic meeting took place between Sir Winston Churchill and Harry Hopkins, the emissary of FDR. The café serves an array of tasty hot and cold bar food, chili, lasagne, a choice of sandwiches, a wide array of international beers, and many different teas and coffee.

PICNIC SUPPLIES & WHERE TO EAT THEM

You'll find any number of deli-like places around the **Central Station** where you can get the makings of a picnic. You can also go to several fast-food places that will pack you a picnic bag to go. **McDonalds,** 209–215 Argyle St., will prepare a bag filled with burgers, french fries, and cold drinks for a family picnic. It's open Sunday through Thursday from 8am to 11pm and on Friday and Saturday from 8am to midnight.

Glasgow abounds in parks where you can enjoy your picnic, including the **Botanic Gardens** on Great Western Road. The **Finlaystone Estate and Country Park** at Langbank has special areas set aside for picnics, and you can even pick fruit. **Queen's Park** on Victoria Road is one of the most beautiful places for a picnic, as it's famed for its fine floral displays. Picnic sites are also found at **Gleniffer Braes Country Park,** Glenfield Road, in Paisley, covering 1,300 acres of woodland and moorland. Later kids can enjoy the adventure play area.

5. ATTRACTIONS

If time is limited, plan your visit carefully, and arm yourself with a good map. Many points of interest, such as the Burrell Collection, are outside the city center. If you're dependent on public transportation, you'll need to figure in transfer times between sights. The tourist office is most helpful in advising you. Those with limited time can always opt for an organized tour.

SUGGESTED ITINERARIES

IF YOU HAVE 1 DAY   Not enough time, but if that's all you've got to spare, head for the Burrell Collection on the city's outskirts and see this dazzling 8,000-piece collection of world-class masterpieces along with tapestries and sculptures. Take our walking tour of historic Glasgow, and have dinner in a typical Glaswegian restaurant, perhaps visiting a pub later.

IF YOU HAVE 2 DAYS   Spend your first day as suggested above. Then, on Day 2, visit the Old Town in the morning, and explore the Gothic Glasgow Cathedral, and later take a look at the Necropolis, one of the most famed Victorian cemeteries anywhere. In the afternoon, visit the Hunterian Museum and the Hunterian Art Gallery.

IF YOU HAVE 3 DAYS   Use your first 2 days as recommended above. On your third day see more of Glasgow, including visits to the Tenement House and the Glasgow Art Gallery and Museum, the latter a collection with everything from Rembrandt to Dalí.

IF YOU HAVE 5 DAYS   Spend Days 1 through 3 as suggested above, but on Day 4 take an excursion to Loch Lomond, less than an hour's drive north of Glasgow along the scenic A82 (two trains serve the loch from Glasgow's Queen Street Station); a tour of this lake will easily fill your day. On the fifth day, see a lot more of Glasgow, as your feet will allow, including visits to Haggs Castle, Pollock House (ancestral home of the Maxwells), and the Museum of Transport. Cap your visit, if time remains, with a late-afternoon call at Paisley Abbey.

THE TOP ATTRACTIONS

GLASGOW ART GALLERY AND MUSEUM, Kelvingrove. Tel. 041/ 3573929.

⭐   The headquarters of Glasgow Museums and Art Galleries, this is the finest municipal gallery in Britain. The art gallery contains a superb collection of Dutch and Italian old masters and French 19th-century paintings, such as Giorgione's *Adulteress Brought Before Christ*, Rembrandt's *Man in Armour*, Millet's *Going to Work*, and Derain's *Blackfriars*. Salvador Dalí's *Christ of St. John of the Cross* is on display. Scottish painting is well represented in the four galleries of British painting from the 17th century to the present day.

One of the gallery's major paintings is *Whistler's Arrangement in Grey and Black no. 2: Portrait of Thomas Carlyle*, the first Whistler to be hung in a British gallery. The artist took great pride in his Scottish background. The James McNeill Whistler collection was given to Glasgow by the artist's nephew. It includes the contents of his studio.

The museum has an outstanding collection of European arms and armor, displays from the ethnography collections featuring the Eskimo and North American Indians, Africa, and Oceania, as well as a large section devoted to natural history. There are major new exhibits on the natural history of Scotland, featuring plant life, animal life, and geology. There are also small, regularly changing displays from the decorative art collections of silver (especially Scottish), ceramics, glass, and jewelry, plus furniture and other decorative art items by Charles Rennie Mackintosh and his contemporaries. Teas and light lunches are available in the museum.

Admission: Free.
Open: Mon–Sat 10am–5pm; Sun 11am–5pm. **Underground:** Kelvin Hall.

BURRELL COLLECTION, Pollok Country Park, 2060 Pollokshaws Rd. Tel. 041/6497151.

⭐   This collection, the single most popular tourist attraction in Scotland, is housed in a building opened in 1983 to display the mind-boggling treasures left to Glasgow by Sir William Burrell, a wealthy shipowner who had a life-long passion for art collecting. A vast aggregation of furniture, textiles, ceramics, stained glass, silver, art objects, and pictures—especially 19th-century French art—can be seen in the dining room, hall, and drawing room reconstructed from Sir William's home, Hutton Castle at Berwick-upon-Tweed. Ancient artifacts, Asian art, and European decorative arts and paintings are featured. There's a restaurant, and you can roam through the surrounding park, which is 3 miles south of Glasgow Bridge.

Admission: Free.
Open: Mon–Sat 10am–5pm, Sun 11am–5pm. **Closed:** Jan 1 and Dec 25. **Bus:** 45, 48, or 57.

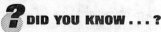

- A former employee of the Glasgow post office, John Kenmuir, holds the world's fast stamp-licking record (328 stamps in 4 minutes), according to the *Guinness Book of World Records.*
- After St. Mungo in 543 founded "Glasgu" and built his little church, the next 600 years of the city's history is a void.
- Glasgow's popular 19th-century refrain was "The hammer's ding-dong is the song of the Clyde"—but now 85% of the population works in the service industry.
- Glasgow plays host to more tourists than Edinburgh, a goal once dismissed as "impossible."
- The great Glaswegian architect, Charles Rennie Mackintosh, was celebrated around the world—"the greatest since the Gothic"—but scoffed at locally.
- The women of Glasgow still have the right to do their laundry in the city's first park, Glasgow Green, beside the Clyde.

POLLOK HOUSE, Pollok Country Park, 2060 Pollokshaws Rd. Tel. 041/6320274.

The ancestral home of the Maxwells, Pollok House was built circa 1750, with additions from 1890 to 1908 designed by Robert Rowand Anderson. The house and its 360 acres of parkland were given to the city of Glasgow in 1966. Today a branch of the Glasgow Museums and Art Galleries, it contains one of the finest collections of Spanish paintings in Britain, with works by El Greco, Goya, and Murillo, among others. There are displays of silver, ceramics, and glass from the Maxwell family's and the city's collections.

Admission: Free.

Open: Mon–Sat 10am–5pm, Sun 11am–5pm. **Bus:** 57 or 57A.

PEOPLE'S PALACE, Glasgow Green. Tel. 041/5540223.

A branch of the Glasgow Museums and Art Galleries, the People's Palace provides a visual record of the rise of Glasgow. The palace was built originally as a cultural center for the people of the East End of Glasgow, between 1895 and 1897. Exhibitions trace the foundation of the city in 1175–1178. Personal relics of Mary Queen of Scots represent her reign. The bulk of the collections are from the Victorian 19th-century Glasgow, including posters, programs, and props from the music-hall era. Items relating to trades and industries, such as the Glasgow potteries and stained-glass studios, trade unions, newspapers, and similar matters are also featured. Paintings of Glasgow by John Knox and others may be seen, plus portraits of Glaswegians, even St. Mungo.

There is a tea room in the Winter Gardens. The palace is situated in **Glasgow Green,** the oldest public park in the city. Seek out, in particular, Nelson's monument, the first of its kind in Britain; the Saracen Fountain, opposite the palace; and Templeton's Carpet Factory, modeled on the Doge's Palace in Venice.

Admission: Free.

Open: Mon–Sat 10am–5pm, Sun 11am–5pm; Apr–Sept additional hours on Thurs, 10am–9pm. **Bus:** 14, 14A, 18, 18A, 18B, 20, or 62.

HUNTERIAN ART GALLERY, University of Glasgow, University Avenue. Tel. 041/3305431.

This art gallery owns the artistic estate of James McNeill Whistler, with some 60 paintings on display. It is also known for its Charles Rennie Mackintosh collection, including the architect's home on three levels, with his own furniture and decorated in the original style. The main gallery exhibits 17th- and 18th-century paintings (Rembrandt to Rubens) and 19th- and 20th-century Scottish painters (McTaggart, Scottish Colourists, Gillies, Philipson, and others). Temporary exhibitions, selected from the largest collection of artists' prints in Scotland, are presented in the print gallery, which also houses a permanent display of print-making techniques. Contemporary sculpture is displayed in an outdoor courtyard.

Admission: Free.

Open: Mon–Sat 9:30am–5pm. **Closed:** Mackintosh House closed 12:30–1:30pm. **Underground:** Hillhead.

HUNTERIAN MUSEUM, University of Glasgow, Gilmorehill. Tel. 041/3398855, ext. 4221.

This is Glasgow's oldest museum, having opened its doors in 1807; it's in the main Glasgow University buildings 2 miles west of the heart of the city. The museum is named after William Hunter, its early benefactor who donated his private collections to get the museum going. The museum is wide-ranging, from fossils of dinosaurs, to coins. There are relics of the Roman occupation, and many rich clues from the past of Scotland, including plunder by the Vikings. The story of Captain Cook's voyages is pieced together in ethnographic material from the South Seas. The museum has a bookstall, a coffeehouse in 18th-century style, and temporary exhibitions.

Admission: Free.
Open: Mon–Sat 9:30am–5pm. **Closed:** Public holidays. **Underground:** Hillhead.

MUSEUM OF TRANSPORT, Kelvin Hall, 1 Bunhouse Rd. Tel. 041/3573929.

This museum contains a fascinating collection of all forms of transportation and related technology. Displays include a simulated Glasgow street of 1938 with period shopfronts and appropriate vehicles and a reconstruction of one of the Glasgow Underground stations. An authentic motor-car showroom has a display of mass-produced automobiles. Superb and varied ship models in the Clyde Room reflect the significance of Glasgow and the River Clyde as one of the world's foremost areas of shipbuilding and engineering. There is a self-service cafeteria.

Admission: Free.
Open: Mon–Sat 10am–5pm, Sun 11am–5pm. **Underground:** Hillhead.

THE TENEMENT HOUSE, 145 Buccleuch St. Tel. 041/3330183.

This house has been called a "Glasgow flat that time passed by." Until her death, Agnes Toward was an inveterate hoarder of domestic trivia. She lived in an 1892 building on Garnethill, not far from the main shopping street, Sauchiehall Street. For 54 years she lived in this flat that is stuffed with the artifacts of her era, everything from a porcelain "jawbox" sink to such household aids as Monkey Brand soap. After her death, the property came into the care of the National Trust for Scotland, which realized that it was a virtual museum of a vanished era.

Admission: £2 ($3) adults, £1 ($1.50) children.
Open: Apr–Oct, daily 2–5pm; Nov–Mar, Sat–Sun 2–4pm. **Underground:** Cowcaddens.

PROVAND'S LORDSHIP, Castle and McLeod Sts. Tel. 041/3341134.

The oldest house in Glasgow, this building stands just opposite the cathedral, across Cathedral Square. It was built around 1471 by Bishop Andrew Muirhead. Mary Queen of Scots is believed to have lived here when she visited Glasgow in 1566 to see Lord Darnley, and some of the "Casket Letters" were probably written here. The house contains 17th- and 18th-century furniture and domestic utensils. It is in the care of Glasgow Museums and Art Galleries.

Admission: Free.
Open: Mon–Sat 10am–5pm, Sun 2–5pm. **Underground:** Queen Street Station.

MORE ATTRACTIONS

The center of Glasgow is **George Square,** dominated by the City Chambers that Queen Victoria opened in 1888. Of the statues in the square, the most imposing is that of Sir Walter Scott, on an 80-foot column. Naturally, you'll find Victoria along with her beloved Albert, plus Robert Burns. The Banqueting Hall, lavishly decorated, is open to the public on most weekdays.

The **Cathedral of St. Kentigern,** Cathedral Street (tel. 041/5528198), originally consecrated in 1136, burned down in 1192. It was rebuilt soon after, and the Laigh Kirk (Lower Church), whose vaulted crypt said to be the finest in Europe, remains to this day. Visit the tomb of St. Mungo in the crypt, where a light always burns. The edifice is mainland Scotland's only complete medieval cathedral, dating from the 12th and 13th centuries. Formerly a place of pilgrimage, 16th-century zeal purged it of all "monuments of idolatry."

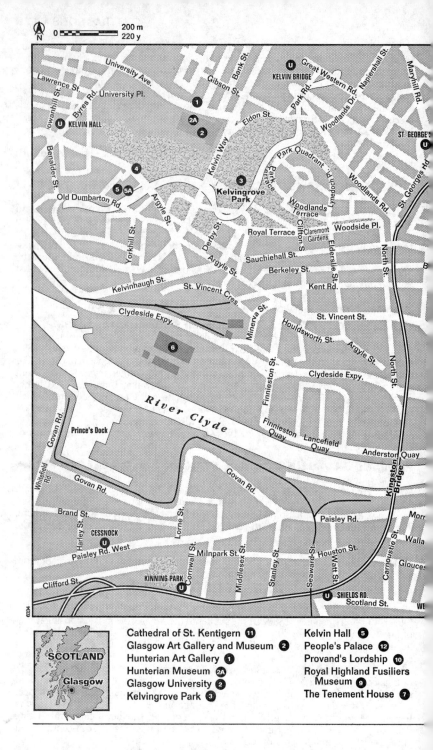

Cathedral of St. Kentigern ⑪

Glasgow Art Gallery and Museum ②

Hunterian Art Gallery ①

Hunterian Museum ②A

Glasgow University ②

Kelvingrove Park ③

Kelvin Hall ⑤

People's Palace ⑫

Provand's Lordship ⑩

Royal Highland Fusiliers
  Museum ⑨

The Tenement House ⑦

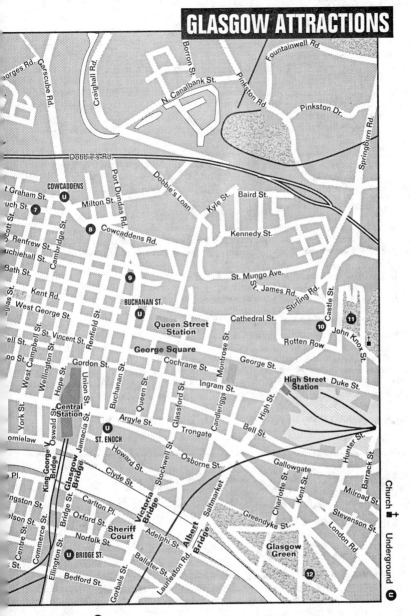

useum of Transport ⑤A
eatre Royal ⑧
ottish Exhibition Centre ⑥

To approach the cathedral, go to the eastern end of Cathedral Street, in back of the Queen Street Station (the nearest Underground stop). It's open April through September, Monday to Saturday from 9:30am to 6pm and on Sunday from 2 to 5pm; October through March, Monday to Saturday from 9:30am to 4pm, and on Sunday from 2 to 4pm. Admission is free.

For the best view of the cathedral, cross the Bridge of Sighs into the **Necropolis,** the graveyard containing almost every type of architecture in the world. The graveyard is built on a rocky hill and dominated by a statue of John Knox. It was opened in 1832, and, typical of the mixing of all races in this tolerant cosmopolitan city, the first person to be buried there was a Jew.

Glasgow's **Botanic Garden,** Great Western Road (tel. 041/3342422), covers 40 acres—an extensive collection of tropical plants and herb gardens. The gardens are acclaimed especially for their collection of orchids and begonias. It is open all year, daily from 7am to dusk. Admission is free. Underground: Hillhead.

COOL FOR KIDS

Many of the attractions already mentioned appeal especially to kids. Children like the **People's Palace,** the dinosaur fossils at the **Hunterian Museum,** and the **Museum of Transport.**

Linn Park, on Clarkston Road, is 212 acres of pine and woodland, with many lovely walks along the river. Here you'll find a nature trail, pony rides for children, an old snuff mill, and a children's zoo. The park is open all year, daily from 8am to dusk.

HAGGS CASTLE, 100 St. Andrews Dr. Tel. 041/4272725.

Haggs Castle is a branch of the Glasgow Museums and Art Galleries designed especially for children. It explores changing life-styles of the 400 years of the castle's existence. In the castle is a reconstructed kitchen from 1585, a room that shows how inhabitants lived in the 17th century, and a Victorian nursery. An 18th-century cottage on the grounds is used as an activities workshop where children can take part in sessions that include weaving, archery, buttermaking, and sampler sewing.

Admission: Free.

Open: Mon–Sat 10am–5pm, Sun 2–5pm. **Underground:** Shiels Road.

FROMMER'S FAVORITE GLASGOW EXPERIENCES

Touring the Burrell Collection   The pièce de résistance of Glasgow (some say of Scotland), this gallery is the city's major attraction. See what good taste and an unlimited pocketbook of a shipowner, Sir William Burrell, can acquire in a lifetime.

Following Walkways and Cycle Paths   Greater Glasgow has an array of trails and cycle paths cutting through areas of historic interest and scenic beauty, including the Paisley/Irvine Cycle and Walkway, 17 miles of unused railway line converted to a trail. Tourist leaflets outline these trails.

Riding the World's Last Seagoing Paddle Steamer   From spring until early fall, the *Waverley* makes day trips to scenic spots on the Firth of Clyde, past docks that once supplied more than half the tonnage of oceangoing ships. (Call 041/2218152 for more details.)

Shopping Paddy's Market   This daily market by the railway arches on Shipbank Lane gives you a real flavor for the almost-vanished Glaswegian style of street vending.

NEARBY ATTRACTIONS

IN PAISLEY

The largest town in the district, Paisley, 7 miles west of Glasgow, became a famous name for the weaving trade in the days of the Industrial Revolution. The Paisley shawl was born here. Actually the inspiration for the pattern came from India, but no matter—it is forever associated with this industrial town.

PAISLEY ABBEY, Abbey Close. Tel. 041/8897654.

This is one of the great attractions of Strathclyde. The church grew out of a Cluniac abbey founded in 1163. Nearly demolished in 1307 on orders of Edward I of England, it was subsequently reconstructed. In the mid-16th century a tower fell in, causing great damage to the transept and choir. For 3½ centuries the nave served as the parish church. New work began around the turn of this century, and by 1928 Paisley Abbey was restored, including a superb stone-vaulted roof. It shelters the tomb of King Robert III. A chapel is dedicated to the monk, Saint Mirin, who founded the town. You can also see an 11-foot-high Celtic cross from the 10th century.

Admission: Free.
Open: Mon–Sat 10am–3:30pm. **Transportation:** The Paisley-bound train leaves from Glasgow's Central Station.

PAISLEY MUSEUM AND ART GALLERIES, High St. Tel. 041/8893151.

This museum is visited mainly because of its famous collection of Paisley shawls. This teardrop pattern dominated the world of fashion for some 70-odd years, and today the shawls are extremely valuable as collector's items. The museum has collected these colorful textiles since 1905, and now has more than 700 examples. The museum also has a collection relating to the history of Strathclyde, along with some fine art and natural history displays.

Admission: Free.
Open: Mon–Sat 10am–5pm. **Transportation:** The Paisley-bound train leaves from Glasgow's Central Station.

ORGANIZED TOURS

The *Waverley* is the last of the seagoing paddle-steamers in the world, and from spring until early fall (depending on weather conditions), the Paddle Steamer Preservation Society conducts 1-day trips from Anderston Quay in Glasgow to historic and scenic places beyond the Firth of Clyde. As you go along, you can take in what was once vast shipyards, turning out more than half the earth's tonnage of oceangoing liners. You're allowed to bring your own sandwiches for a picnic aboard or you can enjoy lunch in the Waverley Restaurant. For more information, call **Waverley Excursions,** Waverley Terminal, Anderston Quay, Broomielaw (tel. 041/2218152).

Many organized tours in Glasgow are possible from April to October. The best are **City Tours,** operated from the Strathclyde Buses Travel Centre at St. Enoch Square (tel. 041/2264826); call for schedules, which can change from week to week.

WALKING TOUR — HISTORIC GLASGOW

Start: Cathedral Square.
Finish: Glasgow Green.
Time: 2 hours.
Best Time: Any sunny day.
Worst Time: Rush hour Monday through Saturday.

Begin the tour in Cathedral Square, where, in 543, St. Mungo arrived in "Glasgu" (meaning "the beloved green place"). There, out of timber and wattle he built his first house of worship, opening onto the banks of Molendinar Burn.

Today, in its place, is the:

1. **Cathedral of St. Kentigern,** Cathedral Square, dating from the 12th century. It has been called "a splendid example of pre-Reformation Gothic architecture."

   After viewing the cathedral, turn left upon leaving it, then take another left to go into the:

2. **Necropolis,** reached by crossing the Bridge of Sighs. This has been called one of the greatest Victorian cemeteries in the world, and has been compared to Père Lachaise in Paris. An example of every type of architecture, from Egyptian vaults to tombs designed by Charles Rennie Mackintosh, can be viewed here. A monumental Doric column holding an effigy of John Knox towers over the cemetery.

   Cut back across Cathedral Square and Castle Street to reach:

3. **Provand's Lordship,** at Castle Street and McLeod Street, dating from 1471, making it the oldest house of Glasgow. It is said that in 1567 Mary Queen of Scots stayed here.

   On leaving Provand's Lordship, cut right and go down Castle Street, which leads to:

4. **High Street,** which, along with Castle Street, is one of the oldest thoroughfares in Scotland. In the 6th century it was called "King's Highway," although it could hardly have been more than a pathway then.

   At the intersection of Duke Street, note the plaque marking the:

5. **Site of the old University of Glasgow,** which was moved here from Rotterdam in 1470. It flourished until its move to Gilmorehill in 1870, the height of the Victorian era. Part of the area is now used by the University of Strathclyde.

   Continue down High Street to Glasgow Cross, dominated by the steeple of:

6. **Tolbooth,** a seven-story stone "traffic cop" placed at the intersection of five streets. The tower was constructed in 1636 and rises 126 feet. Originally, visitors to the city had to pay a toll here—hence, the name. The gaol (jail) in Sir Walter Scott's *Rob Roy* once stood here.

   Directly south of Tolbooth stands the:

7. **Mercat Cross,** which in 1929 replaced the original that had stood here until 1659. It marks the site of Glasgow's first market from the Middle Ages. It was also a place where the condemned were sent to be hanged.

   At Glasgow Cross turn west onto:

REFUELING STOP On the southeast corner of Glasgow Cross, the: **8. Tolbooth Bar** introduced the *hauf an' hauf*—a half measure of a single-malt scotch whisky which is then "chased down" by a half pint of draft lager. If you'd like to be authentically Glaswegian about this, take the glass and turn it upside down over the mug of lager. Tap the glass firmly on its bottom into the beer. That way, a true imbiber knows that "ne'er a drap is lost."

---

9. **Trongate,** dominated by Tron Steeple, a four-tier steeple that is what remains from a church constructed in the late 1500s, a building destroyed by members of the Hell Fire Club who were attempting to show that they were immune to the fires of hell. The fire got out of hand and burnt the church. A new church in 1793 was built by John Adam.

   Trongate leads into:

10. **Argyle Street,** one of the city's major shopping thoroughfares.

   Along Argyle Street, take a left onto Maxwell Street, which will lead to the:

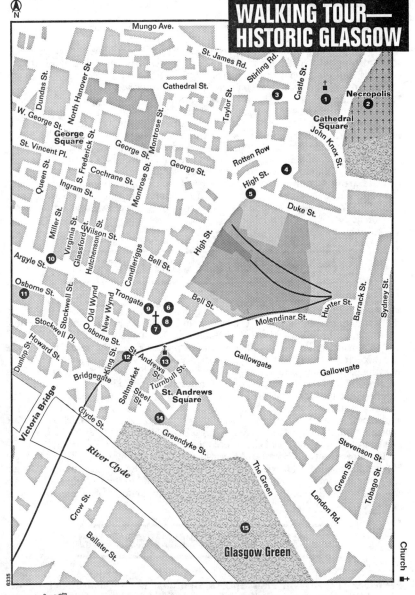

WALKING TOUR—
HISTORIC GLASGOW

N

Mungo Ave.

St. James Rd.

Cathedral St.

Stirling Rd.

Castle St.

Necropolis

3

1

2

Cathedral Square

John Knox St.

Dundas St.

W. George St.

North Hanover St.

George Square

St. Vincent Pl.

St. Frederick St.

S. Frederick St.

Queen St.

Taylor St.

George St.

Montrose St.

Cochrane St.

Ingram St.

George St.

Rotten Row

4

Miller St.

Virginia St.

Glassford St.

St.

Wilson St.

Hutchenson St.

High St.

High St.

5

Duke St.

Argyle St.

10

Candleriggs

Bell St.

Bell St.

Osborne St.

11

Stockwell St.

Old Wynd

New Wynd

Trongate

9

6

8

7

Hunter St.

Barrack St.

Sydney St.

Molendinar St.

Stockwell Pl.

Osborne St.

Howard St.

Dunlop St.

Bridgegate

King St.

St. Andrews St.

12

13

Turnbull St.

Gallowgate

Gallowgate

Victoria Bridge

Saltmarket

Steel St.

St. Andrews Square

Clyde St.

14

Greendyke St.

The Green

Stevenson St.

Green St.

Tobago St.

London Rd.

River Clyde

Crow St.

Ballater St.

15

Glasgow Green

Church

6335

SCOTLAND

Glasgow

1 Cathedral of St. Kentigern
2 Necropolis
3 Provand's Lordship
4 High Street
5 Site of the old University of Glasgow
6 Tolbooth
7 Mercat Cross
8 Tolbooth Bar
9 Trongate
10 Argyle Street
11 St. Enoch Shopping Centre
12 Saltmarket
13 St. Andrew's Parish Church
14 St. Andrew's-by-the-Green
15 Glasgow Green

11. **St. Enoch Shopping Centre,** one of the major venues for shopping in Glasgow.

    After leaving the center, head east again along Osborne Street until you reach:

12. **Saltmarket,** where, it is said, there once stood 200 whorehouses and 150 illicit stills (called shebeens by the Scots).

    At St. Andrews Street, continue east to St. Andrew's Square, site of:

13. **St. Andrew's Parish Church,** dating from 1739 and reminding many visitors of the more famous St. Martin-in-the-Fields in London. From the south side of the square, approached by about a 110-yard walk, you come to:

14. **St. Andrew's-by-the-Green,** opening onto Greendyke Street, the fourth oldest building in Glasgow, and a splendid example of Georgian architecture from the 1750s. This was the first Episcopalian church in Scotland.

    At Greendyke Street you're on the threshold of:

15. **Glasgow Green,** bordering the River Clyde. This is Britain's oldest public park, dating from 1662. Sheep grazed here until the end of Queen Victoria's reign. Everything from political rallies to pop concerts is staged on the green today.

6. SPECIAL & FREE EVENTS

Mayfest is a 3-week event launched on May Day, with an excellent cultural program of local and international music concerts and theatrical performances. For more details, get in touch with Mayfest, 18 Albion St., in Glasgow (tel. 041/5528000).

After an absence of some 120 years, the **Glasgow Fair** (held during most of the month of July—actual dates vary) returned in 1990. The fair is likely to contain everything, including carnivals, tea dances, European circuses, Victorian rides, even a country-and-western stampede. For information, call 041/5547020.

The **Glasgow International Jazz Festival** opens in the last days of June and usually runs through the first week of July. This festival has attracted some big names in the past, including the late Miles Davis and also Dizzy Gillespie. Tickets are available from the Ticket Centre, Candleriggs (tel. 041/2275511), although some free events are always announced. For more information, call 041/2263262.

The **Carmunnock Highland Games** are held at Carmunnock village and at the Hughenden playing field, Anniesland Road, Glasgow. Throwing events test strength and technique, and piping and dancing competitions add to the festivities. The games are usually held the second week in June (consult the tourist office for more details).

7. SPORTS & RECREATION

SPORTS The **Kelvin Hall Sports Complex** is on Dumbarton Road (tel. 041/3371806), near the River Kelvin (Underground: Kelvin Hall). It offers volleyball and basketball courts, as well as an indoor track. Visitors can come here and use the weight room daily from 9am to 9:30pm for £2.20 ($3.30). This is also the major venue in Scotland for national and international sports competitions. Look in the newspapers or check with the tourist office for any events that might be planned at the time of your visit.

The **Crownpoint Sports Complex,** 183 Crownpoint Rd. (tel. 041/5548274), is another major venue for national and international tournaments. This outdoor sports complex has two artificial turf parks, an athletics park, and a track.

RECREATION Glasgow has many gardens and open spaces. Chief among these is

Bellahouston Park, Paisley Road West, 171 acres of beauty with a sunken wall and rock gardens as well as wildlife. It's open all year, daily from 8am to dusk. Here you'll find the **Bellahouston Sports Centre** (tel. 041/4275454), which is a base for a variety of indicated trails that make up runners' training courses.

GOLF Golf courses are found at **Barshaw,** Glasgow Road, Paisley (tel. 041/8892908) and at **Cawder,** Bishopbriggs (tel. 041/7727101).

WATER SPORTS The **Lagoon Leisure Centre,** Mill Street, Paisley (tel. 041/8894000), offers indoor facilities with a free-form leisure pool with a wave machine, fountains, and flume. Sauna suites with sunbeds are also offered, along with Jacuzzis and a Finnish steam room. The ice rink boasts an international ice pad with six curling lanes, and is home to the Paisley Pirates ice hockey team. The center also offers bar and catering facilities.

8. SAVVY SHOPPING

One of the principal shopping districts is **Sauchiehall Street,** Glasgow's fashion center, containing many shops and department stores where you'll often find quite good bargains, particularly in woolen goods. The major shopping area, about three blocks long, has been made into a pedestrian mall. **Argyle Street,** which runs by the Central Station, is another major shopping artery.

All dedicated world shoppers know of **Buchanan Street,** a premier shopping venue and also pedestrianized for the convenience of strollers. This is the street of the famed Fraser's Department Store (see below). From Buchanan Street you can also enter **Princes Square,** an excellent shopping complex with many specialty stores, restaurants, and cafés.

The Barras, the weekend market of Glasgow, takes place about a quarter of a mile east of Glasgow Cross. Admission free, it is held all year on Saturday and Sunday from 9am to 5pm. Rich in stalls and shops, this century-old market has some 800 traders selling their wares. You can not only browse for that special treasure, but can become a part of Glasgow life and be amused by the buskers.

The **Argyll Arcade** stands at 30 Buchanan St. Even if the year of its construction (1827) were not set in mosaic tiles above the entrance, you'd still know that this is an old collection of shops beneath a curved glass ceiling. Most of the establishments sell watches and jewelry, both antique and modern. In fact, the arcade contains what is said to be the largest single concentration of retail jewelers in Europe, surpassing even those of Amsterdam. The fame of the arcade has traveled far beyond Glasgow. It seems to be a Scottish tradition that a wedding ring becomes lucky when purchased in the arcade's narrow confines.

The rents charged here are higher than comparable stores elsewhere in Glasgow, even exceeding the exorbitant rents charged along London's fashionable Bond Street. Since the arcade is officially classified as a historic building, a portion of its rents go toward maintaining it in mint condition. The arcade maintains an impressive security system to protect the area's shops and multi-million-pound inventories.

Antiques lovers will want to browse through **Victorian Village,** 57 West Regent St. (tel. 041/3320703), a warren of tiny shops in a slightly claustrophobic cluster. Much of the merchandise isn't particularly noteworthy, but there are many exceptional pieces. Several of the owners stock reasonably priced 19th-century articles; others sell old jewelry and clothing, a helter-skelter of artifacts.

Paddy's Market, by the railway arches in Shipbank Lane, operates daily if you'd like to see an old-fashioned slice of Glaswegian street vending.

In the heart of Glasgow is the city's latest and most innovative shopping complex, **St. Enoch Centre.** Open year-round, it is climatically controlled. You can shop under the biggest glass roof in Europe, making your selections in stores that have the widest range of both Scottish and international merchandise in the country. The center lies to the east of Central Station on St. Enoch Square.

HIGHLAND HOUSE OF LAWRIE, 110 Buchanan St. Tel. 041/2210217.
There's possibly no more prestigious store in Scotland than this elegant haberdashery. The welcome of the experienced sales staff is genuinely warm-hearted. Crystal and gift items are sold on the street level, but the real heart and soul of the establishment is on the lower level where you will find impeccably crafted and reasonably priced tweed jackets, tartan-patterned accessories, waistcoats, and sweaters of top-quality wool for men and women. Men's kilts contain as much as 8 yards of material. Women's and children's hand-stitched kilts are also available. The establishment was founded in 1881, and is the oldest established kilt maker in Scotland. Open Monday through Saturday from 9am to 5:30pm.

FRASER'S DEPARTMENT STORE, Buchanan St. Tel. 041/2213880.
This is Glasgow's version of Harrods. A soaring Victorian-era glass arcade rises four stories, and inside you'll find everything ranging from clothing to Oriental rugs, from crystal to handmade local artifacts of all kinds.

HENRY BURTON & CO., 111 Buchanan St. Tel. 041/2217380.
One of the city's most prestigious men's outfitters is in a slightly cramped two-story building laden with well-crafted clothes. Established in 1847, the store has a most helpful staff ready to offer their competent advice. Most of the garments are for men, but you can also find some knitwear for women.

VIRGIN RETAIL MUSIC, 28–32 Union St. Tel. 041/2210103.
The staff here is both knowledgeable and charming, eager to pass on their love of Scottish music to interested newcomers. This outlet offers the biggest and best selections of records and tapes in the city. Its special strengths and insights are in both traditional and contemporary Scottish music.

BAG AND BAGGAGE, 11 Royal Exchange Sq. Tel. 041/2218005.
If the other purchases you couldn't resist place you in the market for a new suitcase, this store has a wide selection of reasonably priced but high-quality merchandise. Most of the valises and briefcases were designed for women.

9. EVENING ENTERTAINMENT

Glasgow, not Edinburgh, is the cultural center of Scotland, and the city is alive with presentations. Still, for many a Glaswegian, the best evening ever is to be spent drinking in his or her favorite pub (my selection coming up).

Go to the tourist office and request a copy of **Culture City** or **What's On**. Both these publications are free, are published monthly, and usually contain complete listings of what's happening in Scotland's largest city.

At most newsstands, you can also purchase a copy of **The List,** which is published every other week and sells for 80p ($1.20). It details arts and other events planned not only for Glasgow but for Edinburgh as well.

Instead of rushing from box office to box office, you can purchase tickets to most cultural events by going to the **Ticket Centre,** City Hall, Candleriggs (tel. 041/2275511). The box office there sells tickets to at least a dozen theaters in the city.

THE PERFORMING ARTS

In the winter season, the **Scottish National Orchestra** offers Saturday-evening concerts in Glasgow and the **BBC Scottish Symphony Orchestra** presents

Friday-evening concerts. In the summer months, the Scottish National Orchestra has a short Promenade season (dates and venues are announced in the papers and information is also available at the tourist office). The **Scottish Ballet,** a Glasgow-based touring company, and the **Scottish Opera** perform regularly at both the Theatre Royal and at the Robin Anderson Auditorium on West Princes Street.

CITIZENS THEATRE, Gorbals and Ballater sts. Tel. 041/4290022.

The Citizens Theatre was founded after World War II by James Bridie, a famous Glaswegian whose plays are still produced. It is home to a repertory theater.
Admission: Tickets, £6–£20 ($9–$30).

GLASGOW ARTS CENTRE, 12 Washington St. Tel. 041/2214526.

Directed by Graeme McKinnon, this center always seems to be doing or presenting something interesting, including productions aimed at children. The activities range from theatrical productions to folk concerts. It is open Monday through Saturday from 9:30am to 5pm and 6:30 to 10pm; in summer it's closed in the evening. Tickets to presentations can be reserved over the phone.
Admission: Tickets, £10–£16 ($15–$24).

KINGS THEATRE, 294 Bath St. Tel. 041/2485153.

The Kings Theatre has a wide range of productions, including straight plays, musicals, and comedies. During the winter season it is noted for its spectacular pantomine.
Admission: Tickets, £6–£15 ($9–$22.50).

MITCHELL THEATRE, Granville St. Tel. 041/2213198.

This theater has earned a reputation for small-scale entertainment, ranging from dark drama to dance, as well as conferences and seminars. A modern little theater, it adjoins the well-known Mitchell Library.
Admission: Ticket prices vary with each production.

PAVILION THEATRE, Renfield St. Tel. 041/3321846.

The Pavilion is still alive and well, specializing in modern versions of vaudeville which, as they will assure you around here, isn't dead. The Pavilion sells its own tickets, which are not available at City Centre.
Admission: Tickets, £9–£12.50 ($13.50–$18.80).

THEATRE ROYAL, Hope St. and Cowcaddens Rd. Tel. 041/3311234.

This is the home of the Scottish Opera, which long ago attracted attention on the world scene, as well as of the Scottish Ballet, a national company with an international reputation, and it also hosts visiting theater and dance companies from around the world. The building, designed by C. J. Phipps, first opened in 1895. It was completely refurbished for the Scottish Opera, reopening in 1975. It offers 1,547 comfortable seats, including spacious bars and buffets on all four levels. It has been

---

THE MAJOR CONCERT & PERFORMANCE HALLS

Citizens Theatre, Gorbals Street and Ballater Street (tel. 4290022).
Glasgow Arts Centre, 12 Washington St. (tel. 2214526).
Kings Theatre, 294 Bath St. (tel. 2485153).
Mitchell Theatre, Granville Street (tel. 2213198).
Pavilion Theatre, Renfield Street (tel. 3321846).
Theatre Royal, Hope Street and Cowcaddens Road (tel. 3311234).
Tron Theatre, 63 Trongate (tel. 5524267).

called "the most beautiful opera theatre in the kingdom" by the *Daily Telegraph,* which noted its splendid Victorian Italian Renaissance plasterwork and glittering chandeliers. But it is not the decor that attracts opera-goers; rather, the ambitious repertoire. The box office is open Monday through Saturday from 10am to 7:30pm.

Admission: Tickets, £5–£36 ($7.50–$54).

TRON THEATRE, 63 Trongate. Tel. 041/5524267.

The Tron occupies one of the three oldest buildings in Glasgow, the former Tron Church. The Tron Theatre has transformed the old structure, with its famous Adam dome and checkered history, into a small theater presenting the best of contemporary drama, dance, and music events.

The Tron also has a beautifully restored Victorian café/bar serving traditional home-cooked meals, including vegetarian dishes, and a fine selection of beer and wine. The box office is open on Monday from 10am to 5pm, Tuesday through Saturday from 10am to curtain time, and on Sunday from 5pm to curtain time.

Admission: Tickets, £5–£6.50 ($7.50–$9.80) adults, £3–£3.50 ($4.50–$5.30) children.

THE CLUB & BAR SCENE

THE LEADING DANCE CLUBS

FURY MURRYS, 96 Maxwell St. Tel. 041/2216511.

At least 95% of its clientele is college and university students, who look for nothing more complicated than to have a good, and sometimes rowdy, time in a Glaswegian disco. Opened in 1986, and a 2-minute walk from the very central St. Enoch's Centre, it's in a cellar that was originally built around 1900 as a supply depot for a local printing factory. The disco music is upbeat, and deliberately not geared to the ultra-trendy and avant-garde tastes in new wave. There's one very busy bar, a single dance floor, and ample opportunities to meet the best and brightest of Scotland's university system. Jeans and T-shirts are the most popular garb, and almost no one here wears a necktie. It's open Thursday through Sunday from 10:30pm to 3:30am; other nights are reserved for private parties. A pint of lager runs £1.70 ($2.60).

Admission: £2–£4 ($3–$6), depending on the night of the week.

GRAND OLE OPRY, 2–4 Govan Rd., Paisley Toll Road (tel. 041/4295396).

In a sprawling sandstone building originally built long ago as a movie theater, 1½ miles south of Glasgow's center, it serves today as the largest club in Europe devoted exclusively to country-western music. Visiting it might present something of a cultural shock to North Americans who assume (incorrectly) that country-western is a uniquely new-world phenomenon.

Scattered over two floors of the building, there is a bar and dancing arena on each level, and a "chuck wagon" eatery serving steaks and other such fare on the upper level. Live music is always performed from a large stage at the front, which is visible from everywhere in the club. Performers are usually country-western singers from the U.K., although a handful of visiting artists from the U.S. are also presented. It's open Friday through Sunday and occasionally on Thursday (if demand warrants it) from 6:30pm to midnight. Tuesday is reserved for exhibitions of marksmanship from cowboys aiming at a series of targets, but there's no music or dancing then. Lager costs £1.20 ($1.80) per pint and a shot of Jack Daniels is 75p ($1.10). A three-course fixed-price steak dinner in the restaurant goes for £7.50 ($11.30).

Admission: £2–£5 ($3–$7.50), depending on the performers.

VICTORIA'S NIGHTCLUB, 98 Sauchiehall St. Tel. 041/3321444.

This relative newcomer to the nightlife scenes of Glasgow prides itself on being the only nightclub with cabaret performances in all of Scotland. Scattered over two floors of high-tech design in the heart of town, it contains a restaurant, two different dance floors, several different bar areas (one of which features a live pianist), and a stage upon which singers, comedians, and cabaret artists amuse and titillate the audience every night between midnight and 3am. Dress is "smart casual," and the crowd tends to be older than age 30, affluent, and sophisticated.

Open: Dinner Tues–Sun 7pm–3am. Nightclub Tues–Sun 10:30pm–3am. Live entertainment Tues–Sun midnight–3am.

Admission: Entrance £7 ($10.50). Drinks from £2.50 ($3.80) each, dinner £12–£16 ($18–$24) per person, without wine.

FAVORITE PUBS

BENNET'S, 90 Glassford St. Tel. 041/5525761.

While this place attracts 90% of the gay and lesbian nightlife activity of Glasgow, on certain nights of the week (especially Tuesday) it's generally acknowledged as the most fun, interesting, and crowded straight disco in all of Scotland. One floor above street level in a building a short walk from the Central Station and George Square, its clientele includes men and women ages 17 to 60. The music plays on and on, interrupted only by the occasional drag show. Performers are usually imported from London or the U.S.; shows last about 45 minutes, and begin after 1am on Wednesday or Saturday night. The club is open Tuesday through Sunday from 11pm to 3:30am. A pint of lager runs £1.60 ($2.40).

Admission: £2–£5 ($3–$7.50), depending on the night of the week.

BON ACCORD, 153 North St. Tel. 041/2484427.

One of the most consistently reliable pubs in Glasgow, the Bon Accord contains a traditional decor and aimiably battered paneling whose nicks and dents offer proof of this establishment's enduring popularity. The bar has a bristling array of almost 20 different hand-pumps, a dozen of which are devoted to different brands of real British ales, the remainder to beers and stouts from Germany, Ireland, and Holland. The pub is likely to satisfy your taste in malt whisky as well. The place is clean and tidy, a safe haven in a big city. Bar snacks cost around £3.50 ($5.30) each. It's open Monday through Saturday from 11am to midnight and on Sunday from 11am to 2:30pm and 6:30pm to 11pm.

CORN EXCHANGE, 88 Gordon St. Tel. 041/2485380.

Located opposite the Central Station, this was the Corn Exchange in the mid-19th century, but since 1988 it has been one of the most popular pubs of Glasgow. Amid dark paneling and high ceilings, guests can enjoy a pint of lager for £1.60 ($2.40). The pub is open Monday through Saturday from 11am to midnight and on Sunday from 11am to 2:30pm and 6:30pm to midnight. Food is served Monday through Saturday from 11:30am to 2:30pm, with a bar platter, including dessert, beginning at £2.75 ($4.10).

L'ATTACHÉ, 27 Waterloo St. Tel. 041/2213210.

This is one of several traditional Scottish pubs within its neighborhood, outfitted with stone floors and rows of decorative barrels that evoke an aura of yesteryear. There's a self-service counter for platters of food (steak pie, lasagne, and salads), and an impressive array of ales and single malts. Expect to pay from £1.60 ($2.40) for a pint of lager and from £3.50–£4 ($5.30–$6) for a platter of food. Hours are Monday to Thursday from 11am to 11pm; Friday and Saturday from 11am to midnight. Closed Sunday.

POTSTILL, 154 Hope St. Tel. 041/3330980.

This is the best place to go in Glasgow to sample malt whisky. A selection of more than 250 single-malt (unblended) whiskies, many at a variety of different strengths, can be tasted (perhaps not on the same night). You can also order malt whiskies at a variety of maturities—that is, years spent in casks. Many prefer the malt whisky that has been aged in a sherry cask. On one shelf is displayed a Dalmore and a Springbank whisky, each bottled more than half a century ago. They are to be looked at—never sampled. You can also enjoy good bar food at lunch, including cold meat salads or sandwiches. Light meals cost £3 ($4.50) and up; a pint of lager goes for £1.50 ($2.30). The "Still" is open Monday through Thursday from 11am to 11pm.

10. EASY EXCURSIONS FROM GLASGOW

As Sir Walter Scott dominates the Borders, so is the influence of Robert Burns felt in the country around Ayr and Prestwick. There is, in addition, a string of famous seaside resorts stretching from Girvan to Largs. Some of the greatest golf courses in Britain, including Turnberry, are found here; and Prestwick, of course, is the site of one of Scotland's airports.

Glasgow makes a good gateway to Burns Country, as it has excellent bus and rail connections to Ayr, which is your best bet for exploring the area. Motorists should take the A77 southwest from Glasgow to Ayr. (Prestwick and Troon link directly north of Ayr along the coastal road.)

AYR

Ayr is the most popular resort on Scotland's west coast, lying 81 miles southwest of Edinburgh, 35 miles southwest of Glasgow, and 5 miles south of Prestwick. A busy market town, it offers 2½ miles of beach. This royal burgh is also noted for the manufacture of fabrics and carpets, so you may want to allow time to browse through its shops. With its steamer cruises, fishing, golf, and racing, it faces the Isle of Arran and the Firth of Clyde.

For centuries Ayr has been associated with horse racing, and it now has the top racecourse in Scotland. One of the main streets of the town is named Racecourse Road for a stretch near the town center.

Ayr was the birthplace of the road builder John L. MacAdam, whose name was immortalized in the road surfacing called macadam.

Trains from Glasgow's Central Station (tel. 041/2042844 24 hours a day for passenger inquiries) service Ayr. From Glasgow, Western Service (express bus no. 501) arrives in Ayr in just 1 hour, 25 minutes. For departure information, phone the Buchanan Street Bus Station (tel. 041/3329192) in Glasgow.

The **Ayr Tourist Information Centre** is at 39 Sandgate (tel. 0292/284196).

WHAT TO SEE & DO

Ayr is full of Burns associations. The 13th-century **Auld Brig o' Ayr,** the poet's "poor narrow footpath of a street/Where two wheelbarrows tremble when they meet," was renovated in 1910.

A Burns museum is housed in the thatched **Tam o'Shanter Inn** on Ayr High Street (tel. 0292/269794), an alehouse in Rabbie's day. It is open April through September, Monday to Saturday from 9:30am to 5:30pm (in summer, also on Sunday from 2:30 to 5pm); off-season, Monday to Saturday from noon to 4pm. Admission is £1 ($1.50) for adults and 50p (80¢) for children. Douglas Graham of Shanter, who furnished malted grain to this brewhouse, was immortalized by Rabbie in *Tam o'Shanter.*

The **Auld Kirk** of Ayr dates from 1654 when it replaced the 12th-century Church of St. John. Burns was baptized in the kirk.

Wallace Tower, on High Street, is another attraction of Ayr, rising some 112 feet. Constructed in 1828, it has a statue of Sir William Wallace.

Another architectural curiosity is **Loudoun Hall,** Boat Vennal, off Cross in the heart of town. A wealthy merchant had this town house constructed in the late 1400s. It is considered one of the oldest examples of "burgh architecture" left in the country. Once it was occupied by the Campbells and later by the earls of Loudoun. It is open from mid-July until the end of August, Monday through Saturday from 11am to 6pm.

On the outskirts, the **Maclaurin Gallery and Rozelle House,** on Monument Road in Rozelle Park, are installed in what had been stables and quarters for servants attached to a manor house. A Henry Moore bronze sculpture and a major collection of contemporary art are on display, as well as changing exhibitions of sculpture, paintings, and crafts. Many residents of Ayr go here for an "outing," and there is also a nature trail through woodland. The location is about 1½ miles south of Ayr off the road to the Burns Cottage at Alloway. Open year-round, it can be visited Monday through Saturday from 10am to 5pm. From April through October, it is also open from 2 to 5pm on Sunday. No admission is charged. For information, call 0292/443708.

Nearby Attractions

In Tarbolton village, 7½ miles northeast of Ayr off the A758, is the **Bachelors' Club,** 7 Sandgate (tel. 0292/541940), a 17th-century house where in 1780 Burns and his friends founded a literary and debating society, now a property of the National Trust for Scotland. In 1779 Burns attended dancing lessons there, against the wishes of his father. There also, in 1781, he was initiated as a Freemason in Lodge St. David. Eleven months later he became a member of Lodge St. James, which continues today in the village. Yule Lithgow says the Bachelors' Club is open for visitors daily from noon to 5pm April until the end of October, and he will arrange to show it at other times if you phone him (tel. 0290/50503). Admission is £1.50 ($2.30) for adults, 80p ($1.20) for children. Tarbolton is 6 miles from Prestwick Airport.

WHERE TO STAY

FAIRFIELD HOUSE, 12 Fairfield Rd., Ayr, Ayrshire KA7 2AR. Tel. 0292/267461. Fax 0292/261456. 31 rms (all with bath), 8 suites. TV TEL
$ **Rates:** £70 ($105) single; £80 ($120) double; £105–£200 ($157.50–$300) suite. Scottish breakfast £10 ($15) extra. AE, DC, MC, V. **Parking:** Free.
On the seafront near Low Green, this former Victorian town house of a Glaswegian tea merchant has been restored to its original elegance and converted into the best hotel in Ayr. The staff is especially attentive and helpful, and can direct you to nearby golfing possibilities. The noted designer of classic British interiors, Lady Henrietta Spencer-Churchill, created the public rooms and bedrooms in a British country-house style. Bedrooms are large, comfortable, and luxurious, and often decorated with chintz. Bedrooms contain such amenities as radio, trouser press, and hairdryer, and most of the bathrooms have a bidet. Children under 7 years of age are only accepted by arrangement with the management.
Dining/Entertainment: The food at Fairfield has been called an "oasis in a culinary desert." The best of Scottish produce—from Highland lamb to Spey salmon—goes into the food. Meals cost anywhere from £18 ($27) to £40 ($60), depending on your selection. Men are requested to wear a jacket and tie at dinner.

IN THEIR FOOTSTEPS

Robert Burns [1759–1796] The greatest Scottish poet after the Middle Ages, Burns is the national poet of Scotland, and he carried Scottish vernacular to its highest point with his satiric, earthy, and bawdy romantic verses. He was a farmer and later an exciseman, but the world knows him for such poems as "Tam O'Shanter" and "A Man's A Man for A' That."
• **Birthplace:** Burns was born at Alloway, Ayrshire, on January 25, 1759, the son of an impoverished farmer.
• **Residences:** Burns' Cottage (now a museum) in Alloway draws some 100,000 fans every year to see such exhibits as the bed in which Burns was born.
• **Favorite Haunts:** Rabbie's Bar, at Ayr, where Burns used to drop in for a pint and friendly chatter with his friends.
• **Resting Place:** Burns Mausoleum in St. Michael's Churchyard, Dumfries.

Services: Room service, laundry/valet.
Facilities: Leisure Club with a luxurious swimming pool.

CALEDONIAN HOTEL, Dalblair Rd., Ayr, Ayrshire KA7 1UG. Tel. 0292/ 269331. Fax 0292/610722. 114 rms (all with bath). TV TEL
$ Rates: £75 ($112.50) single; £99 ($148.50) double. Scottish breakfast £8.50 ($12.80) extra. AE, DC, MC, V. **Parking:** Free.

The Caledonian Hotel is centrally situated, just a few hundred yards from Ayr's seashore and 500 yards from the rail station. It offers refurbished bedrooms with radios, hairdryers, and tea and coffee makers. Many of the rooms open onto views of the sea. The rooms are decorated in pastels with lightwood furniture. Hudson's Bar and Grill is a lively place to meet and eat. There's a selection of freshly roasted joints on the captain's table. The hotel also boasts a fully equipped leisure complex and is located near several championships golf courses.

PICKWICK HOTEL, 19 Racecourse Rd., Ayr, Ayrshire, KA7 2TD. Tel. 0292/260111. Fax 0292/285348. 15 rms (all with bath). MINIBAR TV TEL
$ Rates (including Scottish breakfast): £45 ($67.50) single; £70 ($105) double. AE, DC, MC, V. **Parking:** Free.

It may seem ironic to have a hotel commemorating a character in a Charles Dickens novel in a town noted for its memories of Rabbie Burns. But this early Victorian hotel, set on its own grounds directly east of the Esplanade, does just that. The Pickwick is really a large-size house, renting well-furnished private bedrooms. Each unit bears a Dickensian title. All rooms have radios, trouser presses, and hot-beverage facilities. In the paneled Pickwick Club, you can soak up much Dickensian atmosphere. The food is simple but well prepared, a lunch costing around £8.95 ($13.40); a dinner begins at £15.95 ($23.90).

STATION HOTEL, Burns Statue Sq., Ayr, Ayrshire KA7 3AT Tel. 0292/ 263268. Fax 0292/262293. 74 rms (all with bath). TV TEL
$ Rates: £52–£63 ($78–$94.50) single; £59–£70 ($88.50–$105) double. Scottish breakfast £6.75 ($10.10) extra. AE, DC, MC, V. **Parking:** Free.

The Station hotel has been an Ayr landmark since its original construction in 1888. Interconnected with the town's railway station, it sits behind a red sandstone exterior, and although it isn't the most modern hotel in town, many visitors consider its high ceilings, elaborate detailing, and old-world charm more than enough reason to check in. Bedrooms are conservative and comfortable, many quite spacious, sometimes with minibars. There's an evening restaurant one floor above the lobby level, where table-d'hôte dinners cost £12.50 ($18.80) each, and a piano bar on the ground floor where bar lunches cost around £5 ($7.50) each.

WHERE TO DINE

TUDOR RESTAURANT, 8 Beresford Terrace. Tel. 0292/261404.
Cuisine: SCOTTISH/INTERNATIONAL. **Reservations:** Not needed.
$ Prices: Appetizers 70p–£1.20 ($1.10–$1.80); main courses £3.40–£6.30 ($5.10–$9.50); fixed-price three-course lunch £4.20 ($6.30); high tea £4.50–£7.50 ($6.80–$11.30). MC, V.
Open: Apr–Sept, Mon–Sat 9am–9pm (last order), Sun 4pm–8pm (last order); Oct–Mar, Mon–Sat 9am–8pm.

⑤ Deriving its name from the dark half-timbering that crisscrosses its interior, this is one of the busiest, most popular, and best-recommended family-oriented restaurants in Ayr. About 95% of its clients opt for either the fixed-price lunch or the cost-conscious high tea, served from 3:15pm to closing, which substitutes for quantity and feeling for a traditional dinner. Food items are well prepared and copiously served, and include such rib-sticking specialties as an excellent version of chicken Maryland (breaded and fried breast of chicken with bacon, tomatoes, peaches, and pineapple fritters). White with black trim, the establishment is in a turn-of-the-century building in the commercial heart of town, a 20-yard walk south of Burns Statue Square.

EVENING ENTERTAINMENT

RABBIE'S BAR, Burns Statue Sq. Tel. 0292/262112.
This famous pub might be considered a mixture of Scottish poetry with electronic music. The exposed stone of the walls is highlighted with snippets of pithy verses by one of the establishment's earlier clients, Robert Burns, who used to drop in for a pint of ale and conversation with his friends. Today there's a portrait of Rabbie painted directly onto the wall as a nostalgic reminder of another era. However, don't come here expecting poetry readings in a quiet corner. The crowd, while not particularly literary, is talkative and fun, and they enjoy live music several nights a week. There's a large selection of imported beers, a busy stand-up bar, long rows of crowded banquettes and copper-topped tables, and an extra-large TV screen showing videos of whatever musical group is hot in the English-speaking world. A pint of lager costs £1.40 ($2.10). Bar snacks average 60p (90¢). Open Monday through Thursday from 11am to 12:30am, on Friday from 11am to 1am, on Saturday from 11am to midnight, and on Sunday from 1 to 11pm.

ALLOWAY

Some 2 miles south of Ayr is where Robert Burns, Scotland's national poet, was born on January 25, 1759, in the gardener's cottage—the "auld clay biggin"—that his father, William Burns, built in 1757.

WHAT TO SEE & DO

The **Auld Brig** over the Ayr, mentioned in *Tam o'Shanter,* still spans the river, and **Alloway Auld Kirk,** also mentioned in the poem, stands roofless and "haunted" not far away. The poet's father is buried in the graveyard of the kirk.

BURNS MONUMENT AND GARDENS, Alloway. Tel. 0292/41321.
The monument is a Grecian-style building erected in 1823, containing relics, books, and manuscripts associated with Robert Burns, dating back to the 1820s.
Admission: Included in the entrance fee to Burns Cottage and Museum (see below).
Open: Apr–Oct, daily 9am–7pm; Nov–Mar, daily 10am–5pm. **Directions:** Take the B7024, 2 miles south of Ayr.

BURNS COTTAGE AND MUSEUM, Alloway. Tel. 0292/41215.
More than 80,000 people visit this place annually. It still retains some of its original furniture, including the bed in which the poet was born. Chairs displayed here were said to have been used by Tam o'Shanter and Souter Johnnie. Beside the cottage in which the poet lived is a museum.
Admission: £1.80 ($2.70) adults, 90p ($1.40) children.
Open: June–Aug, Mon–Sat 9am–7pm, Sun 10am–7pm; Sept–Oct, Mon–Sat 10am–5pm, Sun 2–5pm; Nov–Mar, Mon–Sat 10am–4pm; Apr–May, Mon–Sat 10am–5pm, Sun 2–5pm. **Directions:** Take the B7024, 2 miles south of Ayr.

LAND O'BURNS CENTRE, Murdoch's Lane, Tel. 0292/443700.
Here you can watch a multiscreen film on Burns's life, his friends, and his poetry. Information is available from the personnel, and a well-stocked gift shop is here, plus a tea room. The Russians are particularly fond of Burns and his poetry, and many come annually to visit the cottage and pore over his original manuscripts.
Admission: 50p (80¢) adults, 30p (50¢) children.
Open: July–Aug, daily 10am–5:30pm; Sept–June, daily 10am–5pm. **Directions:** Take the B7024, 2 miles south of Ayr.

WHERE TO STAY & DINE

BELLEISLE HOUSE HOTEL, Belleisle Park, Doonfoot Rd., Alloway, Ayr, Ayrshire KA7 4DU. Tel. 0292/442331. Fax 0292/445325. 16 rms (14 with bath), 1 suite. TV TEL
$ Rates (including Scottish breakfast): £41.50 ($62.30) single without bath, £50

($75) single with bath; £61 ($91.50) double without bath, £70 ($105) double with bath. Bridal suite £75 ($112.50). AE, DC, MC, V. **Parking:** Free.

This imposing country house was built in 1755 on lands that had been ceded by the magistrates of Ayr to the descendants of a family of writers and doctors whose fortune derived from a plantation in the West Indies. Set beside the A719, in the suburb of Alloway, about 2 miles south of Ayr, it stands in a public park noted for its two golf courses. Today functioning as a country-house hotel, it's noted for its stone exterior and its interior paneling whose ornate carvings sometimes depict scenes in *Tam O'Shanter,* by Robert Burns. Blazing fireplaces add to the traditional Scottish country-house ambience. The hotel has two dining rooms, one inspired by the music room of Marie Antoinette at Versailles, the other by her bedroom. The Scottish cooking is excellent, with table d'hôte lunches priced at £7.95 ($11.90); dinners at £13.95 ($20.90). Open all year, the establishment extends a special welcome to children.

BURNS MONUMENT HOTEL, Alloway, Ayr, Ayrshire, KA7 4PQ. Tel. 0292/442466. Fax 0292/443174. 9 rms (all with bath). MINIBAR TV TEL

$ Rates (including Scottish breakfast): £30–£40 ($45–$60) single; £60–£70 ($90–$105) double. AE, DC, MC, V. **Parking:** Free.

One of the most famous footbridges in Scotland, Brig o'Doon (immortalized by Robert Burns in *Tam o'Shanter*) lies a few steps from the 2 acres of lovely gardens which surround this hotel. So famous are the gardens, in fact, that much of the hotel's income derives from the wedding receptions that book its premises many months in advance. Built 200 years ago on the east bank of the Doon River, this white-painted hotel contains recently refurbished bedrooms awash in flowered chintz and solidly traditional furniture. There's a cocktail lounge/pub on the premises, and a comfortable dining room where fixed-price dinners are available for £16.25 ($24.40) for three courses. The hotel is 2 miles south of Alloway, a quarter mile from the hamlet of Doonfoot, beside the B7024.

MAYBOLE & CULZEAN

Some 12 miles south-southwest of Ayr and 4 miles west of Maybole on the A719 is ✪ **Culzean Castle** (tel. 06556/274). Built by the famous Scottish architect Robert Adam at the end of the 18th century, this magnificent clifftop creation is a fine example of his castellated style. Essentially a dwelling place, Culzean (pronounced cul-LANE) Castle replaced an earlier Scots tower house as the family seat of the powerful Kennedy clan. In 1945 the castle and grounds were given to the National Trust for Scotland. With a view of Ailsa Craig, a 1,100-foot-high rounded rock 10 miles offshore, a nesting ground and sanctuary for seabirds, to the south and overlooking the Firth of Clyde, the castle is well worth a visit, and is of special interest to Americans because of General Eisenhower's connection with its National Guest Flat. In 1946 the guest apartment was given to the general for his lifetime in gratitude for his services as Supreme Commander of Allied Forces in World War II. An exhibition of Eisenhower memorabilia, sponsored by the Scottish Heritage U.S.A., Inc., and Mobil Oil, is incorporated in the tour of the castle. Mementos of Eisenhower include his North African campaign desk and a replica of the Steuben glass bowl given him by his cabinet when he retired from the presidency. Culzean stands near the famous golf courses of Turnberry and Troon, a fact that particularly pleased the golf-loving Eisenhower. The tour also includes the celebrated round drawing room, delicately painted ceilings, and Adam's outstanding oval staircase.

The castle is open May through September, daily from 10am to 6pm; in April and October, Monday to Friday from noon to 5pm and on Saturday and Sunday and Easter from 10:30am to 5:30pm. Last admission is half an hour before closing. The charge is £3 ($4.50) for adults, £1.50 ($2.30) for children.

On the castle grounds is **Culzean Country Park,** which in 1969 became the first such park in Scotland. The 565-acre grounds include a walled garden, an aviary, a swan pond, a camellia house, and an orangery, as well as a deer park, miles of woodland paths, and beaches. It has gained an international reputation for its Visitor Centre (Adam's home farm) and related visitor and educational services. Up to

300,000 people visit the country park annually. The park is open from April through September, daily from 10am to 6pm; in October, daily from 10am to 4pm; November through March, daily from 9am to dusk. Admission is £3 ($4.50) adults, £1.50 ($2.30) children. For information, phone 06556/269.

You can reach Culzean Castle from Ayr. Maidens Bus (no. 60) from the Sandgate Bus Station in Ayr runs to Culzean six times per day; a 1-day round-trip ticket costs £3.50 ($5.30).

TURNBERRY

On the Firth of Clyde, the little town of Turnberry, south of the castle, was originally part of the Culzean Estate owned by the Marquess of Ailsa. It began to flourish after the marquis consented early in this century to allow the Glasgow and South Western Railway to develop golfing facilities, resulting in railway service, a recognized golfing center, and a first-class hotel. From the original two 13-hole **golf courses,** the complex has developed into the two 18-hole courses, Ailsa and Arran, known worldwide. The Ailsa, one of the most exacting courses yet devised, has been the scene of numerous championship tournaments and PGA events. Call 0655/31000 for information.

There was once a **Turnberry Castle** about 6 miles south of this golfing locale. Only scant remains exist to mark the place many historians say was the birthplace of Robert the Bruce in 1274. Turnberry lies 97 miles northwest of Edinburgh and 15 miles south of Ayr.

Just to the east of Turnberry, you might want to take a short drive to see **Souter Johnnie's Cottage** in Kirkoswald (tel. 06556/603), 4 miles west of Maybole on the A77. This was the 18th-century home of the village cobbler, John Davidson (Souter Johnnie), who, with his friend, Douglas Graham of Shanter Farm, was immortalized by Burns in his poem *Tam o'Shanter*. The cottage contains Burnsiana and contemporary cobblers' tools. In the churchyard are the graves of Tam o'Shanter and Souter Johnnie. The cottage is open April through October, Saturday to Thursday from noon to 5pm; other months, by appointment. Admission is £1.50 ($2.30) for adults, 90p ($1.40) for children.

Only about a mile from Souter Johnnie's Cottage is the 16th-century **Kilochan Castle,** stronghold of the Cathcarts of Carleton in the valley of the Water of Girvan.

A final sight is **Carleton Castle,** along the A77 some 14 miles south of Culzean Castle, 6 miles along the coast from the little seaside town of Girvan. In its heyday it was a watchtower, built to guard the coastline against invaders. A famous ballad grew out of a legend surrounding this castle. It was said to be the headquarters of a baron who married eight times. When he got tired of a wife, he pushed her over the cliff and found himself another spouse. However, he proved no match for his eighth wife, May Cullean. She outlived him.

WHERE TO STAY & DINE

TURNBERRY HOTEL AND GOLF COURSES, Maidens Rd., Turnberry, Ayrshire KA26 9LT. Tel. 0655/31000. Fax 0655/31706. 122 rms (all with bath), 10 suites. MINIBAR TV TEL

$ Rates (including Scottish breakfast): £160–£190 ($240–$285) single; £190–£220 ($285–$330) double; £250–£450 ($375–$675) suite. AE, DC, MC, V. **Parking:** Free.

The Turnberry Hotel and Golf Courses, 1 hour south of Glasgow on the A77, is a remarkable Edwardian property that has undergone one of the most complete glamourizations of any hotel in Scotland. The owners spent millions of dollars on the infrastructure and decor without diminishing the aura of the more opulent era of 1908 when the hotel was built. From afar, one can see the hotel's white facade, its red-tile roof and its dozens of gables. In World War II the corridors of the structure were transformed into a military hospital, but today the property is once again one of the grand hotels of Britain. The public rooms contain Waterford crystal chandeliers, Ionic columns, molded ceilings, and well-polished oak paneling. Each suite and bedroom is furnished in an elegant 19th-century style, with a marble-sheathed bath; the rooms include radios and open onto views of the surrounding lawns and forests.

Dining/Entertainment: The hotel maintains three different eating areas with differing degrees of formality. Most elegant of all is the Turnberry Restaurant, serving traditional Scottish and French recipes. Fixed-price dinners cost £35 ($52.50) for five courses. Lunches are more frequently consumed in The Bay at Turnberry, a restaurant that is part of the resort's spa facilities and serves light food; or in the Clubhouse, a headquarters for the golf facilities, built in 1993.

Facilities: Gym equipment, tennis, and Country Club and Spa with leisure center, Turkish bath, sauna, steam rooms, and squash courts.

PRESTWICK

Prestwick is the oldest recorded baronial burgh in Scotland, lying 2 miles north of Ayr, 32 miles southwest of Glasgow, and 78 miles southwest of Edinburgh. But most visitors know it for Prestwick Airport, which used to be a popular local sightseeing attraction, until the volume of international traffic was curtailed. Today it is used mainly for charter flights.

Behind St. Ninian's Episcopal Church is **Bruce's Well,** the water from which is reputed to have cured Robert the Bruce of leprosy. The **Mercat Cross** still stands outside what used to be the Registry Office and marks the center of the oldest part of Prestwick, whose existence goes back to at least 983.

Prestwick is a popular holiday town, and is considered one of Scotland's most attractive resorts, with its splendid sands and golf courses. Prestwick opens onto views of Ayr Bay and the Isle of Arran.

Trains from the Central Station in Glasgow leave hourly from Prestwick. Phone 041/2042844 in Glasgow for more data. Buses from the Buchanan Street Station in Glasgow leave hourly for Prestwick. Phone the station at 041/3329191 for more information. From Glasgow, motorists take the A77 southwest.

A **tourist information office** is at Boydfield Gardens (tel. 0292/79946). It is open only in summer.

WHERE TO STAY & DINE

PARKSTONE HOTEL, Central Esplanade, Prestwick, Ayrshire KA9 1QN. Tel. 0292/77286. 15 rms (all with bath). TV TEL
$ Rates (including Scottish breakfast): £38 ($57) single; £48 ($72) double. AE, MC, V. **Parking:** Free.

The Parkstone is a white-walled Victorian building with cookie-cutter gingerbread set under its steep eaves. Opposite the beach, a 2-minute walk west of the center, the hotel is the property of Stewart and Sandra Clarkson, who maintain their bedrooms in good order. Its modernized interior has a pub in back, with a view of the sea, that attracts a busy lunchtime crowd. A fixed-price dinner starts at £13.50 ($20.30) per person.

ST. NICHOLAS HOTEL, 41 Ayr Rd., Prestwick, Ayrshire KA9 1SY. Tel. 0292/79568. 18 rms (15 with shower). TV TEL
$ Rates (including Scottish breakfast): £24 ($36) single without bath, £32 ($48) single with bath; £40 ($60) double without bath, double £52 ($78) with bath. AE, DC, MC, V. **Parking:** Free.

This comfortable, spotless hostelry on the main road from Prestwick Airport to the train station is within a 5-minute walk of tennis courts, a swimming pool, and indoor bowling. All bedrooms are comfortably furnished and have tea/coffee makers. The hotel has full central heating and double-glazed windows. Good food and service prevail in the dining room, where lunch, high tea, and dinner are available. Margaret Preston, the congenial host, goes out of her way to make guests feel at home.

TOWANS HOTEL AND MOTEL, Powmill Road, Prestwick, Ayrshire KA9 2NY. Tel. 0292/77831. Fax 0292/671485. 53 rms (all with bath). TV TEL
$ Rates (including Scottish breakfast): £25.75–£33.50 ($38.60–$50.30) single;

£40.50–£50.50 ($60.80–$75.80) double; £56.75–£75 ($85.10–$112.50) family rooms. MC, V. **Parking:** Free.

Close to the airport, the original building faces a side lawn and then looks out over the Firth of Clyde to the Isle of Arran. Much of the accommodation is in a modern hotel/motel block that blends with the old. The owners, conscious of the needs of travelers passing through Prestwick Airport, are geared to catering for early and late arrivals. The well-furnished rooms have tea and coffee makers. Breakfast is served from 4am, and the dining room has a local reputation for well-cooked meals. Dinner costs £15.75 ($23.60).

TROON

This holiday resort looks out across the Firth of Clyde to the Isle of Arran, lying 7 miles north of Ayr, 31 miles southwest of Glasgow, and 77 miles southwest of Edinburgh. It offers several golf links, including the "Old Troon" course. In summer, bathers find plenty of room on its 2 miles of sandy beaches, stretching along both sides of its harbor; the broad sands and shallow waters make it a safe haven. From here you can take steamer trips to Arran and the Kyles of Bute.

Troon is a 20th-century town, its earlier history having gone unrecorded. It takes its name from the curiously shaped promontory that juts out into the Clyde estuary on which the old town and the harbor stand. The promontory was called Trwyn, Cymric word for nose, and later this became the Trone and then Troon.

The **Fullarton Estate,** on the edge of Troon beyond the municipal golf course, is the ancestral seat of the dukes of Portland.

A massive **statue of *Britannia*** stands on the seafront as a memorial to the dead of the two world wars. On her breastplate is the lion of Scotland emerging from the sea.

Trains from Glasgow's Central Station arrive at the station several times daily (trip time: 40 minutes). Call 041/2042844 in Glasgow for 24-hour information about departures. Trains also connect Ayr with Troon, a 10-minute ride. From the Ayr bus station, you can reach Troon and other parts of the area by bus. Call the tourist office in Ayr (tel. 0292/284196 for more details). From Prestwick, motorists head north along the B749.

A summer-only **tourist information office** is in the Municipal Buildings, South Beach (tel. 0292/317696).

WHERE TO STAY

MARINE HIGHLAND HOTEL, 8 Crobie Rd., Troon, Ayrshire KA10 6HE. Tel. 0292/314444. Fax 0292/316922. 66 rms (all with bath), 6 suites. TV TEL
$ Rates (including Scottish breakfast): £88 ($132) single; £138–£168 ($207–$252) double; £188 ($282) suite. AE, DC, MC, V. **Parking:** Free.

The hotel's red sandstone exterior rises from flat grasslands, a short stroll from the sea. With dozens of turrets, chimneys, and gables, it resembles a Victorian village, especially since the surrounding Royal Troon Golf Course prevents any significant building nearby. Inside, the comfortably modernized interior still offers glimpses of Victoriana. There are two restaurants, Fairways and Crosbie's Brasserie, offering some of the best food in Troon. The hotel was upgraded and refurbished in 1987, when a leisure and sports center, available to guests, was added.

PIERSLAND HOUSE HOTEL, 15 Craigend Rd., Troon, Ayrshire KA10 6HD. Tel. 0292/314747. Fax 0292/315613. 19 rms (all with bath), 1 cottage suite. TV TEL
$ Rates (including Scottish breakfast): £56 ($84) single; £89.50–£115 ($134.30–$172.50) double or suite. AE, DC, MC, V. **Parking:** Free.

Located beside the B749, a 3-minute drive south of the town center, this house was built a century ago by Sir Alexander Walker of the Johnnie Walker whisky family. Its 4 acres of gardens required the importation of 17,000 tons of topsoil to transform its marshy surface into the lushness that visitors see on a summer day. The most expensive prices for a double indicated above are for a superior twin or a four-poster double, or else for a cottage suite adjacent to the hotel, with a bedroom, sitting room, and private bath. All the bedrooms contain traditional Scottish country-house styling, and have such modern amenities as hairdryers and radios in addition to those cited above. Full room service is available upon request.

At lunchtime and in the evening, pub lovers around Troon flock here for a drink or buffet lunch near one of the hand-carved fireplaces. On sunny days the staff sets tables up at the edge of the formal garden, turning it into an outdoor version of a neighborhood pub. Frankly, this establishment is better known as a social center than as a hotel. The food is considered among the best in the area. A fixed-price dinner costs from £15.50 ($23.30) and might include such dishes as locally caught scallops and chicken in a white wine sauce. The hotel and its public rooms are popular as a place to celebrate large birthday parties and wedding receptions for residents of the surrounding region.

WHERE TO DINE

MARINE HIGHLAND HOTEL, 8 Crosbie Rd. Tel. 0292/314444.

Cuisine: SCOTTISH/INTERNATIONAL. **Reservations:** Required.

$ Prices: Crosbie's, appetizers £1.25–£3.50 ($1.90–$5.30); main courses £4.50–£12 ($6.80–$18). Fairways, appetizers £2.50–£4 ($3.80–$6); main courses £10–£14 ($15–$21); three-course lunch £13.50 ($20.30); four-course dinner £20–£21 ($30–$31.50). AE, DC, MC, V.

Open: Crosbie's, lunch daily noon–2:30pm; dinner daily 6–10pm; drinks daily 11am–10:30pm. Fairways, lunch daily noon–2pm; dinner daily 7–10pm.

This landmark hotel stands on the Ayrshire coastline, overlooking the Royal Troon Golf Course. It is ideal for dining in a choice of rooms. Crosbie's Brasserie is the more informal and fun of the two. In this lively all-day restaurant, the day begins with morning coffee, croissants, and pastries, continuing on to a selection of pastas, steaks, and chicken.

The other, more formal restaurant, Fairways, provides the proper setting for panoramic views of the Isle of Arran. Here you can enjoy traditional Scottish and French cuisine. Try "pillows" of smoked Scottish salmon, followed by rosettes of filet of Scottish beef.

RICHARD'S PLACE, 3 South Beach. Tel. 0292/314421.

Cuisine: SCOTTISH/INTERNATIONAL. **Reservations:** Required.

$ Prices: Appetizers £2.25–£3.50 ($3.40–$5.30); main courses £3.50–£7.50 ($5.30–$11.30); lunch specials £3.75–£5.75 ($5.60–$8.60) per platter. MC, V.

Open: Tues–Sun 10am–9pm (last order).

In a 150-year-old building on the town's main square, this restaurant is run by the mother-son team of Joan and Richard Allison. Simple and pleasant, it contains mahogany-topped tables on wrought-iron legs, mahogany chairs, and a culinary format that includes everything from simple cups of tea with pastries to full-fledged meals. Specialties include chicken in a cranberry and red wine sauce, several different versions of Stroganoff, and pork in an orange sauce. Lunches tend to be somewhat simpler than dinner, and include steak pies, baked potatoes stuffed with a choice of fillings, salads, and lasagne.

CHAPTER 6
ARGYLL & THE ISLES

- **WHAT'S SPECIAL ABOUT ARGYLL & THE ISLES**
1. **OBAN**
2. **DALMALLY & LOCH AWE**
3. **INVERARAY**
4. **THE KINTYRE PENINSULA**
5. **THE ISLE OF ARRAN**
6. **THE ISLE OF GIGHA**
7. **THE ISLE OF ISLAY**
8. **THE ISLE OF JURA**

For those who want to sample a bygone era, the old county of Argyll off the coastline of western Scotland is one of the most rewarding journeys.

The boundaries of Argyll have shifted and changed over the years. Part of it was once an independent kingdom known as Dalriada. It has always been an important area of Scotland. In Gaelic, Argyll is known as *Earraghaidheal,* "coastland of the Gael." Argyll takes up a lot of the deeply dissected western Highlands, its rivers flowing into the Atlantic. Its summers along the coast are usually cool and damp, and its winters are relatively mild but wet, with little snow.

In the southeast the ✪ **Argyll Forest Park,** stretching almost to Loch Fyne, and made up of Benmore, Ardgartan, and Glenbranter, covers an area of 60,000 acres. It contains some of the most magnificent scenery in Scotland, and there are dozens of forest walks for trail blazers. Sometimes these walks lead through forests to lofty peaks, and as such, they are strenuous except for the most skilled and hearty of folk. Others, however, are tamer, including paths from the Younger Botanic Garden by Loch Eck leading to Puck's Glen.

The major center for this district is Oban, meaning "small bay." It is a great port for the Western Isles and a center of Gaelic culture. It is the gateway to Mull, largest of the Inner Hebrides; to the island of Iona, the cradle of Scottish Christianity; and to Staffa, where Fingal's Cave inspired Mendelssohn to write the *Hebrides* Overture. These islands are reviewed in Chapter 10. The ferries to the offshore islands run only twice a day until summer; then there are cruises to Iona from early June to late September. For information about island ferry services to Mull, Iona, and the Outer Hebrides, get in touch with **MacBrayne Steamers** at their office in Oban (tel. 0631/62285).

A number of colorful sites are near the port town, including Port Appin and Inveraray, where visitors can soak up the atmosphere of the district away from the major towns.

After leaving Fort William (see Chapter 9) our trail around the entire length of the Scottish mainland picks up again after crossing the Ballachulish Bridge. If you've already seen Glencoe (reached along the A82), you can hug the coastal road (the A828) which will eventually take you into Oban.

Before you begin your exploration of the Hebridean Islands coming up, there are several island destinations off the Argyll Coast meriting your time. The long peninsula of Kintyre separates the islands of the Firth of Clyde, including Arran, from the islands of the Inner Hebrides, notably Mull, Islay, and Jura. (For information on Mull, see Chapter 10).

WHAT'S SPECIAL ABOUT ARGYLL & THE ISLES

Great Towns/Villages

☐ Oban, a bustling port town of the western Highlands and one of Scotland's leading coastal resorts.

☐ Inveraray, a small resort and royal burgh in a panoramic setting on the upper shores of Loch Fyne.

Great Islands/Peninsulas

☐ Kintyre, longest peninsula in Scotland, more than 60 miles of beautiful scenery, sleepy villages, and sandy beaches.

☐ Isle of Arran, called "Scotland in miniature," with wild, varied scenery of glens, moors, lochs, sandy bays, and rocky coasts.

☐ Isle of Islay, southernmost of the Inner Hebrides, with moors, lochs, sandy bays, and wild rocky cliffs.

☐ Isle of Jura, the fourth largest of the Inner Hebrides, known for its red deer, where Orwell wrote his masterpiece *1984*.

Ace Attractions

☐ Argyll Forest Park, actually three forests—Benmore, Ardgartan, and Glenbranter—covering some 60,000 acres in Argyll.

☐ Loch Awe, a natural moat that protected the Campbells of Inveraray from their enemies to the north, with many reminders of its fortified past.

Ancient Monuments

☐ Dunadd, once the capital of Dalriada, ancient kingdom of the Scots, with numerous Bronze Age stone circles in its vicinity.

☐ Skipness Castle and Chapel, at Skipness, opening onto Loch Fyne, the ruins of an ancient chapel and a 13th-century castle.

Historic Castles

☐ Dunstaffnage Castle, outside Oban, capital of the medieval Dalriada kingdom, site of coronation of Scottish kings until the 10th century.

☐ Castle Stalker, outside Oban, ancient seat of the Stewarts of Appin, depicted in *Monty Python and the Holy Grail.*

☐ Inveraray Castle, headquarters of the Clan Campbell since the early 15th century.

☐ Brodick Castle, antique-filled home of the dukes of Hamilton, dating from the 13th century.

Parks and Gardens

☐ Carradale House Gardens, northeast of Campbeltown, a walled garden from 1870 famed for its azaleas and rhododendrons in spring.

☐ Achamore House Gardens, Isle of Gigha, considered the finest in Scotland, a 50-acre site laid out by one of the world's greatest gardeners.

☐ Crarae Garden, south along Loch Fyne, spreading across 50 acres, considered one of the most beautiful gardens of Scotland.

Museums

☐ Auchindrain Museum of Country Life, outside Inveraray, open-air museum of traditional Highland farming life.

From the Isle of Islay to the Mull of Kintyre, the climate is mild and the land is rich and lush, especially on Arran, giving way on Islay to peat deposits that lend flavor to the making of such fine malt whiskies as Lagavulin, Bruichladdick, and Laproaig. There is a diversity of scenic beauty: hills and glens, fast-rushing streams, and little roads that eventually lead to coastal villages that display their B&B signs in summer.

Yachters are drawn to the sheltered harbors of the Argyll coast. This is active, sports-oriented country, offering golfing, walking, sea angling, and fishing. The best golf is at Machrie and Machrihanish.

The unspoiled and remote island of Jura is easily reached from Islay. And the best news for last: These islands, as well as Kintyre, Scotland's longest peninsula, are among the most economical places to visit in the British isles.

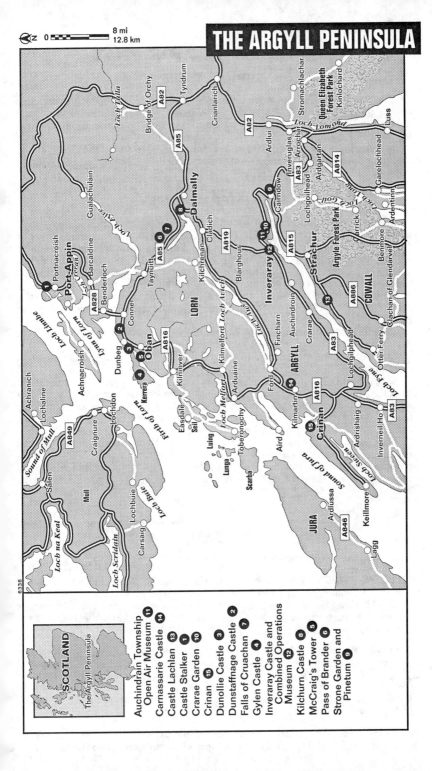

THE ARGYLL PENINSULA

8 mi
0
12.8 km

SCOTLAND

The Argyll Peninsula

Auchindrain Township
Open Air Museum ⑪
Carnassarie Castle ⑭
Castle Lachlan ⑬
Castle Stalker ①
Crarae Garden ⑩
Crinan ⑮
Dunollie Castle ③
Dunstaffnage Castle ②
Falls of Cruachan ⑦
Gylen Castle ④
Inveraray Castle and
Combined Operations
Museum ⑫
Kilchurn Castle ⑧
McCraig's Tower ⑤
Pass of Brander ⑥
Strone Garden and
Pinetum ⑨

SEEING ARGYLL & THE ISLES

GETTING THERE

Oban is the major rail terminus. After that, one must rely on local country buses to get about. The ideal way to tour the Argyll Peninsula is by car, because of inadequate public transportation. Motorists head northwest from Glasgow to the western Highlands by taking the A82.

Motorists can drive to the Kintyre Peninsula (the A816 from Oban leads south). The other destinations that follow Kintyre can only be reached by one of the ferries operated by Caledonian MacBrayne.

SUGGESTED ITINERARY

Day 1: From the Scottish mainland at Ardrossan, southwest of Glasgow, head west on a car-ferry to Brodick, capital of the Isle of Arran. Either overnight there or pick one of the adjoining villages. See the island's major attraction, Brodick Castle.

Day 2: Cross the Kilbrannan Sound by car-ferry leaving from the north of Arran, landing at Claonaig on the Kintyre Peninsula. Head south for the capital, Campbeltown, for an overnight, and explore the Mull of Kintyre at the southern tip.

Day 3: Take another ferry from Kintyre to the Isle of Gigha to explore this ancient island and its famous gardens. Return to Kintyre for the night and overnight in the fishing port of Tarbert.

Day 4: From Kennacraig on the Kintyre Peninsula, cross to Port Ellen. Spend the day exploring the Isle of Islay and overnight there.

Day 5: Take the short ferry crossing and spend a day on Jura. You can overnight there in the one hotel or return to Islay.

Days 6 and 7: From Islay return to the peninsula of Kintyre and drive north to Inveraray, and see its castle, using that town as a base for a motor tour of the western shore of Loch Fyne. You can drive as far south as Lochgilphead. Return to Inveraray for the night. While still based in Inveraray, continue to the east of Cairndow, then drive down the eastern shore of Loch Fyne and have lunch at Creggans.

Day 8: Head northeast from Inveraray for an overnight stay at Dalmally. Use this day to explore both the eastern and western shores of Loch Awe.

Day 9: Head west to Oban and spend the day viewing its numerous attractions, exploring some of the environs (if you have time), including the Crinan Canal and the old capital of Dunadd.

---

1. OBAN

85 miles NW of Glasgow, 50 miles SW of Fort William

GETTING THERE **By Train** From Glasgow, the West Highland lines run directly to Oban with departures from Glasgow's Queen Street Station (tel. 041/2042844 in Glasgow for 24-hour information about tickets and schedules). Four trains per day (only three on Sunday) during the summer months make the three-hour run to Oban at a one-way fare of £14.70 ($22.10).

By Bus Frequent coaches depart from Buchanan Station in Glasgow, taking about the same time as the train, although a one-way fare is only £8.50 ($12.80). Call Scottish Citylink (tel. 041/3327133 in Glasgow) for more information.

By Car From Glasgow, head northwest along the A82 until you reach Tyndrum, then go west along the A85 until you come to Oban.

ESSENTIALS The **tourist information office** is at the Boswell House on Argyll Square (tel. 0631/63122). The **telephone area code** is 0631.

SPECIAL EVENTS   In August the **Oban Highland Games** are held, with massed pipe bands marching through the streets. Ask at the tourist office (see above) for more information. The Oban Pipe Band plays regularly throughout the summer, parading up and down the main street.

One of Scotland's leading coastal resorts, the bustling port town of Oban is set in a sheltered bay that is almost landlocked by the island of Kerrera. A busy fishing port in the 18th century, Oban is now heavily dependent on tourism for its economic base.

WHAT TO SEE & DO

From Pulpit Hill in Oban there is a fine view across the Firth of Lorn and the Sound of Mull. Overlooking the town is an unfinished replica of the Colosseum of Rome, **McCaig's Tower,** built by a banker, John Stuart McCaig, in 1897–1900 as a memorial to his family and to try to curb local unemployment during a slump. Its walls are 2 feet thick and from 37 to 40 feet high. The courtyard within is landscaped and the tower is floodlit at night. Outsiders have been heard to refer to the tower as "McCaig's Folly," but Obanites are proud of the structure and deplore this term.

Near the little granite **Cathedral of the Isles,** 1 mile north of the end of the bay, is the ruin of the 13th-century **Dunollie Castle,** seat of the lords of Lorn, who once owned a third of Scotland.

On the island of Kerrera stands **Gylen Castle,** home of the MacDougalls, dating back to 1587.

You can visit ✪ **Dunstaffnage Castle,** 3½ miles to the north, which was believed to have been the royal seat of the Dalriadic monarchy in the 8th century. The site is believed to have been the location of the Scots court until the unification under Kenneth McAlpine and the transfer to Scone of the seat of Scottish government in the 10th century. The present castle was probably built in 1263. The castle is open from April through September, Monday to Wednesday and Saturday from 9:30am to 7pm, and on Sunday from 2 to 7pm (closed Thursday and Friday); from October through March, it closes at 4pm. Admission is £1.50 ($2.30) for adults, 75p ($1.10) for children. You can take a bus from the Oban Rail Station to Dunbeg, but it's still a 1½-mile walk to the castle.

WHERE TO STAY

MODERATE

ALEXANDRA, Corran Esplanade, Oban, Argyll PA34 5AA. Tel. 0631/ 62381. Fax 0631/64497. 60 rms (all with bath). TV TEL
$ Rates (including Scottish breakfast): £30–£55 ($45–$82.50) single; £60–£90 ($90–$135) double. AE, DC, MC, V. **Parking:** Free.
The Alexandra is a stone hotel with gables and a tower, plus a Regency front veranda, enjoying a sunny perch on the promenade a mile from the train station. From its public room, you can look out onto Oban Bay, and two sun lounges overlook the seafront. The bedrooms are substantial and pleasing, offering comfort and conveniences. The

---

IMPRESSIONS

*Once you get the hang of it, and apprehend the type, it is a most
beautiful and admirable little country—fit, for 'distinction' etc., to make up
a trio with Italy and Greece.*
—Henry James, *Letter to Miss Alice James,* 1878

restaurant, serving good food, also opens onto the panorama. A complete dinner in the evening costs £14.75 ($22.10).

CALEDONIAN HOTEL, Station Square, Oban, Argyll PA34 5RT. Tel. 0631/63133. Fax 0631/62998. 70 rms (all with bath). TV TEL

$ Rates (including Scottish breakfast): £39–£59 ($58.50–$88.50) single; £59–£79 ($88.50–$118.50) double. AE, DC, MC, V. **Parking:** Free.

The Caledonian Hotel makes good on its promise of giving you a "taste of the Highlands." A fine example of Scottish 19th-century architecture, it occupies a landmark position, with a good view opening onto the harbor and Oban Bay looking toward the Mull of Kintyre. This convenient location puts you close to the rail, bus, and ferry terminals from which you can book passage to the Isles. The bedrooms are up-to-date with their amenities, and they all have beverage-making equipment. Good, reasonably priced Scottish fare is served in the dining room, with meals beginning at £13 ($19.50).

COLUMBA HOTEL, The Esplanade, North Pier, Oban, Argyll PA34 5QD. Tel. 0631/62183. Fax 0631/64683. 51 rms (all with bath). TV TEL **Bus:** Scottish Midland Bus Company's Ganavan bus passes by.

$ Rates (including half board): £39.50 ($59.30) single; £79 ($118.50) double. AE, MC, V. **Parking:** Free.

One of the most impressive Victorian buildings in Oban, the Columba was built in 1870 by the same McCaig who constructed the hilltop extravaganza known as McCaig's Tower. The location is among the best in town. A modernized and big-windowed dining room offers views of the port. Rooms are comfortably furnished and well maintained, and each has a tea maker. An à la carte dinner can be ordered in the restaurant, or you can ask for a bar supper in the Cocktail Bar. Seafood is a specialty. The Poop Deck is a more informal bar where live folk music is sometimes presented.

GREAT WESTERN HOTEL, Corran Esplanade, Oban, Argyll PA34 5PP. Tel. 0631/63101. Fax 0631/63394. 84 rms (all with bath). TV

$ Rates (including Scottish breakfast): £25 ($37.50) single; £50 ($75) double. Half board £32 ($48) single; £64 ($96) double. AE, DC, MC, V. **Parking:** Free. **Closed:** Nov–Mar.

The Great Western Hotel is a warmly old-fashioned hotel set directly on the waterfront across the street from the harborfront promenade. Each of its well-furnished bedrooms has a sweeping view over the interisland ferryboats and fishing vessels bobbing at anchor in the harbor. The hotel, which is owned by one of Britain's well-known chains, offers Scottish entertainment in one of its lounges and a well-appointed dining room and a spacious water-view lounge where drinks are served.

INEXPENSIVE

LANCASTER, Corran Esplanade, Oban, Argyll PA34 5AD. Tel. 0631/62587. 27 rms (24 with bath). TV

$ Rates (including Scottish breakfast): £22.50 ($33.80) single without bath, £27.75 ($41.60) single with bath; £51 ($76.50) double with bath. MC, V. **Parking:** Free.

Lancaster is distinguished by its attractive pseudo-Tudor facade. Along the seafront on the crescent of the bay, it commands views from its public rooms of the islands of Lismore and Kerrera, even the more distant peaks of Mull. Open all year, the hotel welcomes you to one of its well-furnished bedrooms. The fully licensed Lancaster is the only hotel in Oban featuring a heated indoor swimming pool, a sauna, a whirlpool, and a solarium. In its dining room, you can order a table d'hôte lunch for £6.25 ($9.40), a table d'hôte dinner for £9.25 ($13.90).

WELLPARK HOTEL, The Esplanade, Oban, Argyll PA34 5AQ. Tel. 0631/62948. Fax 0631/65808. 17 rms (all with shower). TV TEL

$ Rates (including Scottish breakfast): £28–£29 ($42–$43.50) single; £46–£58 ($69–$87) double. MC, V. **Parking:** Free. **Closed:** Nov–Mar.

This B&B is one of the best bargains in Oban. It's set in a substantial stone house with a gabled bay window, positioned just past the cathedral on the seafront and commanding views of the bay and the islands of Kerrera, Mull, and Lismore. All rooms are centrally heated, comfortable, and quiet at night, and feature radios and hot-beverage facilities.

WHERE TO DINE

BALMORAL HOTEL, Craigard Rd. Tel. 0631/62731.

Cuisine: SCOTTISH/ENGLISH. **Reservations:** Recommended in midsummer.

$ Prices: Appetizers £1.50–£6 ($2.30–$9); main courses £6–£17 ($9–$25.50); average bar meal from £6 ($9). AE, DC, MC, V.

Open: May to mid-Oct, lunch daily noon–2:30pm; dinner daily 5–10pm. From mid-Oct to Apr, lunch only, daily noon–2pm. **Closed:** Jan–Mar.

Set on the second floor of a hotel, at the top of a granite staircase whose corkscrew shape is considered an architectural marvel, this is one of the best-recommended and most popular restaurants in town. Filled with a 19th-century kind of charm, it contains Windsor chairs and reproduction Georgian-style tables crafted from darkly stained wood. Specialties include sliced chateaubriand with mushrooms, Isle of Mull rainbow trout, smoked Tobermory trout, Scottish haggis with cream and whisky, venison casserole, and roast pheasant. Less expensive meals, consisting solely of bar platters, are served in the adjacent bar. The hotel stands on the eastern extension of the town's main commercial street (George Street), a 4-minute walk from the center.

The hotel rents 12 bedrooms, with TV and private bath. Including a Scottish breakfast, singles rent for £25 ($37.50), with doubles costing £50 ($75).

KNIPOCH HOTEL RESTAURANT, along the A816, Kilninver. Tel. 08526/251.

Cuisine: CONTINENTAL. **Reservations:** Essential.

$ Prices: Table d'hôte 3-course dinner £27.50 ($41.30); table d'hôte 5-course dinner £37.50 ($56.30). AE, DC, MC, V.

Open: Dinner only, daily 7:30–9pm. **Closed:** Mid-Nov to mid-Feb.

At last Oban has a truly fine restaurant. The only trouble is, you have to drive 6 miles south on the A816 to enjoy it. Jenny and Colin Craig, a mother-son team, offer a choice of three dining rooms and a daily changing menu of five delectable courses. In their whitewashed Georgian house, the oldest part dating from 1592, they serve food daily. Salmon and halibut are smoked on the premises, and the menu relies heavily on Scottish produce, including fresh fish. Try the cock-a-leekie soup, followed by Sound of Luing scallops or saddle of Scottish lamb stuffed with herbs. The wine cellar is excellent, especially in its selection of bordeaux.

MCTAVISH'S KITCHEN, 34 George St. Tel. 0631/63064.

Cuisine: SCOTTISH. **Reservations:** Not needed.

$ Prices: Appetizers £1.20–£5.25 ($1.80–$7.90); main courses £4.55–£10.95 ($6.80–$16.40); budget two-course lunch £4.95 ($7.40); three-course fixed-price dinner £7 ($10.50). MC, V.

Open: Self-service restaurant, daily 9am–9pm. Licensed restaurant, lunch daily noon–2pm; dinner daily 6–10:30pm. Bars, daily 11am–11pm.

Like its cousin in Fort William, this place is dedicated to preserving the local cuisine. Downstairs is a self-service restaurant that serves breakfast, main meals, shortbread, scones, strawberries, cakes, teas, and coffees. There are two bars, the upstairs Lairds Bar and Ground Floor McTavish's Bar where bar meals are available all day. The licensed second-floor restaurant has a more ambitious Scottish and continental menu with higher prices, but there are also budget lunches. The fixed-price menu includes an appetizer, a main course choice that includes fresh salmon, and a dessert such as strawberries or raspberries in season. The à la carte menu offers haggis, Loch Fyne kippers (oak-smoked herring), prime Scottish steaks, smoked salmon, venison, and local mussels.

From mid-May to the end of September there is entertainment with music by local artists, Scottish dance music, singing, piping, fiddling, and Highland dancing nightly from 8:30 to 10:30pm. Admission is £3.25 ($4.90) for adults, £1.65 ($2.50) for children. Reduced admission for diners is £1.75 ($2.60) for adults, £1 ($1.50) for children.

EASY EXCURSIONS FROM OBAN

THE ISLANDS

Oban is the gateway to Mull, largest of the Inner Hebrides; to the island of Iona, the cradle of Scottish Christianity; and to Staffa, where Fingal's Cave inspired Mendelssohn to write the *Hebrides* Overture. The ferries to the offshore islands run only twice a day until summer; then there are cruises to Iona from early June to late September. For information about island ferry services to Mull, Iona, and the Outer Hebrides, get in touch with **MacBrayne Steamers** at their office in Oban (tel. 631/62285).

PORT APPIN

Some 24 miles north of Oban lies a beautiful lochside district, including Lismore Island. Port Appin is a small village with stone cottages.

On an islet near Port Appin is a famous landmark, **✪ Castle Stalker,** the ancient seat of the Stewarts of Appin, built in the 15th century by Duncan Stewart, son of the first chief of Appin. Dugald, the ninth chief, was forced to sell the estate in 1765, and the castle slowly fell into ruin. It was recently restored by Lt. Col. Stewart Allward and is once again inhabited. It is open March to September by appointment (tel. 08832/3944). The cost is £4.50 ($6.80) for adults, £2.50 ($3.80) for children, including the boat trip. In *Monty Python and the Holy Grail,* this castle was depicted as "Castle Asaaaaaaaaa." It lies at Portnacroish (where it's signposted) 10 miles down the A828.

WHERE TO STAY & DINE

AIRDS HOTEL, Port Appin, Argyll PA38 4DF. Tel. 063173/236. Fax 063173/535. 11 rms (all with bath), 1 suite. TV TEL
$ Rates (including Scottish breakfast): £125 ($187.50) single; £220–£230 ($330–$345) double; £250 ($375) suite. AE, MC, V. **Parking:** Free. **Closed:** Mid-Jan to Feb.

✪ The Airds Hotel is an old ferry inn dating from 1700, in one of the most beautiful spots in the historic district of Appin. Considered one of the outstanding hotels of Scotland, it is a Relais & Châteaux, midway between Oban and Fort William. The hotel, overlooking not only Loch Linnhe but the island of Lismore and the mountains of Morvern, is an ideal center for touring this area of the country. You can take forest walks in many directions, or go pony trekking, sea angling, or trout fishing. Boats can be rented and trips arranged to see the seals and to visit the island of Lismore. The resident proprietors, Eric and Betty Allen, along with their son, Graeme, welcome you to one of their handsomely furnished bedrooms. Everything is immaculately maintained, in a tranquil setting.

Dining/Entertainment: It is the food that makes the Airds such an outstanding place to visit. Betty Allen is one of the great cooks of Scotland. In her repertoire of fine Scottish cuisine, home-baking is a specialty, and fresh produce is used in making up the menus. Specialties include Loch Fyne kippers, smoked-mackerel salad, and an exceptional kidney soup. Sole is often served stuffed with crab mousse, or perhaps you'll sample the roast haunch of venison with rowan jelly if featured. Desserts include such mouth-watering concoctions as baked lemon tart. A meal here will cost £35 ($52.50) and up. Reservations for dinner, served only at 8pm, are absolutely necessary.

Services: All-day room service, babysitting, laundry.

Facilities: Garden.

THE PIERHOUSE, Port Appin, Argyll PA38 4DF. Tel. 063173/302. Fax 063173/521. 11 rms (all with bath) TV TEL.
$ Rates (including Scottish breakfast): £29.50 ($44.30) single; £59 ($88.50) double. MC, V. **Parking:** Free.

Although the restaurant associated with this hotel was established by two generations of the McLeod family in 1988, its overnight accommodations are among the newest in Argyll. In 1993, a two-story wing was added containing simple but comfortable bedrooms, many with views out over the water and anchored fishing boats. The complex lies in the hamlet's center, adjacent to the pier where ferryboats depart every two hours for Lismore Island.

Dining/Entertainment: The white-sided restaurant was originally built as a fisherman's cottage over 200 years ago. Its location at the edge of the pier allows much of its seafood to remain alive in underwater cages until just before consumption, ensuring some of the freshest and purest seafood anywhere. Menu items include several different versions of giant prawns; pan-fried scallops served either with lemon butter or a cream cheese and wine sauce; clam chowder; and delicious versions of whatever local fishermen managed to bring in that day. Appetizers cost £1.80–£5 ($2.70–$7.50); main courses cost £7–£15 ($10.50–$22.50). The restaurant is open every day for lunch (noon–4pm) and dinner (6:30–10pm). Reservations are recommended.

---

2. DALMALLY & LOCH AWE

99 miles NW of Edinburgh, 24 miles E of Oban, 68 miles NW of Glasgow

GETTING THERE By Train Proceed to Oban (see above), then take a connecting bus.

By Bus Scottish Citylink, 1 Queens Park Pl. (tel. 0631/62856), in Oban, has service to Glasgow with stopovers at Loch Awe.

By Car From Oban, head east along the A85.

ESSENTIALS Consult with the tourist office in Oban (see above). The **telephone area code** is 08382.

Twenty-two miles long and in most places only about a mile wide, Loch Awe acted as a natural moat protecting the Campbells of Inveraray from their enemies to the north. Along its banks and on its islands are many reminders of its fortified past.

In this area the Forestry Commission has vast forests, and a modern road makes it possible to travel around Loch Awe, so that it is more than ever a popular angling center.

WHAT TO SEE & DO

To the east of the top of Loch Awe, **Dalmally** is small, but because of its strategic position it has witnessed a lot of Scottish history. Its 18th century church is built in an octagonal shape. The ruins of **Kilchurn Castle,** are at the northern tip of Loch Awe, west of Dalmally. It was built by Sir Colin Campbell in 1440 as one of the strongholds of the Campbells of Glen Orchy. It can be viewed from the outside only.

Among other reminders of the days when the Campbells of Inveraray held supreme power in the Loch Awe region, there is a ruined **castle at Fincharn,** at the southern end of the loch, and another on the island of Fraoch Eilean. The **Isle of Inishail** has an ancient chapel and burial ground. The bulk of Ben Cruachan, rising to 3,689 feet, dominates Loch Awe at its northern end and attracts climbers. On the ben is the world's second largest hydroelectric power station, which pumps water from Loch Awe to a reservoir high up the mountain.

Below the mountain are the **Falls of Cruachan** and the wild **Pass of Brander,** where Robert the Bruce routed the Clan MacDougall in 1308. The Pass of Brander was the scene of many a fierce battle in bygone times, and something of that bloody past seems to brood over the narrow defile. Through it the waters of the Awe flow on their way to Loch Etive. This winding sea loch is 19 miles long, stretching from Dun Dunstaffnage Bay at Oban to Glen Etive, reaching into the Moor of Rannoch at the foot of the 3,000-foot Buachaille Etive (the Shepherd of Etive), into which Glencoe also reaches.

WHERE TO STAY & DINE

ARDANAISEIG, Kilchrenan by Taynuilt, Argyll PA35 1HE. Tel. 08663/ 333, or toll-free 800/548-7790 in the U.S., 800/463-7595 in Canada. Fax 08663/222. 14 rms (all with bath). TV TEL **Directions:** Take the A85 to Taynuilt, then follow a secondary road, the B845, to Kilchrenan and follow the signs to Ardanaiseig.

$ Rates (including half board): £105–£135 ($157.50–$202.50) single; £150–£210 ($225–$315) double. AE, DC, MC, V. **Parking:** Free. **Closed:** Mid-Oct to mid-Apr.

When one of the 19th-century Campbell family patriarchs erected this manorial seat in 1834, he designed its lines more along 18th-century styles. He planted some of the rarest trees in the British islands, many of them exotic conifers. Today, clusters of fruit trees in a walled garden, along with rhododendrons and azaleas, add to the arboreal interest of this elegant gray stone property. The house stands between Loch Awe and the peaks of Cruachan, and a golf course is within a 40-minute drive. Fishing vessels can be rented. Until recently a private home, the hotel has formal sitting rooms graced with big chintzy chairs, fresh flowers, and polished tables. Upstairs, each of the bedrooms is well heated. The price of a room depends on its size, ranging from small to a master bedroom with a loch view. The owners have employed an excellent chef, who makes use of fresh produce, game, and meats with skill and flair.

CARRAIG THURA, Loch Awe by Dalmally, Argyll PA33 1AF. Tel. 08382/ 210. 6 rms (all with bath or shower).

$ Rates (including Scottish breakfast): £20–£30 ($30–$45) per person. MC, V. **Parking:** Free. **Closed:** Late Sept to Easter.

The translation of its name ("Rock Tower") is appropriate for its late-Victorian design. Bristling with granite-sided turrets, towers, and gables, it's an excellent example of the Scottish baronial style which swept through the Highlands around 1880. Originally built as the private home of the owner of the much larger hotel down the road (A85), it retains most of the original dark oak paneling, and an impressive collection of armor and old weapons. The hotel occupies 4½ acres of garden and parkland that teem with rabbits and deer. Because the hotel controls fishing rights along a salmon-rich portion of the nearby Orchy River, guests can fish for free. Bedrooms contain modernized bathrooms, but have kept many of their original Victorian features and much of their charm. Only breakfast is served.

AN EASY EXCURSION FROM DALMALLY

THE CRINAN CANAL

Crinan, a yachtsman's haven on the Sound of Jura, is a charming little village overlooked by the early 11th-century **Duntrune Castle,** one of the oldest in Scotland, still inhabited by the descendants of the original owners, Clan Malcolm.

The 9-mile-long canal, constructed during 1793–1801, was designed to provide water communication between the Firth of Clyde, Argyll, the western Highlands, and the islands. It runs roughly north from Ardrishaig and curves gradually to the west before reaching Loch Crinan on the Sound of Jura. Four miles north of **Cairnbaan,** on the canal, is the ruined hill-fort of **Dunadd,** once capital of Dalriada, kingdom of the Scots. This is the spot where God is said to have invested early kings with royal power. In the vicinity are numerous Bronze Age stone circles.

Carnasserie Castle, also to the north of the canal, built in the late 16th century, was the home of John Carswell, the first post-Reformation bishop of the isles, whose translation of John Knox's liturgy into Gaelic was the first book to be published in that language.

WHERE TO STAY

CRINAN HOTEL, Crinan, Argyll PA31 8SR. Tel. 054683/261. Fax 054683/292. 22 rms (all with bath). TV TEL

$ **Rates:** Apr–Oct (including Scottish breakfast), £75 ($112.50) single; £110–£175 ($165–$262.50) double. Winter (including half board), £60 ($90) single; £120 ($180) double. MC. **Parking:** Free.

Constructed 150 years ago on a promontory jutting out into the estuary 7 miles northwest of Lochgilphead, this comfortable hotel in the hamlet's center has been improved and modernized many times since. It was originally built to feed and house the hundreds of workers who transported goods by steamship along the Crinan Canal during the height of the Industrial Age. Inside, you'll find a bright and attractive decor and many up-to-date conveniences. The more expensive bedrooms contain lakefront balconies that open onto sweeping views of lochs and mountains. On the premises are two restaurants, the Westward, where a five-course fixed-price dinner costs £25.50 ($38.30), and the Lock 16 (see "Where to Dine," below). At lunch, the most prevalent fare is bar lunches, priced at around £7 ($10.50) each.

WHERE TO DINE

LOCK 16 RESTAURANT, in the Crinan Hotel. Tel. 054683/292.
Cuisine: SEAFOOD. **Reservations:** Essential.

$ **Prices:** Fixed-price five-course dinner £37.50 ($56.30). MC, V.
Open: Dinner only, Wed–Sat promptly at 8pm.

Built atop a 150-year-old hotel that is considered one of the most upscale inns in the region, the Lock 16's decor comes almost exclusively from the sweeping and big-windowed view of the waterfront that seems to almost leap into the dining room. Only the freshest fish, caught the morning before they're served, are used to create meals whose ingredients vary with the season. Depending on the catch of the day and the whim of the chef, your meal might include Crinan clams mornay, fresh salmon prepared in a champagne sauce, and any of dozens of different fresh and saltwater fish preparations. Set directly on the Crinan canal (whose waterways contain 15 locks), the restaurant derives its name from the fictitious 16th lock, which was never built.

3. INVERARAY

99 miles NW of Edinburgh, 57 miles NW of Glasgow, 38 miles SE of Oban

GETTING THERE   By Train   The nearest rail station is at Dumbarton, 45 miles to the southeast, where bus connections can be made to Inveraray.

By Bus   The National Express operates buses out of Glasgow, heading for Dumbarton, before continuing to Inveraray. Transit time is 1¾ hours. Monday through Saturday, three buses make this run (only two on Sunday).

By Car   From Oban, head east along the A85 until you reach the junction with the A819, at which point you continue south.

ESSENTIALS   The **tourist information office** is on Front Street (tel. 0499/ 2063). The **telephone area code** is 0499.

This small resort and royal burgh occupies a splendid setting on the upper shores of Loch Fyne. It is particularly attractive when you approach from the east on the A83. Across a little inlet, you can see the town lying peacefully on a bit of land fronting on the loch.

WHAT TO SEE & DO

At one end of the main street of the town is a **Celtic burial cross** from Iona. The parish church is divided by a wall which enables services to be held simultaneously in Gaelic and English.

INVERARAY CASTLE AND COMBINED OPERATIONS MUSEUM, three-quarters of a mile northeast of Inveraray on Loch Fyne. Tel. 0499/2203.

⭐ The hereditary seat of the dukes of Argyll, **Inveraray Castle** has been headquarters of the Clan Campbell since the early 15th century. The castle is among the earliest examples of Gothic Revival in Britain, and offers a fine collection of pictures and 18th-century French furniture, old English and continental porcelain, and a magnificent Armoury Hall, which alone contains 1,300 pieces.

On the grounds of Inveraray Castle is a **Combined Operations Museum,** the only one of its kind in the United Kingdom. It displays the role that No. 1 Combined Training Centre played at Inveraray in World War II. On exhibit are scale models, newspaper reports of the time, campaign maps, photographs, wartime posters and cartoons, training scenes, and other mementos. There is a castle shop for souvenirs and a tea room where homemade cakes and scones are served.

Admission: £3 ($4.50) adults, £1.50 ($2.30) children, £7.50 ($11.30) family ticket.

Open: Apr–June and Sept to mid-Oct, Sat–Thurs 10am–12:30pm and 2–5:30pm; July–Aug, Mon–Sat 10am–5:30pm, Sun 1–5:30pm.

AUCHINDRAIN TOWNSHIP OPEN AIR MUSEUM, 6 miles southwest of Inveraray on the A83, Lochgilphead/Campbeltown Road. Tel. 04995/235.

Auchindrain is an original West Highland township of great antiquity and a unique survivor of the long gone communal tenancy townships that were once common throughout the Highlands. There are more than 20 structures remaining in the township, over half of them now restored and furnished and equipped to illustrate the lifestyle of the Highlander in bygone days. There is also a Visitor Centre containing displays on the lives of the Highlanders, a museum shop, and other visitor facilities.

Admission: £2.20 ($3.30) adults, £1.40 ($2.10) children.

Open: Apr–Sept, daily 10am–5pm, closed Sat during Apr, May, and Sept.

WHERE TO STAY & DINE

THE GREAT INN, Front Street, Inveraray, Argyll PA32 8XB. Tel. 0499/2466. Fax 0499/2389. 24 rms (19 with bath). TV TEL **Directions:** Lies adjacent to the town's only bridge, at the eastern edge of the town center.

$ Rates (including Scottish breakfast): £17.50–£22.50 ($26.30–$33.80) single without bath; £32.50–£42.50 ($48.80–$63.80) single with bath; £35–£45 ($52.50–$67.50) double without bath; £45–£65 ($67.50–$97.50) double with bath. AE, DC, MC, V. **Parking:** Free.

This three-story building, with its view of Loch Fyne and Loch Shira, was first constructed in 1755. Dubbed with several different names during its long and varied life, after a modernization in 1990 it readopted its original and oldest name, the Great Inn. One of its noteworthy attractions is the street-level tea room, where a pot of coffee with pastry will provide a pick-me-up for a cost of around £2 ($3). There's also a residents-only cocktail lounge, and a dignified restaurant where three-course evening meals, with a wide choice of food items, cost £13.50 ($20.30). Bedrooms are comfortable, and include decors that range from flowered chintz to modern rooms with no-nonsense functionality.

EASY EXCURSIONS FROM INVERARAY

CAIRNDOW

Barely visible from the main highway (the A83), the hamlet of Cairndow nestles between a hill and Loch Fyne, on the loch's eastern shore. It is a peaceful haven with a view of the loch and the high mountains. The **Strone Garden and Pinetum,** Cairndow (tel. 04996/284), lies on the A815, 12 miles east of Inveraray. The Pinetum contains the tallest tree in Britain, and the gardens are richly planted with primulas, exotic shrubs, rhododendrons, and daffodils. They are open daily from Easter through October, from 9am to 9pm (or dusk if earlier). Admission is £2 ($3) for adults in April, May, and June; then £1 ($1.50) in other months. Children are admitted free.

Where to Stay & Dine

CAIRNDOW STAGECOACH INN & THE STABLES RESTAURANT, Cairndow, Argyll PA26 8BN. Tel. 04996/286. Fax 04996/220. 12 rms (10 with bath). TEL

$ **Rates** (including Scottish breakfast): £24 ($36) single without bath, £26–£28 ($39–$42) single with bath; £36 ($54) double without bath, £44–£48 ($66–$72) double with bath. Children 3–12 pay half price, and children 12–15 receive discounts of 25%. AE, DC, MC, V. **Parking:** Free.

One of the oldest coaching inns in the Highlands, this place has entertained illustrious guests through the years, including Dorothy Wordsworth in 1803. Even Queen Victoria had her horses changed here in 1875. Today, Douglas and Catherine Fraser welcome you in the best tradition of Scottish hospitality. Their inn lies in the heart of the hamlet just off the A83 on the upper reaches of Loch Fyne. In a relaxed country atmosphere, comfortable rooms are rented, including two family rooms, all with showers and toilets, phones, radios, and baby-listening facilities. Many units open onto a view of the loch.

In the pub and lounge, you can sample an array of malt whiskies and chat with the locals. Dining is provided by the Stables Restaurant, which occupies the thick stone premises that, during stagecoach days, housed the horses. Interconnected with the main building, it serves dinner only, every day from 7 to 8:30pm (last order). A three-course fixed-price dinner costs £11.50 ($17.30), and might include homemade soup, roast lamb with mint sauce, chicken breast stuffed with Brie and deep-fried, and fried filet of trout from Loch Fyne served with butter and almonds.

STRACHUR

If you have a car, you can explore this scenic part of Scotland from Cairndow (see above). Head east along the A83 until you reach the junction with the A815, at which point you proceed south along the western shore of Loch Fyne until you come to the famous inn at Creggans (see below), lying directly to the north of Strachur.

Five miles south from the Creggans Inn (see below) along the loch will take you to the old **Castle Lachlan** at Strathiachian, the 13th-century castle of the MacLachlan clan. Now in romantic ruins, it was besieged by the English in 1745. The MacLachlans were fervent Jacobites and played a major role in the uprising.

Where to Stay & Dine

THE CREGGANS INN, Strachur, Argyll PA27 8BX. Tel. 036986/279. Fax 036986/637. 20 rms (all with bath). TV TEL

$ **Rates** (including Scottish breakfast): £45 ($67.50) single; £49–£55 ($73.50–$82.50) double. AE, DC, MC, V. **Parking:** Free.

★ This famous inn commemorates the spot where Mary Queen of Scots is said to have disembarked from her ship in 1563 on her way through the Highlands. Painted white with green trim, and flanked with gardens, the inn rises across the A815 from the sea, exuding a sense of its very long history. The establishment is owned and managed by Sir Fitzroy and Lady Veronica MacLean, assisted by their son Charles. Lady MacLean is well known as the author of several bestselling cookbooks, most of which are for sale at the inn. Bedrooms are elegant and understated. Guests may use the upstairs sitting room and the garden-style lounge.

The in-house restaurant has a charcoal grill, which produces succulent versions of Aberdeen Angus steaks and lamb kebabs. You can also enjoy fresh jumbo prawns, venison, and the MacLeans' own version of smoked salmon. An à la carte dinner starts at £22 ($33), while tasty lunches are much cheaper. An in-house bar features pub lunches beside an open fire. Lunch is served daily from 12:30 to 2pm, and dinner is daily from 7:30 to 9:30pm. Reservations are a must.

4. THE KINTYRE PENINSULA

The longest peninsula in Scotland, Kintyre is more than 60 miles in length, with beautiful scenery, sleepy villages, and miles of sandy beaches. It is one of the most unspoiled areas of Scotland, owing perhaps to its isolation. Kintyre was ancient Dalriada, the first kingdom of the Scots.

If you drive all the way to the tip of Kintyre, you'll be only 12 miles from Ireland. Kintyre is joined to the mainland of Scotland by a narrow neck of land near the old port of Tarbert. The largest town on the peninsula is the port of Campbeltown, on the southeastern coast.

GETTING THERE   Kintyre is virtually an island unto itself. The most efficient way to travel is by private car if you want to explore the peninsula in any depth. From Glasgow, take the A82 up to the Loch Lomond side and cut across to Arrochar and go over the "Rest and Be Thankful" route to Inveraray (A83). Then cut down along Loch Fyne to Lochgilphead and continue on the A83 south to Tarbert (see below), which can be your gateway to Kintyre. You can take the A83 along the western coast or cut east at the junction of the B8001 and follow it across the peninsula to the B842, which you can take south to Carradale (see below). If your final target is Campbeltown, you can reach it by either the western shore (much faster and a better road) or the eastern shore.

From Glasgow, you can take buses to the peninsula (schedules vary seasonally). Inquire at the Western S.M.T. Co. Ltd., Travel Centre of Scottish Transport Group, Buchanan Street Bus Station, Glasgow (tel. 041/3327133). Loganair (tel. 041/8893181 in Glasgow for flight information) also makes two scheduled flights a day from the Glasgow Airport to Campbeltown, the chief town of Kintyre.

TARBERT

A sheltered harbor protects this fishing port and yachting center, on a narrow neck of land at the northern tip of the Kintyre Peninsula. It's between West Loch Tarbert and the head of herring-filled Loch Fyne, and has been called "the world's prettiest fishing port."

Tarbert means "drawboat" in Norse. It referred to a place where Vikings dragged their boats across land on rollers from one sea to another. In 1093 King Malcolm of Scotland and King Magnus Barelegs of Norway agreed that the Western Isles were to belong to Norway and the mainland to Scotland. An island was defined as anything a Viking ship could sail around. King Magnus proclaimed Kintyre an island by having his dragon ship dragged across the mile of dry land from West Loch Tarbert on the Atlantic to East Loch Tarbert on Loch Fyne. After the Vikings gave way, Kintyre came under the control of the Macdonald lordship of the Isles.

WHAT TO SEE & DO

The ancient **castle** at Tarbert dates from the 13th century, and was later extended by Robert the Bruce. The castle ruins are called "Bruce Castle." They're found on a hillock above the village on the south side of the bay. The oldest part still standing is a keep dating from the 13th century.

One of the major attractions of the peninsula is the remains of **Skipness Castle and Chapel,** at Skipness along the B8001, 10 miles south of Tarbert, opening onto Loch Fyne. The hamlet was once an old Norse village. The ruins of the ancient chapel and 13th-century castle look out onto the sounds of Kilbrannan and Bute. In its heyday it could control shipping along Loch Fyne. A five-story tower remains.

WHERE TO STAY

STONEFIELD CASTLE HOTEL, Tarbert, Argyll PA29 6YJ. Tel. 0880/ 820836. Fax 0880/820929. 33 rms (all with bath), 2 mini-suites. TV TEL

$ Rates (including half board): £41–£64 ($61.50–$96) single; £82–£128 ($123–$192) double; £148 ($222) mini-suite.

Occupying a commanding position, Stonefield Castle Hotel is a well-appointed hotel on 60 acres of wooded grounds and some of the most luxuriant gardens in Britain, lying on Loch Fyne, 2 miles outside Tarbert. The castle, with its turrets and steeply pitched roof, was built in the 19th century by the Campbells, whose laird collected the rarest plants found in every corner of the British Empire. The gardens today are believed to be one of the world's best repositories for more than 20 species of tree-size Himalayan rhododendrons, which in April offer a riot of color. Meals utilize produce from the hotel's own garden. In the kitchen the staff does its own baking. Dinner starts at £22.50 ($33.80). The hotel has many facilities, including a drawing room overlooking the loch, cocktail bar, library, outdoor swimming pool, sauna, even yacht anchorage. Book well in advance, as Stonefield has a large repeat clientele.

WEST LOCH HOTEL, Tarbert, Argyll PA29 6YF. Tel. 0880/820283. 7 rms (all with bath). TV

$ Rates (including Scottish breakfast): £25 ($37.50) single; £50 ($75) double. MC, V. **Parking:** Free. **Closed:** Jan.

Set in a rustically isolated position beside the A83, a mile southwest of town, in low-lying flatlands midway between the forest and the loch, this stone inn was built during the 1700s as a staging post for coaches and for farmers driving their cattle to market. Painted white with black trim, it contains two bars and a handful of open fireplaces and wood-burning stoves. Bedrooms are comfortable, often with views of the estuary and a sense of coziness.

The hotel contains a pub and a restaurant that specializes in local seafood and game, using only the best of local ingredients. In the bar, platters of food cost from £4 ($6) to £7 ($10.50). In the restaurant, à la carte dinners can be ordered, with appetizers costing £1.50 ($2.30) to £5 ($7.50), and main courses going for £8.50 ($12.80) to £13.50 ($20.30). The bar is open daily for food, but the restaurant is closed on Sunday and Monday.

WHERE TO DINE

ANCHORAGE SEAFOOD RESTAURANT, Harbour Street, Quayside. Tel. 0880/820881.

Cuisine: SCOTTISH/SEAFOOD. **Reservations:** Recommended.

$ Prices: Appetizers £1.65–£6.95 ($2.50–$10.40); main courses £7.95–£14.95 ($11.90–$22.40). MC, V.

Open: Dinner daily 5–10pm. **Closed:** Nov–Apr.

The Anchorage retains an unpretentious and natural emphasis despite its many culinary awards. Housed in a stone harborfront building that was originally built in the 1880s as a Customs House, it's run by David and Fiona Evamy. Both escaped from an industrial corner of northern England several years ago to better appreciate the great Scottish outdoors. They prepare fish, which David personally selects from local fishing vessels just hours before they're cooked and served.

Food is completely cholesterol-free, taking advantage of freshly prepared all-natural reductions of fish stock flavored with the freshest of local herbs. Examples of the food include king scallops poached in their natural juices with white wine and herbs, sautéed monkfish with Arran isle mustard and spring onion sauce, and preparations of very fresh Scottish oysters and mussels. A selection French and American of wines are available to accompany your fish.

CARRADALE

On the lusher eastern coast of Kintyre 14 miles north of Campbeltown, Carradale is a small town opening onto the shores of Kilbrannan Sound. People come here to walk and relax; they can also go pony trekking or windsurfing, or picnic in several scenic spots that have log tables and benches. Carradale Beach is equipped with facilities for water sports and for swimming, if you don't mind the chilly waters. The fishing fleet is anchored in the harbor and herring boats set out from here each night.

One beauty spot is the **Carradale House Gardens** (tel. 05833/234), off the B842, 12½ miles northeast of Campbeltown. From April to September, daily from 10am to 5:30pm, you can visit this walled garden from 1870. Because of its outstanding azaleas and rhododendrons, it is best seen in late April, May, and June. The remains of a fort built on an island can be reached by foot except at high tide. Admission is 75p ($1.10).

Those interested in historic sites can seek out the ruins of **Saddell Abbey** along the B842, 9 miles northwest of Campbeltown. This Cistercian abbey was built in the 12th century by one of the Lords of the Isles. The walls of the original building remain, and there are several sculptured grave slabs.

WHERE TO STAY & DINE

CARRADALE HOTEL, Carradale, Argyll PA28 6RY. Tel. 05833/223. Fax 05833/638. 17 rms (all with bath). TV
   $ Rates (including half board): £59 ($88.50) single; £98 ($147) double. MC, V.
   Parking: Free. **Closed:** Jan–Feb.
Built around 1800, the Carradale was the first hotel to open on the eastern side of the peninsula. Set in a garden in the center of this hamlet opposite the War Memorial, the hotel offers a comfortable high-ceilinged dining room, a lounge bar serving pub meals, and squash courts. Rooms are simple but pleasantly furnished. Fresh local produce, often from the hotel's own garden, is used in the kitchen.

CAMPBELTOWN

This is a fishing port and a resort with a shingle beach at the southern tip of the Kintyre Peninsula, 176 miles northwest of Edinburgh and 135 miles northwest of Glasgow. Popularly known as the "wee toon," Campbeltown has long been linked with fishing.

Davaar Island, in Campbeltown Loch, is accessible at low tide by those willing to cross the Dhorlin, a half-mile run of shingle-paved causeway; boat trips are also possible. Once on the island, you can visit a crucifixion cave painting, work of Archibald MacKinnon, a local resident, painted in 1887. It takes about an hour and a half to walk around this tidal island, with its natural rock gardens.

On the quayside in the heart of town is the **Campbeltown Cross,** which dates from the 14th century. This Celtic cross is considered the finest piece of carving from the Middle Ages left in Kintyre.

The **tourist information office** is at MacKinnon House, The Pier (tel. 0586/52056).

WHERE TO STAY & DINE

**ARGYLL ARMS HOTEL, Main Street, Campbeltown, Argyll PA28 6AB.
   Tel. 0586/553431.** Fax 0586/553594. 30 rms (14 with bath). TV TEL
   $ Rates (including Scottish breakfast): £27 ($40.50) single without bath, £31 ($46.50) single with bath; £45–£48 ($67.50–$72) double without bath, £48–£52

($72–$78) double with bath. DC, MC, V. **Parking:** Free.

This imposing stone building was once owned by the Duke of Argyll, who maintained a suite on the second floor even after he sold it as a hotel. It still has an aura of Victorian opulence in its public rooms, although bedrooms are modernized.

The Farmers Bar is a convivial cubbyhole near the entrance. The Cocktail Bar is more sedately formal. Yet a third bar is called Wee Toon. The hotel's restaurant serves lunch and dinner daily, with a three-course shopper's lunch going for £4.95 ($7.40). À la carte dinners specialize in fish fresh from the quay and other local produce. A complete meal goes for £16 ($24) and up.

SEAFIELD HOTEL, Kilkerran Road, Campbeltown, Argyll PA28 6JL. Tel. 0586/554385. 9 rms (all with shower). TV TEL
$ Rates (including Scottish breakfast): £29.95 ($44.90) single; £50 ($75) double. MC, V. **Parking:** Free.

Built around 1900, this white-painted stone house rises from a position across the road from the rocky coastline of a saltwater estuary half a mile southeast of town, beside the Campbeltown Loch. Set in a neighborhood of residential houses, it contains a street-level pub where bar meals are served for around £7 ($10.50) each. The simple but comfortable bedrooms contain curtains and carpeting, and tea-making facilities. There's a garden in back of the house with flowers, tables, and chairs, where clients of the pub can spill outdoors during warm weather.

AN EXCURSION TO SOUTHEND & THE MULL OF KINTYRE

Some 10 miles south of Campbeltown, the village of Southend stands across from the Mull of Kintyre. Three buses a day run from Campbeltown to Southend Monday through Saturday. It has sandy beaches, a golf course, and views across the sea to the Island of Sanda and to Ireland. Legend has it that footprints that can be seen here, imprinted on a rock near the ruin of an old chapel, mark the spot where St. Columba first set foot on Scottish soil. Other historians suggest that the footprints mark the spot where ancient kings were crowned.

Visitors can also go to **Dunaverty Rock,** called "Blood Rock" by the locals, once a MacDonald stronghold, known as Dunaverty Castle. It was the scene in 1647 of a great massacre, where some 300 citizens lost their lives.

Visitors also drive down from Campbeltown, a distance of 11 miles, to see the **Mull of Kintyre.** From Southend you can take a narrow road until you reach the "gap." From there, you walk down to the lighthouse. This is one of the wildest and most remote parts of the peninsula, and it is its desolation that appeals to visitors. The Mull of Kintyre lies only 13 miles from Ireland. When local resident Paul McCartney made it the subject of a song, hundreds of fans flocked to the area.

5. THE ISLE OF ARRAN

Brodick: 74 miles W of Edinburgh, 29 miles W of Glasgow

GETTING THERE By Train New high-speed electric trains operate from Glasgow Central direct to Ardrossan Harbour, taking 1 hour (for 24-hour rail inquiries in Glasgow, call 041/2042844). At Ardrossan you must cross by ferry to Arran (see below), arriving in Brodick on the east coast.

By Car From Glasgow, head southwest along the A737 until you reach the port of Ardrossan, where you can board a car-ferry.

By Ferry Ferries making the 30-minute crossing operate from Ardrossan to Brodick, Arran's major town on the eastern shore. In summer a small ferry runs between Lochranza in the north of Arran across to Claonaig in Argyll, providing a gateway to the Highlands and a visit to Kintyre. For information about ferry departures (which change seasonally) call **Caledonian MacBrayne** (tel. 0475/34531) at the ferry terminal in Gourock.

ESSENTIALS The **Arran Tourist Information Office** is at The Pier, Brodick (tel. 0770/302140). The **telephone area code** is 0770.

At the mouth of the Firth of Clyde, this island is often described as "Scotland in miniature," because of its wild and varied scenery—the glens, moors, lochs, sandy bays, and rocky coasts that have made the country famous. Once on Arran, buses will take you to various villages, each with its own character. A coast road, 60 miles long, runs the length of the island.

WHAT TO SEE & DO

Arran has some splendid mountain scenery, notably the conical peak of **Goatfell** in the north, reaching a height of 2,866 feet, called "the mountain of the winds." Arran is also filled with beautiful glens, especially **Glen Sannox** in the northeast and **Glen Rosa,** directly north of Brodick. The island is only 25 miles long, 10 miles wide, and can be seen in 1 day.

Students of geology flock to Arran to study igneous rocks of the Tertiary Age. Cairns and standing stones at Tormore intrigue archeologists as well.

After the ferry docks at Brodick, you may want to head for Arran's major sight, ✪ **Brodick Castle** (tel. 0770/302202), 1½ miles north of the Brodick pierhead. The historic home of the dukes of Hamilton, the castle dates from the 13th century and contains superb silver, antiques, portraits, and objets d'art. Some castle or other has stood on this site since about the 5th century, when the Dalriad Irish, a Celtic tribe, came here and founded their kingdom. The castle is the property of the National Trust for Scotland. It is open in April after Easter on Monday, Wednesday, and Saturday from 1 to 5pm; May through September, daily from 1 to 5pm. The award-winning gardens and the Country Park are open daily from 10am to 5pm. Admission to both the castle and gardens is £3 ($4.50) for adults, £2 ($3) for children.

South from Brodick lies the village and holiday resort of **Lamlash,** opening onto Lamlash Bay. From here a ferry takes visitors over to **Holy Island** with its 1,000-foot peak. A disciple of St. Columba founded a church on this island.

In the north, **Lochranza** is a village with a unique appeal. It opens onto a bay of pebbles and sand, and in the background lie the ruins of a castle that reputedly was the hunting seat of Robert the Bruce.

WHERE TO STAY & DINE

BRODICK

AUCHRANNIE COUNTRY HOUSE HOTEL, Auchrannie Rd., Brodick, Isle of Arran KA27 8BZ. Tel. 0770/302234. Fax 0770/302812. 28 rms (all with bath). TV TEL

$ Rates (including half board): £50–£80 ($75–$120) per person. MC, V. **Parking:** Free.

✪ Acclaimed as the finest dining or accommodation choice on the island, this period mansion was once the house of the dowager duchess of Hamilton. In its pristine glory, it stands in 6 acres of landscaped gardens and woods, lying about a mile from the Brodick ferry terminal. A hotel of charm and character, it also features the best resort facilities on the island. The people who restored this Victorian period piece did so with taste and imagination. Rooms in the extended new wing are the most comfortable, but each accommodation is furnished with taste, employing select fabrics and decorative accessories.

Dining/Entertainment: Guests enjoy drinks in the cocktail bar or sun lounge before heading for the Garden Restaurant, offering a table d'hôte menu, the finest in Arran. The best of fresh local produce is used. The chef's greatest skill is in the preparation of West Coast seafood. A "Taste of Scotland" is evident in many of the dishes. Outside guests should reserve a table; meals cost from £20 ($30). You can also enjoy Brambles Bistro, offering a wide range of snacks and tasty food throughout the day and evening.

Services: Room service, babysitting, laundry.

Facilities: Indoor pool, turbo spa, Turkish bath, sauna, solarium, snooker room, beauty salon, boutique.

KILMICHAEL COUNTRY HOUSE HOTEL, Glen Cloy by Brodick, Isle of Arran KA27 8BY. Tel. 0770/302219. 7 rms (all with bath). TV **Directions:** Lies 1 mile by the Shore Road (take a left turn opposite the Golf Club).

$ **Rates** (including Scottish breakfast): £45 ($67.50) single; £75 ($112.50) double. No credit cards.

Perhaps the most scenically located house on the island, the Kilmichael is an "oasis of tranquility," a favorite phrase most guests use. It, along with the previously previewed Auchrannie Country House, have set new standards of catering on Arran. Standing on its own extensive grounds, it is said to be the oldest house on the island, perhaps in former days a stamping ground for Robert the Bruce. One room is supposedly haunted.

The bathrooms are beautifully appointed, as are the well-furnished bedrooms. A combination of the tasteful new and the antique are used throughout. There is an aura of gentility, as reflected by the log fires and the fresh flowers from the garden. Most important, the staff is helpful, courteous, and welcoming.

The food is also worthy, using local Scottish produce whenever possible. International dishes are also featured. Fine wines and an attention to detail go into every dinner, costing £16.50 ($24.80) per person.

LAMASH

GLENISLE HOTEL, Shore Rd., Lamlash, Isle of Arran KA27 8LS. Tel. 0770/600559. 13 rms (all with bath). TV TEL **Bus:** Whiting bus from Brodick.

$ **Rates** (including Scottish breakfast): £47 ($70.50) single; £65 ($97.50) double. MC, V. **Parking:** Free.

It is said to be one of the oldest buildings in the village, but no one knows its age or even the century of its construction. Across the road from the waterfront, in the heart of the village, the well-kept gardens of this white-sided country B&B, with a view across the bay to the Holy Isle, have flowerbeds and tall old trees. A reception lounge, a water-view dining room, and a lounge where drinks are available are brightly and cheerfully decorated. Each of the bedrooms has flowered curtains, a radio, electric blankets, tea and coffee makers, and room call. A three-course fixed-price dinner costs £9.50 ($14.30).

CARRAIG MHOR, Lamlash, Isle of Arran KA27 8LS. Tel. 0770/600453. **Cuisine:** CONTINENTAL. **Reservations:** Recommended. **Bus:** Whiting bus from Brodick.

$ **Prices:** Appetizers £3.50–£6 ($5.30–$9); main courses £10–£12 ($15–$18). MC, V.

Open: Dinner only, daily 7–9:30pm. **Closed:** 2 weeks in Nov and 2 weeks in Feb (dates vary); Sun in summer.

Carraig Mhor, in a pebbledash 1700s cottage, serves some of the finest food on the island, and its dinners are imaginatively prepared and beautifully presented (but you should call ahead for a reservation). This modernized cottage, to which you are welcomed by Austrian-born Peter Albrich and his British wife, Penny, stands in the center of the village overlooking the water. The chef, who has had worldwide experience, makes extensive use of local produce—in particular, seafood and game. Lunches are mainly seafood. All bread and ice creams, among other offerings, are homemade on the premises. In the evening, there is an extensive à la carte menu available.

Specialties include such dishes as lightly grilled scallops served with lemon rice and a sauce of yellow split peas, chervil, and butter; or grilled breast of duck with sultanas, apple latkis, and a sauce of fresh black currants and marjoram. They smoke their own salmon and pork on the premises.

WHITING BAY

GRANGE HOUSE HOTEL, Whiting Bay, Isle of Arran KA27 8QH. Tel. 07707/263. 9 rms (7 with bath or shower). TV
$ Rates (including Scottish breakfast): £20 ($30) single without bath, £27.50 ($41.30) single with bath; £40 ($60) double without bath, £55 ($82.50) double with bath. No credit cards. **Parking:** Free.

Only 100 yards from the sea, opening onto views across the Firth of Clyde, this country-house hotel is operated by Janet and Clive Hughes. Both of them take a personal interest in their guests (Janet's the chef), and both have an extensive background in catering. A stone-built, gabled house, standing on landscaped grounds, Grange House offers tastefully furnished and traditionally styled bedrooms. Each unit is unique, although Victoriana predominates. Some of the rooms can be arranged to have family privacy. Eight open onto views of Holy Isle and the Ayrshire coastline. One downstairs bedroom is suitable for the disabled, and the hotel also has a sauna and a spa bath.

ROYAL HOTEL, Whiting Bay, Isle of Arran KA27 8PZ. Tel. 07707/286. 5 rms (all with bath). TV TEL **Bus:** Whiting bus from Brodick.
$ Rates (including Scottish breakfast): £25 ($37.50) single; £50 ($75) double. No credit cards. **Parking:** Free. **Closed:** Nov–Mar.

This pleasingly proportioned granite house, whose upper stories have been sheathed in coats of white stucco, was originally built in 1895 as one of the first hotels on Arran. True to its original function as a temperance hotel, it still does not serve alcohol, although dinner guests can bring bottles of wine or beer into the dining room to consume with their meals. Three-course dinners cost £10 ($15) each. Guests enjoy a vista over the bay and its tidal flats from some of the bedrooms. Although all the rooms are priced the same, one contains a four-poster bed and lots of chintz, while another has a small sitting room adjacent to its sleeping area. The hotel is in the center of the village beside the coastal road.

KILDONAN

KILDONANA HOTEL, Kildonan, Isle of Arran, KA27 8SE. Tel. 0770/820207. 22 rms (6 with bath).
$ Rates (including Scottish breakfast): £18 ($27) single without bath, £22 ($33) single with bath, £36 ($54) double without bath, £44 ($66) double with bath. No credit cards. **Parking:** Free.

Originally built as an inn in 1760, with a newer section added in 1928, this hotel rises a few steps from the best beach on the island. Designed in the Scottish farmhouse style, it has a slate roof, white-painted stone walls, and ample views of sea birds and gray seals basking on the rocks of Pladda Island opposite the hotel. The hotel is owned by Maurice Deighton, his wife, Audrey, their sons, and their daughters-in-law, any of whom you're likely to find cooking, tending one of the two bars, or maintaining the panoramic bedrooms. Beneath six large chandeliers, the spacious dining room presents three-course dinners for £9 ($13.50) to £17 ($25.50). (A specialty is fresh crab or lobster salad, made from freshly netted shellfish caught by one of the Deighton sons, who works as a fisherman.) A crowd of locals is likely to compete in a friendly fashion over the dartboard and billiards tables in the establishment's pub. The staff can arrange such diversions as putting, boating, fishing, table tennis, waterskiing, and scuba diving.

LAGG

LAGG HOTEL, Lagg near Kilmory, Isle of Arran KA27 8PH. Tel. 0770/870255. 17 rms (all with bath).
$ Rates (including half board): £45 ($67.50) single; £95 ($142.50) double. No credit cards. **Parking:** Free. **Closed:** Late Oct to mid-Mar.

Set beside the A841, half a mile south of Kilmory and within half a mile of the sea, in a sheltered hollow where some kind of inn has stood since 1791, this pleasantly embellished inn is popular within the island for its dining facilities. Ronald Stewart and his family maintain the gardens that stretch beside the rocky stream that adjoins the 16-acre property. If the weather is sunny, you might enjoy tea on the lawn under the shade of the palm trees, which seem to thrive in this mild micro-climate. In cooler weather, visitors are likely to be greeted by a log fire blazing in one of the cozy cocktail lounges. Nonresidents are welcome to dine here, although it's wise to phone in advance. Most residents dine within the hotel dining room on the half-board plan. On Friday and Saturday nights only, this becomes a carvery where dinners cost from £15 ($22.50) per person for nonresidents. There is also The Wishing Well Restaurant, an à la carte restaurant on the premises. Bedrooms are artfully decorated with flowering fabrics and solidly traditional furniture.

BLACKWATERFOOT

KINLOCH HOTEL, Blackwaterfoot, Isle of Arran KA27 8ET. Tel. 0770/ 860444. Fax 0770/860447. 49 rms (all with bath) TV TEL **Bus:** Blackwaterfoot bus from Brodick.

$ Rates (including dinner and Scottish breakfast): £55 ($82.50) single; £110 ($165) double. AE, DC, MC, V. **Parking:** Free.

The result of two Victorian buildings that were joined together, this hotel appears deceptively small from the road in front. It's actually the largest building in the hamlet that contains it, set behind a cream-colored stone façade, with a contemporary wing jutting out along the coast. Most of the double rooms have sea views, while singles tend to look out over the gardens in back. On the premises are a sauna, a heated indoor swimming pool, and a large dining room. Bedrooms are comfortable and conservative, each with a radio, intercom, and tea-making facilities.

LOCHRANZA

KINCARDINE LODGE HOTEL, Lochranza, Isle of Arran KA27 8HL. Tel. 077083/267. 6 rms (3 with bath or shower).

$ Rates (including Scottish breakfast): £15 ($22.50) single without bath, £17 ($25.50) single with bath; £30 ($45) double without bath, £34 ($51) double with bath. Half board: £23–£25 ($34.50–$37.50) per person. No credit cards. **Parking:** Free. **Closed:** Oct–Mar.

This place across the street from the waterfront in the hamlet's center, has a well-maintained garden whose fish pond glistens just below the branches of a copper-colored beech. The staff sets out lawn furniture in summer beside the holly trees and rhododendrons, where guests are invited to contemplate the view of the water and the village's ruined castle. The half-timbered lodge was built in 1909. Gladys and Bob Brown, charming hoteliers fond of music and the organ, rent pleasantly furnished bedrooms. In good weather tea is served on the lawn, followed by a tasty dinner prepared with fresh produce. A three-course fixed-price dinner costs £8 ($12).

6. THE ISLE OF GIGHA

3 miles W of Kintyre's western coast

GETTING THERE   By Ferry   Take a ferry for Gigha from Tayinloan, which lies halfway up the west coast of Kintyre. Sailings are daily and take about 20 minutes, depositing you at Ardminish, the main hamlet on Gigha. For ferry times, phone 05835/254.

ESSENTIALS   There is no local tourist office. Ask at Campbeltown on the Kintyre Peninsula (see above). Since you'll arrive most likely without a car, and there is no local bus service, you can either walk or call a taxi at 05835/251. The **telephone area code** is 05835.

One of the southern Hebrides, the 6-mile-long Isle of Gigha is often called "sacred" and "legendary." Little changed over the centuries, it is the innermost island of the Hebrides, lying 3 miles off the Kintyre Peninsula's west coast.

WHAT TO SEE & DO

Gigha is visited mainly by those wishing to explore its famous gardens, arguably the finest in Scotland. The **✪ Achamore House Gardens** (tel. 05835/268), a mile from the ferry dock at Ardminish, contain roses, hydrangeas, rhododendrons, camellias, and azaleas, among other flowering plants. They are open year-round, daily from 9am to dusk, charging an admission of £2 ($3) for adults and £1 ($1.50) for children. Occupying a 50-acre site, they were the creation of the late Sir James Horlick, who was considered one of the great gardeners of the world. The house is not open to the public.

The island has a rich Viking past. Cairns and ruins still remain. The Vikings stored their loot here after plundering the west coast of Scotland. **Creag Bhan,** the highest hill, rises more than 330 feet. From the top you can look out onto the islands of Islay and Jura as well as Kintyre; on a clear day you can also see Ireland. The **Ogham Stone** is always sought out by those interested in antiquity. It is one of only two standing stones in the Hebrides that bears Ogham inscription, a form of script used in the Scottish kingdom of Dalriada. High on a ridge overlooking the village of Ardminish are the ruins of the **Church of Kilchattan,** dating back to the 13th century.

WHERE TO STAY & DINE

GIGHA HOTEL/THE BOATHOUSE, Ardminish, Isle of Gigha, Argyll PA41 7AD. Tel. 05835/254. Fax 05835/282. 13 rms (11 with bath).

$ Rates (including half board): £48.50 ($72.80) single without bath, £48–£52 ($72–$78) single with bath; £90 ($135) double without bath, £96 ($144) double with bath. MC, V. **Parking:** Free.

✪ Rising from a lonely and windswept position devoid of any vegetation except low shrubs and lichens, this white-painted stone house originally built in the 1700s as a farmhouse is within a 5-minute walk from the island's only ferryboat landing. Today it contains the island's only pub, one of its two restaurants, and its only overnight accommodations. The polite staff rents small but cozy and comfortable bedrooms, and serves fixed-price dinners every night between 7 and 9pm. Nonresidents of the hotel often arrive for four-course dinners priced at £18.50 ($27.80). Bar lunches cost around £6 ($9).

Under the same administration is the Boathouse Restaurant, which lies a few steps from the ferryboat pier. Open between April and September, daily from 10am to 8pm, it occupies the stone-sided premises of a 200-year-old building originally intended to store small boats, fishermen's gear, and netting. Appetizers cost £1.40 ($2.10) to £5.90 ($8.90), main dishes run £4 ($6) to £15 ($22.50), and a pot of afternoon coffee or tea goes for around £1.75 ($2.60).

7. THE ISLE OF ISLAY

16 miles W of the Kintyre Peninsula, ¾ mile SW of Jura

GETTING THERE By Ferry MacBrayne steamers operate daily service to Islay—you leave West Tarbert on the Kintyre Peninsula, arriving in Port Askaig on Islay in about 2 hours. There is also service to Port Ellen. For information about ferry departures, call Caledonian MacBrayne, the ferry terminal (tel. 0475/34531), at Gourock.

ESSENTIALS The **tourist information office** is at Bowmore, The Square (tel. 049681/254). The **telephone area code** is 049681.

slay is the southernmost island of the Inner Hebrides, separated only by a narrow sound from Jura. At its maximum, Islay is only 20 miles wide and 25 miles long. Called "the Queen of the Hebrides," it is a peaceful unspoiled island of moors, salmon-filled lochs, sandy bays, and wild rocky cliffs. Islay (pronounced *"eye*-lay") is an island of great beauty.

WHAT TO SEE & DO

Near Port Charlotte are the graves of the U.S. seamen and army troops who lost their lives in 1918 when their carriers, the *Tuscania* and *Otranto,* were torpedoed off the shores of Islay. There's a memorial tower on the Mull of Oa, 8 miles from Port Ellen.

The island is noted for its distilleries producing single-malt Highland whiskies by the antiquated pot-still method. Of these, **Laphroaig Distillery,** 1½ miles along the road from Ardbeg to Port Ellen (tel. 0496/2418), allows guided tours. You should call first for an appointment.

The island's capital is **Bowmore,** on the coast across from Port Askaig. There you can see a fascinating Round Church—no corners for the devil to hide in. But the most important town is **Port Ellen,** on the south coast, a holiday and golfing resort, Islay's principal port. The 18-hole Machrie golf course is 3 miles from Port Ellen.

The ancient seat of the lords of the Isles, the ruins of two castles, and several Celtic crosses can be seen. The ancient **Kildalton Crosses** are about 7½ miles northeast of Port Ellen. In the Kildalton churchyard, they are considered two of the finest Celtic crosses in Scotland. The ruins of the 14th-century fortress, **Dunyvaig Castle,** are just south of Kildalton.

In the southwestern part of Islay in Port Charlotte, the **Museum of Islay Life** (tel. 049685/358) has a wide collection of island artifacts, ranging from unrecorded times to the present day. The museum is open year-round, Monday through Saturday from 10am to 5pm and on Sunday from 2 to 5pm. Admission is £1.20 ($1.80) for adults, 60p (90¢) for children. The Portnahaven bus from Bowmore stops here.

Loch Gruinart cuts into the northern part of Islay. As the winter home for wild geese, it has attracted birdwatchers for decades. In 1984 the 3,000 acres of moors and farmland around the loch were turned into the **Loch Gruinart Nature Reserve.**

At Bridgend, you can visit the **Islay Woollen Mill** (tel. 049681/563), which has been in business for more than a century. They make a wide range of country tweeds and accessories. Their mill shop is open Monday through Saturday from 10am to 5:30pm. They sell tastefully designed Shetland wool ties, mufflers, Jacob mufflers and ties, flat caps, travel rugs, and scarves, among many other items.

WHERE TO STAY & DINE

PORT ASKAIG HOTEL, along A846 at ferry crossing to Jura, Port Askaig, Isle of Islay, Argyll PA46 7RD. Tel. 049684/245. Fax 049684/295. 9 rms (4 with bath). TV

$ Rates (including Scottish breakfast and five-course dinner): £48 ($72) single without bath, £51 ($76.50) single with bath; £84 ($126) double without bath, £96 ($144) double with bath. No credit cards. **Parking:** Free.

This is a genuine old island inn, dating from the 18th century but built on the site of an even older inn. It stands on the Sound of Islay overlooking the pier and offers island hospitality and Scottish fare. The hotel is a favorite of anglers on Islay, and the bar at the inn is popular with local fishermen. All its well-appointed bedrooms have radios and hot-beverage facilities, as well as central heating.

BRIDGEND HOTEL, Bridgend, Isle of Islay, Argyll PA44 7PF. Tel. 049681/212. Fax 049681/673. 10 rms (all with bath). TV TEL

$ Rates (including Scottish breakfast): £35.50 ($53.30) single; £71 ($106.50) double. No credit cards. **Parking:** Free.

Victorian spires cap the slate-covered roofs and roses creep up the stone and stucco walls. The hotel forms part of a complex that includes a roadside barn and one of the most beautiful flower and vegetable gardens in Islay. This is one of the oldest hotels on Islay, with somber charm and country pleasures. Guests enjoy drinks beside open fireplaces in the Victorian cocktail lounge and the rustic pub, where locals gather after a day in the surrounding fields. Many nonresidents opt for a dinner, priced at £17.50 ($26.30) to £19.50 ($29.30) in the hotel's high-ceilinged dining room. Bedrooms are comfortably and conservatively furnished.

8. THE ISLE OF JURA

¾ mile E of Islay

GETTING THERE **By Ferry** From Kennacraig (West Loch Tarbert), you can go to Port Askaig or Port Ellen on Islay (see above) where you have to take a second ferry from Port Askaig to Feolin on Jura. For information on departures, call Caledonian MacBrayne at Kennacraig (tel. 088073/253). Car space must be booked in advance.

ESSENTIALS See Isle of Islay (above) for tourist information. The **telephone area code** is 049682.

This is the fourth-largest island in the Inner Hebrides, 27 miles long and varying from 2 to 8 miles in breadth. It perhaps takes its name from the Norse *jura,* meaning "deer island." The red deer on Jura outnumber the people by about 20 to 1. At 4 feet high, the deer are the largest wild animals roaming Scotland. The hearty islanders number only about 250 brave souls, and most of them live along the east coast. The west coast is virtually uninhabited. Jura is relatively little known or explored. Its mountains, soaring cliffs, snug coves, and moors make it an inviting place to be—and it's not at all crowded. The island has actually suffered a drastic loss of population.

The capital, **Craighouse,** is hardly more than a hamlet. From Islay, you can take a 5-minute ferry ride to Jura from Port Askaig, docking at the Feolin Ferry berth.

The island's landscape is dominated by the **Paps of Jura,** that reach a peak of 2,571 feet at Beinn-an-Oir. An arm of the sea, **Loch Tarbert** nearly divides the island, cutting into it for nearly 6 miles.

The square tower of **Claig Castle,** now in ruins, was the stronghold of the MacDonalds until they were subdued by the Campbells in the 17th century.

Literary historians know that George Orwell lived on Jura in the bitter postwar winters of 1946 and 1947. Even though a sick man, he was plotting his masterpiece *1984,* a satire on modern politics, which was published in 1949. He almost lost his life when he and his adopted son ventured too close to the whirlpool in the Gulf of Corryvreckan. They were saved by local fishermen, and he went on to finish his masterwork, only to die in London of tuberculosis in 1950.

WHERE TO STAY & DINE

JURA, Craighouse, Isle of Jura, Argyll PA60 7XU. Tel. 049682/243. 17 rms (11 with bath), 1 suite. **Transportation:** The hotel will pick up visitors arriving without cars at the ferryboat jetty at Feolin, across from Port Askaig on Islay.

$ Rates (including Scottish breakfast): £26.50 ($39.80) single without bath, £30 ($45) single with bath; £53 ($79.50) double without bath, £60 ($90) double with bath; £65 ($97.50) suite for two. AE, DC, MC, V. **Parking:** Free. **Closed:** 2 weeks at Christmas and New Year's.

The only hotel on the island, the Jura has loyal guests that return year after year. It's a sprawling, gray-walled building near the center of the hamlet (Craighouse lies east of Feolin along the coast). Sections of the building date from the 1600s, but what you see today was built in 1956. Kenya-born Fiona Walton and her husband, Steve, are the managing directors. They personally conduct special excursions via Land Rover and motorboat to such island curiosities as the Corryvreckan whirlpool. The dining room's specialty is Jura-bred venison. A fixed-price dinner goes for £15.50 ($23.30).

CHAPTER 7

FIFE & THE CENTRAL HIGHLANDS

- **WHAT'S SPECIAL ABOUT FIFE & THE CENTRAL HIGHLANDS**
- **1. DUNFERMLINE**
- **2. FALKLAND**
- **3. THE EAST NEUK**
- **4. ST. ANDREWS**
- **5. STIRLING**
- **6. DUNBLANE**
- **7. DOUNE**
- **8. CALLANDER**
- **9. ABERFOYLE**
- **10. ALONG LOCH LOMOND**

North of Forth from Edinburgh, the county of Fife still likes to call itself a "kingdom." Its name, even today, suggests the romantic episodes and pageantry during the reign of the early Stuart kings. Some 14 of Scotland's 66 royal burghs lay within this shire. Many of the former royal palaces and castles, either restored or in colorful ruins, can be visited today.

Many sections of the Central Highlands, which rank with Fife in tourist interest, lie on the doorsteps of both Edinburgh and Glasgow. Some of the most visited targets include Stirling, Loch Lomond, and the Trossachs.

The Trossachs is the collective name given to that wild Highland area east and northeast of Loch Lomond. Both **the Trossachs** and Loch Lomond are said to contain Scotland's finest scenery in moor, mountain, and loch. The area is famed in history and romance ever since Sir Walter Scott's vivid descriptive passages in *The Lady of the Lake* and *Rob Roy*.

Legendary **Loch Lomond** is the largest and most beautiful of Scottish lakes and famed for its "bonnie banks" of the song. At Balloch in the south, the lake is a Lowland loch of gentle hills and islands. But as it moves north, the loch changes to a narrow lake of Highland character, with moody cloud formations and rugged steep hillsides.

SEEING FIFE & THE CENTRAL HIGHLANDS

GETTING THERE

Either Glasgow or Edinburgh can be your gateway if you're arriving by air to explore Fife and the Central Highlands. Dumfermline and St. Andrews are easily reached by rail from Edinburgh. St. Andrews also has good bus connections with Edinburgh. By car, the main motorway is the M9, the express highway that starts on the western outskirts of Edinburgh and is linked to the M80 from Glasgow. The M9 passes close to Stirling. The M90, reached by crossing the Forth Road Bridge, will take you north into the Fife region.

Stirling is the major rail center for the region, with stops at such places as Dunblane, and much of Loch Lomond has rail connections. Towns and some villages have bus service, but connections are too limited or infrequent for the hurried visitor. For bus connections, Stirling is the central point.

However, much of the Trossachs needs to be explored by car, and your best bet for

WHAT'S SPECIAL ABOUT FIFE & THE CENTRAL HIGHLANDS

Great Towns/Villages

- ☐ St. Andrews, called the "Oxford of Scotland" and the capital of golf, opening onto the North Sea.
- ☐ East Neuk Villages, the most unspoiled villages of eastern Scotland.
- ☐ Dunfermline, an ancient town that was once the capital of Scotland, birthplace of Andrew Carnegie.
- ☐ Culross, renovated by the Scottish National Trust, considered the single most beautiful village in Scotland.
- ☐ Stirling, dominated by its castle, standing at the crossroads of central Scotland.
- ☐ Dunblane, a small city on the banks of Allan Water, known for its 13th-century cathedral.
- ☐ Callander, the best base for exploring the Trossachs and Loch Katrine, Loch Achray, and Loch Venachar.

Ace Attractions

- ☐ Loch Lomond, largest of Scottish lochs, whose "bonnie, bonnie banks" encase a lake fed by 10 rivers.
- ☐ The Trossachs, great beauty spot of Scotland, famed in history and romance for its scenery of moor, mountain, and lake.
- ☐ Queen Elizabeth Forest Park, between the eastern shore of Loch Lomond and the Trossachs, some 45,000 acres of moor, trees, and mountain.

Cathedrals and Abbeys

- ☐ St. Andrews Cathedral and Priory, constructed in the Romanesque and Gothic styles, dating from the 1160s.
- ☐ Dunfermline Abbey, burial place of 22 royal personages, including Queen Margaret and King Robert the Bruce.
- ☐ Dunblane Cathedral, in the 13th-century Gothic style, filled with historic relics.
- ☐ Culross Abbey, a Cistercian monastery founded in 1217, with parts of the original nave still intact.

Ancient Monuments

- ☐ Stirling Castle, dating from the Middle Ages, where Mary Queen of Scots lived as an infant monarch.

Palaces and Gardens

- ☐ Falkland Palace and Gardens, favorite seat of the Scottish court—Mary Queen of Scots came here for "hunting and hawking"; James V, to die.

Sports

- ☐ The historic sea town of St. Andrews, home of golf in Great Britain, with four celebrated courses: the Old, the New, the Jubilee, and the Eden.

discovering the hidden villages and scenic lochside roads of the region or the fishing villages of East Neuk is to rent a car and drive.

SUGGESTED ITINERARY

Day 1: Leave Edinburgh and head for a morning's visit to Dunfermline, crossing the Forth Road Bridge. After lunch, head northeast along the coastal route to see the villages of East Neuk, and select one for an overnight stopover, perhaps Anstruther.

Day 2: Continue along the coast, following the A917 until you reach St. Andrews, which deserves at least an overnight stopover. If you're a serious golfer, you'll want to anchor here for several days.

Day 3: From St. Andrews, head west to Stirling to see its castle and many attractions. Plan to overnight there.

Day 4: Go north to Dunblane to see its cathedral in the morning, then spend the rest of the day exploring nearby Doune, with its castle and car museum. Overnight in Doune.

Day 5: Continue northwest to Callander for the night and save time to explore its scenic environs, including Leny Park and Leny Falls.

Day 6: On your way southwest, swing through Aberfoyle before spending a night at one of the villages of Loch Lomond. (Those with another night could spend it well seeing both the western and eastern shores of Loch Lomond.)

1. DUNFERMLINE

14 miles NW of Edinburgh, 39 miles NE of Glasglow, 52 miles SW of Dundee

GETTING THERE By Train   Dunfermline is a stop along the main rail route from London via Edinburgh to Dundee, which means that it has frequent connecotions to the Scottish capital. For rail schedules and fares, call 031/5562451 in Edinburgh.

By Bus   From its station at St. Andrews Square in Edinburgh, Eastern Scottish Omnibuses (tel. 031/5568464 for information) operates frequent service to Dunfermline.

By Car   From Edinburgh, take the A90 west, cross the Forth Road Bridge, and follow the signs north to the center of Dunfermline.

ESSENTIALS   A summer-only **tourist information booth** is found at Abbot House Maygate (tel. 0383/720999). The **telephone area code** is 0383.

This ancient town was once the capital of Scotland. It is easily reached by the Forth Road Bridge, which was opened by Queen Elizabeth II in 1964.

WHAT TO SEE & DO

DUNFERMLINE ABBEY AND PALACE, St. Margaret's Drive. Tel. 0383/ 2443101.

The abbey is on the site of two earlier structures, a Celtic church and an 11th-century house of worship dedicated to the Holy Trinity, under the auspices of Queen Margaret (later St. Margaret). Culdee Church, dating to the 5th and 6th centuries, was rebuilt in 1072. Traces of both buildings are visible beneath gratings in the floor of the old nave. In 1150 the church was replaced with a large abbey, the nave of which remains, an example of Norman architecture. Later, St. Margaret's shrine, the northwest baptismal porch, the spire on the northwest tower, and the flying buttresses were added. While Dunfermline was the capital of Scotland, 22 royal personages were buried in the abbey. However, the only visible memorial or burial places known are those of Queen Margaret and King Robert the Bruce, whose tomb lies beneath the pulpit.

The once royal palace of Dunfermline stands adjacent to the abbey. The palace witnessed the birth of King Charles I and James I. The last king to reside here was Charles II in 1651. But, today, only the southwest wall remains of this once gargantuan edifice.

Admission: £1.20 ($1.80) adults, 60p children.

Open: Apr–Sept, Mon–Sat 9:30am–5pm, Sun 2–5pm; Oct–Mar, Mon–Wed, Fri–Sat 9:30am–4pm, Thurs 9:30am–noon, Sun 2–4pm.

ANDREW CARNEGIE BIRTHPLACE MUSEUM, Moodie St. Tel. 0383/ 724302.

Andrew Carnegie, the American industrialist and philanthropist, was born in 1835 at a site about 200 yards down the hill from the abbey. The museum lies at the corner of Moodie Street and Priory Lane and comprises the 18th-century weaver's cottage in which he was born and a memorial hall provided by his wife. It was completely refurbished in 1984. Displays tell the story of the weaver's son from Dunfermline who immigrated to America to become one of the richest men in the world.

From the fortune he made in steel, Mr. Carnegie gave away more than $400 million before his death in 1919. Dunfermline, his birthplace, received the first of the 2,811 free libraries he provided throughout Britain and the United States. It also received public baths and **Pittencrieff Park and Glen,** so rich in history and natural charm. A statue in the park honors the hometown boy who once worked as a bobbin boy in a cotton factory.

Admission: Free.

Open: Apr–Oct, Mon–Sat 11am–5pm, Sun 2–5pm; Nov–Mar, daily 2–4pm.

WHERE TO STAY

KING MALCOLM THISTLE HOTEL, Queensferry Rd., Dunfermline, Fife KY11 5DS. Tel. 0383/722611. Fax 0383/730865. 48 rms (all with bath). TV TEL **Bus:** 72

$ **Rates:** £65 ($97.50) single; £75 ($112.50) double. Scottish breakfast £8.95 ($13.40) extra. AE, DC, MC, V. **Parking:** Free.

The best choice for either a meal or a bed is the King Malcolm Thistle Hotel. Modern, pastel colored, and fairly stylish, this hotel sits on a roundabout a mile south of Dunfermline on the A823. Named after the medieval king of Fife (and later of Scotland) Malcolm Canmore, it was built in 1972 but thoroughly revamped in 1989. Each of its well-furnished bedrooms contains a color TV with video, trouser press, and hairdryer. On the premises is an elegant, glass-sided bar and restaurant in an appealing design. Meals begin at £14.95 ($22.40). The Canmore Vaults Bar is accessible via a separate entrance.

WHERE TO DINE

NEW VICTORIA, 2 Bruce St. Tel. 0383/724175.
   Cuisine: SCOTTISH. **Reservations:** Not needed.
$ **Prices:** Appetizers 85p–£2.25 ($1.30–$3.40); main courses £3.15–£6.25 ($4.70–$9.40). Scottish "high tea" £4.95 ($7.40). MC, V.
   Open: Mon–Thurs 9am–6:30pm, Fri–Sat 9am–10pm, Sun 10:30am–7pm.

To reach Dunfermline's oldest eating house, established in 1923, you must walk up two flights of stairs. Off High Street, in a pedestrian zone in the center overlooking the abbey, the cozy dining room serves good old-fashioned cookery based on healthy ingredients. There's also plenty of it. You might begin with a robust soup, then follow with steak-and-kidney pie, grilled fish, roast beef, or any of an array of grilled Aberdeen Angus steaks. It's a good choice if you're in the neighborhood seeking a high tea, which costs £4.95 ($7.40).

EASY EXCURSIONS FROM DUNFERMLINE

CULROSS

The old royal burgh of Culross, 6 miles west of Dunfermline, has been renovated by the Scottish National Trust, and is one of the most beautiful in the country. As you walk its cobbled streets, admiring its whitewashed houses with their crow-stepped gables and red pantiled roofs, you'll feel as if you're taking a stroll back into the 17th century.

Set in tranquil walled gardens in the center of the village, **Culross Palace** was built in the village between 1597 and 1611, and contains a most beautiful series of paintings on its wooden walls and ceilings. It has been restored and may be visited from April through September, Monday to Saturday from 9:30am to 7pm and on Sunday from 2 to 7pm; October through March, until 4pm. Admission is £1.25 ($1.90) for adults, 75p ($1.10) for children.

The other important attraction is **Culross Abbey,** a Cistercian monastery whose founding father was Malcolm, Earl of Fife, in 1217. Parts of the nave are still intact, and the choir serves as the Culross parish church. There is also a central tower. The

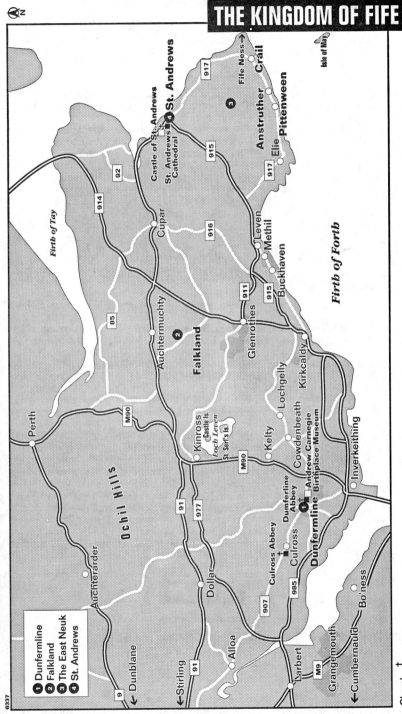

THE KINGDOM OF FIFE

N

St. Andrews

Castle of St. Andrews
St. Andrews Cathedral

Fife Ness →

Crail

Isle of May

Anstruther

Pittenweem

Elie

917

917

915

92

914

916

911

915

Cupar

Leven
Methil
Buckhaven

85

Auchtermuchty

Falkland

Glenrothes

Lochgelly

Kirkcaldy

M90

Perth

Kinross
Castle Is.
Loch Leven
St. Serf's Is.

Cowdenbeath

Kelty

Andrew Carnegie
Birthplace Museum

M90

Ochil Hills

91

977

Dunfermline
Abbey

Dunfermline

Inverkeithing

Auchterarder

Culross Abbey
Culross

985

907

Dollar

Alloa

Larbert

Bo'ness

Grangemouth

M9

← Cumbernauld

← Stirling

91

← Dunblane

9

Firth of Tay

Firth of Forth

① Dunfermline
② Falkland
③ The East Neuk
④ St. Andrews

Church

6337

abbey is open from Easter Saturday to the last Saturday in August, on Saturday and Sunday from 10am to 4pm; at other times, it can be visited by prior arrangement with the Rev. A. Norman, the Abbey Manse, Culross, Fife.

LOCH LEVEN

The loch, 12 miles north of Dunfermline, has seven islands. On St. Serf's, the largest of the islands, are the ruins of the **Priory of Loch Leven,** originally built on the site of one of the oldest Culdee establishments in Scotland.

In Kinross, 25 miles north of Edinburgh, take the ferry over to Castle Island, the only means of access to the ruins of **Loch Leven Castle,** on Castle Island, may be reached by ferry from Kinross. "Those never got luck who came to Loch Leven"— this saying sums up the history of this Douglas fortress. The castle dates from the late 14th century, and among its more ill-fated prisoners, none was more notable than Mary Queen of Scots. Inside its forbidding walls she signed her abdication on July 24, 1567. However, she effected her escape from Loch Leven on May 2, 1568. Thomas Percy, seventh Earl of Northumberland, supported her cause. For his efforts, he, too, was imprisoned and lodged in the castle for 3 years until he was handed over to the English, who beheaded him at York. The castle is open April through September, Monday to Saturday from 9:30am to 7pm, and on Sunday from 2 to 7pm; closed October through March. Admission is £1.50 ($2.30) for adults, and 75p ($1.10) for children. The admission charge for the castle includes the cost of a round-trip by ferry from Kinross to Castle Island.

WHERE TO STAY & DINE

NIVINGSTON HOUSE, Cleish Hills by the B996, Cleish, Kinross-shire KY13 7LS. Tel. 0577/850216. Fax 0577/850238. 17 rms (all with bath). TV TEL

$ Rates (including Scottish breakfast): £67.50 ($101.30) single; £77.50–£87.50 ($116.30–$131.30); double; from £130 ($195) suite. AE, MC, V. **Parking:** Free. Nivingston House lies on the B9097, 2 miles from Exit 5 of the M90 motorway halfway between Edinburgh and Perth, south of Kinross near Cleish. The place is run by Pat and Allan Deeson who offer modernized rooms and serve some of the finest food in Tayside.

Most visitors arrive to sample the wares of the kitchen. Guests rarely have the same meal here twice, as one must depend on the inspiration of the chef. But that's hardly a problem. Meals, costing £15.50 ($23.30) for lunch and £25 ($37.50) for dinner, are concocted principally from local produce, such as fish, Scottish lamb and beef, and veal, as well as charcoal-grilled sardines. Typical dishes include medallions of venison pan-fried with a red currant, paprika, and marsala sauce; rainbow trout sautéed with almonds, capers, and prawns; and Scottish sirloin steak "Hare and Hounds," with a red wine and Dijon mustard sauce, glazed with brown sugar. Desserts are luscious; you make your selection from a trolley wheeled to your table. Service is daily from noon to 2pm and 7 to 9pm. Always reserve a table. The hotel stands on 12 acres of ground.

---

2. FALKLAND

21 miles N of Edinburgh

GETTING THERE   By Train   From Edinburgh, take the train to Markinch, the closest rail link to Falkland. Go the rest of the way by bus.

By Bus   From Markinch, bus no. 36 connects with arriving trains and runs to Falkland.

By Car   Take the A90 northwest of Edinburgh across the Forth Road Bridge, then continue northeast along the A921, which leads into the A92. At the junction with the A912, head northwest to Falkland.

ESSENTIALS The nearest **tourist office** is at Lyon Square, Kingdom Centre at Glenrothes (tel. 0592/610784), 3 miles south of Falkland. In Falkland, the **telephone area code** is 0337.

This royal burgh of cobblestone streets and crooked houses lies at the northern base of the hill of East Lomond. Its notable sight is Falkland Palace and Gardens, now owned by the National Trust of Scotland.

WHAT TO SEE & DO

FALKLAND PALACE AND GARDEN, High St. Tel. 0337/57397.

Since the 14th century Falkland has been connected with Scottish kings. Originally a castle stood on the site of today's palace, but it was replaced in the 16th century. Falkland then became a favorite seat of the Scottish court. James V died here. Mary Queen of Scots used to come to Falkland for "hunting and hawking." It was also here that Francis Stuart, fifth Earl of Bothwell, tried to seize his young cousin, James VI, son of Mary Queen of Scots. The gardens have been laid out to the original royal plans. Falkland also boasts the oldest royal tennis court in the United Kingdom.

Admission: Palace and gardens, £3 ($4.50) adults, £1.50 ($2.30) children.

Open: Apr–Sept, Mon–Sat 10am–6pm, Sun 2–6pm. **Closed:** Oct–Mar. **Bus:** 36 from Markinch.

WHERE TO STAY

COVENANTER HOTEL, The Square, Falkland, Fife KY2 7BU. Tel. 0337/57224. 4 rms (all with bath). TV TEL **Bus:** 36 from Markinch.

$ Rates (including Scottish breakfast): £30–£35 ($45–$52.50) single; £45–£55 ($67.50–$82.50) double. AE, DC, MC, V. **Parking:** Free

Since the early 18th century this has been a popular inn. With modest modernization, it offers a good standard of accommodation. The hotel is built ruggedly of local stone, with high chimneys, wooden shutters, and a Georgian entry, and is on a small square opposite the church and palace. The dining room is strictly "old style" and for the before-dinner drinks there is an intimate pub, the Covenanter Cocktail Bar. Pub luncheons go for £6.50 ($9.80), and a fixed-price evening meal costs £14 ($21).

WHERE TO DINE

KIND KYTTOCK'S KITCHEN, Cross Wynd. Tel 0337/57477.

Cuisine: SCOTTISH. **Bus:** 36 from Markinch.

$ Prices: Appetizers 75p–£1.50 ($1.10–$2.30); main courses £1.40–£4.20 ($2.10–$6.30). AE, V.

Open: Daily 10:30am–5:30pm. **Closed:** Christmas Eve–Jan 5.

Located near the palace, this is also an art gallery that displays local crafts and paintings. A specialty is homemade oatcakes with cheese. The bread is always homemade, very fresh tasting. For a tea, I suggest homemade pancakes with fruit and fresh cream. Even better, however, are the tarts with fresh cream. Salads are also good. A cup of Scotch broth, served with a slice of home-baked whole-meal bread, is a favorite.

3. THE EAST NEUK

Within a half-hour drive south of St. Andrews are some of the most beautiful and unspoiled fishing villages of eastern Scotland. The villages cannot be reached by rail; the nearest stations are Ladybank, Cupar, and Leuchars, where bus connections will take you the rest of the way. The stations mentioned lie on the main London–

Edinburgh–Dundee–Aberdeen rail line serving northeast Fife. Buses from St. Andrews connect the villages.

PITTENWEEM

If you're here in the morning, try to get caught up in the action at the fish auction held under a large shed Monday through Saturday. The actual time depends on the tides. Afterward, you can go for a walk through the village and admire the sturdy stone homes, some of which have been preserved by Scotland's National Trust.

ANSTRUTHER

Once an important herring-fishing port, Anstruther is now a summer resort lying 46 miles northeast of Edinburgh, 34 miles east of Dunfermline, and 23 miles south of Dundee. The **Scottish Fisheries Museum,** St. Ayles, Harbourhead (tel. 0333/310628), is down by the harbor. Here you can follow the fisherfolk through every aspect of the fishing industry—from the days of sail to modern times. See the old herring drifter, *The Reaper,* berthed in the harbor, and don't miss the aquarium. The museum is open April through October, Monday to Saturday from 10am to 4:30pm and on Sunday from 2 to 4:30pm. Admission is £2 ($3) for adults, £1 ($1.50) for children. Take bus no. 95.

From the museum, you can walk to the tiny hamlet of **Cellardyke,** adjoining Anstruther. It has many charming stone houses and its own ancient harbor, where in the year that Victoria took the throne (1837), 140 vessels used to put out to sea.

Across the harbor, you can visit a floating exhibit in the old **North Carr** lightship. Entrance is free.

The **Isle of May,** a nature reserve in the Firth of Forth, is accessible by boat from Anstruther. It is a bird observatory and a field station, and contains the ruins of a 12th-century chapel as well as an early 19th-century lighthouse.

WHERE TO STAY

CRAW'S NEST HOTEL, Bankwell Rd., Anstruther, Fife KY10 3DS. Tel. 0333/310691. Fax 0333/312216. 50 rms (all with bath). TV TEL **Bus:** 95.
$ Rates (including Scottish breakfast): £30–£47 ($45–$70.50) single; £51–£82 ($76.50–$123) double. AE, DC, MC, V. **Parking:** Free.
Originally a Scottish manse, the Craw's Nest Hotel was converted into a popular hotel, with beautiful views over the Firth of Forth and May Island. Many extensions were added to the original building under the direction of the owner, Mrs. Edward Clarke, and her son-in-law, Ian Birrell. The black and white step-gabled building stands behind a high stone wall. The bedrooms are handsomely equipped and appointed. Public areas, including a lounge bar as well as a bustling public bar, are simply decorated and cozy. The food is good, and the wine is priced reasonably in the hotel's dining room. The hotel is just 10 minutes from St. Andrews.

SMUGGLER'S INN, High St., East Anstruther, Fife KY10 3DQ. Tel. 0333/310506. 9 rms (all with bath). TV TEL **Bus:** 95.
$ Rates: £25 ($37.50) per person with Scottish breakfast, £34 ($51) per person with half board. AE, DC, MC, V. **Parking:** Free.
This warmly inviting inn located in the heart of town evokes memories of smuggling days. The original inn that stood on this spot dates back to 1300. In Queen Anne's day it was a well-known tavern. The ceilings are low, the floors uneven, and of course the stairways winding. Bedrooms are pleasantly decorated and comfortably furnished.

À la carte dinners, available for £12 ($18), and bar suppers are served daily from 7 to 10:30pm. Bar lunches or suppers begin at £5 ($7.50). If featured, ask for the local Pittenweem prawns.

WHERE TO DINE

HAVEN, 1 Shore Rd., Cellardyke Anstruther. Tel. 0333/310574.
   Cuisine: SCOTTISH. **Reservations:** Recommended. **Bus:** A James Anderson & Co. bus runs every hour from St. Andrews 8 miles south to the door of the restaurant; local bus no. 95.
$ Prices: Appetizers £1.90–£3.60 ($2.90–$5.40); main courses £5.80–£9.90 ($8.70–$14.90); high tea £5.50–£6.20 ($8.30–$9.30). No credit cards.
   Open: Daily noon–9:30pm (depending on business, the street-level restaurant, but not the upstairs bar, might close several hours earlier during midwinter).

Set directly on the harborfront, this unpretentious establishment serves simple and wholesome food, such as breaded and pan-fried prawns or filets of halibut, Angus steaks, local crabmeat salad, and homemade soups and stews. The stone structure was originally built as two separate fishermen's cottages some 300 years ago and was interconnected when the restaurant was established. The upper floor contains one of the town's most popular bars, where all lunches and inexpensive dinners are served. The street level, more formal and sedate, is the site of high teas and evening meals.

THE CELLAR, 24 East Green. Tel. 0333/310378.
   Cuisine: SEAFOOD. **Reservations:** Recommended. **Bus:** 95
$ Prices: At lunch appetizers £2.50–£5 ($3.80–$7.50), main courses £4.95–£12 ($7.40–$18). At dinner, table-d'hôte meals £22.50–£27.50 ($33.80–$41.30). AE, MC, V.
   Open: Lunch Tues–Sat 12:30–2pm; dinner Mon–Sat 7–9:30pm.
Some visitors consider this well-managed seafood restaurant the best eatery in town. Set within the solid stone walls of a cellar whose age is positively dated from 1875 (but more likely dating from the 16th century) the establishment is illuminated with candlelight—in winter by twin fireplaces at opposite ends of the room. Cuisine derives from very fresh fish hauled in from nearby waters, cooked carefully and delicately, usually with light-textured sauces. Examples include grilled suprême of halibut dredged in bread crumbs and citrus juices, and served with hollandaise sauce; a mixture of turbot with Western Isles scallops served in a chardonnay cream sauce; monkfish with herb and garlic sauce; and flavorful versions of a limited array of meat dishes. The staff is youthful and charming.

ELIE

With its step-gabled houses and little harbor, this is many visitors' favorite village along the coast. Lying only a 25-minute ride from Edinburgh, Elie and its close neighbor, **Earlsferry,** overlook a crescent of golden sand beach, with more swimming possibilities to be found among sheltered coves. The name Elie is believed to be derived from the "ailie," or island, of Ardross, which now forms part of the harbor and is joined to the mainland by a road. A large stone building, a former granary, at the harbor is a reminder of the days when Elie was a busy trading port.
   Earlsferry, to the west, got its name from an ancient ferry crossing, which Macduff, the Thane of Fife, is supposed to have used in his escape from Macbeth.

WHAT TO SEE & DO

East of the harbor at Elie stands a stone structure known as the **Lady's Tower,** used by Lady Janet Anstruther, a noted 18th-century beauty, as a bathing cabaña. Another member of the Anstruther family, Sir John, added the interesting **bell tower** to the parish church that stands in the center of the village.
   Beyond the lighthouse, on a point of land to the east of the harbor, lies **Ruby Bay,** so named because garnets can be found here. Farther along the coast is **Fossil Bay,** where a variety of fossils can be found.

WHERE TO STAY

THE ELMS, 14 Park Pl., Elie, Fife KY9 1DH. Tel. 0333/330404. 7 rms (5 with bath).

$ Rates (including half board) £28.50 ($42.80) per person. No credit cards. **Parking:** Free.

Run by Cameron and Pat Mann, this 1880 building is set on the wide main street behind a conservative stone facade, with a crescent-shaped rose garden in front. The comfortably furnished rooms are centrally heated and contain wash basins, hairdryers, and tea/coffee makers. Home-cooking is a specialty of the house, and dishes include Scottish lamb, Pittenweem haddock, haggis, and Arbroath kippers. The house is licensed, and dinner is available to nonresidents. There is a large conservatory in the walled flower garden behind the house for guests' use.

WHERE TO DINE

BOUQUET GARNI, 51 High St. Tel. 0333/330374.
Cuisine: FRENCH/SCOTTISH. **Reservations:** Required in summer, recommended in winter.
$ Prices: At lunch, appetizers £1.50–£3.90 ($2.30–$5.90), main courses £5.50–£9.50 ($8.30–$14.30); at dinner, appetizers £2.50–£9.50 ($3.80–$14.30), main courses £8.50–£18.50 ($12.80–$27.80). AE, MC, V.
Open: Lunch daily noon–2pm; dinner Mon–Sat 6:45–9:30pm. **Closed:** 2nd week of Nov and second half of Jan.

In a white-painted stone house on the main street of Elie, this restaurant is considered charming enough to justify a culinary excursion from St. Andrews. Run by owner-chef Andrew Keracher and his wife Norah (who will greet you in the dining room), the establishment bases its reputation on French-derived recipes prepared with fresh, all-Scottish ingredients.

Your order will be taken in a small apéritif bar before you're ushered into dining rooms filled with pink linen and fresh flowers. Dishes include lobster and scallops set in a light pastry case with a saffron-flavored brandy sauce; breast of wild pigeon with wild mushrooms and Madeira sauce; and lightly heated crayfish (langoustines) in walnut oil with chives on a bed of bitter lettuces (radicchio, wild oak leaves, frisée, and lollo rosso). Dessert might be a brandy basket with chocolate ganache and seasonal fruits.

THE SHIP INN, The Toft. Tel. 0333/330246.
Cuisine: SCOTTISH. **Reservations:** Unnecessary.
$ Prices: Appetizers 75p–£2.50 ($1.10–$3.80); main courses £2.50–£7.50 ($3.80–$11.30). No credit cards.
Open: Mon–Sat 11am–midnight, Sun 12:30–11pm.

Even if you're not stopping over in Elie, I suggest that you drop in at the Ship on the Toft (from the center, follow the signs marked HARBOUR) and enjoy a pint of lager, real ale, or whisky from a large selection. The building occupied by this pub with nautical atmosphere dates from 1778, and a bar has been in business here since 1830. In summer you can sit out in fair weather and look over the water; in colder months a fireplace burns brightly. In July and August a barbecue operates outside. The menu features such items as pheasant, steaks of Angus beef, and venison, along with such standard items as haddock and "chips" (french fries). Look also for the specials of the day.

CRAIL

Considered the pearl of the East Neuk of Fife, Crail is an artists' colony, and many painters live in cottages around this little harbor. Natural bathing facilities lie at Roome Bay, and many beaches are nearby. The Balcomie Golf Course is one of the oldest in the world and is still in good condition. Crail is 50 miles northeast of Edinburgh, 23 miles south of Dundee, and 9 miles south of St. Andrews.

WHERE TO STAY & DINE

CROMA HOTEL, 33-35 Nethergate, Crail, Fife KY10 3TU. Tel. 0333/ 50239. 11 rms (all with bath). TV TEL

$ Rates (including Scottish breakfast): £15–£17.50 ($22.50–$26.30) per person. No credit cards. **Parking:** Free. **Closed:** Dec–Jan.

This guest house one block off High Street near the harbor features a fully licensed Chart Room bar. The dining room is decorated in green and white, and Windsor chairs are set in front of the bay window. Many of the artists who live in this little fishing village come here for drinks and dinner. A table d'hôte lunch costs £5 ($7.50), and an evening meal goes for £10 ($15). You can also have a bar meal in the Chart Room. Bedrooms are centrally heated, comfortably furnished, and well maintained.

4. ST. ANDREWS

14 miles SE of Dundee, 51 miles NE of Edinburgh

GETTING THERE   By Train   BritRail stops 8 miles away at the town of Leuchars (rhymes with *euchres*) on its London–Edinburgh–Dundee–Aberdeen run to the northeast. About 15 trains per day make the trip. Trip time from Edinburgh to Leuchars is about 1 hour. A one-way fare is £5.80 ($8.70).

By Bus   Once at Leuchars (see above), you can take a bus the rest of the way to St. Andrews. Bus no. 94 or 95 departs about every 30 minutes. Fife Scottish bus nos. 23 and X99 connect St. Andrews to Glasgow and take between 2½ and 3 hours for the journey and depart daily from 7am to midnight. Buses arrive at the St. Andrews Bus Station, Station Road, just off City Road (tel. 0334/74238 for schedules).

By Car   From Edinburgh, head northwest along the A90 and cross the Forth Road Bridge north. Take the A921 to the junction with the A915 and continue northeast until you reach St. Andrews.

ESSENTIALS   The **tourist information office** is on Market Street (tel. 0334/ 72021). The **telephone area code** is 0334.

The medieval royal burgh of St. Andrews was once filled with monasteries and ancient houses that did not survive the pillages of Henry VIII; regrettably, only a few ruins rising in ghostly dignity remain. Most of the town as you'll see it today was built during the 18th, 19th, and early 20th centuries of local stone.

The historic sea town in northeast Fife is also known as the seat wherein the rules of golf in Britain and the world are codified and arbitrated. Golf was played for the first time in the 1400s, probably on the site of St. Andrews' Old Course, and enjoyed by Mary Queen of Scots there in 1567. All six of St. Andrews' golf courses are fully owned by the municipality, and are open to the public on a more-or-less democratic basis whereby ballots are polled one day in advance. This balloting system might be circumvented for players who reserve with the appropriate starters several days or weeks in advance. To play the hallowed Old Course, a current handicap certificate and/or letter of introduction from a bona fide golf club must be presented.

The town's misty and verdant golf courses are the very symbol of the town itself, and a mecca for golfers around the world. They include the above-mentioned Old Course, the New Course (opened in 1896), the Jubilee Course (opened in 1897 in honor of Queen Victoria), the Eden (opened in 1914), the Balgove (a 9-hole course designed for children's golf training in 1972), and the newest and most far-flung of all, the 18-hole Strathtyrum, which opened in 1993. Encircled by all of them is the world's most prestigious golf club, the **Royal and Ancient** (tel. 0334/72112), which was founded in St. Andrews in 1754 and remains more or less rigidly closed as a private-membership men's club. (The Royal and Ancient has traditionally opened its doors to the public only one day a year for views of its legendary trophy room on St. Andrews' day. This usually, but not always, falls around November 30.)

Facilities for golfers in St. Andrews are legion. Beside the 18th hole of the Old Course, within premises owned and operated by The Rusacks Hotel, there are links rooms with lockers, showers, and changing facilities, as well as meals and bar facilities. These might be enlarged and expanded during the lifetime of this edition, but in the meanwhile, virtually every hotel in town maintains some kind of facility to help and assist golfers in their explorations of the region's golf options.

WHAT TO SEE & DO

Founded in 1411, the **University of St. Andrews** is the oldest in Scotland and the third oldest in Britain and has been called the "Oxbridge" of Scotland. At term time you can see the students in their characteristic red gowns. The university grounds stretch west of the St. Andrews Castle between North Street and the Scores.

The university's most interesting buildings include the tower and church of St. Salvator's College and the courtyard of St. Mary's College, dating from 1538. An ancient thorn tree, said to have been planted by Mary Queen of Scots, stands near the college's chapel. The church of St. Leonard's College is also from medieval days. In 1645 the Scottish Parliament met in what was once the University Library and is now a students' reading room. A modern University Library, containing many rare and ancient volumes, was opened in 1976.

HOLY TRINITY CHURCH, opposite St. Mary's College, off South St. Tel. 74494.
Called "the Town Kirk" this beautifully restored medieval church once stood on the grounds of the now-ruined cathedral (see below). The church was moved to its present site in 1410 and considerably altered after the Reformation of 1560. Restored in the early 20th century, the church has much fine stained glass and carvings.
Admission: Free.
Open: Apr–Sept, daily 10am–noon and 2–4pm.

ST. ANDREWS CATHEDRAL AND PRIORY, off Pends Rd. Tel. 72563.
In the area of the Celtic settlement of St. Mary of the Rock, by the sea at the east end of town, is the semi-ruin of St. Andrews Cathedral and Priory. The earlier cathedral Church of St. Rule Regulus may have been built in the late 11th century and modified in the mid-12th century. In the 1160s the cathedral was founded and built in both Romanesque and Gothic styles. The largest church in Scotland, it established St. Andrews as the ecclesiastical capital of the country. Today the ruins can only suggest its former beauty and importance. There is a collection of early Christian and medieval monuments, as well as artifacts discovered on the cathedral site.
Admission: £1.20 ($1.80) adults, 60p (90¢) children.
Open: Apr–Sept, Mon–Sat 9:30am–6pm; Sun 2–6pm; Oct–Mar, Mon–Sat 9:30am–4pm, Sun 2–4pm.

ST. RULES TOWER, near the cathedral.
The 12th-century tower has a 108-foot accessible stairway to the top, where you'll enjoy a fine view of the city.
Admission: Included in cathedral admission (see above).
Open: Apr–Sept, Mon–Sat 9:30am–7pm, Sun 2–7pm; Oct–Mar, Mon–Sat 9:30am–4pm, Sun 2–4pm.

CASTLE OF ST. ANDREWS, northwest of the cathedral.
Also of great interest is the ruined 13th-century castle, with its bottle dungeon and secret passages. Founded in the early part of the 13th century, it was reconstructed several times.

Admission: £1 ($1.50) adults, 50p (80¢) children.
Open: Mid-Mar to mid-Oct, Mon–Sat 9:30am–6:30pm, Sun 2–6:30pm; off-season closing is at 4pm.

WHERE TO STAY

Today you can fare much better than Samuel Johnson and James Boswell, who stopped off here for a meal of "rissered haddocks and mut chops."

EXPENSIVE

RUFFLETS COUNTRY HOUSE HOTEL, Strathkinnes Low Rd. St. Andrews, Fife KY16 9TX. Tel. 0334/72594. Fax 0334/78703. 25 rms (all with bath). TV TEL

$ Rates (including Scottish breakfast): £63–£68 ($94.50–$102) single; £104–£136 ($156–$204) double. AE, DC, MC, V. **Parking:** Free. **Closed:** Jan to mid-Feb.

Some golfers prefer this cozy retreat on the B939, 1½ miles from St. Andrews. Each bedroom is equipped with a radio, hot-beverage facilities, and alarm clock, and all are well furnished in a warm, homelike way. Set in a garden of about 10 acres, this country house is substantial. The furnishings throughout are tasteful, as is the decor. The most modern bedrooms are in the newer wing, although traditionalists request space in the handsome main building, and those in-the-know reserve well in advance, as Rufflets is very popular with the British.

Even if you aren't staying here, you may want to call and reserve a table at the Rufflets Hotel Restaurant, which overlooks a well-designed garden. Excellent, fresh ingredients are used in the continental and Scottish dishes, and everything I've sampled here has been accurately cooked. The service, too, is polite and efficient. A dinner begins at £22 ($33). Lunch is served daily from 12:30 to 2pm; dinner, from 7 to 9:30pm.

ST. ANDREWS GOLF HOTEL, 40 The Scores, St. Andrews, Fife KY16 9AS. Tel. 0334/72611. Fax 0334/72188. 23 rms (all with bath). TV TEL

$ Rates (including Scottish breakfast): £66–£71 ($99–$106.50) single; £105–£116 ($157.50–$174) double. AE, DC, MC, V. **Parking:** Free

A combination of greenery, sea mists, and tradition makes this 19th-century property extremely popular with golfers, despite the fact that many of them confuse it at first glance with the larger and more prestigious St. Andrews Old Course Hotel (see below). Set about 200 yards from the first tee-off of the famous golf course, it was originally built as a private home, and later expanded and transformed into a hotel run by Brian and Maureen Hughes. Redecorated in the early 1990s, it contains a pair of cocktail bars, a sauna, a solarium, and handsome bedrooms. Each contains a radio and several thoughtful extras. Bar lunches are served Monday through Saturday, and table d'hôte dinners, served nightly, begin at £21.50 ($32.30). Tennis courts are nearby.

ST. ANDREWS OLD COURSE HOTEL, Old Station Rd., St. Andrews, Fife KY16 9SP. Tel. 0334/74371. Fax 0334/77668. 125 rms (all with bath), 17 suites. MINIBAR TV TEL

$ Rates: £150–£205 ($225–$307.50) single; £200–£235 ($300–$352.50) double; from £275 ($412.50) suite. Scottish breakfast £12.50 ($18.80) extra. AE, DC, MC, V. **Parking:** Free.

Many dedicated golfers prefer the St. Andrews Old Course Hotel, close to the A91 on the outskirts of town, where it overlooks the 17th fairway, the "Road Hole" of the Old Course. Fortified by finnan haddie and porridge, a real old-fashioned Scottish breakfast, you can face that diabolical stretch of greenery where nearly all the world's golfing greats have played and the Scots have been whacking away since early in the 15th century.

The hotel is not ancient—far from it: It's very contemporary, and its balconies afford top preview seats at all tournaments. Some £16 million has been spent to transform it into one of world-class standard. The facade was altered to keep it in line with the more traditional buildings of St. Andrews and bedrooms and suites were remodeled and refurbished.

Dining/Entertainment: Well-prepared international cuisine is available in the Road Hole Grill, and light meals and afternoon tea are served in a plant-filled room known as the Conservatory. The Jigger Inn serves real ale and wholesome food in a traditional pub atmosphere. A four-course table d'hôte evening meal costs £32.50 ($48.80), and lunch costs £19.50 ($29.30).

Services: Room service, laundry, babysitting.

Facilities: The hotel offers an array of facilities, including health spa, whirlpool, a massage room, steam rooms, beauty therapy salons, pool, changing and locker rooms, and a pro shop.

THE RUSACKS, Pilmour Links, St. Andrews, Fife KY16 9JQ. Tel. 0334/74321, or toll free 800/225-5843 in the U.S. Fax 0334/77896. 48 rms (all with bath), 2 suites. TV TEL

$ Rates: £90 ($135) single; £130 ($195) double; £235 ($352.50) suite. Scottish breakfast £9.50 ($14.30) extra. AE, DC, MC, V. **Parking:** Free

The Rusacks sits at the edge of the famous 18th hole of Pilmour Links. Rusacks was originally built in 1887 by Josef Rusack, a German from Silesia who recognized the potential of St. Andrews as a golf capital. He placed advertisements on the front pages of British newspapers, which at the time was considered revolutionary. The hotel stands behind stone walls capped with neoclassical gables and slate roofs. Inside, chintz picks up the tones from the bouquets of flowers sent in fresh twice a week. Between panels and Ionic columns of the public rooms, racks of lendable books re-create the atmosphere of a private country house library. Fireplaces and armchairs add to the allure. Upstairs, the bedrooms, all with private bath, contain some carved antiques, modern conveniences, and spacious charm.

The nightlife in the hotel partially explains why the crew and actors of *Chariots of Fire* stayed here during filming. The Champions Bar in the basement, overlooking the links, has golf-related photos, trompe-l'oeil racks of books, vested waiters, and evening folksinging. The Chesterfield sofas are full of animated clients from 11am to 11pm, and light meals and snacks are served as well. The hotel's formal restaurant, Strathtyrum, serves daily specials along with local game, meat, and fish, accompanied by a wine list from a well-stocked cellar. In the Strathtyrum, table d'hôte lunches cost £8.50–£9.50 ($12.80–$14.30) during the week (Monday through Saturday) and £12.50 ($18.80) on Sunday; table d'hôte dinners cost £19.95–£24.95 ($29.90–$37.40), depending on the number of courses.

MODERATE

LATHONES HOTEL, By Largoward, St. Andrews, Fife KY9 1JE. Tel. 0334/84494. Fax 0334/84494. 14 rms (all with bath). TV TEL

$ Rates (including Scottish breakfast): £28 ($42) single; £56–£70 ($84–$105) double. Half board £42–£49 ($63–$73.50) per person. MC, V. **Parking:** Free.

Originally a coaching inn, this 200-year-old manor, 5 miles southwest of the center of St. Andrews on the A915 has been thoughtfully restored and given a comfortable aura. All its bedrooms—often decorated with pastels—are furnished to a good standard, with individually controlled central heating, coffee-making equipment, and hairdryers. Each of the two that rent for £88 ($154) has a log-burning stove and a Jacuzzi.

The public rooms reflect Scottish tradition, with open fires and beamed ceilings. Guests enjoy the old-world atmosphere of the Stable Bar (which contains some original artifacts from the coaching inn) and the Manor Bar, with its armchairs placed around an open fire. Chefs make wise use of local produce, as reflected by their filet of beef flavored with cognac, or venison filets in a juniper-and-gin sauce.

RUSSELL HOTEL, 26 The Scores, St. Andrews, Fife KY16 9AS. Tel. 0334/73447. 10 rms (all with bath). TV TEL

$ Rates (including Scottish breakfast): £40–£55 ($60–$82.50) single; £60–£72 ($90–$108) double. MC, V. **Parking:** Free. **Closed:** Dec 24–Jan 14.

Originally built as a private home around 1850, the Russell has one of the most ideal locations for a moderately priced hotel in St. Andrews—overlooking St. Andrews Bay and just a 2-minute walk from the first tee of the Old Course. Of great appeal to golfers, it is well maintained and run by Gordon and Fiona de Vries. The hotel offers fully equipped bedrooms with tea/coffee makers. There's a cozy Victorian pub that serves bar meals, priced at around £7.50 ($11.30) each, and drinks to a loyal local clientele. There's also an à la carte restaurant where lunches cost around £13 ($19.50) and dinners go for around £18 ($27).

INEXPENSIVE

NUMBER TEN, 10 Hope St., St. Andrews, Fife KY16 9HJ. Tel. 0334/ 74601. 10 rms (all with bath).
$ Rates (including Scottish breakfast): £19–£25 ($28.50–$37.50) per person. Children under 12 half price in parents room. No credit cards. **Parking:** Free.

Housed in a classic Georgian building directly south of the Royal & Ancient Golf Club, only a 3-minute walk from the first tee of the Old Course, this guest house is centrally heated and has a lounge with color TV. All rooms have facilities for making hot beverages. The hosts will arrange tee-off times and mini golf packages for guests.

WHERE TO DINE

GRANGE INN, Grange Rd., at Grange. Tel. 0334/72670.
 Cuisine: SCOTTISH/SEAFOOD. **Reservations:** Recommended.
$ Prices: Appetizers £2.50–£5.50 ($3.80–$8.30); main courses £4.95–£7.95 ($7.40–$11.90). AE, DC, MC, V.
 Open: Lunch daily 12:30–2pm; dinner daily 7–9:30pm.

If you're seeking less formality, a favorite eating spot, well established for many years, go to the Grange Inn, about 1½ miles from St. Andrews on the B959. It offers a good choice of dishes made from fresh produce. In this country cottage, with its charming garden, an old-fashioned hospitality prevails. Local beef and lamb always appear on the menu, as do fish and shellfish from the fishing villages of East Neuk. Fruits and herbs come from Cupar. Try, if featured, smoked wild Rannoch venison thinly sliced and served cold with hot gratin dauphinoise; cassoulet of pork, beans, and sausages in a spicy tomato sauce; or a platter of smoked fish and meats with horseradish mayonnaise. A classic opener and an old favorite at the inn is a stew of mussels and onions, or else you might prefer game terrine with a cumberland sauce.

NEARBY PLACES TO STAY & DINE

THE PEAT INN, Cupar, Fife KY15 5LH. Tel. 033484/206. Fax 033484/ 530. 8 suites. TV TEL **Directions:** Take the B940 6 miles southwest of St. Andrews.
$ Rates (including Scottish breakfast): £130 ($195) suite for 2. AE, DC, MC, V. **Parking:** Free. **Closed:** 2 weeks in Jan and 2 weeks in Nov.

The Peat Inn is in an old inn/post office built in 1760, where David Wilson prepares exceptional cuisine. The inn offers accommodation in beautifully furnished suites. The restaurant is run by David and his wife, Patricia, who have built a reputation for serving high-quality meals in comfortable surroundings. The ingredients are almost all locally grown—even the pigeons (a specialty) come from a St. Andrews farm. Pigeon is offered in a pastry case with wild mushrooms, or you can order the plump breasts in an Armagnac-and-juniper sauce. Other dishes are wild duck, crab, and lobster salad, grouse (in season), sometimes even woodcock. One unusual dish David created is a flan of Scottish Abroath smokies (haddock). The inn has a worthy wine selection too. Lunch costs £18.50 ($27.80), and a fixed-price dinner goes for £28 ($42); both are four courses, including coffee. A "tasting menu" of 6 or 7 small courses is offered at £38 ($57), or else you can order à la carte, paying about £30 ($45) for 3 courses. The restaurant is open Tuesday through Saturday at 12:30pm for a set lunch, served at 1pm. Dinner is served daily from 7 to 9:30pm.

5. STIRLING

37 miles NW of Edinburgh, 28 miles NE of Glasgow

GETTING THERE   By Train   Frequent trains run between Glasgow and Stirling and between Edinburgh and Stirling. A 1-day round-trip ticket from Edinburgh costs £4.80 ($7.20), and from Glasgow £4.20 ($6.30). For schedules, call 041/2042844 in Glasgow, and 031/5562451 in Edinburgh. Both information numbers are available 24 hours a day.

By Bus   Frequent buses run to Stirling from both Glasgow and Edinburgh. A 1-day round-trip ticket from Edinburgh costs £4.50 ($6.80); from Glasgow £3 ($4.50). Call Scottish Citylink for information (tel. 031/5575717 in Edinburgh or 041/332-7133 in Glasgow.)

By Car   From Glasgow, head northeast along the A80 to the M80, at which point head north. From Edinburgh, head northwest along the M9.

ESSENTIALS   The **tourist information office** is at 41 Dumbarton Rd. (tel. 0786/475019). The **telephone area code** is 0786.

Stirling is dominated by its impressive castle, perched on a 250-foot basalt rock on the main east-west route across Scotland, formed by the River Forth and the River Clyde and the relatively small section of land between them. The ancient town of Stirling, which grew up around the castle, lies in the heart of an area so turbulent in Scottish history that it was called "the cockpit of Scotland." A memorable battle fought in the area was the Battle of Bannockburn in 1314, when Robert I (the Bruce) defeated the army of Edward II of England.

Stirling is the central crossroads of Scotland, giving easy access by rail and road to all its major towns and cities. If you use it as a base, you'll be only a short distance from many attractions, including Loch Lomond, the Trossachs, and the Highlands.

The town center boasts several shopping facilities, including the Thistle Centre indoor shopping plaza.

WHAT TO SEE & DO

The **Church of the Holy Rude** on St. John Street is said to be the only church in the country still in use that has witnessed a coronation. The date was 1567 when the 13-month-old James VI was crowned. John Knox preached the sermon. The church itself dates from the early 15th century, and in its day it attracted none other than Mary Queen of Scots. It is open May through September, daily from 10am to 5pm.

STIRLING CASTLE, Upper Castle Hill. Tel. 0786/450000.

On the right bank of the Forth, Stirling Castle dates from the Middle Ages, when its location on a dividing line between the Lowlands and the Highlands caused it to become known as "the key to the Highlands." There are traces of earlier (7th-century) royal habitation of the Stirling area. Later the castle became an important seat of Kings James IV and James V, both of whom added to the structures, the latter following classic Renaissance style, then relatively unknown in Britain. Here Mary Queen of Scots lived as an infant monarch for the first 4 years of her life. After its final defeat, Bonnie Prince Charlie's army stopped here in 1746, and later the castle became an army barracks and headquarters of the Argyll and Sutherland Highlanders, one of Britain's most celebrated regiments. An audiovisual presentation explains what you are about to see.

Admission: £2 ($3) adults, £1 ($1.50) children.
Open: Apr–Sept, Mon–Sat 9:30am–6pm, Sun 10:30am–5:30pm; Oct–Mar, Mon–Sat 9:30am–5:30pm, Sun 12:30–4:20pm.

MUSEUM OF THE ARGYLL AND SUTHERLAND HIGHLANDERS, Stirling Castle, Upper Castle Hill. Tel. 0786/475165.
Also at the castle, you can visit this regional museum, which presents an excellent

exhibition of colors, pipe banners, and regimental silver, along with medals (some of which go back to the Battle of Waterloo) won by Scottish soldiers for valor.

Admission: Free.

Open: Easter–Sept, Mon–Sat 10am–5:30pm, Sun 11:30am–5pm; Oct–Easter, Mon–Sat 10am–4pm, Sun 11am–4pm.

A NEARBY ATTRACTION

One of the most interesting excursions is to **Bannockburn,** a name that looms large in Scottish history. It was here that Robert the Bruce, his army of 6,000 outnumbered three to one, defeated the forces of Edward II in 1314. Before nightfall Robert the Bruce had won back the throne of Scotland. The battlefield lies off the M80, 2 miles south of Stirling.

At the **Bannockburn Heritage Centre,** Glasgow Road (tel. 0786/812664), an audiovisual presentation tells the story of these events. The Queen herself came here in 1964 to unveil an equestrian statue of the Scottish hero. An exhibition, "The Kingdom of the Scots," traces the history of Scotland from the earliest times to the Union of Crowns. The site is open all year, but the Heritage Centre and shop are open only from April through October, daily from 10am to 6pm. The last audiovisual showing is at 5:30pm. Admission is £1.50 ($2.30) for adults, 80p ($1.20) for children.

At the **Borestone,** where Robert the Bruce commanded his forces, you can see Stirling Castle and the Forth Valley. The location is off the M80/M9 at Junction 9.

WHERE TO STAY

GOLDEN LION HOTEL, 8–10 King St., Stirling, Stirlingshire FK8 2ND. Tel. 0786/475351. Fax 0786/472755. 71 rms (all with bath). TV TEL

$ Rates: £59 ($88.50) single; £69 ($103.50) double. Continental breakfast £6.50 ($9.80) extra. AE, DC, MC, V. **Parking:** Free.

About a block downhill from Holyrood Church, one of the oldest and largest hotels in town is the beneficiary of a recent refurbishment that improved and modernized most of the bedrooms. Originally built in 1786 as a coaching inn, its sandstone shell was greatly enlarged with the addition of modern wings in 1962. The hotel contains a pleasant and popular cocktail bar and a restaurant. Its bedrooms are simple, "easy on the eye" accommodations, with tea-making facilities and radios. Bar lunches cost from £3 ($4.50) to £7 ($10.50); table d'hôte dinners in the restaurant are £15 ($22.50).

PARK LODGE HOTEL, 32 Park Terrace, Stirling, Stirlingshire FK8 2JS. Tel. 0786/474862. 9 rms (all with bath). TV TEL **Bus:** 51 or 52.

$ Rates (including Scottish breakfast): £45 ($67.50) single; £60 ($90) double. AE, DC, MC, V. **Parking:** Free.

Set across the street from a city park, in a residential neighborhood uphill from the center of town, this hotel is in a 19th-century Italianate mansion. Built of stone blocks and slates, it has a Doric portico, a Georgian-era core dating from 1825, and century-old climbing roses and wisteria, along with Tudor-style chimney pots. The hotel qualifies as the most stylish in town. Anne and Georges Marquetty house guests in one of their nine upstairs bedrooms, and later suggest that they dine at one of the elegant tables of their restaurant, the Heritage (see "Where to Dine," below). Each bedroom contains an array of antique furnishings (Room 6 has a four-poster bed). You might enjoy tea in a walled garden behind the hotel, with its garden room, widely spaced iron benches, and terra-cotta statues. On the other side of tall casement windows are a pair of French-inspired salons with such luxuries as marble fireplaces, elaborate draperies, and cabriole-legged armchairs.

STIRLING HIGHLAND HOTEL, Spittal St., Stirling, Stirlingshire FK8 1DU. Tel. 0786/475444. Fax 0786/462929. 72 rms (all with bath). TV TEL.

$ Rates (including Scottish breakfast): £88–£97 ($132–$145.50) single; £120–£132 ($180–$198) double. AE, DC, MC, V. **Parking:** Free.

Stirling's newest hotel has also become its most important. In the center of town, within what was originally built as the Old High School, this stylish hotel was installed after major renovations to a Victorian building with which almost everyone in town had maintained some kind of emotional link. A respect for the historic atmosphere was maintained, and many of the original architectural features remain. Florals, tartans, and solid wood furnishings dominate both the public rooms and the bedrooms of what is now viewed as the finest hotel in town. The well-furnished bedrooms are contained within a modern new wing, with up-to-date amenities. From its position close to Stirling Castle, the hotel enjoys views over the town and surrounding region.

Dining/Entertainment: Small but charming, the cocktail bar is usually active in the evening, and most guests dine at their hotel rather than face the uncertain cuisine of the town itself. Scottish cuisine is featured in Scholars Restaurant, while Rizzio's restaurant serves the cuisine of Italy.

Services: Room service, babysitting, laundry.

Facilities: Steam room, squash courts, gymnasium, snooker room.

TERRACES HOTEL, 4 Melville Terrace, Stirling, Stirlingshire FK8 2ND. Tel. 0786/472268. Fax 0786/450316. 18 rms (all with bath). TV TEL

$ **Rates** (including Scottish breakfast): £49.95 ($74.90) single; £63.50 ($95.30) double. AE, DC, MC, V. **Parking:** Free.

Originally built as a fine Georgian-inspired house of buff-colored sandstone, this hotel stands on a raised terrace in a quiet residential neighborhood a 5-minute walk south of the center near the town's largest shopping center. Considered one of the best-value hotels in town, it's owned by the Danish-British partnership of Lars and Julie Christiansen. The half-paneled cocktail bar and velvet-upholstered restaurant provide one of the most popular settings in Stirling for local parties and wedding receptions. Melville's Restaurant offers both a Scottish and a continental menu, everything from beef Stroganoff to Wiener schnitzel, from tagliatelle Napolitana to chicken Kiev. A wide array of beef dishes is offered, including pepper steak and homemade beefsteak pie. Main dishes start at £4.50 ($6.80). Each of the bedrooms is comfortably furnished in a country-house motif of flowered curtains and solidly traditional furniture.

WHERE TO DINE

THE HERITAGE, 16 Allan Park, Stirling, Stirlingshire FK8 2QC. Tel. 0786/473660. Fax 0786/451291.

Cuisine: INTERNATIONAL/SCOTTISH. **Reservations:** Recommended.

$ **Prices:** Appetizers £1.85–£7.50 ($2.80–$11.30); main courses £4.50–£8.50 ($6.80–$12.80); two-course fixed-price lunch £10.75 ($16.10); three-course fixed-price dinner £17 ($25.50). MC, V.

Open: Lunch daily noon–2pm; dinner daily 6:30–9:30pm. **Closed:** Sun in winter.

Its culinary sophistication and its beautiful decor rank it as one of the most sought-after restaurants in the entire district (it also rents rooms). Near the center of town, a 5-minute walk east of the railway station, it's located on a quiet residential street. You enter a gentleman's parlor, richly outfitted with somber walls and enviable antiques, for a drink before descending to the low-ceilinged basement restaurant. Amid a French-inspired decor, you'll taste some of the best cuisine in town, prepared with finesse by Georges Marquetty. In his youth he worked as an executive chef in Paris, and later spent 12 years in Cincinnati with his British wife, Anne (there he was voted one of the leading chefs of America). Specialties include scallops, scampi, and prawns in Pernod sauce, filet of wild venison with port and black-currant sauce, scallops with smoked ham in a lemon sauce, and foie gras with truffles.

Upstairs, four handsomely furnished bedrooms, each with private bathroom, TV, and telephone, rent for £45–£50 ($67.50–$75) for a single, and £60 ($90) for a double, with breakfast included.

RIVERWAY RESTAURANT, Kildean, outside Stirling. Tel. 0786/475734.

Cuisine: SCOTTISH. **Reservations:** Not required. **Directions:** Head half a mile from the center of Stirling, just off the M8 beside Junction 10.

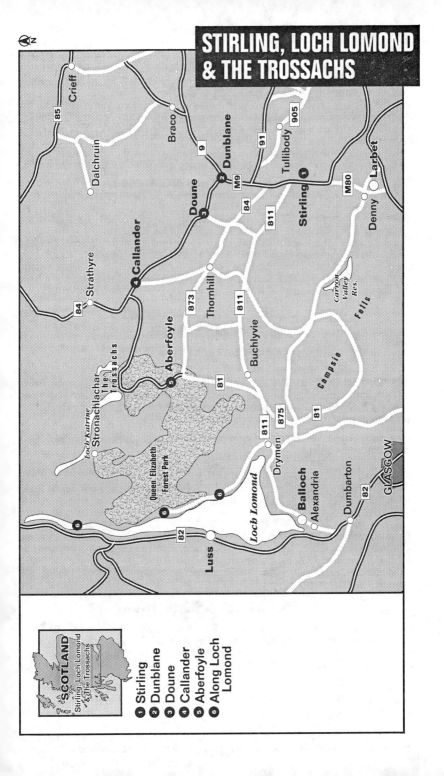

$ Prices: Appetizers 50p–£2.75 (80¢–$4.10); main courses £3.95–£9 ($5.90–$13.50); high tea £5–£8 ($7.50–$12). V.
Open: Daily 10am–noon (coffee and scones); lunch daily noon–3pm; high tea 3–6pm. **Closed:** Mon in summer, Mon–Tues Nov–Easter.

This fully licensed restaurant has a local reputation for good food at moderate tariffs. It has panoramic views of Stirling Castle, the Wallace Monument, and the Ochil Hills. The Riverway offers well-prepared food, such as honeyed lamb cutlets, deep-fried haddock, and grilled sirloin steaks. At lunchtime you can order a real Scottish menu, including haggis, neeps, and tatties. The high-tea menu has such rib-sticking fare as fried liver, bacon, and onions. Wine of the house is sold by the glass or the bottle.

SETTLE INN, 91 St. Mary's Wynd. Tel. 0786/474609.
Cuisine: DRINKS. **Bus:** The bright-red "Heritage Bus" makes frequent runs (May–Sept only) from Stirling's railway station.
$ Prices: Lager £1.45 ($2.20). No credit cards.
Open: Mon–Sat 11am–11pm or midnight, Sun 12:30–11pm.

Established in 1733 inside a thick-walled, low-slung building in the shadow of Stirling Castle, this is believed to be the oldest (and perhaps the most atmospheric) drinking tavern in town. Much rejuvenated, and popular with local residents, it has a stone fireplace that casts a welcome warmth on chilly days. You'll find several kinds of lager and about 15 kinds of single-malt whiskies. No food of any kind is served.

---

6. DUNBLANE

7 miles N of Stirling, 42 miles NW of Edinburgh,
29 miles SW of Perth, 33 miles NE of Glasgow

GETTING THERE By Train Trains run between Glasgow and Dunblane with a stopover at Stirling; for 24-hour rail information about departures from Glasgow, call 041/2042844. Rail connections are also possible through Edinburgh via Stirling; for 24-hour information in Edinburgh, call 031/5562451.

By Bus Buses travel from the Goosecroft Bus Station in Stirling (tel. 0786/73763 in Stirling) to Dunblane.

By Car From Stirling (see above), continue north along the M9 to Dunblane.

ESSENTIALS A summer-only **tourist information office** is on Stirling Road (tel. 0786/824428). The **telephone area code** is 0786.

A small cathedral city on the banks of the Allan Water, Dunblane takes its name from the Celtic Church of St. Blane, which once stood on the site now occupied by the fine 13th-century Gothic cathedral.

Sports enthusiasts are attracted to the area because of its golfing, fishing, and hunting possibilities.

WHAT TO SEE & DO

An excellent example of 13th-century Gothic ecclesiastic architecture, ✪ **Dunblane Cathedral,** Cathedral Close (tel. 0786/824254), was spared the ravages of attackers who destroyed other Scottish worship centers. Altered in the 15th century and restored several times in the 19th and 20th centuries, the cathedral may have suffered the most from neglect subsequent to the Reformation. A Jesse Tree window is in the west end of the building, and of interest are stalls, misericords, a pulpit with carved figures of early ecclesiastical figures, and other striking features, including the wooden, barrel-vaulted roof with colorful armorials. A Celtic stone from about A.D. 900 can be seen in the north aisle.

A 1687 structure on the grounds of the old manse contains a personal library of Bishop Robert Leighton, an outstanding leader of the 17th century who did much to

IMPRESSIONS

The Scots are steadfast—not their clime.
—THOMAS CAMPBELL, *THE PILGRIM OF GLASGOW*, 1842

Nowhere beats the heart so kindly
As beneath the tartan plaid.
—W. E. AYTOUN, *LAYS OF THE SCOTTISH CAVALIERS AND OTHER POEMS*, 1849

resolve religious bickerings. It is of interest because of the bishop's material on the 17th century and the effects of the troubled times on Scotland. The **Cathedral Museum,** on the Square, is in the Dean's House and contains articles and papers pertaining to both the cathedral and the town. Admission is a minimum donation of 50p (80¢) per adult. It is open June through September, Monday to Saturday from 10:30am to 12:30pm and 2:30 to 4:30pm. The story of Dunblane and its ancient cathedral is displayed in the 1624 house, and you can also visit an enclosed garden with a very old (restored) well.

WHERE TO STAY & DINE

CROMLIX HOUSE, Kinbuck, Dunblane, Perthshire FK15 9JT. Tel. 0786/ 822125. Fax 0786/825450. 6 rms (all with bath), 8 suites. TV TEL
$ Rates (including Scottish breakfast): £90–£140 ($135–$210) single; £125–£150 ($187.50–$225) double; £160–£210 ($240–$315) suite. AE, DC, MC, V. **Parking:** Free.

Cromlix House is a fine country-house hotel 3¼ miles north of Dunblane on the B8033 (off the A9), just beyond the village of Kinbuck. The manor, built in 1880 as the seat of a family that has owned the surrounding acreages for the past 500 years, was transformed into an elegant hotel in 1982. (The owners moved into a smaller and more manageable building on the estate, and today derive at least part of their income from organizing of hunting and fishing expeditions in the River Allan and in the surrounding moors and forests.)

Fishing in three private lakes and hunting are available as well as tennis, and guests can walk through the surrounding forests and farmland. The manor has an elegant drawing room with big bow windows, and antiques are among the furnishings of both the public rooms and the bedrooms. Bouquets of fresh flowers and open fires in cool weather add to the comfort of the place. The bedrooms (eight with sitting rooms) are carpeted and have radios. In addition to a second-floor library, guests are invited to visit the chapel and the gun room.

Lunch is served to residents or nonresidents, daily from 12:30 to 1:45pm for between £15 ($22.50) and £22 ($33) for table d'hôte, and dinner is served nightly from 7 to 8:30pm for £32 ($48) per person for five courses.

7. DOUNE

41 miles NW of Edinburgh, 35 miles N of Glasgow, 8 miles NW of Stirling

GETTING THERE By Train Stirling (see above) is the closest rail link to Doune.

By Bus Buses from the Stirling bus station on Goosecroft run throughout the day to Doune.

By Car From Dunblane (see above), continue west along the A820.

ESSENTIALS The nearest **tourist information office** is at Dunblane (see above). The **telephone area code** is 0786.

This small market town with its 15th-century castle is a good center for exploring the Trossachs. The Rivers Teith and Ardoch flow through Doune.

WHAT TO SEE & DO

DOUNE CASTLE, on the A820 4 miles west of Dunblane. Tel. 0786/50000.

This castle, once a royal palace, stands on the banks of the River Teith. Now owned by the Earl of Moray, it was restored in 1883, making it one of the best preserved of the medieval castles of Scotland.

Admission: £1.20 ($1.80) adults, 60p (90¢) children.

Open: Apr–Sept, Mon–Sat 9:30am–6pm, Sun 2–6pm; Oct–Mar, Mon–Thurs 10am–4pm; alternate Sat 10am–4pm; Sun 2–4pm.

DOUNE MOTOR MUSEUM, Carse of Cambus (on the A84). Tel. 0786/841203.

After visiting the castle, guests can drive 1½ miles to the motor museum that contains about 40 vintage motor cars, including the second oldest Rolls-Royce in the world. This is the finest collection of classic and vintage cars in Scotland. Various motoring events are announced throughout the summer.

Admission: £2.50 ($3.80) adults; £1 ($1.50) children.

Open: Apr–May and Sept–Oct, daily 10am–4:30pm; June–Aug, daily 10am–5:30pm. **Closed:** Nov–Mar.

BLAIR DRUMMOND SAFARI AND LEISURE PARK, Blair Drummond. Tel. 0786/841456.

South of Doune is the Blair Drummond Safari and Leisure Park. You meet the typical cast of animal safari characters here, and the park also offers a jungle cruise, a giant astraglide, and an amusement arcade, as well as a pet farm and a performing sea lions show. A safari bus is available for visitors, costing 30p (45¢) extra per person.

You can have refreshments at the Watering Hole Bar or in the Ranch Kitchen (tel. 0786/841430), or use one of the picnic areas. To reach the park, take Exit 10 off the M9 onto the A84 near Stirling.

Admission: £5.80 ($8.70) adults, £3.30 ($5) children 3–14, free for children under 3.

Open: April 3–Oct 4, daily 10am–5pm.

WHERE TO STAY & DINE

WOODSIDE, Stirling Rd., Doune, Perthshire FK16 6AB. Tel. 0786/841237. 12 rms (all with bath). TV TEL

$ Rates (including Scottish breakfast): £30 ($45) single; £44 ($66) double. MC, V. **Parking:** Free.

The Woodside stands on the A84 main Stirling–Oban road. In the heart of Perthshire, it was originally a coaching inn and dates back to the 18th century. Its bedrooms are well furnished. The lounge bar has an open fire and offers a selection of more than 100 malt whiskies. You can enjoy a selection of traditional dishes on the bar luncheon menu, such as soused herring, homemade pâté salads, and grilled Aberdeen Angus steaks. The dining room overlooks the garden, and specialties include venison, salmon, and lobster (in season). Dinner is likely to cost £12 ($18) to £15 ($22.50). On Sunday, dinner is served only to residents.

8. CALLANDER

16 miles NW of Stirling, 43 miles N of Glasgow,
52 miles NW of Edinburgh, 42 miles W of Perth

GETTING THERE **By Train** Stirling (see above) is the nearest rail link.

By Bus Once at Stirling, continue on a Midland Bluebird bus from the Stirling bus station on Goosecroft Road (tel. 0786/73763 for schedules) the rest of the way to Callander.

By Car   From Stirling, head north along the M9, cutting northwest at the junction of the A84 to Callander, bypassing Doune.

ESSENTIALS   The **Rob Roy & Trossachs Visitor Centre** is at Ancaster Square (tel. 0877/30342). The **telephone area code** is 0877.

In Gaelic, the Trossachs means "the bristled country," an allusion to its luxuriant vegetation. The thickly wooded valley contains three lochs—Venachar, Achray, and Katrine. In the summer the steamer on Loch Katrine offers a fine view of the splendid wooded scenery.

For many, the small burgh of Callander makes the best base for exploring the Trossachs and Loch Katrine, Loch Achray, and Loch Venachar. For years, motorists—and before them, passengers traveling by bumpy coach—stopped here to rest up on the once difficult journey between Edinburgh and Oban.

Callander stands at the entrance to the Pass of Leny in the shadow of the Callander Crags. The Rivers Teith and Leny meet to the west of the town.

WHAT TO SEE & DO IN THE ENVIRONS

In the scenic Leny Hills to the west of Callander beyond the Pass of Leny lie **Leny Park** and **Leny Falls.** At one time all the lands in Leny Park were part of the Leny estate, home of the Buchanan clan for more than 1,000 years. In the wild Leny Glen, a naturalist's paradise, deer can be seen grazing. Leny Falls is an impressive sight, near the confluence of the River Leny and the River Teith.

Four miles beyond the Pass of Leny lies **Loch Lubnaig** ("the crooked lake"), divided into two reaches by a rock and considered fine fishing waters. Nearby is **Little Leny,** the ancestral burial ground of the Buchanans.

More falls are found at **Bracklinn,** 1½ miles northeast of Callander. In a gorge above the town, Bracklinn is considered one of the most scenic of the local beauty spots. Other places of interest include the **Roman Camp,** the **Caledonian Fort,** and the **Foundations of St. Bride's Chapel.**

The Visitor Centre (see above) will give you a map that pinpoints the above-recommended sights. While there, you can also get directions for one of the most interesting excursions from Callander, to **Balquhidder Church,** 13 miles to the northwest, the burial place of Rob Roy. Off the A84, the church also has the St. Angus Stone from the 8th century, a 17th-century bell, and some Gaelic Bibles.

WHERE TO STAY

HIGHLAND HOUSE HOTEL, South Church St., Callander, Perthshire FK17 8BN. Tel. 0877/30269. 9 rms (7 with bath). TV TEL **Directions:** In the town center, just off A84, near Ancaster Square.

$ Rates (including Scottish breakfast): £18 ($27) single without bath; £21 ($31.50) single with bath; £36 ($54) double without bath; £42 ($63) double with bath. Half board £31.50–£34.50 ($47.30–$51.80) per person. AE, MC, V. **Parking:** Free.

This Georgian style stone building, full of charm and character, stands on a quiet tree-lined street a few yards from the River Teith and a short walk to the Rob Roy Visitor Centre. All bedrooms have color TV, radio alarms, and hot beverage facilities, and most have private baths or showers. The hotel is owned and managed by David and Dee Shirley, winners of the 1992 Antartex award for the best hotel or guest house in the region. Scottish-style meals are served in the dining room for around £13.95 ($20.90), or in lighter and simpler versions in the bar. The lounge contains many brands of malt whiskies, some of them relatively obscure.

LUBNAIG HOTEL, Leny Fues, Callander, Perthshire FK17 8AS. Tel. 0877/30376. 10 rms (all with showers). TV **Directions:** Proceed on

Callander's Main Street to the western outskirts and turn right into Leny Fues, 25 yards past the Poppies Hotel.

$ Rates (including half board): £38–£45 ($57–$67.50) per person. MC, V. **Parking:** Free. **Closed:** Nov–Mar.

The Lubnaig Hotel, an old-fashioned hostelry with plenty of character, occupies a Victorian stone structure from 1864 with many gables and bay windows in its own acre of garden. The pleasant bedchambers, doubles only, have hot-beverage facilities and central heating. Dinner is prepared fresh daily using only the best of Scottish produce. Salmon, sea trout, grouse, pheasant, venison, and Scottish beef all appear on the menu. A fully stocked bar with a wide selection of malt whiskies and wines is available. Guests can enjoy salmon and trout fishing, canoeing, and pony trekking near the River Lemy and the River Teith.

ROMAN CAMP, Main St., Callander, Perthside FK17 8BG. Tel. 0877/ 30003. Fax 0877/31533. 14 rms (all with bath), 3 suites. TV TEL **Directions:** As you approach Callander on the A84, the entrance to the hotel is signposted between two cottages on Callander's Main Street.

$ Rates (including Scottish breakfast): £65 ($97.50) single; £90–£120 ($135–$180) double; from £145 ($217.50) suite. AE, DC, MC, V. **Parking:** Free.

★ The leading hotel, once a 17th-century hunting lodge with pink walls and small gray-roofed towers, was built on the site of what was believed to have been a Roman camp. The modern-day traveler drives up a 200-yard driveway, with shaggy Highland cattle and sheep grazing on either side. The River Teith runs through the 20-acre estate. In summer, flowerbeds are in bloom. Inside you are welcomed to a country house furnished in a gracious manner. Seven of the units are on the ground floor and one is adapted for use by disabled guests. All have hairdryers, radios, and hot-beverage facilities. The dining room was converted in the '30s from the old kitchen, with a ceiling design based on the old Scottish painted ceilings of the 16th and 17th centuries, which were a feature of houses around the time the Roman Camp hunting lodge was built. The meals—Scottish country-house fare—are served until 8:30 in the evening. A table d'hôte lunch costs £12.50 ($18.80) to £17 ($25.50), with a set dinner going for £30 ($45). There is a small but cozy cocktail bar. The library, with its ornate plasterwork and richly grained paneling, remains as an elegant holdover from yesteryear. The hotel remains open throughout the year.

ON LOCH VOIL

This was an area known to Rob Roy MacGregor, who died in 1734 but lives on in legend as the Robin Hood of Scotland. If you visit Rob Roy's Grave at Balquhidder, you may find this remote part of Scotland so enchanting that you'll want to continue to drive west and explore the Braes o'Balquhidder and the banks of Loch Voil.

STRONVAR COUNTRY HOUSE HOTEL, Balquhidder, Lochearnhead, Perthshire FK19 8PB. Tel. 08774/688. Fax 08774/230. 5 rms (all with bath). TV TEL

$ Rates (including Scottish breakfast): £54.50 ($81.80) single; £79 ($118.50) double. MC, V. **Parking:** Free. **Closed:** Nov–Feb.

Originally built in 1850 as the manorial seat of the entire region, this hotel rises imperially in beige sandstone. Set in 2½ acres of garden, with hundreds of acres of wilderness around it, the hotel opens onto a view of Loch Voil. Stronvar can accommodate a maximum of 10 guests. All rooms have tea-making equipment and trouser presses, among other amenities. Every bedroom has the tartan motif of the clan whose name is marked on the door. All contain antiques and four-poster beds. There are several fireplaces and a "trust bar" where guests help themselves. An evening dinner costs £14 ($21).

To get here, at a point 28 miles north of Stirling along the A84, turn at the signpost to Balquhidder; then continue 2 miles down the glen into the village, where signs point the way to Stronvar House.

WHERE TO DINE

LADE INN, Trossachs Rd. at Kilmahog. Tel. 0877/30152.
    Cuisine: INTERNATIONAL. **Reservations:** Not needed.
$ Prices: Appetizers £1.25–£3.95 ($1.90–$5.90); main courses £4.95–£10.95 ($7.40–$16.40). MC, V.
    Open: Mon–Sat noon–2:30pm and 5:30–11pm, Sun noon–11pm. **Closed:** Mon–Tues Jan–Feb.

Surrounded by fields, within earshot of the Leny River and a short walk to two old woolen mills, this establishment was originally built as a teahouse. Converted after World War II to a pub and restaurant with overnight accommodations, it attracts residents from the surrounding farmlands as well as tourists from afar. You will enjoy Highland scenery in views that incorporate Ben Ledi, one of the region's most prominent peaks and a favorite of visiting hill climbers.

Much of the clientele arrives to sample the inn's wide range of cask-conditioned ales and cider, but if you're hungry, food items include Rob Roy steaks, barbecued pork ribs, Japanese prawns, and "Lade-burgers" garnished in honor of Canada (the homeland of owners David and Libby Stirrup) with strips of Canadian bacon. Also available is Cullen Skink, a smoked haddock chowder whose recipe has been featured in several newspapers throughout Britain. The inn also offers six well-furnished bedrooms, each with private bath, costing £20 ($30) per person nightly, including a full Scottish breakfast.

DALGAIR HOTEL, 113–115 Main St., Callander, Perthshire FK17 8BQ Tel. 0877/30283. Fax 0877/31114.
    Cuisine: SCOTTISH. **Reservations:** Recommended in restaurant, not necessary in the bar.
$ Prices: In bar, appetizers £1.75–£2.50 ($2.60–$3.80); main courses £3.95–£7.95 ($5.90–$11.90). In restaurant, appetizers £1.60–£3.25 ($2.40–$4.90), main courses £7.95–£11.50 ($11.90–$17.30). AE, DC, MC, V.
    Open: Bar, food service daily noon–9pm. Restaurant, dinner only, daily 7:30–9pm.

Although this establishment contains eight overnight accommodations, it's best known for its food and beverage facilities, which are among the most popular in town. The hotel building was constructed in the 19th century as a private home, and later functioned as a shop. Today, its bar is lined with gray bricks, rustic accessories, and flickering candles. Food items are "not the kind of thing you can get at home," in the words of the chef. They include halibut and either Dover or lemon sole, steaks, and game stews. Australian, German, or Austrian wine sold by the glass and priced at from £1 ($1.50) each, imbues the place with the aura of a wine bar.

More formal meals are served after dark within The Restaurant. Menu items might include sliced pork on a bed of cucumber noodles with oregano and ginger sauce; filet of chicken in champagne-butter sauce; and different preparations of salmon and Angus steaks.

The hotel's bedrooms contain private bathrooms, TV, and telephones, and—with Scottish breakfast included—cost £40 ($60) for a single and £52 ($78) for a double.

---

9. ABERFOYLE

56 miles NW of Edinburgh, 27 miles N of Glasgow

GETTING THERE **By Train** The nearest rail link is Stirling (see above).

By Bus Connections are meager. A postal bus leaves from Callander (see above).

By Car This is by far the best means of reaching Aberfoyle. From Stirling (see above), take the A84 west until you reach the junction of the A873 and continue west to Aberfoyle.

ESSENTIALS   A summer-only **tourist information office** is on Main Street (tel. 08772/352). The **telephone area code** is 08772 for 3-figure numbers, 0877 for 6-figure numbers.

———

Looking like an alpine village in the heart of Rob Roy country, this small holiday resort near Loch Ard is the gateway to the Trossachs. Shops offer gift items related to the Highlands.

WHAT TO SEE & DO IN THE ENVIRONS

About 4 miles to the east of Aberfoyle along the A81, **Inchmahome Priory** stands on an island in Lake Menteith. From the Port of Menteith, you can sail to the island if the weather's right. Once there, you'll find the ruins of a 13th-century Augustinian house where Mary Queen of Scots was sent as a baby in 1547. The ferry costs £1.50 ($2.25) for adults, £1 ($1.50) for children, if it's running—everything depends on the weather. For information, call 0786/62421.

A **Queen Elizabeth Park Visitor Centre** is installed in the David Marshall Lodge, off the A821, 1 mile north of Aberfoyle. It is open mid-March through mid-September, daily from 10am to 6pm. Admission is free. From the lodge you'll enjoy views of Ben Lomond, the Menteith Hills, and the Campsie Fells.

The center is a good starting point for walks into the beautiful ۞ **Queen Elizabeth Forest Park,** lying between the eastern shore of Loch Lomond and the Trossachs. Some 45,000 acres of moor, woodland, and mountain have been set aside for walking and exploring. It's a nature lover's delight.

WHERE TO STAY

COVENANTERS INN HOTEL, Duchray Road, Aberfoyle, Perthshire FK8 3XD. Tel. 08772/347. Fax 08772/785. 49 rms (all with bath) TV.
$ Rates (including dinner, bed, and breakfast): £45–£50 ($67.50–$75) single; £90–£100 ($135–$150) double. AE, DC, MC, V. **Parking:** Free.

Set on 6 acres of privately owned land overlooking the headwaters of the River Forth, about a half mile southwest of Aberfoyle, this hotel was originally built as the family home of a local landowner in the early 1800s. Gracefully enlarged during several stages in the 1960s and 1980s, it derives its name from a famous convention held here in the 1950s, when a group of Scots church and political leaders issued a then-famous and much publicized covenant promoting the separation of Scotland from England. On Christmas Eve of 1952, the hotel again became famous (or notorious) after the theft from Westminster Abbey of the Stone of Scone, the medieval throne of the Scottish kings. After nationwide appeals from Buckingham Palace, the Stone was recovered in a Scottish railway station, after having spent a night, it's claimed, in the Covenanter's Inn Hotel. (A controversy continues as to the authenticity of the recovered artifact—some Scots nationalists claim that the object found in the railway station was a clever copy, and that the original lies today on Scottish soil. Conjecture and speculation about the event still goes on, sometimes heatedly, in the in-house bar.)

The bar serves drinks from a wide selection of single malt whisky, as well as bar meals for around £7 ($10.50) each. There's also a more formal restaurant where table d'hôte dinners cost around £16 ($24) each. Bedrooms are dignified and comfortable, evoking something you might find in a Scottish country house. Neil Blackburn is the manager.

WHERE TO DINE

BRAEVAL OLD MILL, Callander Rd. Tel. 08772/711.
   Cuisine: SCOTTISH. **Reservations:** Required.
$ Prices: Fixed-price 4-course dinner £26.50 ($39.80); 4-course Sun lunch £17.50 ($26.30). MC, V.
   Open: Dinner Tues–Sat 7–9:30pm; lunch Sun 12:30–1:30pm. **Closed:** 2 weeks in Nov., 1 week in Feb, 1 week in June (dates vary).

⭐ For dining, Braeval Old Mill, lying a mile east of Aberfoyle on the A81 (the Callander road), is the obvious choice. Overlooking a golf course, this top-notch restaurant is housed in a former stone mill. Owners Fiona and Nick Nairn (he's the chef) kept an antique waterwheel to remind diners of the building's former function. Mr. Nairn's repertoire embraces both traditional and modern British dishes on a changing fixed-price menu based on the availability of fresh produce, which he uses deftly. You might begin with a ginger, honey, and carrot soup, followed by a warm salad of pigeon with green lentils and balsamic dressing, then filet of monkfish and sea bass with a pesto sauce. Or else the dinner might be wild mushroom soup, mousseline of sole with a shellfish sauce, and roast breast of mallard with wild rice and a game and Cassis sauce. Desserts are superb, as reflected by the caramel soufflé with caramel ice cream or the warm banana crêpe with rum cream and chocolate sauce.

AN EXCURSION TO THE TROSSACHS

The **Dukes Pass** (A821) north from Aberfoyle climbs through Achray Forest, past the Queen Elizabeth Forest Park Visitor Centre (see above), operated by Forest Enterprise, where you can stop for snacks and a breathtaking view of the Forth Valley. Information on numerous walks, cycling routes, the Achray scenic forest drive, picnic sites, car parks, and many other activities is available at the center. The road runs to the Trossachs—the "bristly country"—between Lochs Achray and Katrine.

Loch Katrine, at the head of which Rob Roy MacGregor was born, owes its fame to Sir Walter Scott's poem *The Lady of the Lake.* The loch is the principal reservoir of the city of Glasgow. A small steamer, the S.S. *Sir Walter Scott,* plies the waters of the loch, which has submerged the romantic poet's Silver Strand.

Sailings are from early May to late September, between Trossachs Pier and Stronachlachar, at a round-trip fare of £2.95 ($4.40) for adults and £1.70 ($2.60) for children. Complete information about sailing schedules is available from the Strathclyde Water Department, Lower Clyde Division, 419 Balmore Rd., Glasgow, Lanarkshire G22 6NU (tel. 041/3555333). Light refreshments are available at Trossachs Pier.

WHERE TO STAY & DINE

LOCH ACHRAY HOTEL, The Trossachs, Perthshire FK17 3HZ. Tel. 08776/229. Fax 08776/278. 75 rms (all with bath).

$ Rates (including Scottish breakfast): £27 ($40.50) single; £54 ($81) double. No credit cards. **Parking:** Free. **Closed:** Jan–Feb.

This sprawling and very visible white-sided hotel stands 9 miles east of Callander on the A821, a short walk from Loch Achray, in an isolated estate of 45 acres between Callander and Aberfoyle. Although parts of its foundation date from Jacobean times, the bulk of what you'll see today was built around the turn of the century as a resort for the appreciation of the flora and fauna of the Highlands. From the hotel, you can step directly into the Achray Forest, part of the vast Queen Elizabeth National Park, which abounds in wildlife, especially roe deer. Many of the building's original architectural details have been removed during its various modernizations. Bedrooms are simple, contemporary, each with a tea kettle, functional furniture, and views over the forest. The hotel is usually heavily booked with visiting tour groups, who overnight here between bus excursions through the Highlands. A set dinner costs only £8 ($12).

10. ALONG LOCH LOMOND

The largest of Scotland's lochs, ⭐ **Loch Lomond** was the center of the ancient district of Lennox, in the possession of the branch of the Stewart (Stuart) family from which sprang Lord Darnley (second husband of Mary Queen of Scots and father of

James VI of Scotland, who was also James I of England). The ruins of Lennox Castle are on Inchmurrin, one of the 30 islands of the loch—one with ecclesiastical ruins, one noted for its yew trees planted by King Robert the Bruce to ensure a suitable supply of wood for the bows of his archers. The loch is fed by at least 10 rivers from west, east, and north and is about 24 miles long; it stretches 5 miles at its widest point. On the eastern side is **Ben Lomond,** which rises to a height of 3,192 feet.

The song "Loch Lomond" is supposed to have been composed by one of Bonnie Prince Charlie's captured followers on the eve of his execution in Carlisle Jail. The "low road" of the song is the path through the underworld that his spirit will follow to his native land after death, more quickly than his friends can travel to Scotland by the ordinary high road.

The easiest way to see the famous loch is not by car but by the *Silver Marlin,* a 62-foot-long (by 17-foot-wide), 125-passenger cruiser, which began its life hauling river traffic on the Thames. On board are two decks, big windows for viewing the scenery, and an amply stocked bar loaded with Scottish malt whisky. Owned by Sweeney's Cruises Ltd., the ship is based at Sweeney's Shipyard, 26 Balloch Rd., Balloch, Dunbartonshire G83 8LQ (tel. 0389/52376). Cruises last for about an hour, and depart every hour on the half-hour every day of the year between 10:30am and 7:30pm. Cruises sail from Balloch to a wooded island, Inchmurrin, year-round home to five families, several vacation chalets, and a summer-only nudist colony. Although the ship docks at the island for only a moment or two before returning to Balloch, passengers can get off at the island to explore and board again on one of the ship's subsequent returns. Per person round-trip fares cost £3.50 ($5.30).

BALLOCH

At the southern end of Loch Lomond, Balloch is the most touristy of the towns and villages around the lake. The town grew up on the River Leven, where the water leaves Loch Lomond and flows south to the Clyde. Today Balloch is visited chiefly by those wanting to take boat trips on Loch Lomond, which sail in season from Balloch Pier.

WHAT TO SEE & DO

Set on 200 acres, **Balloch Castle Country Park** is on the "bonnie, bonnie banks of Loch Lomond," three-quarters of a mile north of Balloch Station. The present **Balloch Castle** (tel. 0389/58216), replacing one that dated from 1238, was constructed in 1808 for John Buchanan of Ardoch. Built in the "castle-Gothic" style, it has a Visitor Centre that explains the history of the property. The site has a walled garden, and the trees and shrubs, especially the rhododendrons and azaleas, reach the zenith of their beauty in late May and early June. You can also visit a "Fairy Glen." The location is about three-quarters of a mile from the center of Balloch, and it is open all year, daily from 8am to dusk, with no admission.

Dumbarton District's Countryside Ranger Service is based at Balloch Castle and conducts guided walks at various locations around Loch Lomond throughout the summer.

WHERE TO STAY & DINE

BALLOCH HOTEL, Balloch Rd., Balloch, Dunbartonshire G83 8LQ. Tel. 0389/52579. Fax 0389/55604. 14 rms (all with bath). TV TEL
$ Rates (including Scottish breakfast): £42 ($63) single; £63 ($94.50) double. AE, DC, MC, V. **Parking:** Free.
Called the "Grande Dame" hotel of Balloch, this was the first to be erected in the town, and as such, welcomed the Empress Eugénie, wife of Napoléon III, to its premises in 1860 when she was on a tour of Scotland (she slept in the Inchmoan Room). It stands beside the river, in the center of the hamlet.

CAMERON HOUSE HOTEL & COUNTRY ESTATE, Balloch, Loch Lomond,

Dunbartonshire, G83 8QZ. Tel. 0389/55565. Fax 0389/59522. 63 rms (all with bath), 5 suites. TV TEL
$ Rates (including Scottish breakfast): £115 ($172.50) single; £138 ($207) double; £275 ($412.50) suite. AE, DC, MC, V. **Parking:** Free.

⭐ Set beside the A86, this is the finest accommodation and dining choice along Loch Lomond. This turreted mansion, its lawns sweeping down to the "bonnie bonnie banks" itself, has been skillfully converted to receive guests. With its superb facilities (see below), it qualifies as a country club and luxury hotel. Bedrooms have been beautifully decorated, most often in pastel colors, with excellent reproductions of antique furniture, giving it a traditional aura throughout.

Dining/Entertainment: The hotel offers the award-winning Georgian Room, offering a French and Scottish "Auld Alliance" cuisine against a lavish Victorian backdrop. Nonresidents are welcome but reservations are essential. Lunch costs £15.50 ($23.30), with a fixed-price dinner going for £27.50 ($41.30), although you can also order à la carte. No lunch is offered on Saturday and Sunday. The menu changes to reflect the seasons, but you might try such dishes as a terrine of rabbit and hare encased in leeks, followed by medallions of lamb flavored with fresh herbs and served with a Madeira sauce. A more informal Brasserie opens onto the garden. The hotel also has a cocktail bar.

Services: Room service, laundry, babysitting.

Facilities: Swimming pools, a gymnasium, a squash court, sauna, solarium, steamroom, Jacuzzi, badminton.

LUSS

This village on the western side of Loch Lomond is the traditional home of the Colquhouns. Among its stone cottages, on the water's edge, is a branch of the Highland Arts Studios of Seil. Cruises on the loch and boat rentals may be arranged at a nearby jetty.

WHERE TO STAY & DINE

COLQUHOUN ARMS HOTEL, Luss, Alexandria, Dunbartonshire G83 8NY. Tel. 043686/282. 24 rms (6 with bath). TV
$ Rates (including Scottish breakfast): £28 ($42) single without bath; £32 ($48) single with bath; £44 ($66) double without bath; £50 ($75) double with bath. AE, DC, MC, V. **Parking:** Free.

The Colquhoun Arms Hotel is a pale yellow and white former coaching inn, located on the A82 going north, close to the road under a canopy of large trees. It lies a two-minute walk from the edge of a lake. The modernized interior is filled with light-grained paneling, plaid carpeting, a pool table, an attractively lit dining room, a lounge bar, and a pub. Bedrooms are comfortable and traditionally furnished. Lunches and dinners are served both in the bar (where people smoke) and the restaurant (where they cannot). The bar has food platters costing from £3.50 to £4.25 ($5.30–$6.40); the restaurant offers appetizers from £1.50 to £2.85 ($2.30 to $4.30) and main courses from £4 to £9 ($6 to $13.50).

INVERBEG

This hamlet on the western shore of Loch Lomond stands in a beauty spot of Scotland, about 3 miles north of Luss. It can be reached in about 40 minutes from Glasgow. The hamlet is known for its oldtime ferry inn (see below), the second oldest youth hostel in Scotland, and several well-known art galleries. A small fleet of Loch Lomond cruisers can usually be seen in the harbor of Inverbeg Bay, and a ferry to Rowardennan and Ben Lomond plies the route three times a day in summer.

WHERE TO STAY & DINE

INVERBEG INN, on the A82, Luss, Loch Lomond, Dunbartonshire G83 8PD. Tel. 043686/678. Fax 043686/686. 14 rms (7 with bath). TV TEL
$ Rates (including Scottish breakfast): £28 ($42) single without bath, £45 ($67.50)

single with bath; £50 ($75) double without bath, £57 ($85.50) double with bath. AE, MC, V. **Parking:** Free.

The site of this inn, 28 miles north of Glasgow, and a five-minute drive south of Luss, has always been important as the ferryboat landing servicing the western end of Loch Lomond. The building was constructed in 1814, but the first thing a cold-weather visitor might see is a blazing fireplace heating the reception room near the entrance. About half the comfortably furnished bedrooms look out over a garden in the rear. The establishment serves savory pub lunches as well as more formal restaurant meals throughout the year. The same food is offered in both the bar and the restaurant, including breaded prawns, halibut, and T-bone steaks. Appetizers cost from £1.45 to £4.95 ($2.20 to $7.40), with main courses going for £3.95 to £13.50 ($5.90 to $20.30).

TARBET

On the western shores of Loch Lomond, Tarbet is not to be confused with the larger center of Tarbert, headquarters of the Loch Fyne herring industry. Loch Lomond's Tarbet is merely a village and a summer holiday base with limited accommodations. In the distance you can see the majesty of Ben Lomond. King Haakon of Norway came this way in the 13th century and devastated the countryside. To the north, now the site of the Inveruglas power station, the Clan MacFarlane had their rallying point.

Boats can be launched from the pier, and Tarbet is one of the stops on the route of the steamship *Countess Fiona*.

WHERE TO STAY & DINE

TARBET HOTEL, Tarbet, Arrochar, Dunbartonshire G83 7DE. Tel. 03012/228. Fax 03012/673. 88 rms (all with bath). TV

$ Rates (including half board): £38 ($57) single; £76 ($114) double. AE, DC, MC, V. **Parking:** Free. **Closed:** Jan.

Considered a famous and historic hotel, the Tarbet sits in the center of a very small hamlet, at the junction of the A82 and the A83. It stands on the site of a simple inn built more than 400 years ago. A coaching inn was erected on the old foundation in 1760, and during the Victorian era, a baronial facade and mock-fortified crenellations were added. A cozy cocktail lounge looks past a row of very old yew trees onto the lake. Good food is served in the dining room, where a fixed-price dinner costs only £7 ($10.50).

CHAPTER 8

TAYSIDE & GRAMPIAN

- **WHAT'S SPECIAL ABOUT TAYSIDE & GRAMPIAN**
1. **PERTH**
2. **CRIEFF**
3. **COMRIE**
4. **ABERFELDY**
5. **DUNKELD**
6. **PITLOCHRY**
7. **DUNDEE**
8. **BRAEMAR**
9. **BALLATER**
10. **BANCHORY**
11. **ABERDEEN**
12. **WEST GRAMPIAN**

Before you rush to the Highlands (see Chapter 9), consider northeast Scotland, taking in Tayside and Grampian. Although separate entities within themselves, these two history-rich sections comprise a vast array of sightseeing, even though they are relatively small. Tayside, for example, is about 85 miles, east to west, and some 60 miles south to north.

The two regions share the North Sea coast between the Firth of Tay in the south and the Firth of Moray farther north. The so-called "Highland Line" separating the Lowlands in the south from the Highlands in the north crosses both regions. The Grampians, the highest mountain range in Scotland, are to the west of this "Highland Line."

Carved out of the old counties of Perth and Angus, Tayside is named for its major river, the 119-mile-long Tay. The region is easy to explore. Its tributaries and dozens of lochs and highland streams are some of the best salmon and trout waters in Europe. One of the loveliest regions of Scotland, Tayside is filled with heather-clad Highland hills, long blue lochs under tree-clad banks, and miles and miles of walking trails. Perth and Dundee are among the six leading cities of Scotland. Tayside provided the backdrop for many novels by Sir Walter Scott, including *The Fair Maid of Perth, Waverley,* and *The Abbot.* Its golf courses are world famous, ranging from the trio of 18-hole courses at Gleneagles to the open championships links at Carnoustie.

The Grampian region has such centers as Aberdeen, Scotland's third largest city, and Braemar, site of the most famous of the Highland gatherings. The queen herself comes here for holidays, to stay at Balmoral Castle, her private residence, a tradition dating back to the days of Queen Victoria and her consort, Prince Albert. The very word *Balmoral* seems to evoke images of tartans and bagpipes. As you journey on the pleasant roads of Scotland's northeast, you'll pass heather-covered moorland and peaty lochs, wood glens and salmon-filled rivers, granite-stone villages and ancient castles, and fishing harbors as well as North Sea beach resorts.

SEEING TAYSIDE & GRAMPIAN

GETTING THERE

Tayside does have an airport at Dundee but it only receives flights from faraway Wick and the northern islands, so Edinburgh is your best gateway if you're an air passenger. Most visitors arrive by train, as ScotRail offers excellent service from Edinburgh to Perth and Dundee and on to Aberdeen. For example, it takes only 1½ hours to reach Perth from Edinburgh. Once at Perth you have a choice of scenic train trips, into the Highlands via Pitlochry or heading northeast to explore the Scottish coast.

WHAT'S SPECIAL ABOUT TAYSIDE & GRAMPIAN

Great Towns/Villages

☐ Perth, an ancient city and former capital of Scotland, stands where the Highlands meet the Lowlands.

☐ Dundee, old seaport and royal burgh lying on the north shore of the Firth of Tay.

☐ Pitlochry, a popular holiday resort and ideal base for touring the Valley of the Tummel.

☐ Aberdeen, Scotland's third city, often called "the granite city," filled with attractions and the best center for touring "castle country."

Ace Attractions

☐ Pitlochry Festival Theatre, Scotland's "theater in the hills" since 1951.

☐ Pitlochry Dam, a power station known for its famous "Salmon Ladder" to help the struggling fish upstream.

☐ The golf courses of Gleneagles, championship courses that have attracted the world's greatest players and many golfers.

Castles and Palaces

☐ Glamis Castle, linked to British royalty for 10 centuries.

☐ Scone Palace, at Scone, seats of the earls of Mansfield, an art-filled palace dating from 1580.

☐ Blair Castle, Blair Atholl, built in the Scottish baronial style and dating from 1269.

☐ Braemar Castle, a fully furnished 17th-century castle opening onto the River Dee.

☐ Balmoral Castle, beloved "paradise" of Queen Victoria, still the private residence of the British sovereign.

☐ Crathes Castle and Gardens, outside Banchory, with historical associations dating from 1323.

☐ Craigievar Castle, outside Banchory, dating from 1626, where Scottish baronial architecture reached its pinnacle.

☐ Fyvie Castle, on the Aberdeen–Banff road, another grand example of Scottish baronial architecture.

Religious Shrines

☐ Cathedral of Dunkeld, founded in A.D. 815 and converted from a church to a cathedral in 1127 by David I.

Parks and Gardens

☐ Pitmidden Garden, Ellon, a 100-acre garden originally laid out by Sir Alexander Seton in 1675.

Special Events/Festivals

☐ Royal Highland Gathering (late August or early September), ancient games that date from the time of the Norman conquest, in Braemar.

While a train will get you there faster, once in the area you'll find that the villages and towns are well linked by bus. Potential bus travelers should call one of two companies about routes through the area: Stagecoach (tel. 0738/33481) or Strathtay Scottish Omnibuses (tel. 0738/26122). Both are based at Perth.

Major motorways to Tayside and Deeside include the M90 between Edinburgh and Perth via the Forth Road Bridge, the A914 between the Kingdom of Fife and Dundee via the Tay Road Bridge, or the A9 between Glasgow and Perth via Stirling.

The fastest way to reach the Grampian region is to take a flight into Aberdeen, although the city is also reached by ScotRail service on the run between Perth, Dundee, and Aberdeen. There is also good rail service between Aberdeen and Inverness.

Coach and bus travel in the northeast is provided by Northern Scottish Lines, whose headquarters in Aberdeen is located at the bus station on Guild Street (tel. 0224/212266).

SUGGESTED ITINERARY

Day 1: From Edinburgh, head north to Perth for the night, visiting its attractions, especially Scone Palace on the outskirts. (Golfers will want to spend whatever time they have not at Perth but at nearby Gleneagles.)

Day 2: From Perth, head west for 18 miles to Crieff at the edge of the Perthshire Highlands, visiting its distillery, Glenturret, plus other attractions. Overnight there.

Days 3–5: From Crieff, head north to Dunkeld to see its old cathedral and continue northwest to Pitlochry for 3 nights. Since you'll probably spend most of the day reaching Pitlochry, occupy Day 4 viewing its attractions, including Pitlochry Dam. Try to attend a performance at the festival theater in the evening. Reserve Day 5 for exploring the major sights of the environs, including the Pass of Killiecrankie, Queen's View, and Blair Castle.

Day 6: After Pitlochry, head east in the morning for a visit to Glamis Castle and drive south to Dundee for an overnight stopover.

Day 7: From Dundee, continue north to Braemar to take in its beauty spots and major attractions, including Braemar Castle. Overnight there.

Day 8: Head east to Ballater to see Balmoral Castle and the surrounding region. Spend the night.

Day 9: Continue east to Banchory for the night. Occupy the day visiting Crathes Castle and Gardens and Craigievar Castle.

Day 10: For your final night, go to Aberdeen and spend some time exploring its attractions. If time remains, visit the castle country and at least see Fyvie Castle in the environs.

---

1. PERTH

44 miles N of Edinburgh, 22 miles SW of Dundee, 64 miles NE of Glasgow

GETTING THERE   By Train   ScotRail provides service between Edinburgh and Perth, with continuing service to Dundee. Trip time to Perth is 1½ hours. Telephone 031/5562451 in Edinburgh for 24-hour information.

By Bus   Edinburgh and Perth are connected by frequent bus service. You can even go from London's Victoria Station by bus to Perth, but the trip takes 12 long hours. For bus information and schedules, phone Stagecoach (tel. 0738/33481) or Strathtay Scottish Omnibuses (tel. 0738/26122), both in Perth, for information.

By Car   To reach Perth from Edinburgh, head northwest along the A90 and go across the Forth Road Bridge, continuing north along the M90.

ESSENTIALS   The **tourist information center** is at 45 High St. (tel. 0738/38353). The **telephone area code** is 0738.

From its majestic position on the Tay, the ancient city of Perth was the capital of Scotland until the middle of the 15th century. Here the Highlands meet the Lowlands.

WHAT TO SEE & DO

The main sightseeing attraction of "the fair city" is the **Kirk of St. John the Baptist,** St. John Street (tel. 26159); it is believed that the original foundation dates from Pictish times. The present choir dates from 1440 and the nave from 1490. In 1559 John Knox preached his famous sermon here attacking idolatry, which caused a turbulent wave of iconoclasm to sweep across the land. The church was restored as a World War I memorial in the mid-1920s. In the church is the tombstone of James I, who was murdered by Sir Robert Graham.

BLACK WATCH REGIMENTAL MUSEUM, Balhousie Castle, Hay Street. Tel. 21281, ext. 8530.

The museum contains the memorabilia of the 42nd and 73rd Highland Regiments. The 2½ centuries of British military history includes paintings, silver, and uniforms.

Admission: Free, but donations appreciated.

Open: Easter–Sept, Mon–Fri 10am–4:30pm, Sun 2–4:30pm; Oct–Mar, Mon–Fri 10am–3pm.

JOHN DEWAR & SONS, Inveralmond, the A912 (Dunkeld Rd.). Tel. 21231.

The internationally renowned distillers of Dewar's White Label scotch whisky have a massive bottling complex at Inveralmond, on the outskirts of Perth at the junction of the A9 and A912. Inveralmond is one of the largest establishments of its kind in Scotland, and as many as 350,000 bottles are filled here in 1 day. Organized tours are given for visitors wishing to see the bottling and dispatch processes. You are advised to phone for information.

Admission: Free.

Open: Guided tours Mon–Thurs 10am, 11:15am, 2pm, and 3:15pm; Fri 10am, 11:15am. **Bus:** 5, 6, 9, or 10.

THE FAIR MAID'S HOUSE, North Port. Tel. 25976.

Near Charlotte Street, this was the old Glover's Hall that Sir Walter Scott chose as the home of his heroine in *The Fair Maid of Perth*. Now a craft shop, it sells high-quality Scottish crafts, including woolen goods, silver, glass, and pottery.

Open: Mon–Sat 10am–5pm.

BRANKLYN GARDEN, Dundee Rd. (A85), in Branklyn. Tel. 25535.

Branklyn Garden has been called the finest 2 acres of private garden in Scotland. It was bequeathed to the National Trust for Scotland, having been established in 1922 by Mr. and Mrs. John Renton. It has a superb collection of rhododendrons, alpines, and herbaceous and peat-garden plants from all over the world.

Admission: £1.50 ($2.30) adults, 80p ($1.20) children.

Open: Mar–Oct, daily 9:30am–sunset.

CAITHNESS GLASS FACTORY, on the main A9 trunk route at Inveralmond. Tel. 37373.

You can watch glassmakers at work at the Caithness Glass Factory, where there is also a visitor center. Of special interest is the intricate art of paperweight making.

Admission: Free.

Open: Factory (where you observe the glassmaking) Mon–Fri 9am–4:30pm; shop and restaurant Mon–Sat 9am–5pm, Sun 11am–5pm. **Bus:** From Mill Street in the center, take the bus to North Muirton; then it's a 10-minute walk.

WHERE TO STAY

BEAUMONT, 15 St. Johns Place, Perth, Perthshire PH1 5SZ Tel. 0738/441770. Fax 0738/441870. 36 rms (all with bath). TV TEL

$ Rates: £35 ($52.50) single; £50 ($75) double. Continental breakfast £4.95 ($7.40) extra. AE, DC, MC, V. **Parking:** Free.

Acclaimed as the best budget hotel in Perth, this travel lodge–style accommodation in the city center offers mostly twin-bedded rooms, although seven are ideal for families. Only two are rented as singles. Opened in 1991, the hotel is clean and bright, beautifully run, and a good value, a chance to stay overnight in immaculate style and comfort, in contrast to some of Perth's threadbare B&Bs. Around the corner is Timothy's, one of Perth's best and most reasonably priced restaurants.

DUNDEE & TAYSIDE

N
0 — 21 mi
— 35 km

B9128
Forfar
Kirriemuir
A94
A929
Glamis
Glamis Castle
A920
Meigle
Alyth
Coupar Angus
Sidlaw Hills
Blairgowrie
A93
A924
A923
A984
Dunkeld
A822
A926
A827
Pitlochry
Aberfeldy
B846
B8019
B846
Kinloch
Rannoch
Loch Rannoch
Schiehallion
Ben Lawers
A827
Loch Tay
Killin
Lochearnhead
Ben More
Ben More
Comrie
A85
Ben Vorlich
Ben Chonzie
A822
A85
Crieff
Earn
Perth
A94
A93
A85
Newport-on-Tay
Tay
Newburgh
A914
Leuchars
Tayport
Buddon Ness
Monifieth
A930
A92
Carnoustie
Dundee

Carnoustie A92

Carnoustie

7 Dundee

6 Perth
3 Crieff
1 Comrie

2 Aberfeldy
5 Dunkeld
4 Pitlochry
7 Dundee

SCOTLAND
DUNDEE & TAYSIDE

HUNTING TOWER, Crieff Road, Perth, Perthshire PH1 3JT. Tel. 0738/-83771. Fax 0738/83777. 35 rms (all with bath). MINIBAR TV TEL **Directions:** 3½ miles west by A85.

$ Rates (including Scottish breakfast): £79 ($118.50) single; £99 ($148.50) double. AE, DC, MC, V. **Parking:** Free.

This late-Victorian house is set in 3½ acres of well-manicured gardens. A magnificent country house, it is the finest lodging choice in and around Perth. Lying about a 10-minute drive from the city center, it has a mock Tudor facade. Taste and concern went into the public rooms, which have fine wood paneling. The bedrooms are also distinguished, although they range from rather large to smaller and more compact. Such thoughtful amenities as hairdryers, radios, minibars, and trouser presses are included; seven of the accommodations have spa baths.

Dining/Entertainment: The fine cuisine is reason enough to stay here. In the elegant restaurant, both a Scottish cuisine and continental dishes are served. Dinners cost from £18 ($27).

Services: Room service, laundry, babysitting.

Facilities: Leisure complex, sauna, solarium, gymnasium, putting green, Turkish bath.

PARKLANDS HOTEL & RESTAURANT, 1 St. Leonard's Bank, Perth, Perthshire PH2 8EB. Tel. 0783/22451. Fax 0738/22046. 14 rms (all with bath). TV TEL

$ Rates (including Scottish breakfast): £75–£100 ($112.50–$150) single; £85–£125 ($127.50–$187.50) double. AE, MC, V. **Parking:** Free.

Luxuriously overhauled, this hotel near the rail station opened in 1991 and immediately became the most fashionable hotel in Perth. The husband-and-wife team of Pat and Allen Deeson set out to create a country-house hotel in the middle of the city, and they succeeded admirably. The beautifully decorated bedrooms, filled with wood paneling and cornices, overlook the South Inch Park. All the rooms are spacious and contain tea makers and hairdryers.

Dining/Entertainment: Light traditional fare is served in country-house style. Breakfast begins with such classic Scottish dishes as Loch Fyne kippers, deviled kidneys, smoked kedgeree, and smoked salmon. For dinner you can enjoy such specialties as sautéed chicken livers with a ginger dressing, marinated scallops and oysters in citrus juices flavored with dill and garlic, or breast of duck with an apricot sauce. Sweets include an iced honey-and-whisky mousse on a coriander sauce. A fixed-price lunch costs £15.50 ($23.30), and a set dinner costs £22.50 ($33.80).

Services: Room service (from early morning until late in the evening), babysitting, laundry.

Facilities: Victorian conservatory.

ROYAL GEORGE, Tay St., Perth, Perthside PH1 5LD. Tel. 0738/24455. Fax 0738/30345. 39 rms (all with bath). TV TEL **Bus:** 9

$ Rates: £70 ($105) single; £80 ($120) double. Scottish breakfast £9.50 ($14.30) extra. AE, DC, MC, V. **Parking:** Free.

The Royal George gets the "royal" in its name from a long-ago visit by Queen Victoria. The stone facade and landscaped garden you see today, however, date from around 1910. Each bedroom is solidly furnished, evoking the 19th century with high ceilings, big windows, and wood detailing. On the premises is Helen MacGregor's, a bar named after the legendary mistress of Rob Roy. In Manton's Restaurant, traditional cookery, including Scottish beef, is a specialty. A fixed-price dinner costs £15.95 ($23.90) per person.

WHERE TO DINE

NUMBER THIRTY THREE, 33 George St. Tel. 0738/33771.
Cuisine: SEAFOOD. **Reservations:** Required

$ Prices: Appetizers £3.50–£7 ($5.30–$10.50); main courses £8.50–£15 ($12.80–$22.50). AE, MC, V.

Open: Lunch Tues–Sat 12:30–2:30pm; dinner Tues–Sat 6:30–9:30pm. **Closed:** 10 days at Christmas and New Year's.

Acclaimed as the finest dining choice in Perth, this restaurant is the creation of Gavin Billingshurt, who employed a thoughtful, considerate staff. Many patrons come here just to enjoy the treats of the oyster bar. In the art deco dining room beyond, you can sample such dishes as moules (mussels) marinière, which are served like a pyramid. That keeps the shellfish at the bottom hot until the last delicious morsel is consumed. Others prefer to begin with a terrine made from prawns and crabmeat, perhaps ordering sautéed lemon sole flavored with herb butter as a main dish. One dish that might be a first for you is grilled sparlings, which are big spratlike fish caught in the Tay estuary. Baked rock turbot is another specialty, but you can also order meat dishes, including, for example, escalope of veal suédoise. Since the restaurant is small with only seven tables, reservations are vital.

TIMOTHY'S, 24 St. John St. Tel. 0738/26641.
   Cuisine: SCANDINAVIAN. **Reservations:** Required. **Bus:** 9.
   $ Prices: Appetizers 95p–£3 ($1.40–$4.50); smørrebrød £3.45–£8.55 ($5.20–$12.80); cold platters £5.55–£7.95 ($8.30–$11.90). MC, V.
   Open: Lunch Tues–Sat noon–2:30pm; dinner Tues–Sat 7–10pm.

Timothy's has a convivial informality, and serves superior food. Try the Swedish smörgåsbord offered by the owners, Caroline and Athole Laing. Roast beef (rare and tender), smoked trout, tasty sausages, crabmeat wrapped in smoked salmon, and homemade soups (such as nettle or dandelion) are well prepared. Salmon caught in the River Tay, only about 55 yards away, is brought here fresh each morning and served at lunch and dinner during the season. The fresh oysters from Loch Fyne are luscious. Top-quality local produce is used, including garden fruit and vegetables. The menu opens with "snitters," which in Danish means an appetizer, and follows with a selection of smørrebrød, those famous Danish open-faced sandwiches. To complement the sandwiches, cold platters, such as seafood or a health food platter, are offered, along with salads. The hot dish is fondue bourguinonne with six sauces for two or more diners, costing from £10.60 ($15.90) per person. Athole wears his kilt every evening to give visitors to Perth a warm Scottish welcome. Caroline, who does all the cooking, makes a special "pudding" every day, such as fresh raspberry-cream soufflé in summer and a steamy hot, fruit-spiced sponge in winter. She's known for her Scottish trifle, made the old-fashioned way—lots of fruit, sherry, and cream.

EASY EXCURSIONS FROM PERTH
SCONE

Old Scone, 2 miles from Perth on the River Tay, was the ancient capital of the Picts. On a lump of granite called the "Stone of Destiny" the early Scottish monarchs were enthroned. To this day the British sovereign is still crowned on the stone, now in Westminster Abbey. Edward I moved it there in 1296. Charles II was the last king crowned at Scone, in 1651.

The seat of the earls of Mansfield and birthplace of David Douglas of fir-tree fame, **۞ Scone Palace,** Scone, along the A93 (tel. 0783/52300), was largely rebuilt in 1802, incorporating the old palace of 1580. Inside is an impressive collection of French furniture, china, ivories, and 16th-century needlework, including bed hangings executed by Mary Queen of Scots. A fine collection of rare conifers is found on the grounds in the Pinetum. Rhododendrons and azaleas grow profusely in the gardens and woodlands around the palace. To reach the palace, head 2 miles northeast of Perth on the A93. The site is open from Good Friday through mid-October, Monday to Saturday from 9:30am to 5pm and on Sunday from 1:30 to 5pm. Admission is £4 ($6) for adults, £2.20 ($3.30) for children, including entrance to both house and grounds.

Where to Stay & Dine

THE MURRAYSHALL, New Scone, Perthshire PH2 7PH. Tel. 0738/51171. Fax 0738/52595. 16 rms (all with bath), 3 suites. TV TEL **Directions:** Take the A94 1½ miles east of New Scone.
   $ Rates (including Scottish breakfast): £60–£75 ($90–$112.50) single; £105–£125

($157.50–$187.50) double; £105–£185 ($157.50–$277.50) suite. AE, DC, MC, V. **Parking:** Free.

✪ The Murrayshall is an elegant country-house hotel and restaurant. Set in 300 acres of parkland, it was completely refurbished in 1987 and reopened as one of the showpieces of Perthshire. The Victorian mansion offers its own 18-hole, par-73 golf course, interspersed with trees, water hazards, and white-sanded bunkers. The hotel is traditionally styled, in both its public rooms and its bedrooms, each with quality furniture. The size of the rooms varies, as does the decorating.

Dinner is another £25 ($37.50), and it's a worthy choice—in fact, the finest dining in the area. The Old Master's restaurant takes its name from reproduction paintings of the Dutch masters that hang on its walls. The menu provides Scottish flavor and French inspiration in cooking. Main courses might include filet of Shetland Isles farmed salmon, sirloin of Scottish beef, or deep-fried filet of North Sea haddock. Dinner is served in the candlelit restaurant daily from 7 to 9:30pm; lunch is served from noon to 3pm. Nonresidents are welcome, but must reserve.

GLENEAGLES

This famous golfing center and sports complex is on a moor between Strath Earn and Strath Allan. The center gets its name from the Gaelic Gleann-an-Eaglias, meaning "glen of the church." St. Mungo's Chapel, higher up the glen than the internationally known golf courses and hotel, has monuments of the Haldane family, whose ancestral castle ruins provided the stones for the building of the later family seat constructed in 1624.

Gleneagles has four 18-hole golf courses connected with the hotel: King's Course, the longest one; Queen's Course, next in length; Prince's Course, shortest of all; and Glendevon, the newest of the quartet, built in 1980. They are considered the best in Scotland. The sports complex is one of the most splendid in Europe.

Gleneagles provides a good—but far from inexpensive—base from which to explore the major attractions of central Scotland. It is in the ancient royal burgh of Auchterarder of many centuries ago, strategically placed on the road that led from the royal residence at Scone to Stirling Castle. Today it's on the A9, about halfway between Perth and Stirling, a short distance from the village of Auchterarder. It lies 55 miles from Edinburgh and 45 miles from Glasgow. The tourist information center is at 90 High St. (tel. 0764/63450).

Where to Stay & Dine

AUCHTERARDER HOUSE, Auchterarder, Perthshire PH3 1DZ. Tel. 0764/663646. Fax 0764/6622939. 15 rms (all with bath). TV TEL

$ Rates (including Scottish breakfast): £90–£110 ($135–$165) single; £130–£195 ($195–$292.50) double. AE, DC, MC, V. **Parking:** Free.

✪ Auchterarder House, 1 mile from Gleneagles and 1½ miles from Auchterarder, sits in its own grounds off the B8062 between Auchterarder and Crieff. A fine example of 1830s architecture and construction in the Scots Jacobean style, the mansion house has been completely restored and the interior refurbished to a high standard of luxury by its present owners, Ian and Audrey Brown. The house has elegant public rooms and comfortable bedrooms, all with amenities calculated to please a discerning clientele. Afternoon tea is served in the glass conservatory with its marble fountain. The handsome bar was originally designed as the building's chapel. Lunch and dinner are served in the Victorian dining room or in the library. You can choose from both a French and British menu. Dinner will cost £37.50 to £50 ($56.30 to $75), the price including canapés, coffee, and petits fours.

Free courtesy car service is offered from the Gleneagles station, and the staff will help arrange tours of the area as well as sports activities, including golf. You may be content, however, just to browse around the 20 acres of grounds, where a fine collection of rare shrubs, trees, and rhododendrons is nurtured.

GLENEAGLES HOTEL, Auchterarder, Perthshire PH3 1NF. Tel. 0764/ 662231. Fax 0764/662134. 236 rms (all with bath), 20 suites. MINIBAR TV TEL

$ Rates (including Scottish breakfast): £145 ($217.50) single; £205–£280 ($307.50–$420) double; £305–£880 ($457.50–$1,320) suite. AE, DC, MC, V. **Parking:** Free.

The Gleneagles Hotel stands in its own 830-acre estate, 1½ miles southwest of Auchterarder by the A9. Built in isolated grandeur in 1924, it was for many years after its establishment the only five-star hotel in Scotland, a position it maintained until the early 1990s. It is owned by Guinness, PLC, the famous British brewery, and is sought after for its golf course (see facilities, below). The service and decor are considered among the finest in the country. Each of the luxurious bedrooms has in-house video. The rooms contain elegant furnishings, and offer splendid views of hills and glens of the surrounding countryside.

Dining/Entertainment: Guests can dine in the Strathearn Restaurant, paying £25 ($37.50) and up for a table d'hôte lunch, and from £38.50 ($57.80) for a table d'hôte dinner. The emphasis is on regional dishes, and piano music is played in the evening. The gourmet restaurant is the Conservatory Restaurant, which has magnificent views. Both restaurants are open daily from 7:30 to 10pm. The cook uses fresh Scottish and French produce, cooked in a light style while still incorporating traditional flair and imagination. Service is impeccable.

Services: 24-hour room service, laundry/valet, babysitting.

Facilities: The hotel's country club, enclosed in a glass dome to provide a year-round tropical climate, offers to members and hotel guests use of a swimming pool, whirlpool, Turkish bath, saunas, plunge pool, and children's pool. You can have steak and salads at the Brasserie, and there's a cocktail bar. If you're really hardy, you can use the Canadian hot tubs outdoors. Champneys The Health Spa includes treatment rooms for health, beauty, and massages. There are also squash courts, a gym, snooker tables, tennis courts, croquet lawns, and a bowling green, not to mention fishing on the River Tay. In addition, there are the Gleneagles Jackie Stewart Shooting School and the Gleneagles Mark Phillips Equestrian Centre. For the coddling of golfers, the Dormy House (old name for a clubhouse) beside the 18th greens of the King's and Queen's courses has a restaurant and bar, showers, and changing rooms.

The hotel maintains a legendary golf course that is sought after by golfers throughout the summer and winter. (Diehards have been known to brush away piles of light snow to improve their golfing skills even in January.) The course is open only to residents of Gleneagles, who pay £40 ($60) per person to play the course's famous 18 holes.

---

2. CRIEFF

18 miles W of Perth, 60 miles NW of Edinburgh, 50 miles NE of Glasgow

GETTING THERE By Train There is no direct service. The nearest rail stations are at Gleneagles, 9 miles away, and Perth, 18 miles away (see above).

By Bus Once you arrive in Perth, you'll find regular connecting bus service hourly during the day. However, the bus service from Gleneagles is too poor to recommend.

By Car From Perth, continue west along the A85.

ESSENTIALS The year-round **tourist information office** is on High Street (tel. 0764/652578). The **telephone area code** is 0764.

At the edge of the Perthshire Highlands, with good fishing and golf, Crieff makes a pleasant stopover. This small burgh was the seat of the court of the earls of Strathearn until 1747. The gallows in its marketplace once was used to execute Highland cattle rustlers.

You can take a "day trail" into Strathearn, the valley of the River Earn, the very center of Scotland. Highland mountains meet gentle Lowland slopes, and moorland mingles with rich green pastures. North of Crieff, the road to Aberfeldy passes through the narrow pass of the Sma' Glen with hills rising on either side to 2,000 feet. The glen is a famous beauty spot.

WHAT TO SEE & DO

GLENTURRET DISTILLERY LTD., on the A85, Glenturret. Tel. 0764/652424.

Scotland's oldest distillery, Glenturret Distillery was established in 1775 on the banks of the River Turret. Visitors can see the milling of malt, mashing, fermentation, distillation, and cask filling, followed by a free "wee dram" dispensed at the end of the tour. Guided tours leave every 10 minutes and take about 25 minutes. The Glenturret Heritage Centre incorporates a 100-seat audiovisual theater and an Exhibition Display Museum. The presentation lasts about 20 minutes. The distillery shop has the full range of the Glenturret Pure Single Highland Malt scotch whisky and the Glenturret malt liqueur, together with an extensive range of souvenirs. At the Smugglers Restaurant and Whisky Tasting Bar you can taste older Glenturret whiskies, such as 10-year-old, high-proof, 12- and 15-year-old, and the Glenturret malt liqueur.

Admission: Guided tours, £2.80 ($4.20) adults, £1.20 ($1.80) students 12–17, free for children under 12.

Open: Mar–Dec, Mon–Sat 9:30am–6pm, Sun noon–6pm. Jan–Feb, Mon–Fri 11:30am–2:30pm.

Directions: Take the A85 toward Comrie; three-quarters of a mile from Crieff, turn right at the crossroads; the distillery is a quarter mile up the road.

CRIEFF VISITORS CENTRE, 14 Comrie St. Tel. 0764/655151.

This point of interest in the town center off West High Street opened in 1985, built by Buchan's Thistle Potteries and Perthshire Paperweight, two medium-size craft factories, to enable visitors to see their skills in manufacturing pottery and glass. Visitors can go on a free guided tour through the factory Monday through Friday; sometimes tours can be taken on Sunday afternoon in high season.

Admission: Center, free; pottery tours, £1 ($1.50) adults, 50p (80¢) children.

Open: Apr–Oct, daily 9am–6pm; Nov–Mar, daily 9am–5pm.

DRUMMOND CASTLE, Grimsthorpe, Crieff. Tel. 0764/681257.

The gardens of Drummond Castle, first laid out in the early 17th century by John Drummond, second earl of Perth, are said to be among the finest formal gardens in Europe. A spectacular view can be obtained from the upper terrace, overlooking a magnificent example of an early Victorian parterre in the form of St. Andrew's Cross. The multi-faceted sundial by John Mylne, master mason to Charles I, has been the centerpiece since 1630.

Admission: £2 ($3) adults, £1 ($1.50) children.

Open: May–Sept daily 2–6pm. **Closed:** Oct–Apr. **Directions:** Take the A822 3 miles south of Crieff.

WHERE TO STAY & DINE

MURRAYPARK HOTEL, Connaught Terrace, Crieff, Perthshire PH7 3DJ.
Tel. 0764/653731. Fax 0764/655311. 21 rms (all with bath). TV TEL.
Directions: Approaching from Perth, take the first right after the golf club; the hotel will be on your left.

$ Rates (including Scottish breakfast): £45 ($67.50) single; £65 ($97.50) double. AE, DC, MC, V. **Parking:** Free.

Originally built by a sea captain late in the 19th century as a refuge from his trips abroad, this stone-fronted house lies in a residential neighborhood, about a 10-minute walk from Crieff's center. In 1993, a new wing was opened, enlarging the public rooms and the number of guest accommodations. You can drink in the bar before dinner. Recipes are based on Scottish, French, and international inspirations, and cost around £21.75 ($32.60) for table d'hôte dinners.

3. COMRIE

25 miles W of Perth

GETTING THERE By Bus Daily buses run from Crieff to Comrie.

By Car Continue west from Crieff along the A85.

ESSENTIALS The nearest **tourist office** is in Crieff. The **telephone area code** is 0764.

An attractive little village in Strathearn, Comrie stands at the confluence of the Earn, Ruchill, and Lednock rivers. The A85 runs through the village to Lochearnhead, Crianlarich, and on to Oban on the western seaboard. It's convenient as an overnight stop for travelers crossing Scotland. Waterskiing, boating, and sailing are available on Loch Earn.

WHAT TO SEE & DO

SCOTTISH TARTANS MUSEUM, Drummond St. Tel. 0764/70779.
This is the only museum in the world devoted entirely to tartans and Highland dress. There are more than 400 tartans on display, and you can follow the evolution of Highland dress down through the ages. There is a reconstructed weaver's cottage with occasional demonstrations of hand-spinning and hand-weaving, as well as a garden featuring plants, shrubs, and trees used in past times to dye tartan. The Scottish Tartans Society undertakes research inquiries on a fee basis using its archives, *The Register of All Publicly Known Tartans*. There is a shop selling authentic tartan goods, plus a mail-order service.
   Admission: £1.60 ($2.40) adults, £1 ($1.50) children.
   Open: Nov–Mar, Mon–Fri 10am–1pm and 2–5pm, Sat 10am–1pm; Apr–May and Sept–Oct, Mon–Sat 10am–6pm, Sun 11am–5pm; June–Aug, Mon–Sat 9am–6:30pm, Sun 11am–5pm.

WHERE TO STAY & DINE

ROYAL HOTEL, Melville Square, Comrie, Perthshire PH6 2DN. Tel. 0764/670200. Fax 0764/670479. 9 rms (all with bath). TV TEL
$ Rates (including Scottish breakfast): £25 ($37.50) single; £50 ($75) double. AE, MC, V. **Parking:** Free.
The Royal Hotel was awarded the "royal" after the visit of Her Majesty, Queen Victoria. It's not, as you might imagine, a Victorian hotel, but rather an L-shaped stone inn dating back to 1765, with white trim and six bedroom dormers. Its cocktail bar with copper-top tables, furnished and decorated in the Gordon tartan, is noted for its selection of malt whiskies, and on the walls are framed prints and photographs with signatures of numerous famous guests who have stayed here over the years, including that of "Monty," Lloyd George, actress Sarah Bernhardt, and Queen Victoria's faithful servant, John Brown.
   The bedrooms are comfortable, and all have radios, hot-beverage facilities, and electric blankets. The spacious residents' lounge is well appointed, and the cocktail bar has been refurbished. A table d'hôte dinner costs £15 ($22.50). Lunch is served daily from noon to 2pm, and dinner is daily from 7 to 9pm.

---

4. ABERFELDY

76 miles NW of Edinburgh, 73 miles NE of Glasgow, 32 miles NW of Perth

GETTING THERE   By Train There is no direct service into Aberfeldy. You can take a train to either Perth (see above) or Pitlochry (see below), then continue the rest of the way by bus.

By Bus Connecting buses at either Perth or Pitlochry make the final journey to Aberfeldy.

By Car Edinburgh lies about a 1¾-hour drive from Aberfeldy, and it takes about 2 hours to reach Aberfeldy from Glasgow. Take the M9 from Stirling, then the A9 to Perth and continue on the A9 to Ballinluig, then the A827 to Aberfeldy. Or take the scenic route—the M9 from Stirling, then the A9 turning off at Greenloaning onto the A822 to Crieff. Continue on the A822 to Gilmerton, then after going through Amulree, take the A826 to Aberfeldy.

ESSENTIALS A **tourist information office** is at The Square (tel. 0887/820276). The **telephone area code** is 0887.

The "Birks o' Aberfeldy" are among the beauty spots made famous by Robert Burns. Once a Pictish center, this small town makes a fine base for touring Perthshire's glens and lochs. Loch Tay lies 6 miles to the west; Glen Lyon, 15 miles west; and Kinloch Rannoch, 18 miles northwest.

In Aberfeldy, General Wade in 1733 built the bridge spanning the Tay. In the town's shops are good buys in tweeds and tartans, plus other items of Highland dress.

WHERE TO STAY & DINE

ATKINS AT FARLEYER HOUSE, along the B846, Aberfeldy, Perthshire PH15 2JE. Tel. 0887/820332. Fax 0887/829430. 9 rms (all with bath), 2 suites. TV TEL

$ Rates (including Scottish breakfast): £50 ($75) single; £105 ($157.50) double; from £200 ($300) suite. AE, MC, V.

A tranquil oasis, this Scottish hotel of character stands on 70 acres of grounds in the Tay Valley 2 miles west of Aberfeldy on the B846. Dating from the 1500s but much restored and altered over the years, it entertains guests as if they were in a private home. It is a former dower house of the Menzies clan. Castle Menzies, their 16th-century mansion, can be seen in the distance. The public rooms are immaculate and beautifully furnished, and the bedrooms are well maintained and comfortable. Each has a radio and hairdryer.

Dining/Entertainment: The internationally renowned Atkins Restaurant offers a fixed-price menu of five courses (changed daily) for £35 ($52.50). A typical menu might begin with a warm salad of pigeon, goose, and duck with a raspberry vinaigrette, then follow with lobster bisque, stuffed saddle of lamb wrapped in pastry and served with wild mushrooms, a plate of British cheese, and a basket of sorbets and fruits or else a honey and whisky parfait with butterscotch sauce and praline. Only dinner is served, nightly from 7:30 to 8:30pm. Less formal and less expensive is The Scottish Bistro, serving daily from 10am to 2pm and 6:30 to 9:30pm. Typical dishes here include entrecôte of Angus beef, venison steak with red cabbage, and roast grouse with bacon and rowan jelly. Meals here cost from £12 ($18).

Service: Room service, laundry/valet, babysitting.

Facilities: Reception desk will arrange for golf, fishing, sailing, waterskiing, windsurfing, and shooting, as well as tennis and swimming.

---

5. DUNKELD

58 miles N of Edinburgh, 14 miles N of Perth, 98 miles SW of Aberdeen

GETTING THERE By Train Trains from Perth arrive every 2 hours at Dunkeld Station, which is actually in the neighboring town of Birnam.

By Bus Pitlochry-bound buses leaving from Perth make a stopover in Dunkeld, letting you off at the Dunkeld Car Park.

By Car From Perth, continue north on the Pitlochry road (A9) until you reach Dunkeld.

A cathedral town, Dunkeld lies in a thickly wooded valley of the Tay, on the edge of the Perthshire Highlands. Once a major ecclesiastical center, it is one of the seats of ancient Scottish history and an important center of the Celtic church.

WHAT TO SEE & DO

Founded in A.D. 815, the **Cathedral of Dunkeld** was converted from a church to a cathedral in 1127 by David I. It stands on Cathedral Street in a beautiful setting along the River Tay. The 14th and 15th centuries witnessed subsequent additions. The cathedral was first restored in 1815, and traces of the 12th-century structure clearly remain today. It can be visited May through September, daily from 9:30am to 7pm; October through April, daily from 9:30am to 4pm. Admission is free.

The National Trust for Scotland has restored many of the old houses and shops around the marketplace and cathedral that had fallen into decay. The trust owns 20 houses on High Street and Cathedral Street as well. Many of these houses were constructed in the closing years of the 17th century after the rebuilding of the town following the Battle of Dunkeld. The Trust runs the **Ell Shop,** the Cross (tel. 0350/727460), open from Easter weekend to May 31 and September 1 to December 22, Monday through Saturday from 10am to 1pm and 2 to 4:30pm; from June 1 to the end of August, Monday through Saturday from 10am to 6pm and on Sunday from 2 to 5pm.

The **Scottish Horse Museum,** The Cross, has exhibits tracing the history of the Scottish Horse Yeomanry. From the time of the raising of the cavalry force in Scotland and South Africa in 1900 to its amalgamation with the Fife & Forfar Yeomanry in 1956, the Scottish Horse mounted yeomanry regiment was the only such fighting body besides the Lovat Scouts. The museum is open from Easter to the end of September, daily from 10am to noon and 2 to 5pm. Admission is 50p (80¢) for adults, free for children.

Shakespeare fans may want to seek out the oak and sycamore in front of the destroyed **Birnam House,** a mile to the south. This was believed to be a remnant of the Birnam Wood in *Macbeth;* in Shakespeare's drama, you may recall, Macbeth could be defeated only when "Birnam wood came to Dunsinane."

The **Hermitage,** lying off the A9 about 2 miles west of Dunkeld, was called a "folly" when it was constructed in 1758. Today it makes for one of the most scenic woodland walks in the area. The folly was built above the wooded gorge of the River Braan and restored in 1984.

WHERE TO STAY & DINE

KINNAIRD, Kinnaird, Kinnaird Estate, Dunkeld, Perthshire PH8 0LB.
Tel. 0796/482440. Fax 0796/482289. 8 rms (all with bath), 1 suite. TV TEL
Directions: Traveling north on the A9 after passing Dunkeld on your right, turn left on to the B898 (sign posted Balnaguard and Dalguise). Follow this road for 4½ miles and the main gate of Kinnaird will be on your right.
$ Rates (including Scottish breakfast): £170–£190 ($255–$285) double; £230 ($345) suite. MC, V. **Parking:** Free.

✪ Opened in 1990, Kinnaird, set on a 9,000-acre private estate, is a small hotel of great warmth, charm, and comfort. All the beautifully furnished bedrooms have king-size beds, private baths, and splendid views. Some rooms overlook the valley of the River Tay, and others open onto gardens and woodlands. Built originally in 1770 as a hunting lodge for the Duke of Atholl, the house was purchased in 1927 by the Ward family. Today, its present owner, American-born Constance Cluett Ward, has lovingly restored the house to its previous grandeur.

Dining/Entertainment: Kinnaird House Restaurant brings a high-caliber cuisine to the area. The chef cooks in the modern, post-nouvelle British and continental style, depending on fresh ingredients with changing menus based on the

red meals for some of the golden palates of Europe, mer seat of Lady Astor. Lobster, Scottish salmon, the poultry go into his kitchen and turn up like delicate ced at £19.50 ($29.30) for two courses and £24 ($36) ur-course dinner goes for £38 ($57) per person.
dry/valet, babysitting.
n the estate include salmon and trout fishing, roe t, grouse, and duck. All equipment is provided kennels for gun dogs.

ORT HOTEL, Dunkeld, Perthshire PH8
0350/728924. 92 rms (all with bath), 3 suites.

DUNKELD · 267 (tel. 0350/727688).

River at the one of the rch.

breakfast): £72.50 ($108.80) single; £108 ($162) ..8 ($192–$237) suite. AE, DC, MC, V. **Parking:** Free.

in 1903 as the private home for the Duke and Duchess of Atholl, this property was acquired by the Stakis chain and much enlarged in 1988. Today, it offers the quiet dignity of life in a Scottish country house, about a mile northwest of Dunkeld on the road leading to Pitlochry (signposted). It is ranked as one of the leading leisure and sports hotels in the area. On the banks of the Tay, the surrounding grounds—280 acres in all—are planted with trees and flowering bushes, making for a parklike setting. The house is beautifully kept, and accommodations come in a wide range of styles, space, and furnishings. The hotel, extensively restored and expanded, now offers first-class bedrooms.

Dining/Entertainment: Its restaurant is one of the finest in the area, paying homage to its "Taste of Scotland" dishes, but also serving an international cuisine as well. Fixed-price lunches cost £14.50 ($21.80); fixed-price dinners go for £22.50 ($33.80).

Services: Room service, laundry/valet, babysitting.

Facilities: Guests can fish for trout and salmon right on the grounds. Facilities include all-weather tennis courts and an indoor swimming pool. Archery and fishing are also popular.

---

6. PITLOCHRY

71 miles NW of Edinburgh, 27 miles NW of Perth

GETTING THERE By Train Seven trains per day (tel. 0796/472513 in Pitlochry for information) arrive from Edinburgh and an additional seven per day arrive from Glasgow (trip time from each: 2 hours). A one-way fare is £14 ($21) from either city.

By Bus Buses to Pitlochry arrive hourly from Perth (see above). The one-way fare is £3.90 ($5.90).

By Car From Perth, continue northwest along the A9.

ESSENTIALS The **tourist information office** is at 22 Atholl Rd. (tel. 0796/472215). The **telephone area code** is 0796.

After leaving Edinburgh, many motorists stop here for the night before continuing on the Highland road to Inverness, 85 miles to the north. This charming and popular holiday resort center is a touring headquarters for the Valley of the Tummel.

Pitlochry doesn't just entertain tourists, although it would appear that way in summer; it also produces scotch whisky and tweeds.

WHAT TO SEE & DO

The town is renowned for its **Pitlochry Festival Theatre,** Scotland's "theater in the hills" (tel. 0796/472680 for information). Founded in 1951, the festival theater draws people from all over the world to its repertory of plays, which change daily, its Sunday concerts, and varying art exhibitions, presented from April 30 to October 9. Performances in the evening begin at 8pm, and on Wednesday and Saturday there is a matinee at 2pm. The theater complex opened in 1981 on the banks of the River Tummel near the dam and fish ladder, with a parking area, a restaurant serving coffee, lunch, and dinner, and other facilities for visitors. Tickets for plays and concerts cost £8–£13 ($12–$19.50). For details by mail, address correspondence to the Pitlochry Festival Theatre, Pitlochry PH16 5DR.

The **Pitlochry Dam** was created because a power station was needed, but in effect, the engineers created a new loch. The famous "Salmon Ladder" was built to help the struggling salmon upstream. An underwater portion of the ladder—a salmon observation chamber—has been enclosed in glass to give fascinated sightseers a look. An exhibition (tel. 0796/473152) is open here from Easter to late October, daily from 9:45am to 5:30pm, costing £1.50 ($2.30) for adults and 60p (90¢) for children.

WHERE TO STAY

GREEN PARK HOTEL, Clunie Bridge Rd., Pitlochry, Perthside PH16 5JY. Tel. 0796/473248. Fax 0796/473520. 37 rms (all with bath). TV TEL
$ **Rates** (including half board): £53 ($79.50) per person. MC, V. **Parking:** Free. **Closed:** Nov to mid-Mar.
The Green Park Hotel lies about half a mile from the center, at the northwest end of Pitlochry. Against a backdrop of woodland, the white-painted mansion with its carved eaves enjoys a scenic position; its lawn reaches to the shores of Loch Faskally. Visitors who reserve well in advance get one of the half dozen or so rooms in the garden wing, which all enjoy a view of the loch. Guests order drinks in a half-moon-shaped lounge overlooking the water. Many diners come here during festival season to enjoy the good food and wine. Dinner is served until 8:30pm, and many traditional Scottish dishes are featured. The hotel is supervised by Anne and Graham Brown.

PINE TREES HOTEL, Strathview Terrace, Pitlochry, Perthshire PH16 5QR. Tel. 0796/472121. Fax 0796/472460. 20 rms (all with bath). TV TEL
Directions: On the north side of Pitlochry; turn right up Larchwood Road, below the golf course.
$ **Rates** (including Scottish breakfast): £43–£49 ($64.50–$73.50) single; £78–£90 ($117–$135) double. MC, V. **Parking:** Free.
The Pine Trees Hotel is a charming, country-house hotel built in 1892 by a French woman on 14 acres of private grounds. It's only about a 15-minute walk to the town center and 5 minutes to the golf course, home of the Highland Open Championships. A well-appointed family-run hotel, the Pine Trees has spacious, comfortable public rooms, an atmosphere of warmth and relaxation, and an enviable reputation for good food and wine. Bar lunches and full luncheon and dinner menus are offered, with fresh and smoked salmon always on the menu. Trout and salmon fishing can usually be arranged.

PITLOCHRY HYDRO HOTEL, Knockard Rd., Pitlochry, Perthshire PH16 5JH. Tel. 0796/472666. Fax 0796/472238. 64 rms (all with bath). TV TEL
$ **Rates** (including Scottish breakfast): £57 ($85.50) single; £98 ($147) double. AE, DC, MC, V. **Parking:** Free. **Closed:** Jan–Feb 7.
This hotel was originally known by the English gentry who came here in summer to enjoy the fresh air of the Perthshire Highlands. Built in the Scottish-baronial-mansion style in the 1890s, the hotel has kept up with modern improvements. It stands on large, well-manicured grounds. Ask for one of the turreted corner rooms when making a reservation. A fixed-price dinner costs £15 ($22.50). The hotel has an indoor swimming pool and other leisure facilities.

WHERE TO DINE

EAST HAUGHT HOUSE, Old Perth Rd., East Haught, Pitlochry, Perthshire PH16 5JS. Tel. 0796/473121. Fax 0796/472473.

Cuisine: MODERN BRITISH. **Reservations:** Recommended.

$ Prices: In bar, platters £5–£10 ($7.50–$15); in restaurant, table d'hôte dinner £25 ($37.50). MC, V.

Open: Bar lunches daily noon–2:30pm; bar suppers daily 6–10:30pm; in restaurant, dinner only, 7–10:30pm. **Closed:** One week in early March.

Although it contains eight comfortably furnished bedrooms, this establishment is best known for its sophisticated and well-prepared cuisine. Set within a Teutonic-looking granite house originally commissioned in the 1600s by the Duke of Atholl for one of his tenant farmers, it offers a menu that relies exclusively on fresh Scottish ingredients and that changes every two days. Meals in the cozy bar area might include mixed grills, Scottish lamb, steaks, and haggis. Meals in the more elegant restaurant are more adventurous, featuring such dishes as zucchini flowers stuffed with a duxelle of wild mushrooms; grilled and marinated Scottish goat cheese with a mixed leaf and pine nut salad; terrine of local pigeon with orange salad and *mange tout;* and many different variations of salmon. Dessert might include a dark chocolate torte with crème fraîche, or a hot thin apple flan with caramel sauce. Scottish-born Neil McGown and his English wife Lesley are the hardworking and gracious owners.

Bedrooms are outfitted like rooms in a Scottish country mansion, with conservative dignity, private bathrooms, telephones, and TVs. Depending on the season, with Scottish breakfast included, singles range from £35 ($52.50) to £55 ($82.50); doubles from £60 ($90) to £80 ($120).

The establishment lies about a mile south of Pitlochry, across the road from the Tummell River, beside the A9 leading to Inverness.

EASY EXCURSIONS FROM PITLOCHRY

PASS OF KILLIECRANKIE   Heading northwest for 3 miles along the B8019, you come to the Pass of Killiecrankie, where "Bonnie Dundee" and his Jacobites won their famous victory over King William's armies led by General Mackay in 1689. A **Visitors Centre** (tel. 0796/473233) stands near the site of the famous battle. Dedicated Scots will answer questions on walks, which are possible in the area. The exhibition, Visitors Centre, shop, and snack bar are open from Easter weekend to May and September to the end of October, daily from 10am to 5pm; from June to August, daily from 9:30am to 6pm. It costs 50p (80¢) to enter.

QUEEN'S VIEW   If time remains, try to see another attraction, Queen's View, where Victoria herself picnicked, in 1844. At the eastern end, Victoria looked down the length of the loch toward Schiehallion. To reach the view, take the B8019 for 2½ miles northwest of Pitlochry. An obelisk commemorates the visit of the queen. The beauty spot, the **Linn of Tummel,** along with 50 acres, came to the National Trust for Scotland during World War II. It is filled with magnificent woodland walks, in which you can enjoy the Douglas fir, spruce, larch, oak, and sycamore.

BLAIR ATHOLL   Eight miles northwest of Pitlochry—well signposted from the A9—stands the gleaming white ○ **Blair Castle** (tel. 0796/481207), home of the dukes of Atholl, just off the A9. Built in the Scottish baronial style and dating from 1269, the castle allows you to view more than 30 rooms. Inside is an impressive collection of paintings, furniture, china, lace, arms and armor, and Masonic regalia, along with many family portraits. It is open daily from the first of April to the last Friday in October from 10am to 6pm. Admission is £4 ($6) for adults, £3 ($4.50) for children. The Duke of Atholl has the only official private army in Great Britain, known as the Atholl Highlanders.

Where to Stay & Dine

ATHOLL ARMS HOTEL, Main St., Blair Atholl, Perthshire PH18 5SG. Tel. 0796/481205. Fax 0796/481550. 30 rms (all with bath). TV TEL

$ Rates (including Scottish breakfast): £32.50 ($48.80) single; £53 ($79.50) double. MC, V. **Parking:** Free.

Once lords and ladies who couldn't find room at Blair Castle stayed at the Atholl Arms, where some of the grand balls of old Perthshire were held. Now the Atholl Arms is a stately gabled stone roadside inn, attracting motorists en route to Inverness (it stands adjacent to the town's railway station, just north of the center, beside the road leading to Pitlochry). The bedrooms are individually styled and well fitted.

A cocktail lounge has been created, and the grandiose ballroom has been turned into a dinner and dance restaurant, complete with a minstrels' gallery. There's also a more intimate dining room. Bar snacks are served at lunch, and a four-course table d'hôte dinner, costing £14 ($21) per person, is offered in the evening.

7. DUNDEE

63 miles N of Edinburgh, 67 SW of Aberdeen, 83 miles NE of Glasgow

GETTING THERE   By Train   ScotRail offers frequent service between Perth, Dundee, and Aberdeen. Phone 0738/37117 in Perth for schedules and departure times.

By Bus   National Express buses from both Edinburgh and Glasgow offer frequent bus service from those cities to Dundee. In Glasgow, phone 041/3324100 for information; in Edinburgh, 031/4528777.

By Car   From Edinburgh, take the M90 north to Perth, then cut northeast along the A85.

ESSENTIALS   The **tourist information office** is at 4 City Square (tel. 0382/ 27723). The **telephone area code** is 0382.

This royal burgh and old seaport is an industrial city on the north shore of the Firth of Tay. When steamers took over the whaling industry from sailing vessels, Dundee took the lead as home port for the ships from the 1860s until World War I. Long known for its jute and flax operations, Dundee today is linked with the production of the rich Dundee fruitcakes and Dundee marmalades and jams. This was also the home of the man who invented stick-on postage stamps, James Chalmers.

Spanning the Firth of Tay is the **Tay Railway Bridge,** opened in 1888. Constructed over the tidal estuary, the bridge is some 2 miles long, one of the longest in Europe. There is also a road bridge 1¼ miles long, with four traffic lanes and a walkway in the center.

WHAT TO SEE & DO

For a spectacular view of Dundee, the Tay bridges across to Fife, and mountains to the north, go to **Dundee Law,** a 572-foot hill a mile north of the city. The hill is an ancient volcanic plug.

THE UNICORN, Victoria Dock. Tel. 0382/200900.

This 46-gun ship of war commissioned in 1824 by the Royal Navy, now the oldest British-built ship afloat, has been in large part restored and visitors can explore all four decks: the quarterdeck with 32-pound carronades, the gundeck with its battery of 18-pound cannons and the captain's quarters, the berth deck with officers' cabins and crew's hammocks, and the orlop deck and hold. Various displays portraying life in the sailing navy and the history of the *Unicorn* make this a rewarding visit.

Admission: £2 ($3) adults, £1.50 ($2.30) children.
Open: Daily 10am–5pm. **Bus:** 6, 23, or 78.

MCMANUS GALLERIES, Albert Square. Tel. 0382/23141.

Designed by Sir George Gilbert Scott and built in 1867, the galleries house an art collection of national importance, including fine examples of 19th- and 20th-century Scottish paintings, prints, drawing, sculptures, furniture, clocks, glass, ceramics, and silver. Three galleries show the history of life in Tayside. The building is one of Scotland's finest examples of Victorian Gothic architecture.

Admission: Free.

Open: Mon–Sat 10am–5pm. **Bus:** 6, 23, or 78.

BROUGHTY CASTLE, Castle Green, Broughty Ferry. Tel. 0382/76121.

About 4 miles east of the city center on the seafront, at Broughty Ferry, a little fishing hamlet and once the terminus for ferries crossing the Firth of Tay until the bridges were built, is Broughty Castle, a 15th-century estuary fort. Besieged by the English in the 16th century and attacked by Cromwell's army under General Monk in the 17th, it was eventually restored as part of Britain's coastal defenses in 1861. Its gun battery was dismantled in 1956, and it is now a museum with displays on local history, arms and armor, seashore life, and Dundee's whaling story. The observation area at the top of the castle provides fine views of the Tay estuary and northeast Fife.

Admission: Free.

Open: July–Sept, Mon–Thurs 10am–1pm and 2–5pm, Sun 2–5pm; Oct–June, Mon–Thurs 10am–1pm and 2–5pm. **Bus:** 7, 9, 11, or 24.

WHERE TO STAY

ANGUS THISTLE, 101 Marketgait, Dundee, Angus DD1 IQU. Tel. 0382/ 26874. Fax 0382/22564. 53 rms (all with bath), 5 suites. TV TEL

$ Rates (including Scottish breakfast): £72 ($108) single; £89 ($133.50) double; from £115 ($172.50) suite. AE, DC, MC, V. **Parking:** Free.

A modern hotel in the city center, the Angus, part of the Thistle chain, attracts both visitors and business clients. Rising six stories, the hotel is up-to-date, efficient, and functional in both its public areas and its well-furnished bedrooms. The hotel offers a choice of bars, and a table d'hôte four-course dinner can be ordered for £17.45 ($26.20).

INVERCARSE HOTEL, 371 Perth Rd., Dundee, Angus DD2 1PG. Tel. 0382/69231. Fax 0382/644112. 39 rms (all with bath). TV TEL

$ Rates (including Scottish breakfast): £30–£55 ($45–$82.50) single; £57–£80 ($85.50–$120) double. AE, MC, V. **Parking:** Free.

In landscaped gardens overlooking the River Tay, this privately owned hotel lies 3 miles west of the heart of Dundee. Many prefer it for its fresh air, tranquil location, and Victorian country-house aura. Rooms open onto views across the Tay to the hills of the Kingdom of Fife. A frequent venue for conferences and local banquets, the hotel with its large car park is also suitable as a center for exploring the nearby region, not just Dundee. Most rooms are singles. Accommodations come in a variety of sizes, but all are well maintained and furnished, often with pieces crafted from light-grained wood. Guests enjoy drinks in the bar, furnished in red leather, later ordering both a continental or Scottish cuisine.

STAKIS EARL GREY HOTEL, Earl Grey Place, Dundee, Angus DD1 4DE. Tel. 0382/29271. Fax 0382/200072. 102 rms (all with bath), 2 suites. TV TEL **Bus:** 1A, 1B, or 20.

$ Rates: £85 ($127.50) single; £110 ($165) double; £155 ($232.50) suite. Scottish breakfast £8.95 ($13.40) extra. AE, DC, MC, V. **Parking:** Free.

Along the waterfront, this chain hotel helped rejuvenate the once-seedy waterfront of Dundee. Built in an extremely modern style, it takes its name from a famous English tea, which most often accompanies marmalade and Dundee fruitcakes, the city's two most famous products. Some of the well-furnished bedrooms overlook the Firth, the river, or the Tay Bridge. It's an easy walk from the hotel to the *Unicorn,* a wooden frigate, now a museum, or to Captain Scott's R.S.S. *Discovery.*

Dining/Entertainment: Guests can dine at either Juliana's Table Restaurant or the à la carte restaurant, Epicures. In Juliana's Table, a table d'hôte lunch begins at £10 ($15), and a table d'hôte dinner goes for £16.50 ($24.80). In Epicures, meals start at £20 ($30).

Services: Room service, babysitting, laundry/valet.
Facilities: Indoor heated swimming pool, exercise equipment, sauna, whirlpool.

WHERE TO DINE

JAHANGIR TANDOORI, 1 Sessions St. (corner of Hawk Hill). Tel. 202022.
Cuisine: INDIAN. **Reservations:** Recommended.
$ Prices: Appetizers £1.50–£4.50 ($2.30–$6.80); main courses £5.50–£14.95 ($8.30–$22.40). AE, MC, V.
Open: Dinner only, 5pm–midnight.

Built around an indoor fish pond, within a dining room draped with the soft folds of an embroidered tent, this is considered the best Indian restaurant in Dundee, and one of the most exotic in the region. Meals are prepared with fresh ingredients, and cover the gamut of recipes from both north and south India. Meals are sometimes slow-cooked in clay pots (tandoori), and seasoned to the degree of spiciness you prefer. Both meat and meatless dishes are available, and the staff is polite and discreet.

AN EASY EXCURSION TO GLAMIS

The little village of Glamis (pronounced without the "i") grew up around ✿ **Glamis Castle,** Estate Office, Glamis (tel. 030/784242). After Balmoral Castle, visitors to Scotland most want to see Glamis Castle for its architecture and its link with the Crown. For six centuries it has been connected to members of the British royal family. Queen Elizabeth, the Queen Mother, was brought up here; and Princess Margaret was born here, becoming the first royal princess born in Scotland in three centuries. The present owner, the queen's great nephew, is the 18th earl of Strathmore and Kinghorne and the direct descendant of the first earl. The castle contains Duncan's Hall, supposedly the setting for Shakespeare's *Macbeth,* the thane of Glamis.

The present Glamis Castle dates from the early 15th century, but there are records of a castle having been in existence in the 11th century, a hunting lodge of the kings of Scotland. King Malcolm II was carried there mortally wounded in 1034 after having been attacked by his enemies while hunting in a nearby forest.

Glamis Castle has been in the possession of the Lyon family since 1372, when it was given to Sir John Lyon by King Robert II. Four years later Sir John married the king's daughter, Princess Joanna. The castle was altered in the 16th century and restored and enlarged in the 17th, 18th, and 19th centuries. It contains some fine plaster ceilings, furniture, and paintings.

The castle is open to the public, who have access to the Royal Apartments and many other rooms, and also the fine gardens, daily from noon to 5:30pm (open from early April to mid-October). Admission to the castle and gardens is £4 ($6) for adults, £2.20 ($3.30) for children. If you wish to visit the grounds only, the charge is £2 ($3) for adults, £1 ($1.50) for children. Buses run between Dundee and Glamis.

WHERE TO STAY

CASTLETON HOUSE, Eassie by Glamis, Forfar, Tayside DD8 1SJ. Tel. 030/784340. Fax 030/784506. 6 rms (all with bath). TV TEL **Directions:** 3¾ miles west of center along A94.
$ Rates (including Scottish breakfast): £70 ($105) single; £100 ($150) double. AE, MC, V.

Only 3 miles from Glamis Castle, this Victorian hotel has been restored with love and care by its owners, Maureen and William Little. In cool weather (often the case around here), you're greeted by welcoming coal fires in both the bar and public lounge, and a youthful staff that's the most considerate we've encountered in the area. Bedrooms of various sizes are beautifully furnished with reproduction antiques. Children can stay free in a room shared with parents.

Dining/Entertainment: Guests can select either the high-ceilinged dining room or else the plant-filled conservatory as settings for their meals. Chef William Little features a set luncheon for £12 ($18), with a fixed-price dinner going for £22 ($33).

The menu changes daily but is based on the freshest produce in any given season. Dishes usually include, among others, tender Angus steak, and grilled or roasted Highland lamb. Fresh fish, such as North Sea monkfish, regularly appears on the menu.

WHERE TO DINE

STRATHOMORE ARMS, Glamis. Tel. 030784/248.
   Cuisine: FRENCH/SCOTTISH. **Reservations:** Recommended.
$ Prices: Appetizers £1.50–£2.20 ($2.30–$3.30); main courses £5.75–£8.70 ($8.60–$13.10); fixed-price menus £11.50–£15.50 ($17.30–$23.30). AE, MC, V.
   Open: Lunch daily noon–2pm; dinner daily 6:30–9pm.

Try this place, near the castle, for one of the best lunches in the area. You might begin with a freshly made soup of the day or else Cheddar-filled mushrooms wrapped in bacon and grilled. Another appetizer is warm breast of pigeon on a bed of tossed salad leaves. Grilled lamb cutlets are regularly featured, as is poached sole with prawns and mushrooms in a light curry sauce. You might also try filet of Angus beef in a whisky sauce.

8. BRAEMAR

85 miles N of Edinburgh, 58 miles W of Aberdeen, 51 miles N of Perth

GETTING THERE   By Train   Take the train to Aberdeen (see below), then continue the rest of the way by bus (see below).

By Bus   Regular buses run daily from Aberdeen west to Braemar. The bus station in Aberdeen is on Guild Street (tel. 0224/212266 for information about schedules), beside the train station.

By Car   Two excellent routes extend from the south, the M6 and the A1. Head for Perth and follow the Braemar signs from the M90.

ESSENTIALS   The **telephone area code** is 03397. The summer-only **Braemar Tourist Office** is in The Mews, Mar Road (tel. 03397/41600).

SPECIAL EVENTS   This is the site of the spectacular **Royal Highland Gathering,** which takes place annually in the Princess Royal and Duke of Fife Memorial Park, in either late August or early September. For more information, call the tourist office (see above). Braemar is overrun with visitors during the gathering—anyone thinking of attending would be wise to reserve accommodations anywhere within a 20-mile radius of Braemar not later than early April.

In the heart of some of Grampian's most beautiful scenery, Braemar is not only known for its own castle, but it also makes a good center from which to explore Balmoral Castle (see "Ballater," below). In this Highland village, set against a massive backdrop of hills covered with heather in summer, Clunie Water joins the River Dee. The massive Cairn Toul towers over Braemar, reaching a height of 4,241 feet.

The queen herself often attends the Royal Highland Gathering, ancient games thought to have been originated by King Malcolm Canmore. That chieftain ruled much of Scotland at the time of the Norman conquest in the south, and he selected his hardiest warriors from all the clans for a "keen and fair contest."

WHAT TO SEE & DO

If you're a royal family watcher, you might be able to see members of the family, even the Queen, at **Crathie Church** (tel. 03397/422208), 9 miles east of Braemar on the

A93. They attend Sunday services here when they're in residence. Services are at 11:30am; otherwise the church is open to view April through October, Monday to Saturday from 9:30am to 5:30pm and on Sunday from 2 to 5:30pm.

Nature lovers may want to drive to the **Linn of Dee,** 6 miles west of Braemar, a narrow chasm on the River Dee, which is considered a local beauty spot.

Other beauty spots include **Glen Muick, Loch Muick,** and **Lochnagar.** A Scottish Wildlife Trust Visitor Centre, reached by a minor road, is located in this Highland glen, off the South Deeside road. An access road joins the B976 at a point 16 miles east of Braemar. The tourist office (see above) will give you a map pinpointing these beauty spots.

BRAEMAR CASTLE, on the Aberdeen–Ballater–Perth Rd. (A93). Tel. 03397/41219.

⭐ This romantic 17th-century castle is a fully furnished private residence of architectural grace, scenic charm, and historical interest. It is the seat of Capt. A. A. C. Farquharson of Invercauld. Opening onto the Dee River, it was built in 1628 by the earl of Mar. John Farquharson of Inveraray, the "Black Colonel," attacked and burned it in 1689. The castle has barrel-vaulted ceilings and an underground prison and is known for its remarkable star-shaped defensive curtain wall. There is a gift shop and a free parking area.

Admission: £1.70 ($2.60) adults, 90p ($1.40) children.

Open: May–Oct 15, Sat–Thurs 10am–6pm. **Closed:** Oct 16–Apr. **Directions:** On the A93 half a mile northeast of Braemar.

WHERE TO STAY & DINE

BRAEMAR LODGE HOTEL, Glenshee Rd., Braemar, Aberdeenshire AB35 5YQ. Tel. 03397/41627. 5 rms (all with shower). TV **Bus:** 201.

$ Rates (including Scottish breakfast): £37 ($55.50) single; £70 ($105) double. MC, V. **Parking:** Free. **Closed:** Nov–Easter.

This hotel, popular with skiers at the nearby Glenshee slopes, was originally built in 1870 as a hunting lodge. Set on 2 acres of grounds at the head of Glen Clunie, it contains a bar, lounge, and reading room for guests. All bedrooms have tea/coffee makers. Dinner, served in the restaurant from 7pm, includes "Taste of Scotland" dishes on the à la carte menu, with meals costing £18.50 ($27.80) and up. Lunch is not served. The food is excellent. A typical dinner might begin with smoked venison, followed with fennel and green pepper soup, then noisettes of Scottish lamb grilled with fresh rosemary for a main course. Guests should indicate their intention of dining at the hotel in advance, so that a table can be reserved and menus planned. The hotel is on the road to the Glenshee ski slopes, near the cottage where Robert Louis Stevenson wrote *Treasure Island.*

INVERCAULD ARMS HOTEL, Braemar, Aberdeenshire AB35 5YR. Tel. 03397/41605. Fax 03397/41428. 68 rms (all with bath or shower). **Bus:** 201.

$ Rates (including Scottish breakfast): £60 ($90) single; £90 ($135) double. AE, DC, MC, V. **Parking:** Free.

The Invercauld Arms Hotel is a lovely old granite building of which the original part dates back to the 18th century. In cool weather there's a roaring log fire on the hearth, and the staff offers you traditional Highland hospitality. You can go hill walking and see deer, golden eagles, and other wildlife. Fishing and, in winter, skiing are other pursuits in the nearby area. Bedrooms are comfortably furnished.

In the pub close by you'll meet the "ghilles" and "stalkers" and then return to the Scottish and international fare with fresh Dee salmon, Aberdeen Angus beef, venison, and grouse. Of course, you'll find kippers and porridge with the full Scottish breakfast that is included in the room rates.

SHIEHALLION GUEST HOUSE, Glenshee Road, Braemar. Aberdeenshire AB35 5YQ. Tel. 03397/41679. 11 rms (5 with bath). TEL

$ Rates (including Scottish breakfast): £14 ($21) single without bath; £28 ($42) double without bath, £32 ($48) double with bath. Half board £23.50–£25.50 ($35.30–$38.30) per person. MC, V. **Parking:** Free.

Ⓢ A family-run guest house on the A93 to Glenshee, this is one of the best-value guest houses in the area. Owners Neil and Alison Vaughan welcome international guests to their traditional house and shelter them in comfortably furnished bedrooms, many of which open onto views of mountain scenery. Rooms have beverage-making equipment, and although not all have private baths, each has hot and cold running water. Furnishings are in a style appropriate to the building's Victorian origins. Ground-floor rooms are suitable for the disabled. Freshly prepared Scottish food is served at the lodge, including trout, salmon, beef, haggis, and venison.

9. BALLATER

111 miles N of Edinburgh, 41 miles W of Aberdeen,
67 miles NE of Perth, 70 miles SE of Inverness

GETTING THERE   By Train   Go to Aberdeen (see below) and continue the rest of the way by connecting bus.

By Bus   Regular buses run daily from Aberdeen west to Ballater. The bus station in Aberdeen is on Guild Street (tel. 0224/212266 for information about schedules), beside the train station. Bus no. 201 from Braemar runs to Ballater.

By Car   From Aberdeen, head west along the A93. From Braemar, head east along the A93 to reach Ballater.

ESSENTIALS   The summer-only **tourist information office** is at Station Square (tel. 03397/55306). The **telephone area code** is 03397.

Ⓞn the Dee River, with the Grampian mountains in the background, Ballater is a holiday resort center. The town still centers around its Station Square, where the royal family used to be photographed as they arrived to spend holidays. The railway is now closed. From Ballater you can drive west to view the magnificent scenery of Glen Muick and Lochnagar, where you'll see herds of deer.

WHAT TO SEE & DO IN THE ENVIRONS

BALMORAL CASTLE, Balmoral, Ballater. Tel. 03397/42334.

✪ "This dear paradise" is how Queen Victoria described Balmoral Castle, rebuilt in the Scottish baronial style by her beloved Albert. It was completed in 1855. Today Balmoral, 8 miles west of Ballater, is still a private residence of the British sovereign. Albert, the prince consort, leased the property in 1848 and bought it in 1852. As the original castle of the Farquharsons proved too small, the present edifice was built in its place. Its principal feature is a 100-foot tower. On the grounds are many memorials to the royal family. In addition to the gardens there are country walks, pony trekking, souvenir shops, and a refreshment room. Of the actual castle, only the ballroom is open to the public. It houses an exhibition of pictures, porcelain, and works of art.

   Admission: £1.50 ($2.30) adults, free for children.
   Open: May–July Mon–Sat 10am–5pm. **Bus:** Crathie bus from Aberdeen to the Crathie station; Balmoral Castle is signposted from there (a quarter-mile walk).

WHERE TO STAY

CRAIGENDARROCH HOTEL AND COUNTRY CLUB, Braemar Rd., Ballater, Aberdeenshire AB35 5XA. Tel. 03397/55858. Fax 03397/55447. 49 rms (all with bath). TV TEL
$ Rates (including Scottish breakfast): £99 ($148.50) single; £125 ($187.50) double. AE, DC, MC, V. **Parking:** Free.
The hotel, built in the Scottish baronial style, is set amid old trees on a 28-acre estate a few minutes' drive outside Ballater along the A93 in the direction of Braemar. The 20th-century comfort has been added, but the owners have tried to maintain a

19th-century aura. The public rooms include a regal oaken staircase and a large sitting room. Bedroom views open onto the village of Ballater and the River Dee.

Each of the accommodations is furnished in an individual style, and all have radios, hairdryers, trouser presses, private baths and showers, and small refrigerators (not minibars). The public facilities are luxurious, especially the study with oak paneling, a log fire, and book-lined shelves.

Dining/Entertainment: See "Where to Dine," below.

Services: 24-hour room service, laundry/dry cleaning, babysitting.

Facilities: The Leisure Club includes a spa pool, two swimming pools, a sauna, and a solarium, along with various games and a beauty salon. Tennis courts are outside, and there's a dry ski slope.

TULLICH LODGE, along the A93, Ballater, Aberdeenshire AB35 5SB. Tel. 03397/55406. Fax 03397/55397. 10 rms (all with bath). TEL

$ Rates (including half board): £95 ($142.50) per person. £37 ($55.50) additional charge for single occupancy of double room. AE, DC, MC, V. **Parking:** Free.

Closed: Dec–Mar.

Tullich Lodge, 1½ miles east of Ballater on the A93, is a turreted country house built in the Scottish-baronial style, standing in 5 acres of its own gardens and woods above Royal Deeside and Ballater. The attractive hotel is tastefully decorated and furnished, often with antiques, and brass fittings and wood paneling. Your pleasant hosts, Hector Macdonald and Neil Bannister, offer only a handful of bedrooms, but the accommodations are of generous size and are beautifully furnished. To get the most out of the surrounding countryside, as well as this special hotel, I'd recommend a stay of at least 2 nights.

Dining/Entertainment: Its dining room, commanding panoramic views of the "royal valley," serves some of the finest food along Royal Deeside. One of the chef's specialties is casseroles, although he does all the standard dishes with above-average flair, including locally caught trout and salmon, game and especially venison (in season), as well as crab and lobster. A table d'hôte dinner, served from 7:30 to 8:30pm daily, goes for £23 ($34.50). A bar luncheon is at 1pm with no fried foods. It's essential to make a reservation. In an amusing bar, you can order from a good selection of malt whiskies.

Services: Limited room service, laundry.

Facilities: Garden.

MONALTRIE HOTEL, 5 Bridge Square, Ballater, Aberdeenshire AB35 5QJ. Tel. 03397/55417. Fax 03397/55180. 25 rms (all with bath). TV TEL

$ Rates (including Scottish breakfast): £27.50 ($41.30) single; £55 ($82.50) double. AE, DC, MC, V. **Parking:** Free.

Built in 1835 of Aberdeen granite during the reign of William IV, this was the first hotel in the region. It accommodated the clients of a now-defunct spa, which during the 19th century lay at the opposite end of the Royal Bridge. Today this hotel, a 4-minute walk east of the center of town, bustles with a contemporary clientele who come for the live music occasionally presented in its pub and for the savory food served in its two restaurants. The more unusual of the two is a Thai restaurant, which serves dinner only Thursday through Tuesday from 7 to 10pm. Maintained by the Thai-born wife (Laddawan) of the Scottish owner, James Anderson, it offers a four-course fixed-price Thai meal for £18.95 ($28.40). Each of the bedrooms contains an unobtrusive monochromatic decor and comfortable beds.

WHERE TO DINE

OAKS RESTAURANT, in the Craigendarroch Hotel & Country Club, Braemar Road, Tel. 03397/55858.

Cuisine: BRITISH. **Reservations:** Strongly recommended.

$ Prices: Appetizers £3–£9.50 ($4.50–$14.30); main courses £13–£19.50 ($19.50–$29.30); fixed-price 4-course dinner £24.50 ($36.80); fixed-price Sun lunch £13.50–£17.50 ($20.30–$26.30). AE, DC, MC, V.

Open: Dinner daily 7–10:30pm; lunch, Sun only, 12:30–2:30pm.

⭐ Considered the most glamorous and sophisticated restaurant in the region, the Oaks, 1 mile west of Ballater beside the A93, is in the century-old mansion that was originally built by the "marmalade kings" of Britain, the Keiller family. (The company's marmalade is still a household word throughout the U.K.) This is the most upscale of the three restaurants in a resort complex that includes hotel rooms, time-share villas, and access to a nearby golf course. Translated from the Gaelic, Craigendarroch means "Hill of the Oaks," from which the restaurant's name is derived. Specialties include filets of beef and veal on a bed of parsnips with red wine sauce; wild duck with assorted sweetbreads in a chive dressing; poached lobster with tomato ravioli; or pan-fried rack of lamb with rosemary, watercress, poppyseed, and sesame-seed dressing.

GREEN INN, 9 Victoria Rd., Ballater, Aberdeenshire AB35 5QQ. Tel. 03397/55701.

Cuisine: SCOTTISH. **Reservations:** Required. **Bus:** 201 from Braemar goes by.

$ Prices: Appetizers £2.75–£4.50 ($4.10–$6.80); main courses £10.50–£14.50 ($15.80–$21.80); fixed-price lunch £10.25 ($15.40). MC, V.

Open: Lunch daily 12:30–1:30pm; dinner daily 7–9:30pm. **Closed:** 2 weeks in Oct., first week in Jan.

In the heart of town, this establishment was once a temperance hotel (a no-alcohol hostelry). That condition has now been rectified, and the pink-granite Green Inn, built in 1840, is one of the finest dining rooms in town, especially for traditional Scottish dishes. The chef places his emphasis on local produce, including home-grown vegetables when available. In season, loin of venison is served with a bramble sauce, and you can always count on fresh salmon and the best of Angus beef.

Three double bedrooms are rented here, all with private bath/shower and TV. B&B costs £20 ($30) per person.

---

10. BANCHORY

118 miles NE of Edinburgh, 17 miles W of Aberdeen, 55 miles NE of Dundee

GETTING THERE By Train Go to Aberdeen (see below), then take a connecting bus the rest of the way.

By Bus A Bluebird bus runs between Aberdeen and Braemar, going via Banchory. For more information, call 0224/212266 in Aberdeen. Departures are from the bus station on Guild Street in Aberdeen.

By Car From Aberdeen, head west along the A93; or from Braemar, head east along the A93.

ESSENTIALS A year-round **tourist information office** is on Bridge Street (tel. 03302/2000). The **telephone area code** is 03302.

On lower Deeside, this pleasant resort is rich in woodland and river scenery. From this base, you can take excursions to two of the most popular castles in the Grampian region, Crathes and Craigievar.

WHAT TO SEE & DO

CRATHES CASTLE AND GARDENS, Banchory. Tel. 033044/525.

⭐ This castle 2 miles east of Banchory has royal historical associations dating from 1323, when the lands of Leys were granted to the Burnett family by King Robert the Bruce. The Horn of Leys, said to have been given by the Bruce to symbolize the gift, is in the Great Hall. The castle's features include remarkable late 16th-century painted ceilings. The garden is a composite of eight gardens that give a display all year. The great yew hedges date from 1702. The grounds are ideal for nature study, and there are five trails, including a long-distance layout with ranger service. The complex includes a licensed restaurant, a Visitor Centre with permanent exhibitions, a souvenir shop, a wayfaring course, picnic areas, and a parking lot.

Admission: £3.50 ($5.30); adults, £1.80 ($2.70) children.

Open: Grounds and park, daily 9:30am–sunset; castle, Visitor Centre, shop, restaurant, and adventure area, Apr–Oct daily 11am–6pm.

CRAIGIEVAR CASTLE, Hwy. A980, 6 miles south of Alford. Tel. 03398/ 83635.

Structurally unchanged since its completion in 1626, Craigievar Castle is an exceptional tower house where Scottish baronial architecture reached its pinnacle of achievement. It has magnificent contemporary plaster ceilings in nearly all its rooms. The castle had been continuously lived in by the descendants of the builder, William Forbes, until it came under the care of the National Trust for Scotland in 1963. The family collection of furnishings is complete.

Some 4 miles from the castle, near Lumphanan, is **Macbeth's Cairn,** where the historical Macbeth is supposed to have fought his last battle.

Admission: £3 ($4.50) adults, £1.50 ($2.30) children.

Open: Castle, May–Sept, daily 2–6pm. **Closed:** Oct–Apr. Grounds, daily 9:30am–sunset.

WHERE TO STAY & DINE

BANCHORY LODGE, Dee St., Banchory, Kincardineshire AB31 3HS. Tel. 03302/2625. Fax 03302/5019. 22 rms (all with bath). TV TEL

$ Rates (including half board): £78.75 ($118.10) single; £120.75–£131.25 ($181.10–$196.90) double. AE, DC, MC, V. **Parking:** Free.

Banchory Lodge, built in 1738, was once the home of a well-known Deeside family. It's an 18th-century country house with much Georgian charm. On the banks of the Dee, where it is joined by the Water of the Feugh, the lodge is open all year. Guests are accommodated in well-furnished bedrooms, some of which overlook the river. In the dining room, furnishings and decor are in period style. Specialties include fresh Dee salmon and Aberdeen Angus roast beef. Guests can fish from the lawn or in one of the hotel's boats by arrangement.

INVERY HOUSE, High St., Bridge of Feugh. Banchory, Kincardineshire AB31 3NJ. Tel. 03302/4782, or toll free 800/525-4800 in the U.S. and Canada. Fax 03302/4712. 14 rms (all with bath). 1 suite. TV TEL

$ Rates (including Scottish breakfast): £105–£140 ($157.50–$210) single; £120–£175 ($180–$262.50) double; £240 ($360) suite. AE, DC, MC, V. **Parking:** Free.

The premier place to stay is Invery House, a Georgian mansion of great charm standing on 40 acres of gardens and woodland opening onto the banks of the River Feugh. It's small, but its reputation as one of the leading hotels of Scotland is big. It hosted the wedding dinner of Princess Anne in September of 1992. Former guests have included actor Charlton Heston and rock singer Rod Stewart.

The proprietors, Sheila and Stewart Spence, have sensitively and painstakingly restored this mansion, and today it is one of the grand addresses of the Grampian region. Antiques and oil paintings add to the Scottish country-house atmosphere, but all the modern necessities are here, too.

Mr. and Mrs. Spence have paid particular care to their beautifully furnished bedrooms, each one named after one of the novels of Sir Walter Scott, who worked on his romance *Marmion* here.

Dining/Entertainment: The hotel is the outstanding dining choice in the area. Fresh produce goes into the imaginative dishes, which are handled skillfully in the kitchen and served with a certain formality. Dining is daily from 12:15 to 2:15pm and 7:15 to 9:45pm. A three-course lunch costs £19.50 ($29.30); a five-course dinner costs £35.50 ($53.30).

Services: 24-hour room service, laundry, babysitting.

Facilities: Garden, putting, tennis, game fishing, helipad, snooker.

RAEMOIR HOUSE, along the A980, Banchory, Kincardineshire AB31 4ED. Tel. 03302/4884. Fax 03302/2171. 28 rms (all with bath). 4 suites. TV TEL **Directions:** Turn off the A93 at the eastern end of Banchory onto the A980 (Raemoir Road): the hotel entrance is at the junction 2 miles down the road.

$ Rates (including Scottish breakfast): £65–£85 ($97.50–$127.50) single; £110–£120 ($165–$180) double; from £130 ($195) suite. AE, DC, MC, V. **Parking:** Free.

Raemoir House is an 18th-century manor standing on 3,500 acres of grounds with such sporting attractions as shooting, fishing, and riding. It lies 2½ miles north of Banchory on the A980. A journey into nostalgia, the hotel has a ballroom, antiques, fine tapestries, and log fires burning in the colder months. The rooms are handsomely decorated, and most of them are quite large.

What is so lovely about Scotland is its curious mixtures—in this case, an 18th-century manor house with its own helipad. The hotel is run just like a private house. The adjoining 16th-century Ha' House was once used by Mary Queen of Scots.

Dining/Entertainment: Meals are served in an attractive Georgian dining room and feature a standard repertoire of familiar dishes, rather well done. Service is informal and prompt. Bar lunches are offered Monday through Saturday. A fixed-price dinner in the evening costs £23.50 ($35.30), and you can also order à la carte.

Services: All-day room service, laundry, babysitting.

Facilities: Helipad, garden, solarium, sauna, an all-weather tennis court, a nine-hole pitch-a-putt course on the grounds.

TOR-NA-COILLE, Inchmarlo Rd., Banchory, Kincardieshire AB31 4AB. Tel. 03302/2242. Fax 03302/4012. 24 rms (all with bath). TV TEL

$ Rates (including Scottish breakfast): £59 ($88.50) single; £95 ($142.50) double. AE, DC, MC, V. **Parking:** Free.

Tor-Na-Coille is a country-house hotel—really a Victorian mansion—standing on its own wooded grounds of about 6 acres. Public rooms are suitably spacious and comfortable, and the whisky always tastes good in the modern bar. If you're on your way to see Balmoral Castle or to attend the Highland gathering at Braemar, you can relax here and enjoy the gracious hospitality, as did Charlie Chaplin and his family, who once used the place as a retreat. The bedrooms, many of which are quite large and restful, have radios and coffee makers. The hotel is interesting architecturally, and the room you may be assigned could have much character.

Dining/Entertainment: Lunches are light meals in the bar, including smoked venison sausage blended with rum and red wine. You can enjoy Sunday brunch accompanied by an accordion player. Food at night is accompanied by music from an accordion player. Here might be your chance to try real Scottish salmon (the salmon leap at the Falls of Feugh nearby). Dinner is likely to feature the chef's special pheasant. The hotel has a high reputation for its food. Dinner costs £22 ($33) and up.

Services: All-day room service, babysitting, laundry.

Facilities: Deeside Indoor Sporting Club, with two indoor bowling alleys and four snooker tables, plus two squash courts outdoors.

11. ABERDEEN

130 miles NE of Edinburgh, 67 miles N of Dundee

GETTING THERE By Plane Aberdeen is served by a number of carriers, including British Airways and Air Ecosse. If you're flying directly from North America to Scotland, there is an air link from Glasgow to Aberdeen. For flight information, phone 0224/722331. The airport is about 6 miles away from the heart of town and is connected to it by a bus service.

By Train Aberdeen has direct rail links to the major cities of Britain. Special fares are offered on most routes, both to holders of Rail-Cards and to those with the

"InterCity Saver," along with weekend round-trip tickets. Eighteen trains per day arrive from Edinburgh; a one-way ticket costs £24.50 ($36.80) but a round-trip ticket is just £29 ($43.50). Some 15 trains per day arrive from Glasgow, costing £28 ($42) one way or £32 ($48) round-trip. Some 4 trains per day arrive from London as well. For rail information concerning Aberdeen, call 0224/594222.

By Bus   Coach is the least expensive way. Several coach companies have express routes serving Aberdeen, and many offer special round-trip fares and low-cost "standby" tickets on long-distance routes. Frequent buses arrive from both Glasgow and Edinburgh via Dundee. There are also frequent arrivals from Inverness. For bus information and schedules in Aberdeen, call 0224/212266.

By Car   It's also easy to drive to the northeast. From the south, drive via Edinburgh, the Forth and Tay Road bridges, and take the coastal road. From the north and west, approach the area from the much improved A9, which links Perth, Inverness, and Wick.

ESSENTIALS   The **tourist information center** is at St. Nicholas House, Broad Street, Aberdeen, Aberdeenshire AB9 1DE (tel. 0224/632727). The **telephone area code** is 0224.

The harbor in this seaport is one of the largest fishing ports in the country, and is filled with kipper and deep-sea trawlers. The **Fish Market** on Market Street near Palmerston Road is well worth a visit; it's the liveliest in Britain.

Bordered by fine sandy beaches (delightful if you're a polar bear), Scotland's third city is often called "the granite city," as its buildings are constructed largely of pink or gray granite, hewn from the Rubislaw quarries.

Aberdeen is the capital of the oil workers of six North Sea oilfields. Their numbers have dwindled in recent years, however. The city lies on the banks of the salmon- and trout-filled Don and Dee rivers. Spanning the Don is Brig o'Balgownie, a steep Gothic arch, begun in 1285.

WHAT TO SEE & DO

THE TOP ATTRACTIONS

ABERDEEN ART GALLERY, Schoolhill. Tel. 0224/646333.

Built in 1884 in a neoclassical design by A. Marshall MacKenzie, this building houses one of the most important art collections in Great Britain. It contains 18th-century portraits by Raeburn, Hogarth, Ramsay, and Reynolds, and acclaimed 20th-century artworks by Paul Nash, Ben Nicholson, and Francis Bacon. The exhibits also include excellent works by impressionists, such as Monet, Pissarro, Sisley, and Bonnard. There is a collection of Scottish domestic silver and examples of other decorative arts. Special exhibitions and events are frequently offered.
   Admission: Free.
   Open: Mon–Wed and Fri–Sat 10am–5pm, Thurs 10am–8pm, Sun 2–5pm. **Bus:** 20.

ABERDEEN MARITIME MUSEUM, Shiprow. Tel. 0224/585788.

This museum is housed in Provost Ross's House, the oldest surviving building in the city, built in 1593. Its exhibitions begin with the development of Aberdeen harbor and extend through the Arctic whaling trade right up to the present North Sea oil adventure. In whatever way, the point is made repeatedly of a people who had to earn a living from a turbulent sea.
   Admission: Free.
   Open: Mon–Sat 10am–5pm. **Bus:** 20.

GORDON HIGHLANDERS REGIMENTAL MUSEUM, Regimental Headquarters, Viewfield Rd. Tel. 0224/318174.

The Gordon Highlanders Regimental Museum offers exhibitions of the many battle campaigns of the regiment, including colors and banners, medals, and uniforms. The museum depicts the history of the regiment from its creation in 1794 to the present day.

Admission: Free.
Open: May 1–Oct Tues–Thurs 1–4:30pm.

JAMES DUN'S HOUSE, 61 Schoolhill. Tel. 0224/646333.

This museum offers a program of special exhibitions. An 18th-century house, it was once the residence of James Dun, master of the Aberdeen Grammar School.

Admission: Free.
Open: Mon–Sat 10am–5pm. **Bus:** 20.

PROVOST SKENE HOUSE, 45 Guestrow. Tel. 0224/641086.

The Provost Skene House is named for a rich merchant who was Lord Provost of Aberdeen during 1676–1685. Off Broad Street, it's a museum with period rooms and artifacts of domestic life. Provost Skene's kitchen has been converted into a café.

Admission: Free.
Open: Mon–Sat 10am–5pm. **Bus:** 20.

MORE ATTRACTIONS

In Castlegate is the **Mercat Cross,** a hexagonally shaped structure built in 1686 and considered the most handsome of the old crosses in Scotland. **Aberdeen University,** St. Machar Drive, is a fusion of two separate colleges. King's College is older, dating from 1483, and it contains the oldest school of medicine in Great Britain. A stately tower from 1505 crowns the chapel of King's College. Marischal College, founded in 1593, is recognized as one of the finest granite buildings in the world.

The university is in Old Aberdeen, as is the **Cathedral of St. Machar,** Chanonry (tel. 0224/485988), founded in 1131. The present structure dates from the 15th century. Its splendid heraldic ceiling contains three rows of shields representing the kings and princes of Europe along with the Scottish ecclesiastical and aristocratic hierarchy. The modern stained-glass windows are magnificent; they're the work of Douglas Strachan. The cathedral is open daily from 9am to 5pm. Take bus no. 1, 2, 3, 4, 6, 7, or 25.

Aberdeen also has several beautiful gardens, including the **Cruickshank Botanic Garden,** St. Machar Drive (tel. 0224/272704), under the auspices of the University of Aberdeen. Here you'll find alpines, shrubs, and many herbaceous plants, along with rock and water gardens. It's open all year, Monday through Friday from 9am to 4:30pm; in summer, it is also open on Saturday and Sunday from 2 to 5pm. No admission is charged. Take bus no. 6.

WHERE TO STAY

Because of increasing numbers of tourists and business visitors to the Granite City, now established as Europe's offshore oil capital, hotels are likely to be heavily booked any time of year. It's best to go to the **Aberdeen Tourist Information Centre,** at St. Nicholas House on Broad Street (tel. 0224/632727). There's a wide range of accommodation, whether you prefer to stay in a family-run B&B, a guest house, or a hotel, and the center's staff can usually find just the right kind of lodging.

EXPENSIVE

ARDOE HOUSE, South Deeside Rd., Blairs, Aberdeen, Aberdeenshire AB1 5YP. Tel. 0224/867355. Fax 0224/861283. 69 rms (all with bath), 2 suites. TV TEL **Directions:** Lies 5 miles SW on B9077.
$ Rates (including Scottish breakfast): £87.50 ($131.30) single; £109 ($163.50) double; £128 ($192) suite. AE, DC, MC, V. **Parking:** Free.

Known for its tranquil, scenic setting at the end of a winding drive, this Scottish baronial house stands on large grounds on the south bank of the River Dee. Imbued with charm and character, its architecture is graced with soaring turrets. Constructed back in 1878 of silver granite, it still retains much of its original

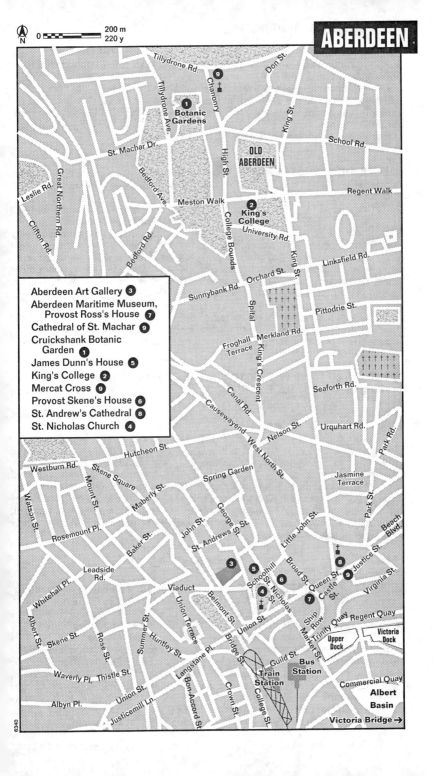

ABERDEEN

0 | 200 m
220 y

N

Tillydrone Rd.

Don St.

Chanonry

King St.

School Rd.

Tillydrone Ave.

Botanic Gardens ❶

St. Machar Dr.

High St.

OLD ABERDEEN

Regent Walk

Bedford Ave.

Great Northern Rd.

Leslie Rd.

Clifton Rd.

Meston Walk

King's College ❷

University Rd.

Linksfield Rd.

Bedford Rd.

Sunnybank Rd.

Orchard St.

King St.

Pittodrie St.

Aberdeen Art Gallery ❸
Aberdeen Maritime Museum, Provost Ross's House ❼
Cathedral of St. Machar ❾
Cruickshank Botanic Garden ❶
James Dunn's House ❺
King's College ❷
Mercat Cross ❾
Provost Skene's House ❻
St. Andrew's Cathedral ❽
St. Nicholas Church ❹

Spital

Froghall Terrace

Merkland Rd.

King's Crescent

Seaforth Rd.

Canal Rd.

Causewayend

Nelson St.

Urquhart Rd.

West North St.

Park Rd.

Hutcheon St.

Westburn Rd.

Skene Square

Spring Garden

Jasmine Terrace

Mount St.

Maberly St.

Watson St.

Rosemount Pl.

Baker St.

John St.

George St.

St. Andrews St.

Little John St.

Broad St.

Park St.

Beach Blvd.

Leadside Rd.

Whitehall Pl.

Viaduct

Belmont St.

Union Terrace

Schoolhill

St. Nicholas St.

❸ ❺ ❻ ❹ ❼

Queen St.

Castle St.

❽ ❾ Justice St.

Virginia St.

Albert St.

Skene St.

Rose St.

Summer St.

Huntley St.

Langstane Pl.

Bon-Accord St.

Bridge St.

Union St.

Ship Row

Market St.

Trinity Quay

Regent Quay

Upper Dock

Victoria Dock

Waverly Pl.

Thistle St.

Union St.

Albyn Pl.

Justicemill Ln.

Crown St.

College St.

Guild St.

Train Station

Bus Station

Commercial Quay

Albert Basin

Victoria Bridge →

6340

design, as exemplified by its carved oak paneling. Guests can opt for the more traditional rooms in the old house or else be sheltered in a large extension with more modern units.

Dining/Entertainment: Guests relax in the drawing room and cocktail bar before going in to dinner in either the Drawing Room or the Garden Room annex. Naturally, salmon freshly caught in the Dee is the chef's specialty. Dinners cost about £28 ($42).

Services: Room service, laundry, babysitting.

Facilities: Garden, pétanque.

CALEDONIAN THISTLE HOTEL, 10–14 Union Terrace, Aberdeen, Aberdeenshire AB9 1HE. Tel. 0224/640233. Fax 0224/641627. 71 rms (all with bath), 6 suites. MINIBAR TV TEL **Bus:** 23.

$ **Rates:** £98 ($147) single; £115 ($172.50) double; £138 ($207) suite. Scottish breakfast £9.95 ($14.90) extra. AE, DC, MC, V. **Parking:** Free.

The Caledonian Thistle Hotel sits in a grandly detailed, stone-fronted, 19th-century building in the center of Aberdeen off Union Street. Recent restorations have added a veneer of Georgian-era gloss, which contributes to one of the most elegant series of public rooms in town. The hotel offers Elronds (see "Where to Dine"), plus a more formal dining area, The Restaurant on the Terrace, which serves dinner nightly, charges £19.50 ($29.30) for a table d'hôte. Lunch is also served, Monday through Friday only, ranging in price from £9.50 to £11.95 ($14.30 to $17.90). The hotel offers free parking in a walled-in lot on a street paralleling the hotel. The rooms are at the top of a 19th-century stairwell, with Corinthian columns and a free-standing atrium. There is also elevator service. Each bedroom contains a radio and warmly upholstered furniture.

STAKIS TREE TOPS HOTEL, 161 Springfield Rd., Aberdeen, Aberdeenshire AB9 2QH. Tel. 0224/313377. Fax 0224/312028. 110 rms (all with bath), 2 suites. TV TEL **Bus:** 11.

$ **Rates:** £99 ($148.50) single; £109 ($163.50) double; £129 ($193.50) suite. Scottish breakfast £9.50 ($14.30) extra. AE, DC, MC, V. **Parking:** Free.

A 10-minute drive west of the center of Aberdeen, this comfortable hotel built in the 1960s and renovated in 1991 has a sweeping white facade of traditional design. The windows of its 112 contemporary bedrooms look over landscaped grounds. Each accommodation contains a tile-lined bath and many other extras. The leather-covered chairs of the paneled main bar offer a cozy conversation spot. You can dine in the elegant Garden Room or in Rocco's Ristorante, the bistro-style Italian restaurant. The hotel invites guests to take advantage of the Leisure Club, with swimming pool, whirlpool, multi-gym, sauna, jogging machine, sunbeds, two all-weather tennis courts, and sports training.

MODERATE

MANNOFIELD HOTEL, 447 Great Western Rd. Aberdeen, Aberdeenshire AB1 6NL. Tel. 0224/315888. Fax 0224/208971. 9 rms (7 with shower). TV TEL **Bus:** 17, 18, or 19.

$ **Rates** (including Scottish breakfast): £36 ($54) single with or without shower; £49 ($73.50) double with or without shower. MC, V. **Parking:** Free.

Built of silver-toned Aberdeen granite as an opulent private house around 1880, this hotel looks like a Victorian architectural fantasy, with step-shaped gables, turrets, spires, and protruding bay windows. Inside, a mahogany and teakwood staircase, slightly modified to satisfy building codes, sweeps upstairs. Each of the bedrooms was modernized into a no-nonsense monochromatic design in 1990, and each contains tea-making facilities and a TV. The hotel, a favorite of visiting businesspeople from other parts of Britain, contains a well-used cocktail bar and a restaurant that charges around £10 ($15) for a fixed-price three-course dinner.

The hotel stands 1 mile west of the city center with good transportation links.

Bruce and Dorothy Cryle are joint owners, offering a warm Scottish welcome to visitors.

INEXPENSIVE

JAYS GUEST HOUSE, 422 King St., Aberdeen, Aberdeenshire AB2 3BR. Tel. 0224/638295. 6 rms (1 with bath). TV **Bus:** 1, 2, 3, or 4.

$ **Rates** (including Scottish breakfast): £18–£20 ($27–$30) single without bath; £30 ($45) double without bath; £36 ($54) double with bath. No credit cards. **Parking:** Free.

Ⓢ This is one of the nicer guest houses in Aberdeen, mainly because of the high standards of the owner, Mrs. Alice Jennings. It's near the university and the Offshore Survival Centre. Everything runs smoothly, and the rooms are bright and airy. All accommodations have hot- and cold-water basins, hot-beverage facilities, and central heating. Plans call for the house to be extended and private baths installed in all rooms during the lifetime of this edition.

NEARBY PLACES TO STAY

KILDRUMMY CASTLE HOTEL, Kildrummy by Alford, Aberdeenshire AB33 8RA. Tel. 09755/71288. Fax 09755/71345. 16 rms (all with bath). TV TEL

$ **Rates** (including Scottish breakfast): £65 ($97.50) single; £104–£120 ($156–$180) double. AE, MC, V. **Parking:** Free. **Closed:** Jan–Feb.

✪ Kildrummy Castle Hotel, about 1½ miles south of the village of Kildrummy on the A97, overlooks the ruined castle of Kildrummy, 35 miles west of Aberdeen. This 19th-century gray stone mansion, set in acres of landscaped gardens, has well-equipped bedrooms, all with hairdryers and tea and coffee makers. The public rooms have oak-paneled walls and ceilings, mullioned windows, and cushioned windowseats. The drawing room and bar open onto a flagstone terrace from which you can see the gardens of the castle. Traditional Scottish food is served in the handsome dining room, including Cullen skink (smoked haddock soup), filet of sole stuffed with smoked Scottish salmon, and Aberdeen Angus steaks. Meals cost £13.50 ($20.30) and up for lunch, £25 ($37.50) and up for dinner.

MUCHALLS CASTLE, Muchalls by Stonehaven, Kincardineshire AB3 2RS. Tel. 0569/31170. Fax 0569/31480. 7 rms (all with bath). TV **Directions:** From the main Aberdeen-Dundee Road (A92/A94), turn off the A92 at Bridge of Muchalls—signposted Netherley, 3 miles north of Stonehaven. From Netherley Road, go for 1 mile up the hill and turn right at the top.

$ **Rates** (including Scottish breakfast): £35–£50 ($52.50–$75) per person. No credit cards. **Parking:** Free.

Ⓢ "Every feature has its purpose, angle turrets, towers, dormer windows, crow-stepped gables, vaulted basements, shot-holes and heraldry"—that's how Nigel Tranter, the historian, saw this castle. Built in 1619 this is an unaltered example of a Scottish laird's house from the 1600s. The house stands in five acres of grounds overlooking the North Sea. Its plaster ceilings are from 1624, and its Great Hall has an ornamented fireplace with a Royal coat-of-arms. Lived in for four centuries without interruption, this is a rare historic place and it provides an unusual way to visit northeast Scotland.

Bedrooms are traditional, and some have four-poster beds. All accommodations have private baths, except one that has private (but not *en suite*) facilities. The Turret Room is a favorite, named in honor of its matched pair of towers and its large bed canopied in jade silk. The original laird's bedroom has a gold and crimson canopy over the bed, reputedly slept under by James II. Ground-floor bedrooms are in a series of vaulted store rooms. The original 17th-century vaulted kitchen is now the main dining room. A four-course dinner, including Scottish and continental cuisine, is served every evening by candlelight.

PITTODRIE HOUSE HOTEL, Chapel of Garioch Rd., Pitcaple, Aberdeenshire AB5 9HS. Tel. 0467/681444. Fax 0467/681648. 27 rms (all with bath). TV TEL

$ Rates (including Scottish breakfast): £85 ($127.50) single; £105 ($157.50) double. AE, DC, MC, V. **Parking:** Free.

⭐ The Pittodrie House Hotel was originally one of the castles in the area. Dating from 1490, it was burned down and rebuilt in 1675, as a family home that changed into a country-house hotel when Royal Deeside came into prominence through Queen Victoria's adoption of Balmoral as her holiday retreat. The public rooms have antiques, oil paintings and open fires. The elegant restaurant serves venison, grouse, partridge, pheasant, or woodcock, depending on the season, and fresh fish, such as turbot, sea trout, and salmon. Dinners begin at £25 ($37.50) and are served daily from 7:30pm to last orders at 8:45pm. Bar lunches are served Monday through Saturday from 12:30 to 1:30pm. The hotel is 21 miles northwest of Aberdeen, 1¾ miles southwest of Pitcaple near Inverurie.

THAINSTONE HOUSE HOTEL & COUNTRY CLUB, Inverurie, Aberdeenshire, AB51 9NT, Tel. 0467/21643. Fax 0467/25084. 47 rms (all with bath). TV TEL **Directions:** Lies 14 miles northwest of Aberdeen.

$ Rates: £85 ($127.50) single; £100 ($150) double. Scottish breakfast £9.25 ($13.90) extra. AE, DC, MC, V. **Parking:** Free.

⭐ One of the most elegant country hotels in northeast Scotland, set on 40 acres of ground, Thainstone House Hotel can be both a retreat and a center for exploring this history-rich part of Scotland, including the Malt Whisky Trail. A four-star luxury hotel, this establishment is housed in a Palladian-style mansion whose adornments give it the air of a country club. Entrance is through a grand portal up an elegant stairway. The estate has dim origins in the Dark Ages, and a property that stood here in the 1700s was torched by the Jacobites. James Wilson, the owner, not only escaped the fire but fled to America where he was later to sign the Declaration of Independence. Today's mansion was designed by Archibald Simpson, the famed architect of many of Aberdeen's public buildings. The high ceilings, columns, neoclassical plaster reliefs, and cornices evoke Simpson's trip to Italy. To the original house a new development was added, and the old has been skillfully blended with the new. Rooms are elegantly furnished and contain many amenities including direct-dial phones, TV, radio, beverage-making equipment, hairdryer, and trouser press. Several rooms have original four-poster beds.

Dining/Entertainment: In the Georgian ambience of Simpson's Restaurant, an award-winning chef turns out a continental and a "Taste of Scotland" menu with a light, inventive touch. Dining is more informal in the Cammie's Grill, where local game is served along with Aberdeen Angus beef, seafood from the coast, and fresh salmon and trout from the Rivers Spey or Don.

Services: Room service, laundry, babysitting.

Facilities: Country Club Jacuzzi and steam room, fully equipped "trimnasium," snooker room, and a swimming pool designed in the style of an ancient Roman bath.

WHERE TO DINE

ATLANTIS, 16–17 Bon Accord Crescent. Tel. 0224/591403.
Cuisine: SEAFOOD. **Reservations:** Recommended. **Bus:** 23.
$ Prices: Appetizers £4.50–£7.50 ($6.80–$11.30); main courses £12.50–£16 ($18.80–$24). AE, DC, MC, V.
Open: Lunch Mon–Fri noon–2pm; dinner Mon–Sat 7–10pm. **Closed:** Some holidays and 2 weeks at Christmas.

Atlantis is one of the best seafood restaurants in Aberdeen. It's in a comfortably furnished basement near the center of town. You can enjoy several preparations of lobster, fish chowder, and an array of sole, scampi, and halibut. Some meat dishes are offered, and the fresh vegetables, salads, and desserts will complete your meal.

ELROND'S CAFÉ BAR AND RESTAURANT, in the Caledonian Thistle Hotel. 10–14 Union Terrace. Tel. 0224/640233.

Cuisine: INTERNATIONAL. **Reservations:** Not needed. **Bus.** 23.

$ **Prices:** Appetizers £2.50–£6 ($3.80–$9); main courses £10–£18 ($15–$27); pot of tea with a pastry £3 ($4.50); pint of lager £1.60–£1.70 ($2.40–$2.60). AE, DC, MC, V.

Open: Café bar Mon–Sat 10am–midnight; Sun 10am–11pm; restaurant Mon–Sat lunch 11:30am–2:30pm; dinner Mon–Sat 5:30–11:45pm; Sun dinner 5:30–11pm.

White marble floors, a long oak-capped bar, evening candlelight, and a garden-inspired decor create an ambience that caters to many different tastes. No one will mind if you show up just for a drink, a pot of tea, a midday salad or snack, or a full-blown feast. Specialties include burgers, steaks, pastas, fresh fish, lemon chicken suprême, chicken Kiev, and such vegetarian dishes as vegetables Cantonese. Although it's in one of Aberdeen's well-known hotels, it has a separate entrance set about 10 steps uphill from the street.

FARADAY'S, 2 Kirk Brae, Cults. On the A93 Aberdeen-Braemar Road. Tel. 0224/869666.

Cuisine: INTERNATIONAL. **Reservations:** Recommended.

$ **Prices:** Appetizers £3.50–£4.50 ($5.30–$6.80); main courses £9.50–£15 ($14.30–$22.50). Fixed-price dinner Fri–Sat £24.90 ($37.40). MC, V.

Open: Lunch Tues–Sat 12:15–2pm; dinner Mon–Sat 7–9:30pm. **Closed:** 2 weeks Jan.

In a granite-built converted generating station, this restaurant is now pure Victorian inside. John Inches is the chef-patron, and his menu is international, including perhaps a Malaysian pork and fruit curry or even a gratin of rock turbot with mushroom-studded pasta. His skill in the kitchen is reflected by dishes such as grilled eggplant with a pesto sauce. Stews and casseroles are excellent. Vegetarian meals can also be ordered, as can children's portions.

FERRYHILL HOUSE, Bon Accord St. Aberdeen, Aberdeenshire AB1 5NL. Tel. 0224/590867. Fax 0224/590867.

Cuisine: INTERNATIONAL. **Reservations:** Recommended Sat–Sun only. **Bus:** 22.

$ **Prices:** Appetizers £1.50–£2.40 ($2.30–$3.60); main courses £5.50–£7.50 ($8.30–$11.30); pint of lager £1.60 ($2.40); single-malt whiskies from £1.50 ($2.30) per shot. AE, DC, MC, V.

In its own park and garden on the city's southern outskirts, half a mile from the center, Ferryhill House was built 250 years ago by the region's most successful brickmaker and quarrymaster. It has Georgian detailing and an interior whose rich panels and ceiling beams have accumulated many decades of patina. It has one of the largest collections of single-malt whiskies in the region—more than 140 brands. There's also a fireplace for chilly afternoons, a bevy of waitresses who carry food to the scattered dining tables, and an outdoor beer garden for midsummer. Food items include shrimp or vegetable tempura, steak jambalaya, ploughman's platters, fried filet of haddock or plaice, pastas, and chili. The establishment also rents 10 bedrooms, all with bath, TV, and phone. The single rate is £48 ($72) Sunday through Thursday, only £20 ($30) on Friday and Saturday. The double rate is £65 ($97.50) Sunday through Thursday, or else £40 ($60) Friday and Saturday. A Scottish breakfast is included.

SILVER DARLING, Pocra Quay, Footdee. Tel. 0224/576229.

Cuisine: FRENCH/SEAFOOD. **Reservations:** Required. **Bus:** 14 or 15.

$ **Prices:** Appetizers £4.50–£7.25 ($6.80–$10.90); main courses £13.25–£15.75 ($19.90–$23.60); 2-course fixed-price lunch £13.90–£16.80 ($20.90–$25.20). AE, MC, V.

Open: Lunch Mon–Fri noon–2pm; dinner Mon–Sat 7–9:30pm. **Closed:** Dec 23–Jan 8.

The Silver Darling (local nickname for herring) is a definite asset to the dining picture in Aberdeen. Occupying a former Customs House at the mouth of the harbor, it spins a culinary fantasy around the freshest catch of the day. You might begin with a savory fish soup, almost Mediterranean in flavor, then go on to one of the barbecued fish dishes. Salmon is the invariable favorite of the more discriminating diners.

EASY EXCURSIONS FROM ABERDEEN
CASTLE COUNTRY

Aberdeen is the center of "castle country," as 40 inhabited castles lie within a 40-mile radius. Some of the most popular castle excursions are previewed below.

DRUM CASTLE, off the A93 (signposted). Tel. 0330/811204.

The handsome mansion was added in 1619, but the great square tower dates from the late 13th century. That makes this one of the three oldest tower houses in the country. There is also a garden of historic roses.

Admission: Castle, £3.30 ($5) adults, £1.70 ($2.60) children; grounds, free or by donation.

Open: Castle, Apr and Oct, Sat–Sunday 2–5pm. May–Sept, daily 2–6pm; grounds, daily 9:30am–dusk. **Directions:** Head 10 miles west of Aberdeen, off the A93.

CASTLE FRASER, Sauchen, near Kemnay. Tel. 03303/463.

One of the most impressive of the fortresslike castles of Mar, Castle Fraser stands in a 25-acre parkland and woodsy setting. The sixth laird, Michael Fraser, began the structure in 1575, and his son finished it in 1636. The castle is attractively furnished with such pieces as Jamie Fleeman's chest. Its Great Hall is spectacular, and you can wander around the grounds, which include an 18th-century walled garden.

Admission: £3.30 ($5) adults, £1.70 ($2.60) children.

Open: Apr, Sat–Sun 2–5pm; May–June, daily 2–6pm; July–Aug, daily 11am–6pm; Sept, daily 2–6pm; Oct, Sat–Sun 2–5pm. **Closed:** Nov–Mar. **Directions:** Head 3 miles south of Kemnay, 16 miles west of Aberdeen, off the A944.

KILDRUMMY CASTLE, on the A97, Kildrummy. Tel. 09755/71331.

The ruins of the ancient seat of the earls of Mar, this is the most extensive example of a 13th-century castle in Scotland. You can see the four round towers, the hall, and the chapel from the original structure. The great gatehouse and other remains date from the 16th century. The castle played a major role in Scottish history up to 1715, when it was dismantled.

Admission: £1.20 ($1.80) adults, 60p (90¢) children.

Open: Apr–Sept, Mon–Sat 9:30am–6pm, Sun 2–6pm; Oct–Mar, Mon–Sat 9:30am–4pm, Sun 2–4pm. **Directions:** Take the A97, 35 miles west of Aberdeen; it's signposted off the A97, 10 miles west of Alford.

FYVIE CASTLE, Turriff, on the Aberdeen-Banff Rd. Tel. 065/16266.

⭐ The National Trust for Scotland opened this castle to the public in 1986. The oldest part of the castle, dating from the 13th century, has been called the grandest existing example of Scottish baronial architecture. There are five towers, named after Fyvie's five families—the Prestons, Melddrums, Setons, Gordons, and Leiths—who lived here over five centuries. Originally built in a royal hunting forest, Fyvie means "deer hill" in Gaelic. The interior, created by the first Lord Leith of Fyvie, a steel magnate, reflects the opulence of the Edwardian era. His collections contain arms and armor, 16th-century tapestries, and important artworks by Raeburn, Gainsborough, and Romney. The castle is rich in ghosts, curses, and legends.

Admission: £3 ($4.50) adults, £1.50 ($2.30) children.

Open: May, daily 2–6pm; June–Sept, daily 11am–6pm. **Closed:** Oct–Apr. **Directions:** The castle is off the A947, 2 miles northwest of Aberdeen.

HADDO HOUSE, 10 miles NW of Ellon. Tel. 0651/851440.

In 1731, William Adam turned the Place of Kellie into Haddo House. This Palladian structure has been the home of the Gordons of Haddo for more than five centuries. The Marchioness of Aberdeen and Temair lives in the south wing of this property, which is owned by the National Trust for Scotland. The house is impressive, yet it also looks homelike. The country park of some 180 acres surrounding the house is maintained by the Grampian Regional Council.

Admission: £3.30 ($5) adults, £1.70 ($2.60) children.

Open: Apr 3–25 and Oct 2–31, Sat–Sun 2–5pm; May and Sept, daily 2–6pm; June–Aug, daily 11am–6pm. **Closed:** Nov–Mar. **Directions:** Head 19 miles north of Aberdeen along the A92 to the junction with the B999; take the B999 for another 15 miles.

12. WEST GRAMPIAN

Much of the region covered in this section is in the Moray district, on the southern shore of the Moray Firth, a great inlet cutting into the northeastern coast of Scotland. The district stretches in a triangular shape south from the coast to the wild heart of the Cairngorm Mountains near Aviemore. It's a land steeped in history, as its many castles, battle sites, and ancient monuments testify. It is also very sports oriented, attracting not only fishermen but also golfers. Golfers can purchase a 5-day ticket from tourist information centers that will allow them to play at more than 11 courses in the area.

The major tourist attraction is the **Whisky Trail,** running through the glens of Speyside. Here distilleries, many of which can be visited, are known for their production of *uisge beatha* or "water of life." Whisky (note the spelling without the *e*) is its more familiar name.

Half the malt distilleries in the country lie along the River Spey and its tributaries. Here peat smoke and Highland water are used to turn out single-malt (unblended) whisky. The Whisky Trail is 70 miles long. There are five malt distilleries in the area: Glenlivet, Glenfiddich, Glenfarclas, Strathisla, and Tamdhu. Allow about an hour each to visit them.

If you're traveling north on the A9 road from Perth and Pitlochry, your first stop might be at **Dalwhinnie,** which has the highest whisky distillery in the world at 1,888 feet. It's not in the Spey Valley but is at the northeastern end of Loch Ericht, with views of lochs and forests.

GLENLIVET

To reach your first distillery on the designated Whisky Trail, you leave Grantown-on-Spey (see Chapter 9) and head east along the A95 until you come to the junction with the B9008. Go south along this route and you can't miss it. The location of the **Glenlivet Reception Centre** is 10 miles north of the nearest town, Tomintoul. For information, call 08073/427. Near the River Livet, a Spey tributary, this distillery is one of the most famous in Scotland, and it's open to visitors from Easter through October, Monday to Saturday from 10am to 4pm. In July and August it remains open to 7pm.

Back on the A95, you can visit the **Glenfarclas Distillery** at Ballindalloch (tel. 08072/245), one of the few malt-whisky distilleries that's still independent of the giants. Glenfarclas is managed by the fifth generation of the Grant family. Founded in 1836, it is open all year, Monday to Friday from 9am to 4:30pm, and from June through September, also on Saturday from 10am to 4pm. There is a small craft shop, and each visitor is offered a dram of Glenfarclas Malt Whisky.

WHERE TO STAY & DINE

MINMORE HOUSE HOTEL, Glinlivet, Ballindalloch, Banffshire AB3 9DB.
Tel. 08073/378. Fax 08073/472. 10 rms (all with bath).
$ Rates (including Scottish breakfast): £32 ($48) per person. Half board £48 ($72) per person, 50% discount for children 5–14 staying in parents' room. MC, V.
Parking: Free. **Closed:** Nov–Mar.

Standing on 7 acres of private grounds adjacent to the Glenlivet Distillery, this is an impressive country house. Guests are welcomed to one of the well-furnished bedrooms, all with tea/coffee makers. Before being converted into a hotel, the Minmore was the home of the Glenlivet Distillery owners. The hotel operators have elegantly furnished their drawing room, which opens onto views of the Ladder Hills and an outdoor swimming pool. Guests enjoy drinks in the oak-paneled lounge bar, with an open log fire on chilly nights. The Scottish food is excellent, served in a Regency-style dining room with mahogany tables and matching chairs.

DUFFTOWN

James Duff, the fourth Earl of Fife, founded this town in 1817. The four main streets of town converge at the battlemented clock tower, which is also the tourist information center.

WHAT TO SEE & DO

Dufftown, a center of the whisky-distilling industry, is surrounded by seven malt distilleries. The major one is the family-owned **Glenfiddich Distillery,** on the A941, half a mile north of Dufftown (tel. 0340/20373). It is open Monday to Friday from 9:30am to 4:30pm. In addition, from Easter through mid-October, it is open on Saturday from 9:30am to 4:30pm and on Sunday from noon to 4:30pm. Guides in kilts show visitors around the plant and explain the process of distilling. A film of the history of distilling is also shown. At the finish of the tour, you're given a dram of malt whisky. The tour is free. There's a souvenir shop. The first whisky was produced on Christmas Day back in 1887.

Other sights include **Balvenie Castle,** along the A941, the ruins of a moated stronghold from the 14th century that lie on the south side of the Glenfiddich Distillery. During her northern campaign against the Earl of Huntly, Mary Queen of Scots spent two nights here. From 1459 to the 17th century the earls of Atholl retained Balvenie. It is open from April through September, Monday to Saturday from 9:30am to 7pm and on Sunday from 2 to 6pm; closed off-season. Admission is £1 ($1.50) for adults, 50p (80¢) for children.

The **Mortlach Parish Church** in Dufftown is one of the oldest places of Christian worship in the country. It is reputed to have been founded in 566 by St. Moluag. A Pictish cross stands in the graveyard. The present church was reconstructed in 1931 and incorporates portions of an older building.

WHERE TO DINE

TASTE OF SPEYSIDE, 10 Balvenie St. Tel. 0340/20860.
   Cuisine: SCOTTISH. **Reservations:** Recommended in the evening.
$ Prices: Appetizers £3.30–£4.30 ($5–$6.50); main courses £4.50–£6 ($6.80–$9). Speyside platter £5.70 ($8.60). MC, V.
   Open: Lunch daily 11am–6pm; dinner daily 6–9pm. **Closed:** Nov–Feb.

True to its name, this restaurant in the town center, just off the main square, avidly promotes a Speyside cuisine as well as Speyside malt whiskies, and in the bar you can buy the product of each of Speyside's 46 distilleries. A platter including a slice of smoked salmon, smoked venison, a slice of smoked trout, pâté flavored with malt whisky, locally made cheese (cow or goat), salads, and homemade oatcakes is offered at noon and at night. Nourishing soup is made fresh daily and is served with homemade bread. There's also a choice of meat pies, including venison with red wine and herbs or rabbit. A small but limited selection of hot dishes is offered, too. For dessert, try Scotch Mist, which contains fresh cream, malt whisky, and crumbled meringue.

KEITH

Keith, 11 miles northwest of Huntly, grew up because of its strategic location, where the main road and rail routes between Inverness and Aberdeen cross the River Isla. It has an ancient history, but owes its present look to the "town planning" of the late

18th and early 19th centuries. Today it is a major stopover along the Malt Whisky Trail.

The oldest operating distillery in the Scottish Highlands, the **Strathisla Distillery,** on Seafield Avenue (tel. 05422/7471), was established in 1786. It offers guided tours from Easter through the end of September, Monday to Friday from 9am to 4:30pm.

There is also a fine woolen mill in the town, **G. & G. Kynoch,** Isla Bank Mills, Station Road (tel. 05422/2648), which has been in business since 1788 producing high-quality tweeds and woolens. The mill shop is open daily from 8:30am to 4:15pm, and mill tours are conducted on Tuesday and Thursday at 2:30pm.

WHERE TO STAY & DINE

ROYAL HOTEL, Church Rd., Keith, Banffshire AB5 5BQ. Tel. 05422/ 2528. 12 rms (3 with bath).

$ Rates (including Scottish breakfast): £18.50 ($27.80) single without bath, £29.50 ($44.30) single with bath; £31 ($46.50) double without bath, £42 ($63) double with bath. AE, MC, V. **Parking:** Free.

In addition to being a cozy and comfortable hotel, this stone establishment a quarter mile north of town beside the A96 serves as the village pub and social center. Built beside the road in 1883, it has probably welcomed the grandparents and parents of virtually every longtime resident of Keith. A handful of the more expensive bedrooms contain TV sets and tea-making facilities. On the premises is a restaurant; inexpensive platters are served as bar snacks in the lounge.

ROTHES

A Speyside town with five distilleries, Rothes is just to the south of the lovely Glen of Rothes, 49 miles east of Inverness and 62 miles northwest of Aberdeen. Founded in 1766, the town lies between Ben Aigan and Conerock Hill. A little settlement, the basis of the town today, grew up around Rothes Castle, ancient stronghold of the Leslie family, who lived here until 1622. Only a single massive wall of the castle remains.

Among the several distilleries bearing the name of, or having been launched by, the Grant family is the **Glen Grant Distillery,** opened in the mid-19th century. It's located right outside town (signposted from the center) and can be visited anytime from mid-April through September, Monday to Friday from 10am to 4pm. A Visitor Reception Centre offers guided tours. Call 03403/413 for information.

WHERE TO STAY & DINE

ROTHES GLEN HOTEL, Rothes, Morayshire AB38 7AH. Tel. 03403/254. Fax 03403/566. 16 rms (all with bath). TV TEL

$ Rates (including Scottish breakfast): £68 ($102) single; £105 ($157.50) double. AE, DC, MC, V. **Parking:** Free.

For food and lodging, the Rothes Glen Hotel lies 3 miles north of Rothes on the A941. The old turreted house, with many of its original pieces of furniture, stands back from the road and is surrounded by about 40 acres of fields with grazing Highland cattle. This historic, castlelike building was designed by the architect who built Balmoral. The dining room is paneled in wood, and good wholesome meals are served in true Scottish tradition. Bar lunches are popular, with a wide choice offered. A fixed-price four-course dinner costs £26 ($39).

ELGIN

The center of local government in the Moray district, an ancient royal burgh, this cathedral city lies on the Lossie River, 38 miles east of Inverness and 68 miles northwest of Aberdeen. The city's medieval plan has been retained, with "wynds" and "pends" connecting the main artery with other streets. The castle, as was customary in medieval town layouts, stood at one end of the main thoroughfare, with the cathedral at the other. Nothing remains of the castle.

Samuel Johnson and James Boswell came this way on their Highland tour and reported a "vile dinner" at the Red Lion Inn in 1773.

WHAT TO SEE & DO

Lady Hill stands on High Street, opposite the post office. This is the hilltop location of what was once the royal castle of Elgin. Edward I of England stayed here in 1296 during the Wars of Independence. Only a fragment of the mighty castle now remains. A column, put up in 1839 in memory of the last duke of Gordon, surmounts the hill.

Birnie Kirk, at Birnie, 3 miles south of Elgin and west of the A941 to Rothes, was for a time the seat of a bishopric. It dates from about 1140 when it was constructed on the site of a much earlier church founded by St. Brendan. One of the few Norman churches in Scotland still in regular use, it is open daily from 10am to 4pm.

On King Street is the ✪ **Cathedral of Moray** (tel. 0343/547171). Now in ruins, once called the "lantern of the north," the cathedral was founded in 1224 but destroyed in 1390 by the "wolf of Badenoch," the natural son of Robert II. After its destruction, the citizens of Elgin rebuilt their beloved cathedral and turned it into one of the most attractive and graceful buildings in Scotland. The architect's plan was that of a Jerusalem cross. However, when the central tower fell in 1711, the cathedral was allowed to fall into decay. Today tourists can wander among its ruins and snap pictures. Best preserved is the 15th-century chapter house. The cathedral stands beside the river in the town center, off North College Street near the A96. Admission is 60p (90¢) for adults, 30p (50¢) for children. It is open from April through September, Monday to Saturday from 9:30am to 7pm, Sunday from 2pm to 7pm; October through March, Monday to Saturday from 9:30am to 4pm, Sunday from 2pm to 4pm.

WHERE TO STAY

MANSION HOUSE HOTEL, The Haugh, Elgin, Morayshire IV10 1AW. Tel. 0343/548811. Fax 0343/547916. 22 rms (all with bath). MINIBAR TV TEL
Directions: Follow the A96 onto Alexandra Road to the turnoff onto Haugh Road.
$ Rates (including Scottish breakfast): £70–£85 ($105–$127.50) single; £100–£130 ($150–$195) double. AE, DC, MC, V. **Parking:** Free.

The Mansion House Hotel is an elegantly appointed hotel, where the baronial proportions of the original design remain intact. Public rooms include a bistro, a lounge bar, a residents' lounge, and a dining room. Each bedroom contains a radio alarm clock and hot-beverage equipment; most have four-poster beds. The establishment lies at the edge of the River Lossie, about a quarter of a mile from the center of Elgin. The hotel has a country club with a swimming pool, Jacuzzi, sauna, Turkish bath, and gym.

EIGHT ACRES HOTEL, Sheriffmill, Elgin, Morayshire IV30 3UN. Tel. 0343/543077. Fax 0343/540001. 56 rms (all with bath), 1 suite. TV TEL.
$ Rates (including Scottish breakfast): £48.50–£55 ($72.80–$82.50) single; £68 ($102) double; £80 ($120) suite. AE, DC, MC, V. **Parking:** Free.

This hotel was built in the 1970s in a low-slung motel-inspired format about a mile west of the center of Elgin, beside the main A96 road leading to Inverness. Rooms, though streamlined and functionally furnished, are warm and clean, attracting motorists from England on their way to Inverness and the Highlands. There's a restaurant and bar on the premises, as well as a swimming pool, gym, and squash courts.

WHERE TO DINE

ABBEY COURT RESTAURANT, 15 Greyfriars St. Tel. 0343/542849.
Cuisine: SCOTTISH. **Reservations:** Required.
$ Prices: Appetizers £1.60–£7.95 ($2.40–$11.90); main courses £6–£14.75 ($9–$22.10). AE, DC, MC, V.
Open: Lunch Mon–Sat noon–2pm; dinner Mon–Sat 6:30–9:45pm.

The Abbey Court, in the center of town behind the County Building, is an excellent

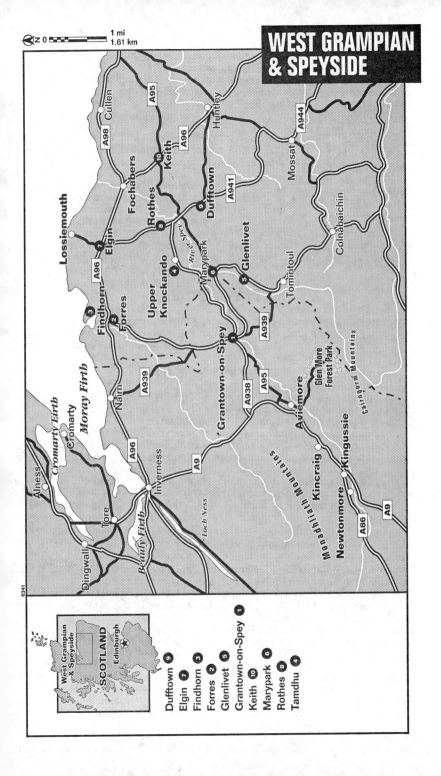

WEST GRAMPIAN & SPEYSIDE

1 mi
1.61 km

Dufftown **9**
Elgin **7**
Findhorn **3**
Forres **2**
Glenlivet **5**
Grantown-on-Spey **1**
Keith **10**
Marypark **6**
Rothes **8**
Tamdhu **4**

SCOTLAND
Edinburgh

West Grampian
& Speyside

and sophisticated restaurant decorated with lots of stone- and earth-colored quarry tile, along with an artificial pergola, a separate bistro corner, and a more formal dining area in the rear with lots of plants. Fresh pasta is homemade, and fresh fish is delivered daily. Game is also a feature. The owner is a local wine importer, and he stocks more than 150 varieties.

THE OAKWOOD, Forres Rd. Tel. 0343/542688.
  Cuisine: BRITISH. **Reservations:** Not necessary.
$ Prices: Appetizers £1–£4 ($1.50–$6); main courses £3.50–£7.50 ($5.30–$11.30); snacks and sandwiches £1.50–£3.50 ($2.30–$5.30). AE, DC, MC, V.
  Open: Daily 9am–6:30pm.

Built in 1932 to cater to automobile traffic, the Oakwood lies about 2½ miles west of Elgin on the A96 leading to Inverness. Its facade is crafted from an interlocking mosaic of pinewood logs. Inside, amid the light reflected from acres of pinewood paneling and stained-glass windows, you'll find a wishing well and a staff well accustomed to serving everything from cups of coffee and sandwiches to full-blown lunches and teas. No hard liquor is served, although beer and light wines are available. Menu items include casseroles, salads, burgers, steaks, and fried filets of haddock and plaice.

FINDHORN

As you travel westward from Elgin to Forres, a turn to the right and then to the left will bring you to Findhorn, a tiny village that used to be a busy commercial fishing port. Findhorn lies at the end of the B9011, and a local bus from Forres stops here.

WHAT TO SEE & DO

These days, the unique tidal bay at the mouth of the River Findhorn makes the village an ideal center for yacht racing, sailing, and windsurfing. Across the bay from Findhorn is the Culbin Sands, under which lies a buried village.

Just before Findhorn village, you'll see the home of the **Findhorn Foundation,** The Park (tel. 0309/690311), an international education community based on spiritual principles, founded in 1962. It owns and runs the Findhorn Bay Caravan Park (tel. 0309/30203) and the Phoenix Shop, where you can purchase health foods, books, and crafts. Tours of the complex are given every afternoon from April to September. If you're interested in residential courses, write or call 0309/73655.

Not far away is the RAF airfield of Kinloss. Here **Kinloss Abbey** was founded in 1150 by David I, but after the Reformation it fell into ruins.

WHERE TO STAY & DINE

CULBIN SANDS HOTEL, Findhorn Rd. Findhorn, Morayshire IV36 0YE. Tel. 0309/690252. 16 rms (9 with shower, none with toilet). TEL
$ Rates (including Scottish breakfast): £17 ($25.50) single without bath, £19 ($28.50) single with shower; £30 ($45) double without bath, £34 ($51) double with bath. AE, MC, V. **Parking:** Free.

Solidly built of stone during the Victorian era and later painted with coats of black and white paint, this once private house a quarter mile west of Findhorn's center, beside the A96, enjoys panoramic views of the Moray Firth, Findhorn Bay, and the Culbin Forest. It's solidly booked throughout most of each summer, partly because of its proximity to many desirable beaches, and partly because of its status as one of the most convivial spots in the region. It boasts several well-stocked bars that rock every weekend to live and recorded music, and a disco that many local residents welcome as a rare relief in these otherwise quiet climes. Bar lunches and suppers are served every day. Three-course dinners in the restaurant cost £12.50 ($18.80). Bedrooms are simple and unpretentious but comfortable, and all have tea-making facilities and radios. Residents can congregate in an upstairs sitting room usually reserved for their private use. Fishing, pony trekking, and waterskiing are all within easy reach. Findley and Amanda McNaughton are your hosts.

CROWN & ANCHOR INN, Findhorn, Morayshire IV36 0YF. Tel. 0309/ 690243. 6 rms (all with shower). TV

$ Rates (including Scottish breakfast): £18 ($27) single; £36 ($54) double. No credit cards. **Parking:** Free.

The stone-built Crown & Anchor dates from 1739 when it was constructed to cater to travelers making the run between Edinburgh and Inverness. On the seafront near the pier, bar snacks and meals are served all day 7 days a week. Locals drop in to enjoy the real ales and malt whiskies served in the bar. Rooms are simply but comfortably furnished.

CHAPTER 9

THE WEST HIGHLANDS

- **WHAT'S SPECIAL ABOUT THE WEST HIGHLANDS**
1. **AROUND LOCH LINNHE & LOCH LEVEN**
2. **FORT WILLIAM**
3. **MALLAIG**
4. **INVERGARRY**
5. **AVIEMORE**
6. **SPEYSIDE**
7. **ALONG LOCH NESS**
8. **INVERNESS**
9. **NAIRN**
10. **THE BLACK ISLE**
11. **SUTHERLAND**
12. **CAITHNESS**

From their romantic glens and their rugged mountainous landscapes, the West Highlands suggest a timeless antiquity. You can see deer grazing only yards from the highway in remote parts, and you can stop by a secluded loch for a picnic or fish for trout and salmon. The region's beauty has been praised by such authorities as Robert Burns, Dr. Johnson, and Daniel Defoe. The shadow of Macbeth still stalks the land, and locals will tell you that this 11th-century king was much maligned by Shakespeare. The area's most famous resident, however, is said to live in mysterious Loch Ness. First sighted by St. Columba in the 6th century, "Nessie" has evaded searchers ever since.

Centuries of invasions, rebellions, and clan feuds are but distant memories now, and the Highlands are among the most peaceful and tranquil parts of Great Britain. They're not as remote as they once were, when many Londoners seriously believed that the men of the Highlands had tails.

SEEING THE WEST HIGHLANDS

Your entrance into the Highlands might be Fort William and the surrounding area, including Loch Linnhe and Loch Leven. The famous Glencoe is on the shores of Loch Leven. In the south, Fort William, capital of Lochaber, is the major touring center for the West Highlands. In the north, of course, Inverness makes the best base.

Fort William is surrounded by wildly beautiful Lochaber, called "the land of bens, glens, and heroes." Dominating the area is Ben Nevis, Britain's highest mountain, rising 4,406 feet. In summer when it's clear of snow, there's a good path to the summit, although rapidly changing weather conditions can alter the safety here. A cable car takes visitors to a height of 2,300 feet where they can view the mountain. This district is the western end of what is known as Glen Mor—the Great Glen, geologically a fissure that divides the northwest of Scotland from the southeast and contains Loch Lochy, Loch Oich, and Loch Ness. The Caledonian Canal, opened in 1847, linked these lochs, the River Ness, and Moray Firth. It provided sailing boats a safe alternative to the stormy route around the north of Scotland. Larger steamships made the canal out of date commercially, but fishing boats and pleasure steamers still use it. Good roads run the length of the Great Glen, partly following the line of General Wade's military road. From Fort William you can take steamer trips to Staffa and Iona. See Chapter 10.

WHAT'S SPECIAL ABOUT THE WEST HIGHLANDS

Great Towns/Villages

☐ Fort William, on the shores of Loch Linnhe, one of the best bases for touring the western Highlands.

☐ Aviemore, in the heart of the Highlands, a winter and summer sports mecca.

☐ Grantown-on-Spey, holiday resort near the Cairngorm mountains and best center for exploring Speyside.

☐ Inverness, capital of the Highlands, one of the oldest inhabited localities in Scotland.

☐ Nairn, old-time royal burgh and seaside resort on Moray Firth at the mouth of the Nairn River.

☐ Ullapool, an 18th-century fishing village on the shores of Loch Broom—for some, a gateway to the Outer Hebrides.

Ace Attractions

☐ Loch Ness, home of the legendary "Nessie," the elusive denizen of the deep that fascinates the world and Scotland's most famous "resident."

☐ Caledonian Canal, launched in 1803, a 60-mile stretch of man-made canal and natural lochs.

☐ The Black Isle, not an island really (and certainly not black), but a history-rich peninsula of beauty and mystery.

☐ Speyside, the valley of the second longest river in Scotland, lying both north and south of Aviemore.

☐ Ben Nevis, highest mountain in Britain, rising 4,406 feet, with a path to summit in summer.

☐ Lochaber, a wildly beautiful part of west Scotland, "land of bens, glens, and heroes."

☐ "Road to the Isles" (A830), a famous highway that begins at Invergarry, running through the western Highland glens and mountains to the Kyle of Lochalsh.

☐ Glencoe, Scotland's most famous— and, to many, its most beautiful glen—site of the 1692 massacre of the Clan MacDonald by the Campbells.

☐ Loch Leven, one of two such named lakes in Scotland, this one considered by many as the loveliest of all the western Highland lochs.

Historic Castles

☐ Cawdor Castle, considered the most romantic castle in the Highlands, linked by Shakespeare with Macbeth.

☐ Dunrobin Castle, Golspie, the northernmost of the great houses of Scotland, seat of the Countess of Sutherland.

☐ Urquhart Castle, on Loch Ness, one of the largest in Scotland (now in colorful ruins).

Parks and Gardens

☐ Inverewe Gardens, near Ullapool, an exotic mixture of plants from many parts of the world, including the Himalayas.

Special Events/Festivals

☐ Highland Games in July at Inverness, with their sporting competitions and festival balls.

If you have time before heading to Inverness and Loch Ness, you can take a detour northeast to visit Aviemore and the villages and towns of the Spey Valley, which offer much activity for the visitor. In the Spey Valley you're at the doorway to the "Malt Whisky Trail" (See West Grampian in Chapter 8). Aviemore is also the winter sports capital of Britain. Aviemore Centre has a multitude of outdoor pursuits: golfing, angling, skiing, and ice skating. Those seeking a more traditional Scottish ambience will gravitate to one of the many Speyside villages, each with its own attractions and atmosphere. Ranking next to Aviemore, Grantown-on-Spey is a major sports center.

Inverness and legendary Loch Ness are the most popular attractions of the West Highlands and consequently are overcrowded in summer, but they are surrounded by villages and towns, which also make good centers, especially if you are driving. If you're dependent on public transportation, make Inverness your base, as it has good rail and bus connections to the rest of Scotland and also to England.

Finally, if you've caught Highland fever, and you have the time, you can extend your stay in the region by visiting the far north of Britain, where the mainland of Scotland comes to an end. This section of the Highlands, Sutherland and Caithness, is not for everyone. It's the loneliest part of Scotland. But for some, that is part of its undeniable charm. Crumbling watchtowers no longer stand guard over anything except the sheep-cropped wilderness. Moss-green glens give way to inland lochs and sea fjords. In summer the deep-blue lochs and towering cliffs, as well as the gentle glens, are to be enjoyed in the sun. Many relics of Scotland's turbulent past dot the landscape. Castles are left in ruins. Today potteries, and craft centers encourage visitors; crafts include silversmithing, stone polishing, glassmaking, and most definitely weaving.

GETTING THERE

The northernmost rail line throughout the Highlands goes toward the Isle of Skye and stops at Fort William (which has good connections from Glasgow), ending at Mallaig. If you're depending on public transportation, it's better to go by rail, then rely on local buses once you've arrived at your Highland destination. Motorists head north from Glasgow along the A82, which eventually leads to Inverness, passing through Fort William.

Aviemore and the villages of the Spey Valley are easily reached by car from Fort William. If you plan to fly to the Highlands from England, the fastest way is to fly to Inverness (see Section 8), then go to your ultimate destination by rail, bus, or car. Trains to Inverness leave from London's King's Cross Station (tel. 071/278-2477), but if you're already in Scotland you'll find good rail connections from both Glasgow and Edinburgh.

By road, rail, and bus, getting to Inverness and Loch Ness is relatively easy today. From the south, you can take fast roads through either Edinburgh or Glasgow, heading for your ultimate destination. If you don't want to drive, there are Motorrail terminals at Edinburgh, Stirling, and Inverness. Direct rail service operates from London to Inverness. You can also go by coach or plane.

Most of the main arteries are good, but other roads in the Highlands are single lane, slowing you down considerably. Remember that sheep have the right-of-way. The A9 along the east coast, which leads from Perth to Inverness, continues all the way to John o'Groats, at the end of mainland Britain.

The fastest way to reach the Far North is to fly to Wick. British Airways flies into Wick Airport (tel. 0955/3914), as does Loganair Ltd. (tel. 0955/2294). There is also rail service between Inverness and Wick and Thurso on the north coast.

SUGGESTED ITINERARY

Days 1 and 2: Spend Day 1 at Fort William and its immediate environs, then occupy Day 2 by touring around Loch Leven, including Glencoe. You can do this while still based in Fort William.

Day 3: Take the A830 west to Mallaig, one of the most scenic drives in Scotland.

Day 4: Return toward Fort William, then head northeast to Aviemore to visit its attractions.

Day 5: Using Grantown-on-Spey as your hotel base, explore the River Spey valley and its many sights.

Day 6: Head west again and get on the A82 going north to Inverness. Drive along Loch Ness hoping for a sighting of "Nessie." Instead of pressing north to Inverness, stay overnight at one of the inns along the lake. Drummnadrochit makes a good center.

Day 7: Continue north to Inverness and view that city and its attractions. Enjoy a Highland dinner in the evening.

Day 8: Continue east to the seaside resort of Nairn and use it as an overnight base, exploring nearby Cawdor Castle during your stay.

Day 9: Explore the Black Isle west of Inverness, planning an overnight stopover in the region, perhaps at Beauly.

Day 10: Continue north through Dornoch, visiting Dornoch Cathedral, then continuing north to Golspie to see Dunrobin Castle. Overnight in Golspie.

Day 11: Continue north exploring the coastline, overnighting in either Wick or Thurso with a side trip to John o'Groats, the most northerly point on the British mainland.

Day 12–13: Continue driving west around the coast, taking the A836 via Tongue (where you can have lunch), and continuing to Ullapool for 2 nights. On the second day, while based in Ullapool, take as many of the scenic excursions in the environs as time allows.

1. AROUND LOCH LINNHE & LOCH LEVEN

To the south of Fort William (see Section 2, below) is one of the most history-rich sections of Scotland, a group of settlements around Loch Linnhe and Loch Leven (not the also-famous Loch Leven near Dunfermline). The best-known hamlet here is Glencoe, site of the famous 1692 massacre when the Campbells massacred the MacDonalds. Glencoe is considered the most beautiful glen in Scotland.

Around both lochs are impressive landscapes and moorland, with various flora and fauna unique to the western Highlands. Many people prefer to find lodgings in this area instead of at Fort William. Robert Louis Stevenson captured much of the essence of this moorland and wilderness in the novel *Kidnapped*.

ONICH

On the shores of Loch Linnhe, this charming little village lies to the north of Ballachulish Bridge, 9 miles southwest of Fort William. It's a good center if you're taking the western route to Inverness, or going to Skye and Fort William.

WHERE TO STAY & DINE

CREAG DHU (THE LODGE ON THE LOCH), Creag Dhu, Onich, Inverness-shire PH33 6RY. Tel. 08553/238. Fax 08553/463. 21 rms (18 with private bath). TV TEL

$ Rates (including half board): £40.50 ($60.80) single without bath, £65.50 ($98.30) single with bath; £81 ($121.50) double without bath, £131 ($196.50) double with bath. MC, V. **Parking:** Free. **Closed:** Mid-Nov to Christmas and Jan 3 to mid-Mar.

This house was originally built in 1860 and transformed into a hotel by the Young family about a century later. Now a family-run hotel, it lies on the A82, 10 miles south of Fort William between Ben Nevis and Glencoe, with expansive lochside and mountain views. The loch views are of prawn-filled Linnhe and Leven. The bedrooms have radios, hairdryers, trouser presses, and tea and coffee makers. Under the supervision of the Young family, the hotel kitchen offers several traditional Scottish dishes, among other fare. Ceilidhs, evenings of Scottish music and song, as well as talks and slide shows, are among events held at the hotel. Lunches are bar meals, with platters priced from £3 ($4.50) to £6 ($9), and a table d'hôte dinner is offered for £21.50 ($32.30). Boating, sailing, waterskiing, and aqualung diving are offered nearby, along with good sea and freshwater fishing, pony trekking, riding, golfing, swimming, and tennis. The hotel has an enthusiastic repeat clientele.

BALLACHULISH

This small village enjoys a splendid scenic position on the shores of Loch Leven at the entrance to Glencoe, and is a good center for touring the western Highlands. It's located 117 miles northwest of Edinburgh and 13 miles south of Fort William. Take the A82 south from Fort William to reach it.

WHERE TO STAY & DINE

BALLACHULISH HOTEL, on the A828, Ballachulish, Argyll PA39 4JY. Tel. 08552/606. Fax 08552/629. 30 rms (all with bath). TV TEL
$ Rates (including Scottish breakfast): £45–£56 ($67.50–$84) single; £60–£86 ($90–$129) double. MC, V. **Parking:** Free.

Although it served for a brief period of its life as a school, it was custom built in 1850 as one of the first hotels in this region of Scotland. Alluringly located 2 miles northwest of Ballachulish at the junction of Loch Leven and Loch Linnhe, it offers hospitality, warmth, and old-style elegance. All bedrooms have a high standard of comfort and convenience, and all are equipped with tea/coffee makers. A handful of them contain four-poster beds. The staff will arrange boat trips or fishing expeditions on the lochs.

GLENCOE

On the shores of Loch Leven, near where it joins Loch Linnhe, the Ballachulish Bridge now links the villages of North and South Ballachulish, at the entrance to Glencoe. The bridge saves a long drive to the head of the loch if you're coming from the north, but many visitors enjoy the scenic drive to Kinlochleven to come upon the wild and celebrated Glencoe from the east.

Glencoe runs from Rannoch Moor to Loch Leven between some magnificent mountains, including 3,766-foot Bidean nam Bian. Known as the "Glen of Weeping," Glencoe is where, on February 11, 1692, Campbells massacred MacDonalds—men, women, and children—who had been their hosts for 12 days. Although massacres were not uncommon in those times, this one shocked even the Highlanders because of the breach of hospitality. When the killing was done, the crime of "murder under trust" was regarded by law as an aggravated form of murder, and carried the same penalties as treason. The **Monument to the Massacre of Glencoe** at Carnoch was erected by the chief of the MacDonald clan to commemorate the massacre.

The glen, much of which now belongs to the National Trust for Scotland, is full of history and legend. A tiny lochan is known as "the pool of blood" because by its side some men are said to have quarreled over a piece of cheese, and all were killed.

This is an area of massive splendor, with towering peaks and mysterious glens where you can well imagine the fierce battle among the kilted Highlanders to the skirl of the pipes and the beat of the drums.

Glen Orchy, to the south, is well worth a visit too, for the wild river and mountain scenery is beautiful and photogenic. It was the birthplace of the Gaelic bard Duncan Ban MacIntyre, whose song "In Praise of Ben Doran" is considered a masterpiece.

WHERE TO STAY & DINE

In the Glen

CLACHAIG INN, Glencoe, Ballachulish, Argyll PA39 4HX. Tel. 08552/252. Fax 08552/679. 19 rms (16 with bath or shower).
$ Rates (including Scottish breakfast): £24 ($36) single without bath; £36 ($54) double without bath. £48–£52 ($72–$78) double with bath. MC, V. **Parking:** Free.

After the bleakness of Glencoe, the trees ringing this place—the only hotel in the glen (look for the signs on the highway)—make it seem like an oasis. The Daynes family offers Highland hospitality and good food and an excellent selection of British ales in their informal hotel, reached by taking a winding gravel-covered road off the main highway. They rent some contemporary chalets in the back garden, plus several bedrooms in the main house. Live folk music now brings the place alive every night during the winter season and three to four times a week during the summer season.

KING'S HOUSE HOTEL, Glencoe, Argyll PA39 4HZ. Tel. 08556/259. Fax 08556/250. 22 rms (12 with bath). TEL. **Transportation:** Guests can arrange to be met at the Bridge of Orchy railway station.

$ Rates: £16–£18 ($24–$27) single without bath; £36 ($54) double without bath, £42 ($63) double with bath. Scottish breakfast £6.50 ($9.80) extra. MC, V. **Parking:** Free.

The solid walls of this historic inn were built on a windswept plateau beside the A82 12 miles southeast of Glencoe village, at the strategic point where Glencoe joins the Glen Etive near a famous and jagged mountain known as Buachaille Etive Mor. Built during the 1600s, the establishment is believed to be one of the oldest licensed inns in Scotland, although many modernizations have upgraded its interior into a streamlined version of its original rustic format. The hotel is considered a ski center, and maintains a ski lift a short walk from its entrance. Warm, comfortably furnished bedrooms usually offer sweeping views of majestic scenery. There's a lounge with comfortable modern chairs, and a dining room with a fine wine cellar and freshly prepared meals. A three-course table d'hôte dinner costs £16.50 ($24.80).

In Glencoe Village

GLENCOE HOTEL, Glencoe, Argyll PA39 4HW. Tel. 08552/245. Fax 08552/492. 15 rms (all with bath).

$ Rates (including Scottish breakfast): £37–£42 ($55.50–$63) single; £50–£60 ($75–$90) double. AE, DC, MC, V. **Parking:** Free. **Closed:** 1 week at Christmas.

This white-fronted, slate-roofed building was originally built in 1932, and is today the only hotel in Glencoe still owned by the descendants of the people who built it. The McConnacher family, who renovated it in 1989, retained much of the pinewood paneling inside and outside, and imbue its drinking facilities with spirit and life. The hotel boasts a flowering outdoor patio overlooking the Pape of Glencoe and the islands in Loch Leven. Each room contains tea-making facilities and simple but comfortable furnishings. The hotel contains a restaurant, where table d'hôte dinners cost £14.75 ($22.10), and two bars where platters are served at lunch and dinner every day for around £4 ($6) to £6 ($9).

---

2. FORT WILLIAM

133 miles NW of Edinburgh, 68 miles S of Inverness, 104 miles N of Glasgow

GETTING THERE By Train Fort William is a major stop on the West Highland rail line that begins its run at the Queen Street Station in Glasgow, ending at Mallaig on the west coast of Scotland. Six trains a day make this trip to Fort William (two or three on Sunday), at a one-way cost of £18.50 ($27.80). For information about schedules, call 0397/703791 in Fort William.

By Bus Six buses run from Glasgow to Fort William per day, taking 3 hours and costing £7.10 ($10.70) for a one-way ticket. Call Scottish Cityline at 041/3327133 in Glasgow for information about departures and tickets.

By Car From Glasgow, head north along the A82.

ESSENTIALS The **tourist information office** (tel. 0397/703781) is at Cameron Centre, Cameron Square. The **telephone area code** is 0397.

This town, on the shores of Loch Linnhe, is a good center for exploring the western Highlands. Fort William stands on the site of a fort built by General Monk in 1655, to help crush any rebellion Highlanders might have been plotting. After several reconstructions, it was finally torn down in 1864 to make way for the railroad, and little remains of it today. During the notorious Highland Clearances, many starving and evicted people were shipped from here to America.

Today Fort William is a bustling town, thriving very well on the summer tourist trade. It is filled with shops, many selling tartans and tweeds, as well as hotels and cafés.

WHAT TO SEE & DO

Neptune's Staircase is a series of nine locks that were constructed at the same time as the Caledonian Canal, raising Telford's canal 64 feet. The location of the "staircase" is 3 miles northwest of Fort William off the A830 at Banavie.

WEST HIGHLAND MUSEUM, Cameron Sq. Tel. 0397/702169.
The collection of this museum sheds light on all aspects of local history, especially the 1745 Jacobite Rising, plus sections on tartans and folk life. It lies in the center of town next to the tourist office.
Admission: £1 ($1.50) adults, 40p (60¢) children.
Open: Mon–Sat 10am–1pm and 2–5pm (also Sun—same hours—July–Aug).

NEARBY ATTRACTIONS

The ruins of **Old Inverlochy Castle,** scene of the famous battle in 1645, can be reached by driving on the A82, 2 miles north of Fort William. At a point just 1 mile north of Fort William is **Glen Nevis,** one of the most beautiful glens in Scotland.

About 14 miles west of Fort William, on the A830 toward Mallaig, at Glenfinnan at the head of Loch Shiel is the **Glenfinnan Monument,** which marks the spot where Bonnie Prince Charlie unfurled his proud red-and-white silk banner on August 19, 1745 in his ill-fated attempt to restore the Stuarts to the British throne. The figure of a kilted Highlander tops the monument. At a Visitor's Centre you can learn of the prince's campaign from Glenfinnan to Derby that ended in his defeat at Culloden.

WHERE TO STAY

There is no shortage of B&B accommodations in Fort William, most with a good view of Loch Linnhe or Ben Nevis. The tourist information office can supply you with a list. The area also contains some substantial hotels.

VERY EXPENSIVE

INVERLOCHY CASTLE, Torlundy, Fort William, Inverness-shire PH33 6SN. Tel. 0397/702177. Fax 0397/702953. 14 rms (all with bath), 4 suites. TV TEL **Directions:** Take the A82, 3 miles northeast of town.
$ Rates (including Scottish breakfast): £180 ($270) single; £240 ($360) double; from £280 ($420) suite. AE, MC, V. **Parking:** Free. **Closed:** Late Nov to early Mar.

Inverlochy Castle is another place where Queen Victoria stayed. In her time it was newly built (completed in 1870), a Scottish mansion belonging to Baron Abinger. The monarch claimed in her diary, "I never saw a lovelier or more romantic spot." The seventh Baron of Abinger sold the estate to the Hobbs family, who transformed it into one of the premier places of Scotland for food and accommodations. Mrs. Grete Hobbs, who was born in Denmark, is a delightful hostess, assisted by a large staff. Against the scenic backdrop of Ben Nevis, the castle hotel, a Relais & Châteaux, has a mood of elegance and refinement, luxurious appointments and antiques, artwork, and crystal, plus a profusion of flowers. Prices reflect this opulence.

Dining/Entertainment: The cuisine is one of the finest in Scotland, with food cooked to order and served on silver platters. Guests enjoy such fare as salmon from the Spean or crayfish from Loch Linnhe, even produce from the hotel's own farm garden. Partridge and grouse are offered in season. A table d'hôte lunch costs £27.50 ($41.30), with a set dinner going for £39.95 ($59.90). Men are required to wear jackets and ties, and no smoking is permitted in the dining room. Outsiders can dine here if there's room, but reservations are mandatory. Meals are served daily from 12:30pm to 1:45pm and 7:30 to 9pm.

Services: 24-hour room service, laundry, babysitting.

Facilities: Garden, tennis, game fishing.

MODERATE

THE MOORINGS HOTEL, Banavie, Fort William, Inverness-shire PH33 7LY. Tel. 0397/772797. Fax 0397/772441. 24 rms (all with bath). TV TEL

$ Rates (including Scottish breakfast): £40–£76 ($60–$114) single; £70–£90 ($105–$135) double. AE, DC, MC, V. **Parking:** Free.

One of the most modern and up-to-date hotels in the region, the Moorings was built by its present owners, the Sinclair family, in the mid-1970s. Designed in a traditional style with bay and dormer windows and a painted black and white facade, the hotel is 3 miles north of Fort William in the hamlet of Banavie, beside the B8004 and the Caledonian Canal, and offers easy access to the many lakes and forests of the surrounding region.

Most of the interior is richly paneled in the Jacobean style, while bedrooms are attractive modern entities in monochromatic color schemes. Bar lunches and suppers are served in the cellar in the Mariner Wine Bar, where 40 kinds of wine from around the world sell for between £1.50 ($2.30) and £2.50 ($3.80) a glass. More formal meals are served in the Moorings Restaurant, where an even greater selection of wine (more than 200 types) accompanies such dishes as smoked venison, Scottish oysters, homemade terrines, cullen skink (the traditional smoked-haddock soup of Scotland), wild salmon in a lemon butter sauce, and halibut in a wild mushroom sauce. Four-course fixed-price dinners in the restaurant cost £23 ($34.50) each.

INEXPENSIVE

ALEXANDRA, The Parade, Fort William, Inverness-shire PH33 6AZ. Tel. 0397/702241. Fax 0397/705554. 98 rms (all with bath). TV TEL

$ Rates (including Scottish breakfast): £58 ($87) single; £58–£89 ($87–$133.50) double. AE, DC, MC, V. **Parking:** Free.

Directly across from the rail terminal, the Alexandra is a familiar sight, a hotel with tall gables and formidable granite walls, so common in this part of the Highlands. It has been completely modernized, offering rooms that are pleasantly and attractively furnished, each with tea and coffee maker. Service and housekeeping standards are good. The chef makes excellent use of fresh fish, and the wine cellar is amply endowed. The vegetables are simply cooked with enjoyable results. A fixed-price dinner begins at £15 ($22.50).

CROIT ANNA HOTEL, Druimarbin, Fort William, Inverness-shire PH33 6RR. Tel. 0397/702268. Fax 0397/704099. 92 rms (74 with bath). TV. **Directions:** Take the A82, 2½ miles south of town.

$ Rates (including Scottish breakfast): £18–£22 ($27–$33) single without bath, £25–£33 ($37.50–$49.50) single with bath; £36–£44 ($54–$66) double without bath, £50–£66 ($75–$99) double with bath. MC, V. **Parking:** Free. **Closed:** Nov–Mar.

The Croit Anna Hotel overlooks Loch Linnhe, with fine views of the Ardgour Hills. All rooms have tea and coffee makers. In the hotel dining room, a four-course à la carte meal costs £17 ($25.50). Hotel facilities include a games room, panoramic lounge, gift shop, lounge bar, and guest launderette. It's open from April to October, and entertainment is provided on most evenings in season. The hotel is owned and managed by the same family who designed and built it on a traditional Highland croft that has been in their possession for more than 250 years.

NEVIS BANK HOTEL, Belford Rd., Fort William, Inverness-shire PH33 6BY. Tel. 0397/705721. Fax 0397/706275. 31 rms (all with bath). TV TEL

$ Rates (including continental breakfast): £45 ($67.50) single; £68 ($102) double. AE, DC, MC, V. **Parking:** Free.

The Nevis Bank is a popular choice, especially if you're arriving in Fort William by train. It's a modern building with a somewhat older core in the eastern part of town, about a 12-minute stroll to the center, at the intersection with the access road to Ben Nevis. The home features traditional Scottish fare, a table d'hôte dinner costing £13.95 ($20.90). On weekends the hotel is host to a Highland cabaret in the Ceilidh bar, and in summer it's possible to book motor launches for cruises on Loch Linnhe. The traditionally furnished bedrooms contain such amenities as hairdryers, trouser presses, radios, and tea makers.

WHERE TO DINE

CRANNOG SEAFOOD RESTAURANT, Town Pier. Tel. 0397/705589.
Cuisine: SEAFOOD. **Reservations:** Recommended.
$ Prices: Appetizers £2.20–£5 ($3.30–$7.50); fixed-price lunch £7.50 ($11.30); main courses £6.50–£10 ($9.80–$15). MC, V.
Open: Lunch daily noon–2:30pm; dinner daily 6–9:30pm. **Closed:** Nov and Tues–Wed in winter.

In a converted ticket office and bait store in a quayside setting overlooking Loche Linnhe, this restaurant serves seafood so fresh that locals claim "it fairly leaps at you." Much of the fish comes from the owner's own fishing vessels, and they also have their own fish smokehouse, turning out smoked salmon, mussels, and trout. Bouillabaisse is a chef's specialty, as are freshly caught Loch Linnhe prawns or langoustines. A vegetarian dish of the day is invariably featured. Look also for the daily specials listed on the blackboard.

FACTOR'S HOUSE, Torlundy, Fort William, Inverness-shire PH33 6SN.
Tel. 0397/705767. Fax 0397/702953.
Cuisine: BRITISH/INTERNATIONAL. **Reservations:** Required. **Directions:** Take the A82, 3½ miles northeast of Fort William.
$ Prices: Fixed-price dinner £20 ($30). AE, MC, V.
Open: Dinner only, Tues–Sun 7–9:30pm. **Closed:** Mid-Nov to mid-Mar.

The Factor's House is a restaurant *avec chambres*. The establishment lies on the grounds of the previously recommended, and much more expensive, Inverlochy Castle. The building that contains it was originally built as a home for the estate's overseer. Guests at the Factor's House are welcome to visit the main house's restaurant and gardens, although many choose to dine in-house because of the relatively cheaper prices. Six well-furnished bedrooms, each with bath or shower, phone, and TV, are rented at a cost of £58.50 ($87.80) daily in a single, rising to £70.50 ($105.80) in a double.

But the Factor's House is mainly known as a restaurant. The owner, Peter Hobbs (likely to be wearing a kilt), is the host. The cooking here is honest, without unnecessary adornments, and only good fresh British produce seems to be used. Try the mussels marinara or the smoked trout, followed by such dishes as venison with wild mushrooms or pork Normandie. The charcoal-grilled Scottish steaks are excellent.

EASY EXCURSIONS

ARDNAMURCHAN PENINSULA

One of the loveliest spots in the western Highlands, this peninsula lies about an hour's drive west from Fort William. Much of it remains an unspoiled wilderness. The peninsula begins on the northern shores of Loch Sunart, and it faces the Isle of Mull.

Where to Stay & Dine

GLENBORRODALE CASTLE, Glenborrodale, near Acharacle, Argyll PH36 4JP. Tel. 09724/266. Fax 09724/224. 16 rms (all with bath). TV TEL.
Directions: From Fort William, take the A82, 8 miles south to the ferry crossing near Keppanach; cross to Corran and continue along the A861 until you reach the junction with the B8807, which takes you southwest to Glenborrodale.

$ Rates (including continental breakfast): £160–£260 ($240–$390) double. AE, MC, V. **Parking:** Free.

Here, in this tranquil setting, America's Cup yachtsman Peter de Savary has created one of the premier hotels of the Highlands, restoring a century-old Victorian castle built by a mining tycoon. Set on 1,000 acres, Glenborrodale looks like one of those castles where you could imagine Sleeping Beauty slumbering for all those years. Overlooking the loch, the turreted castle offers only 16 bedrooms and staterooms, each sumptuously furnished with luxurious fabrics and carpets, and Edwardian-style tubs in the bathrooms. Mr. de Savary has filled the hotel with antiques and period pieces, and decorated it with objects of art and the finest of British furnishings. State rooms have four-poster beds. Comfort, in fact, seems to be the keynote here.

Dining/Entertainment: The cuisine is one of the reasons to stay here. Lunch is offered only to residents, but nonresidents who call to reserve are welcome for dinner, served nightly from 7 to 9pm. A fixed-price dinner costs £32.50 ($48.80) per person. Vegetables come fresh from the gardens, and both traditional Scottish and modern British dishes are served in the elegantly appointed restaurant, including venison, fresh salmon, grouse, and pheasant.

Services: Daytime room service, beauty salon, babysitting, laundry/valet.
Facilities: Garden, solarium, sauna, gym equipment, tennis, sea fishing, riding.

3. MALLAIG

179 miles NW of Edinburgh, 47 miles NW of Fort William,
96 miles NW of Oban

GETTING THERE By Train Trains from Fort William to Mallaig take you along one of the most panoramic routes in Scotland, well worth experiencing even if you don't want to go to Mallaig. From mid-May through September, four or five trains per day make the run, cut to two trains per day on Sunday; off-season, only two trains run daily. A round-trip ticket costs £9.20 ($13.80).

By Bus One to three buses per day run to Mallaig from Fort William.

By Car From Fort William, take the A830, the scenic road west to Mallaig.

ESSENTIALS A summer-only **tourist information office** is in the center of Mallaig; look for the signs (tel. 0687/2170 for tourist information). The **telephone area code** is 0687.

This small fishing village is a good touring center for the western Highlands and the islands. Steamers call here for the Kyle of Lochalsh, the Isle of Skye, the Outer Hebrides, and the sea lochs of the northwest coast. At the tip of a peninsula, Mallaig is surrounded by moody lochs and hills. The distance between Morat and Mallaig is just 3 miles.

WHERE TO STAY & DINE

MARINE HOTEL, 10 Station Rd., Mallaig, Inverness-shire PH41 4PY. Tel. 0687/2217. 21 rms (15 with bath). TV
$ Rates (including Scottish breakfast): £22–£24 ($33–$36) single without bath, £30–£35 ($45–$52.50) single with bath; £44–£48 ($66–$72) double without bath, £48–£58 ($72–$87) double with bath. Half board £35–£40 ($52.50–$60) per person. AE, DC, MC, V. **Parking:** Free.

This family-owned business is located in the vicinity of the train station. All the comfortably furnished rooms are heated and contain beverage-making facilities. Guests gather in the cocktail bar or TV lounge after enjoying a home-cooked meal, usually locally caught seafood. The Marine stays open all year.

4. INVERGARRY

25 miles NE of Fort William, 158 miles NW of Edinburgh

GETTING THERE   By Train   Go to Fort William (see below) and proceed the rest of the way by a connecting bus.

By Bus   Highland Omnibuses service the area from Fort William. Since there's no bus station to go to for information in Fort William, the tourist office there (see below) will provide a list of schedules and departures.

By Car   In Fort William, proceed north on the Inverness road (A82) to Invergarry.

ESSENTIALS   For tourist information, ask at Fort William. The **telephone area code** is 08093.

A Highland center for fishing and deer stalking, Invergarry is noted for its fine scenery. It is a good center for exploring Glen Mor and Loch Ness. At Invergarry the road through the western Highland glens and mountains begins, forming one part of the famous **"Road to the Isles"** that terminates at Kyle of Lochalsh.

WHAT TO SEE & DO

Near Invergarry, you can visit the **Well of the Heads,** on the west side of Loch Oich near its southern tip, erected in 1812 by MacDonnell of Glengarry to commemorate the decapitation of seven brothers who had murdered the two sons of a 17th-century chief of Clan Keppoch, a branch of the MacDonnell clan. The seven heads were washed in the well before being presented to the chief of the MacDonnells at Glengarry.

You can also see the ruins of the **Invergarry Castle,** the stronghold of the MacDonnells of Glengarry. The situation of the castle on Raven's Rock, overlooking Loch Oich in the Great Glen, was a strategic one in the days of clan feuds and Jacobite risings. Because the castle ruins are not considered safe, you should view them only from the outside.

WHERE TO STAY & DINE

GLENGARRY CASTLE HOTEL, Invergarry, Inverness-shire PH35 4HW. Tel. 08093/254. Fax 08093/207. 26 rms (all with bath). TV TEL
$ Rates (including Scottish breakfast): £39 ($58.50) single; £65–£80 ($97.50–$120) double. MC, V. **Parking:** Free.
This is a mansion built between 1866 and 1869 on extensive grounds that contain the ruins of Invergarry Castle. With its gables and chimneys, it is an impressive sight, lying on the River Garry, which runs into Loch Oich. Glengarry makes a pleasant base for a holiday, combining fishing, tennis, walking, and rowing. There are two lounges where drinks are served to residents, and the dining room offers good home-cooked meals made from local produce. Lunches cost £8.50 ($12.80) and up, with dinners going for £15.50 ($23.30). Rooms are comfortably old-fashioned.

---

5. AVIEMORE

129 miles N of Edinburgh, 29 miles SE of Inverness, 85 miles N of Perth

GETTING THERE   By Train   Aviemore lies on the main Inverness–Edinburgh rail line, and is the major transportation hub of the area. For rail schedules and information in Aviemore, call 0479/810221. Some 10 to 13 trains a day from Inverness pass through here (trip time: 45 minutes), at £5.90 ($8.90) for a one-way ticket. Some 5 to 7 trains per day arrive from either Glasgow or Edinburgh. Trip time from each city is 3 hours and a one-way ticket from each destination is £9.90 ($14.90).

By Bus Aviemore lies on the main Inverness–Edinburgh bus line. Service is frequent throughout the day and the trip from Edinburgh takes about 3 hours (call 031/452-8777 in Edinburgh for schedules and information). Frequent buses throughout the day also arrive from Inverness (trip time: 40 minutes).

By Car From Edinburgh, after crossing the Forth Bridge Road, take the M90 to Perth, then continue the rest of the way along the A9 into Aviemore.

ESSENTIALS The **tourist information office** is on Grampian Road (tel. 0479/810363). The **telephone area code** is 0479.

This year-round holiday complex on the Spey was opened in 1966 in the heart of the Highlands, at the foot of the historic rock of Craigellachie. This rock was the rallying place for Clan Grant.

WHAT TO SEE & DO

In the heart of the resort, **Stakis Aviemore Centre** (tel. 0479/810624) is an all-purpose cultural, sports, and entertainment complex. Built nearly a quarter of a century ago, inside a loop road, it contains four hotels and their grounds. The center's activities are suitable for everyone and include ice skating, a dry ski slope, swimming, saunas, solarium, squash, table tennis, snooker, discos, putting, go-karting, and much more. Most sports facilities are open daily from 10am to 1pm, 2 to 5pm, and 6 to 9pm. The Speyside Theatre, seating 710, changes its film programs weekly, and often is host to live shows and concerts. Also on the grounds is the Highland Craft Centre, a small shopping emporium.

In winter, ski runs are available for both beginners and experts (four chair lifts and seven T-bar tows). The ice rink is the second largest indoor ice rink in Britain, with seven curling lanes and ice skating on a separate 4,000-square-foot pad. At night, younger people are attracted to the many pubs, while others seek out one of the Scottish nights, folk singing, country dancing, supper dances, or dancing in the large Osprey Ballroom with a sprung maple floor. In summer, sailing, canoeing, pony trekking, hill walking, and mountain climbing, as well as golf and fishing, are just some of the many activities. You can also swim in a heated indoor pool 82 feet long.

NEARBY ATTRACTIONS

You can journey to the sky on the **Cairngorm Chair Lift** (tel. 0479/861261), whose lowest section lies 10 miles east of Aviemore. A round-trip passage on this longest chair lift in Scotland costs £4 ($6) per person during working hours, 9am to 4pm daily in winter and summer. In winter, the uppermost reaches are closed during periods of high wind. The highest section is 4,084 feet above sea level. In summer, on a clear day you can see Ben Nevis in the west, and the vista of Strathspey from here is spectacular, from Loch Morlich set in the Rothiemurchus Forest to the Spey Valley.

Skiers are attracted to the area anytime after October, when snow can be expected. Ski equipment and clothing can be rented at the Day Lodge at the main Cairngorm parking area. Weather patterns can change quickly in the Cairngorm massif. Call the number above for a report on the latest weather conditions. To reach the area, take the A951 branching off from the A9 at Aviemore, then head for the car park near Loch Morlich.

North of Aviemore, the **Strathspey Railway,** Dalfaber Road (tel. 0479/810725), is billed as providing "a trip into nostalgia." The railway follows the valley of the River Spey between Boat of Garten and Aviemore, a distance of 5 miles. The train is drawn by a coal-burning steam locomotive. The newest locomotive used was made some 35 years ago, the oldest being of 1899 vintage. The round-trip takes about an hour. Only two service designations—first class and third class, in conformity with railroad tradition—are offered. Round-trip passage costs £6 ($9) in first class, £3.80 ($5.70) in third class. Schedules change frequently, but from June through the end of September trains make five round-trip journeys daily except on Saturday. In spring and fall, the trains run only on Wednesday and Sunday, making four round-trip journeys each day. The trains do not run in winter.

The backers of this railway, which takes you through scenes unchanged in a century, set out to re-create the total experience of travel on a Scottish steam railway that once carried wealthy Victorians toward their hunting lodges in "North Britain." The rail station at Boat of Garten, where you can board the train, has also been restored. To complete the experience, you can wine and dine aboard on Saturday, when a single-seating dinner is served, costing £21 ($31.50), and at a single-seating lunch on Sunday, when the price is £12.50 ($18.80). Reservations must be made for the meals. The dining car is a replica of a Pullman parlor car, the *Amethyst*. For reservations and hours of departure, call 0479/83258.

WHERE TO STAY

AVIEMORE HIGHLANDS HOTEL, Aviemore Centre, Aviemore, Inverness-shire PH22 1PJ. Tel. 0479/810771. Fax 0479/811473. 103 rms (all with bath). TV TEL

$ Rates: £32.50 ($48.80) single; £45 ($67.50) double. Scottish breakfast £7.50 ($11.30) extra. AE, DC, MC, V. **Parking:** Free.

This resort hotel caters to winter and summer sports enthusiasts. Originally built by Trusthouse Forte in the 1970s, it was taken over by another chain, Principal Hotels, in 1990. Its beige-brick, two-story exterior rambles in a labyrinthine progression of wings, staircases, and long hallways, which funnel into the public rooms illuminated with big windows overlooking the countryside. In summer, doors open to reveal flagstone outdoor terraces ringed with viburnum and juniper. You can drink in the Illicit Still Bar, which has an antique whisky still and copper-top tables. The main restaurant is capped with a soaring ceiling, trussed with beams. Lunches are always bar snacks, priced at from £3 ($4.50) to £6 ($9). Dinner is served in the more formal restaurant, and costs £12.50 ($18.80) for table d'hôte. In the games room is a resident nanny—so if you have children, you're free to head for the slopes in winter without them. The bedrooms are well furnished, and some family rooms are available.

STAKIS FOUR SEASONS, Aviemore Centre, Inverness-shire PH22 1PF. Tel. 0479/810681. Fax 0479/810534. 87 rms (all with bath), 1 suite. TV TEL

$ Rates: £73 ($109.50) single; £83 ($124.50) double; £123 ($184.50) suite. Scottish breakfast £8.75 ($13.10) extra. AE, DC, MC, V. **Parking:** Free.

The Stakis Four Seasons, built in the 1960s, is an ideal holiday hotel offering excellent facilities for a comfortable, relaxed stay. The bedrooms all have radios, hot-beverage facilities, trouser presses, hairdryers, baby-listening devices, and views of the surrounding hills and mountains. The hotel has a first-class cocktail bar, a coffeehouse, and its own leisure complex with an indoor swimming pool, sauna, solarium, whirlpool spa, steam room, and gym.

STAKIS COYLUMBRIDGE RESORT HOTEL, Rothiemurchus, Aviemore, Inverness-shire PH22 1QN. Tel. 0479/810661. Fax 0479/811309. 175 rms (all with bath), 4 suites. TV TEL

$ Rates: £73 ($109.50) single; £83 ($124.50) double; £123 ($184.50) suite. Scottish breakfast £8.75 ($13.10) extra. AE, DC, MC, V. **Parking:** Free.

The Stakis Coylumbridge Resort Hotel, christened by the Duke of Edinburgh in the 1960s, stands in 65 acres of tree-studded grounds facing the slopes of the Cairngorms, and has extensive sports and leisure facilities. The bedrooms are well appointed, each with in-house films, hot-beverage equipment, fresh fruit, and daily newspaper. Meals are served either in Walker's Restaurant where a table d'hôte costs £12.95 ($19.40), or else in the Grant Room, serving a table d'hôte dinner for £14.95 ($22.40). In the hotel are two heated swimming pools, a sauna, whirlpool, steambath, gym, hairdressing salon, gift shop, and games room. House entertainment is a regular feature during the evening, particularly on weekends. In winter, downhill and cross-country skiing equipment and training are available.

STAKIS AVIEMORE BADENOCH HOTEL, Aviemore Centre, Av **Inverness-shire PH22 1PF. Tel. 0479/810261.** Fax 0479/810671. 6 (all with bath) TV TEL

$ **Rates** (including Scottish breakfast): £45 ($67.50) single; £64 ($96) double. AE, DC, MC, V. **Parking:** Free.

Operated as the least expensive of the Stakis hotels at Aviemore, this modern, simply designed establishment makes special efforts to attract families with children. Modern and monochromatic, and set on the circumference road encircling Aviemore Centre, it was refurbished in 1991. A bar, a restaurant, and a snack bar are on the premises.

WHERE TO DINE

THE BAR/THE RESTAURANT, in the Dalfaber Golf and Country Club. Tel. 0479/811244.

Cuisine: SCOTTISH/STEAKS. **Reservations:** Not necessary in the bar, necessary in the restaurant.

$ **Prices:** Bar platters £4–£6 ($6–$9); in restaurant, appetizers £1.50–£3.65 ($2.30–$5.50), main courses £5.50–£12 ($8.30–$18). MC, V.

Open: Bar, daily noon–9pm. Restaurant, dinner only, 6–9:30pm.

Although the golf course, the health club, and the leisure facilities of this country club are open only to members, it maintains a cozy and well-managed bar and restaurant where drinkers and diners are welcome. Set about a mile north of the center of Aviemore, the establishment is outfitted in a Scottish inspiration of tartan carpets and upholstery, with heavy brocade curtains and views from big windows over the surrounding conifers and tundra.

In the bar, the fare includes venison casseroles, scampi, sandwiches, homemade steak pies, and any of a variety of malt whiskies. In the restaurant, grilled Angus steaks are the specialty, including mixed grills, salads, such fish dishes as salmon filet with dill sauce, and a limited number of vegetarian dishes as well.

A NEARBY PLACE TO DINE

THE DAY LODGE RESTAURANT/PTARMIGAN SNACK BAR, Cairngorm Mountain. Tel. 0479/861161.

Cuisine: BRITISH. **Bus:** The Ski Bus from Aviemore makes frequent runs during ski season and less frequent runs July–Aug.

$ **Prices:** Snacks, burgers, and sandwiches £2–£4.50 ($3–$6.80); appetizers 90p–£2 ($1.40–$3); main courses £2.50–£8 ($3.80–$12). No credit cards.

Open: Lunch, daily 11:30am–3pm. Drinks, daily 11:30am–4pm at Ptarmigan Snack Bar; daily 11:30am–6pm at The Day Lodge Restaurant.

Owned and operated by the Cairngorm Chair Lift Company, these two eateries 9 miles southeast of Aviemore along the "Ski Road" provide a welcome relief from the cold, the wind, and the sometimes agoraphobic fear of the wide and blustering open spaces. The Day Lodge Restaurant has an open fireplace and easy access from the nearby parking lot. It has a full bar facility, and food items that include fish and chips, burgers, and platters of such items as roast beef and fried plaice.

The Ptarmigan Snack Bar lies at the uppermost stop of the region's most famous chair lift. Round-trip passage from the car park costs £4 ($6) and provides a 10-minute, slightly windblown aerial ride of great beauty. Once at the terminus, you can hike another 20 minutes uphill to reach the summit of Cairngorm Mountain, or stop at the Ptarmigan for a view of the valley and a sandwich, cup of soup or coffee, or a chocolate biscuit.

6. SPEYSIDE

The valley of the second largest river in Scotland, the Spey, lies north and south of Aviemore. A journey north through Speyside will take you toward the Malt Whisky

at natural beauty, the river is born in the Highlands above Loch
s 40 miles south of Inverness. Little more than a creek at its
in force as it is fed by many "burns" that drain water from the
. It is one of Scotland's great rivers for salmon fishing, and it runs
ering Cairngorms on the east and the Monadhliath mountains on the
center is Grantown-on-Spey.

NEWTONMORE

This Highland resort on Speyside is a good center for the Grampian and Monadhliath
mountains, and it offers excellent fishing, golf, pony trekking, and hill walking. A
track from the village climbs past the Calder River to Loch Dubh and the massive
Carn Ban (3,087 ft.), where eagles fly. Castle Cluny, ancient seat of the MacPherson
chiefs, is 6 miles west of Newtonmore.

Newtonmore lies 113 miles northwest of Edinburgh and 43 miles south of
Inverness.

WHAT TO SEE & DO

CLAN MACPHERSON HOUSE & MUSEUM, Main St. Tel. 0540/673332.
Most motorists zip through on the way to Aviemore, but sightseers may want to
stop off and visit this museum at the south end of the village. Displayed are clan relics
and memorials, including the Black Chanter and Green Banner as well as a "charmed
sword," and the broken fiddle of the freebooter, James MacPherson—a Scottish
Robin Hood. Relics associated with Bonnie Prince Charlie are also here. An annual
clan rally is held in August.

Admission: Free.

Open: Mon–Sat 10am–5:30pm, Sun 2:30–5:30pm. **Bus:** The Edinburgh-
Inverness bus stops by.

WHERE TO STAY & DINE

**ARD-NA-COILLE, Kingussie Rd., Newtonmore, Inverness-shire PH20
1AY. Tel. 0540/673214.** Fax 0540/673453. 7 rms (all with bath).
$ Rates (including Scottish breakfast and 5-course dinner): £60 ($90) single;
£120–£140 ($180–$210) double. MC, V. **Parking:** Free. **Closed:** Nov–Dec.
Half a mile north of town beside the A86, Ard-Na-Coille translates from the Gaelic as
"High in the Woods." It was originally built around 1920 as a hunting lodge. Antique
furniture, English engravings, racks of heirloom porcelain, and lots of colorful chintz
fill both the bedrooms and the public rooms of this elegant house. Partners Nancy
Ferrier and Barry Cottam (who doubles as the chef) welcome residents and
nonresidents alike for the modern British cuisine served every evening. Nonresidents
pay £27.50 ($41.30) for the fixed-price meal. Fresh and mostly Scottish ingredients are
used for such dishes as saddle of venison with a port wine and blaeberry (a smaller,
bog-raised version of a North American blueberry) sauce. Other specialties include
breast of guinea fowl with chanterelle sauce or char-grilled filet of salmon with a
shellfish and whisky sauce. The house is ringed by 2 acres of pinewood forest suitable
for extended rambles by restless guests.

KINGUSSIE

Your next stop along the Spey might be at the little summer holiday resort and winter
ski center of Kingussie (it's pronounced "King-you-see), just off the A9, the so-called
capital of Badenoch, a district known as "the drowned land" because the Spey can
flood the valley when the snows of a severe winter melt in the spring.

Kingussie practically adjoins Newtonmore (see above), for it lies directly northeast
along the A86. The location is 117 miles northwest of Edinburgh, 41 miles south of
Inverness, and 11 miles southwest of Aviemore.

A summer-only tourist information center is on King Street (tel. 0540/661297).

WHAT TO SEE & DO

HIGHLAND FOLK MUSEUM, Duke St. Tel. 0540/661307.
This is the first folk museum established in Scotland (1934), and collections are based on the life of the Highlanders. You'll see domestic, agricultural, and industrial items. Open-air exhibits are a turf kailyard (kitchen garden), a Lewis "black house," and old vehicles and carts. Traditional events such as spinning, music-making, and showing of handcrafts are held throughout the summer.
Admission: £2 ($3) adults, £1 ($1.50) children.
Open: Apr–Oct, Mon–Sat 10am–6pm, Sun 2–6pm; Nov–Mar, Mon–Fri 10am–3pm.

WHERE TO STAY

HOMEWOOD LODGE, Newtonmore Road, Kingussie, Inverness-shire PH21 1HD. Tel. 0540/661507. 3 rms (all with bath).
$ Rates (including Scottish breakfast): £17.50 ($26.30) per person. Half board £28.25 ($42.40) per person. No credit cards. **Parking:** Free.
One of the best B&Bs in the area, this small Highland house offers large, comfortable rooms for either doubles or families. Rooms are pleasantly furnished with beverage-making equipment. Set on a half acre of garden and woodland, the house has a sitting room with an open fire and TV. Good traditional local fare is served in the evening, and summer barbecues are also offered. Children are welcome, and they can be served "high teas" if they can't wait for the regular dinner hour.

OSPREY HOTEL, Ruthven Rd., Kingussie, Inverness-shire PH21 1EN. Tel. 0540/661510. 8 rms (6 with bath or shower).
$ Rates (including half board): £36 ($54) single without bath, £41 ($61.50) single with shower; £36 ($54) double without bath, £39–£42 ($58.50–$63) double with bath or shower. MC, V. **Parking:** Free. **Closed:** Nov 1–14.
The Osprey Hotel, at the corner of Ruthven Road and High Street, 300 yards from the rail station, is a convenient place to stay, with comfortable bedrooms, all with hot and cold running water, central heating, electric blankets, electric fires, and heated towel racks. The hotel has a licensed bar, residents' lounge, and a TV lounge. Babysitting and baby-listening service is provided. Laundry and ironing facilities are available. The place is known for its pure, fresh, 100% homemade food. Prime Scottish meats are served; in summer, salmon and trout from local rivers are offered either fresh or peat-smoked. The wine list is extensive.

WHERE TO DINE

THE CROSS, Tweed Mill Brae, Ardbroilach Road, Kingussie, Inverness-shire PH21 1HX. Tel. 0540/661166. Fax 0540/661080.
Cuisine: SCOTTISH. **Reservations:** Recommended.
$ Prices: Weekday dinner £25 ($37.50); Sat dinner £32.50 ($48.80).
Open: Lunch Wed–Mon 12:30–2pm; dinner Wed–Mon 7–9pm. **Closed:** Dec–Feb.
This chic restaurant comes as a surprise: In an out-of-the-way setting in a remote Highland village, it serves superlative food that involves theater as much as it does fine food. The restaurant stands on four acres, with the Gynack Burn running through the grounds. The main building of the complex is an old tweed mill, and the restaurant has an open beam ceiling and French doors leading out onto a terrace over the water's edge where al fresco lunches or dinners are served, depending on the weather. Specialties depend on the availability of produce in the local markets and might include venison Francatelli, wild pigeon with grapes, or Highland lamb with sorrel. A selection from more than 300 wines rounds out any menu, and sorbets are served between courses. A seven-course gastronomic "extravaganza" is served on Saturday night. Dinner other nights is a four-course, fixed-price meal.
Rooms are rented in a new building, which has been designed in the old style. Each room is different in size and style—for example, two rooms have canopied beds, and

another has a balcony overlooking the mill pond. Personal service and attention to detail go into the running of this place, operated by Ruth and Tony Hadley, and Ruth's cooking has put it on the gastronomic map of Scotland.

KINCRAIG

Kincraig enjoys a scenic spot at the northern end of Loch Insh, overlooking the Spey Valley to the west and the Cairngorm mountains to the east. From Kingussie, continue northeast along the A9 (the route north to Aviemore) to reach Kincraig. Kincraig lies 37 miles south of Inverness and 119 miles northwest of Edinburgh.

WHAT TO SEE & DO

Near Kincraig, the most notable sight is the **Highland Wildlife Park** (tel. 0540/651270), a natural area of parkland with a collection of Highlands wildlife, some of which is extinct elsewhere in Scotland. Herds of European bison, red deer, shaggy Highland cattle, wild horses, St. Kilda Soay sheep, and roe deer range the park.

In enclosures are wolves, polecats, wildcats, beavers, badgers, and pine martens. Protected birds to see are golden eagles and grouse species—of special interest is the capercaillie ("horse of the woods"), a large Eurasian grouse that is a native of Scotland's pine forests. There is a visitor center with gift shop, café, and exhibition areas. Ample parking and a picnic site are also available.

The park is open from April through October, daily from 10am to 4pm. Admission is £10 ($15) per car.

GRANTOWN-ON-SPEY

This holiday resort, with its gray granite buildings, is 34 miles southeast of Inverness, in a wooded valley from which it commands views of the Cairngorm mountains. It's a key center of winter sports in Scotland. Fishermen are also attracted to this setting, because the Spey is renowned for its salmon. Grantown, one of Scotland's many 18th-century planned towns, was founded on a heather-covered moor in 1765 by Sir James Grant of Grant and became the seat of that ancient family. Grantown became famous in the 19th century as a Highland tourist center, enticing visitors with its planned concept, the beauty of surrounding pine forests, the Spey River, and the mountains around it.

From a base here, you can explore the valleys of the Don and Dee, the Cairngorms, and Culloden Moor, scene of the historic battle in 1746.

A summer-only tourist information office is on High Street (tel. 0479/2773).

WHERE TO STAY

TULCHAN LODGE, Advie, Grantown-on-Spey, Morayshire PH26 3PW. **Tel. 08075/510200.** Fax 08075/510234. 9 rms (all with bath). TEL.

$ **Rates** (including full board): £215 ($322.50) single; £350 ($525) double. No credit cards. **Parking:** Free. **Closed:** Feb–Mar.

The Tulchan Lodge, built in 1906 to serve as the 22,000-acre Tulchan Estate's fishing and shooting lodge, is a place for both sports-oriented visitors and travelers who want to experience a place designed with the elegance required by King Edward VII, who came here for the sports. The lodge, has splendid views of the Spey Valley. Each of the bedrooms is different in size and furnishings, and all have private baths. In the two elegant dining rooms, Scottish and international dishes are served, with particular attention to Scottish beef, lamb, game, and fresh local seafood. The vegetables are grown in the lodge's garden. Only full-board residents are accepted. Tulchan Lodge, open from April to January, lies 9 miles northeast of Grantown on the B9102.

GARTH HOTEL, The Square, Castle Rd., Grantown-on-Spey, Morayshire PH26 3HN. Tel. 0479/2836. Fax 0479/2116. 14 rms (all with bath). TV TEL

$ **Rates** (including Scottish breakfast): £43 ($64.50) single; £68 ($102) double; half board £56 ($84) per person. DC, MC, V. **Parking:** Free.

The elegant, comfortable Garth was built as a private house in the 17th century standing on 4 acres of grounds beside the town square. Guests enjoy the use of a spacious upstairs lounge, whose thick walls, high ceilings, wood-burning stove, and vine-covered veranda make it the perfect place for morning coffee or afternoon tea. This attractive hotel features comfortable and handsomely furnished bedrooms, with all the necessary amenities. Extensive and selective meals are presented in an attractive dining room. "Taste of Scotland" dishes are featured, with emphasis on fresh local produce, including seafood, salmon, venison, game, and beef.

WHERE TO DINE

CRAGGAN MILL, on the A95 three-quarters of a mile south of Grantown-on-Spey. Tel. 0479/2288.
Cuisine: BRITISH/ITALIAN. **Reservations:** Recommended.
$ Prices: Appetizers £2–£5.95 ($3–$8.90); main courses £6.95–£11.95 ($10.40–$17.90). MC, V.
Open: June–Sept, lunch daily noon–2pm; dinner daily 6–10pm. Oct–May, dinner only, Tues–Sun 7–10pm.
This licensed restaurant and lounge bar a 10-minute walk south of the town center is housed in a restored ruined granite mill whose water wheel is still visible. The owners offer British or Italian cuisine at attractive prices. Therefore your appetizer might be smoked trout in deference to Scotland, or ravioli, inspired by sunny Italy. For a main course the selection might be breast of chicken with cream or chicken cacciatore, followed by a dessert of either rum-raisin ice cream or peach Melba. A good selection of Italian wines is also offered.

FI'S CONTINENTAL BAR, in the Rosehall Hotel, The Square, Grantown-on-Spey, Morayshire PH26 3JU. Tel. 0479/2721.
Cuisine: INTERNATIONAL. **Reservations:** Not required.
$ Prices: Appetizers £1.20–£2.75 ($1.80–$4.10); main courses £3.95–£11.95 ($5.90–$17.90). MC, V.
Open: Lunch daily 11am–2:30pm; dinner daily 5–11pm.
Named after Fiona, its manager and the daughter of the owners of the building that contains it, this restaurant occupies a late-Victorian stone-fronted building whose almost perfect symmetry makes it one of the prettiest in town. Inside, a decor mixing elements of a Parisian bistro with a Scottish pub seems to encourage visitors to linger over coffee or a drink or two. An international array of wines is sold by the glass, bottle, or carafe, and menu choices include such perennial favorites as pastas, burgers, terrines of smoked salmon, grilled fish, salads, and steaks. They also have single malt whiskies and a collection of real ales.

Julia and Uisdean Morrison maintain 10 comfortable bedrooms upstairs, each with private bath, TV, and a reproduction Victorian decor. At least one contains a four-poster bed, and a handful offer big-windowed views over the historic square outside. With Scottish breakfast included, singles cost £22 ($33); doubles from £44 ($66) to £50 ($75).

7. ALONG LOCH NESS

Sir Peter Scott's *Nessitera rhombopteryx* continues to elude her pursuers. "Nessie," as she's more familiarly known, has captured the imagination of the world, drawing thousands of visitors yearly to Loch Ness. The Loch Ness monster has been described as the world's greatest mystery. Half a century ago the A82 was built alongside the banks of the loch's western shores. Since that time many more sightings have been claimed.

Midget yellow submarines and all types of high-tech underwater contraptions have gone in after the Loch Ness monster, but no one can find her in spite of the photographs that have appeared. Dr. Robert Rines and his associates at the Academy of Applied Science in Massachusetts maintain an all-year watch with sonar-triggered cameras and strobe lights suspended from a raft in Urquhart Bay.

Some people in Inverness aren't very keen on collaring the monster, and you can't blame them. An old prophecy predicts a violent end for Inverness if the monster is ever captured.

The loch is 24 miles long, a mile wide, and some 754 feet deep. If you'd like to stay along the loch and monster-watch, instead of seeking lodgings at Inverness, you can do so at the centers mentioned below. Even if the monster doesn't put in an appearance, you can enjoy the splendid scenery. In summer, from both Fort Augustus and Inverness, you can take boat cruises across Loch Ness.

Motorists should take the A82 between Fort Augustus and Inverness running along Loch Ness. Buses from either Fort Augustus or Inverness also traverse the A82, taking you to Drumnadrochit.

DRUMNADROCHIT

This pleasant hamlet lies about a mile from Loch Ness at the entrance to Glen Urquhart. It's the nearest village to the part of the loch in which the sighting of the monster has been reported most frequently.

WHAT TO SEE & DO

LOCH NESS MONSTER EXHIBITION, Drumnadrochit. Tel. 04562/573.

This official exhibition is Drumnadrochit's big attraction, featuring a scale replica of Nessie. It opened in 1980 and has been packing 'em in ever since. You can follow the story from A.D. 565 to the present in photographs, audio, and video, as well as climbing aboard the sonar research vessel *John Murray*. The Exhibition Centre is the most visited place in the Highlands of Scotland, with more than 200,000 visitors annually.

Admission: £4 ($6) adults, £2.50 ($3.80) children.

Open: Mid–June to Aug, daily 9am–9:30pm; Sept–Oct and Apr to mid-June, daily 9:30am–5:30pm; Nov–Mar, daily 10am–4pm.

URQUHART CASTLE, Loch Ness along the A82.

This ruined castle, one of Scotland's largest, is 1½ miles southeast of Drumnadrochit on a promontory overlooking Loch Ness. The chief of Clan Grant owned the castle in 1509, and most of the existing building dates from that period. In 1692 the castle was blown up by the Grants to prevent its becoming a Jacobite stronghold. It is here at Urquhart Castle that sightings of the Loch Ness monster are most often reported.

Admission: £1.50 ($2.30) adults, £1 ($1.50) children.

Open: Apr–Sept, Mon–Sat 9:30am–7pm, Sun 2–7pm; Oct–Mar, Mon–Sat 9:30am–4pm, Sun 2–4pm.

WHERE TO STAY & DINE

LEWISTON ARMS, Lewiston, near Drumnadrochit, Inverness-shire IV3 6UN. Tel. 04562/225. 9 rms (all with bath). TV

$ Rates (including Scottish breakfast): £25 ($37.50) single; £50 ($75) double. MC, V. **Parking:** Free.

The bulk of its white-painted stone walls were originally built in the mid-1700s as a brewery. A century ago the brewery was interconnected with an adjacent farmer's cottage, which resulted in an L-shaped building whose wings today embrace a charming garden. (The ghost of a 19th-century former resident is said to make occasional appearances in the garden, feeding her ghostly chickens.) Owned by members of the Quinn family for many generations, the establishment incorporates a thriving pub managed by the Quinn family's latest scion, Nicky. His wife, Helen, prepares food for the establishment's well-flavored bar lunches and dinners. Each of the bedrooms was completely renovated in 1991, and include country-rustic accessories, flowered curtains, and matching bedspreads. The Lewiston Arms is near the center of the hamlet beside the A82.

POLMAILY HOUSE HOTEL, Drumnadrochit, Inverness-shire IV3 6XT.
Tel. 04562/343. 9 rms (7 with bath).
$ Rates (including Scottish breakfast): £45 ($67.50) single without bath; £100 ($150) double or twin with bath. MC, V. **Parking:** Free.

⭐ The Palmaily House graciously re-creates the pleasures of manorial country-house living. According to letters discovered by the owners, the house was probably built in 1776. The 18-acre estate is 2 miles west of Drumnadrochit on the A831. Spacious and elegant bedrooms tastefully filled with antiques have high ceilings, leaded-glass windows, and flowered wallpaper. The hotel has a tennis court, a swimming pool, and a croquet lawn flanked with garden statuary.

The restaurant attracts locals as well as hotel residents. Most exquisite dishes are prepared using the best of fresh local ingredients. A fixed-price four-course dinner costs £23 ($34.50).

INVERMORISTON

If you stop at this hamlet, 168 miles northwest of Edinburgh and 29 miles south of Inverness, you'll be in one of the beauty spots along Loch Ness. Glenmoriston is one of the loveliest glens in the Highlands. You can take walks along the riverbanks, with views of Loch Ness. The location is at the junction of the Loch Ness Highway (A82) and the road to the Isle of Skye (A887).

WHERE TO STAY & DINE

GLENMORISTON ARMS HOTEL, Invermoriston, Inverness-shire IV3
6YA. Tel. 0320/51206. 8 rms (all with bath). TV TEL
$ Rates (including Scottish breakfast): £29–£39 ($43.50–$58.50) single; £50–£60 ($75–$90) double. MC, V. **Parking:** Free.
This has been a roadside inn for two centuries. It's a lot like a woodsy, intimate hunting lodge, with antique weapons, old trophies, well-polished paneling, and more than 160 varieties of single-malt whisky. À la carte meals are served nightly, costing around £14 ($21) per person. You'll find the hotel at the junction of the A82 and the A887.

FORT AUGUSTUS

This Highland touring center stands at the head (the southernmost end) of Loch Ness. The town took its name from a fort named for a Duke of Cumberland, built after 1715. The present Benedictine abbey stands on its site. The location is 36 miles south of Inverness along the A82 and 166 miles northwest of Edinburgh.

WHAT TO SEE & DO

Bisecting the actual village of Fort Augustus is the **Caledonian Canal,** and the locks are a popular attraction when boats are passing through. Running across the loftiest sections of Scotland, the canal was constructed between 1803 and 1822. Almost in a straight line, it makes its way from Inverness in the north to Corpach in the vicinity of Fort William. The canal is 60 miles long: 22 man-made miles and the rest natural lochs. In summer you can take several pleasure craft along this canal, leaving from Fort Augustus.

WHERE TO STAY & DINE

INCHNACARDOCH LODGE, along the A82, Fort Augustus, Inverness-
shire PH32 4BL. Tel. 0320/6258. 15 rms (all with bath). TEL
$ Rates (including Scottish breakfast): £30–£45 ($45–$67.50) single; £45–£60 ($67.50–$90) double. AE, DC, MC, V. **Parking:** Free. **Closed:** Jan–Feb.
The Inchnacardoch Lodge, a family-run hotel in a beautiful setting overlooking Loch Ness, is half a mile north of Fort Augustus on the A82. The house of many gables, a country residence of a 19th-century Lord Lovat of Lovat, chief of the Fraser clan,

offers comfortable bedrooms with private bath. You can relax over coffee or drinks in the cocktail bar—but be careful. A wee dram of malt over your limit might cause you to see the Loch Ness monster. A table d'hôte dinner costs £15 ($22.50).

LOVAT ARMS, along the A82, Fort Augustus, Inverness-shire PH32 4DU. Tel. 0320/6206. Fax 0320/6677. 21 rms (all with bath). TV TEL
$ Rates (including Scottish breakfast): £29.50–£33.50 ($44.30–$50.30) single; £53.50–£67 ($80.30–$100.50) double. MC, V. **Parking:** Free.

Built between 1840 and 1860, and later enlarged with wings added in the 1890s and 1990s, it was reputedly owned long ago by Lord Lovat, scion of one of the oldest Norman lineages of Scotland, the Fraser family. Stucco-covered, with sandstone window and door frames, the house is well known in the region for its convivial pub, where tasty meals are served at lunch and dinner. Also on the premises is a spacious lounge bar where good food is available at lunch and in the evening at reasonable prices and a dining room where an à la carte menu features Scottish fish and meat. Each of the comfortable bedrooms is carpeted and very clean. On cold days a fire burns in an area reserved for residents. The Lovat Arms stands beside one of the two major roads through the Highlands and is an ideal base from which to explore Loch Ness.

---

8. INVERNESS

156 miles NW of Edinburgh, 134 miles NW of Dundee,
134 miles W of Aberdeen

GETTING THERE   By Plane   Inverness makes for the best serial gateway into the Highlands. Domestic flights from various parts of Britain arrive at the Inverness airport. Flight time from London's Heathrow to the **Inverness/Dalcross Airport** (tel. 0463/232471 locally) is 75 minutes.

By Train   Some five to seven trains per day arrive from Glasgow and Edinburgh (on Sunday, two or three trains). A one-way fare from either Edinburgh or Glasgow is £20 ($30). Trains pull into Station Square, off Academy Street in Inverness (tel. 0463/238924 in Inverness for schedules and information).

By Bus   Scottish Citylink Coaches (tel. 0463/710555) provides service for the area. Frequent service through the day is possible from either Edinburgh or Glasgow, at a one-way fare of £10.30 ($15.50) to £10.60 ($15.90), respectively. There's also daily service from Aberdeen in the east; a one-way fare is £8.30 ($12.50).

By Car   From Edinburgh, take the M9 north to Perth, then follow along the Great North Road (A9) until you reach Inverness.

ESSENTIALS   The **information office** of the Inverness, Loch Ness, and Nairn Tourist Board is at Castle Wynd (tel. 0463/234353). In an emergency, dial 999 to summon police, an ambulance, or firefighters. For exchanging currency and other banking affairs, you can go to the **Bank of Scotland,** 9 High St. (tel. 0463/230907), open Monday through Wednesday from 9:30am to 12:30pm and 1:30 to 3:30pm, on Thursday from 9:30am to 12:30pm, 1:30 to 3:30pm, and 4:30 to 6pm, and on Friday from 9:30am to 3:30pm. The head **post office** is at Queensgate (tel. 0463/234111), open Monday through Friday from 9am to 5:30pm and on Saturday from 9am to 12:30pm. The **telephone area code** is 0463.

SPECIAL EVENTS   At the **Highland Games** in July, with their sporting competitions and festive balls, the season in Inverness reaches its social peak. For more information and exact dates, consult the tourist office (see above).

The capital of the Highlands, Inverness is a royal burgh and seaport lying at the north end of Great Glen on both sides of the Ness River. It is considered the best base for touring the north.

GETTING AROUND   For transportation facilities and information, the **bus station** is at Farraline Park, off Academy Street (tel. 0463/233371), and the **railway station** is on Academy Street (tel. 0463/238924). **Taxis** are also found off Academy Street by the Station Square (tel. 0461/238924). If you'd like to park your car and tour the center of Inverness, there is a multistory **parking lot** on Rose Street, charging reasonable rates.

WHAT TO SEE & DO
ATTRACTIONS

Inverness is one of the oldest inhabited localities in Scotland. On **Craig Phadrig** are the remains of a vitrified fort, believed to date from the 4th century B.C. The old castle of Inverness stood to the east of the present Castlehill, the site still retaining the name **Auld Castlehill.**

King David built the first stone castle in Inverness around 1141. The **Clock Tower** is all that remains of a fort erected by Cromwell's army between 1652 and 1657. The 16th-century **Abertarff House,** Church Street, is now the headquarters of An Comunn Gaidhealach, the Highland association that preserves the Gaelic language and culture.

Opposite the town hall is the **Old Mercat Cross,** with its **Stone of the Tubs,** an Inverness landmark, said to be the stone on which women rested their washtubs as they ascended from the river. Known as "Clachnacudainn," the lozenge-shaped stone was the spot where the early kings were crowned.

West of the river rises the wooded hill of **Tomnahurich,** known as "the hill of the fairies." It is now a cemetery, and from here the views are magnificent. In the Ness are wooded islands, linked to Inverness by suspension bridges and turned into parks.

St. Andrews Cathedral, Ardross Street, is open to visitors daily from 9am to 6pm, and this northernmost diocese of the Scottish Episcopal Church boasts a fine example of Victorian architecture. The icons given to Bishop Eden by the tsar of Russia should be viewed. For information, get in touch with the Provost, 15 Ardross St. (tel. 0463/233535).

INVERNESS MUSEUM AND ART GALLERY, Castle Wynd. Tel. 0463/ 237114.

This museum in the town center, off Bridge Street, is a top attraction. It has displays representing the social and natural history, archeology, art, and culture of the Scottish Highlands, with special emphasis on the Inverness district. There is an important collection of Highland silver, with a reconstructed silversmith's workshop; displays on the "Life of the Clans"; a reconstruction of a local taxidermist's workshop; a reconstructed Inverness kitchen of the 1920s; and an art gallery. There is also a permanent exhibition on the story of the Inverness district, from local geology and archeology to the present day. Other facilities include a souvenir shop, a coffee shop, a regular program of temporary exhibitions and events, and an information service.

Admission: Free.
Open: Mon–Sat 9am–5pm.

TOURS

If you're interested in bus tours of the Highlands and pleasure cruises, particularly of Loch Ness, go to **Highland Omnibuses,** Farraline Park (tel. 0463/237575). In summer, cruises go along the Caledonian Canal from Inverness into Loch Ness.

NEARBY ATTRACTIONS

From Inverness, you can visit **Culloden Battlefield,** Culloden Moor, 6 miles to the southeast, where Bonnie Prince Charlie and the Jacobite army were finally crushed on April 16, 1746. Leanach Cottage, around which the battle took place, still stands and was inhabited until 1912. A path leads from the Visitor Centre through the Field of the English, where 76 men of the Duke of Cumberland's forces who died during the battle are said to be buried. Features of interest include the Graves of the Clans, communal burial places with simple stones bearing individual clan names; the great memorial cairn, erected in 1881; the Well of the Dead; and the huge Cumberland Stone, from which the victorious "Butcher" Cumberland is said to have reviewed the scene. The battle lasted only 40 minutes; the prince's army lost some 1,200 men out of 5,000, and the king's army 300 out of 9,000.

A **Visitor Centre** (tel. 0463/790607) is open from February 2 to March 28 and October 28 to December 30, daily from 10am to 4pm; March 29 to May 24 and September 16 to October 27, daily from 9:30am to 5:30pm; and May 25 to September 15, daily from 9am to 6:30pm. Admission of £1.50 ($2.30) for adults, 80p ($1.20) for children, includes a visit to an audiovisual presentation of the background and history of the famous battle.

Between Inverness and Nairn, about 6 miles east of Inverness, are the **Stones of Clava,** one of the most important prehistoric monuments in the north. These cairns and standing stones are from the Bronze Age.

On the Moray Firth by the village of Ardersier, 11 miles northeast of Inverness, **Fort George** (tel. 0463/224380) was called "the most considerable fortress and best situated in Great Britain" in 1748 by Lt. Col. James Wolfe, who went on to fame as Wolfe of Québec. Built following the Battle of Culloden, the fort was occupied by the Hanoverian army of King George II and is still an active army barracks. The rampart, almost a mile around, encloses some 42 acres. Dr. Samuel Johnson and James Boswell visited here in 1773 on their Highland trek.

The fort contains the **Queen's Own Highlanders Regimental Museum,** with regimental exhibits from 1778 to today, representing the 72nd and 78th Highlanders, Seaforth Highlanders, 79th and Queen's Own Cameron Highlanders, Lovat Scouts, militia, volunteers, and territorial army, as well as the Queen's Own Highlanders. The public can visit some parts of the fort as well as the museum from April through September, Monday to Friday from 10am to 6pm and on Sunday from 2 to 6pm; October through March, Monday to Friday from 10am to 4pm. Admission to the fort is £1.75 ($2.60) for adults, 50p (80¢) for children. Once inside, you can visit the museum free.

About midway between Inverness and Nairn on the A96 lies the **Culloden Pottery Restaurant and Gift Shop,** the Old Smiddy, Gollanfield (tel. 0667/ 462340), where a meal is usually combined with a browse through an adjacent gift shop and pottery studio that specializes in stoneware. Visitors can watch potters at work, and their products and other Scottish handcrafted items are sold in the gift shop. You can make your own pot. The restaurant serves light vegetarian whole-food meals with two fish dishes. Meals are served daily from 9:30am to 5:30pm (in July, August, and September, the place accepts orders until 7:30pm, Friday and Saturday nights until 8:30pm). A full meal begins at £7 ($10.50). The restaurant is open daily all year except Christmas and New Year.

WHERE TO STAY
VERY EXPENSIVE

CULLODEN HOUSE, Culloden, Inverness, Inverness-shire IV1 2NZ. Tel. 0463/790461. Fax 0463/792181. 21 rms (all with bath), 4 suites. TV TEL. **Directions:** Take the A96, 3 miles east of Inverness.

$ **Rates** (including Scottish breakfast): £110 ($165) single; £150 ($225) double; from £190 ($285) suite. AE, DC, MC, V. **Parking:** Free.

Culloden House is a Georgian mansion with a much-photographed Adam facade. It includes part of the Renaissance castle in which Bonnie Prince Charlie slept the night before Culloden, the last great battle on British soil. Superbly isolated, with extensive gardens and parkland, it's perfect for a relaxed Highland holiday. At the iron gates to the broad front lawn, a piper in full Highland garb plays at sundown, the skirl of the bagpipe accompanied by the barking of house dogs. Such notables as the Prince of Wales and Crown Prince of Japan have stayed here, perfectly at home among the exquisite furnishings and handsome plaster friezes. Guests are welcomed to spacious and comfortable public rooms, beautifully painted and furnished, and to the cozy bedrooms with sylvan views and history-laden atmosphere. The hotel maintains traditional ideas of personal service.

Dining/Entertainment: In the elegant Adam Dining Room, beautifully presented meals are a combination of traditional Scottish country-house cooking and a classical French cuisine. All the produce is fresh, and game is featured in season. The selection of food appeals both to the hearty eater and the vegetarian. Lunch, served daily from 12:30 to 2pm, is à la carte, but a fixed-price dinner, at £29.50 ($44.30), consists of five courses in the evening, and it's offered nightly from 7 to 9pm.

Services: All-day room service, laundry service.

Facilities: Tennis, sauna, solarium.

EXPENSIVE

BUNCHREW HOUSE HOTEL AND RESTAURANT, Bunchrew, Inverness, Inverness-shire IV3 6TA. Tel. 0463/234917. Fax 0463/710620. 11 suites (all with bath). MINIBAR TV TEL **Directions:** Take the A862, 3 miles west of Inverness.

$ Rates (including Scottish breakfast): £55–£82 ($82.50–$123) single; £105–£115 ($157.50–$172.50) double. AE, MC, V. **Parking:** Free.

The Bunchrew House Hotel and Restaurant is a fine Scottish mansion on the shores of Beauly Firth. The ancestral home of both the Fraser and the McKenzie clans, the house built by Simon Fraser, the eighth Lord Lovat, dates to 1621, the same year he married into the Stewart family. Set in 15 acres of landscaped gardens, the house has been restored as a country-house hotel. Guests get a glimpse of a bygone era when they relax in the paneled drawing room with roaring log fires in winter. The staff welcomes travelers to the individually designed and decorated bedrooms. The Lovat Suite has a fully canopied four-poster bed, and the Wyvis Suite boasts a half-tester bed and Jacuzzi.

Dining/Entertainment: You can dine in the candlelit restaurant on prime Scottish beef, fresh lobster and crayfish, local game and venison, and fresh vegetables. Try such dishes as a terrine of venison with gooseberry sauce, followed by poached salmon in a lemon-flavored sauce with parsley. Lunch, beginning at £10.50 ($15.80), is served daily from noon to 2pm. Dinner is offered Monday through Saturday from 7:30 to 9:15pm and on Sunday from 8:30 to 10pm. A fixed-price dinner costs £20 ($30).

Services: All-day room service, laundry, babysitting.

Facilities: Clay pigeon shooting, free salmon fishing on the estate.

DUNAIN PARK HOTEL, Dunain Park, Inverness, Inverness-shire IV3 6JN. Tel. 0463/230512. Fax 0463/224532. 6 rms (all with bath), 8 suites and cottages. TV TEL

$ Rates (including Scottish breakfast): £120–£140 ($180–$210) double; from £140 ($210) suite or cottage. AE, DC, MC, V. **Parking:** Free.

Located 2½ miles southwest of Inverness on the A82, the Dunain Park Hotel stands in 6 acres of garden and woods, between Loch Ness and Inverness. This 18th-century house was opened as a hotel in 1974, and is furnished with fine antiques, china, and clocks, allowing it to retain its atmosphere of a private country house. Although Dunain Park has won its fame mainly as a restaurant, it does offer bedrooms. A host of thoughtful details and pretty, soft furnishings have gone into the bedrooms. There are no singles.

Dining/Entertainment: The breakfast served here is exceptional. You can order a simple lunch (in the garden, if you prefer), and snack meals are served daily from 12:30 to 2pm, but it is at dinner that the chef really delivers, offering a fixed-price meal for £21 ($31.50). Ann Nicholl, who enjoys an enviable reputation for her cooking, compiles her menus from the local venison, grouse, pheasant, pigeon, salmon, scallops, and lobster, as well as prime Scottish beef and lamb. Her dessert presentation is noteworthy. You'll definitely want to consider having dinner here, and you can do so daily 7 to 9pm.

Services: All-day room service, babysitting, laundry.

Facilities: Indoor heated swimming pool and sauna.

KINGSMILLS HOTEL, Culcabock Rd., Inverness, Inverness-shire IV2 3LP. Tel. 0463/237166. Fax 0463/225209. 79 rms (all with bath), 6 suites. TV TEL.

$ Rates (including Scottish breakfast): £85 ($127.50) single; £110 ($165) double; from £130 ($195) suite. AE, DC, MC, V. **Parking:** Free.

This hotel is an 18th-century house of much charm set in 4 acres of woodland garden only a mile east of the center of Inverness (take Kingsmill Road). Once a private mansion, it stands adjacent to an 18-hole golf course. The owner maintains a country-house atmosphere with an informal and hospitable Highland staff. Furnishings throughout the hotel are of a high quality, and all the bedrooms are attractively furnished.

Dining/Entertainment: Dinner, offered nightly from 7 to 10pm, begins at £19.50 ($29.30). The fish dishes are exceptional. Bar lunches and snack meals offer a wide choice, including Scottish fare. A notice in the lobby tells you that Robert Burns dined here in 1787, and the "Charles" who signed the guest register in 1982 was (you guessed it) the Prince of Wales. His sister, Princess Anne, has also stayed here.

Services: 24-hour room service, laundry/valet, babysitting.

Facilities: Indoor pool and health spa (comprising a sauna, steam room, spa bath, fitness room, and sun bed), hairdressing salon, and a three-hole minigolf course.

MODERATE

GLEN MHOR HOTEL, 9–12 Ness Bank, Inverness, Inverness-shire IV1 4SG. Tel. 0463/234308. Fax 0463/713170. 30 rms (all with bath or shower). TV TEL

$ Rates (including Scottish breakfast): £53 ($79.50) single; £59–£94 ($88.50–$141) double. AE, DC, MC, V. **Parking:** Free.

⑤ This hotel looks out onto the River Ness. A house of gables and bay windows, the Glen Mhor is a hospitable, family-run hotel with an endearing charm. The owners provide many thoughtful touches, such as a log fire blazing in the entrance lounge. From many of the individually styled bedrooms you have views of the river, castle, and cathedral. Some of these are suitable for families, and children sharing a room with two adults are accommodated free. Amenities in the rooms include trouser presses, hairdryers, and baby-listening service. Ten of the hotel's bedrooms are in an annex called "The Cottage." These fully modernized rooms are small by American standards but comfortable and well equipped. Two of the ground-floor rooms are suitable for disabled persons.

In the Riverview Restaurant overlooking the river and specializing in Scottish dishes, you can enjoy such fine food as salmon caught in the river outside, shellfish, lamb, game, and beef. The wine list is considered one of the best in the country. In addition to the cozy cocktail lounge, there's a charming European Bistro bar called Nico's, which is open at lunch and in the evening. It's a popular nightspot, serving traditional Scottish meals and Italian pastas. Members of the royal family have eaten at the hotel. Nicky Tams is called a "stable bar," serving a wide range of beer and ale.

THE STATION HOTEL, 16–18 Academy St., Inverness, Inverness-shire IV1 1LG. Tel. 0463/231926. 67 rms (with bath). TV TEL.

$ Rates (including Scottish breakfast): £42 ($63) single without bath, £62 ($93) single with bath; £70 ($105) double without bath, £95 ($142.50) double with bath. AE, DC, MC, V. **Parking:** Free.

The Station Hotel, adjacent to the railway station, offers a high standard of first-class service, comfortable accommodations, and well-prepared food. The occupants of those baronial Highland mansions like to stop here when they're in Inverness on shopping or social expeditions, gathering for somewhat lively chats in the conservatory lounge. Grandly Victorian, the bedrooms are tastefully decorated and welcoming. The dining room is one of the finest in Inverness, serving good-quality Scottish dishes, plus some excellently cooked continental favorites. Lunch is served in the bar/lounge for £5–£7 ($7.50–$10.50) per person. High tea is offered in the restaurant (light food daily from 5:30 to 7pm, scampi and filets of fish). Dinner is served in the restaurant daily from 7 to 9:15pm, and is a table d'hôte affair at £14.95 ($22.40) per person.

INEXPENSIVE

BALLIFEARY HOUSE HOTEL, 10 Ballifeary Rd., Inverness, Inverness-shire IV3 5PJ. Tel. 0463/235572. Fax 0463/235572. 8 rms (all with bath).
$ Rates (including Scottish breakfast): £28 ($42) single; £56 ($84) double. MC, V.
Parking: Free. **Closed:** Mid-Oct to Easter.

This well-maintained stone villa with a pleasant garden, 300 yards from the Eden Court Theatre, is one of the better B&Bs in the area. Mr. and Mrs. Luscombe, the owners, offer their guests individual attention. Bedroom facilities include hairdryers, clock radios, and beverage-making equipment. You get good home-cooking, a sampling of traditional Scottish fare; a four-course table d'hôte costs £13.50 ($20.30). It is a no-smoking establishment.

CUCHULLIN LODGE HOTEL, 43 Culduthel Rd., Inverness, Inverness-shire IV2 4HQ. Tel. 0463/231945. 13 rms (all with bath).
$ Rates (including Scottish breakfast): £38 ($57) single; £56 ($84) double. DC, MC, V. **Parking:** Free.

Set on three-quarters of an acre of prime residential real estate, two-thirds of a mile west of the train station, this sandstone house was built in the 1870s as the private home of one of the chairmen of the Highland Railways. Later it was sold to a whisky distiller, and in 1946 it became one of the first private houses in Inverness to accept paying overnight guests. Hamish Sutherland, a retired major in the British army, is the conscientious owner. Bedrooms are comfortable, decorated in a mixture of styles, usually with chintz curtains and solidly traditional furniture. An elegant fixed-price dinner in the dignified dining room costs £15.95 ($23.90) per person.

IVYBANK, 28 Old Edinburgh Rd., Inverness, Inverness-shire IV2 3HJ. Tel. 0463/232796. 5 rms (2 with bath).
$ Rates (including Scottish breakfast): £18 ($27) single without bath, £20 ($30) single with bath; £36 ($54) double without bath, £40 ($60) double with bath. No credit cards. **Parking:** Free.

The Ivybank, off Castle Road about a 10-minute walk north of the town center, was originally built in 1836, and today retains its original fireplaces and an oak-paneled and beamed hall with a rosewood staircase. It has a walled and landscaped garden, and comfortably furnished bedrooms, each with hot and cold running water, central heating, and beverage-making equipment. Mrs. Catherine Cameron is the gracious hostess, making guests feel at ease and welcome. There is ample parking within the walled garden, and although no meals other than breakfast are served, the staff offers advice and directions to many of the city's restaurants.

RIVERSIDE HOUSE HOTEL, 8 Ness Bank, Inverness, Inverness-shire IV2 4SF. Tel. 0463/231052. 11 rms (6 with bath). TV
$ Rates (including Scottish breakfast): £22 ($33) single without bath; £44 ($66) double without bath, £48 ($72) double with bath. No credit cards. **Parking:** Free.
This immaculate place occupies perhaps the most scenic spot on the Ness River, opposite St. Andrews Cathedral and the Eden Court Theatre, only a 3-minute walk from the city center. All bedrooms in this refurbished and centrally heated hotel have hot-beverage facilities, electric blankets, and hot- and cold-water basins. The tastefully decorated residents' lounge is open all day. Good Scottish home-cooked food with a choice of menu is featured in the dining room, and the hotel has a liquor license.

WHERE TO DINE

DICKENS INTERNATIONAL RESTAURANT, 77–79 Church St. Tel. 0463/713111.
Cuisine: INTERNATIONAL. **Reservations:** Not needed.
$ Prices: Appetizers £2.10–£5.90 ($3.20–$8.90); main courses £6–£20 ($9–$30). AE, DC, MC, V.

Open: Lunch daily noon–2pm; dinner daily 5:30–11pm.

The decor of this establishment, with its Ionic columns, rattan furniture, and potted palms, looks almost like an English colonial bar in Singapore. On a downtown street near the tourist office, between Bank Street and Academy Street, this restaurant offers a wide selection of European, Chinese, and international dishes, including vegetarian dishes. On the menu are Dickens's own steak, Peking duck, fresh local salmon, and chateaubriand. The widest choice of side dishes in Inverness is found here.

PIERRE VICTOIRE, 75 Castle St. Tel. 0463/225662.

Cuisine: CONTINENTAL. **Reservations:** Required only on weekends.

$ Prices: Appetizers 90p–£3.90 ($1.40–$5.90); main courses £5.90–£8.10 ($8.90–$12.20). Three-course fixed-price lunch £4.90 ($7.40). MC.

Open: Lunch daily 11:45–3pm; dinner daily 5:30–10pm. **Closed:** Nov–Mar.

This is the Inverness branch of one of the most successful restaurant chains to ever hit Scotland. Decorated with deliberately mismatched secondhand furniture, and staffed with an engaging crew who are wryly amused by the wobbly tables and chairs, the restaurant serves some of the most copious portions in town. The fixed-price lunch is one of the best bargains in Inverness, while dinners are candlelit and served in a format you might expect within a working-class bistrot in France. Menu items change every two days, but might include grilled mussels in garlic and Pinot-butter sauce; smoked salmon; brioches stuffed with mushrooms and a whisky cream sauce; roast lamb in a rosemary and red wine sauce; and venison in a celeriac and port wine sauce. Glasses of wine begin at £1.50 ($2.30) each, and comprise a learned array of unusual vintages.

STAKIS STEAKHOUSE, Bank St. Tel. 0463/236577.

Cuisine: BRITISH. **Reservations:** Not needed.

$ Prices: Appetizers £1.10–£3.45 ($1.70–$5.20); main courses £4.95–£10.95 ($7.40–$16.40); fixed-price meal (served at lunch and 5–7pm) £4.95 ($7.40). AE, DC, MC, V.

Open: Lunch Mon–Sat noon–2:30pm; dinner daily 5–10:30pm.

A member of a chain, this is one of the most attractive restaurants in the center, lying on the banks of the River Ness beside the main bridge, with a garden-style decor of big windows and padded banquettes. There's plenty of space for everyone. Steaks, fish such as salmon, and poultry are featured. Main courses include roast chicken, and a full assortment of prime Angus steaks, some weighing in at your choice of 8 or 16 ounces.

WHINPARK HOTEL, 17 Ardross St., Inverness, Inverness-shire IV3 5NS. Tel. 0463/232549.

Cuisine: MODERN BRITISH. **Reservations:** Recommended.

$ Prices: Appetizers £3.50–£5 ($5.30–$7.50); main courses £9.75–£14.35 ($14.60–$21.50). Fixed-price lunch £7.50 ($11.30), fixed-price dinners £16.75–£18.75 ($25.10–$28.10). V.

Open: Lunch Mon–Fri noon–2pm; dinner daily 6:30–9pm.

Although it contains 9 comfortable bedrooms upstairs, nearly everyone in Inverness refers to this establishment as "a restaurant with rooms" rather than as a hotel with dining facilities. Its food is prepared by John McCruden under the supervision of Ms. Jackie McKintosh, and features the best of Scottish ingredients in innovative combinations. This includes shellfish lasagne with white wine sauce; fresh mussels and watercress soup; a tartlet of home-smoked salmon with dill-flavored hollandaise; croissants stuffed with sautéed vegetables and ginger; grilled monkfish with saffron noodles and a sauce made from Pernod, fennel, and double cream; and an antique recipe for a dish much noted by culinary historians, venison Mary Stuart, marinated in red currant jelly, red wine, and honey, and covered with a rich madeira sauce.

The restaurant lies within a 19th-century, stone-fronted building on the southern periphery of town, close to the edge of the River Ness. Only four of the nine bedrooms contain bath or shower, although all have TV, telephone, and hairdryer. With Scottish breakfast included, rooms with bath cost £27.50 ($41.30) for a single,

£37 ($55.50) for a double. Rooms without bathroom cost £22 ($33) for a single and £33 ($49.50) for a double.

EVENING ENTERTAINMENT

EDEN COURT THEATRE, Bishops Rd. Tel. 0463/221718.

The city has a luxurious theater complex on the bank of the River Ness, the Eden Court Theatre, which has a superb restaurant, bars, and an art gallery. Included in the repertoire are variety shows, drama, ballet, pop music, movies, opera, and rock and folk concerts. The theater, which opened in 1976, has a horseshoe-shaped auditorium. Programs are advertised in most hotels and guesthouses. Ticket prices can vary widely depending on the event (call the box office). The box office is open Monday through Saturday from 10:30am to 8:30pm.

SCOTTISH SHOWTIME, in the Cummings Hotel, 70 Church St. Tel. 0463/232531.

For an evening of fun, try this place. It has become a Highland tradition that the best of the region's entertainers appear at least once at this hotel in the center of Inverness. A bekilted and bagpiped evening here combines Scottish songs with music, dancing, and Highland humor into an enthusiastic *ceilidh* (a Highland hoedown) that many guests remember for a long time. Showtime is Monday through Saturday at 8:30pm, beginning in early June and running into the autumn. Tickets can be purchased at the door just before showtime or at the hotel reception desk. On Saturday and Sunday, it's a good idea to phone ahead for a reservation.

Admission: Tickets, £7 ($10.50) adults, £3.50 ($5.30) children.

9. NAIRN

172 miles N of Edinburgh, 91 miles NW of Aberdeen,
16 miles E of Inverness

GETTING THERE   By Train   Nairn can be reached by train from the south, with a change at either Aberdeen or Inverness. The services between Inverness and Nairn are particularly frequent, and this is the most popular route of travel for most visitors. For information, call the Inverness train station at Station Square (tel. 0463/238924).

By Bus   From Inverness, Inverness Traction runs daily buses to Nairn.

By Car   From Inverness, take the A96 east to Nairn.

ESSENTIALS   The summer-only **tourist information office** is at 62 King St. (tel. 0667/52753). The **telephone area code** is 0667.

A favorite family seaside resort on the sheltered Moray Firth, Nairn is a royal burgh at the mouth of the Nairn River. Its fishing harbor was constructed in 1820, and golf has been played here since 1672, as it still is today. A large uncrowded beach and angling also draw a horde of vacationers in summer.

Nairn is great walking country, and the tourist office will give you a map and details about the various possibilities, including along the banks of the River Nairn (from the Gaelic for "Water of Alders").

Since 1855 Nairn has been a popular seaside resort of the north, brought about by the completion of the Inverness–Nairn rail line. It was also the center of a thriving fishing settlement, and its old Fishertown provides an insight into those past times.

WHAT TO SEE & DO

To the south of Nairn, you encounter 600 years of Highland history at   ✪ **Cawdor Castle,** Cawdor (tel. 06677/615), between Inverness and Nairn on the B9090 off the

A96. Since the early 14th century it has been the home of the thanes of Cawdor. Although not constructed until four centuries after the time of Macbeth, Cawdor was nevertheless romantically linked to Macbeth by Shakespeare. The castle has all the architectural ingredients you associate with the medieval: a drawbridge, an ancient tower (this one built around a tree), and fortified walls. The severity is softened by the handsome gardens, flowers, trees, and rolling lawns. The castle is open to the public from May 1 to October 3, daily from 10am to 5:30pm; last admission at 5pm. Admission is £3.50 ($5.30) for adults, £1.90 ($2.90) for children.

The castle has beautiful gardens, extensive nature trails, a nine-hole golf course, putting green, licensed restaurant that serves hot meals, teas, coffees, and home baking all day, snack bar, and picnic area. There are three shops at Cawdor.

Car and coach parking is free. Inverness Traction, a local bus company, runs regular buses to Cawdor from both Inverness and Nairn. For details about these connections, ask at the tourist office in either Inverness or Nairn.

WHERE TO STAY

CLIFTON HOUSE, 1–3 Viewfield St., Nairn, Nairnshire IV12 4HW. Tel. 0667/53119. Fax 0667/53119. 16 rms (all with bath). **Directions:** Turn east of the town roundabout on A96.

$ Rates (including Scottish breakfast): £54 ($81) single; £91–£106 ($136.50–$159) double. AE, DC, MC, V. **Parking:** Free.

Clifton House reflects the dynamic personality of J. Gordon Macintyre, the owner of this honey-colored sandstone, vine-covered Victorian mansion. Clifton House has been "home" to the present owner for the last 61 years. Fully licensed, it stands on the sea front, 3 minutes from the beach and equidistant to both Golf Links. Mr. Macintyre has spent a great deal of time and care in decorating, refurbishing, and preserving the house. Most of the furniture is antique. The collection of paintings, prints, etchings, engravings, and drawings is unusual and extensive, not only in the Red Drawing Room, the Yellow Sitting Room, and the Green Room, but also in the long corridor and on the staircases. Each of the bedrooms is pleasantly appointed. Gordon Macintyre organizes in the hotel, which is licensed as a theater, a series of concerts, chamber opera, plays, and recitals but only from October until March.

Dining/Entertainment: The Clifton has the most extensive wine list in the north of Scotland and also serves the best food in Nairn, using only basic raw ingredients with nothing packaged. The cooking is very traditional using the best of local Highland food but cooked using classic techniques—for instance, game pie, double stuffed chicken, lamb in mustard, mallard duck, wild salmon, brill, turbot, and sole. Dinner hours are from 7 to 9:30pm daily. Lunch is from 12:30 to 1pm. Reservations are necessary. Breakfast is very traditionally Scottish with no allowance for packaged cereals. Juice is squeezed while you wait; homemade oatcakes and marmalade, and local honey are served from 8am until lunch time.

Services: All-day room service, laundry, babysitting.
Facilities: Garden.

GREENLAWNS PRIVATE HOTEL, 13 Seafield St., Nairn, Nairnshire IV12 4HG. Tel. 0667/52738. 7 rms (4 with bath). TV **Directions:** Turn down Albert Street from the A96.

$ Rates (including Scottish breakfast): £20 ($30) single without bath, £25 ($37.50) single with bath; £34 ($51) double without bath, £40 ($60) double with bath. MC, V. **Parking:** Free.

This is a small but thriving B&B, a Victorian house within easy reach of many sporting activities. Guests are surrounded by paintings and antiques, many of which are for sale in the gallery. All bedrooms have electric blankets, heating, and coffee- and tea-making facilities. Bill and Isabell Caldwell do much to see that their guests have a comfortable stay. The hotel lies close to the beaches and two golf courses, and is within easy reach of Loch Ness if you want to use it as a tourist center.

NEWTON, Inverness Rd., Nairn, Nairnshire IV12 4RX. Tel. 0667/ 53144. Fax 0667/54026. 44 rms (all with bath or shower). TV TEL

$ Rates (including Scottish breakfast): £42–£55 ($63–$82.50) single; £55–£95 ($82.50–$142.50) double. AE, DC, MC, V. **Parking:** Free.

A castlelike hotel, Newton stands just outside town in an attractive park of 27 acres, overlooking the Nairn Golf Course and offering views across sweeping lawns and the golf course to the sea. Considered one of the finest of the "manor house" hotels of Scotland, it is spacious and sumptuous, drawing a clientele likely to include everybody from a prime minister to a Glasgow industrialist. The public rooms are furnished with taste, and the Moray Firth, viewed on a day when the sun is shining brightly, forms a spectacle of beauty from many of the Newton's windows. The bedrooms have many fine appointments. There is a high standard of maintenance and personal service.

WHERE TO DINE

TASTE BUD BAR & RESTAURANT, 44 Harbour St. Tel. 0667/52743.
  Cuisine: SEAFOOD/SCOTTISH. **Reservations:** Recommended.
$ Prices: In bar, appetizers £1.20–£3.95 ($1.80–$5.90), main courses £4–£8 ($6–$12). In restaurant, appetizers £1.35–£4.10 ($2–$6.20), main courses £6.30–£12.50 ($9.50–$18.80). DC, MC, V.
  Open: Lunch daily noon–2pm; dinner daily 5–9:30pm. Sat–Sun open throughout the afternoon.

The Taste Bud is set within what was once a fisherman's cottage, built more than 300 years ago. Some of its original stone walls and ceiling beams still remain. On the town's main street leading down to the harbor, it's known for its simple but flavorful preparations of very fresh fish, brought in the same day by local fishing boats. Although some sauces are available, and are usually proposed as optional dressings on the side, most fish here is simply grilled or sautéed with oil or butter, and served with locally grown vegetables. The best choice might be a fish platter with portions of simply prepared mackerel, trout, scampi, and prawns, served with salad. Other options include trout with a courgette, tomato, and cream sauce; salmon with dill; a selection of Taste of Scotland dishes (including haggis, in summertime only); and several types of Angus steaks. Children are welcome, and it's very much a family place, although fully licensed.

10. THE BLACK ISLE

Cromarty: 23 miles NW of Inverness (via Kessock Bridge)

GETTING THERE By Train Go to Inverness (see section 8 of this chapter), then proceed the rest of the way west by bus.

By Bus The Highland Bus and Coach company from Inverness services the peninsula (nos. 26, 26A, and 126), making stops at North Kessock, Munlochy, Avoch, Fortrose, Rosemarkie, and Cromarty. Buses depart from Farraline Park in Inverness (tel. 0463/233371 for information and schedules).

By Car Making Fortrose your first stopover (see below), take the A9 north from Inverness (signposted Wick). Follow the A9 for 4 miles until you see the Kessock Bridge. Go over the bridge and take the second road to the right, signposted Munlocky (Fortrose is 8 miles from this turnoff). Follow the A832 through the village of Munlochy and at the junction take the road right, signposted Fortrose. Continue straight on through Avoch (pronounced "och") to Fortrose.

ESSENTIALS Ask at the Inverness Tourist Office (see above) for any information on Black Isle, as the peninsula is most often included on a day tour from that city. The **telephone area code** is 03817.

This is, in my opinion, one of the most enchanting peninsulas of Scotland, a land rich in history, beauty, and mystery. Part of Ross and Cromarty County, it lies north of Inverness, and a car tour of it is about 37 miles. But allow plenty of time for stopovers along the way. It's reached after a 20-minute car or bus ride west from Inverness.

There is much confusion about its name, because it is neither black nor an island. In summer the land is actually green and fertile, and tropical plants flourish. It's filled with forests, fields of broom and whin, and scattered coastal villages. No one seems to agree on how it got its name.

What is known is that the "isle" or peninsula has been inhabited for 7,000 years, as 60-odd prehistoric sites testify to this day. Pictish kings, whose thrones passed down through the female line, once ruled this land. The Vikings held sway, and the evidence of many Gallows Hills testify that justice was harsh.

WHAT TO SEE & DO

If you're touring the island, your first goal might be **Fortrose.** Along the way you'll pass a celebrated wishing well or "clootie well," which is festooned with rags. Dedicated to St. Boniface, the well has a long tradition, dating back to pagan times. It is said that anyone removing a rag will inherit the misfortunes of the person who placed it there.

In the sleepy village of Fortrose stand the ruins of **Fortrose Cathedral,** which can be visited free April through September, Monday to Saturday from 9:30am to 7pm and on Sunday from 2 to 7pm; off-season Monday through Saturday from 9:30am to 4pm and on Sunday from 2 to 4pm. Founded in the 13th century, it was dedicated to St. Peter and St. Boniface. There is still some fine detailing from the 14th century. Cromwell's men removed many of its stones to help build a fort at Inverness.

Fortrose adjoins **Rosemarkie,** up the road. The site has been inhabited since the Bronze Age. A center of Pictish culture, it saw the arrival of the first Christian missionaries. It is reported that St. Moluag founded a monastery here in the 6th century. Rosemarkie became a royal burgh in 1216. The twin hamlets share a golf course today, and they are the site of the Chanonry Sailing Club, whose annual regatta brings entries from all over Scotland. Right beyond Rosemarkie is the mysterious **Fairy Glen,** signposted at the end of the village.

Cromarty stands at the tip of the peninsula where the North and South Sutars guard the entrance to the Cromarty Firth, the second-deepest inland waterway estuary in Europe, always considered of strategic importance to the Royal Navy. Once a flourishing port and a former royal burgh, the town gave the world a famous son: Hugh Miller. Born here in 1802, Miller was a stonemason as a young man. But in time he became a recognized expert in the field of geology, as well as a powerful man of letters in Scotland. His thatched cottage was built in 1711. **Hugh Miller's Cottage,** on Church Street (tel. 03817/245), is on view to the public today, containing many of his personal belongings and collections of geological specimens. It is open only from April 1 through September 27, Monday to Saturday from 10am to 1pm and 2 to 5pm; Sunday, 2 to 5pm. Admission is £1.50 ($2.30) for adults, 80p ($1.20) for children.

WHERE TO STAY & DINE
FORTROSE

ROYAL HOTEL, at the corner of Union and High streets, Fortrose, Ross-shire IV10 8SU. Tel. 0381/620236. 10 rms (5 with bath).

$ Rates (including Scottish breakfast): £18–£20 ($27–$30) single without bath; £24–£28 ($36–$42) single with bath; £32–£36 ($48–$54) double without bath, £38–£42 ($57–$63) double with bath. MC, V. **Parking:** Free.

S The Royal Hotel overlooks the ancient monument of Fortrose Cathedral. Despite the traditional Victorian exterior, the establishment has been tastefully redecorated inside, with two bars, a dining room, a residents' lounge, and guest rooms. Family rooms are also available. Resident proprietors of this hotel are Eoin and Jean MacLennan, who provide meals for residents and nonresidents alike.

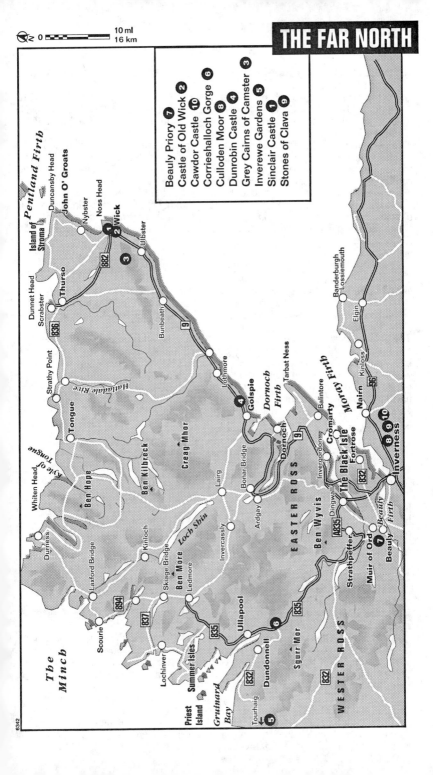

THE FAR NORTH

10 ml
16 km

Beauly Priory **7**
Castle of Old Wick **2**
Cawdor Castle **10**
Corrieshalloch Gorge **6**
Culloden Moor **8**
Dunrobin Castle **4**
Grey Cairns of Camster **3**
Inverewe Gardens **5**
Sinclair Castle **1**
Stones of Clava **9**

Pentland Firth

Duncansby Head
John O' Groats
Island of Stroma
Dunnet Head
Noss Head
Nybster
Wick
Ulbster
Thurso
Scrabster
Strathy Point
882
336
9
Bunbeath
Lothmore
Lothmore
Tongue
Whiten Head
Kyle of Tongue
Ben Hope
Ben Kilbreck
Creag Mhor
Halladale Rive
Dornoch Firth
Tarbat Ness
Golspie
Balintore
Cromarty Firth
Moray Firth
Nairn
Kinloss
Elgin
Banderburgh
Lossiemouth
96
Dornoch
Bonar Bridge
Lairg
Invergordon
Fortrose
The Black Isle
Inverness
9
832
Dingwall
Ardgay
Invercassly
EASTER ROSS
Ben Wyvis
A835
Strathpeffer
Muir of Ord
Beauly
Beauly Firth
Duness
Laxford Bridge
Kinloch
Loch Shin
Skiage Bridge
Ben More
Ledmore
894
837
Scourie
Lochinver
Summer Isles
Priest Island
Gruinard Bay
Tourhaig
Dundonnell
832
832
835
835
Ullapool
Sgurr Mor
WESTER ROSS
The Minch

Balblair

6

5

1
2

3

4

7

8 9 10

ROSEMARKIE

MARINE HOTEL, Rosemarkie, Ross-shire IV10 8UL. Tel. 0381/620253.
50 rms (25 with bath).
$ Rates (including Scottish breakfast): £24.50 ($36.80) single without bath, £30 ($45) single with bath; £49 ($73.50) double without bath, £60 ($90) double with bath. Discounts of up to 50% for children under 12. MC, V. **Parking:** Free. **Closed:** Oct–Mar.

This palatial building on the seafront was constructed of red sandstone around 1830 by a local landowner. Since then it has been enlarged and adapted into an old-world kind of hotel, rich with Victorian proportions and awash with sea breezes and sunlight from its panoramic windows. At the bottom of the hotel's garden, you'll find a converted garage that now functions under separate management as a pub. You'll also have the option of drinking and dining within the hotel's cocktail lounge on bar platters, priced at from £3.50 ($5.30) each. Also available are more formal meals that are served at nighttime within the hotel's restaurant. Table d'hôte dinners cost £14.50 ($21.80) each.

CROMARTY

ROYAL HOTEL, Marine Terrace, Cromarty, Ross-shire IV11 8YN. Tel. 03817/217. 10 rms (all with bath). TV **Bus:** 26, 26A, or 126 from Inverness.
$ Rates (including Scottish breakfast): £28 ($42) single; £50 ($75) double. AE, MC, V. **Parking:** Free.

The only hotel in town, it sits on an embankment near one of the deepest estuaries in Europe. Around 1940 the British navy combined a series of waterfront buildings into living quarters for sailors. Today the hotel is a comfortably cozy enclave alive with wood-burning stoves and open fireplaces. There's a comfortable lounge bar, plus a public bar and a dining room that spills onto a glassed-in extension opening onto the harbor. A fixed-price evening meal is another £14.95 ($22.40). You can also enjoy a good bar menu, with a tempting list of burgers, crêpes, and salads; light meals begin at £5 ($7.50).

EASY EXCURSIONS

MUIR OF ORD

This small town, 10 miles west of Inverness, near Beauly, makes a good touring center for a history-rich part of Scotland. If you stay at the recommendation below, you can branch out on day excursions in many directions. Sportsmen are attracted to the region as it offers good fishing, roe and red deer stalking, golfing, and shooting.

Where to Stay & Dine

THE DOWER HOUSE, Highfield, Muir of Ord, Ross-shire IV6 7XN. Tel. 0463/870090. Fax 0463/870090. 4 rms (all with bath), 1 suite. TV TEL **Directions:** 1 miles north of A862.
$ Rates (including half board): £95 ($142.50) single; £140 ($210) double; £160 ($240) suite. MC, V. **Parking:** Free.

Open all year, this is the most charming place to stay in the area, although it has only five units so you should reserve as far in advance as possible. Bedrooms are decorated in the fine tradition of a Scottish country house, with a tasteful decor. Each room is well furnished and cozily comfortable, with Victorian-style bathrooms.

Even if you don't stay there, call ahead for a dinner reservation. Costing £25 ($37.50) and up, a fixed-price menu is served nightly at 7:30pm. Guests gather for an apéritif in the charming lounge, followed by a four-course table d'hôte. Robyn Aitchison is an inspired chef, turning out Scottish or French-style dishes with equal flair. The menu, followed by rich coffee, is changed daily.

BEAULY

The French monks who settled here in the 13th century named it literally "beautiful place," and it still is. The ruins of Beauly Priory, which the monks built, can still be visited. You'll see the Highland Craftpoint on your left as you come from Inverness. In summer, they have an interesting exhibition of Scottish handcrafts. Beauly is 12 miles west of Inverness on the A862.

A local bus company, Inverness Traction, has bus service to Beauly from Inverness, a bus arriving during the day at the rate of one per hour.

What to See & Do

Dating from 1230, the **Beauly Priory** (tel. 0463/782309) is the only remaining one of three priories constructed for the Valliscaulian order, an austere body drawing its main components from the Cistercians and the Carthusians. Some notable windows and window arcading can still be seen in the ruins. Hugh Fraser of Lovat erected the Chapel of the Holy Cross on the nave's north side in the early 15th century. The ruins are open April through September, daily from 9:30am to 7pm. If the priory is locked, ask for a key from the Priory Hotel across the way. Admission is free.

On the south bank of the River Beauly southwest of the town is **Beaufort Castle,** a 19th-century baronial mansion which is the seat of the Frasers of Lovat, whose ancestor was Simon, Lord Lovat, a Jacobite agent, known as the "Lovat of the Forty-five." The original seat of the Lovats was Castle Dounie, built about 1400, but it was destroyed after "Butcher" Cumberland after his victory at Culloden.

If you're interested in tweeds, don't miss **Campbell's of Beauly,** Highland Tweed House (tel. 0463/782239), operated by the same family since 1858. An excellent selection of fine tweeds and tartans is offered, and you can have your material tailored if you wish. Blankets, travel rugs, tweed hats (deer-stalkers and fishing hats), and kilts are sold here, as well as sweaters in cashmere and lambswool. Shetland knits can be found here also. The establishment is open from 9am to 1pm and 2 to 5:30pm Monday through Saturday (closing at 1pm on Thursday). It's on the main street at the south end of the village square, next to the Royal Bank of Scotland.

Where to Stay & Dine

PRIORY HOTEL, The Square, Beauly, Inverness-shire IV4 7BX. Tel. 0463/782309. Fax 0463/783531. 24 rms (all with bath). TV TEL
$ Rates (including Scottish breakfast): £37.50 ($56.30) single; £59.50 ($89.30) double. AE, DC, MC, V. **Parking:** Free.
The Priory Hotel is directly on the historic main square of town, a short walk from the ruins of the priory. The century-old building's attractively modernized interior houses comfortably furnished bedrooms. The highlight of your stay is likely to be the choice of food available in the restaurant and the bars. Full meals begin at £10 ($15). The atmosphere is unusually homelike.

11. SUTHERLAND

It's been called the "gem of Scotland." It's got more sheep than people (20 to 1), and is probably the least-written-about area of Scotland, but its devotees (and not just the local residents) maintain that it's the most beautiful county in Scotland. Adding to the scenic sweep of haunting beauty are lochs and rivers, heather-covered moors and mountains—in all, 2,000 square miles of territory. The Duke of Sutherland used to own most of it.

It's a country of quiet pleasures, as it offers few amusements in the conventional sense, except such sporting activities as golf and fishing. It is an ancient unspoiled landscape that has witnessed a turbulent history.

To the northwest of Inverness, Sutherland has three coastlines—to the north and west, the Atlantic; to the east, the North Sea. Most villages have populations of only a hundred or so hearty souls. Sutherland was the scene of the notorious Highland Clearances when many of its residents were driven out and made their way to the New World where they went on to greater prosperity. The sheep, known as "the white plague," took over after their departure. One critic called the dislocation of the people of Sutherland in the 19th century "an orgy of ruthless social engineering." In many a deserted glen you can still see traces of former crofting villages.

DORNOCH

The ancient cathedral city of Dornoch, 63 miles northwest of Inverness and 219 miles northwest of Edinburgh, is the most interesting stopover in Sutherland, and the major sightseeing attraction nearby is **Dunrobin Castle** (see Golspie, below). The turf of the **Royal Dornoch Golf Club,** Golf Road (tel. 0862/810219), has been called "sacred" by aficionados. Golf was first played there in 1616!

Villagelike Dornoch is the major town of Sutherland, and has long been known for its Royal Dornoch Golf Club, the northernmost first-class course in the world. On the sheltered shores of Dornoch Firth, the cathedral town also attracts tourists in summer to its beaches.

A **tourist information office** is found at The Square (tel. 0862/810400).

From the Inverness bus station (tel. 0463/233371), three different local companies run daily buses to Dornoch: Stagecoach, Caledonian Express, and Scottish Citylink.

WHAT TO SEE & DO

Built in the 13th century, **Dornoch Cathedral,** Castle Street, was partially destroyed by fire in 1570. It has had many restorations, including one in 1924, but its fine 13th-century stonework can still be seen. The cathedral is famous for its magnificent stained-glass windows—three of which are in memory of Andrew Carnegie, the American "steel king." The cathedral is open daily from 9am to dusk.

For food or shopping, try the **Dornoch Craft Centre,** Town Jail, Castle Street (tel. 0862/810555), next to the Dornoch Castle Hotel in the center of town and opposite the cathedral. The present-day center occupies the floors of what was the town jail dating from 1844. You can wander through the selection of Scottish crafts, jewelry, and pottery, then visit the Textile Hall and browse through the range of knitwear, tartans, mohair goods, and tweeds. On the top floor is a small coffee shop selling sandwiches and drinks. The center is open Monday through Saturday from 9am to 5pm, and stays open on Sunday from July to the end of September.

WHERE TO STAY & DINE

DORNOCH CASTLE HOTEL, Castle Street, Dornoch, Sutherland IV25 3SD. Tel. 0862/810216. Fax 0862/810981. 19 rms (all with bath). TV TEL
$ Rates (including Scottish breakfast): £36 ($54) single; £63–£76 ($94.50–$114) double. AE, MC, V. **Parking:** Free.

★ This unusual hotel close to the Royal Dornoch Golf Course is inside the massive walls of what used to be the residence of the bishops of Caithness. It was built of local stone in the center of town in the late 15th or early 16th century. Today its winding stairs, labyrinthine corridors, and impenetrable cellars have been converted into a well-directed hotel and restaurant. All the accommodations contain private baths. You can enjoy a fixed-price dinner for £16.50 ($24.80) in the stone-walled dining room. Menu specialties include filet of Angus beef Balmoral style (in a red wine and whisky sauce with asparagus) and Sutherland lobster Hebridean style in a cheese and Drambuie sauce. Table reservations are suggested.

GOLSPIE

Today a family resort with a golf course, Golspie was once part of the vast holdings of the earls and dukes of Sutherland. The town, lying on the A9, looks out across the water to the Dornoch Firth. A crescent of sandy beach is an attraction to visitors. Golspie lies 228 miles northwest of Edinburgh and 72 miles northwest of Inverness.

WHAT TO SEE & DO

Golspie is visited chiefly because of a towering attraction half a mile northeast on the A9, **۞ Dunrobin Castle** (tel. 0408/633177), home of the earls and dukes of Sutherland. It is the most northerly of the great houses of Scotland, and also the biggest in the northern Highlands, and dates in part from the early 13th century. Formal gardens are laid out in the manner of Versailles. On the grounds is a museum overlooking these gardens, containing many relics from the Sutherland family. Trophies and regimental colors of the 93rd Sutherland Highlanders are on view. Some of the castle's 180 rooms are open to the public, others form the apartments of the Countess of Sutherland, while many rooms are empty. Among the sections to be seen are an ornately furnished dining room, a billiard room–cum–family museum, and the room and gilded four-poster bed where Queen Victoria slept when she visited in 1872.

The castle is open from June through mid-September, Monday to Saturday from 10:30am to 5:30pm and on Sunday from 1 to 5:30pm; in May, Monday to Thursday from 10:30am to 12:30pm. Admission is £3.20 ($4.80) for adults and £1.60 ($2.40) for children.

WHERE TO STAY & DINE

GOLF LINKS HOTEL, Church St., Golspie, Sutherland KW10 6TT. Tel. 0408/633408. 8 rms (all with bath). TV
$ Rates (including Scottish breakfast): £28 ($42) single; £50 ($75) double. Half board £40 ($60) per person. MC, V. **Parking:** Free.
Constructed of stone, this hotel at the southern edge of town contains well-furnished bedrooms, all doubles. A first-class chef prepares the varied Scottish and continental menu served in a dining room opening onto a view of Ben Bhraggie. A fixed-price dinner goes for £15 ($22.50), or you can order à la carte. The contemporary lounge bar looks through big plate-glass windows onto Dornoch Firth. Bar lunches are served daily around noon, for £6 ($9) and up. Much of the establishment's clientele is made up of golfers drawn to the nearby Golspie, Royal Dornoch, and Brora courses. A handful of self-service units is in the annex, which also has a hairdressing salon.

TONGUE

North along the A836 you cross high moors and brooding peaks until you come to Tongue, 257 miles northwest of Edinburgh and 101 miles northwest of Inverness. For the nature lover there is much here, ranging from the mighty cliffs of Clo Mor, near Cape Wrath (known for its large colonies of puffins), to waterfalls such as Eas-Coul-Aulin (the highest in Britain) and the Falls of Shin, where you can see salmon leap. Masses of land suddenly rise from a barren landscape, including Ben Loyal, known as the "queen of Scottish mountains."

West of Tongue on a promontory stand the ruins of **Castle Varrich,** said to have been built by the Vikings. Possibly dating from the 14th century, this castle was the Mackay stronghold. Mackays from North America visit Tongue annually, seeking lore about their ancestral roots.

Tongue House, from 1678, was also a home base for the chief of the Mackays, but it now belongs to the estate of the Duke of Sutherland. On the shores of the Kyle of Tongue, it has a walled garden and is open to the public only on a Sunday in August.

WHERE TO STAY & DINE

BEN LOYAL HOTEL, Main St., Tongue, Sutherland, IV27 4XE. Tel. 0847/55216. 18 rms (9 with bath). TV
$ Rates (including Scottish breakfast): £23.50 ($35.30) single without bath; £30 ($45) single with bath; £47 ($70.50) double without bath, £60 ($90) double with bath. MC, V. **Parking:** Free.

This is a good choice, with everything under the careful attention of Mel and Pauline Brook. There are 18 pleasant rooms, including six units in a bungalow annex. All accommodations have hot- and cold-water basins, electric blankets, and shaver points. Rooms are furnished in attractive traditional styling. Good home-cooking is served, with emphasis on local meat and fish, plus the hotel's own garden produce in season. A fine wine list complements meals. The Ben Loyal Hotel structures incorporate 19th-century stables, a former post office, a shop, and a village bakery.

TONGUE HOTEL, Tongue, Sutherland IV27 4XD. Tel. 0847/55206. Fax 0847/55345. 20 rms (all with bath). TV TEL
$ Rates (including Scottish breakfast): £30 ($45) single; £60 ($90) double. MC, V.
Parking: Free.

Ever since Queen Victoria's day, the best place to stay in town has been the Tongue Hotel, a mile north of the village center, beside the road leading to Durness. Built of gray stone in the baronial style, it opens onto the Kyle of Tongue and still possesses much of its initial character and many of its antiques. It was built around 1850 as a hunting lodge for the Duke of Sutherland. To identify its builder, an S is carved into the stonework high above one of the doorways. The establishment is known for the quality of its food. A hearty three-course dinner, which usually includes a choice of game or fresh fish caught within the region, costs from £15 ($22.50) on an à la carte menu. Accessible through a separate entrance is a paneled and popular pub with its own open fireplace and impressive collection of whiskies. There's also a more sedate cocktail lounge. Both the bedrooms and the public rooms are decorated in the Victorian style, with flowered curtains and well-upholstered furniture.

12. CAITHNESS

It doesn't look like the Highlands at all, but Caithness is the northernmost county of mainland Scotland. The landscape is gentle and rolling.

Caithness is ancient—in fact, within its 700 square miles you'll find signs of the Stone Age. The enigmatic Grey Cairns of Camster date from 4,000 B.C. The county is filled with cairns, mysterious stone rows and circles, and standing stones. The Vikings once occupied this place, with its rock stacks, old harbors, craggy cliffs, and quiet coves, and many place names are in Old Norse. It has churches from the Middle Ages, as well as towering castles on cliff tops. The Queen Mother's home, Castle of Mey, dating from 1570, lies between John o' Groats and Thurso.

Rich in bird and animal life, Caithness is unspoiled country. Sportsmen are drawn to the area, finding the wild brown trout in some 100 lochs, along with salmon in the Thurso and the Wick rivers.

Most people head for Caithness with John o' Groats as their final destination. John o' Groats, with its many souvenir shops, is popularly called the extreme northern tip of the British mainland. Actually, Dunnet Head is farther north by a few miles.

Others drive all the way to Scrabster where there's a ferry harbor. This is the main car-and-passenger service which operates all year to the Orkney Islands. There are day trips in summer.

WICK

This famous old herring port on the eastern coastline of Caithness is a popular stopping-over point for those heading north to explore what is often called the John o' Groats Peninsula. Wick has some claim as a holiday resort as well. Robert Louis Stevenson spent part of his boyhood in Wick when his father worked here on a project. Today a sleepy nostalgia hangs over the town.

Wick lies 287 miles northwest of Edinburgh and 126 miles northwest of Inverness. There is daily bus and rail service from Inverness, from which train connections are possible via Edinburgh, Glasgow, or Stirling.

WHAT TO SEE & DO

At **Caithness Glass,** Harrowhill (tel. 0955/2286), you can watch the glass blowing and tour the factory Monday through Friday from 9am to 4:30pm. The shop and cafeteria are open Monday to Friday from 9am to 5pm and on Saturday from 9am to 1pm (to 4pm on Saturday June through September).

The **Wick Heritage Centre,** 20 Bank Row (tel. 0955/5393), has many exhibitions pertaining to the herring-fishing industry in Wick in days of yore. You can also see farm implements from Caithness. It is open June through September, Monday to Saturday from 10am to 5pm. Admission is £1 ($1.50) for adults, 50p (80¢) for children.

In the environs you can visit the **Grey Cairns of Camster.** These two megalithic cairns lie 6 miles north of Lybster on the Watten Road, off the A9.

The ruins of the **Castle of Old Wick** are also worth exploring. The location is off the A9, a mile and a half south of Wick. Once known as Castle Olipant, the ruined structure dates back to the 14th century. You may also want to seek out the **Castles Sinclair and Girnigoe,** 3 miles north of Wick (follow the airport road in the direction of the Noss Head Lighthouse). These adjacent castles were built on the edge of a cliff overlooking the Bay of Sinclair. At one time they were the strongholds of the Sinclairs, the earls of Caithness. The older structure, Girnigoe, dates from the latter 1400s; Sinclair was constructed in the early years of the 17th century. By 1679 both castles had been deserted and allowed to fall into ruins.

WHERE TO STAY & DINE

BREADALBANE HOUSE HOTEL, 20 Breadalbane Crescent, Wick, Caithness KW1 5AT. Tel. 0955/3911. 10 rms (9 with bath). TV

$ Rates (including Scottish breakfast): £26.50 ($39.80) single without bath; £29.50 ($44.30) single with bath; £47–£53 ($70.50–$79.50) double with bath. MC, V. **Parking:** Free.

The stone walls of this building on the southern outskirts of town, a 5-minute walk from the center, were originally built a century ago as the private home of a local furnituremaker. (Most of the interior woodwork, including the door and window frames and the staircase, are reputed to have been built by the owner personally.) Extensively renovated in 1990, the building now operates as an unpretentious guesthouse with an in-house pub and restaurant. Each of the bedrooms has uncomplicated furnishings with traditional accessories.

HARBOUR GUEST HOUSE, 6 Rose St., Wick, Caithness KW1 5EX. Tel. 0955/3276. 10 rms (none with bath).

$ Rates (including Scottish breakfast): £15 ($22.50) single; £30 ($45) double. No credit cards. **Parking:** Free.

Adjacent to the town's harbor and Wick's Heritage Centre, a 5-minute walk east of the center, this hostelry was built of local stones a century ago to house an employee of the fishing industry, whose efforts probably contributed to Wick's status at that time as the largest port for herring fishing in Europe. The guest house offers cozy and comfortable bedrooms. Only breakfast is served, although owners Olive and Ronald Ross direct residents to the handful of nearby restaurants.

JOHN O' GROATS

For those who wanted to go to Land's End at the tip of the Cornish peninsula in England, John o' Groats is the northern equivalent. The southern tip of England, Land's End in Cornwall, is 878 miles south of John o' Groats. John o'Groats lies 17 miles north of Wick. Tourists are fond of having their pictures taken at the "Last House," standing at the end of the A9. From John o' Groats there are views north to the Orkney Islands and the Pentland Firth.

John o' Groats is named after a Dutch ferryman, Jan de Groot. His tombstone can still be seen at Cabisbay Church. Many visitors like to walk along the coast, to Duncansby Head and to the great Stacks. The town abounds in souvenir shops, some selling Groatie buckies, or small Arctic cowrie shells once used as decoration by the first settlers on Caithness.

In the summer months you can take a 7-day passenger-only ferry service to Orkney. Bus tours of the island are included. The Orkney Islands are just a 45-minute sail from John o' Groats across the Pentland Firth.

WHERE TO STAY & DINE

SEAVIEW HOTEL, John o' Groats, Caithness KW1 4YR. Tel. 095581/ 220. 9 rms (5 with bath).
$ Rates (including Scottish breakfast): £15 ($22.50) single without bath, £21 ($31.50) single with bath (available only in winter); £30 ($45) double without bath, £42 ($63) double with bath. No credit cards. **Parking:** Free.

One of the most northerly hotels on the British mainland, the Seaview is a family-run hotel whose severe and streamlined sides rise abruptly from a flat and windswept landscape beside the town's only highway near the hamlet's center. Built in the 1950s, and enlarged in 1991, it's covered with a roughly textured white stucco that locals refer to as "pebble dash." Each accommodation is comfortably spacious and conservatively furnished, with tea/coffee makers, electric blankets, and a TV on request. There's a pub on the premises, where bar lunches and dinners draw an appreciative clientele.

THURSO

Motorists pass through this northern port heading for Scrabster where they can board ferries year round for the Orkney Islands. In Thurso you can visit the ruins of St. Peter's Church, near the harbor in the old restored district of Thurso.

There is a golf course nearby, and to the west the cliffs of Holborn Head and Dunnet Head, which boasts a lighthouse. A nuclear energy establishment was installed to the west at Dounreay. The town lies 289 miles northwest of Edinburgh, 133 miles northwest of Inverness, and 21 miles northwest of Wick.

WHERE TO STAY & DINE

PENTLAND HOTEL, Princes St., Thurso, Caithness KW14 7AA. Tel. 0847/63202. Fax 0847/62761. 56 rms (34 with bath). TV TEL
$ Rates (including Scottish breakfast): £20 ($30) single without bath, £25 ($37.50) single with bath; £38 ($57) double without bath, £46 ($69) double with bath. MC, V.
Parking: Free on the streets ringing the hotel.

This is a relatively modern hotel with cream-colored walls, bay and dormer windows, and a revolving glass door giving access to a streamlined lobby. It occupies most of a full city block a short walk from the center of the village. Uisdean and Flora Maclean take some of the chill off the weather with their central heating and their welcome. Fully licensed, the hotel contains its own bar as well as a dining room. Food is served nightly until 8:30pm, and features fresh fish, local lamb, and Scottish beef.

ULLAPOOL

Ullapool is an interesting village, the largest in Wester Ross, lying 215 miles northwest of Edinburgh, 59 miles northwest of Inverness. It was built by the British Fishery Society in 1788 as a port for herring fishermen, and is still a busy harbor. The original town plan has not been changed, and many of the buildings stand much as they were at the time of their construction, although mellower and more weatherbeaten. Ullapool has long been an embarkation point for travelers crossing the Minch, a section of the North Atlantic separating Scotland from the Outer Hebrides.

A short drive south to Gairloch takes you into the heart of Wester Ross, with its splendid scenery, mountains, and Atlantic seascape.

WHERE TO STAY & DINE

ALTANAHARRIE INN, Loch Broom, Ullapool, Ross-shire IV26 2SS. Tel. 085483/230. Fax 085483/303. 8 rms (all with bath). **Transportation:** Private ferry.

$ Rates (including half board): £130 ($195) per person. No credit cards. **Closed:** Nov–Easter.

This is one of those places you feel you shouldn't tell anyone about, for fear they won't have room for you when you get there. The Altanaharrie was once a 17th-century drover's inn on the banks of Loch Broom. There is no access by road, so guests are brought over the loch by private launch. Once you've landed, you are greeted with a warm log fire in a lounge and a dram before dinner, which is likely to consist of locally caught seafood. The owners make their own bread, and they like to know beforehand if you're "eating in" so that they can cater accordingly.

ROYAL HOTEL, Garve Rd., Ullapool, Ross-shire IV26 2SY. Tel. 0854/ 612181. Fax 0854/612951. 52 rms (all with bath). TV TEL

$ Rates (including half board): £38–£41 ($57–$61.50) single; £76–£82 ($114–$123) double. AE, DC, MC, V. **Parking:** Free. **Closed:** Late Oct to mid-Mar.

The Royal Hotel sits on a knoll on the "Inverness side" of town, overlooking the harborfront. Graced with curved walls and large sheets of glass, it was rebuilt in 1961 from an older building, with an east wing added in the 1970s. It offers well-furnished bedrooms, 21 of which have balconies opening onto views over Loch Broom. Live entertainment in season is offered, and home-cooked bar meals are a feature. If someone wants to show up for a fixed-price dinner, a table d'hôte in the dining room costs only £7 ($10.50); bar meals begin at £4 ($6). Later, guests sit around a log fire in the well-appointed lounge. The hotel is a special favorite with families, offering bunk beds where required, a babysitting and baby-listening service, and other amenities.

EASY EXCURSIONS FROM ULLAPOOL

There are a number of excursions that can be made from Ullapool, including a trip to the **Corrieshalloch Gorge,** 12 miles southeast of town, a national nature reserve along the A835 at Braemore. From this point, the Falls of Measach plunge 150 feet into a mile-long wooded gorge.

Another interesting excursion is to the **Inverewe Gardens** (tel. 044586/200). Osgood MacKenzie created these gardens a century and a quarter ago, when he planted species from many countries. An exotic mixture of plants from the South Pacific, the Himalayas, and South America allows the gardens to have color year-round. The gardens can be reached along the A832, 6 miles northeast of Gairloch. Open all year, they can be visited Monday through Saturday from 9:30am to sunset and on Sunday from noon to sunset (in the off-season watch for 5pm closings). Admission is £2.50 ($3.80) for adults and £1.25 ($1.90) for children.

From either Ullapool or Achiltibuie, it's possible to take excursions in season to the **Summer Isles,** a beautiful group of uninhabited islands off the coast. The islands get their names because sheep are transported there in summer for grazing. The largest is Tanera More. The islands are a mecca for birdwatchers. Information about how to reach the islands is available from the summer-only tourist information office on West Shore Street (tel. 2135). Boat schedules can vary, depending on weather conditions.

Dundonnell, 29 miles south of Ullapool, at the head of Little Lochbroom, can be reached by car from Braemore junction along the "destination road," so called because it was built to help relieve the distress and poverty among Scots of the parish during the potato famine of 1846. After Braemore junction, the road goes toward **Loch-a-Bhraoln,** a 4-mile-long freshwater lake, near which are the graves of a group of Lochaber men who were cattle rustling in the strath. A Lochbroom man disguised as a beggar followed them, and when they were asleep, he killed them all except the one they had left on guard.

CHAPTER 10
THE HEBRIDEAN ISLANDS

- **WHAT'S SPECIAL ABOUT THE HEBRIDEAN ISLANDS**
1. **DORNIE**
2. **THE KYLE OF LOCHALSH**
3. **THE ISLE OF SKYE**
4. **RHUM (ALSO RUM)**
5. **EIGG & MUCK**
6. **COLL & TYREE**
7. **MULL**
8. **IONA & STAFFA**
9. **THE ISLE OF COLONSAY**
10. **LEWIS**
11. **HARRIS**
12. **NORTH & SOUTH UIST**
13. **BARRA**

Geologists wandering through bog and bracken used to mingle with painters and birdwatchers and an occasional sea angler or mountain climber on the Hebridean Islands. Today, however, these special-interest groups are likely to encounter more and more general tourists.

In visiting the Inner Hebridean islands, you'll be following a worthy tradition in the footsteps of Samuel Johnson and his faithful Boswell. Just off the shores of Mull is Iona, the isle that played a major part in the spread of Christianity in Britain. A trip there usually includes a visit to Staffa, a tiny uninhabited volcanic island where Fingal's Cave inspired Mendelssohn. (See Chapter 6 for the southernmost islands, Arran and Islay, and the Isle of Jura.)

What about the Outer Hebrides? One of the lesser-known parts of western Europe, these are a splintered sweep of islands that stretch for some 130 miles, from the Butt of Lewis in the north all the way to Barra Head at the southernmost tip. With rugged cliffs, clean beaches, archeological treasures, and tiny bays, the Outer Hebrides are just beginning to awaken to their touristic possibilities.

From Gourock, the ferry terminal near Glasgow (tel. 0475/33755 for information, 0475/34531 for reservations), **Caledonian MacBrayne** sails to 23 Scottish islands in the Firth of Clyde and the Western Isles, including Skye and Mull, as well as the Outer Hebrides. The company also offers inclusive tours for people and cars to "island-hop" between islands. This is an ideal opportunity to visit places well away from the beaten track. The information office at Gourock is most helpful, and will assist you in planning a trip if you wish to plan your own journey.

If you're driving from the mainland—say, from Fort William or Inverness—you can take the "Road to the Isles," heading for the Kyle of Lochalsh if your destination is Skye (for Mull and Iona, Oban is your port).

SEEING THE HEBRIDEAN ISLANDS
GETTING THERE

The most popular islands to visit are the Isle of Skye and the Isle of Mull, both reached by car-ferries from Oban, the Kyle of Lochalsh, or Mallaig. Iona can be explored by taking a ferry from Mull (see below). These islands are part of the Inner

WHAT'S SPECIAL ABOUT THE HEBRIDEAN ISLANDS

Great Islands

☐ The Isle of Skye, a mystical island off the northwestern coast of Scotland, the largest of the Inner Hebrides.

☐ The Isle of Mull, third largest of the Inner Hebrides, rich in legend and folklore (ghosts, monsters, and the "wee folk").

☐ Iona, off the coast of Mull, known for its "Grave of the Kings" and its abbey from the 13th century.

Ace Attractions

☐ Fingal's Cave on Staffa, its crashing waves and swirling waters inspired Mendelssohn's *Fingal's Cave Overture*.

Historic Castles

☐ Dunvegan Castle, Isle of Skye, seat of the chiefs of Clan MacLeod for 750 years.

☐ Torosay Castle, Craignure, Isle of Mull, the only privately lived-in castle in the western Highlands open to the public.

Cool for Kids

☐ Mull Railway, the only passenger railway in the Hebrides.

Special Events

☐ Mull Highland Games, in July, with all the traditional events, including bagpipes, caber tossing, and dancing.

☐ The Tour of Mull Rally, in October, car-racing drivers take over the island's 120 miles of twisting, tortuous roads.

Hebrides, and enjoy fairly good connections with mainland Scotland. More remote, the Outer Hebrides, a windswept chain, are also linked by car-ferries from such mainland ports as Ullapool (tel. 0851/3088 for schedules). The main islands to visit here are Lewis and Harris. Air service from Glasgow includes the airport at Stornoway on Lewis (tel. 041/3329666 in Glasgow for more information).

SUGGESTED ITINERARY

Days 1 and 2: From Oban, sail to the Isle of Mull for a day of exploration. While still based on Mull, schedule Day 2 to visit Iona and Fingal's Cave on the nearby island of Staffa.

Days 3 and 4: From Craignure on Mull, take the 45-minute crossing back to Oban. From Oban, take the A828 northeast to Fort William, then head west along A830 to Mallaig, where frequent ferries depart for Skye. Sail to the Isle of Skye and spend that time (too little, really) exploring one of the western Highland's most fascinating islands.

Day 5: Transfer to Lewis in the Outer Hebrides and overnight at its capital, Stornoway.

Day 6: Continue south to Harris (there's a road connection) for a look at this island, famed for its tweeds. Overnight in its main village, Tarbert.

---

1. DORNIE

212 miles NW of Edinburgh, 63 miles SW of Inverness, 8 miles E of Kyle of Lochalsh

GETTING THERE By Train The nearest rail station is at the Kyle of Lochalsh (see below), within a 15-minute drive away. Most trains to Kyle require a change at

Inverness from whatever their origin happens to have been (Glasgow or Edinburgh, for example).

By Bus   A bus originating on the Isle of Skye travels from there to either Inverness or Fort William, and then eventually to Glasgow. There are two to four of these buses every day, depending on the season, and they stop in Dornie along the way. They are run by Citylink/National Express. Phone 0463/233371 in Inverness for schedules.

By Car   From Invergarry, head northwest along the A87 to the Kyle of Lochalsh.

ESSENTIALS   The nearest tourist office is in the Kyle of Lochalsh (see below). The **telephone area code** is 059985.

This small crofting village on the road to the Isle of Skye is the meeting place of three lochs—Duich, Long, and Alsh. On a rocky islet stands Eilean Donan Castle at Dornie, 8 miles east of the Kyle of Lochalsh on the A87.

WHAT TO SEE & DO

South of Dornie and Eilean Donan Castle is Shiel Bridge. From here, an "unclassified road" leads to **Glenelg,** after a twisting climb over Ratagan Pass with a fine view of the mountain range known as the **Five Sisters of Kintail,** which is dominated by Sgurr Fhuaran, 3,505 feet high. In summer a car-ferry crosses the Sound of Sleat to Skye. It was from Glenelg that Dr. Johnson and James Boswell crossed to Skye in 1773. In Gleann Beag, 2 miles to the southeast, stand two of the best-preserved Iron Age brochs on the Scottish mainland—**Dun Telve** and **Dun Troddan.** Brochs are stone towers with double walls, probably built more than 2,000 years ago by the Picts for protection against raiders. The walls of the two brochs are more than 30 feet high.

EILEAN DONAN CASTLE, Dornie. Tel. 059985/202.

This romantic castle, 8 miles east of the Kyle of Lochalsh on A87, was built in 1220 as a defense against the Danes. In 1719 it was shelled by the British frigate *Worcester.* In ruins for 200 years, it was restored by Colonel MacRae of Clan MacRae in 1932 and is now a clan war memorial and museum, containing Jacobite relics, mostly with clan connections. There is a shop that sells kilts, woolens, and souvenirs. You can arrange to have your selections mailed home.

   Admission: £1 ($1.50) adults, 50p (80¢) children.
   Open: Apr–Sept, daily 10am–12:30pm and 2–6pm. **Closed:** Oct–Mar.

WHERE TO STAY & DINE

LOCH DUICH HOTEL, Ardelve, Dornie, near Kyle of Lochalsh, Ross-shire IV40 8DY. Tel. 059985/213. Fax 059985/214. 18 rms (5 with shower).
$ Rates (including Scottish breakfast): £22–£26.50 ($33–$39.80) single; £44–£53 ($66–$79.50) double. MC, V. **Parking:** Free.
Just outside Dornie, about a quarter mile west of the center, close to the town's only bridge and near the confluence of Loch Duich and Loch Long, this hotel overlooks one of the Highland's most photogenic castles, Eilean Donan. The hotel was originally built as a private home late in the 19th century, and today its white-painted stone walls contain comfortable and simply decorated bedrooms.

   On the premises is a small lounge and bar where you can wait for dinner, which will cost £17 ($25.50). It's likely to be a magnificent meal of fresh chowder or pâté, followed by venison or fresh local fish.

---

2. THE KYLE OF LOCHALSH

204 miles NW of Edinburgh, 82 miles SW of Inverness, 125 miles N of Oban

GETTING THERE   By Train   Four trains per day (two on Sunday) arrive from Inverness daily, taking 2½ hours.

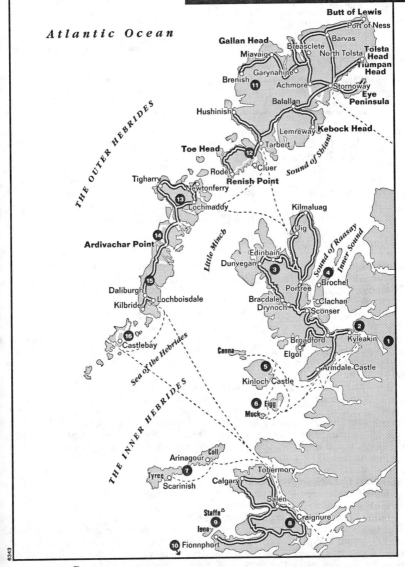

THE HEBRIDEAN ISLANDS

0 ——— 50 km
——— 31.25 mi

Atlantic Ocean

Butt of Lewis
Port of Ness
Gallan Head
Barvas
Breasclete
Tolsta
Miavaig
North Tolsta
Head
Garynahine
Stornoway
Tiumpan
Head
Brenish
11
Achmore
Balallan
Eye
Peninsula

THE OUTER HEBRIDES

Hushinish
Lemreway
Kebock Head
Toe Head
12
Tarbert
Rodel
Cluer
Sound of Shiant
Tigharry
Renish Point
Newtonferry
13
Kilmaluag
Lochmaddy
Uig
Sound of Raasay
Ardivachar Point
14
Edinbain
Dunvegan
3
Inner Sound
Portree
4
Brochel
Daliburgh
15
Bracadale
Clachan
Kilbride
Lochboisdale
Drynoch
Sconser
Little Minch

16
Broadford
Castlebay
2
Kyleakin
Canna
Elgol
1
Sea of the Hebrides
5
Armdale Castle
Kinloch Castle
THE INNER HEBRIDES
6 Eigg
Muck

Coll
Arinagour
Tobermory
Tyree
7
Calgary
Scarinish
Salen
Staffa
9
Craignure
Iona
8
10 Fionnphort

SCOTLAND

Glasgow ☆

1 Dornie	**9** Iona & Staffa
2 Kyle of Lochalsh	**10** Isle of Colonsay
3 Isle of Skye	**11** Lewis
4 Isle of Raasay	**12** Harris
5 Rhum	**13** North Uist
6 Eigg & Muck	**14** Benbecula
7 Coll & Tyree	**15** South Uist
8 Mull	**16** Barra

6343

By Bus   Both Scottish Citylink and Skye-Ways coaches arrive daily from Glasgow to the Kyle of Lochalsh (trip time: 5 hours). Skye-Ways also operates two buses a day from Inverness (trip time: 2 hours).

By Car   From Fort William, head north along the A82 to Invergarry, where you cut west onto the A87 to the Kyle of Lochalsh.

ESSENTIALS   A summer-only **tourist information center** is at the Kyle of Lochalsh Car Park (tel. 0599/4276). The **telephone area code** is 0599.

This popular center is a good jumping-off point to the islands. A car-ferry leaves for Kyleakin on the Isle of Skye (see below). There is no need to book in advance—the journey is only 10 minutes. The ferry shuttles back and forth all day, and you will have plenty of time to drive the length of Skye in a day, returning to the mainland by night if you want to. Plans have been approved for a bridge linking mainland Scotland to the Isle of Skye, but that may take some time.

WHERE TO STAY & DINE

Lodgings are limited, just barely adequate to meet the demand for rooms.

LOCHALSH HOTEL, Ferry Road, Kyle of Lochalsh, Ross-shire IV40 8AF. Tel. 0599/4202. Fax 0599/4881. 38 rms (all with bath). TV TEL
$ Rates (including Scottish breakfast): £67–£80 ($100.50–$120) single; £87–£110 ($130.50–$165) double. AE, DC, MC, V. **Parking:** Free.
There's no way a visitor can talk about the Kyle of Lochalsh without mentioning this landmark hotel. It was built as a luxury oasis when the British Railway finally extended its tracks in this direction. During World War II it served as the headquarters of a branch of the Royal Navy, which had mined the coastline. Today, in memory of that period, a large (defused) mine sits near the flagpole on the seaside lawn. The south shore of the Isle of Skye and the rock-studded inlet are visible through crafted, small-paned windows, whose full-grain hardwood and brass fittings are similar to those on an oceangoing yacht. The bedrooms have been stylishly overhauled. Evening meals begin at £21.50 ($32.30) and include the best of Scottish cuisine and ingredients. The ground-floor bar stocks a variety of malt whiskies, and the dining room has a panoramic view. On a hillside above the hotel, the Ferry Boat Inn, run by the hotel, is one of the most popular pubs in the area, attracting locals as well as visitors.

HOTEL KYLE, Main Street, Kyle of Lochalsh, Ross-shire IV40 8AB. Tel. 0599/4204. Fax 0599/4932. 32 rms (all with bath). TV TEL
$ Rates (including Scottish breakfast): £25–£37 ($37.50–$55.50) single; £50–£70 ($75–$105) double. MC, V. **Parking:** Free.
This modernized stone hotel in the center of town, a 5-minute walk from the train station, is your best all-around bet in the moderate category. Bedrooms are furnished in a functional modern style, with shaver points and tea makers. The hotel serves reasonably priced dinners in the lounge nightly from 6 to 9:30pm.

AN EXCURSION TO BALMACARA

Those planning to stay in the Kyle of Lochalsh district, taking the car and passenger ferry to Skye, may prefer a more peaceful oasis for a day or two.

WHERE TO STAY & DINE

BALMACARA HOTEL, Balmacara, Ross-shire IV40 8DH. Tel. 059986/ 283. Fax 059986/329. 30 rms (all with bath). TV TEL

$ Rates (including Scottish breakfast): £38 ($57) single; £57.50–£62.75 ($86.30–$94.10) double. AE, DC, MC, V. **Parking:** Free.

Balmacara lies 3 miles east of the Kyle of Lochalsh along the A87. Its windows present a panoramic waterside view of Loch Alsh and forests and the island of Skye. Comfortable bedrooms have a contemporary design. Most guests congregate in the TV lounge or cocktail bar just before being served a tasty dinner. A fixed-price evening meal runs £16.50 ($24.80), while a lighter lunch averages around £5 ($7.50).

THE INNER HEBRIDES

The chain of Inner Hebridean islands lies just off the west coast of the Scottish mainland. The Isle of Skye is the largest of the Inner Hebrides. Mull has wild scenery, golf courses, and is a treasure-trove of tradition. Adventurous readers will also seek out Coll and Tyree as well as the Isle of Colonsay and Rhum, Eigg, or the tiny island of Raasay, off the Isle of Skye.

3. THE ISLE OF SKYE

83 miles W of Inverness, 176 miles NW of Edinburgh,
146 miles NW of Glasgow

GETTING THERE By Ferry and Car Ferry service from the Kyle of Lochalsh is available 24 hours a day. From Skye, take ferry service back to Kyle or to Mallaig from Armadale. The Armadale ferry transports cars, but the service is less frequent than the one to Kyle. If you're planning to take your car, reservations are recommended. The ferry crossing is only 5 minutes from the Kyle of Lochalsh or 30 minutes between Mallaig and Armadale. For ferry information, call Caledonian MacBrayne (tel. 0599/4482 in the Kyle of Lochalsh or 047/14248 in Armadale for Mallaig). Passengers go free on the ferry to Kyleakin from the Kyle of Lochalsh, although an average car is transported for £4.75 ($7.10). Passengers between Armadale and Mallaig pay £2 ($3), with cars transported for £10 ($15).

ESSENTIALS There's a **tourist information center** at Mealle House in Portree (tel. 0478/2137). The **telephone area code** for Portree is 0478.

Located off the northwest coast of Scotland, the mystical Isle of Skye, largest of the Inner Hebrides, is 48 miles long and between 3 and 25 miles wide. It is separated from the mainland by the Sound of Sleat (pronounced "Slate"). At Kyleakin, on the eastern end, the channel is only a quarter of a mile wide. The ferry docks there.

Dominating the land of summer seas, streams, woodland glens, mountain passes, cliffs, and waterfalls are the Cuillin Hills, a range of jagged black mountains. The Peninsula of Sleat, the island's southernmost arm, is known as "The Garden of Skye." There are many stories as to the origin of the name Skye. Some believe it is from the Norse *ski,* meaning a cloud, while others say it is from the Gaelic word for winged. There are Norse names on the island, however, as the Norsemen held sway for four centuries before 1263. Overlooking the Kyle is the ruined Castle Moal, once the home of a Norwegian princess.

The island has inspired many of the best-loved and best-known of Scottish ballads such as "Over the Sea to Skye" and "Will Ye Not Come Back Again." On the island you can explore castle ruins, duns, and brochs, enjoying a Highland welcome. For the Scots, the island will forever evoke images of Flora MacDonald, who conducted the disguised Bonnie Prince Charlie to Skye after the Culloden defeat.

KYLEAKIN

The ferry from the Kyle of Lochalsh docks at this tiny waterfront village. There are a few quiet, well-kept places to stay.

WHERE TO STAY

DUNRINGELL HOTEL, Kyleakin, Isle of Skye, Inverness-shire IV41 8PR. Tel. 0599/4180. 17 rms (10 with bath).
$ Rates (including Scottish breakfast): £15–£18 ($22.50–$27) single without bath; £30 ($45) double without bath, £40–£46 ($60–$69) double with bath. No credit cards. **Parking:** Free.

This hotel three-quarters of a mile from the ferry terminal sits in 4½ acres of extensive lawns in which rhododendrons, azaleas, and other flowering shrubs provide a riot of color from March to July. Dunringell is a spacious structure, built in 1912. Both smoking and no-smoking lounges are maintained for guests. Many of the well-furnished bedrooms open onto scenic views. For those who wish to participate, the proprietors, Mr. and Mrs. MacPherson, hold a short worship service in one of the lounges each evening. Dinner costs an additional £10 ($15).

WHITE HEATHER HOTEL, Kyleakin, Isle of Skye, Inverness-shire IV41 8PL. Tel. 0599/4577. 20 rms (4 with bath or shower).
$ Rates (including Scottish breakfast): £20 ($30) single; £38 ($57) double. MC, V. **Parking:** Free. **Closed:** Dec–Feb.

This licensed hotel with up-to-date amenities consists of three interconnected buildings. Bedrooms are simply but comfortably furnished, with tea makers. From its lounges you can enjoy a view of Castle Moil. The hotel sits close to the edge of the road, near ferryboat and bus terminals.

SLIGACHAN

This village sits at the head of a sea loch in a setting of scenic beauty, that opens onto views of the Cuillin Hills. It is one of the best centers for exploring Skye because of its central location. Visitors enjoy sea-trout fishing (with an occasional salmon caught) on the Sligachan River. It's also possible to rent a boat from the hotel below to explore the Storr Lochs, 15 miles from Sligachan and known for their good brown-trout fishing from May until September.

WHERE TO STAY & DINE

SLIGACHAN HOTEL, Sligachan, Isle of Skye, Inverness-shire IV47 8SW. Tel. 0478/650204. Fax 0478/650204. 19 rms (all with bath).
$ Rates (including Scottish breakfast): £25–£30 ($37.50–$45) single; £50–£60 ($75–$90) double. MC, V. **Parking:** Free.

The Sligachan Hotel nestles at the foot of the Cuillin Mountains on the main road between Portree and Kyleakin, and is an ideal touring center from which to explore Skye. This family-run hotel is one of Skye's oldest coaching inns, built sometime in the 19th century. The cuisine consists of such local fare as venison, lamb, salmon, oysters, and vegetarian dishes, and a three-course dinner goes for £18 ($27). The open fires and fine selection of malt whiskies will warm the cockles of your heart.

PORTREE

Skye's capital, Portree, is the port for steamers making trips around the island and linking Skye with the 15-mile-long island of Raasay. Sligachan, 9 miles south, and Glenbrittle, 7 miles farther southwest, are centers for climbing the Cuillin (Coolin) Hills.

WHERE TO STAY & DINE

ROYAL HOTEL, Bank St., Portree, Isle of Skye, Inverness-shire IV51 9LU. Tel. 0478/612525. Fax 0478/613198. 25 rms (all with bath). TV TEL
$ Rates (including Scottish breakfast): £38–£40 ($57–$60) single; £70–£84 ($105–$126) double. MC, V. **Parking:** Free.

The Royal Hotel stands on a hill facing the water and is said to have extended hospitality to Bonnie Prince Charlie during his flight in 1746. In less dramatic and rushed circumstances, you can book one of its comfortable bedrooms; the preferred ones open onto the sea. All the accommodations have tea and coffee makers, and central heating. À la carte meals and bar snacks are offered; a dinner in the restaurant averages £15 ($22.50).

ROSEDALE HOTEL, Beaumont Crescent, Portree, Isle of Skye, Inverness-shire IV51 9DB. Tel. 0478/613131. Fax 0478/612531. 23 rms (all with bath). TV TEL

$ Rates (including Scottish breakfast): £33–£37 ($49.50–$55.50) single; £66–£74 ($99–$111) double. MC, V. **Parking:** Free. **Closed:** Oct to mid-May.

In one of the more secluded parts of Portree, on the harbor 100 yards from the village square, the Rosedale opens directly onto the sea. It was created from a row of fishermen's dwellings dating from the reign of William IV. Bedrooms in this warm and welcoming place are decorated in modern style and all have radios and other amenities. In a lounge, you can be served a good range of Highland malt whiskies. The food is good too, a five-course dinner costing £18.50 ($27.80).

UIG

This village is on Trotternish, the largest Skye peninsula, ferry port for Harris and Uist in the Outer Hebrides. It's 15 miles north of Portree and 49 miles from the Kyle of Lochalsh. **Monkstadt House,** 1½ miles north, is where Flora MacDonald brought Prince Charles after their escape flight from Benbecula. In **Kilmuir** churchyard, 5 miles north, Flora was buried, wrapped in a sheet used by the prince. Her grave is marked by a Celtic cross.

WHERE TO STAY

FERRY INN, Uig, Isle of Skye, Inverness-shire IV51 9XP. Tel. 047042/ 242. 6 rms (all with bath). TV.

$ Rates (including Scottish breakfast): £26–£30 ($39–$45) single; £52–£60 ($78–$90) double. MC, V. **Parking:** Free.

The main energies of this establishment are focused on its popular pub, which is probably the busier of the hamlet's two watering holes. John and Betty Campbell maintain the building, which was originally constructed late in the 19th century as a bank; later, it served as the post office. Today, there are a handful of cozy and pleasantly furnished bedrooms upstairs. You'll recognize this place in the town center by its roadside design of late-Victorian gables. There's a modern TV lounge on the premises. In summer, full three-course dinners are served in the dining room for £14 ($21). In winter, lunches and dinners are served less expensively in the pub, and cost £5 ($7.50) to £8 ($12) each.

DUNVEGAN

The village of Dunvegan, northwest of Portree, grew up around ✪ **Dunvegan Castle** (tel. 047022/206), the principal sight on the Isle of Skye, seat of the chiefs of Clan MacLeod who have lived there for 750 years. The castle, which stands on a rocky promontory, was once accessible only by boat, but now the moat is bridged and the castle open to the public. It holds many fascinating relics, including a "fairy flag." It is reputed to be the oldest inhabited castle in Britain. It is open from Easter through the end of September, Monday to Saturday from 10am to 5pm and from 2 to 5pm during October. The castle is also open on Sunday during this period from 1 to 5pm. Admission to the castle is £3.80 ($5.70) for adults, £2.10 ($3.20) for children. The entry fee to the gardens only is £2.20 ($3.30) for adults, £1.40 ($2.10) for children.

Boats leave the castle jetty at frequent intervals every day from May through the end of September going to the **Seal Colony.** The seals in Loch Dunvegan, both brown and gray varieties, aren't bothered by the approach of people in boats and can be studied at close range. The 20-minute round-trip costs £3.20 ($4.80) for adults, £2.20 ($3.30) for children.

At **Trumpan,** 9 miles north of Dunvegan, are the remains of a church that was set afire in 1597 by MacDonald raiders while the congregation, all MacLeods, were inside at worship. Only one woman survived. The MacLeods of Dunvegan rushed to the defense, and only two MacDonalds escaped death.

WHERE TO STAY

ATHOLL HOUSE HOTEL, Dunvegan, Isle of Skye, Inverness-shire IV55 8WA. Tel. 047022/219. 9 rms (6 with bath).
$ **Rates** (including Scottish breakfast): £20 ($30) single; £40 ($60) double. MC, V. **Parking:** Free. **Closed:** Oct–Mar.

This hotel stands right in the village of Dunvegan, opposite the post office and near Dunvegan Castle. Built in 1908 as a private home, it was converted to a guest house in 1923. Well-furnished units contain facilities for making hot beverages. In the dining room, emphasis is placed on friendly service and well-prepared local produce, including lamb, venison, salmon, and shellfish (in season). A three-course dinner costs £15 ($22.50). It has a residents-only license. From the hotel, you have views over mountain moorland and Loch Dunvegan.

WHERE TO DINE

THREE CHIMNEYS RESTAURANT, Colbost. Tel. 047081/258.
Cuisine: SCOTTISH. **Reservations:** Essential at dinner, recommended at lunch.
$ **Prices:** Appetizers £2.50–£10 ($3.80–$15) at lunch, main courses £5–£20 ($7.50–$30) at lunch; fixed-price dinner £25–£30 ($37.50–$45). MC, V.
Open: Lunch Mon–Sat noon–2pm (last order); dinner Mon–Sat 7–9pm (last order). **Closed:** Nov–Feb.

Winner of several culinary awards, including one in 1990 that dubbed it the best restaurant in Scotland, the Three Chimneys is in a stone crofter's house that replaced an earlier thatch-roofed building around 1900. Two of the establishment's three chimneys funnel smoke from a pair of blazing fireplaces during cold and foggy weather.

Cuisine is prepared by Edinburgh-born Shirley Speare and served by her London-born husband, Edward. Specialties include fresh seafood and shellfish, and Highland game dishes. Examples include traditional dishes as well as such modern cuisine as wild salmon from Skye grilled with strawberries and champagne sauce, or a trio of Highland game (venison, wild hare, and breast of pigeon) served with a sauce of bitter chocolate and raspberries. More than 100 vintages from one of the most complete wine lists on Skye is available to accompany your meal.

The restaurant is 4 miles west of Dunvegan beside the B884.

SKEABOST BRIDGE

Eastward from Dunvegan, Skeabost Bridge has an island cemetery of great antiquity. The graves of four Crusaders are here.

WHERE TO STAY

SKEABOST HOUSE HOTEL, Skeabost Bridge, Isle of Skye, Inverness-shire IV51 9NP. Tel. 047032/202. Fax 047032/451. 26 rms (all with bath). TV TEL
$ **Rates** (including Scottish breakfast): £35–£38 ($52.50–$57) single; £64–£90 ($96–$135) double. MC, V. **Parking:** Free. **Closed:** Mid-Oct to Mar.

This is one of the most inviting country homes of Skye. It is thoroughly modernized and interesting architecturally with its dormers, chimneys, tower, and gables. Once a private estate built in 1870, it has been converted into a lochside hotel, standing on grounds studded with flowering bushes. The location is 35 miles west of the Kyle of Lochalsh and 6 miles north of Portree. Sports people are attracted to the hotel, and the atmosphere is of hardy tweeds. The loch outside is well stocked with salmon and trout, and a short par-three golf course has been constructed. The hotel owns 8 miles on both banks of the River Snizort. A bar buffet lunch goes for £6.50 ($9.80) and a four-course dinner runs £22 ($33). The Scottish fare, featuring smoked salmon, is served on fine china with elegant silver.

THE SLEAT PENINSULA

A lot of Skye can look melancholy and forlorn, especially in misty weather. For a change of landscape, head for the Peninsula of Sleat, the southeastern section of the island. Because of the lushness of its vegetation, it has long been known as the "Garden of Skye." Shores here are washed by the warmer waters of the Gulf Stream.

WHAT TO SEE & DO

A ruined stronghold of the MacDonalds, **Knock Castle** lies off the A851 some 12 miles south of Broadford. It can be visited, admission-free, throughout the day.

Another MacDonald stronghold, **Dunsgiath Castle** has some well-preserved ruins open to view. They are found at Tokavaig on an unclassified road (a sign directs you) at a point 20 miles south and southwest of Broadford.

CLAN DONALD CENTRE, Armadale. Tel. 04714/305.

At Armadale, you don't have to have MacDonald as your last name to enjoy a visit to Skye's award-winning Clan Donald Centre, with its historical exhibition, "The Headship of the Gael," woodland gardens, restaurant, and gift shop. From Broadford, travel along a winding seaside road to the recently restored and well-kept grounds surrounding the sculptured ruins of Armadale Castle and the rebuilt baronial stables. The multimedia exhibition is in part of the castle and tells of the lost culture of the ancient Gaelic world under the MacDonalds as lords of the Isles.

There is a countryside ranger service with a full summer program of guided walks and talks to introduce you to several miles of trails and the history and workings of the adjacent Highland estate. There is also a program of evening arts and theater events. The licensed restaurant in the stables offers home-baking and good local food, from teas and coffees to a full meal.

The drive from the ferryboat at Kyleakin is about 30 minutes, and the center is along the A851 (follow the signs) near the Armadale–Mallaig ferry.

Admission: £3 ($4.50) adults, £2 ($3) children.
Open: Apr–Oct, daily 9:30am–5:30pm.

WHERE TO STAY & DINE

FIORDHEM, Ord, Sleat, Isle of Skye, Inverness-shire IV44 8RN. Tel. 04715/226. 4 rms (3 with bath). Directions: See below.
$ **Rates** (including half board): £30–£34 ($45–$51) per person. No credit cards. **Parking:** Free. **Closed:** Mid-Oct to mid-March.
Some kind of stone-sided house has stood in this spot for hundreds of years. The present version is a rebuilt fisherman's cottage, enlarged in 1990, within 20 feet of the edge of Loch Eishort. Bedrooms are on the upper floor, with striking panoramic views of the Cuillin Mountains and the islands of Canna and Rhum. It's a place to stop and linger a bit, and booking must be for a minimum of three nights. Fresh fish and seafood, along with lamb and venison, are featured on the menu. The dining room is pleasantly furnished with antiques, and the welcome is warm and hearty. In the sitting room are comfortable armchairs, gleaming copper and brass, and an open fireplace for peat and log fires.

To find the place, take the A852 south along the eastern coast of Skye, but cut west along an unclassified road signposted Ord to the west coast of the island.

KINLOCH LODGE, Isleornsay, Sleat, Isle of Skye, Inverness-shire IV43 8QY. Tel. 04713/333. Fax 04713/277. 10 rms (all with bath). Directions: Take the A851, 3½ miles north of Sleat.
$ **Rates** (including Scottish breakfast): £25–£75 ($37.50–$112.50) single; £50–£150 ($75–$225) double. MC, V. **Parking:** Free. **Closed:** Mid-Jan to Feb.

★ The white stone walls of this dignified manor house are visible from across the scrub- and pine-covered hillsides bordering the edges of this historic property. When it was built in 1680, it was a hunting lodge for the MacDonald estates. Today, after much rebuilding and expansion, the linden-flanked manor house is the private residence of Lord and Lady MacDonald, who welcome discriminating guests into the confines of their very elegant home. Portraits of the family's 18th-century forebears are a striking feature of the reception rooms, where open fireplaces illuminate the burnished patina of scores of family antiques. Many of the bedrooms have been freshly papered and painted and contain private baths. From the windows of some of the bedrooms, guests sometimes catch glimpses of the sea, which washes up to the edge of the property's sloping gardens.

Every evening guests enjoy drinks in a peach-colored drawing room before consuming one of the well-prepared meals for which Lady MacDonald is justifiably famous. The author of eight bestselling cookbooks, she applies her techniques to imaginative recipes, for which the ingredients are usually shot, trapped, netted, or grown on the Isle of Skye. Dinner costs £30 ($45) and up per person.

ARDVASAR HOTEL, Ardvasar, Isle of Skye, Inverness-shire IV48 8RS. Tel. 04714/223. 10 rms (all with bath). TV

$ Rates (including Scottish breakfast): £31 ($46.50) single; £55–£65 ($82.50–$97.50) double. MC, V. **Parking:** Free. **Closed:** Jan–Feb.

★ This 250-year-old coaching inn has as its oldest part a stone-trimmed pub in what was originally a stable. Today virtually every off-duty resident in the area heads here for a mug of lager and perhaps a taste of the cuisine prepared by Bill Fowler, the owner and chef, and his wife, Greta. Fixed-price evening meals are offered for £17 ($25.50) and up, and might include flavorful preparations of very fresh local fish as well as homemade pâté with tomato vinaigrette, fresh halibut with hollandaise, or Scottish sirloin steak with local prawns and Drambuie. Dessert might consist of a chocolate rum pot with cream. Bar meals at lunch and suppertime begin at £6 ($9) each.

In 1990 a major renovation added private baths to each of the bedrooms, and a "cottage cozy" decor that includes pastel colors, flowered chintz, and pinewood furniture. Guests are free to congregate in their own residents' lounge, which contains separate sections for TV watching and reading, and a fireplace.

4. RHUM (RUM)

9 miles SW of Isle of Skye

GETTING THERE By Ferry To reach Rhum, you can take a passenger ferry from Mallaig, on the western coast of Scotland. It leaves about four times a week, and no cars are allowed on the island.

For information about departures, call **Caledonian MacBrayne** (tel. 0687/2403 in Mallaig). Sailings are only from May through September on Monday and Wednesday at 11am, on Friday at 5am, and on Saturday at 5am and 12:30pm. A round-trip costs £10.50 ($15.80). **Murdo Grant** (tel. 06875/224) sails to Rhum on Tuesday and Thursday at 11am from Arisaig. A round-trip costs £15.50 ($23.30). Schedules can vary, so it's best to call for confirmations. It takes about 3 hours to reach Rhum from one of these ports.

This enticingly named island is only about 8 miles wide and 8 miles long. There are those who will tell you not to go. "If you like a barren desert, where it rains all the time, you'll love Rhum," a skipper in Mallaig recently told me. It's stark all right. And very wet. In fact, with more than 90 inches of rainfall recorded annually, it is said to be the "wettest" island of the Inner Hebrides.

Since the mid-1950s Rhum has been owned by the Edinburgh-based Nature Conservancy Council, an ecological conservation group. Conservation is of paramount importance on the island, and attempts are being made to bring back the sea eagle, which used to inhabit the island in Victoria's day.

On this storm-tossed outpost in summer, mountain climbers meet challenging peaks, and anglers are attracted to its good trout fishing. Bird lovers seek out the Manx shearwaters which live on the island in great numbers. Red deer and ponies add color, along with the wildflowers of summer, to an otherwise bleak landscape.

WHERE TO STAY & DINE

KINLOCH CASTLE, Kinloch, Isle of Rhum, Inverness-shire PH43 4RR. Tel. 0687/2037. 9 rms, 30 hostel beds (none with bath).
$ Rates: Castle (including half board), £92 ($138) single, £144 ($216) double. Hostel (with no meals included), £8.50 ($12.80) per person, in accommodations containing between 2 and 5 beds each. No credit cards.

Quite astonishingly in such a forbidding place, you come upon a hotel that has been called "Britain's most intact example of an Edwardian Country House." On the seafront in the center of Rhum's biggest hamlet, Kinloch, its very inaccessibility may have kept this mansion of imposing stature and grandeur unchanged over the years. It was completed in 1901 for Sir George Boullough, a wealthy Lancashire textile magnate, and decorated under the direction of his wife, Lady Monica (both are buried in the family mausoleum on the island's west coast.) The castle still contains their ballroom, with its gold curtains and upholstery, a massive inglenook, Adam-style fireplace, and the monumental paintings and stuffed animals that were *de rigueur* in such mansions when Kinloch Castle was in its heyday.

The showplace rooms are in the front of the building, and although the original plans have not been altered, the shared bathrooms are spacious, with elaborate lavatories that still flush as well as they did when they were installed 80 years ago. The former servants' quarters are now a simple and uncomplicated hostel.

Because residents almost always spend the days tramping or trekking around the island, all lunches are packed picnics, priced at £4 ($6) per person. Occupants of the showplace rooms dine dinner-party style, promptly at 7pm, around a dining table. The food is good, and in season you are likely to be served Scottish salmon and venison. Hostel residents eat at night in the Bistro for £5 ($7.50) to £10 ($15) for a full meal.

---

5. EIGG & MUCK

Eigg: 4 miles SE of Rhum; Muck: 7 miles SW of Eigg

GETTING THERE   By Ferry   Caledonian MacBrayne ferries (tel. 0687/2403) go from Mallaig to Eigg. Sailings are on Monday and Wednesday at 11am, on Friday at 5am, and on Saturday at 5am and 12:30pm. Only Wednesday and Saturday sailings stop at Muck. From Airsaig, another ferry line, **Murdo Grant** (tel. 06875/224), sails to Muck on Monday, Wednesday, and Friday (but departure days and times can vary, so always call first). Sailings to Eigg are on Friday and Saturday and Monday through Wednesday. Most departures are at either 11 or 11:30am (subject to change, based on weather conditions).

ESSENTIALS   For details about a possible holiday on the island of Eigg, phone the estate office at Eigg (tel. 0687/82413) or on mainland Scotland (tel. 06513/2367).

The tiny islands of Eigg and Muck lie in the Sea of the Hebrides, which separates the Inner from the Outer Hebrides.

EIGG

Eigg, about 4½ miles by 3 miles in size, lies some 12 miles out in the Atlantic. The laird of the island purchased Eigg in 1975 at a reported cost of half a million dollars.

He is Keith Schellenberg, who drives vintage Bentleys, owns powerboats, and is known as a rugged rugby football player. He was formerly the captain of the British Olympic bobsled team. A dedicated conservationist, he doesn't allow blood sports on Eigg, except for some fishing. Visitors are welcome here to see the Sgurr of Eigg, a tall column of lava, said to be the biggest such pitchstone mass in the United Kingdom. Climbers on its north side try to reach its impressive height of 1,300 feet. It is said that the last of the pterodactyls roosted there. The bones of this towering, bat-winged and beaked flying dinosaur were discovered, or so it is reported, by St. Donnan, a Christian missionary, in the 7th century.

After your arrival at Galmisdale, the principal hamlet and pier, you can take an antique omnibus to Cleadale. Once there, you walk across moors to Camas Sgiotaig, with its well-known beach of the Singing Sands (its black and white quartz grains are decidedly off-key).

MUCK

Lying 7 miles to the southwest of Eigg, **Muck** has such an unappetizing name that visitors may turn away. However, the name of this little 2½-square-mile island is based on a Gaelic word, *muic,* meaning the "island of the sow." Naturalists come here looking for everything from rare butterflies to otters. The large colonies of nesting seabirds in May and June should be viewed.

Often storm-tossed by the ocean, Muck is actually a farm. There are hardly more than two dozen people on Muck, and all are concerned with the running of the farm. Visitors are welcome.

The entire island is owned by two brothers, including the Laird of Muck, Lawrence MacEwan, and his younger brother, Ewen MacEwan. There are no vehicles on the island, except for bicycles and tractors.

WHERE TO STAY & DINE

PORT MHOR HOUSE, Port Mhor, Isle of Muck, Inverness-shire PH42 4RP. Tel. 0687/2365. 8 rms (none with bath).
$ Rates (including half board): £27 ($40.50) single; £54 ($81) double. No credit cards. **Closed:** Oct–Mar.
Heavily accented with varnished planks of Scots pine, this solidly weatherproof hotel was personally built by Ewen MacEwan. Its construction required 5 years (1975–1980), and most of its building materials were barged in from the mainland. Almost everyone checks in here on the half-board plan. For daytime visitors to the island, a fixed-price evening meal is offered for £12 ($18). Residents can get a drink in the cocktail lounge, and during cold weather there's likely to be a log fire blazing. The kitchen uses produce from the island's farm for plain and wholesome fare well suited to the brisk climate. Bedrooms are functional, clean, and comfortable, with lots of pinewood trim. The hostelry is only a few steps from the island's only ferryboat landing.

6. COLL & TYREE

90 miles NW of Glasgow; 48 miles W of Fort William

GETTING THERE By Plane Loganair (tel. 041/8871111 in Glasgow for flight information) also flies directly to Tyree from Glasgow, with about six scheduled flights weekly (none on Sunday).

By Ferry and Car The car-ferry sails from Oban to Mull and then, if conditions are right, goes on to Coll and Tyree, although sometimes gales may force you to cancel the trip. You can be stranded on an island for a while, waiting for the next departure. Details and bookings, essential for cars, are available from **Caledonian MacBrayne,** Ferry Terminal (tel. 0631/62285) at Oban.

If you like your scenery stark and tranquil, try Coll and Tyree, tiny islands that attract visitors seeking remoteness. Coll and Tyree are very much sibling islands, exposed to the open Atlantic. The outermost of the Inner Hebrides, they are said to have the highest sunshine records in Britain. On Tyree (also spelled Tiree), the shell-sand machair increases the arable area, differentiating it from the other inner isles.

Trees are rare on either island, but that doesn't mean that they're bleak. Both are rich in flora, with some 500 species, along with a fascinating bird life. It is estimated that some 150 species are found here, including Arctic skuas and razorbills. Both common and gray seals have breeding colonies on the islands.

If that sun does come out in midsummer, you'll find silver beaches. Boat rentals and sea angling can be arranged on both Coll and Tyree. Many visitors bicycle around the island, and there are a few cars for rent. Tyree has the least expensive method of transport: A mail bus serves most of the island.

Both islands have accommodations, but there are no officially designated campsites. Campers must ask a local farmer for permission, and it's usually granted.

COLL

Lying in the seemingly timeless world of the Celtic west, the little island of Coll, with a population of some 130 hearty souls, is rich in history, even prehistory. Distances from one place to another are short on Coll, as the island averages about 3 miles in breadth; at its longest point, it stretches for some 13 miles.

WHAT TO SEE & DO

Coll has a restored castle, **Breacachadh,** from the Middle Ages. In the 15th century this was a stronghold of the Macleans. This is a private residence but also a center for Project Trust, which prepares young people for voluntary service overseas. On some occasions it is open to the public.

The so-called **New Castle,** ordered built for Hector Maclean in 1750, provided shelter for Samuel Johnson and James Boswell when they were stranded on the island for 10 days because of storms at sea. The castle was altered considerably by the Stewart family, who in the mid-19th century added many embellishments, including pepperpot turrets and parapets.

In the western part of the island at Totronald are two standing stones called **Na Sgeulachan** ("the teller of tales"). The stones predate the Druids and are thought to have been the site of a temple. Another idea is that they may have been an astronomical laboratory, recording the movements of the sun and moon.

The highest point on Coll is **Ben Hogh,** which many hearty visitors climb (340 feet) for a panoramic view. The boulder on the hill, supported by smaller stones, is believed to have been left that way from the Ice Age.

On the road to Sorisdale, at **Killunaig,** stand the ruins of a church from the late Middle Ages and a burial ground. Going on to **Sorisdale,** you'll see the ruins of several houses occupied by crofters earlier in this century. Hundreds of families once lived here. Some were chased away in the wake of the potato famine, and many crofters were forced out in Land Clearance programs. Enduring great hardships at sea, including disease, they went to Canada, Australia, the United States, and New Zealand.

WHERE TO STAY & DINE

ISLE OF COLL HOTEL, Arinagour, Isle of Coll, Argyll PA78 6SZ. Tel. 08793/334. 6 rms (3 with bath). MINIBAR TV
$ Rates (including Scottish breakfast): £20 ($30) single without bath, £25 ($37.50) single with bath; £40 ($60) double without bath, £50 ($75) double with bath. DC, MC, V. **Parking:** Free.
Originally built in the early 1700s of local stone, it enjoys the dubious honor of being immediately rejected by Samuel Johnson and James Boswell as an appropriate place to spend the night during their 18th-century tour of Scotland. (They eventually succeeded in securing accommodations with the Laird of Coll instead.) Today the

establishment's rooms are far more comfortable, with wood sheathing in at least four of them, electric blankets, tea-making facilities, and simple but functional furniture. A good dinner will cost £15 ($22.50) in the dining room. The hotel contains the town's only pub, so you're likely to meet the locals over a pint of ale and a platter of bar food.

Painted white, the hotel sits on a hilltop at the end of the Arinagour estuary about a 10-minute walk north of town, beside the B8071. Its facilities include a sauna, solarium, and a games room.

TYREE [TIREE]

A fertile island, one of the richest in the Hebrides, flat Tyree earned the Gaelic nickname "the land below the wave-tops." Filled with farming communities, Tyree has a population of some 800 residents who enjoy its gentle landscape, sandy beaches, and rolling hills. At Vaul is a nine-hole golf course open to visitors.

WHAT TO SEE & DO

As you travel about the island, you'll see many Hebridean crofters' houses with thatched roofs, constructed in the early 1800s. The Duke of Argyll in 1886 caused a scandal when he sent in marines and police to clear the crofters off the land. Many were sent destitute to Canada. But crofters once again occupy the land.

Most of the population is centered around **Scarinish,** with its little stone harbor where lobster boats put in. Fishing isn't what it used to be, when the appearance of fast and dangerous squalls and storms are said to scatter the fishing fleet as far as the shores of North America.

Birdwatchers are drawn to the shores of **Loch Bhasapoll,** a favorite gathering place of wild geese and ducks. Another sightseeing target for birdwatchers is a cave on the coast at Kenavara, where many seabirds can be observed. The Reef was an important air base for the Royal Air Force in World War II, and is still in use.

Ancient duns and forts are scattered around Tyree. The best of these is a broch at **Vaul Bay,** which has walls more than 12 feet thick. It is 30 feet in diameter. At **Balephetrish,** on the northern rim of the island, stands a huge granite boulder. Locals call it "The Ringing Stone," because when struck it gives off a metallic sound. In the western part of the island, at **Kilkenneth,** are the ruins of the Chapel of St. Kenneth, a comrade of St. Columba.

WHERE TO STAY & DINE

TIREE LODGE HOTEL, Kirkatol, Isle of Tiree, Argyll PA77 6TW. Tel. 08792/368. 11 rms (7 with bath). TV
$ **Rates** (including Scottish breakfast): £24.50 ($36.80) single without bath, £31.75 ($47.60) single with bath; £42 ($63) double without bath, £47 ($70.50) double with bath. MC, V. **Parking:** Free.

Originally built as a simple island hunting lodge around 1790 for the Duke of Argyll, it was greatly enlarged in the 1970s with a modern addition, and the interior brought severely up-to-date. Today, a mile east of the island's only ferryboat landing, the establishment's big plate-glass windows benefit from the views of the emerald-green fields and the beach surrounding it. The hotel, run by Kenneth and Irene Hutchinson, contains one of the island's two pubs (the other is almost 3 miles away) and as such is sometimes crowded with local residents. Substantial bar meals are available, as well as fixed-price evening meals in the dining room that cost around £11 ($16.50) each. Bedrooms are comfortable, clean, and unpretentious.

7. MULL

121 miles NW of Edinburgh, 90 miles NW of Glasgow

GETTING THERE By Ferry and Car It's a 45-minute car-ferry trip from Oban to Craignure on Mull. For times of departure, contact **Caledonian**

MacBrayne, the ferry terminal (tel. 0631/62285), Oban. It's a roll-on/roll-off operation for your car. From Oban, there are about five or six sailings per day at a cost of £2.40 ($3.60) for a one-way ticket.

GETTING AROUND   By Bus   Take the ferry to get there (see above), then use a local bus service, **Bowman's Coaches** (tel. 06802/313) to get around the island. Coaches connect with the ferry daily at 8am, noon, and 4pm, and will take you to Fionnphort in 80 minutes for £1.60 ($2.40) or to Tobermory in 50 minutes for £1.30 ($2).

ESSENTIALS   The **tourist information center** is on Main Street in Tobermory (tel. 0688/2182). The **telephone area code** for the capital, Tobermory, is 0688.

SPECIAL EVENTS   The **Mull Highland Games** are held annually in July, filled with all the traditional events such as bagpipes, caber tossing, and dancing. The **Tour of Mull Rally** is held in early October of every year. Ask at the tourist office for exact dates.

The third largest island in the Hebrides, Mull is rich in legend and folklore, a land of ghosts, monsters, and the wee folk. Over open fires that burn on cold winter evenings, the talk is of myths and ancient times. The island is wild and mountainous, characterized by sea lochs and sandy bars. If you come to Mull, be sure to bring a raincoat, as it is known as the wettest island in the Hebrides, a fact that upset Dr. Johnson, who visited here in 1773. Actually, Dr. Johnson was a latecomer to Mull, which has an ancient history. It was, in fact, known to the classical Greeks, and its prehistoric past is recalled in forts, duns, and stone circles.

Many visitors consider Mull more beautiful than Skye, a controversy I don't choose to get involved in, as both the islands are different, each with many attractions. However, Mull is made additionally enticing in that it can be used as a launching pad from which to explore the famed islands of Iona and Staffa. Mull has a varied scenery, with many waterfalls. Its highest peak is Ben More at 3,169 feet, but it also has many flat areas. It is rich in wildlife, including roe deer, golden eagles, polecats, seabirds, and feral goats.

Guarding the bay (you'll see it as you cross on the ferry) is Duart Castle, restored just before World War I, once the seat of the fiery Macleans, who shed much blood in and around the castle during their battles with the lords of the Isles. In the bay—somewhere—lies the *Florencia,* a Spanish galleon that went down laden with treasure. Many attempts have been made to bring it up, but so far all have failed.

To the southeast, near Salen, are the ruins of **Aros Castle,** once the stronghold of the MacDonalds, Lords of the Isles. Its ruins date from the 14th century, and it was last occupied in the 17th century. On the far south coast at Lochbuie, **Moy Castle** has a water-filled dungeon.

The wild countryside of Mull was the scene of many of David Balfour's adventures in *Kidnapped* by Robert Louis Stevenson.

If you're driving along any of the single-track roads of Mull, remember to take your time and let the sheep and cattle have the right-of-way. Also, a car coming downhill toward you has preference, so seek a spot to pull off.

There are two nine-hole golf courses on the island. The Western Isles Golf Course at Tobermory, the island's capital, dates from the 1930s and is said to have possibly the best views of any course in the world. A newer course, flat and tight, opened in 1980 at Craignure. Sea fishing and river fishing are also popular on Mull, where anglers seek salmon and three kinds of trout: rainbow, sea, and brown. The trout is found in the fast-flowing rivers and hill lochs of the island. Some sports lovers take to the sea in pursuit of sharks and monster skate. Stalking, hiking, and hill walking are other activities for the fit.

At the end of the day, you might enjoy a dram of malt whisky from the Tobermory Malt Whisky Distillery, which has had a troubled history but is now back in business. Incidentally, visitors are welcome to visit the distillery in Tobermory, established in 1823. Call 0688/2119 for an appointment.

CRAIGNURE
WHAT TO SEE & DO

Even passengers who arrive on Mull with a car might want to take an excursion on the **Mull Railway,** Old Pier Station, Craignure (tel. 06802/494), the only passenger railway in the Hebrides. It was inaugurated in 1983, and its puffing engine and narrow-gauge tracks give the impression of a frontier-style excursion into the past. The tracks begin at the Old Pier in Craignure, running 1½ miles to Torosay Castle and its famous gardens. Some of the engines are powered by steam, others by diesel. The view is one of unspoiled mountains, glens, and seaside; otters, eagles, and deer can sometimes be seen in the course of the 20-minute journey.

Trains operate between late April and mid-October. The most frequent service occurs between June and mid-September, when it begins Monday to Friday at 11:10am and on Saturday and Sunday at 11:15am. Most visitors use the train as an opportunity to spend a few hours to explore Torosay Castle before returning to the Oban ferryboat at Craignure. One-way fares are £1.50 ($2.30) for adults and £1 ($1.50) for children. A special round-trip ticket is available for families of two parents and two children, costing £4 ($6).

For more information, call the **Mull and West Highland Railway Co.** in Craignure (tel. 0680/300389).

TOROSAY CASTLE AND GARDENS, Craignure. Tel. 06802/421.

✪ This Victorian mansion, 1½ miles south of Craignure on the A849, was constructed in the mid-19th century by David Bryce, a famous Scottish architect. In his early years Churchill was a frequent visitor. It is set in gardens designed at the turn of the century and attributed to Sir Robert Lorimer. One writer said that a visit here is like returning to "the Edwardian age of leisure," and so it is. To the surprise of hundreds of visitors, the armchairs are labeled "Please sit down" instead of "Please keep off." This is very much a family place, home to four generations. It is the only privately occupied castle and garden open daily to the public in the western Highlands. The castle has family portraits by such famous artists as Sargent, along with wildlife pictures. It has numerous exhibits to intrigue its visitors, including evidence for the Loch Ness monster. You can wander through 12 acres of Italian-style terraced gardens; a water garden with shrubs that grow in the Gulf Stream climate, and a Japanese garden and life-size figures by Antonio Bonazza. You can enjoy extensive views of the Appin coastline from Ben Nevis to Ben Cruachen.

Admission: £3.50 ($5.30) adults, £2.75 ($4.10) children.
Open: May to mid-Oct, daily 10:30am–5:30pm.

DUART CASTLE, off the A849, on the eastern point of Mull. Tel. 06802/309.

Both Torosay Castle and Duart Castle can ideally be visited on the same day. Located 3 miles west of Torosay, this castle dates from the 13th century and was the home of the Maclean clan. An imposing and majestic structure, it was sacked in 1791 by the dukes of Argyll in retaliation for the Macleans' support of the Stuarts in 1715 and 1745. It was allowed to fall into ruins. However, Sir Fitzroy Maclean, the 26th chief of the clan and grandfather of the present occupant, began restoration in 1911 when he was 76, spending a considerable fortune. It had been his ambition since he was a boy to see his ancestral home restored. He lived until he was 102. Many relics of clan history are found inside. Visitors can wander about, taking in such rooms as the Banqueting Hall, which is in the keep, the great tower that is the heart of the castle.

Admission: £3 ($4.50) adults, £1.50 ($2.30) children under 14.
Open: May–Sept, daily 10:30am–6pm.

WHERE TO STAY & DINE

ISLE OF MULL, Craignure, Isle of Mull, Argyll PA65 6BB. Tel. 06802/ 351. Fax 06802/462. 60 rms (all with bath). TV TEL
$ Rates (including half board): £25 ($37.50) single; £50 ($75) double. MC, V.
Parking: Free. **Closed:** Mid-Oct to mid-Mar.

Opened in 1971, the Isle of Mull stands near the ferry and the meeting point of the Sound of Mull and Loch Linnhe. From the picture windows of its public rooms you'll have panoramic vistas of mountains and the island of Lismore. Each of its bedrooms, all handsomely furnished, comes equipped with tea/coffee makers. The food is good and served in the attractive dining room, which faces both sea and hills. The chef does both British and continental dishes. The sea trout is superb. Hopefully, you'll be there on a night when the specialty is roast haunch of venison with gooseberry sauce. A fixed-price dinner begins at £11.65 ($17.50). Other facilities include a cocktail bar and a resident's lounge.

SALEN

Near Salen are the ruins of **Aros Castle,** once the stronghold of the lords of the Isles, the MacDonalds. It dates from the 14th century, and it was last occupied in the 17th century.

WHERE TO STAY

GLENFORSA HOTEL, By Salen, Aros, Isle of Mull, Argyll PA72 6JN. Tel. 0680/300377. Fax 0680/300535. 16 rms (all with bath).
$ **Rates** (including Scottish breakfast): £29.50 ($44.30) single; £59 ($88.50) double. AE, MC, V. **Parking:** Free.
This Norwegian pine log construction, in secluded grounds by the Sound of Mull and the River Forsa 11 miles southeast of Tobermory, is known in late summer for its seafront and salmon. Rooms are well appointed and spacious. The bar serves an array of tempting pub food, with venison, trout, and salmon offered in season for guests and nonresidents alike. Dinner costs £15 ($22.50). The hotel has a grass airstrip adjacent to which Dakotas and other private and charter planes can land from dawn to dusk. A parking area is alongside.

WHERE TO DINE

PUFFER AGROUND RESTAURANT, Salen. Tel. 0680/300389.
Cuisine: SCOTTISH. **Reservations:** Recommended. **Transportation:** Craignure–Tobermory bus.
$ **Prices:** Appetizers £3.75–£5.90 ($5.60–$8.90); main courses £9.50–£12.95 ($14.30–$19.40); fixed-price dinner £5.90 ($8.90). MC, V.
Open: Lunch Mon–Sat 11am–2:30pm; dinner Mon–Sat 7–9:30pm.
After exploring the ruins of Aros Castle, this is a good luncheon stop. The design of this restaurant is based on the old steamships that used to ply the River Clyde. Exhibitions of marine paintings are presented in summer. This is a licensed table-service restaurant. It provides home-style typically Scottish cookery, and whenever possible fresh Mull produce is used. You get seafood-stuffed crêpes, fish casseroles, salads, and homemade pies. To begin your meal, try the local shellfish soup laced with brandy and cream, and for dessert, the traditional "baked sponge." Next to the restaurant is a craft shop. Both the restaurant and shop are located in a row of country cottages along the roadside.

TOBERMORY
WHAT TO SEE & DO

The **Mull Museum** has local exhibitions relating to the island, displayed in an old bakery building on Main Street, open April through September, Monday to Friday from 10:30am to 4:30pm, charging 50p (80¢) for adults and 10p (20¢) for children.
The **Western Isle Golf Course** dates from the 1930s and is said to have possibly the best views of any golf course in the world.

WHERE TO STAY

The capital of Mull, Tobermory (or Tobar Mhoire, "well of Mary," in Gaelic) is the best equipped in accommodations.

WESTERN ISLES, Tobermory, Isle of Mull, Argyll PA75 6PR. Tel. 0688/ 2012. Fax 0688/2297. 21 rms (all with bath). TV TEL

$ Rates (including Scottish breakfast): £33–£40 ($49.50–$60) single; £40–£65 ($60–$97.50) double. MC, V. **Parking:** Free. **Closed:** Jan and part of Feb.

In a beautiful location above the harbor, the Western Isles is a large gray stone country inn on a bluff above Tobermory. It was constructed by the Sandeman sherry company in the late 1880s as a hunting and fishing lodge for their top-level staff and customers, and was owned for a number of years by the MacBrayne shipping company. The current owners welcome visitors to rooms decorated in a mixture of styles, but they're homelike and spotless, and have electric heaters. You get good meals here, especially fish dishes. A four-course dinner goes for £19 ($28.50).

TOBERMORY HOTEL, 53 Main St., Tobermory, Isle of Mull, Argyll PA75 6NT. Tel. 0688/2091. Fax 0688/2140. 15 rms (7 with bath).

$ Rates (including Scottish breakfast): £25 ($37.50) single without bath, £30 ($45) single with bath; £50 ($75) double without bath, £60 ($90) double with bath. 10% discounts offered Oct–Mar. MC, V. **Parking:** Free on nearby streets.

Originally built around 1900, when a trio of three-story houses were interconnected and covered with a salmon-colored coat of stucco, this hotel on the upper end of the town's main street, a minute's walk from the center, retains a sense of privacy and intimacy. Many of the bedrooms were renovated in 1991, and contain color-coordinated fabrics and comfortable furnishings. Twelve have views of the fishing boats bobbing at anchor in the harbor just across the road; the remaining three have views of the steep and tree-dotted cliff that rises abruptly behind the hotel. There are a number of bathrooms scattered in the hallways upstairs, so several of the bathless rooms offer exclusive use of a particular one to its occupants. A fixed-price dinner in the dining room costs £16 ($24) for three courses.

HARBOUR HOUSE, 59 Main St., Tobermory, Isle of Mull, Argyll PA75 6NT. Tel. 0688/2209. 9 rms (1 with bath).

$ Rates (including Scottish breakfast): £17–£20 ($25.50–$30) per person. MC, V. **Parking:** Free.

Situated on the seafront overlooking Tobermory Bay, the Harbour House is a warm and welcoming family-run guest house. Your hosts are Donald and Lorna MacLean. The bedrooms have tea- and coffee-making facilities, washbasins, shaverpoints, and heaters.

WHERE TO DINE

GANNET'S RESTAURANT, 25 Main St. Tel. 0688/2203.
Cuisine: FRENCH/ITALIAN.
$ Prices: Appetizers £1.15–£3.95 ($1.70–$5.90); main courses £3–£9.50 ($4.50–$14.30). MC, V.
Open: Daily 9am–10pm. **Closed:** Sun Nov–Easter.

This eatery enjoys a quayside setting in one of the stone-fronted 200-year-old buildings along Main Street. It is one of the best of the independent restaurants operating in this port. You get the freshest of seafood, much of it caught locally, along with fresh salads, roast venison, tender and juicy steaks, and some fine vegetable dishes, finished off by creamy desserts. During the day you might stop in for sandwiches and fresh coffee.

DERVAIG

Considered the most charming village of Mull, Dervaig or "The Little Grove" lies an 8-mile drive west from Tobermory. A Maclean built the town in the closing year of the 18th century.

WHAT TO SEE & DO

The **Mull Little Theatre** (tel. 06884/267), founded in 1966, seats 40 viewers which, according to the *Guinness Book of World Records,* makes it the smallest professional theater in Great Britain. The theater group tours during the winter but comes home in summer for the season. See local posters for details of its latest productions.

From Dervaig, you can take cruises to the lonely **Treshnish Isles,** a sanctuary for seabirds and seals. These islands form a group unto themselves, including Fladda (is flatter) and Lunga (is longer), along with the well-named Dutchman's Cap or Bac Mor.

OLD BYRE HERITAGE CENTRE, Dervaig. Tel. 06884/229.

This center houses one of the most charming museums you could hope to find. Although programs are subject to change, the 1993 exhibit covered the history of Mull from the first settlers to the Highland clearances, using scale models, painstakingly made and researched by a local historian. Performances are every 30 minutes.

Admission: £2 ($3) adults, £1 ($1.50) children.

Open: Easter–Oct, daily 10:30am–6:30pm. **Transportation:** Twice-daily bus from Tobermory.

WHERE TO STAY & DINE

DRUIMNACROISH COUNTRY HOUSE HOTEL, Dervaig, Isle of Mull, Argyll PA75 6QW. Tel. 06884/274. Fax 06884/311. 6 rms (all with bath). TV TEL

$ Rates (including Scottish breakfast): £50 ($75) per person. £70 ($105) per person half board. AE, DC, MC, V. **Parking:** Free. **Closed:** Mid-Oct to mid-Apr.

This hotel owes its personality and charm to Wendy and Donald Maclean. Located in Bellart Glen, 1½ miles south of Dervaig, handsomely furnished and well appointed, it now occupies what had once been listed as a "ruin" on an ordnance survey map. As you enter your beautifully furnished room, you'll find a welcoming miniature bottle of Tobermory whisky. At dinner, you get not only produce from the owners' 3-acre garden, but some of the finest lamb, Angus steak, venison, and salmon that Scotland has to offer. Wendy is a superb cook. One reader wrote, "I could cover a page about the gourmet quality of the food so graciously served by Donald."

BUNESSAN

In the center of the Ross of Mull, the southwestern section, you'll come across this hamlet on the way to the Iona ferry.

NEARBY ATTRACTIONS

On the Ross of Mull, as you proceed to the southwestern corner of the island in the direction of the ferry to Iona, you will see a sign pointing south to the little village of Carsaig. The most adventurous may want to go on a 3-mile hike from here to the **Carsaig Arches,** a group of tunnels formed by the sea in the basaltic rock. Along the way you'll pass **Nuns' Cave,** with strange carvings. It is said that sisters chased out of Iona at the time of the Reformation found refuge in this cave.

Another attraction lies opposite the Ross of Mull on the northern rim of Loch Scridain. Called **"The Burg,"** it is only for the stout of foot and heart, or followers of the trail of Dr. Johnson and Boswell. The Burg lies 5 miles west on a track road from the B8035. The trail to it is extremely rough and requires boots. At the extremity of this Ardmeanach Peninsula—an area appropriately called "The Wilderness"—stands a fossil tree, **MacCulloch's Tree,** said to be 50 million years old. Standing 40 feet tall and about 5 feet broad, it was trapped in a flow of lava. The tree is named after the geologist who discovered it in 1819. The tree can be visited only at half tide on a falling tide, or you will find yourself cut off on a turbulent shore.

Other athletes seek out **MacKinnon's Cave,** Dr. Johnson's "greatest natural marvel," which lies north along the coast. You can leave your car at Balmeanach Farm, then walk about a mile to the mouth of the cave across wet slippery boulders and through some murky mud. The cave is deeper than the more famed Fingal's Cave at Staffa. The cave can only be entered when the tide is right, and torches are used to penetrate the blackness.

WHERE TO STAY & DINE

ARDFENAIG HOUSE, Bunessan, Isle of Mull, Argyll PA67 6DX. Tel. 06817/210. Fax 06817/210. 5 rms (all with bath).

$ Rates (including half board): £65–£78 ($97.50–$117) per person. V. **Parking:** Free. **Closed:** Nov–Mar.

For discriminating readers, a stay here can represent a perfect retreat in a cozily proportioned country house, where the thick stone walls and the blazing fireplace ward off any chill mists rising from the nearby Loch Caol. The slate-roofed house was originally built as a Georgian-era farmhouse by the Duke of Argyll as a residence for his chamberlain. In 1875 it was expanded into a hunting lodge. The house is small enough to cater for just nine guests and is the home of ex-merchant banker Malcolm Davidson and his wife Jane. Reservations are strongly recommended. It is the nearest licensed hotel to Iona.

Ardfenaig House is three miles west of Bunessan by the A849 and 2 miles from the Iona ferry, just off the main road from Craignure. You pass through two gates set into a private road, taking care not to let grazing sheep escape in the process.

TIRORAN

This hamlet opens onto the shores of Loch Scridain and is ideal for those seeking tranquility. It's only a 40-minute drive from the ferry terminal at Craignure, and is convenient for visiting not only Mull, but Iona and Staffa (see below).

WHERE TO STAY & DINE

TIRORAN HOUSE, Tiroran, Isle of Mull, Argyll PA69 6ES. Tel. 06815/232. Fax 06815/232. 9 rms (all with bath). **Directions:** From Craignure, take the A849 to Fionnphort (see below); at the head of Loch Scridain, turn right onto the B8035 to Gruline; after 5 miles, take a left to Tiroran, which is 1 mile down the road.

$ Rates (including half board): £86–£105 ($129–$157.50) per person. No credit cards. **Parking:** Free. **Closed:** Oct to mid-May.

About a mile off the B8035, Tiroran House stands in wooded grounds sweeping down to Loch Scridain. Flowering shrubs abound and golden pheasants frequent the 12 acres that make up the property of the serenely remote country house. Guests in the house are made to feel at ease, as if they were personal friends of the owners. The bedrooms are individually decorated with charm and taste. The house has fine art and antiques, and fresh flowers brighten the interior. Meals are served in the dining room, gleaming with polished wood, which has a vine-covered porch adjacent, also used for serving. Dinners may include such dishes as steak-and-kidney pie with oyster or mushroom sauce, crab mornay, or kidneys in wine and orange. This is a good base for seeing the attractions of Mull.

IN THEIR FOOTSTEPS

Robert Louis Stevenson [1850–1894] This Scottish novelist, essayist, and poet is best remembered for such works as *Treasure Island*, *Kidnapped*, and *The Strange Case of Dr. Jekyll and Mr. Hyde*. Although burdened by physical weakness and tuberculosis, he had great personal charm. For much of the 20th century, he was dismissed as a writer of children's books, but today he is viewed as a writer of power and originality.

• **Birthplace:** He was born at Edinburgh on November 13, 1850, the son of a prosperous civil engineer.

• **Residences:** Eight Howard Place in Edinburgh was the Stevenson family home. He spent several years wandering the South Seas and in California.

• **Final Days:** In October 1890, Stevenson arrived in Samoa because the climate suited him. He died suddenly on December 3, 1894, of a cerebral hemorrhage.

FIONNPHORT

Lying at the western tip of the Ross of Mull, Fionnphort is a tiny port that sees a lot of traffic. This is where the road ends and regular ferry passage is available across the mile-long Sound of Iona to the Isle of Iona, one of the most visited attractions in Scotland (see the next section). Iona is clearly visible from Fionnphort. Less than 2 miles to the south is the tidal island of Erraid, where David Balfour had adventures in Stevenson's *Kidnapped*.

WHERE TO STAY

ACHABAN HOUSE, Fionnphort, Isle of Mull, Argyll PA66 6BL. Tel. 06817/205. 7 rms (none with bath).
$ Rates (including Scottish breakfast): £16.50 ($24.80) per person. Half board £25 ($37.50) per person. No credit cards. **Parking:** Free.

Its almost indestructible walls, which in many places measure almost 3 feet thick, were built in 1820 of pink granite for the supervisor of the local quarry. Shortly thereafter the building was converted into the manse (pastor's residence) for the local church. Today it sits beside the town's only highway, a 10-minute walk (or a 1-minute drive) east of the ferryboat landing servicing Iona, in a windswept, treeless, and isolated position. Thirty feet from the hotel's entrance stands a Druidic dolmen, 10 feet tall, erected by prehistoric inhabitants of Mull several thousand years ago.

Bedrooms have pinewood furniture and are cozy and comfortable. Public rooms include a scattering of family antiques, and the succulent aromas from the cuisine prepared by German-born Camilla Baigent and her husband, Chris. Fixed-price evening meals are offered for £15.50 ($23.30) each, and might include excellent preparations of poached local salmon wrapped in a sheath of herbs, and such local game dishes as wild hare or venison.

WHERE TO DINE

KEEL ROW, at the harborfront. Tel. 06817/458.
Cuisine: SCOTTISH/INTERNATIONAL.
$ Prices: Appetizers £1.50–£3 ($2.30–$4.50); main courses £4–£6 ($6–$9); sandwiches £1.20 ($1.80). AE, MC, V.
Open: Apr–Sept, lunch daily noon–3pm; dinner daily 6–9pm (last order); snacks and drinks daily 11am–midnight. Oct–Mar, lunch Thurs–Sun noon–2pm; dinner Thurs–Sun 6–9pm (last order); snacks and drinks daily 11am–midnight.

The undisputed leader in the efficient and friendly dispensation of food and drink to passengers waiting for a ferryboat to Iona, this establishment occupies two interconnected buildings near the pier, at the end of the A849. Food is served in a box-shaped cedar-sided building with big windows overlooking the waterfront. Drinks are served in a 19th-century stone cottage whose rustic walls and blazing fireplace add cheer to many a gray day. Meals include filet of salmon poached in a tangy lemon sauce and grilled venison served with a rich herb sauce. Lighter fare includes sandwiches, steaming pots of tea, and pastries. Andrew Macdonald is your world-traveled host.

8. IONA & STAFFA

Iona, ⅛ mile W of Mull; Staffa, 6 miles NE of Iona

GETTING THERE   By Ferry   Iona is accessible only by passenger ferry from the Island of Mull (cars must remain on Mull). Service is informal, although fairly frequent in summer. It operates Monday through Saturday from 7am to 7pm and on Sunday from 10am to 5pm. The round-trip fare is £1.80 ($2.70). In the off-season, transport depends entirely on the weather, but is usually every 30 minutes from 10am to 5pm.

A remote, low-lying, green and treeless island with high cliffs and rolling meadows, Iona lies off the southwestern coast of Mull across the Sound of Iona. It is only 1 mile by 3½ miles in size.

Staffa, with its famous musical cave, is a 75-acre island in the Inner Hebrides, lying to the west of Mull. For transportation to Staffa, see below.

IONA

Someone once said, "When Edinburgh was but a barren rock and Oxford but a swamp, Iona was famous." It has been known as a place of spiritual power and pilgrimage for centuries. It was the site of the first Christian settlement in Scotland.

The island was owned by the dukes of Argyll from 1695, but the 12th duke was forced to sell it to pay $1 million in real estate taxes. The island was purchased by Sir Hugh Fraser, former owner of Harrods. He secured Iona's future and made it possible for money raised by the National Trust for Scotland to be turned over to the trustees of the restored abbey. The only village, Baille Mor, on Iona sits in the island's most sheltered spot, thus allowing some trees and garden plots to be cultivated.

The best way to get around Iona is to walk. If that's not for you, you can take **horse-drawn-carriage tours** (for information about these, phone 06814/230).

WHAT TO SEE & DO

Iona is known for its ☆ **"Graves of the Kings."** A total of 48 Scottish kings, including Macbeth and his supposed victim, Duncan, were buried on Iona, as were four Irish kings and eight Norwegian kings.

Today the island attracts nearly 1,000 visitors a week in high season. Most of them come to see the ☆ **Abbey of Iona,** part of which dates back to the 13th century. But they also visit relics of the settlement founded there by St. Columba in 563, from which Celtic Christianity spread through Scotland. The abbey has been restored by the Iona Community (see below), which conducts workshops on Christianity, sponsors a youth camp, offers tours of the abbey, and each Wednesday leads a 7-mile hike to the various holy and historic spots on the island.

Despite the many visitors to the abbey, the atmosphere on the island remains very peaceful and spiritual. It's possible to walk off among the sheep and cows that wander freely everywhere to the top of Dun-I, a small mountain, and contemplate the ocean and the landscape as if you were the only person on earth.

One reader, Capt. Robert Haggart of Laguna, California, described his experience this way: "I was enchanted by the place. It really has a mystic atmosphere—one feels something ancient here, something spiritual, sacred, long struggles, and wonderment about the strength of religion."

WHERE TO STAY & DINE

Most of the islanders live by crofting and fishing. In addition, they supplement their income by taking in paying guests in season, usually charging very low or at least fair prices. You can, of course, check into the hotels recommended below, but a stay here in a private home may be an altogether rewarding travel adventure. If you don't stay on Iona, you must catch one of the ferries back to Mull.

ARGYLL HOTEL, Isle of Iona, Argyll PA76 6SJ. Tel. 06817/334. 19 rms (10 with bath).

$ Rates (including Scottish breakfast): £26.50–£30 ($39.80–$45) single without bath, £30.50–£34 ($45.80–$51) single with bath; £49–£51 ($73.50–$76.50) double without bath, £57–£60 ($85.50–$90) double with bath. MC, V. **Parking:** Free. **Closed:** Mid-Oct to Easter.

This pleasant hotel, well run by Mrs. Fiona Menzies, stands in the village 200 yards from the ferry dock, overlooking the Sound of Iona and Mull in the distance. The rooms are attractively furnished. You get good home-cooking and baking, and vegetarian meals are available. In summer, vegetables are home-grown, and there is a nice selection of wines. The hotel is licensed to serve alcoholic drinks to residents.

ST. COLUMBA HOTEL, Isle of Iona, Argyll PA76 6SL. Tel. 06817/304.
Fax 06817/335. 23 rms (19 with bath or shower).
$ Rates (including half board): £42–£44 ($63–$66) single; £78–£84 ($117–$126)
double. No credit cards. **Parking:** Free. **Closed:** Nov–Mar.

$ This hotel, built of clapboard and white stone, is just uphill from the village about a quarter of a mile from the jetty, a two-minute walk from the abbey. Originally built as a manse for Presbyterian clergy in 1847, it was transformed into a hotel in 1868, and continues to attract a stream of pilgrims. The food is good, especially the fish dishes, but remember that the last order is taken at 7pm (people turn in early on Iona). Try to get a room overlooking the sea, but keep in mind that it's virtually impossible to secure an accommodation here in summer without a reservation made well in advance.

STAYING AT IONA ABBEY

Some travelers consider a visit to Iona the highlight of their trip to Scotland. Aside from viewing it as an unusual historical and archeological site, many people come back with a renewed interest in both their faith and the power of religion. The Iona Community is an ecumenical religious group who maintain a communal lifestyle in the ancient abbey. They offer full board and accommodation to visitors who want to share in the community's daily life. The only ordained members of the group are its two "wardens," who are members of either the Presbyterian Church of Scotland or the Scottish Episcopal Church.

During the peak summer months, between June and September, the community leads a series of discussion seminars, each of which lasts a week, stretching from Saturday to Saturday. The cost of a week's full board during one of these seminars is £151 ($226.50) per person. During one of the off-season months, except at Easter, guests can share in the daily life of the community if they stay for a minimum of three nights. Full board begins at £17.50 ($26.30) per day. The abbey closes in January and February. Guests are expected to contribute a small portion of their day—about 30 minutes—to the execution of some kind of household chore. The daily schedule involves a wakeup call at 8am, communal breakfast at 8:20am, a morning religious service, and plenty of unscheduled time for conversation, study, and contemplation. Up to 44 guests can be accommodated at one time in bathless, bunk-bedded twin rooms. In addition to the abbey, there is the Iona Community's center for reconciliation, the MacLeod Centre, built for youth, the disabled, and families. It also accommodates up to 50 guests. For further details, phone 06817/404.

For day visitors, the community leads tours through the rebuilt Benedictine abbey, maintains a gift and book shop, and runs a coffee shop. Each is open daily from 10am to 4:30pm.

STAFFA

The attraction of this island, 6 miles north of Iona, is **Fingal's Cave,** a lure to visitors for more than 200 years and the inspiration for music, poetry, paintings, and prose. Its Gaelic name, An Uamh Ehinn, means "musical cave." The place is unique in that it is the only known such formation in the world with basalt columns. Over the centuries the sea has carved a huge cavern in the basalt, leaving massive hexagonal columns to create what Queen Victoria described, after a visit in the 19th century: "The effect is splendid, like a great entrance into a vaulted hall. The sea is immensely deep in the cave. The rocks under water were all colors—pink, blue and green." The sound of the crashing waves and swirling waters caused Mendelssohn to write the *Fingal's Cave Overture.* Turner painted the cave on canvas, and Keats, Wordsworth, and Tennyson all praised it in their poetry.

The island of Staffa has not been inhabited for more than 170 years. Visitors can still explore the cave, which is strictly protected from development by the National Trust. Entrance to the cave is free, requiring only payment for boat passage from Mull or Iona. Boat trips from Mull or Iona cost £7.50 ($11.30) for adults and £4 ($6) for children. You're taken to Staffa's only pier, which was enlarged and rebuilt in 1992, near a lesser attraction known as *Clamshell Cave.* Visitors then walk along a basalt path into Fingal's Cave, where a guardrail separates them from the water and waves below. Inside, the noise of the pounding surf is deafening. The boat carries 67 passengers, and contains both open-air and covered areas upon its decks. It runs from Iona and Mull twice a day, every day, between March and October, departing from Iona at 9:45am and 1:45pm, stopping briefly at Fionnphort, on Mull, just across the channel, to pick up additional passengers. Tours last from 60 to 75 minutes each, depending on weather conditions. During violent storms, no tours are offered, and reservations are important. Rubber-soled shoes and warm clothing are recommended for this excursion.

Phone Mrs. Carol Kirkpatrick, whose husband, David, operates the boat, at Tigh-na-Traigh (House by the Shore), Isle of Iona (tel. 06817/358), for reservations and departure information.

9. THE ISLE OF COLONSAY

15 miles S of the Isle of Mull

GETTING THERE   By Ferry and Car   A ferry, operated by **Caledonian MacBrayne** (tel. 0631/62285 in Oban), sails between Oban and Colonsay three times a week. The 37-mile crossing takes 2½ hours.

The most remote of the islands of Argyll, Colonsay with Oransay, a tidal neighbor, shares some of the same characteristics as Iona, Tyree, and Coll. To the west it faces nothing but the open Atlantic—only a lighthouse stands between Colonsay and Canada. The island is more tranquil than Mull or Skye because it does not accommodate "day trippers."

WHAT TO SEE & DO

The island encompasses 20 square miles, enjoying an equable climate because of the warming waters of the Gulf Stream. Plants do well here. It is estimated that there are some 500 species of flora, which are best seen in the **gardens of Colonsay House,** filled with rare rhododendrons, magnolias, and eucalyptus, even palm trees. Colonsay House, dating from 1722 and seat of the laird, Lord Strathcona, is not open to the public. There is also an 18-hole golf course.

All parts of the island can be explored along its one-lane roads. Many visitors prefer to rent a bicycle rather than drive. You can rent sailing dinghies and rowboats and sail around the island, following in the grand tradition of the Vikings. The Vikings also held several ship burials on the island. Some of the sites have been excavated, but, regrettably, the ships had decayed.

Wildlife abounds, including golden eagles, falcons, gray seals, otters, and wild goats with elegant horns and long shaggy hair. Prehistoric forts, stone circles, and single standing stones attest to the antiquity of Colonsay, which has been occupied since the Stone Age.

The little island of **Oransay** was named for Oran, a disciple of St. Columba. It is joined at low tide by the Strand, and visitors can wade across the sands during a 2-hour period. The ancient monastic ruins seen here date from the 6th century, and tradition has it that they were founded by St. Columba. You can see some splendid tombstones of carved stone. The most notable is the Great Cross of Prior Colin, from the early 16th century.

Back at your hotel, if you're lucky you might join in a *ceilidh* on a summer evening.

WHERE TO STAY & DINE

ISLE OF COLONSAY HOTEL, Isle of Colonsay, Argyll PA61 7XP. Tel. 09512/316. Fax 09512/353. 11 rms (8 with bath), 3 cottages. (all with bath).

$ Rates (including half board): £40–£68 ($60–$102) per person; cottages £190–£395 ($285–$592.50) weekly. AE, DC, MC, V. **Parking:** Free.

Dating from the 18th century, this place is considered the most isolated hotel in Great Britain. Above the harbor, 400 yards from the ferryboat landing, it is the social center of Colonsay. Its solidly constructed gables and chimneys rise above its surrounding herb and vegetable gardens at a point within 5 miles of everything on the island. Many guests check in here for closeup views of the island's abundant flora and fauna. The owners provide bicycles free to guests or drop them by courtesy car to go on rambles.

There are three self-contained cottages; each has a combined living room and kitchen, veranda, double bedroom, an upper level with three single beds, and maid service. The cottages are suitable for up to six people. Electricity (which is metered at cost) is not included in the weekly rate.

A meal in the hotel's dining room is considered an event for the local residents, who appreciate the ambience of the cocktail lounge and the public bar. The inn is licensed, serving lunch daily from noon to 1:30pm and dinner at 7:30pm. A meal is likely to include a homemade soup, fresh mussels, trout, scallops, and prawns, with vegetables from the garden. Fixed-price dinners cost £18 ($27) and up.

THE OUTER HEBRIDES

At first you may feel that you've come to a lunar landscape where there is a sense of infinite time. The character of the Outer Hebrides islands is unique, quite different from the chain of the Inner Hebrides that we have just visited. The string of islands lie some 30 to 40 miles off the northwest coast of Scotland. The main islands to visit are Lewis and Harris (parts of the same island in spite of different names), North Uist, Benbecula, South Uist, and Barra. The archipelago also takes in some minor offshore islands. From the Butt of Lewis in the north to Barra Head in the south, the chain stretches for some 130 miles.

Gaelic is spoken here; its gentle cadence is said to have been the language spoken in the Garden of Eden. Presbyterianism is still very strong (in one B&B house, for example, watching TV on Sunday is forbidden). Before you go, you might read Compton Mackenzie's novel *Whisky Galore.*

The islands today, which knew two centuries of Viking invasions, are the retreat of many a disenchanted artist from the mainland. They come here, take over old crofters' cottages, and devote their days to such pursuits as pottery making and weaving.

Birdwatchers flock to the islands to see the habitats along cliffs, in peat bog, and farmland of the red-necked phalarope, the corncrake, the golden eagle, the Arctic skua, and the grayleg goose. Golfers come here just to play golf on these far-northern courses, including one at Stornoway (Lewis) and at Askernish (South Uist). Anglers also come here to fish for salmon, brown trout, and sea trout among the fishing lochs found throughout the island chain.

Much of the dim past can be seen on these islands, including a version of Stonehenge. A good time to visit is in June and July when adults' and children's choirs compete for honors. You can attend these festivals celebrating Gaelic music and poetry.

Each of the main islands has tourist accommodations (and reservations are important). Most are small family-run guest houses and hotels, and many are crofters' cottages that take in B&B guests, mainly in summer.

---

10. LEWIS

209 miles NW of Edinburgh, 213 miles NW of Glasgow

GETTING THERE By Plane An airport, which doubles as an RAF base, lies about 3½ miles from the center of **Stornoway.** Stornoway receives daily flights from

Glasgow and Inverness, as well as Benbecula and Barra. The operators are British Airways and Loganair. Phone 041/3329666 in Glasgow to confirm schedules or to make reservations.

By Ferry and Car From Monday to Saturday, **Caledonian MacBrayne** operates two or three ferries from Ullapool to Stornoway. One-way passage costs £8.80 ($13.20). For reservations and general information, call Caledonian MacBrayne at the ferry terminal (tel. 0475/34531) in Gourock. Cars can be transported as well. Trip time is 3½ hours.

ESSENTIALS The **Western Isles Tourist Board,** which has information about all the Outer Hebrides, is at 4 South Beach, Stornoway (tel. 0851/703088). The **telephone area code** for Stornoway is 0851.

The most northerly of the islands of the Outer Hebrides, and also the largest, Lewis is easily reached by ferry from Ullapool (see Chapter 9). The island was once known as "Lews," or more poetically, "the island of heather." The sweetness of the lamb grown here is said to come from the heather diet. Lewis and Harris form part of the same island, stretching for a combined length of some 95 miles. Lewis is about 60 miles long and from 18 to 28 miles across. Even though the whole world has heard of "Harris tweed," it might as well be called "Lewis tweed," as Stornoway has taken over the industry. There are some 600 weavers on the island, and one of the attractions of this rather bleak port is to visit a mill shop or a weaver's cottage.

With a population of some 5,000 souls, Stornoway is the only town in the Outer Hebrides. On the eastern side of the island, it is a land-locked harbor where you can see gray seals along with fishing boats setting out.

Filled with marshy peat bogs, the landscape is relatively treeless, thanks in part to the Norse raider, Magnus Barelegs. Although Lewis used to have trees, Barelegs and his tree-burning Viking warriors left much of Lewis as bare as his shanks. Efforts at reforestation have been unsuccessful.

WHAT TO SEE & DO

The major attraction is the Neolithic temple of Callanish, called the ✪ **Standing Stones of Callanish.** This unique cruciform setting of megaliths, off the A858, 16 miles west of Stornoway, is outranked in prehistoric archeological splendor only by Stonehenge. From a circle of 13 stones, a road of 19 monoliths leads north. Branching off to the south, east, and west are rows of more stones. A tiny chambered tomb is inside the circle.

In the more immediate vicinity, you can visit the grounds of **Lews Castle** (the old spelling), west of the harbor at Stornoway. The castle, built in 1818 in **Lady Lever Park,** is not open to the public. Lord Leverhulme of Sunlight soap fame left the grounds to the public. You can wander among a stunning collection of rhododendrons, at their best in May.

At Amol, 15 miles northwest of Stornoway, off the A858, you can visit the **Lewis Black House,** a thatched house that has been preserved to show visitors what a typical Hebridean dwelling looked like. It's called a "black house" because it was believed that the smoke from the open peat fires was good for the thatched roof; therefore the Leodhasach (as the islanders are called) built their houses with no chimneys so the smoke could go through the thatch. The house was constructed without mortar. Many of its original furnishings are intact. It is open June through September, Monday to Saturday from 9:30am to 6pm, closing at 5pm in winter. Admission is £1 ($1.50) for adults, 50p (80¢) for children.

Shawbost School Museum, Shawbost (tel. 085171/212), has Hebridean artifacts, each piece something discovered locally and preserved. The museum is admission-free, but a donation is appreciated. On the A858, 19 miles northwest of Stornoway, it is open April through October, Monday to Saturday from 10am to 6pm.

For the serious student of history and ancient monuments, the **Steinacleit Cairn and Stone Circle** are the ruined fragments of what was once a rather substantial house built in the mists of prehistory. The house was found beneath huge layers of peat. At the southern end of Loch an Duin, Shader, 12 miles north of Stornoway, it can be visited throughout the day for no fee.

The **Clach an Trushal** at Balanthrushal, Barvas, is the largest single monolith in northern Scotland. It is 19 feet tall and 6 feet wide. Near this same site was the field of the last battle fought between the Macaulays of Uig and the Morrisons of Ness.

Dun Carloway Broch is a broch tower, about 30 feet high, left over from the Iron Age. It stands along the A858, 20 miles west and northwest of Stornoway. It can be visited throughout the day for no fee. At Arnish, near Stornoway, is the **Bonnie Prince Charlie monument.**

At Dun Borranish, near the village of Ardroil, the famous Lewis Chessmen were dug up in 1831 outside Uig Sands. Made of walrus tusks, they now form an outstanding exhibit in the British Museum in London. If you're a chess player, you may want to purchase a reproduction set in Lewis.

Ui Church, at Aignish, off the A866, 2 miles east of Stornoway, is now in ruins. Pronounced "eye," it was the burial grounds of the Macleods of Lewis. You can see their carved tombs. The ruins are on the Eye Peninsula, also known as "The Point." At Ness, toward that northerly outpost, the Butt of Lewis, is **St. Moluag's Church,** a Scottish Episcopal church. You can attend an occasional service here. The chapel, known in Gaelic is *Teampull Mhor* or "big temple," is circa 12th century, founded by Olav the Black during the Norse occupation of the island. The original church is said to have been founded in the 6th century by a companion of St. Columba.

WHERE TO STAY

CABERFEIDH HOTEL, Manor Park, Stornoway, Lewis, Outer Hebrides PA87 2EU. Tel. 0851/702604, or toll free in the U.S. 800/528-1234. Fax 0851/705572. 47 rms (all with bath). TV TEL

$ Rates (including Scottish breakfast): £65 ($97.50) single; £85 ($127.50) double. AE, DC, MC, V. **Parking:** Free.

About a mile north of Stornoway, midway between the hamlets of Laxdale and Newmarket, the Caberfeidh, the best hotel on Lewis, shelters guests from the chilly winds behind unadorned white walls designed like large building blocks in a contemporary arrangement of cubes. A member of the Best Western reservations chain, the hotel is considered the most luxurious in the Outer Hebrides. It was built by a Mackenzie, who named it after the battle cry of his fighting clan. (Translated from Gaelic, the name means "stag antlers.") It was completely renovated in 1990; the decor includes a collection of stag's heads and a convivial bar shaped like a Viking longship. Each of the comfortable bedrooms has a radio, trouser press, and hairdryer, along with other amenities. The dining room offers the best of local produce, fresh fish (especially trout and salmon), local beef and lamb, and scallops. Meals are savory and well prepared, costing £17 ($25.50) for a table d'hôte dinner.

CALEDONIAN HOTEL, 6 S. Beach St., Stornoway, Lewis, Outer Hebrides PA87 2XY. Tel. 0851/702411. Fax 0851/702610. 10 rms (all with bath). TV TEL

$ Rates (including Scottish breakfast): £34 ($51) single; £52 ($78) double. MC, V. **Parking:** Free.

Built during the darkest days of Britain's involvement in World War II, this hotel burned to the ground in a tragic fire in the 1970s. It was immediately reconstructed in an uncomplicated modern format, but continues to display within its interior the yellowing photographs of its original, stone-fronted manifestation. Today, it prides itself on offering throughout the year some of the most reasonable overnight rates in Stornoway. Each of the simple but comfortable bedrooms contains a tea-making facility. Dining is within a restaurant with a panoramic view of Stornoway Harbour, with platters priced at from £3 ($4.50) to around £10 ($15) each. The hotel also contains two bars serving sandwiches and snacks from noon to 10am daily.

SEAFORTH HOTEL, 9 James St., Stornoway, Lewis, Outer Hebrides PA87 2QN. Tel. 0851/702740. Fax 0851/703900. 65 rms (all with bath or shower). TV TEL

$ Rates (including Scottish breakfast): £57 ($85.50) single; £79 ($118.50) double. AE, MC, V. **Parking:** Free.

A 5-minute walk from the town center, the Seaforth is one of the most modern hotels in the Outer Hebrides. The accommodations cost more than most of its nearby competitors, but many visitors to Lewis are willing to spend the extra money for better amenities. Each comfortable bedroom has a radio and a tea/coffee maker. The public rooms have several full-size snooker tables, as well as a bar/lounge. There's even an in-house cinema, the only one in town. La Terrazza restaurant specializes in both traditional Scottish and Italian cuisines. Open until 9:30pm every day for lunch and dinner, the restaurant provides value for money in comfortable surroundings.

COUNTY HOTEL, Francis St., Stornoway, Lewis, Outer Hebrides PA87 2XB. Tel. 0851/703250. Fax 0851/706008. 17 rms (all with bath). TV TEL
$ Rates (including Scottish breakfast): £38 ($57) single; £50 ($75) double. MC, V. **Parking:** Free.

Some of the details about this hotel's locally patronized pub—the copper-plated foot railing, the cubbyhole beside the fireplace, the exposed wood—might be remembered after you leave. Since it's in the center of town next door to the post office and the offices of a local newspaper, some of the editorial staff might be seen raising a mug next to yours. The reception area has open fires and oak paneling in the lounge bar. Rooms are comfortably furnished.

WHERE TO DINE

COFFEE POT, 5 Kenneth St., Tel. 0851/703270.
Cuisine: BRITISH. **Reservations:** Not needed.
$ Prices: Appetizers 90p–£1.75 ($1.40–$2.60); main courses £2.50–£4 ($3.80–$6). No credit cards.
Open: Mon–Sat 7:30am–6pm.

From its windows, you'll have a view of the sea, the source of livelihood for husbands and brothers of many of this establishment's waitresses. It's very much a "caff" in the British sense, serving sandwiches, baps, lasagne, shepherd's pie, breaded haddock, and even some stew-like dishes inspired by the cuisine of India. Despite its coffee-shop format, it offers a warm and welcome refuge from the cold and wet winds that often whip through the streets of Stornaway. Strictly nonalcoholic, it caters to the schedules and appetites of local residents throughout the day, serving breakfasts, lunches, high teas, snacks, and endless cups of strong black coffee and tea.

PARK GUEST HOUSE, 30 James St., Stornoway, Lewis, Outer Hebrides PA87 2QN. Tel. 0851/702485.
Cuisine: SEAFOOD AND GAME. **Reservations:** Necessary.
$ Prices: Appetizers £1.70–£5.45 ($2.60–$8.20); main courses £12.75–£21 ($19.10–$31.50). Fixed-price 3-course dinner £11 ($16.50), served only 5:30–6:30pm. No credit cards.
Open: Dinner only, Tues–Sat 5:30–9pm. **Closed:** Oct.

Set within a stone-built, century-old house cheek by jowl with rows of very similar neighbors, about a 10-minute walk north of the ferryboat terminal, this is considered one of the best dining rooms in town, a favorite of many local residents. Owned and operated by island-born Roddy and Catherine Afrin, it contains a dignified fireplace in the style of Charles Rennie Mackintosh, and a country-house decor designed by Catherine, a graduate of the Glasgow School of Art. Menu items include seasonal game (grouse, partridge, and venison) and choices from the rich bounties of the nearby seas. They might include, depending on arrivals of ingredients, grilled lobster served thermidor style with brandy sauce; oysters, served either raw or au gratin; pan-fried scallops in lemon butter and herbs; and filet of turbot grilled with herb butter. The establishment is fully licensed, serving beer, wine, and whisky, and is at its most elegant and appealing between 7 and 9pm.

Upstairs are five simple bedrooms, none with private bath, shower, TV, or telephone. With breakfast included, they cost £19 ($28.50) per person, single or double occupancy.

11. HARRIS

218 miles NW of Glasgow, 56 miles NW of Mallaig,
246 miles NW of Edinburgh, 34 miles S of Stornoway

GETTING THERE   By Ferry   You can take a ferry to Tarbert (capital of Harris) from Uig on the Isle of Skye, Monday through Saturday. There are one or two ferries per day, and a one-way ticket costs £6.25 ($9.40). Call **Caledonian MacBrayne** in Tarbert (tel. 0859/2444) for schedules and more information.

By Bus   Buses run from Stornoway to Tarbert daily. Phone 0859/2441 for schedules. At least one bus per day—perhaps three in summer—makes the run Monday through Saturday only.

By Car   From Stornoway on Lewis in the north, drive south along the A859 to reach Tarbert.

ESSENTIALS   A summer-only **tourist information center** operates from the port at Tarbert (tel. 0859/2011). The **telephone area code** for Tarbert is 0859.

Harris, south of Lewis, might share the same island with Lewis, but its geography is different. North Harris is full of mountains, dominated by the Clisham, which at 2,600 feet is the highest mountain peak in the Outer Hebrides. Harris may not have as many ancient relics as Lewis, but, most visitors agree, the mountains, beaches, and scenic vistas make up for that lack. Explorers can seek out the beaches in the west, either for swimming or camping, or go to the bays in the east, which are ideal for fishing and sailing.

The local people, some 3,000 in all, are called Hearach, and they, too, are different from the people of Lewis, even speaking with a different accent. If you've arrived in Lewis, you can drive to Harris, as the two "islands" are connected by a small single-lane road, going from pass to pass. As you go along the rugged terrain, you might see a fell walker. Occasionally you'll meet another car. If you do, "passing places" have been provided. In any case, you should drive slowly, because sheep might suddenly scamper in front of your wheels. The distance from Stornoway, the capital of Lewis, to Tarbert, the capital of Harris, is 34 miles.

Many visitors, however, prefer to take the ferryboat from the little port of Uig on the Isle of Skye that heads for Harris daily except Sunday. Even in the busiest season Harris is not overrun with visitors. From Harris you can also make connections to Lochmaddy on North Uist (see below).

Harris has long been known for its hand-weaving and tweed. Though that industry has now passed to Stornoway, it is still possible to buy Harris tweed jackets in Harris. In summer you'll see them displayed on the walls of corrugated iron sheds along the road. You get very good prices here.

The main village of Harris is **Tarbert,** a one-street town. The island is bisected by two long sea lochs that meet at Tarbert, which is surrounded by rocky hills. Whatever you need in the way of supplies, you should pick up here. Otherwise you'll be out of luck. If you're touring by private car, also fill up with "petrol" (gas) at Tarbert. Ask at the information center about the bus tours that are conducted in summer around Harris, and for an adventure, take the car-ferry that runs regularly across the sound to the little fishing community of Scalpay, an offshore island.

WHAT TO SEE & DO

Because of the lack of roads, you can't make a circular tour of Harris. However, using Tarbert as your base, you can set out northwest along the coastline of West Loch Tarbert, with the Forest of Harris to your north. Or you can go south from Tarbert, hugging the western coastal road along the Sound of Taransay, with Rodel as your final destination.

Taking the northwesterly route first, you come to an **Old Whaling Station** at Bunavoneadar. Norwegians set up a whaling station here in the early 20th century, but because of dwindling profits it was abandoned in 1930. Slipways and a chimney can still be seen. Continuing north along the B887, you will arrive at the **Amhuinnsuidhe Estate,** a Scottish baronial castle constructed by the Earl of Dunmore in 1868. Sir James Barrie stayed here while working on his novel *Mary Rose.* The river to the left has one of the most beautiful salmon leaps in Scotland.

The road beyond the castle continues to **Hushinish Point.** In addition to machair, the area in springtime becomes a bed of wildflowers. At Hushinish you can see the little offshore island of **Scarp,** which was once inhabited. Returning to Tarbert, you can take the A859 south. Some of the South Harris coastline will remind you of Norway, with its sea lochs and "fjord fingers." The main road to Rodel is mostly two lane and well surfaced; however, if you take the east-coast road, you'll find it not only single lane, but tortuous and winding.

Along the way you'll pass the Clach Mhicleoid, or standing stone. The locals call it **MacLeod's Stone.** This monolith, placed above the Nisabost Sands, stands as a lonely sentinel at night, a silent witness to what it has seen over the centuries.

From here you can look out across the Sound of Taransay to the **Island of Taransay,** which was named after St. Tarran. The island has several ancient sites, including the remains of St. Tarran's Chapel. Like Scarp, it was once populated, but now its grazing fields are turned over to sheep. Continuing on the coastal road along the wild Atlantic—actually the Sound of Taransay—you'll see another ancient stone, the **Scarista Standing Stone.** But before reaching it you'll pass **Borve Lodge,** the former home of Lord Leverhulme, the soap tycoon.

The road south passes the little promontory of Toe Head jutting out into the Atlantic. An ancient chapel, **Rudh'an Teampull,** stands about three-quarters of a mile west of Northton, reached by a sand track. Many prehistoric sites were uncovered and excavated on the machair-studded tiny peninsula of Toe Head. Bone tools and Neolithic pottery were found, the earliest recorded habitations of the Western Isles.

The next hamlet is **Leverburgh,** named after the soap magnate. He is credited with trying to bring the people of the area into the 20th century, but his efforts to rejuvenate the economy largely failed. From here you can take a small passenger ferry to North Uist and Berneray. You can also visit the **An Clachan Centre** at Leverburgh, where you can purchase many items of local craftware.

Finally, you drive east to Rodel, where ✪ **St. Clement's Church** stands high in the village. Overlooking Loch Rodel, this church is one of the most important monuments in the Western Isles. Cruciform in plan, it has a western tower, a nave, and two cross aisles. Some of the masonry work in freestone is similar to that used at Iona Abbey. The church is believed to have been built around the closing years of the 15th century or the very early years of the 16th century. There are three tombs inside, including one that is considered among the finest in the islands. The tomb contains part of the MacLeod coat-of-arms.

In the Sound of Harris, separating Harris from North Uist, lie the islands of **Ensay, Killegray,** and **Pabbay.** Once they were populated, but now they have been turned over to grazing sheep.

WHERE TO STAY & DINE

TARBERT

HARRIS HOTEL, Tarbert, Harris, Outer Hebrides PA85 3DL. Tel. 0859/ 2154. Fax 0859/2281. 24 rms (16 with bath).

$ Rates (including Scottish breakfast): £28.85 ($43.30) single without bath; £55 ($82.50) double without bath, £62.50 ($93.80) double with bath. MC, V. **Parking:** Free.

Built in the mid-1800s as a private house, this hotel has been a local landmark since it first accepted customers in 1904. Today it's one of the most popular and best-established places for eating, drinking, and sleeping in the Outer Hebrides. Each accommodation has hot and cold running water, lots of old-fashioned comfort, and modern amenities. Some family rooms are available, many looking out over the garden, one of the largest in Harris.

Dinner is offered for £14.25 ($21.40) to £15.50 ($23.30), and the food is good and plentiful. This hotel houses the most popular pub in Tarbert, the social center of town, attracting many locals, including some "ghillies" who show guests who are here for fishing holidays how it's done. You can order pub grub at midday.

SCARISTA

SCARISTA HOUSE, Scarista, Harris, Outer Hebrides PA85 3HX. Tel. 085985/238. 7 rms (all with bath). TEL
$ Rates (including Scottish breakfast): £56 ($84) single; £82–£90 ($123–$135) double; £64–£69 ($96–$103.50) per person with half board. No credit cards. **Parking:** Free. **Closed:** Mid-Oct to Mar.

This is a lovely hotel on the A859, about 15 miles southwest of Tarbert on the west coast of Harris. It was constructed long ago as a Georgian vicarage. Each handsomely decorated bedroom is centrally heated. A few of the summer guests enjoy an occasional bracing dip in the 55° water of nearby Scarista Beach. Others prefer to enjoy the well-stocked library.

Here you get the best breakfast in the Outer Hebrides: freshly squeezed orange juice and a compote of fresh and dried fruits, along with organic oatmeal porridge with cream and kippers from Lewis—and that's only the beginning. These dishes are followed by Stornoway black pudding, bacon, sausage, and fresh eggs, plus fresh herring rolled in oatmeal. There's also homemade whole-wheat bread and a variety of other baked items. If you plan to burn off this morning feast, a packed lunch will be provided. Most guests return to a spot near the fireplace of the hotel's beautifully appointed drawing room for a drink before a five-course dinner. A full dinner featuring locally caught shellfish and heather-fed lamb, among other ingredients, begins at £24 ($36). Meals are served at 8pm.

12. NORTH & SOUTH UIST

90–100 miles NW of Glasgow

GETTING THERE By Plane British Airways flies daily except Sunday to and from Benbecula Airport (the nearest connection for North Uist) and Glasgow. Phone the Glasgow Airport (tel. 041/8871111) for flight information.

By Car North Uist is linked with Benbecula and South Uist by causeways and bridges, so you can travel to or from either of these islands by car along the A867, which becomes the A865.

By Ferry For information about car-ferry services, consult Caledonian MacBrayne at Lochmaddy (tel. 08763/337). One ferry per day runs from Oban to Lochmaddy on North Uist from Monday to Saturday. The trip takes anywhere from 5 to 7 hours and a one-way ticket costs £13.65 ($20.50). Some of these ferries stop at Castlebay on Barra. Other ferries run from Uig on the Isle of Skye to Lochmaddy at the rate of one to three per day, including Sunday. The most popular connection, this ferry trip takes anywhere from 2 to 4 hours and a one-way ticket costs £6.25 ($9.40).

Lochboisdale is the site of the ferry terminal, which provides a link between South Uist and the mainland at Oban, taking 5½ hours. Call 0631/62285 in Oban for more details.

ESSENTIALS Consult with the Western Isles Tourist Board in Stornoway (see above). There's also a **tourist information center** in the center of Lochmaddy (tel. 08763/321), open Monday to Saturday from 9am to 5pm, which can arrange accommodations if you have arrived without a reservation. The **telephone area code** is 08763.

At Lochboisdale the **tourist information center** is found at the pier (tel. 08784/286), open Easter through October, Monday to Saturday from 9am to 5pm. Accommodations can be arranged through this office. The **telephone area code** is 08784.

Standing stones and chambered cairns, ruins and fortresses, tell of a history-rich past on these two old islands, connected by the smaller island of Benbecula.

NORTH UIST

A real bogland—where hardy crofters try to wrestle a living from both a turbulent sea and disappointing land, North Uist is one of the least-frequented islands in the Outer Hebrides. That's a pity, because it's so beautiful. Its antiquity is reflected in its brochs, duns, wheelhouses, and stark monoliths, all left by the island's prehistoric dwellers.

The population of North Uist is about 2,000, and the island is about 12½ miles wide by 35 miles at its longest point. North Uist is served by a circular road, most often the single-lane variety with passing places, and there are several feeder routes branching east and west. Road surfaces are usually good.

The main village is **Lochmaddy,** on the eastern shoreline. Whatever you need, if it's available in North Uist at all you're likely to find it here, from a post office to a petrol station. Lochmaddy is the site of the ferry terminal. In addition to the ferries from Oban and Uig, a small private ferry runs from Newton Ferry, north of Lochmaddy, to Leverburgh on Harris. This is not a car-ferry, but allows small motorcycles or bicycles. A small vehicular ferry will also take you to the island of Berneray. In keeping with the strict religious tradition of these islands, the ferry doesn't operate on Sunday, and neither, seemingly, does anything else.

WHAT TO SEE & DO

For such a small island, the scenery of North Uist is extremely varied. The eastern shores have an untamed beauty. The coastline is dotted with lochs filled with trout, and everything is set against a backdrop of darkened, rolling, heather-clad hills. Nights come on fast in winter; sunsets linger in summer. The western side of North Uist is a land of rich meadows filled with wildflowers. Here you find long white beaches, where Atlantic rollers attract the hardier surfers.

Heading northwest from Lochmaddy for 2½ miles you come to Blashaval, where you will find the Three Standing Stones of the False Men. Local tradition has it that this trio of stones, known in Gaelic as *Na Fir Bhreige,* actually were men, wife deserters from Skye turned into stone by a witch.

Continuing along the road for 4 miles, you approach an island on the west side of Loch an Duin where access is possible on foot only at periods of low tide. Caution should be exercised. Dun Torcuill is a fine example of a broch that provided defense for the villagers against raiders.

Turning north on the B893, you come to Newton Ferry (see above). A 15-minute crossing will take you to the little offshore island of **Berneray,** which has some ancient sites, including the Borve Standing Stone. There is a privately run hostel here. The 140 or so people who live on the island are mainly engaged in crofting and fishing, and may regard you as a sightseeing attraction.

After you return to Newton Ferry, head south on the same road. A left-hand fork takes you to **Trumisgarry** to see the ruins of an old chapel where an early Christian settlement was founded. **St. Columba's Well** (*Tobar Chaluim Chille,* in Gaelic) is named after the saint.

Returning to the main road, head west toward Sollas. On both sides of the road are cairns and standing stones, many from 2000 B.C.—some hard to reach, including those on uninhabited islands. Pass through Hosta, site of the Highland Games, heading for the **Balranaid Nature Reserve,** 3 miles northwest of Bayhead. At a reception cottage at Goulat, near Hougharty, you can learn more about the bird inhabiting the Outer Hebrides. It is open between April and September, daily from 10am to 4pm, charging no admission.

Back on the main road again, you'll pass through Bayhead heading to the southeast. Again, the area is filled with an astonishing number of ancient monuments; many more have disappeared since the 1920s, reclaimed by the Atlantic. At the junction, take the A867 back toward Lochmaddy. You'll see a sign pointing to **Barpa Langass.** On the slopes of Ben Langass is a chambered cairn thought to be at least 3,000 years old, one of the best preserved on the island. Some historians believe a warrior chieftain was buried here, but others suggest it was a communal burial ground. Bones and pottery fragments removed from excavations here were sent to the National Museum in Edinburgh.

Returning to the main road again, retrace your trail and head south for Carinish, a hamlet known for the **Carinish Stone Circle** and the **Barpa Carinish,** the site of the major attraction on the island, **Trinity Temple** (*Teampull na Trionad,* in Gaelic), lying off the A865 some 8 miles southwest of Lochmaddy. Admission-free, it is open at all times. The monastery is said to have been founded in the 13th century by Beathag, the first prioress of Iona, daughter of Somerland, an Irish mercenary and the founding father of the MacDonalds. In the Middle Ages, on this site was a great college that the Franciscan scholar, Duns Scotus (1265–1308), was said to have attended. He later became one of the most influential of medieval philosophers and theologians.

Nearby is **Teampull Clann A'Phlocair,** the chapel of the MacVicars. You can see a number of ancient "cup and ring" markings. The site of a clan battle is also nearby. Appropriately called the "Field of Blood," it is where the MacLeods of Harris and the MacDonalds of Uist met in 1601.

You can continue southeast to the island of **Grimsay,** connected by a causeway, and known for its lobster ponds. You'll also find the remains of Michael's Chapel and the ruins of Dun Bay Grimsay, an ancient fortification.

WHERE TO STAY & DINE

LOCHMADDY HOTEL, Lochmaddy, North Uist, Outer Hebrides PA82 5AA. Tel. 08763/331. Fax 08763/210. 15 rms (all with bath), TV TEL.
$ Rates (including Scottish breakfast): £33 ($49.50) single; £62 ($93) double. MC, V. **Parking:** Free.

You can't miss the peaked gables of this white-walled hotel a few steps from the ferry terminal. It frequently hosts fishermen who come for the area's brown trout, sea trout and salmon—anyone wishing to weigh his or her catch of the day is welcome to make use of the hotel's set of scales. The hotel offers one of the few outlets on the island for the sale of fishing permits, with prices varying from £5 ($7.50) to £35 ($52.50) a day, according to what kind of fish you're seeking and the season. The establishment contains an accommodating pub, a cocktail bar, and a dining room, serving a table d'hôte dinner for £16 ($24). At dinner you are likely to be offered heather-fed North Uist lamb, and bar meals are served both at lunch and in the evening. The bar also offers about the best collection of single-malt whiskies in the Outer Hebrides. Bedrooms are comfortable, uncluttered, and tasteful, having benefitted from a renovation in 1992.

LANGASS LODGE, Locheport, North Uist, Outer Hebrides PA82 5AE. Tel. 08764/285. 6 rms (all with bath).
$ Rates (including Scottish breakfast): £29.50 ($44.30) single; £59 ($88.50) double. MC, V. **Parking:** Free. **Closed:** Feb.

Its spaciousness and comfort comes as a welcome surprise after the miles of windswept and barren countryside you'll traverse before you reach it. Its multiple chimneys and mint-green-colored facade are softened by the nearby presence of half a dozen sycamore trees, cited by the staff as among the few trees on all of North Uist. Originally built as a hunting lodge in 1876, the hotel has been comfortably modernized, and today accepts a clientele of hunters, fishers, and nature lovers from Britain, Europe, and North America. The modernized bedrooms are appointed with flowered curtains, solid furnishings, and views of the nearby loch. A three-course evening meal costs £15 ($22.50) per person. The lodge is 2 miles north of Locheport and 6 miles south of Lochmaddy, beside the highway.

BENBECULA

For many visitors Benbecula is a mere causeway linking North Uist with South Uist, or an airport useful for reaching other destinations (see "Getting There" "By Plane" above).

Benbecula is small, only about 6 miles in diameter. Nearly all the population lives in the west. Most of the eastern part, real bogland, is without roads except for a narrow single-track "path" along the southeastern part. If you're planning to spend time on the island, **Creagorry** might be your center, as you'll find facilities there, including accommodations, shops, and a post office. The main center of the island is **Balivanich,** which is near the Benbecula Airport and a Royal Artillery base.

Going south on the road from the airport you'll come to the ruins of an ancient chapel at Nunton. A nunnery was here, but at the time of the Reformation the sisters were massacred. A large house nearby was the 18th-century residence of the Clan Ranalf chieftains.

In the southwestern part of the island you can see the ruins of **Borve Castle,** the seat of the cadet chiefs of the MacDonalds of Clan Ranald of Benbecula. It was occupied in the 17th century. Near the shore, close to the castle, you can see the ruins of a small chapel, **Teampull Bhuirgh.**

Where to Stay & Dine

CREAGORRY HOTEL, Creagorry, Benbecula, Outer Hebrides PA88 5PG. Tel. 0870/602024. Fax 0870/603108. 15 rms (5 with bath, 10 with shower, no toilet). TV
$ Rates (including Scottish breakfast): £27 ($40.50) single with shower, £35 ($52.50) single with bath; £44 ($66) double with shower, £54 ($81) double with bath. MC, V. **Parking:** Free.

Its solidly weatherproof walls were originally built in 1870 as the island's branch of the City of Glasgow Bank, in the center of a very small town. After it went bankrupt in 1878, local entrepreneurs transformed it into a simple but convenient hotel in 1884. Today, much modernized and covered in a sheathing of cream-colored stucco, the hotel offers a handful of uncomplicated bedrooms and the welcome relief of the island's busiest pub, a favorite of local off-duty fishermen. The hotel owns fishing rights to some of the nearby lochs, so sportsmen are also attracted. An evening meal in the dining room costs around £14 ($21) for three courses. A table d'hôte lunch costs £7.75 ($11.60) and a table d'hôte dinner goes for £15.75 ($23.60).

DARK ISLAND HOTEL, Liniclate, Benbecula, Uist, Outer Hebrides PA88 5PJ. Tel. 0870/602414. Fax 0870/602347. 43 rms (41 with bath). TV TEL.
$ Rates (including Scottish breakfast): £24 ($36) single without bath, £45 ($67.50) single with bath; £39 ($58.50) double without bath, £65 ($97.50) double with bath. MC, V. **Parking:** Free.

Capped with a series of skylights and reddish tiles, this is one of the most up-to-date and best-appointed hotels in the Outer Hebrides. It lies within a 10-minute walk of the sea on the island's west coast, midway between Craegorry and Nunton, amid a treeless, wind-battered landscape overlooking dramatically sculpted sand dunes. Bedrooms are modern, functional, and comfortable. The hotel has three different dining areas, that function according to season and their advance bookings. The fish and lamb dishes are ultra-fresh and well prepared. There is also a pub.

SOUTH UIST

A rich treasure trove of antiquity can be found on South Uist, which has a number of ecclesiastical remains scattered along its shores. Clan Ranald, who ruled the island, left many ruins and fortresses known as "duns." Ornithologists and anglers are also attracted here. Part bogland, the island is 20 miles long and 6 miles wide at its broadest point. A main road, the A865, bisects the island, with feeder roads, single-track lanes with passing places, branching off east and west. Some of the most interesting sights, all ruins, lie off these little roads.

WHAT TO SEE & DO

The biggest village in South Uist is **Lochboisdale,** at the head of a deep-sea loch in the southeastern part of the island. It was settled in the 19th century by crofters who had been forced off their land in the notorious Land Clearances of those troubled years. However, the ruins of a small medieval castle can also be seen at the head of the loch on the island of Calvay, one of the many places where Bonnie Prince Charlie hid out.

Leaving Lochboisdale, the A865 goes west for 3 miles to Daliburgh, from where you can take the B888 south to **Pollachar** on the southern shore, a distance of 6 miles, a hamlet named for the Pollachar Standing Stone. Continue east along a minor road for 2½ miles to the Ludag jetty, where a private ferry goes to **Eriskay** and to **Barra.** Then head north again in the direction of Daliburgh to visit the contemporary **Church of Our Lady of Sorrows,** at Garrynamonie, a short drive north of Pollachar. Consecrated in 1964, it has a mosaic of "Our Lady," and can be visited from 9am to 7pm.

The next stop is at **Klipheder Wheelhouse,** 2 miles west of the A865, the meager ruins of a circular building from A.D. 200. Back on the main road again, you come to Askernish, site of a nine-hole golf course. At Mingarry are the remains of a big chambered cairn.

Three miles north from Daliburgh, at Airidh Mhuilinn, is a **Flora MacDonald memorial.** West of the A865, about 200 yards up a little farm track half a mile north of Milton, a cairn on top of a little hill marks the spot where this woman, so revered in legend, was born in 1722. Staying on the minor roads, you'll see the dramatic machair-fringed shoreline and pass through the hamlets of Bornish, Ormiclete, and Stoneybridge. At Ormiclete are the ruins of **Ormiclete Castle,** constructed by the Clan Ranald chieftains in the early 18th century.

Rejoin the main road at Howbeg. The part of the island directly north of Howbeg is rich in archeological remains. Ruins of several medieval chapels are all that is left of a major South Uist ecclesiastical center. An ancient graveyard nearby was the burial ground of the Clan Ranald chieftains.

Farther north, the A865 passes the **Loch Druidibeg National Nature Reserve,** the most significant breeding ground for the native grayleg goose in the country. Attracting the dedicated birdwatcher, it is a setting of machair and brackish lochs. At Drimsdale lie the ruins of a big dun, a fortification in a loch where the villagers retreated when under attack. It continued as a stronghold for the Clan Ranald until the early 1500s.

The road continues past the Royal Artillery Rocket Range (heed those warning signs). On the flank of a Reuval Hill, called "the mountain of miracles," stands **Our Lady of the Isles,** a 30-foot statue of the Virgin and Child. Erected in 1957, the statue was the creation of artist Hew Lorimer, and Catholic contributions from around the world financed the project. It is the largest religious statue in Britain.

Loch Bee, inhabited by mute swans, nearly bisects the northern part of South Uist.

WHERE TO STAY & DINE

LOCHBOISDALE HOTEL, Lochboisdale, South Uist, Outer Hebrides PA81 5TH. Tel. 08784/332. Fax 08784/367. 20 rms (11 with bath).
$ Rates (including Scottish breakfast): £24–£34 ($36–$51) single without bath, £27–£40 ($40.50–$60) single with bath; £48–£58 ($72–$87) double without bath, £54–£70 ($81–$105) double with bath. MC, V. **Parking:** Free.
This hotel is the quintessential fisherman's refuge. Solidly built of local stone in 1892, in center of town, a half-minute walk from the ferryboat terminal, it proudly displays tile-covered tables and scales near its entrance to prepare and weigh the daily catch of its residents. Boasting a strongly international clientele, the hotel estimates that 75% of its visitors come to fish in the local waters. Many of their trophies and much of their

memorabilia decorate the half-paneled walls of the cocktail lounge and restaurant. Each of these areas has its own blazing fireplace and an international sense of sportsman's conviviality. A three-course à la carte dinner costs £17 ($25.50). Also in the hotel is a public bar—the only one within 4 miles—frequented by local residents. Bedrooms are outfitted with an English country-house look of chintz curtains and solidly comfortable furniture.

BORRODALE HOTEL, Daliburgh, South Uist, Outer Hebrides PA81 5SS. Tel. 08784/444. Fax 08784/611. 14 rms (12 with bath). TV
$ Rates (including Scottish breakfast): £30 ($45) single without bath, £32 ($48) single with bath; £50 ($75) double without bath, £52 ($78) double with bath. MC, V.
Parking: Free.

Set near the center of the island, 2½ miles west of Loch Boisdale along the A865, this hotel stands amid a landscape of freshwater lakes, heather, and gorse. Originally built long ago as a doctor's surgery, it was enlarged and modernized in the late 1970s. Today a row of gables runs across the building's second floor, and the interior contains a cocktail bar, a pub, and a restaurant where table d'hôte lunches cost £7.50 ($11.30), and table d'hôte dinners go for £14.50 ($21.80). The owners will assist to arrange fishing and golf expeditions.

AN EASY EXCURSION TO ERISKAY

Eriskay, the small island lying at the southern tip of South Uist, is reached by car-ferry from Ludag. Departure times depend on tides and the weather. If you want to see a staunchly independent Scottish island filled with hardworking, industrious people (some 200 in all), go to Eriskay. You may learn more about Hebridean life here than elsewhere.

The major settlement was founded in the hard days of the notorious Land Clearances. Eriskay was given to crofters because the land was bad. Many or most of today's residents are descended from those evicted crofters who were cleared off their lands along the coasts of Barra and South Uist. The crofters turned to fishing, an occupation followed by the residents today. Father Alan Macdonald is said to have built the island's church, St. Michael's, from the profits of a single night's fishing back in 1903. At the island's cooperative store, you can buy hand-knitted sweaters of excellent quality. Once their design patterns were commonplace, but now they are made only on Eriskay.

The island has a herd of ponies, a rare breed that was barely saved from extinction by a preservation society. Usually measuring only 12 hands, this small pony is found only on Eriskay.

It was here that Bonnie Prince Charlie first landed in his attempt to win back the crown from the Hanoverians. Apparently he got the cold shoulder from the natives and was forced to fish for his supper, spending the night in a hovel before leaving for more hospitable islands. However, to commemorate his memory to this day, a sea bindweed called the Prince's flower, was named after him.

Between Eriskay and South Uist, in the sound, lies the wreck of the S. S. *Politician*. It sank in 1941, carrying 24,000 cases of whisky. This event formed the plot of Compton MacKenzie's novel *Whisky Galore.*

Eriskay, whose two peaks are Ben Stack at 400 feet and Ben Scrien at 600 feet, makes for a rare travel experience, but you must return to South Uist to find accommodation.

13. BARRA

118 miles NW of Edinburgh, 88 miles NW of Glasgow

GETTING THERE   By Plane   At the northern end of Barra is Cockle Strand, the airport. Loganair, the Scottish airline, lands craft here from Glasgow, or from Benbecula and Stornoway on Lewis. Phone 041/8871111 in Glasgow for flight information.

By Ferry From the mainland at Oban, Barra can be reached by Caledonian MacBrayne car-ferry, which docks at Castlebay. Subject to weather conditions, departures from Oban are on Monday, Wednesday, Thursday, and Saturday, with a return on Tuesday, Thursday, Friday, and Sunday. Sailing time is 5 hours, and a one-way ticket costs £13.65 ($20.50). In Oban, call 0631/62285 for sailing information.

From South Uist you can also take a car-ferry from Lochboisdale to Castlebay.

A privately operated 12-passenger ferry will take you from Eoligarry, north of the Cockle Strand airport, to Ludag on South Uist. It operates only Monday through Saturday (tel. 08784/216 for schedules).

ESSENTIALS The **Castlebay Tourist Information Centre** (tel. 08784/336) is found near the pier where the ferryboat docks. It is open Easter through September, Monday to Friday from 9am to 5pm and on Saturday from 9am to 3:30pm. The staff there will help you locate a room should you arrive in Barra without a reservation. The **telephone area code** is 08784.

Called "the garden of the Hebrides," Barra lies at the southern end of the Outer Hebrides. Locals claim that here are some 1,000 varieties of wildflowers. Once occupied by Vikings, the island is one of the most beautiful in the Hebridean chain, with heather-clad meadows, beaches, sandy grasslands, peaks, rocky bays, and lofty headlands. Since the days of the conquering Norsemen it has been associated with the Clan MacNeil.

A circular road of 10 miles will take you around Barra, which is about 4 by 8 miles. Cockle Strand, the airport, is a long and wide beach of white sand, said to be the only runway in Britain washed twice daily by sea tides.

Most of the 200 inhabitants of Barra are centered at **Castlebay,** its capital, a 19th-century herring port and the best place to stock up on supplies. In the background of the port is **Ben Heaval,** at 1,250 feet the highest mountain on Barra. On its slopes you'll see a Virgin and Child carved of Carrara marble.

WHAT TO SEE & DO

The most important sightseeing attraction of Barra is in the bay. **Kismul Castle** (tel. 08714/336) was built for strategic purposes on a small islet, the longtime stronghold of the notorious MacNeils of Barra, a clan known for piracy and lawlessness. Their 35th chieftain, Ruari the Turbulent, was so bold as to seize one of Elizabeth I's ships. When the direct male line died out in 1863, leadership of the clan reverted to the Canadian branch.

The oldest part of the castle is a tower dating from 1120. An accidental fire swept through the 15th- and 16th-century part of the structure in 1795. In 1938, the 45th chieftain of the clan, the late Robert Lister Macneil of Barra, an architect, began restoration work on his ancestral home. After many interruptions, including World War II, the job was completed in 1970. The castle may be visited from May to September only on Monday, Wednesday, and Saturday afternoons. A boatman will take you over and back at 2pm. Entrance is £2.50 ($3.80), including the boat ride.

To drive around the island, head west from Castlebay until you reach Kinloch. On the left is Loch St. Clair, reached by a tiny track road. In the loch on an islet stand the ruins of St. Clair Castle, called **MacLeod's Fort.** In the vicinity you can also see **St. Columba's Well,** named for the saint.

Continuing north to Borve, you will see the **Borve Standing Stones** on your left. At Borve, the north fork leads to a chambered cairn and the hamlet of **Craigston,** which has a church dedicated to St. Brendan, the Irish navigator whom many cite as the discoverer of America. In the area are two interesting ruins, **Dun Bharpa,** a collection of stones encircled by standing stones, and **Tigh Talamhanta,** a ruined wheelhouse.

Continue north to Allasdale. **Dun Cuier** is one of the few excavated Hebridean Iron Age forts, better preserved than most. Opposite Allasdale is **Seal Bay,** a beauty spot where the seals do as much inspection of you as you do of them.

At **Northbay** at Loch an Duin, the remains of an old dun protrude from the water. Continue north to **Eoligarry,** site of a small ferry terminal taking passengers to Ludag on South Uist. Eoligarry's proud possession is **St. Barr's Church,** named after St. Findbarr of Cork (A.D. 550–623), who is said to have converted the islanders to Christianity after finding many of them practicing cannibalism when he arrived. The original 12th-century chapel was restored by Fr. Callum MacNeil. The Celtic stones in the churchyard are called "Crusader stones." This was the old burial ground of the MacNeil chieftains. Novelist Compton MacKenzie is buried here. Near Eoligarry, on the summit of a small hill, is **Dun Scurrival,** another ruined fort, this one measuring 39 by 52 feet.

WHERE TO STAY & DINE

CASTLEBAY HOTEL, Castlebay, Barra, Outer Hebrides PA80 5XD. Tel. 08714/223. 13 rms (all with bath). TV
$ Rates (including Scottish breakfast): £27.50 ($41.30) single; £55 ($82.50) double. MC, V. **Parking:** Free. **Closed:** Dec 22–Jan 5.
Originally built around 1890, its gables overlook the bay and the ferryboat terminal where most of the island's visitors disembark. Its cocktail bar has a quiet corner reserved for dining. A four-course dinner costs £15 ($22.50) and might feature the fruits of the sea for which the island derives much of its income. Adjacent to the hotel, and under the same management, is the Castlebay Bar, one of the island's most consistently popular gathering places (its open fireplace is particularly welcome on a cold night). The bedrooms are simply but comfortably furnished.

CRAIGARD HOTEL, Castlebay, Barra, Outer Hebrides PA80 5XD. Tel. 08714/200. 7 rms (3 with shower). TV.
$ Rates (including Scottish breakfast): £24 ($36) single without bath, £30 ($45) single with shower; £40 ($60) double without bath, £52 ($78) double with shower. MC, V. **Parking:** Free.
Built originally as a private house, this establishment became a hotel in 1940, and was upgraded in 1993. The white-walled gables of this hotel command a handsome view of the bay and Kismul Castle. The hotel offers clean, efficient, and functional rooms. Table d'hôte dinners cost £15.95 ($23.90) and bar meals (three courses) go for £8 ($12) each.

ISLE OF BARRA HOTEL, Tangusdale, Castlebay, Barra, Outer Hebrides PA80 5XY. Tel. 08714/383. Fax 08714/385. 30 rms (all with bath). TV.
$ Rates (including Scottish breakfast): £35 ($52.50) single; £65 ($97.50) double. MC, V. **Parking:** Free. **Closed:** Oct–Mar.
The low-slung rooflines of this seashore hotel are part of a design by an architect who won an award in the late 1970s for this hotel. For the Outer Hebrides, it is a luxury selection. It was erected as a project of the Highlands and Islands Development Board, which adorned its brick walls with nautical paraphernalia and contemporary tapestries. It commands a view of the tranquil less-populated western shore of the island.

Its pub, the most westerly in Scotland, is widely touted as "the last dram before America." From the dining room and many of the well-furnished bedrooms you can see everything that's coming and going at sea. At the suggestion of their Scottish nanny, the shah of Iran used this hotel as a safe haven for his children when he was threatened by a revolution knocking at his door. The shah and his retinue are long gone, but the hotel remains a favorite with the yachting crowd. Some of the best food on Barra is served here. A set dinner costs £15.50 ($23.30).

NORTHBAY GUEST HOUSE, Northbay, Barra, Outer Hebrides PA80 5YH. Tel. 08715/255. 3 rms (one with bath).
$ Rates (including Scottish breakfast): £15 ($22.50) per person single or double without bath; £17 ($25.50) per person single or double with bath. No credit cards. **Parking:** Free. **Closed:** Nov–Mar.
Dramatically situated on the northeastern shore of the island, midway between Castlebay and the Cockle Strand Airport, at the top of a loch, it was originally built

around 1882 as one of the island's first schools. Today its churchlike belfries and steeply inclined roofs lie within a short walk of one of the island's oldest structures, a ruined mill whose origins seem shrouded in mystery, and a jagged and unusual rock nearby whose side resembles, it's said, the craggy profile of Queen Victoria herself. Run by Marion and Donald Galbraith, the hotel caters to a clientele of fishers and nature lovers. Guests appreciate the simple, very clean bedrooms.

AN EASY EXCURSION TO VATERSAY

Across the bay from Barra stands the little island of Vatersay; ferry goes there from Castlebay, running once a day except Sunday. Vatersay is visited mostly on sunny days fot its beautiful beaches. The island is less than 4 miles long and wide, with a broad isthmus of shell sand. Points on the island are connected by a little single-lane roadway, stretching for about 5 miles. It's inhabited by about 100 tranquil souls who like to live near their cattle, as Vatersay is known for its excellent grazing. Many local inhabitants are descendants who from the "Vatersay Raiders," crofters from Barra who took over the island. They established homesteads, faced a legal challenge, and won the right to stay on the land.

Food can be purchased at the island's community center, and the rest of the day can be spent on one of the beaches. A monument on West Beach is in memory of the *Annie Jane,* an emigrant ship wrecked off the coastline in 1853. The most significant remain on the island is **Dun a'Chaolais,** in the western part. Built on a rocky knoll about 100 feet high, this circular broch has an internal diameter of about 30 feet.

CHAPTER 11

THE ORKNEY & SHETLAND ISLANDS

- **WHAT'S SPECIAL ABOUT THE ORKNEY & SHETLAND ISLANDS**
- **1. THE ORKNEY ISLANDS**
- **2. FAIR ISLE**
- **3. THE SHETLAND ISLANDS**

Northern outposts of civilization, the Orkney and Shetland archipelagos consist of about 200 islands, about 40 of which are inhabited. "Go to Shetland for scenery, Orkney for antiquities," or so the saying goes. That doesn't mean that Orkney doesn't have scenery, too. It does, in abundance.

These far-flung and scattered islands are rich in a great Viking heritage. Ceded to Scotland by Norway as part of the dowry of Princess Margaret in 1472 (she'd married a Scottish king), the islands were part of the great Norse earldoms. They were a gathering place for Norse fleets, and celebrated in the *Orkneyinga Saga,* which detailed the exploits of the Viking warriors.

The Vikings did not settle the islands. Tribes of Stone Age people occupied both Shetland and Orkney. The Picts came later, and ruins of their round forts can still be seen dotting the coastlines. The handcraft of prehistoric people still stands in stark contrast to the rich rolling hills and landscape.

The island chains are not part of the Highlands, and totally differ from both the Inner and Outer Hebrides. Clans, Gaelic, and kilts were unfamiliar to the Orcadians and the Shetlanders—until the Scots arrived. At first these merchants and newcomer landlords were bitterly resented. Even today the islanders are fiercely independent. They speak of themselves as Orcadians and Shetlanders instead of as Scots. Not only are Orkney and Shetland different from the Highlands, they are different from each other, as we will soon see.

Change, as was inevitable, has come to Orkney and Shetland in the way of oil and modern conveniences. But tradition is still strong. It has a lot to do with climate and with ancestry.

SEEING THE ORKNEY & SHETLAND ISLANDS

GETTING THERE

P&O Ferries run between Scrabster (near Thurso) on Scotland's north coast to the Orkneys in just 2 hours; call 0856/850655 for information. A passenger ferry operates two to four times a day in summer from John o' Groats; call 095581/353 for information. This connection takes only 45 minutes. British Airways and Loganair also fly into the Orkneys, as they do to Sumburgh, 26 miles south of Lerwick, the most important center on the Shetland Islands. P&O Ferries provide overnight ferry service three times weekly between Aberdeen in northeast Scotland and Lerwick (tel. 0224/572615 in Aberdeen for more information).

WHAT'S SPECIAL ABOUT THE ORKNEY & SHETLAND ISLANDS

Great Towns/Villages
- ☐ Kirkwall, established by Norse invaders, the capital of the Orkneys for nine centuries.
- ☐ Stromness, in Orkney, the main port of the archipelago and once the last port of call before the New World.
- ☐ Fair Isle, "the most isolated part of Britain," an important staging point for migrating birds.
- ☐ Lerwick, capital of Shetland since the 17th century, once the herring capital of northern Europe.

Ancient Monuments
- ☐ Midhowe Broch and Tombs, on Rousay, dating from the Iron Age, called "the great ship of death."
- ☐ Quoyness Chambered Tomb, Sanday, a spectacular chambered cairn dating from 2,900 B.C.

- ☐ The Ring of Brodgar, between Loch and Stenness, a stone circle of some 36 stones, dating from 1,560 B.C., called "the Stonehenge of Scotland."
- ☐ Unstan Chambered Tomb, northeast of Stromness, a burial mound from 2,500 B.C., unsurpassed in western Europe.
- ☐ Skara Brae, a Neolithic village joined by covered passages, last occupied about 2,500 B.C.

Religious Shrines
- ☐ St. Magnus Cathedral, Kirkwall, burial place of the saint of the Orkneys, founded in 1137.

SUGGESTED ITINERARY

Days 1 and 2: Head for Kirkwall in the Orkneys. You'll spend a good part of the day getting there, so save Day 2 for exploring the nearby attractions, including the Ring of Brodgar and Unstan Chambered Tomb.

Day 3: Transfer to Stromness for the night and explore the Neolithic village of Skara Brae to the north.

Day 4: Spend a day on Rousay—called "Egypt of the North"—and explore some of its prehistoric monuments, including the Midhowe Broch and Tombs.

Days 5 and 6: Transfer to Lerwick in the Shetland Islands and discover as much of the mainland there as time allows.

---

1. THE ORKNEY ISLANDS

6 miles N of John o' Groats (mainland Scotland) across Pentland Firth, 280 miles N of Edinburgh

GETTING THERE   By Plane   British Airways (tel. 041/329666) and Loganair (tel. 041/8893181) have daily scheduled service to **Kirkwall Airport** on Mainland Orkney. British Airways flies from Glasgow, Inverness, and Aberdeen, with connections from London, Birmingham, and Manchester. Loganair operates from Glasgow, Edinburgh, Inverness, and Wick.

By Car and Ferry   If you're driving over, head for Scrabster, near Thurso, in the northern province of Caithness. There, **P&O's St. Ola** operates a roll-on/roll-off ferry service with 2-hour sailings to Stromness on Mainland Orkney. The ferry sails two or three times a day in summer. A round-trip fare is about £85 ($127.50), including a car. A single fare (passenger only) is £12 ($18) per person. For more information, phone P&O Ferries in Stromness (tel. 0856/850655).

By Ferry If you don't have a car, it's faster and cheaper to go from "end-of-the-line" John o' Groats to Burwick. The time is only 45 minutes and the fare is £10 ($15). This ferry operates only in summer, Monday through Saturday. Departures from Scrabster are usually at noon, and from John o'Groats at 10:30am and 4:15pm. However, in July, August, and September, the ferries leave four times a day in both directions (check locally for accurate times of departure). **Thomas & Bews,** the John o'Groats operator, can be reached by phoning 095581/353.

ESSENTIALS If you want to know what events are taking place at the time of your visit, you will have to consult **The Orcadian,** a weekly published since 1854. There are **tourist information centers** at both Kirkwall, on 10 Broad St. (tel. 0856/872856), and Stromness, the two principal "towns" of Orkney. In winter the office in Stromness (tel. 0856/850716) stays open for only 2 hours a day to meet the ferry coming from Scrabster on the mainland (the information booth is in the ferry terminal building).

The **telephone area code** for both Kirkwall and Stromness is 0856.

SPECIAL EVENTS The last week in May at Stromness the **Orkney Traditional Folk Festival** attracts musicians from Scandinavia. For information write to the Festival Office, P.O. Box 4, Stromness, Orkney KW16 3AA.

To visit the Orkney Islands is to look at a thousand years of history. Orkney is an archipelago of islands extending for about 50 miles north and northeast. Covering a land area of 376 square miles, they lie some 6 miles north of the Scottish mainland. The terrain has a lot of rich and fertile farmland, but also some dramatic scenery: Britain's highest perpendicular cliffs rise to 1,140 feet.

The population of the entire chain is less than 20,000, spread sparsely across about 29 inhabited islands. The people are somewhat suspicious of strangers, and if you meet an Orcadian in a local pub, you will have to break the ice.

The climate is far milder than the location would suggest because of the warming currents of the Gulf Stream. There are few extremes in temperature. From May through July you get some astonishing sunsets, with the midsummer sun over the horizon for 18¼ hours a day. The Orcadians call their midsummer sky "Grimlins" from the old Norse word *grimla,* which means to twinkle or glimmer. There's enough light for golfers to play at midnight.

Who comes here other than the golfer? The archeologist, the artist, the walker, the climber, and the birdwatcher are likely to share your breakfast table. Many history students come here. They've read the *Orkneyinga Saga,* that product of the "golden age" of Orkney in which the pomp and heraldry of the archipelago were recorded. Orkney is a virtual archeological garden, as some 100 of the 500 known brochs—often called "the castles of the Picts"—are found here. Built by Orkney chiefs, these brochs were fortified structures where islanders could find refuge from invaders. Wells inside the structure provided water.

Divers are attracted to Orkney, some drawn by the remains of the warships of the German Imperial Navy that were scuttled here on June 21, 1919, on orders of Rear Admiral Ludwig von Reuter. Most of the vessels have been salvaged, but there are still plenty lying down there in the deep.

Anglers come in droves. Unlike other parts of Scotland, fishing is free in Orkney, because of old Norse law and ancient Udal tradition. The wild brown trout is said to be the best in Britain. The season runs from mid-March until the first week in October.

A large percentage of the world's gray seal population visits Orkney to breed and molt. The islanders call the seal a "selkie." Wildfowl migrate from Iceland and northern Europe in winter, including the goldeneye, the red-throated diver, known locally as the "rain goose," and the short-eared owl or "cattieface," as well as such breeding seabirds as kittiwakes, puffins (called "tammie-honies" locally), and guillemoats. The resident bird of prey on the island is the hen harrier. Some 300 species have been identified in the islands.

Orkney is also known for its flora, including the Scottish primrose, which is no

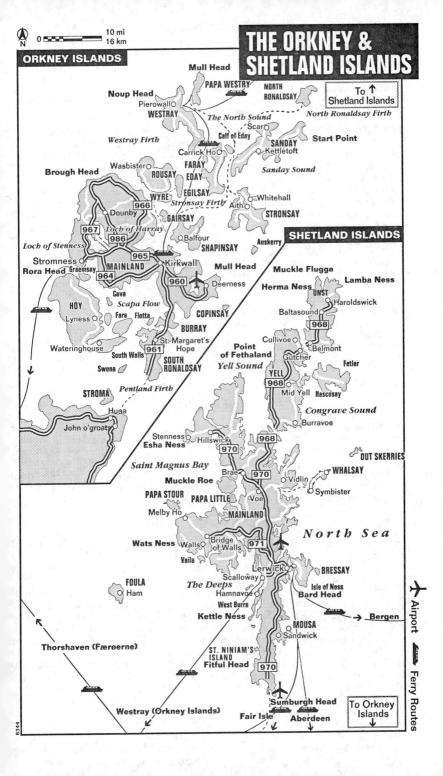

more than 2 inches in height and is believed to have survived the Ice Age by growing in small ice-free areas. The amethyst, with a pale-yellow eye, is found only in Orkney and parts of northern Scotland.

Accommodations are few in the Orkneys; the greatest number are found in Kirkwall and Stromness, both on the same island, which is called "the Mainland." Stromness is in the west, Kirkwall in the east.

GETTING AROUND   Island-hopping is common in the north of Scotland. In fact, Scots take to the air more often than anywhere else in Britain. **Loganair** operates scheduled flights from Kirkwall Airport on Mainland to the isles of Sanday, Stronsay, Westray, Eday, North Ronaldsay, and Papa Westray. To reach them, call 0856/ 872494, at the Kirkwall Airport.

The **Orkney Islands Shipping Co.** operates scheduled ferry service from Kirkwall to Orkney's north and south islands: Eday, Papa Westray, Sanday, Stronsay, Westray, North Ronaldsay, and Shapinsay. From Houton there is service to the south isles: Flotta, Graemsay, and Hoy at Longhope and Lyness; and from Tingwall to Rousay, Egilsay, and Wyre. The headquarters of the shipping line is at 4 Ayre Rd. in Kirkwall (tel. 0856/872921).

There is also a private ferry service to take you to Hoy, departing from Stromness. The tourist office will have the latest details on departures.

The Churchill Barriers, erected to impede enemy shipping in World War II, have been turned into a road link between the islands of Mainland and South Ronaldsay. **Bus tours** operate from March through the end of October, visiting the major sights. One reliable operator is **"Go Orkney,"** South Cannigall, St. Ola (tel. 0856/874260). You can go aboard naturalist David Lea's luxury coach, taking in such attractions as prehistoric monuments and seals. He knows Orkney better than anybody. The tours are popular, and it's wise to book seats with the **Kirkwall Tourist Office** (tel. 0856/872856). Tours range from £5 ($7.50) to £12 ($18). The trips usually begin at 9:45am. Some island tours start earlier.

KIRKWALL

On the bay of Firth, Kirkwall, established by Norse invaders, has been the capital of the Orkney Islands for at least 900 years. It used to be called Kirkjuvagr or "church bay," after a church built around 1040 honoring the memory of King Olaf Harraldsson, later the patron saint of Norway. That church no longer stands.

The old Norse streets of Kirkwall are very narrow to protect the buildings from galelike winds. But don't get the idea they're pedestrian walkways. That myth is dispelled when a car comes roaring down the street.

WHAT TO SEE & DO

For the best view of Kirkwall and the North Isles, head up **Wideford Hill,** about 2 miles west of town. There you will enjoy a panoramic sweep. On the western slope of this hill, 2½ miles west of Kirkwall, is the **Wideford Hill Cairn,** a trio of concentric walls built around a passage and a megalithic chamber.

Kirkwall was granted a royal charter from James III in 1486. "The Pride of Orkney" is   ✪ **St. Magnus Cathedral,** Broad Street, burial place of the martyred St. Magnus, patron saint of the island chain. The cathedral was founded in 1137 by Jarl Rognvald in honor of his uncle, the martyred saint to whom the cathedral is dedicated. The remains of both the saint and Jarl Rognvald were interred between the two large central piers. It's a "Norman" building, constructed of gray and pinkish rose sandstone. Work went on over centuries, and additions were made in the transitional and very early Gothic styles. It is still in regular use as a church, and can be visited Monday through Saturday from 9am to 5pm (closed Sunday except for services).

Across the cathedral are the ruins of a 12th-century **Bishop's Palace,** Broad Street, with a round tower dating from the 16th century. King Haakon came here to die in 1263, following the Battle of Largs and his attempt to invade Scotland. The ruins can be visited April through September, Monday to Saturday from 9:30am to 6pm and on Sunday from 2 to 6pm. Admission is £1 ($1.50) adults, 50p (80¢) children

The palace was originally constructed for William the Old, a bishop who died in 1168.

An easy walk will take you to the impressive ruins of **Earl Patrick's Palace,** on Watergate. Built in 1607, it has been called "the most mature and accomplished piece of Renaissance architecture left in Scotland." Earl Patrick Stewart was the illegitimate son of the brother of Mary Queen of Scots. The palace figured in the novel by Sir Walter Scott, *The Pirate.* It keeps the same hours as the Bishop's Palace, charging an admission of £1 ($1.50) for adults and 50p (80¢) for children.

Nearby is **Tankerness House,** on Broad Street, dating from 1574. This is an example of a merchant-laird's mansion, with crow-stepped gables, complete with courtyard and gardens. A museum here depicts life in Orkney over the past 5,000 years. Exhibitions range from the bones of the earliest prehistoric inhabitants to Neolithic pottery to farming and domestic utensils. You'll see, among other items, a Pictish stone symbol, bronze jewelry, and temporary exhibitions as well. It is open all year, Monday to Saturday from 10:30am to 1pm and 2 to 5pm; from May through September, it is also open on Sunday from 2 to 5pm. Admission is £1 ($1.50) for adults, free for children.

In the environs, you can visit the **Grain Earth Houses** at Hatson, near Kirkwall. This is an Iron Age souterrain, with stairs leading to an underground chamber. Another Iron Age souterrain, **Rennibister Earth House,** lies about 4½ miles west and northwest of Kirkwall. This excavation also has an underground chamber that has supporting roof pillars.

At Holm, on the road south to the island of South Ronaldsay (see the section on Burray and South Ronaldsay below) you can visit Graemeshall House. Its outstanding collection of **Norwood Antiques** has many rare and unusual pieces of furniture. The collection was started by Norris Wood, described as a "working man," just after World War II when many valuable pieces of Orkney Islands furniture were available for "very little" money. Over the years he added to his treasures, buying both island and European antiques. Norwood Antiques is today directed by his daughter-in-law, Mrs. Cilla Wood, who advises allowing at least an hour to view the entire collection. It is open May through September on Tuesday, Wednesday, Thursday, and Sunday from 2 to 5pm and 6 to 8pm. Admission is £1.75 ($2.60) for adults, £1 ($1.50) for children. For information, phone 0856/78217.

Shopping

You may not think of the Orkney Islands as a place to shop, but there are many interesting purchases to be made here. **The Longship,** 7 Broad St. (tel. 0856/873251) is the retail outlet of Ola Gorie, the Orkney jewelry in Kirkwall. Now in its third decade, it has a wide range of high-quality jewelry, including some inspired by stone carvings found at archeological digs, others by the rich flora and fauna of the islands. A collection based on designs by Charles Rennie Mackintosh has proved popular, as have some art nouveau pieces and a range of enamel jewelry with traditional Paisley pattern designs.

Scott's Fish Shop, 3 Bridge St. (tel. 0856/873170) is known throughout Britain for its earthy but elegant curing of salmon from local waters with oak smoke. It also sells yellow and white Orkney Islands farm cheese, including flavorful versions of local varieties known as Claymore and Swanney. The staff is delightful.

Robert Tower's Workshop, Rosegarth House, St. Ola (tel. 0856/873521), located in the village of St. Ola, 1½ miles from Kirkwall, displays the Orkney chair, a famous design created by a crofter and fisherman. Made from prime oak, it is fumed and finished with raw linseed oil. A favorite design is a hooded chair with drawers underneath the seat.

WHERE TO STAY & DINE

AYRE HOTEL, Ayre Road, Kirkwall, Orkney KW15 1QX. Tel. 0856/ 873001. Fax 0856/876289. 34 rms (all with bath). TV TEL
$ Rates (including Scottish breakfast): £46 ($69) single; £68–£75 ($102–$112.50) double. MC, V. **Parking:** Free.

Set midway between the town's copper-spired church and the harborfront, within a 2-minute walk of the town center, this white-sided hotel contains a stone core built in 1792, and a sprawling modern addition added during the 1970s. When it was originally built, its owners considered it a social showcase for the town, hosting dances and bridge parties that became famous in the region. Today guests congregate in the establishment's popular bar, where lunches and dinners begin at £4 ($6) each. A fixed-price dinner in the hotel's dining room costs around £16 ($24). About half the bedrooms were refurbished in 1991, and all are comfortable and functionally modern.

FOVERAN HOTEL, St. Ola, Kirkwall, Orkney KW15 1SF. Tel. 0856/ 872389. Fax 0856/876430.
   Cuisine: SCOTTISH. **Reservations:** Recommended.
$ Prices: Appetizers £2.50–£5 ($3.80–$7.50); main courses £9.75–£15 ($14.60– $22.50). MC, V.
   Open: Dinner only Tues–Sat 7–9pm.
Located 2 miles west of Kirkwall, overlooking the Scapa Flow, site of the sinking of the German Imperial Fleet in 1919, the Foveran looks like a modern hotel of Scandinavian design. Fully licensed, its restaurant offers the best cuisine in the area, and emphasizes "Taste of Scotland" menus. You get tasty homemade soups, along with pâtés and a rich array of seafood. The catch of the day might turn out to be lobster, grilled salmon, deep-fried squid, giant crab claws (known locally as "partan toes"), scallops, prawns, or brown trout. Vegetarian meals are also offered, as well as succulent portions of Orkney Island beef, lamb, and farm-made cheeses.
   The hotel also rents eight pleasantly furnished bedrooms, all with private baths. The price for B&B in a single is £40 ($60) daily, while doubles cost £65 ($97.50).

KIRKWALL HOTEL, Harbour St., Kirkwall, Orkney KW15 1LF. Tel. 0856/2232. Fax 0856/2812. 44 rms (all with bath or shower). TV TEL
$ Rates (including Scottish breakfast): £40–£45 ($60–$67.50) single; £60–£68 ($90–$102) double. No credit cards. **Parking:** Free.
The Kirkwall's four-story brick facade is one of the most visible structures in town. Its well-crafted design includes windows trimmed in yellow-beige stone, along with a comfortably modernized interior. All bedrooms have hot-beverage facilities, among other amenities. The preferred rooms overlook the harbor.

LECKMELM, Annfield, Crescent, Kirkwall, Orkney KW15 1NS. Tel. 0856/873917. 3 rms (none with bath). TV TEL
$ Rates (including Scottish breakfast): £13 ($19.50) single; £24 ($36) double. No credit cards. **Parking:** Free.
   ⑤ In this comfortable guest house home-baking can be sampled at a light supper, served at about 9:30pm. Visitors like the lovely view of the North Isles from the house, and Mrs. Margaret A. Scott, the owner, has a fairly extensive range of books on Orkney and local ornithological interests. Leckmelm is a 10-minute walk from the harbor, going uphill on East Road.

ROYAL HOTEL, Victoria St., Kirkwall, Orkney KW15 1DN. Tel. 0856/ 873477. 32 rms (16 with bath). TV
$ Rates (including Scottish breakfast): £15–£21 ($22.50–$31.50) single without bath, £30–£35 ($45–$52.50) single with bath; £30–£42 ($45–$63) double without bath, £60–£70 ($90–$105) double with bath. MC, V. **Parking:** Free.
The Royal Hotel occupies a pair of centrally located houses, one of which opens onto the main street 50 yards from St. Magnum's Cathedral, the other fronting a nearby courtyard. The lintel over the main entrance is dated 1670, but the bedrooms have been modernized. The hotel also operates two bars, the Public Bar and the Lounge Bar. The hotel's restaurant serves a Scottish/Orcadian cuisine based on local meats and seafood products. A table d'hôte dinner costs £8.95 ($13.40).

WEST END HOTEL, 14 Main St., Kirkwall, Orkney KW15 1BU. Tel. 0856/872368. 16 rms (all with bath). TV TEL

$ Rates (including Scottish breakfast): £30 ($45) single; £48 ($72) double. MC, V. **Parking:** Free.

Set in dignified isolation just outside the town center, its solid stone walls and three stories were originally built in 1837 by a retired sea captain who had made his fortune running contraband goods between Britain and the Baltic during the Napoleonic wars. Today longtime Orkney resident Mrs. Eva Currie extends a warm welcome to guests. Bedrooms are comfortable but simple, each containing tea-making facilities. Mrs. Currie charges from £11 ($16.50) to £13 ($19.50) for a supper in her dining room, and from £4 ($6) to £9 ($13.50) for suppers in her bar. The lounge bar on the premises is licensed to sell drinks to residents and their visitors.

EXPLORING MAINLAND FROM KIRKWALL TO STROMNESS

Heading south from Kirkwall along the southern coastal road toward Stromness, we come first to the hamlet of Orphir. **Orphir Church,** along the A964, is 6 miles southwest of Kirkwall. The ruins here are of the country's only circular medieval church. It was constructed in the first part of the 1100s and dedicated to St. Nicholas. In the vicinity is the site of **Earl's Bu,** a great banqueting hall of the earls of Orkney.

At Orphir, you can see vast tracts of land set aside for birdwatching. If you're an angler, the fishing is free on Kirbister Loch. Ferries leave the **Houton Terminal** for Hoy and Flotta five or six times a day.

In the area is the **Cuween Hill Cairn,** along the A965, half a mile south of Finstown and 6 miles west and northwest of Kirkwall. The owner of a nearby farmhouse has the key that will open a door to reveal a low mound over a megalithic passage tomb, probably dating from the third millennium B.C. Ancient men's bones, along with those of their oxen and dogs, were excavated here.

Bypassing Stromness for the moment, a visitor can continue with a circular tour of the island. In the vicinity of Stromness, lying off the A965, is **Maes Howe,** 10 miles west of Kirkwall. Dating from 2700 B.C., this is a superb achievement of prehistoric architecture. There is a passageway through which the sun shines only at the winter solstice. Constructed with precise masonry, it was built from single slabs more than 18 feet long and some 4 feet wide. It also contains the largest collection of Viking runes in the world, the inscriptions the work of marauding Norsemen who broke into the chambered cairn in search of buried treasure.

The ✪ **Ring of Brodgar,** between Loch and Stenness and Loch of Harray, is found 5 miles to the northwest of Stromness. A stone circle of some 36 stones is surrounded by a deep ditch carved out of solid bedrock. The best stone circle in Scotland, it has been dated 1560 B.C. It has been suggested that it was a lunar observatory. Like Stonehenge, its exact purpose remains a mystery. In the vicinity, the **Stenness Standing Stones** are a quartet of four upright stones, all that's left from a stone circle from 3000 B.C.

The ✪ **Unstan Chambered Tomb,** 2 miles northeast of Stromness along the A965, 10 miles west of Kirkwall, is a big (115 feet in diameter) burial mound dating from 2500 B.C. For its type, it is unsurpassed in western Europe. There is a chambered tomb more than 6 feet high. It is open throughout the day; admission is free. The key can be picked up at Diamond Cottage, near the cairn. For information, telephone 0856/850570. Unstan Ware is a name given to pottery discovered in the tomb.

Last occupied about 2500 B.C., ✪ **Skara Brae,** 7½ miles north of Stromness, was a collection of Neolithic village houses joined by covered passages. It was believed to have sheltered farmers and herders. The housing colony remained buried in the sands for 4,500 years, until a storm in 1850 revealed the ruins. You can see the remains of six houses and a workshop. Once there were 10 dwellings. The walls were made from flagstone rock, the roofs were skins laid on wooden or whalebone rafters. A fireplace was in the center; beds were placed against the side walls. The bed "linen" was bracken or heather, and the "quilts" were animal skins. This prehistoric village is considered the best preserved of its type in Europe. It is open April through September, Monday to Saturday from 9:30am to 6pm and on Sunday from 11:30am to 6pm; October through March, Monday to Saturday from 9:30am to 4pm, Sunday from 2 to 4pm. Admission is £1.70 ($2.60) for adults, 90p ($1.40) for children.

The **Brough of Birsay,** at Birsay, at the northern end of Mainland about 11 miles north of Stromness, is the ruin of a Norse settlement and Romanesque church on an islet that can only be reached at low tide. You can see a replica of a Pictish sculptured stone (the original was removed for safekeeping to a museum). The site is open April through September, Monday to Saturday from 9:30am to 6pm. From October through March, hours are Monday and Tuesday from noon to 4pm, Wednesday to Saturday from 9:30am to 4pm, and on Sunday from 2 to 4pm. Admission is £1 ($1.50) for adults and 50p (80¢) for children. Nearby are the ruins of **Earl's Palace at Birsay,** a mansion constructed in the 16th century for the earls of Orkney.

Click Mill, off the B9057, 2 miles northeast of Dounby, is the only still-functioning example of an old horizontal watermill on the island.

WHERE TO STAY & DINE IN BIRSAY PARISH

BARONY HOTEL, Birsay, Orkney KW17 2LS. Tel. 0856/72327. Fax 0856/72302. 10 rms (8 with bath). TEL TV

$ Rates (including Scottish breakfast): £20 ($30) single without bath, £25 ($37.50) single with bath; £39 ($58.50) double without bath, £45 ($67.50) double with bath. No credit cards. **Closed:** Oct–Mar.

One of the more isolated hotels in the Orkneys, it sits more than half a mile from its nearest neighbor, amid a sea of grasslands and farmlands. Originally built as a pair of stone cottages around 1870, it has been enlarged so often that the original plans have been obliterated in favor of something that resembles an angular civic building. Sheathed in a coat of "pebble dash" (roughly textured stucco), the hotel contains simple but comfortable bedrooms, a dining room and cocktail lounge, and the possibility for such sporting diversions as nearby fishing and golf. A table d'hôte dinner costs £12 ($18).

The Barony Hotel is in the open countryside of Birsay Parish, 25 miles west of Kirkwall and 20 miles north of Stromness. From either of the roads connecting the towns, follow the signs to Birsay.

WHERE TO DINE AT ORPHIR

SCORRABRAE INN, Orphir. Tel. 0856/81262.
Cuisine: BRITISH. **Reservations:** Recommended.

$ Prices: Appetizers £1–£1.50 ($1.50–$2.30); main courses £4–£6 ($6–$9). No credit cards.

Open: May 1–Aug 31, lunch daily noon–2:30pm; dinner daily 5–10pm. Sept 1–Apr 30, dinner only, daily 6–10pm.

In a 10-year-old extension built onto the side of what was originally a 19th-century grocer's shop, this simple but convenient restaurant also contains the town's only pub. In addition to whiskies and beer, it dispenses platters of such time-tested dishes as fried filet of plaice with lemon butter, sandwiches, steaks, prawn salads, platters of roasted pork, and omelets.

STROMNESS

Set against a hill, Brinkie's Brae, Stromness was once known as Hamnavoe or "haven bay" in Old Norse. With its sheltered anchorage, it is the main port of Orkney. Its stone-flagged main street is said to "uncoil like a sailor's rope." It's really about three-quarters of a mile of narrow street and not much else. The ferryboat *St. Ola* comes in here from the mainland, having left from Scrabster. Fishing boats find shelter here from storms in the North Atlantic.

With its waterfront gables, *nousts* (slipways), and jetties, Stromness on the west coast of Mainland strikes many visitors as more interesting than Kirkwall. In the old days you could see whaling ships in port, along with vessels belonging to the Hudson's Bay Company. Some young men of Orkney left with them to man lonely fur stations in the far outposts of Canada. For many transatlantic vessels, Stromness was the last port of call before the New World. At Login's Well, many ships were outfitted for Arctic expeditions.

WHAT TO SEE & DO

A small but well-planned bookshop, **Stromness Books and Prints,** 1 Graham Pl. (tel. 0856/850565), specializes in books about Orkney and has in stock copies of the *Orkneyinga Saga.*

PIER ARTS CENTRE, Victoria Street, Tel. 0856/850209.

This complex opened on a restored pier, and has dazzled Orcadians with its "St. Ives school" of art, including works displayed by Barbara Hepworth and Ben Nicholson. Temporary exhibitions are also presented here.

Admission: Free.

Open: Tues–Sat 10:30am–12:30pm and 1:30–5pm; June–Aug, also Sun 2–5pm.

STROMNESS MUSEUM, 52 Alfred St. Tel. 0856/850025.

Here you can see a collection of artifacts relating to the history of Orkney, especially a gallery devoted to maritime subjects, such as the Hudson's Bay Company and the story of the sinking of the German Imperial Fleet. Founded in 1837, the year Victoria became queen, the museum has been much changed and altered over the years. There is also a natural-history section, with excellent collections of local birds and their eggs, fossils, shells, butterflies, and moths.

Admission: 40p (60¢) adults, 20p (30¢) children under 14.

Open: Mon–Sat 10:30am–12:30pm and 1:30–5pm.

WHERE TO STAY & DINE

STROMNESS HOTEL, Victoria St., Stromness, Orkney KW16 3AA. Tel. 0856/850298. Fax 0856/850610. 40 rms (all with bath). TV TEL

$ Rates (including Scottish breakfast): £20–£28 ($30–$42) single; £40–£56 ($60–$84) double. MC, V. **Parking:** Free.

Considered the most important hotel within the Orkneys' second most important community, the Stromness rises in charming but slightly dowdy dignity from a position about a hundred yards from the ferry terminal in the town center. Built in 1901, with a gradual but complete refurbishment of rooms scheduled for sometime during the lifetime of this edition, this hotel is the largest in the Orkneys. (British TV personality and humorist Cilla Black made it her base in 1993 during the filming of one of her sketches on the Orkneys.) Today, the hotel sits behind an elaborately Victorian facade of symmetrical bay windows and beige sandstone blocks. A cocktail lounge is on the premises. Rooms are comfortable, often with views of the water. Lunch is served daily from noon to 2pm; dinner, from 6:30 to 9pm. A table d'hôte dinner costs £15 ($22.50); a bar lunch from £3 ($4.50) to £6 ($9). They feature seafood dishes and local Orkney produce.

BRAES HOTEL, Hellihole Rd., Stromness, Orkney KW16 3AA. Tel. 0856/850495. 7 rms (all with shower). TV

$ Rates (including Scottish breakfast): £25 ($37.50) single; £36–£40 ($54–$60) double. MC, V. **Parking:** Free.

A solidly constructed stone building with a modern extension, the hotel contains a pub, a sun terrace, a dining room, central heating, and a TV lounge, and provides easy access to golf, riding, sailing, fishing, and hunting. All bedrooms have hot-beverage facilities. The hotel overlooks Scapa Flow.

FERRY INN, John St., Stromness, Orkney KW16 3AA. Tel. 0856/850280. Fax 0856/851332. 17 rms (12 with private bath or shower). TV

$ Rates (including Scottish breakfast): £16 ($24) single without bath, £19–£22 ($28.50–$33) single with bath; £30 ($45) double without bath, £34–£40 ($51–$60) double with bath or shower. MC, V. **Parking:** Public with daytime meter.

As its name implies, this hotel is close to the ferryboat. Its three-story white walls were originally constructed with a collection of working chimneys. Today its format has been modernized and central heating added. The bedrooms are simply but adequately set out along utilitarian designs. A pub on the premises serves typical Scottish fare including haggis, smoked salmon, and steak pie. To finish, try a cloutie dumpling with cream. Meals start at £8 ($12), and meal hours are noon to 2pm and 6 to 10pm daily.

BURRAY & SOUTH RONALDSAY

These are two of the most visited of the southeastern isles, lying within an easy drive of Kirkwall on Mainland. Both are connected to Mainland by the "Churchill Barriers" causeway linking the islands of Glims Holm, Burray, and South Ronaldsay.

BURRAY

Where to Stay & Dine

WATERSOUND RESTAURANT/SANDS MOTEL, Burray Village, Burray, Orkney KW17 2SS. Tel. 0856/73298. 4 apts (all with bath and kitchenette). TV

$ Rates: £240 ($360) per week for one to six occupants in summer; £80 ($120) per week in winter. MC, V.

Considered one of the most prominent structures on the island, this three-story, stone-fronted building was originally built around 1860 as a fish-processing plant. Today the building's ground floor contains a reputable restaurant, the Watersound, and a quartet of upper-story apartments that are rented on a self-catering basis for weekly intervals. Each apartment contains three rooms and a kitchenette, and can be rented, if space is available, for less than a week if it's not fully booked. (Bookings of less than a week are not very likely during midsummer, but more probable in low season.)

In addition to food, the Watersound Restaurant contains the island's only pub, open daily from 11am to 11:30pm. Lunch is served every day from noon to 1:45pm; dinner, from 7 to 9:45pm. Appetizers range from £1 ($1.50) to £2.50 ($3.80); main courses run £3.50–£9 ($5.30–$13.50) and might include different preparations of local trout, salmon, lamb, and beef dishes, as well as such bar snacks as sandwiches and lasagne. Mr. and Mrs. David Watt are the resident proprietors.

The hostelry sits in the center of Burray Village, 8 miles north of the passenger ferry at Burwick, on South Ronaldsay.

ST. MARGARET'S HOPE

Also joined by the barrier, the island of South Ronaldsay is unspoiled fertile countryside. St. Margaret's Hope, a hamlet, was named after a young Norwegian princess. Called the "Maid of Norway," she was Edward II's child bride. Had she lived, she was slated to become queen of both England and Scotland.

What to See & Do

ORKNEY WIRELESS MUSEUM, Church Road.

This is a museum of wartime communications used at Scapa Flow, 11 miles south of Kirkwall, which was a major naval anchorage in both World War I and World War II. Today this sea area, enclosed by Mainland and several other islands, has developed as a pipeline landfall and tanker terminal for North Sea oil. You can also see a large collection of early domestic radios.

Admission: £1 ($1.50) adults, 50p (80¢) children.
Open: Apr–Sept. daily 10am–5pm.

THE WORKSHOP, Back Road. Tel. 0856/83587.

This workshop is a craft producers' cooperative in the center of the village of St. Margaret's Hope. It sells a wide range of locally produced crafts, including pottery, jewelry, baskets, rugs, and fine-quality handknits.

Open: Easter–June Mon–Sat 10am–1pm and 2–5pm; July–Aug Mon–Sat 9:30am–5:30pm; Oct–Christmas Mon–Sat 10am–1pm and 2–5pm; Jan–Easter Mon–Sat 10am–1pm.

Where to Dine

CREEL RESTAURANT, Front Road, St. Margaret's Hope, Orkney KW17 2SL. Tel. 0856/83311.
Cuisine: SCOTTISH. **Reservations:** Recommended.
$ Prices: Appetizers £2–£5 ($3–$7.50); main courses £8–£16 ($12–$24). MC, V.
Open: Tues–Sun daily 7–9pm.

This small, cozy eating place overlooking the bay uses fresh local produce and offers a large selection of fresh seafood as well as Orkney beef, chicken, pork, and lamb. This restaurant was a Scottish winner of the "Taste of Britain" award. Specialties include Orkney crab soup, followed by filet steak in a green-peppercorn sauce. You can also try salmon baked in puff pastry with ginger and currants, served with mild tarragon sauce, or haddock and scallops (filets of haddock filled with a mousseline of scallops served on a sauce of fresh tomato and cucumber). For dessert, the authentic specialty is a clootie dumpling, individual dumplings made from an old Orkney recipe, boiled and served with a "double cream." The restaurant also rents three bedrooms, each with private bath. Charges are £20 ($30) in a single and £40 ($60) in a double, including a Scottish breakfast.

HOY

If you crossed the Pentland Firth from Scrabster, you have already seen the most famous sightseeing attraction of this island, stretching for some 13 miles. It's the **"Old Man of Hoy."** Lying off the cliffs of the northwestern part of the island, this high isolated pillar, climbed for the first time in 1966, is 450 feet high. Rock climbers everywhere view it as one of their biggest challenges.

Hoy, or "high island" in Old Norse, has one of the most dramatic coastlines in Scotland; when the sun hits its cliffs of red sandstone they seem to burst into flame. **Ward Hill,** rising to some 1,570 feet, is the highest hill in Orkney. One of the highest vertical cliffs in Britain, **St. John's Head** rises some 1,140 feet.

Hoy, too, has its prehistoric monuments. The red-sandstone **Dwarfie Stane,** unique in Britain, was a burial chamber dating from the third millennium B.C. The location is near Rackwich. This vast megalithic monument consists of two cells, entered by a passageway. Many legends, including one of a giant said to have inhabited this place, grew up around this monument.

The **Martello Towers** at Hackness can be seen only from the exterior. Originally constructed as a deterrent to the U.S. Navy should it threaten British shipping to the Baltic in the War of 1812, they were used again in World War I.

From Stromness a passenger-only ferry departs daily at 9:30am and 4pm Monday to Friday, arriving at Moaness Pier in North Hoy after a 30-minute journey. In summer, there are additional sailings from Stromness on weekdays at 10:30am and Saturday and Sunday sailings at 9:30am and 6pm. Bookings, although not essential, can be made through Hoy Sailings on 0856/850624 or 0856/850678.

From Houton Orkney Islands Shipping Company operates a roll-on/roll-off car and passenger ferry service from Houton on the Orkney Mainland to Lyness on Hoy. Departure times vary according to days of the week but are normally early morning. A Sunday service operates in the summer season only. Journey time is normally 35 minutes. Bookings are advisable and can be made by telephoning 0856/81397.

SHAPINSAY

If you don't have time to inspect many islands, Shapinsay will give you an idea of what one is like. Getting there is fairly easy if you're based on Kirkwall. The **Orkney Islands Shipping Co.,** 4 Ayre Rd. (tel. 0856/872044), in Wyre, goes there twice a day except on Sunday. The crossing takes less than half an hour.

The island was the seat of the Balfours of Trenabie. John Balfour was a nabob, making his fortune in India before becoming the M.P. (Member of Parliament) for Orkney and Shetland in 1790. He launched the Scottish baronial castle, Balfour.

Washington Irving's father was born on Shapinsay. There are several Neolithic sites on the island, but most remain unexcavated. Visitors come here mainly for Shapinsay's secluded beaches, its many walking trails, and its wildlife, including seals, which can be seen often.

WHERE TO STAY & DINE

BALFOUR CASTLE, Balfour Village, Shapinsay, Orkney KW17 2DY. Tel. 0856/71282. Fax 0856/71235. 6 rms (all with bath).

$ Rates (including full board with wine): £58.75 ($88.10) per person, 30% discount for children under 15. MC, V.

⭐ The region's most important benefactors were the worldwide shipping magnates, the Balfour family. John Balfour began work on this castle, but it was completed by his heir in 1847. In the southwest corner of Shapinsay, it dominates the approach to the island. When in the 1950s the last Balfour died without an heir, the castle was purchased by a former Polish officer, Tadeusz Zawadski, and his Scottish wife, Catherine, along with 800 acres of farmland.

Today the castle accepts no more than 12 guests at a time. The widow Catherine, with her family, runs the place and guests are treated to conversation and entertainment provided by the family. The cuisine relies on such tempting ingredients as local wild duck and freshly caught scallops, crabmeat, and lobster. If they're patient enough, guests can also catch their own dinner, which will cheerfully be prepared for them. The estate shelters the only forest in the Orkney Islands. Composed chiefly of sycamores, it was planted in the 19th century by the Balfours. In its center, a 12-foot stone wall surrounds the kitchen gardens, where greenhouses produce peaches, figs, and grapes. Strawberries, cabbages, and salad greens grow well within the shelter of the wall, providing a constant summertime supply of fresh produce.

The estate is still a working farm, involved with beef cattle, sheep, and grain production. The hosts will take the time to tour the property with guests, and will also arrange fishing trips or birdwatching tours, as well as photographic and ornithological trips with guide and boat. Between May and July, the birdlife here is unbelievably profuse. Guests may also be taken to the family's privately owned 100-acre uninhabited island where a colony of gray seals and puffins like to say hello to visitors.

ROUSAY

Called the "Egypt of the North," the island of Rousay lies off the northwest coast of Mainland. Almost moon-shaped, and measuring about 6 miles across, it is known for its trout lochs, which draw anglers from all over Europe. Much of the land is heather-covered moors. Part of the island has hills, including **Ward Hill,** which many people walk up for a panoramic sweep of Orcadian seascape. In the northwestern part of the island is **Hellia Spur,** one of the most important seabird colonies in Europe. Here you can see the much photographed puffin.

But where does the Egypt come in? Rousay has nearly 200 prehistoric monuments, including one of the most significant, the ✪ **Midhowe Broch and Tombs,** in the west of the island. Excavated in the 1930s, it dates from the Iron Age. The walled enclosure on a promontory is cut off by a deep rock-cut ditch. The cairn is more than 75 feet long and was split among a dozen stalls or compartments. The graves of some two dozen settlers, along with their cattle, were found inside. One writer called the cairn "the great ship of death." The other major sight, the **Blackhammer Cairn,** lies north of the B9064 on the southern coast. This megalithic burial chamber is believed to date from the third millennium B.C. It was separated into about half a dozen different compartments for the dead.

Excavation began in 1978 on a Viking site at Westness. The place figured in the *Orkneyinga Saga.* A farmer digging a hole to bury a dead cow came across an old Norse grave site. Three silver brooches, shipped to the National Museum of Antiquities at Edinburgh, were discovered among the ruins. The earliest one dated from the 9th century.

To reach Rousay, you can rely on the service provided by the **Orkney Islands**

Shipping Co., 4 Ayre Rd. (tel. 0856/872044), in Wyre, which gets you just about anywhere on the Orkneys. Call for details about departure times.

WHERE TO STAY & DINE

THE TAVERSOE HOTEL, Frotoft, Rousay, Orkney KW17 2PT. Tel. 085682/325. 3 rms (none with bath, 1 with shower).
$ Rates: £18 ($27) per person with Scottish breakfast, £25 ($37.50) per person with half board. No credit cards.

On a treeless landscape, this little guest house provides shelter from the storm in its unpretentious accommodations. Open all year, it offers clean and comfortable bedrooms. The hotel offers two bedrooms overlooking the sea, the occupants of which share a bathroom, plus a third bedroom without a view but with a private shower. The hotel has a dining room serving good food, including fresh fish caught in local waters. Dinner is nightly from 6 to 9pm.

EGILSAY

Only a mile east of Rousay, and often visited on a boat trip from there, this little 3-mile-long island, shaped like an arrowhead, is forever linked to the legend of St. Magnus, the martyr who became the patron saint of the Orkney Islands. Visitors come here to see the ruins of **St. Magnus Church,** dating from the 12th century. Its round tower was of the type built by monks in Ireland. It reaches a height of some 50 feet, and once was even taller. An ecclesiastical center may have existed here long before the arrival of the Norse invaders. The chancel with barrel vaulting is more than a dozen feet long. Magnus fell into a trap, and was killed here around Easter in 1116 with a fatal axe blow to his skull.

Many varieties of seabirds and marsh fowl live on the island, which mainly attracts visitors on day trips because of its lack of adequate accommodations. A weekly steamer service, operated by the **Orkney Islands Shipping Co.,** 4 Ayre Rd. (tel. 0856/872044), in Kirkwall, goes to Egilsay. More frequent service is provided from the Tingwall Jetty in Evie on the northern coast of Mainland.

STRONSAY

One of the North Isles, Stronsay lies to the northeast of Mainland. Sanday is to its north and Eday to its northwest (see below). This island is not as rich in attractions as some of those previously visited. Mostly flat land with gentle bays, it has a number of lovely sand beaches and is known for its farming. From the 1600s until around 1920 it was also known for its fishing. The herring catch here was the greatest in Orkney. Whaling, especially in the 19th century, was an important source of revenue.

The main village on Stronsay is **Whitehall,** in the northeast of the island near a small promontory jutting out into the sea. In the "great day of the herring," as it is referred to, this was a boomtown. Now it peacefully overlooks the little offshore island of Papa Stronsay, an ecclesiastical center in Viking days, recounted in the *Orkneyinga Saga.*

Birdwatchers also flock to the island, going to such cliffs as **Odin Ness** in the north. The puffin, everybody's favorite seabird, is fond of visiting the island. Along some of the shores you can see the remains of kelp kilns, which began in 1722 as a controversial industry introduced by James Fea of Whitehall. The industry fell on bad days in 1832.

The little island of **Auskerry** lies directly south of Stronsay. It has a lighthouse—now automatic—and sheep are sent to pasture here in warm weather. The island was once inhabited, as a standing stone, a prehistoric cairn, and a chapel ruin reveal. Some of the islanders still engage in weaving.

Because of the scarcity of accommodations, Stronsay is best visited on a day trip. You can fly there from Kirkwall two or three times a day Monday through Saturday.

Loganair, the Scottish airline, operates the service (tel. 0856/872494 in Kirkwall for flight data). **Orkney Islands Shipping Co.,** 4 Ayre Rd. (tel. 0856/872044), in Kirkwall, also crosses there by sea three times a week, departing from Kirkwall.

EDAY

Called the "Isthmus Isle of the Norsemen," Eday is the center of a hardworking and traditional crofting community. Life is not easy, for most of this north isle is barren, with heather-clad and hilly moorlands that often lead to sheer cliffs or give way to sand dunes with long sweeping beaches. Chambered cairns and standing stones speak of ancient settlements. In the 18th and 19th centuries the island was a major supplier of peat.

Today most of the population derives its income from cattle and dairy farming, although other products include hand-knit sweaters, cheesemaking, and the brewing of a highly rated beer within individual crofts by local farmers and their families.

People come to this almost-forgotten oasis today for birdwatching, beachcombing, and sea angling. Others prefer the peaceful walks to the Red Head cliffs, likely to be filled with guillemots and kittiwakes. The cliffs rise to a height of 200 feet, and on a clear day you can see Fair Isle.

On its eastern coastline, Eday opens onto Eday Sound where John Gow, the pirate, was captured. After a trial in London, he was hanged in 1725; his exploits are detailed in *The Pirate* by Sir Walter Scott. Gow, following his capture, was held prisoner at Carrick House, in the northern part of the island. **Carrick House** was built in 1633 by James Stewart, the second son of Robert Stewart, who had been named Earl of Carrick.

Despite the sale of various parcels of land to the island's 130 to 140 inhabitants, most of the island is owned by the Laird of Eday, Mrs. Rosemary Hebdon Joy, whose link to the island dates back to around 1900, when her grandfather bought the island from his London Club. Interestingly, the circumstances since then that surround the island's inheritance have made it one of the few matriarchal lairdships in Scotland because of its ownership which, for several generations, has passed from mother to daughter. Mrs. Joy and her husband, retired from Britain's diplomatic corps, spend their winters in Worcestershire, but the warm-weather months on Eday.

Again, because of limited accommodations Eday is most often visited on a day trip. **Loganair** (tel. 0856/872492) in Kirkwall on Mainland flies in twice a day, except on Sunday and Wednesday. The **Orkney Islands Shipping Co.,** 4 Ayre Rd. (tel. 0856/872044), in Kirkwall, also crosses to Eday three times a week.

WHERE TO STAY & DINE

If you'd like to find lodgings on the island, you can get in touch with the **Eday Tourist Information Centre** (tel. 08572/248), which will supply you with details about farmhouses and B&B cottages offering meals. You can also visit the studios of working artists, and can travel about by bicycle or car, even boat, and can also hire a pony.

GREENTOFT FARM, Isle of Eday. Tel. 08572/269. 3 rms (none with bath) TV.
$ Rates (including half-board): £15 ($22.50) single; £30 ($45) double. No credit cards.

Mrs. Ena Hewison accepts overnight guests within her stone-built 1894 farmhouse, one of several buildings on lands known for their herds of cattle and sheep. Her husband, George (Geordie to everyone on the island) is overseer of the local laird's farms, and welcomes strangers to his table with warmth. Bedrooms are accessible via a steeply inclined staircase, and are simple affairs that share a communal bathroom. Nonetheless, the welcome is genuine and an overnight here offers insights into island life. Meals are fresh, rustic, and healthy, often made with island meats and fish and produce from the farm's extensive garden.

SKAILL FARM, Skaill, Eday, Orkney KW17 2AB. Tel. 08572/271. 2 rms (neither with bath).
$ Rates (including half board): £22 ($33) single; £44 ($66) double. No credit cards.

Operated by a pair of English expatriates fleeing the congestion of the London suburbs, this establishment is the centerpiece for the island's third largest farm. Set upon 800 acres of windswept grazing land, midway along the length of the island near its narrowest point, 4 miles from both Calfsound and Backaland, it's in a stone building whose 18th-century core was built on the foundations of the island's medieval *skaill*. (A skaill is the honorific home of an earl, designed to shelter him during his visits from other parts of his realm.) Part of the farmstead dates from the Victorian age, when it was nearly doubled in size around 1850. Michael and Dee Cockram welcome visitors to their home, providing them with well-prepared evening meals and comfortable overnight accommodations. Nonresidents are welcome to come for three-course dinners, although a telephone call is requested for reservations in advance. Meals to nonresidents cost £15 ($22.50) per person, and are usually served between 7 and 8pm. Menus might include freshly grown vegetables from the family's garden, lobsters, scallops, and lamb.

WHERE TO DINE

BLETT CROFT, Eday. Tel. 08572/248.
Cuisine: SCOTTISH. **Reservations:** Absolutely necessary with as much advanced warning as possible.
$ Prices: £15 ($22.50) per person. No credit cards.
Open: To be arranged when making reservations.

One of the most charming possibilities for a meal on Eday is provided by Yorkshire-born Mrs. Emma Popplewell, who, if notified in advance, will prepare table d'hôte lunches and dinners. Most repasts cost around £15 ($22.50) per person, and are served to a loyal following of "off-island" yacht owners enjoying the nautical challenges of the local waters. The setting is within a croft cottage whose 30-inch-thick stone walls were originally built around 1900. Its flower and vegetable garden slopes down to the edge of the sea, source of some of the kelp and seaweed that Mrs. Popplewell uses to flavor her succulent versions of Orkney lamb. Depending on what's available that day, menu items might include grilled halibut with scallops and local dill and fennel, salads made with wild greens gathered from the nearby hills, homemade versions of raspberry bramble sorbet, locally made cheeses and beers, and aromatic crusty bread that is freshly baked every morning.

Within one of the croft's outbuildings (a former boathouse), Mrs. Popplewell sells sweaters, accessories, and caftans that are hand-knit on Eday by local women. (In recent years, this merchandise has found an enthusiastic market in such places as Colorado, New Hampshire, and Texas.) Also for sale are paintings and sculpture by island artists, among which are included the watercolors of Mrs. Popplewell's husband, Geoffrey.

SANDAY

This island, meaning "sand island," is aptly named. The sand banks seem to keep growing, because the island was much smaller in the mid-18th century. Among the North Isles, it is part of the eastern archipelago. Its long white sandy beaches are nearly deserted, even on the sunniest day in summer.

One of the largest of the North Isles, some 16 miles in length, Sanday has one of the most spectacular chambered cairns found in the Orkney Island chain, the **Quoyness Chambered Tomb,** and it lies on the tidal island of Elsness. The tomb and its principal chamber date from around 2900 B.C., reaching a height of some 13 feet. Access is by key, which is available at the local post office in Lady Village. Other ancient monuments, including Viking burial grounds and broch sites, have been found on Sanday.

Rare migrant birds and terns can be seen at the **Start Point Lighthouse.** The early 19th-century lighthouse is one of the oldest in the country, but since the early 1960s it has been on "automatic pilot." The number of ships wrecked off Sanday's shore is topped only by North Ronaldsay; the wreck of a German destroyer can be seen on the Sand of Langamay.

While on the island you may visit the **Isle of Sanday Knitters,** which has a large selection of high-quality knitwear in both classic and modern design. A display and a sales room is found in the Wool Hall at Lady Village. For information, you can call 08575/367. This cooperative, the largest of its kind in the North Isles, employs more than 100 women.

Accommodations are extremely limited, so arrive with a reservation if you're planning to stay over. **Loganair** from the Kirkwall Airport (tel. 0856/872494) flies in at least two times a day except on Sunday. Also the **Orkney Islands Shipping Co.,** 4 Ayre Rd. (tel. 0856/872044), in Kirkwall, crosses to the island about three times a week.

WHERE TO STAY & DINE

BELSAIR GUEST HOUSE, Kettletoft, Sanday, Orkney KW17 2BJ. Tel. 08575/206. 6 rms (3 with bath). TV
$ Rates (including half board): £23.50 ($35.30) single without shower, £30.55 ($45.80) single with shower; £47 ($70.50) double without shower; £61 ($91.50) double with shower. No credit cards.

Located in the hamlet of Kettletoft, site of about 15 buildings and the most central of the island's four communities, this guest house contains one of the island's two pubs and its only restaurant. Originally built of stone and clapboards in 1879 by the ancestors of its present owners, it was upgraded and renovated in 1992. Gardens across the road produce many of the vegetables used in preparing the cuisine served within. Dishes include straightforward but flavorful preparations of fish, beef, and lamb. Most residents check in on half board, although nonresidents are welcome to call ahead for table d'hôte dinners priced at £10 ($15), and bar lunches priced at from £3 ($4.50) to £6.50 ($9.80). The owner and manager is Mrs. Joy Foubister, whose husband, Kenneth, is the island's postmaster. The establishment lies about 6 miles northeast of Sanday's new roll-on, roll-off ferryboat pier, which was erected in 1992.

WESTRAY

One of the biggest of the North Isles, Westray is a fertile island with a closely knit community, many of whom are said to have Spanish blood, owing to shipwrecks of the Armada off its stormy shores. The western shoreline is the steepest, rising in parts to some 200 feet, from which panoramic vistas can be enjoyed. Seabirds such as guillemots can be seen around Noup Head, with its red sandstone cliffs. The island is a birdwatcher's paradise. Along the lochs are many sandy beaches.

Below these cliffs is the so-called **Gentleman's Cave.** A Balfour of Trenabie is said to have found refuge in this cave, along with his comrades after the defeat at Culloden in 1746. As winter winds howled outside, they drank to the welfare of the "king over the water," Bonnie Prince Charlie.

At **Pierowall,** the major hamlet, you can see Pierowall Church, a ruin with a chancel and a nave. There are also some finely lettered grave slabs.

The most famous attraction is **Noltland Castle,** a former fortress overlooking Pierowall. A governor of the island, Thomas de Tulloch, had this castle built in 1420. Eventually it was occupied by Gilbert Balfour of Westray, and its present ruins date from around the mid-1500s. It was destroyed in part by a fire in 1746. A kitchen, a stately hall, and a winding staircase can still be seen. Gilbert Balfour had it designed as a fortress, constructed in a "three-stepped" or Z plan, which provided complete all-round visibility against attack. It was never finished. One of John Knox's "men without God," Gilbert Balfour was involved in many intrigues around Mary Queen of Scots—he was perhaps implicated in the murder of Darnley. Eventually he fled to Sweden, but more intrigues there led to his hanging in 1576.

The **Orkney Islands Shipping Company** sails to Pierowall, Westray, three times per week. This is a passenger/cargo service. Bookings are required for cars. Phone 0856/872044 in Kirkwall. During the summer months OISC also operates a passenger service three days per week from Kirkwall to Rapness Jetty at the south end of the island with a bus link to Pierowall. Phone 0856/872044 in Kirkwall. **Loganair** flies to Westray twice daily except Sunday throughout the year. Phone 0856/872494 in Kirkwall.

WHERE TO STAY & DINE

Since accommodations are very limited on the island, always go armed with reservation.

PIEROWALL HOTEL, Pierowall Village, Westray, Orkney KW17 2BZ. Tel. 08577/206. 5 rms (none with bath). TV
$ Rates (including Scottish breakfast): £14.50 ($21.80) single; £24 ($36) double. No credit cards. **Parking:** Free.

Originally built a century ago as a manse (clergyman's residence) for a nearby Presbyterian church, this cozy hotel is the domain of Mrs. Jean Fergus. It lies 7¼ miles north of the roll-on, roll-off ferryboat terminal (newly built in 1992), adjacent to the old ferryboat terminal, which now for the most part services the island's fishing boats. Open year-round, the hotel is secure and snug, offering food and drink to anyone who shows up for a meal. (It's wise to phone in advance, if possible.) Table d'hôte lunches cost £4.70 ($7.10); table d'hôte dinners cost £7 ($10.50). Freshly caught fish and local lamb are often served.

PAPA WESTRAY

Both the birdwatcher and the student of history are drawn to Papa Westray, which was believed to have been settled at least by 3500 B.C. One of the most northerly isles in the Orkney archipelago, it is rich in archeological sites. In the fertile farmland around Holland, the **Knap of Howar** was discovered, the earliest standing dwelling house in northwestern Europe, dating from before 3000 B.C.

On the eastern shore of Loch Treadwell, visits are possible to **St. Treadwell's Chapel,** which is believed to have marked the arrival of Christianity in the Orkney Islands. The chapel, now in ruins, was dedicated to Triduana, a Celtic saint. When a Pictish king, Nechtan, admired her lovely eyes, she is said to have plucked them out and sent them by messenger to the king. She reportedly hoped he would learn that it was foolish to admire physical beauty. After that she went to a nunnery. For many decades the chapel was a place of pilgrimage for those suffering from eye problems.

St. Boniface Church is also a Celtic site. Stone Celtic crosses were found here on a location north of the airfield. Grave slabs were carved of red sandstone. This is believed to have been a Christian Viking burial ground.

A major attraction is **Holland House,** formerly the home of the Traills of Holland. Dating from the 17th century, the house is a fine example of a circular "Horse Engine House," which was driven by 11 horses and a dovecote. At one time the Traills owned most of Papa Westray.

The northern end of the island has been turned into a nature reserve. Along with colonies of guillemots and kittiwakes, **North Hill** is a site for one of the largest breeding colonies of the Arctic tern. Once the great auk flew over this island, but the last male was shot in 1813. If you'd like to see what an auk looked like, you'll find a typical one stuffed in the British Museum in London.

Air connections are made from Kirkwall on Mainland, stopping at Westray. Flights are twice daily on Tuesday, Thursday, and Saturday. For information, call **Loganair** at the Kirkwall Airport (tel. 0856/872494). The **Orkney Islands Shipping Co.,** 4 Ayre Road (tel. 0856/872044), in Kirkwall, also sails to Papa Westray three times a week from Kirkwall.

WHERE TO STAY & DINE

BELTANE HOUSE, Papa Westray, Orkney KW17 2BU. Tel. 08574/267. 4 rms (all with shower).
$ Rates (including Scottish breakfast): £25 ($37.50) single; £42 ($63) double. MC, V. **Parking:** Free.

Originally built in 1983 about 2 miles from the island's main pier, this all-purpose accommodation was developed by the island's local farm cooperative. A row of stone-sided farm worker's cottages was renovated to form a complex of shops, a guest house (whose prices are quoted above), and two dormitories (male and female) containing a bare-bones youth hostel with bunk beds. June and July are the busiest months, requiring advance reservations. Prices for overnights in the youth hostel are £6.50 ($9.80) per person for residents age 18 and over; £5.20 ($7.80) for anyone under 18. Breakfast is included in the price paid by residents of the four guest rooms (see above), but costs £5 ($7.50) extra for residents of the youth hostel. An evening meal in the simple and functional dining room costs £10.50 ($15.80).

2. FAIR ISLE

27 miles S of Lerwick, Shetland Islands

GETTING THERE By Plane Loganair operates scheduled services in a seven-seater "Islander" (flight time: 25 minutes). From Sumburgh Airport, there is a flight only on Saturday. This flight links with incoming Loganair flights from both Glasgow and Edinburgh. From Lerwick Airport, there are flights twice daily on Monday, Wednesday, and Friday. The standard air fare from Lerwick to Fair Isle is £60 ($90) round-trip. Call Loganair at 059584/246 in the Shetlands for more information.

By Boat The mailboat, *Good Shepherd,* sails on Tuesday, plus alternate Thursdays and Fridays, from Grutness Pier, Sumburgh Head, on Shetland. It is advisable to check sailing times from Grutness by telephoning before 9:30am on the morning of the scheduled departure for Fair Isle, in case of weather delay (which is frequent). Bookings for the trips to Fair Isle can be made through **J. W. Stout,** Skerryholm, Fair Isle (tel. 03512/222). A one-way fare is £1.20 ($1.80), and the trip takes 2½ hours.

ESSENTIALS Ask at Lerwick (see "The Shetlands Islands," below). The **telephone area code** is 03512.

Called the "most isolated inhabited part of Britain," Fair Isle lies on the same latitude as Bergen, Norway. Measuring only about 1 mile by 3½ miles, it sits in the lonely sea, about midway between Orkney and Shetland, administered by the latter. Relentless seas pound its 20-mile coastline in winter, and powerful westerly winds fling Atlantic spray from one side of the island to the other. It is home to fewer than 100 hearty, rugged, and self-reliant souls.

An important staging point for migrating birds, Fair Isle is even better known for the patterned pullovers produced here. These pullovers came into fashion again in the 1970s, and they greatly aid the island's economy. In the chic boutiques of London, Milan, New York, and Paris, you'll see these garments retailing at high prices. But the home-grown product is sold on Fair Isle at half the price. Fair Isle knitting is even a part of the curriculum at all primary schools, and many jobless men have turned to knitting.

Originally the fame of this intricate pattern was spread in the 1920s by the then Prince of Wales. The pattern is of mysterious origin. Some suggest that it was derived from Celtic sources, others that it came from the island's Viking heritage. A more daring theory maintains that the themes were Moorish, learned from Spanish sailors shipwrecked off Fair Isle from the Armada in 1588.

In 1954 the island was acquired by the National Trust for Scotland. The bird observatory installed here is considered the most remarkable in the country. Since work began in 1948, some 200 different species have been ringed. Fair Isle is an important breeding ground for everything from the puffin to the Arctic skua, from the razorbill to the storm petrel.

WHERE TO STAY & DINE

FAIR ISLE LODGE AND BIRD OBSERVATORY, Fair Isle, Shetland ZE2 9JU. Tel. 03512/258. Fax 03512/258. 14 rms (none with bath).

$ Rates (including full board): £34–£38 ($51–$57) single; £56–£66 ($84–$99) double; £20–£24 ($30–$36) dormitory bed. MC, V. **Closed:** Nov–Mar.

Even if you're not a birdwatcher, you might stay at this low-slung, big-windowed isolated building in the shelter of treeless hillsides, near the sea at the northern end of the island. This establishment was the dream of a well-respected ornithologist, George Waterson, who bought Fair Isle in 1948, creating the observatory. It is now administered by the Fair Isle Bird Observatory Trust. The establishment is most popular during the spring and autumn bird migrations. It's always wise to reserve well in advance, especially during those seasons. On the premises you'll find a superb collection of reference books on birds. Sometimes the wardens will take guests on before-breakfast tours of bird traps which, for tagging purposes, are placed in strategic points along the stone dikes surrounding the island.

Adjacent accommodations were constructed to provide housing for visitors. There are 32 beds for rent. It is also possible to stay here in a dormitory room, with 4 or 5, maybe even 6 beds.

3. THE SHETLAND ISLANDS

60 miles N and NE of the Orkneys

GETTING THERE   By Plane   It's a 2½-hour flight from London. By air or sea, Aberdeen is the major departure point from Scotland. **British Airways** (tel. toll free 800/247-9297 in the U.S. or 0224/722331) flies four times per day to Shetland from Aberdeen between 9:30am and 5pm, with reduced service on Saturday and Sunday. The flight takes less than an hour. **Loganair** (tel. 0595/84246 at Lerwick), the Scottish airline, also operates a direct service from Edinburgh to Tingwall, which lies only 5 miles from Lerwick. This flight takes about 2 hours. If booking on British Airways, ask about their "Saver" fares, but this has to be done in advance. You might also ask about BA's "Airpass."

By Ferry   Roll-on/roll-off car-ferries operate to Shetland from Aberdeen five times a week, carrying up to 600 passengers and 240 automobiles. On-board facilities include restaurants, cafeterias, bars, lounges, and gift shops. Departure time from Aberdeen is usually 6pm on Monday through Friday. The trip takes about 14 hours. For more information, get in touch with **P&O Ferries,** Jamieson's Quay, in Aberdeen (tel. 0224/572615).

P&O offers ferry service once a week, departing on Sunday at noon from Stromness, Orkney, heading for Lerwick in the Shetlands. Service is in both summer and winter. For information in Stromness, call 0856/850655.

A modern 1,000-passenger car-ferry, the *Noronna,* operates from the end of May until the beginning of September, carrying passengers on a weekly schedule, calling at Lerwick en route from Norway, Denmark, Iceland, and Faroe. Information can be obtained, along with a Smyril line brochure, from P&O.

ESSENTIALS   The **tourist information center** is at the Market Cross in Lerwick (tel. 0595/3434). The **telephone area code** for Lerwick is 0595.

SPECIAL EVENTS   The **Shetland Folk Festival** takes place around the end of April and the beginning of May at Lerwick. Young fiddlers on the island take part, and international artists fly in for 4 days of concerts, musical workshops, and informal jam sessions, climaxed by what they call their "Final Foy."

Up Helly Aa, a Viking tradition left over from pagan days, is celebrated at Lerwick with great relish in January. The festival celebrates the return of the sun after a long winter's absence. Blazing torches light up the dark winter sky, as a replica of a Viking longship is paraded through the streets of Lerwick, then ceremonially burned.

The northernmost part of the British Isles, the rugged Shetland Islands, with their spectacular coastline, includes some 500 square miles of islands, 100 in all. Many are merely islets or rocks, but 17 are inhabited. The major island is called **Mainland,** as in Orkney. This island, on which the capital, **Lerwick,** is located, is about 55 miles long and 20 miles wide. It has been turned into what some critics have called "a gargantuan oil terminal," but it contains much scenic beauty. Shetland handles about half of Britain's oil.

Nature in the way of fjordlike "voes" or sheer rock cliffs makes Shetland beautiful in both seascape and landscape. But it is a stark beauty, a wild, rugged look as you wander across windswept moors. Because there are few trees, the landscape at first looks barren. But after a while it begins to take on a fascination, especially when you come upon a typical Shetlander, in his sturdy Wellington boots and thick woolen sweater, cutting peat along a bog as his ancestors did before him. Shetlanders are proud, warm, and hospitable, and often eager to share the treasures of their island chain with you. At no point in Shetland are you more than 3 miles from the sea, as the coastline stretches for some 3,000 miles.

The islands have been called that "long string of peat and gneiss that stand precariously where three seas—the Atlantic Ocean, the North Sea, and the Arctic Ocean—meet." The major airport is at **Sumburgh** on the southern tip of the southernmost island of Mainland, but even it is on a level with St. Petersburg, Russia.

The far-northern outpost of Shetland, **Muckle Flugga Lighthouse,** is a stunning achievement of engineering. Standing poised on near-vertical rock, it is called "the last window on the world" through which Great Britain looks out to the north. It's not as cold here as you might think, as the Shetland archipelago benefits from the warming influence of the Gulf Stream. But even in summer the weather tends to be chilly, so dress the way you would in early spring in a northern clime such as New York. It does not rain all the time in Shetland; actually, it has less than half the annual rainfall recorded in the western Highlands. In summer there is almost continuous daylight. The Shetlanders call it "Simmer Dim." Conversely in midwinter there is no more than 5 hours of daylight.

Shetland civilization is old, dating back some 5,000 years. Shetland was inhabited more than 2,000 years before the Romans, who called it "Ultima Thule." Through these islands paraded Neolithic people, followed by the people of the Iron and Bronze Ages, who gave way to the Picts and the Celts. But the most enduring influence of all came from the Vikings, who ruled Shetland until some 500 years ago. The Norse established an influence that was not only to last for centuries, but is still evident today in language, culture, and customs.

The Vikings ruled from A.D. 800. But the islands were given to Scotland in 1469 as part of the wedding dowry of Princess Margaret when she married King James III. Scotland's takeover of Shetland marked a sad period in the life of the islanders, who found themselves ruled by often cruel and unreasonable feudal barons. Earl Patrick Stewart was assigned the dubious task of imposing Scottish custom on people who up to then had known only Viking law. He became one of the most hated of rulers, and his son was "a chip off the old block." Eventually both earls were executed in Edinburgh for their crimes.

Shetlanders still think of themselves as separate from Scots, though today the fisherman who lives on his croft is likely to be seen on Commercial Street in Lerwick picking up supplies and rubbing shoulders with North Sea oilmen. The impact of the oilmen on this traditionally strait-laced community is noticeable in overcrowding and other ways. It is imperative to have advance reservations if you're contemplating a visit especially in midsummer when most of the visitors arrive.

Away from all this oil activity, life in the Shetland Islands goes on much as it always did, except for the profusion of modern conveniences and foodstuff. However, the food on Shetland tastes better when it's from Shetland. You don't have to stick just to fish; other local delicacies are served, including Reestit mutton (salted and smoked mutton with a distinctive flavor).

The islands are famous for their short ponies and their wool. The island craftspeople are noted for their creativity, reflected in their handcrafts, jewelry, and knitware. In some places you can watch these items being made in the workshops of the artists. Hand-knitted sweaters are still produced in great numbers on the island and anyone contemplating a visit might want to return with at least one.

Shetland ponies roam freely among the hills and common grazing lands in the island chain. Some are shipped south to England where they are popular as childrens mounts. Once the pony was a "workhorse," bred to work in British coal mines. The intention was to make them have as "much strength as possible" and to be "as near the ground as it can be got." Now this beautiful pony has an easier life.

Shetland also has 10% of all the seabirds in the British Isles, and several of the smaller islands or islets have nature reserves. There are 300 recorded species.

Seals are protected and welcomed here. You can see them drifting among the waves, sliding down in pursuit of a fish dinner, or lounging about on the rocks and beaches, enjoying a sunny day. You'll recognize most of them as the Atlantic gray seal, with its big angular head. The common seal, with a dog-shaped head, is most often found on the islet of Mousa. If you want to see the otter, you have a better chance in Shetland than anywhere else in Britain.

Fishermen find some 200 freshwater lochs in Shetland, and deep-sea angling makes for a memorable sport. Many world fishing records have been set in Shetland. "Ton-up" fish are common.

GETTING AROUND If you have a problem about transportation either to or around the islands, you can always check with the tourist office in Lerwick at the Market Cross (tel. 0595/3434) and the Shetland Islands Council, Grantfield, Lerwick (tel. 0595/2024).

By Plane A daily interisland air service operates from Tingwall Airport (tel. 0595/84306) on Mainland to the islands of Whalsay, Fetlar, and Unst. There are weekly flights to Foula and Out Skerries in summer.

By Ferry Most of the inhabited islands are reached from the Shetland "Mainland," and passenger fares are nominal as they are heavily subsidized by the government. Service is 13 to 16 times a day to the islands of Unst, Yell, Whalsay, Fetlar, and Bressay. Passenger/cargo vessels service the islands of Fair Isle, Foula, the Skerries, and Papa Stour. Scheduled services to the little-visited places only operate once or twice a week, however. Boat trips to the islands of Mousa and Noss can be arranged in summer. Call 0595/5252 for more information.

By Bus In summer, buses travel around Mainland to all the major places of interest. Call the leading bus company, **John Leask & Son** (tel. 0595/3162), or pick up a copy of **Inter-Shetland Transport Timetable,** costing 60p (90¢) at the tourist office and seek the assistance there if you're planning to tour by public transport.

By Car It's easier than you think, as there are some 500 miles of passable roads—no traffic jams, no traffic lights. Many of the islands are connected by road bridges, and for those that aren't, car-ferries provide frequent service. Renting a car might be the best solution if you want to cover a lot of ground in the shortest possible time. You can either bring a car from mainland Scotland or pick one up in Lerwick. No major international car-rental firm as yet maintains an office in the Shetlands. However, Avis and Europcar have, as their on-island agents, **Bolts Car Hire,** North Road in Lerwick (tel. 0595/2855); a competitor is **Grantsfield Garage,** North Road (tel. 0595/2709).

By Bicycle In Lerwick, **Shetland Cycle Hire,** 19 Market St. (tel. 0595/4797), rents touring bikes for £8 ($12) per day.

LERWICK

The capital of Shetland since the 17th century, Lerwick, on the eastern coast of "Mainland," is sheltered by the little offshore island of Bressay. In the 19th century it was the herring capital of northern Europe, and before that, a haven for smugglers. The fishing fleet of the Netherlands put in here after combing the North Sea. Even before Victoria came to the throne in 1837, Lerwick had a bustling, cosmopolitan atmosphere. That's even truer today, with the influx of foreign visitors.

Believe it or not, Lerwick is sometimes the sunniest place in Britain, experiencing some 12 hours of sunshine a day in the early summer. Commercial Street is the town's principal artery, and it is said that beneath the steep and narrow lanes runs a network of passages used by smugglers. Lerwick today is the main port and shopping center of Shetland.

WHAT TO SEE & DO

Your first stop might be at the **Shetland Tourist Organization,** the Market Cross in Lerwick (tel. 0595/3434). The helpful staff does many things, such as arranging rooms, and providing information about ferries, boat trips, car rentals, what to see and do, and local events. You can even rent fishing tackle there. They're used to unusual requests: Sometimes visitors from Canada or America drop in here wanting their ancestors traced. You might find out details about a 40-foot replica of a Viking longboat, *Dim Riv* ("Morning Light"), anchored in the harbor of Lerwick. It's available for a tour of the harbor on a summer evening. The boat was constructed by Lerwick craftsmen in 1980, and has been a popular tourist attraction ever since.

The **Shetland Library and Museum,** Lower Hillhead (tel. 0595/3868), has, in addition to a reading room, four galleries devoted to such themes as art and textiles, shipping, archeological digs, and oil exploration. Admission-free, it is open on Monday, Wednesday, and Friday from 10am to 7pm and on Tuesday, Thursday, and Saturday from 10am to 5pm.

Fort Charlotte, built in 1665, is pentagonal in shape, containing high walls with gun points pointing, naturally, at the sea. Eight years after it was constructed, it was burned by the Dutch. Restoration came in 1781. It is open daily from April through September, Monday to Saturday from 9:30am to 6pm, Sunday from 2 to 6pm. From October through March, hours are Monday to Saturday from 9:30am to 4pm, Sunday from 2 to 4pm. Admission is free, and entrance is via Market Street.

At the north end of Hillhead stands the 1882 **Town Hall,** from whose clock tower a panoramic vista unfolds. The stained-glass windows depict a host of Vikings, and a rose window, if seen in the right light, becomes a blaze of colors. Some of the coats-of-arms are from such old cities as Christiana, now known as Oslo.

Clickhimin Broch, about a quarter of a mile southwest of Lerwick, was fortified at the beginning of the Iron Age. Excavated in the 1950s, the site revealed 1,000 years of history. It was at one time turned into a broch, rising 17 feet and built inside the fort. Admission is free. It is open April through September, Monday to Saturday from 9:30am to 6pm, Sunday from 2 to 6pm. From October through March, hours are Monday to Saturday from 9:30am to 4pm, Sunday from 2 to 4pm.

SHOPPING

Shopping is so interesting in Lerwick that it might be termed a sightseeing attraction. Of the many shops, you may want to drop in at **L. & M. Anderson,** 56 Commercial Street (tel. 0595/3007), which has a good assortment of Icelandic woolens, knitwear, silvercraft, local handcrafts, and Shetland souvenirs.

Another knitware store is **Kloo Knit,** 10 Commercial Rd. (tel. 0595/5597), which sells handmade crofter and designer sweaters.

J. G. Rae Ltd., 92 Commercial St. (tel. 0595/3686), has one of the best assortments of silvercraft in all the islands. Both silver and gold jewelry are produced entirely in Shetland. Designs are often based on Viking motifs.

The **Shetland Workshop Gallery,** 4 Burns Lane (tel. 0595/3343), is two old dwellings joined on one of the oldest lanes in town. Nowadays it's a gift shop of character, selling an exclusive range of hand-cast wildlife figurines and original knitwear in a wide range of color patterns exclusive to the shop. It is open daily except Wednesday from 9:30am to 1pm and 2:15 to 5pm.

WHERE TO STAY

SHETLAND HOTEL, Holmsgarth Rd., Lerwick, Shetland ZE1 0PW. Tel. 0595/5515. Fax 0595/5828. 66 rms (all with bath), 1 suite. TV TEL
$ Rates (including Scottish breakfast): £64.95 ($97.40) single; £73 ($109.50) double; £96 ($144) suite. AE, DC, MC, V. **Parking:** Free.
Built in 1984, this four-floor brick, stone, and concrete structure with square windows

is one of the most modern hotels in Shetland. It is close to the center of town, opposite the ferry terminal, with a good view of the harbor. Many guests seem to prefer all the amenities in this far-northern clime, including a choice of three different cocktail bars, a heated indoor swimming pool, a sauna, a solarium, an exercise room, and a first-class restaurant. They have a sprinkling of family rooms along with some units for disabled guests. Rooms are well furnished and contain trouser presses, radios, tea makers, and hairdryers. There's free use of laundry facilities.

QUEENS HOTEL, 24 Commercial St., Lerwick, Shetland ZE1 0AB. Tel. 0595/2826. Fax 0595/4048. 26 rms (all with bath or shower). TV TEL
$ Rates (including Scottish breakfast): £56 ($84) single; £75 ($112.50) double. AE, DC, MC, V. **Parking:** Free in a nearby public parking lot.

Its foundations rise directly from the sea at the harborfront, in the town center, so that on blustery nights, fine sprays of saltwater sometimes coat the windowpanes of the lower floors. Originally built of natural stone around 1900, the Queens rivals the nearby Grand Hotel (see below) as the best established and most prestigious hotel in Lerwick. (Both hotels, in fact, share the same reservations staff.) Inexpensive bar lunches are served in the cocktail lounge, while more formal dinners are served every night in the dining room. Bedrooms are conservatively and comfortably furnished.

LERWICK HOTEL, South Rd., Shetland ZE1 0RB. Tel. 0595/2166. Fax 0595/4419. 31 rms (all with bath). TV TEL **Directions:** Take Scalloway Road west from the center for 5 minutes.
$ Rates (including Scottish breakfast): £56.50 ($84.80) single; £72–£95 ($108–$142.50) double. AE, MC, V. **Parking:** Free.

This is one of the biggest and most up-to-date hotels in Shetland, sprawling beside a gravel- and kelp-covered beach. Its comfortably streamlined bedrooms offer various amenities, including radios and hairdryers. Dinner dances are held frequently in summer. The decor of some of the public rooms is in a modernized marine style. Bar meals provide an inexpensive alternative to the full-service restaurant.

GRAND HOTEL, 149 Commercial St., Lerwick, Shetland ZE1 0AB. Tel. 0595/2826. Fax 0595/4048. 23 rms (18 with bath). TV TEL
$ Rates (including Scottish breakfast): £38 ($57) single without bath, £48 ($72) single with bath; £50 ($75) double without bath, £64 ($96) double with bath; £90 ($135) family room (quad) with bath. AE, DC, MC, V. **Parking:** Free in nearby public parking lot.

As its name implies, a grander hotel would be hard to find anywhere in Shetland. With its pointed turrets, weather vanes, crow's-step gables, and solid stone walls, it's one of the most ornate buildings in Lerwick. It lies a block from the waterfront, in the town center. All the bedrooms have hot-beverage facilities, among other necessities. The extensively modernized hotel has a hairdressing salon, beauty parlor, coffee shop, two lounge bars, a dining room, and a nightclub (Poser's Disco) whose premises open their doors three nights a week to every night-owl in Lerwick. The Grand Hotel shares its reservations facilities and some of its staff with the Queens Hotel (see above).

GLEN ORCHY GUEST HOUSE, 20 Knab Rd., Lerwick, Shetland ZE1 0AX. Tel. 0595/2031. 8 rms (1 with bath) TV.
$ Rates (including Scottish breakfast): £19.50 ($29.30) single without bath, £26 ($39) single with bath; £37 ($55.50) double without bath, £44 ($66) double with bath. No credit cards. **Parking:** Free.

($) Set near the top of a brae (gently sloping hill) near a nine-hole golf course, a 4-minute walk uphill from the center of town, this white-sided building was built in 1904 as an Episcopalian nunnery. The English and Scottish family who own it will prepare a three-course evening meal for £8.50 ($12.80) to clients who request it in advance. Bedrooms are cozy and comfortable, each decorated in coordinated tones of pink.

WHERE TO DINE

FERRY INN, in the Shetland Hotel, Holmsgarth Road. Tel. 0595/5515.

Cuisine: SCOTTISH. **Reservations:** Recommended.
$ Prices: Appetizers £2.95–£6.75 ($4.40–$10.10); main courses £10–£15 ($15–$22.50). AE, DC, MC, V.
Open: Lunch daily 12:30–2pm; dinner daily 7–9:30pm.

On the third floor of a four-story hotel that was built in the early 1980s across the road from the Holmsgarth ferryboat terminal, about half a mile north of the town center, this comfortable and unpretentious restaurant enjoys a sweeping panoramic view over the ferryboats that depart from Lerwick for both Aberdeen and Iceland. Amid a blue-toned decor accented with natural wood and stone, you'll enjoy traditional preparations of Scottish food, with a heavy emphasis on fresh seafood. The restaurant has its own entrance which accesses directly to the street.

GOLDEN COACH, 17 Hillhead. Tel. 0595/3848.
Cuisine: CHINESE. **Reservations:** Required Sat–Sun.
$ Prices: Appetizers £1.80–£3.70 ($2.70–$5.60); main courses £7–£15 ($10.50–$22.50); 2-course fixed-price lunch £8 ($12). MC, V.
Open: Mon–Fri noon–2pm and 5:30–11pm, Sat noon–11pm, Sun 1–11pm.

The only Chinese restaurant in the Shetlands, this intimate place is softly lit and contemporary in decor. The cuisine is basically Peking, with a wide array of poultry, pork, seafood, duckling, and beef dishes. Try the barbecued Peking duck or deep-fried shredded beef in a hot sweet-and-sour sauce. Malaysian chicken comes in a peanut sauce, or you can order king prawns Peking with garlic sauce.

QUEENS HOTEL, 24 Commercial St. Tel. 0595/2826.
Cuisine: BRITISH. **Reservations:** Recommended.
$ Prices: Appetizers £2.25–£5 ($3.40–$7.50); main courses £7–£14 ($10.50–$21); fixed-price three-course dinner £14.50 ($21.80). AE, DC, MC, V.
Open: Lunch daily noon–2pm; dinner daily 6–9pm.

Located on the lobby level of a previously recommended hotel (see "Where to Stay," above), its pink and white premises overlook the sea, the wharves, and the many fishing boats bobbing at anchor. It caters to families, many of whom seem to arrive in groups as part of scheduled reunions. Many residents consider it the best and most solidly entrenched restaurant in Lerwick—a staple on the island's culinary scene. Menu specialties include goujons of haddock with tartar sauce, roast sirloin of beef with Yorkshire pudding, chicken Caribbean (with pineapple sauce), braised lamb cutlets, surf and turf, and conservative preparations of fish dishes.

THE NOOST, 86 Commercial St. Tel. 0595/3377.
Cuisine: SCOTTISH. **Reservations:** Not needed.
$ Prices: Scottish breakfast £5 ($7.50); appetizers £1–£2.50 ($1.50–$3.80); main courses £3.50–£4.75 ($5.30–$7.10). MC, V.
Open: Mon–Tues and Thurs–Sat 9:30am–5pm; Wed lunch 11:45am–2pm.

Set behind the pale-blue facade of a 200-year-old stone building in the town center, near the waterfront, this all-purpose restaurant serves filling and cost-conscious meals to a loyal clientele of Lerwick residents and itinerant fishermen. Amid half-paneling and wallpaper, you can order copious breakfasts, steaming cups of coffee and soups, sandwiches, afternoon tea, and meals that include such time-tested specialties as filets of haddock and sole, Scottish steaks, hamburgers, and scampi. *Noost* translates from the Gaelic as "small, sandy-bottomed harbor."

SCALLOWAY

On the western coast, 6 miles west of Lerwick, Scalloway was once the capital of Shetland. In recent years this town was the base for rescue operations in Norway during the darkest days of World War II. Still an important fishing port, Scalloway has been altered because of the oil boom.

WHAT TO SEE & DO

The ruins of **Scalloway Castle,** commissioned by the dreaded Earl Patrick at the beginning of the 17th century, dominate the town. The castle was allowed to deteriorate after the earl was executed in Edinburgh (no one in Scalloway wanted to perpetuate his memory). The castle was built in the corbel-turreted medieval style. Admission-free, it is open April through September, Monday to Saturday from 9:30am to 6pm, Sunday from 2 to 6pm. From October through March, hours are Monday to Saturday from 9:30am to 4pm, Sunday from 2 to 4pm.

The **Scalloway Woollen Company** (tel. 059588/243) is open to visitors Monday through Friday from 9am to 1pm and 2 to 5pm. You can see the processing and finishing of Shetland knitware. Later you can visit the showroom where a selection of garments made locally is sold, along with Icelandic knitwear.

North of Scalloway, and 5 miles northwest of Lerwick, you can visit the **Tingwall Agricultural Museum** (tel. 059588/344) in the hamlet of Veensgarth, off the A971. Set in the surroundings of a working farmstead, Mrs. Jeanie Sandison's private collection on Shetland's agricultural and domestic past is unequaled in the islands. All the buildings date from the mid-1700s—a granary, stable, bothy, smithy, and dairy. There is a slide room, where a 25-minute documentary is shown. The museum is open on Tuesday, Thursday, and Saturday from 10am to 1pm and 2 to 5pm, on Wednesday from 10am to 1pm, and on Sunday from 2 to 5pm. Admission is £1 ($1.50) for adults, 50p (80¢) for children.

Shetland folklore evenings are held at the museum in summer, followed by food and entertainment at the Tingwall Public Hall. Visitors can see something of Shetland history, taste traditional island food, and be entertained by local musicians and storytellers. There are usually two folklore evenings in June, two in July, and two in August. Dates vary, but information and tickets can be picked up at the tourist office in Lerwick.

WEST MAINLAND

It is said that you can see more of Shetland from the Scord of Weisdale than from any other vantage point in the archipelago. But West Mainland has many more attractions than panoramic vistas.

NEAR WHITENESS
What to See & Do

Shetland's only stone-polishing business operates at **Hjaltasteyn,** Whiteness (tel. 059584/351), 9 miles west of Lerwick. Here gemstones are turned out from raw materials in fetching hand-wrought silver settings. The workshop is open Monday and Wednesday through Friday from 11am to noon. The admission-free showroom is open Monday through Friday from 9am to 5pm, Saturday, 9am to 4:30pm.

Continuing north at Weisdale, you can watch high-quality jewelry being made at **Shetland Silvercraft,** Soundside, Weisdale (tel. 0595/72275), where the artisans base many of their designs on ancient Celtic and Viking patterns. Visitors may go through the workrooms, and later stop in for an inspection of the stocks available in the showroom. It is open Monday through Friday from 9am to 1pm and 2 to 5pm.

Where to Stay

WESTINGS HOTEL, Wormadale, West Mainland, Shetland ZE2 9LJ. Tel. 059584/242. Fax 059584/500. 6 rms (all with shower). TV
$ Rates (including half board) £49 ($73.50) single; £72 ($108) double. MC, V.
Parking: Free.
Set just below the summit of one of the region's tallest hills, in an isolated position 9 miles west of Lerwick, this hotel was originally built by the British army as an observation post during World War II. On clear days, it offers views of up to 40 miles from the east to the southwest, and if you climb to the hill's summit, you can enjoy simultaneous views of the Atlantic and the North Sea. Today, much modified and improved since its original construction, it has a Scandinavian look, with asymmetrical roofs and low-slung horizontal lines. Each of the half-dozen rooms contains a radio and tea-making facilities. The hotel contains a restaurant, where table d'hôte evening meals cost £16 ($24), and a pub where bar meals cost around £7.50 ($11.30) each.

The owners will organize pony treks on the backs of Shetland ponies or indicate which of the nearby spots to seek out for the best sea fishing or hill walks.

Where to Dine

DA BRIG-STANES TEAROOM, Hjaltasteyn, Whiteness. Tel. 059584/351.

Cuisine: SCOTTISH. **Reservations:** Not needed.
$ Prices: Average light lunch from £2.50 ($3.80).
Open: Mon–Sat 11am–4:30pm.

Here, in summer, you will get a good "cuppa" along with some Shetland hospitality. The scones and cakes are homemade, and you can also order homemade soup and well-stuffed sandwiches. The team room is part of Hjaltasteyn, a larger business manufacturing jewelry by hand from silver, gold, enamel, and Shetland gemstones. A full range of the products can be seen on display and for purchase. It's 9 miles north of Lerwick.

NORSEMAN'S INN, Voehead, Weisdale Parish. Tel. 059572/304.

Cuisine: SCOTTISH. **Reservations:** Not required.
$ Prices: Appetizers £1.40–£3 ($2.10–$4.50); main courses £4–£9.50 ($6–$14.30). No credit cards.
Open: Lunch daily noon–2pm; dinner daily 6:30–8:30pm (until 9:30pm on Fri and Sat). **Closed:** Nov–Mar Mon–Thurs.

Built in 1981 at the head of one of the most dramatic estuaries in the Shetlands, this is one of the most popular pubs and informal restaurants in the region. It welcomes roadside passengers on the main A970 highway, 12 miles northwest of Lerwick. Inside, you'll find a rustic and cozy ambience containing two different drinking areas, a gas-lit fireplace to remove the humid chill from the air, and such culinary specialties as fresh salmon in butter sauce, different preparations of local trout, Shetland lamb, and an array of sandwiches, malts, and beers.

NEAR WALLS

What to See & Do

You can continue your tour of West Mainland by heading west along the A971 toward Walls. You come first to **Staneydale Temple,** 2¾ miles outside Walls. This early Bronze Age hall—perhaps Neolithic—once had a timbered roof. It is called a temple because it bears a remarkable resemblance to such sites in Malta. This lends support to the theory that the early settlers of Shetland came from the Mediterranean.

Continuing past several lochs and sea inlets, you come to **Walls,** a hamlet built on the periphery of two voes. Its natural harbor is sheltered by the offshore islet of Vaila.

Where to Stay & Dine

BURRASTOW HOUSE, Walls, West Mainland, Shetland. ZE2 9PB. Tel. 059571/307. 3 rms (all with bath).

$ Rates (including half board): £56–£61 ($84–$91.50) single; £112 ($168) double. No credit cards. **Closed:** Oct 15–Nov 15 and Christmas–Mar 21. **Parking:** Free.

Set about 3 miles southwest of the hamlet of Walls, a 40-minute drive northwest of Lerwick, this simple but comfortable building was originally built in 1759 as a Haa house (home of the farm manager of a laird's estate). Set amid lands still used in summer for grazing sheep, it lies at the widest section of a windswept peninsula whose views encompass a cluster of rocky and sparsely inhabited islands. Bedrooms are well furnished and evocative of country-house living. At presstime, additional rooms were being added, which might be available by the time of your visit.

The food is among the best on the island. The daily menu in the oak-paneled dining room is likely to include nettle and oatmeal fritters, mussel brose (a stew of mussels thickened with oatmeal), and frequent presentations of fish (including monkfish with anchovy stuffing), lamb, and Scottish beef. Food is served daily from 12:30 to 2pm (lunch), 3:30 to 5:30pm (high tea), and 7:30 to 9pm (dinner). Lunches and high teas cost from £4.50 ($6.80) to £9 ($13.50); fixed-price dinners cost £25 ($37.50). The restaurant is closed Sunday evening and all day Monday to nonresidents of the hotel.

PAPA STOUR

The "great island of priests," in the shape of a large starfish, lies off the west coast of Mainland, 25 miles northwest of Lerwick. Legend has it that its profusion of wildflowers had such a strong scent that old fishermen could use the perfume—borne far out on the wind—to fix their positions. Papa Stour is very isolated, and once it was feared that the island might be depopulated, but about 26 settlers live there now. In the darkest days of winter, bad weather can cut it off for days. But if you see it on a sunny day, it's beautiful.

Encircled by pillars of rock and reefs, it is known for its sea caves, sculpted by turbulent winds and raging seas, among the most impressive in Britain. The largest of these is **Kirstan's Hole**, extending some 80 yards. Papa Stour, as its name indicates, was an early base for monks. Two centuries ago there was a leper colony here on the little offshore islet of Brei Holm.

Boats go to Papa Stour about five times a week from West Burrafirth on Mainland. Call 0595/873335 for information about these constantly changing details.

Where to Stay & Dine

A. AND S. HOLT-BROOK, Longhouse, Papa Stour, Shetland ZE2 9PW. Tel. 0595/873238. 3 rms (none with bath).

$ Rates (including full board): £21 ($31.50) single; £42 ($63) double. No credit cards. **Parking:** Free.

Set within walking distance of the island's only pier, just outside Housa Voe (the island's only hamlet, which contains only seven buildings), this stone-built croft is one of the most archeologically unusual buildings on the island. Built on Viking foundations atop soil where Dutch coins have been unearthed dating from the 1620s, it's the domain of Andrew and Sabina Holt-Brook, who moved from the mainland of Scotland 20 years ago in search of affordable land. Owners of 30 acres of windswept peninsula (whose makeup geologists define as an ancient Devonian fish bed), they are the only establishment offering overnight accommodations and/or meals on Papa Stour. If requested, lunches can be packed as picnics for consumption amid the island's wild landscapes. The house is centrally heated and is available for accommodation throughout the year.

FOULA

This tiny remote island—only 3 miles by 5 miles—with five high peaks is an "Edge of the World" place. Called the "Island West of the Sun," Foula may have been the Romans' legendary Thule. In local dialect, *foula* means "bird island," and the name fits. Uncountable numbers of birds haunt the isle and its towering sea cliffs, including the second highest cliff face in Britain, the **Kame** at 1,220 feet. About 3,000 pairs of the world's great skuas live here. They're known as a "bonxie." The highest peak, however, is the **Sneug**, at 1,370 feet. On the island you'll hear many stories about the rock-climbing prowess of locals who go in search of gulls' eggs, facing dangerous falls.

The island lies 27 miles west of Scalloway on the west coast of Mainland. Until the beginning of the 19th century, Old Norse was the language spoken here. Its 400 people remain very traditional, and count yourself lucky if you get to see them dance the Foula reel, considered a classic dance in Shetland. The locals are vastly outnumbered by sheep.

If the weather's right, a weekly mailboat sails to Foula from Walls on Mainland. Even in summer the seas are likely to be turbulent, and in winter Foula has been known to be cut off from the rest of Britain for weeks. The trip takes 2½ hours. Loganair also operates a summer service from Tingwall on Monday, Wednesday, and Friday (trip time: 15 minutes).

Where to Stay & Dine

Because of the interest by visitors in recent years, some islanders have taken to doing B&B.

MRS. MARION TAYLOR, Leraback, Isle of Foula, Shetland ZE2 2PN. Tel. 03933/3226. 3 rms (none with bath), 2 cottages (both with bath).
$ Rates (including half board): £18 ($27) single; £36 ($54) double; £20 ($30) cottage for up to 4 occupants. No credit cards.

This cozy farmhouse near the geographical center of the island, within walking distance of everything, offers some of the only overnight accommodations on the island. A modern and weathertight house, it was erected in 1990 on 7 acres of land belonging to Bryan and Marion Taylor, both of whom emigrated from Edinburgh 12 years ago. Comfortable rooms in the main house have easy access to the large kitchen whose brick hearth is the focal point of the farm. Two outlying cottages, each suitable for one to four occupants, are available (no meals included) on a self-catering basis. In addition to housing overnight guests, the Taylors' income derives from sheep farming, knitting, and spinning (you can order a custom-made hand-knit sweater).

NORTH MAINLAND

The most rugged and spectacular scenery Shetland has to offer is in the northern part of the island. Some writers have found the area similar to Norway, and I concur. That is especially true in the tiny village of **Voe,** with its little wooden houses.

The most "touristic" thing to do in North Mainland is to pause at **Mavis Grind.** There, take a couple of stones, throw one to your right into the North Sea and the other to your left into the Atlantic Ocean. You can drive north along the A970 until you reach the secondary road heading west to **Esha Ness.** I suggest that you take this exciting detour, for at Esha Ness you will come upon what many consider to be the most beautiful and dramatic cliff scenery not only in Shetland, but in all of Britain.

VIDLIN
What to See & Do

But before reaching these sights, you may want to take an earlier detour, going along the A970 until you reach the eastern junction of the B9071, which will take you to Vidlin, where **Lunna Kirk,** one of the oldest churches in the archipelago, is still used by its congregation. Construction began in 1753. The church has a "leper hole," from which the poor victims could listen to the sermon without being seen.

Where to Stay & Dine

MRS. BARBARA FORD, Skeo Green, Lunning, Vidlin, Shetland ZE2 9QB. Tel. 08067/302. 1 rm (without bath).
$ Rates (including Scottish breakfast): £14 ($21) per person. No credit cards.
Mrs. Ford has only one double family room to rent. If arrangements are made, she'll also prepare an evening meal for you for £8 ($12). Vegetarians are especially welcome. Paintings of the Shetland islands are for sale.

BRAE & BUSTA

Heading west back to the A970, continue north toward the sightseeing attraction of **Mavis Grind.** In the vicinity of the hamlets of Brae and Busta, you'll find some of the best food and hotels in Shetland.

Where to Stay & Dine

BRAE HOTEL, Brae, North Mainland, Shetland ZE2 9QJ. Tel. 080622/456. Fax 080622/456. 28 rms (all with bath). TV TEL
$ Rates (including Scottish breakfast): £55 ($82.50) single; £70 ($105) double; discounts offered for stays of 4 days or more. AE, DC, MC, V. **Parking:** Free.
Built in 1979, this earth-toned modern building lies in the center of the hamlet, 28

miles north of Lerwick beside the main A970 highway about a mile south of the narrow isthmus that separates North from South Mainland. Most of the clientele are oil contractors, helicopter pilots, and shipping executives sent by mainland companies to service the nearby Sullom Voe, site of the largest oil terminal in Europe. The interior is appealingly paneled, and the restaurant serves generous portions in fixed-price meals costing £10.50 ($15.80) for three courses. Bedrooms are wallpapered and painted in pastels, and reassuringly warm. On the premises is a bank, a billiard room, and a unisex hairstyling salon.

BUSTA HOUSE, Busta, near Brae, North Mainland, Shetland ZE2 9QN. Tel. 080622/506. Fax 080622/588. 20 rms (all with bath). TV TEL
$ Rates (including Scottish breakfast): £59 ($88.50) single; £77 ($115.50) double. MC, V. **Parking:** Free.

Busta House is said to be the oldest continuously inhabited house in the Shetland Islands. Originally built in 1580, with ample extensions added in 1714 and 1983, it was the original *busta* (homestead) of the medieval Norwegian rulers of the island. Later inhabited by the island's laird, and considered the region's political centerpiece, it once welcomed Queen Elizabeth II at teatime during her tour of the Shetlands on the royal yacht *Brittania*. The estate's long and tormented history includes episodes of multiple drownings, impoverished and impregnated local girls claiming to have secretly married the heir to the estates, a handful of resident ghosts, and some of the most famous lawsuits in Britain. Some literary enthusiasts claim that the house in all its drama was the inspiration for Dickens's *Bleak House*.

In recent times, the most important economic agreement in the history of the Shetlands (the Busta House Agreement) was signed here between the local government and Britain's multinational oil companies. This agreement paved the way for the construction of the massive Sullom Voe oil terminal.

Painted white, and rising above its own small harbor a short drive from the A970, a 10-minute drive south of the hamlet of Sullom, 1½ miles from Brae, the hotel has crow's-foot gables, stone walls measuring 6 feet thick, and an appearance of a fortified manor house. Peter and Judith Jones, the resident proprietors, prepare four-course evening meals for £20.50 ($30.80) each, and maintain the antique allure of both the public rooms and the chintz-filled bedrooms. Each of these contains a trouser press, tea-making facilities, a radio, and same-day laundry facilities. There's a cocktail lounge with an impressive array of malt whiskies, a quiet library, and an ambience much like that of a prestigious country-house hotel.

HILLSWICK

On the way to the spectacular scenery at Esha Ness, 15 miles northwest of Brae, you come to the little fishing hamlet of Hillswick, opening onto the bay in Ura Firth.

Where to Stay & Dine

ST. MAGNUS BAY HOTEL, Hillswick, Shetland ZE2 9RW. Tel. 080623/ 372. Fax 080623/373. 27 rms (all with bath). TV TEL
$ Rates (including Scottish breakfast): £37.50 ($56.30) single; £65 ($97.50) double. MC, V. **Parking:** Free.

Set in a grandly isolated position at the head of St. Magnus Bay, this establishment was prefabricated of solid pine in Norway, barged across the North Sea and assembled as part of Glasgow's Great Exhibition of 1896, then floated to Hillswick around 1900 and reassembled as one of the terminals for the old North of Scotland Shipping Co. (The person responsible for its construction was the now-legendary Arthur Anderson, co-founder of the line that eventually became P & O.) Despite its black-with-white-trim double-gabled severity, it's considered one of the most lavish Edwardian buildings in the Shetlands, and one of the most boisterously popular pubs in the islands. Meal service in the pleasingly old-fashioned dining room is daily from 12:30 to 2pm and 7:30 to 9pm. Specialties include fresh lobster (in season), fresh haddock, sea trout, Aberdeen Angus beef, local salmon, a local and distinctively flavored Shetland lamb, and a traditional Scottish version of cullen skink.

SOUTH MAINLAND

This part of Shetland, reached by heading south along the A970, is both ancient and modern. On the one hand there is the gleaming **Sumburgh Airport** (tel. 0950/60654), but nearby you stumble on the ruins of Jarlshof, which may have been inhabited for some 3,000 years.

WHAT TO SEE & DO

As you go down the "long leg" of Shetland, as it is called, heading due south, passing a peaty moorland and fresh meadows, the first attraction is not on Mainland at all but on an offshore island called **Mousa**, to see the famous ✪ **Broch of Mousa**, a Pictish broch that was a defense tower guarding the little islet for some 2,000 years. It reached the then-incredible height of some 40 feet and was constructed of local stones, with two circular walls, one within the other. They enclose a staircase that led to sleeping quarters. It is considered the best preserved example of an Iron Age broch in Britain. The ferry point for reaching Mousa is in the hamlet of Sandwick, 7 miles south of Lerwick. There is daily bus service between Lerwick and Sandwick. A local boatman will often take you across to Mousa at a price to be negotiated. It takes about 15 minutes to cross from Mainland to Mousa. Visiting hours are from April through September, Monday to Saturday from 9:30am to 6pm, Sunday from 2 to 6pm. From October through March, hours are Monday to Saturday from 9:30am to 4pm, Sunday from 2 to 4pm.

South of Sandwick, you reach the parish of Dunrossness. At Boddam is the **Shetland Croft House Museum** (tel. 0595/5057), east of the A970 on an unmarked road 25 miles south of Lerwick. Rural Shetland life comes alive here in this thatched croft house from the mid-1800s. The house is authentically furnished, including such items as box beds and butter churns. The museum also has some outbuildings and a functioning watermill. It is open from May through September, daily from 10am to 1pm and from 2 to 5pm. Adults pay an admission of £1 ($1.50); children 50p (80¢).

Continuing south, you reach the outstanding man-made attraction in Shetland, ✪ **Jarlshof**, Sumburgh (tel. 0950/60112), near the Sumburgh Airport. It has been called "the most remarkable archeological discovery in Britain." A violent storm in 1897 performed the first archeological dig. Washing away sections of the large mound, it revealed huge stone walls. Excavations that followed turned up an astonishing array of seven distinct civilizations. The earliest was from the Bronze Age, but habitation continued at the site through the 1500s. Everybody over the centuries lived here from wheelhouse people to Vikings, from broch builders to medieval settlers. A manor house was built here in the 16th century by the treacherous earl, Patrick Stewart, referred to earlier, but it was sacked in 1609. It is open April through September, Monday to Saturday from 9:30am to 6pm; October through March, Monday to Saturday from 9:30am to 4pm; and year-round, on Sunday from 2 to 4pm. Admission is £1.50 ($2.30) for adults and 80p ($1.20) for children.

In the vicinity is **Sumburgh Lighthouse,** one of the many Scottish lighthouses that was constructed by the grandfather of novelist Robert Louis Stevenson. Built in 1821, it can be visited by the public, but you must phone 0950/60374 for an appointment.

The terminal at **Sumburgh Airport** opened in 1979 and has played a major role in the North Sea oilfields development. It services many of the offshore rigs today.

On the coast at the tip of Scatness, about a mile southwest of Jarlshof at the end of the Mainland, you come upon the **Ness of Burgi,** which was a defensive Iron Age structure related to a broch.

Heading back north in the direction of Lerwick, you can veer to the west for a trip to **St. Ninian's Island** in the southwestern corner of Shetland. It is reached by going along the B9122. The island is approached by what is called a *tombolo* or bridging sandbar. An early monastery once stood on this island, but it was not uncovered until 1958. Puffins with their orange beaks often favor the islet, which has a pure white sandy beach on each side.

The island became famous in 1958 when a group of students from Aberdeen came upon a spectacular cache of Celtic artifacts, mainly silverware, including brooches and other valuable pieces. Monks are believed to have hidden the treasure trove, perhaps fearing a Viking attack. The St. Ninian treasure is in the National Museum of Antiquities at Edinburgh.

WHERE TO STAY & DINE

SUMBURGH HOTEL, Sumburgh Head, Virkie Parish, Shetland ZE3 1JN. Tel. 0950/60201. Fax 0950/60394. 24 rms (all with bath). TV TEL

$ Rates (including Scottish breakfast): £32–£50 ($48–$75) single; £46–£62 ($69–$93) double. MC, V. **Parking:** Free.

Its turrets and towers were originally built in 1857 of local stone for the Laird of Virkie, the Victorian descendant of Robert the Bruce. Set on 12 barren acres of land jutting dramatically out to sea, it lies at the southernmost end of the Shetland Islands, at the end of the A970. A modern addition completed in the 1960s doubled the size of the establishment, which contains the Voe Room restaurant and two very popular bars. Bedrooms in the old part of the house have a country-house look with chintz curtains and solidly traditional furniture. Bedrooms in the newer section contain monochromatic decors of comfortable but severe modernity.

WHALSAY

The island is reached by car-ferry from Laxo, north of Lerwick. Take the A970, then turn east along the B9071. The crossing takes less than an hour; call 08066/376 to reserve space. Loganair (tel. 059584/246 also flies into Whalsay's small airfield.

Three miles off the eastern coast of Mainland, Whalsay and its some 1,000 people are concerned mainly with fishing, including excellent wild trout fishing. Fishermen in the 19th century dubbed it "The Bonnie Isle," and the name has stuck. Once it was an important trading post for the Hanseatic League, the Baltic traders coming here to exchange such items as muslin and brandy for salted and dried fish. Their decaying storage warehouse, the Bremen Bod, can still be seen close to the pier at Symbister. The island is also know for its homemade knitware, most often "paneled jerseys" that come in a wide range of colors and designs.

The most important building on the island, **Symbister House,** is now a school. A historic ruin, believed to have been a temple, dates from 2000 B.C. The island has an 18-hole golf course.

Sometimes, if the weather is right, boat trips from Whalsay leave for the **Out Skerries.** These are the most easterly inhabited outcrop of rocks in the North Isles, occupied by some 100 hearty souls who somehow manage to eke out a living on Bruray and Housay, which are connected by a causeway. Before 1852 when a lighthouse was built, many ships were wrecked on the treacherous rocks here. Birdwatchers come here in spring and autumn to enjoy the flocks of rare and exotic migratory birds.

UNST

The northernmost point of Britain, remote and beautiful Unst is easy to reach. After crossing over to Yell, you can drive along the A968 to the little harbor at Gutcher in the northeast of Yell. The ferry to Unst crosses from there about every hour. If you want to bring your car over, phone 095782/259 for a reservation. Loganair (tel. 059584/246) also flies to Unst on Wednesday.

WHAT TO SEE & DO

Robert Louis Stevenson stayed here for a time right before he wrote *Treasure Island.* Alan Stevenson was designing and building the Muckle Flugga lighthouse on an outermost skerry, which is even farther north than Labrador.

Unst is steeped in folklore and legend. An Old Norse longhouse, believed to date from the 9th century, was excavated at Underhoull. The best beach is at Skaw, set against the backdrop of **Saxa Vord,** legendary home of the giant Saxi. A drive to the top will reward you with a view of the Burra Firth. Visitors go to **Haroldswick** to post their cards and letters in the northernmost post office in the British Isles.

The roll-on/roll-off car-ferry from Yell will come into Belmont. Nearby is **Muness Castle,** constructed in 1598 by Laurence Bruce, a relative of the notorious Earl Patrick Stewart who ruled Shetland so harshly. Adam Crawford, who designed Scalloway Castle for the ruling earls on Mainland, also drew up the plans for Muness. Built with rubble and known for its fine architectural detail, the castle was inhabited for less than a century. Normally it is open April through September, daily from 9:30am to 7pm; if it is closed, ask for the key at the cottage across the way. For information, phone 095785/215.

The ruins of the **Kirk of Lund,** dating from the Middle Ages, can also be seen on Unst. Like Lunna Kirk in Vidlin, it, too, had a "leper hole" through which victims could hear the service.

Unst is home of the **Hermaness Bird Reserve,** one of the most important ornithological sites in Britain. Its 600-foot cliffs are filled with kittiwakes, razorbills, guillemots, and the inevitable puffins.

WHERE TO STAY & DINE

BALTASOUND HOTEL, Baltasound, Unst, Shetland ZE2 9DS. Tel. 095781/584. 28 rms (25 with shower) TV TEL
$ Rates (including Scottish breakfast): £36 ($54) single without bath, £40 ($60) single with bath; £50 ($75) double without bath, £54 ($81) double with bath. No credit cards. **Parking:** Free.

Originally built 150 years ago for the family of the local laird, and converted into a hotel in 1939, this granite house sits in lonely isolation on an acre of its own land beside the sea about a quarter mile from the hamlet of Baltasound. Because the building's two upper stories are reserved for the owners, its rentable bedrooms are in what local residents call a "Scandinavian extension" jutting to the building's side. Sheathed on the outside with blackened wood siding and decorated inside with strips of pine, it contains simple and uncluttered bedrooms carefully sealed against the blustering winds.

Late in 1992, the hotel was enlarged with a series of motel-like "chalet" rooms, fully attached to the main building and very similar to conventional bedrooms except that their entrances open directly into the great outdoors.

Many of this hotel's clients are birdwatchers and geologists who stay for as much as a week to observe the island's natural attractions. There's a bar and a restaurant on the premises, serving fixed-price three-course evening meals for £11 ($16.50) per person.

A. GLOSSARY

aber river mouth
ach field
alt stream
baillie magistrate
bal hamlet or tiny village
ben peak, often rugged
birk birch tree
brae hillside, especially along a river
brig bridge
broch circular stone tower of ancient or unknown origin
burn stream
cairn a heap of stones piled up as a memorial or landmark
clach stone
clachan hamlet
close narrow passage leading from the street to a court or tenement
craig rock
creel basket
croft a small farm worked by a tenant, often with hereditary rights
cromlech, dolmen prehistoric tomb or monument consisting of a large, flat stone laid across upright stones
drum ridge
dun fortress, often in a lake, for refuge in times of trouble
factor manager of an estate
fell hill
firth an arm of the sea reaching inland
gate, gait street (in proper names)
glen a small valley
haugh water meadow
inver mouth of a river
kil, kin, kirk church
kyle narrows
loch lake
machair a sand dune, sometimes covered with sea grass
mon hill
muir moor
mull cape or promontory
ness headland
pend vaulted passage
provost mayor
ross cape
strath valley
tolbooth old town hall (often with prison)
way bay
wynd street

B. MEASURES & CONVERSIONS

METRIC MEASURES

LENGTH

1 millimeter (mm)	=	.04 inches (*or* less than ¹⁄₁₆ in.)
1 centimeter (cm)	=	.39 inches (*or* just under ½ in.)
1 meter (m)	=	39 inches (*or* about 1.1 yards)
1 kilometer (km)	=	.62 miles (*or* about ⅔ of a mile)

To convert kilometers to miles, multiply the number of kilometers by .62. Also use to convert kilometers per hour (kmph) to miles per hour (m.p.h.).

To convert miles to kilometers, multiply the number of miles by 1.61. Also use to convert from m.p.h. to kmph.

CAPACITY

1 liter (1)	=	33.92 fluid ounces	=	2.1 pints	=	1.06 quarts
	=	.26 U.S. gallons				
1 imperial gallon	=	U.S. gallons				

To convert liters to U.S. gallons, multiply the number of liters by .26.

To convert U.S. gallons to liters, multiply the number of gallons by 3.79.

To convert Imperial gallons to U.S. gallons, multiply the number of Imperial gallons by 1.2.

To convert U.S. gallons to Imperial gallons, multiply the number of U.S. gallons by .83.

WEIGHT

1 gram (g)	=	.035 ounces (*or* about a paperclip's weight)
1 kilogram (kg)	=	35.2 ounces
	=	2.2 pounds
1 metric ton	=	2,205 pounds (1.1 short ton)

To convert kilograms to pounds, multiply the number of kilograms by 2.2.

To convert pounds to kilograms, multiply the number of pounds by .45.

TEMPERATURE

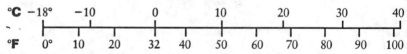

To convert degrees Celsius to degrees Fahrenheit, multiply °C by 9, divide by 5, and add 32 (example: 20°C × 9/5 + 32 = 68°F).

To convert degress Fahrenheit to degrees Celsius, subtract 32 from °F, multiply by 5, then divide by 9 (example: 85°F − 32 × 5/9 = 29.4°C).

C. MILEAGE CHART

	Aberdeen	Ayr	Berwick-on-Tweed	Braemar	Dundee	EDINBURGH	Fort William	Glasgow	Inverness	John o' Groats	Kyle of Lochalsh	LONDON	Oban	Southampton	Stranraer
Stranraer	228	51	158	194	167	124	184	84	250	379	263	402	176	425	
Southampton	547	417	388	512	477	421	520	420	579	706	599	77	512		425
Oban	178	125	180	141	117	123	49	92	134	244	147	489		512	176
LONDON	503	394	338	482	434	378	497	397	536	663	576		489	77	402
Kyle of Lochalsh	189	212	243	159	186.	216	79	179	84	189		576	147	599	263
John o' Groats	232	328	342	202	259	285	195	295	129		189	663	244	706	379
Inverness	105	199	215	75	132	158	66	166		129	84	536	134	579	250
Glasgow	145	33	101	110	83	44	101		166	295	179	397	92	420	84
Fort William	165	133	190	125	127	144		101	66	195	79	497	49	520	184
EDINBURGH	125	73	57	91	56		144	44	158	285	216	378	123	421	124
Dundee	67	117	113	52		56	127	83	132	259	186	434	117	477	167
Braemar	59	143	148		52	91	125	110	75	202	159	482	141	512	194
Ayr	177		134	143	117	73	133	33	199	328	212	394	125	417	51
Aberdeen		177	182	59	67	125	165	145	105	232	189	503	178	547	228

INDEX

This index is organized by destinations (regions and towns) in alphabetical order. General information, major sightseeing attractions, and important people are also listed alphabetically.

For tourist attractions of specific interest, see the following categories: Castles; Gardens; Golf courses; Highland Gatherings; Historical and cultural museums; Historic sites; Monuments and memorials; Nature reserves; Natural spectacles; Parks.

Abbeys, 6, 11. *See also specific places*
Abbey of Iona (Iona), 358–59
Abbotsford (Melrose), 68
ABERDEEN, 4, 32, 34, 280–88
  Aberdeen Art Gallery, 281
  accommodations, 282–86
  excursions, 288–89
  restaurants, 286–88
  sightseeing, 281–82
  traveling to, 280–81
ABERFELDY, 265–66
ABERFOYLE, 249–51
Achamore House Gardens (Isle of Gigha), **222**
Adam, James, 13, 15
Adam, John, 184
Adam, Robert, 13, 15, 67, 129, 196
Adam, William, 15, 66, 288
Adam style, 142–43, 318
Air travel, 42–46, 50
ALLOWAY, 195–96
Alternative and adventure travel, 39–42
Ancestral roots, tracing your, 40–41
ANSTRUTHER, 232–33
Architecture, 15. *See also specific architects*
ARDNAMURCHAN PENINSULA, 303–4
ARGYLL, 4, 5, 201–14. *See also specific places*
Argyll Forest Park, 201, 202
ARMADALE (ISLE OF SKYE), 345
Art, 14–15, 24
AUSKERRY, 389
AVIEMORE, 305–9
AYR, 192–95

BALIVANICH, 370
BALLACHULISH, 298–99
BALLATER, 276–78
Balliol, Devorgilla, 76, 78
BALLOCH, 252–53
BALMACARA, 340–41
Balmoral Castle (Ballater), 255, 276
BANCHORY, 278–80
BANNOCKBURN, 241
BARRA, 372–75
Barrie, Sir James Matthew, 13, 16, 75
Beaches, 199, 216–17, 233–34, 365, 407
BEARSDEN, 173
BEAULY, 329
Bell, Alexander Graham, 13
BENBECULA, 370
Birdwatching, 146, 223, 232, 331, 335, 347–50, 361, 368–69, 371, 378, 383, 388–94, 403, 407
BIRSAY PARISH (ORKNEY ISLANDS), 384
BLACK ISLE, THE, 325–29
BLACKWATERFOOT (ISLE OF ARRAN), 221
Blair Castle (Pitlochry), 270

Bonnie Prince Charlie. *See* Stuart, Charles
BONNYRIGG, 108–9
Books about Scotland, 23–24
BORDERS, THE, 4, 61–69. *See also specific places*
Boswell, James, 13, 16, 23–24, 336, 349, 351, 355
BOWMORE (ISLE OF ISLAY), 223
BRAEMAR, 274–76
Braemar Castle (Braemar), 275
BRAE (SHETLAND ISLANDS), 404–5
Brendan, Saint, 292
Broch of Mousa (Shetland Islands), 406
Brochs, 363, 388, 398, 406.
Brodick Castle (Brodick), 218
BRODICK (ISLE OF ARRAN), 218–19
Bruce, Robert the. *See* Robert I
Buchan, Sir John, 16, 72
Buchanan clan, 247
BUNESSAN (ISLE OF MULL), 355–56
Burns, Robert ("Rabbie"), 16, 32, 56, 74, 80, 84, 179, 192–97, 266, 296
  Burns Cottage and Museum (Alloway), 195
  Burns House (Dumfries), 76
  Burns Monument and Gardens (Alloway), 195
  Land o' Burns Center (Alloway), 195
  Robert Burns Centre (Dumfries), 76, 78
  Souter Johnnie's Cottage (Turnberry), 197
  Tam o' Shanter Inn (museum, Ayr), 192
BURRAY (ORKNEY ISLANDS), 386
Burrell Collection (Glasgow), 177, 182
BUSTA (SHETLAND ISLANDS), 404–5
Bus travel, 47, 51

CAIRNDOW, 213
CAITHNESS, 332–35
Calendar of events, 32–35. *See also* Highland Gatherings; *and specific events*
CALLANDER, 246–47
Campbell clan, 209–10, 212, 224, 299
CARDROSS, 167
Carlyle, Jane Welsh, 144
Carlyle, Thomas, 16
Carnegie, Andrew, 13, 227–28, 330
Cars and driving, 47, 52–53
CASTLEBAY (BARRA), 373–74
CASTLE DOUGLAS, 80–82
Castles
  Amhuinnsuidhe Estate (Harris), 366
  Aros Castle (Isle of Mull), 351, 353
  Balloch Castle (Balloch), 252
  Balmoral Castle (Ballater), 255, 276
  Balvenie Castle (Dufftown), 290
  Beaufort Castle (Beauly), 329
  Blair Castle (Pitlochry), 270
  Borve Castle (Benbecula), 370
  Braemar Castle (Braemar), 275
  Breacachadh (Coll), 349

Castles (cont'd)
Brodick Castle (Brodick), 218
Broughty Castle (Broughty Ferry), 272
Bruce Castle (Tarbert), 215
Cardoness Castle (Gatehouse-of-Fleet), 84
Carleton Castle (Turnberry), 197
Carnasserie Castle (Crinan Canal), 211
Castle Varrich (Tongue), 331
Cawdor Castle (Cawdor), 323–24
Claig Castle (Isle of Jura), 224
Craigievar Castle (Alford), 279
Craigmillar Castle (Edinburgh), 128
Crathes Castle and Gardens (Banchory), 278–79
Culzean Castle (Maybole), 196–97
Dirleton Castle (Dirleton), 148
Doune Castle (Dunblane), 246
Drum Castle (Aberdeen), 288
Drumlanrig Castle (Thornhill), 78–79
Drummond Castle (Crieff), 264
Duart Castle (Isle of Mull), 352
Dunbar Castle (Dunbar), 145
Dunollie Castle (Oban), 205
Dunrobin Castle (Golspie), 331
Dunsgiath Castle (Sleat Peninsula), 345
Dunstaffnage Castle (Oban), 205
Duntrune Castle (Crinan), 210
Dunvegan Castle (Dunvegan), 343
Dunyvaig Castle (Isle of Islay), 223
Edinburgh Castle (Edinburgh), 124–25, 130
Eilean Donan Castle (Dornie), 338
Fincharn, castle at (Loch Awe), 206
Floors Castle (Kelso), 66
Frasier, Castle (Kemnay), 288
Fyvie Castle (Turriff), 288
Glamis Castle (Glamis), 273
Gylen Castle (Kerrera), 205
Haddo House (Ellon), 288–89
Hailes Castle (Dunbar), 145
Inveraray Castle (Inveraray), 212
Invergarry Castle (Invergarry), 305
Kilchurn Castle (Loch Awe), 209
Kildrummy Castle (Kildrummy), 288
Kilochan Castle (Carleton), 197
Kismul Castle (Barra), 373
Knock Castle (Sleat Peninsula), 345
Lachlan, Castle (Strathlachlan), 213
Lauriston Castle (Edinburgh), 128
Loch Leven Castle (Castle Island), 230
McLellan's Castle (Kirkcudbright), 82
Moy Castle (Isle of Mull), 351
Muness Castle (Shetland Islands), 407
Neidpath Castle (Peebles), 72
New Castle (Coll), 349
Noltland Castle (Westray), 392
Old Inverlochy Castle (Fort William), 301
Old Wick, Castle of (Wick), 333
St. Andrews, Castle of (St. Andrews), 236–37
St. John, Castle of (Stranraer), 86–87
Scalloway Castle (Shetland Islands), 400–401
Sinclair and Girnigoe, Castles (Wick), 333
Skipness Castle (Skipness), 215
Stalker, Castle (Portnacroish), 208
Stirling Castle (Stirling), 240
Tantallon Castle (North Berwick), 146
Thirlestane Castle (Lauder), 71
Threave Castle (Castle Douglas), 81
Torosay Castle and Gardens (Isle of Mull), 352
Turnberry Castle (Turnberry), 197
Urquhart Castle (Drumnadrochit), 314
CELLARDYKE, 232

Celts, 5, 11–12, 15, 216, 223, 267, 358, 393, 396
CENTRAL HIGHLANDS, 225–27, 240–54.
    See also specific places
Churches. See individual destinations and specific
    entries
Clans, 6, 11, 17–19, 25, 310, 317, 376. See also
    specific clans
Climate, 31
Clothing, 36. See also Kilts; Knitwear and woolens;
    Tartans; Tweeds; Woolens
COLL, 348–50
Columba, Saint, 6, 217, 218, 296, 350, 358, 360, 369
Combined Operations Museum (Inveraray), 212
COMRIE, 34, 265
Consulates, 57
Country houses. See Castles; Historic houses
CRAIGHOUSE (ISLE OF JURA), 224
Craigievar Castle (Alford), 279
CRAIGNURE (ISLE OF MULL), 352–53
CRAIL, 234–35
Crathes Castle and Gardens (Banchory), 278–79
CREAGORRY, 370
CRIEFF, 263–64
CRINAN, 210–11
CROMARTY, 326, 328
Cruises, 49–50, 251–52. See also Tours
Cuisine, 21–22
CULROSS, 228, 230
CULZEAN, 196–97
Culzean Castle (Maybole), 196–97
CUPAR, 239
Currency and exchange, 28–29

DALKEITH, 143–44
DALMALLY, 209
DALWHINNIE, 289
David I, 6, 11, 317
Dean Village, 126, 129
DERVAIG (ISLE OF MULL), 354–55
DIRLETON, 148
Disabled travelers, tips for, 36–37
Distilleries. See Whisky
DORNIE, 337–38
DORNOCH, 330
DOUNE, 245–46
Doyle, Sir Arthur Conan, 16, 126
Drumlanrig Castle (Thornhill), 78–79
DRUMNADROCHIT, 314–15
DRYBURGH, 67
DUFFTOWN, 290
DUMFRIES, 4, 32–33, 75–80
DUNBAR, 145–46
DUNBLANE, 244–45
Dunblane Cathedral (Dunblane), 244–45
DUNDEE, 271–73
DUNDONNELL, 335
DUNFERMLINE, 227–28
DUNKELD, 266–68
Dunrobin Castle (Golspie), 331
Dunstaffnage Castle (Oban), 205
Dunvegan Castle (Dunvegan), 343
DUNVEGAN (ISLE OF SKYE), 343–44

EARLSFERRY, 233
EAST NEUK, 231–35
EDAY (ORKNEY ISLANDS), 390–91
EDINBURGH, 15, 32, 34–35, 90–142
    accommodations, 97–109
        castle and country house hotels, 108–109
        in the center, 97–104

EDINBURGH (cont'd)
  north of the center, 108
  south of the center, 106–108
  west of the center, 104–106
American Express, 95
arriving in, 90–91
bookstores, 135–36
Calton Hill, 128–29, 132
cars and driving, 94
castles, 124–25, 128, 130
cinemas, 142
cost of everyday items, 30
Dean Village, 129
Edinburgh Castle, 124–25, 130
evening entertainment, 138–42
excursion areas, 142–48
Fast facts, 95–97
films, 142
High Kirk of St. Giles, 121
historic sites, 121, 124–25, 129–30, 132
hotels. *See* accommodations
International Arts Festival, 4, 34, 90–91, 133–34,
  139
itineraries, suggested, 121
layout of, 92
museums
  Museum of Childhood, 121, 122
  National Gallery of Scotland, 125, 132
  Royal Museum of Scotland, 127
  Scottish National Gallery of Modern Art, 127
  Scottish National Portrait Gallery, 127
  Scottish United Services Museum, 127–28
music, 138–39, 140
neighborhoods, 92–93
Palace of Holyroodhouse, 125, 132
panoramas, 126–29, 132
parks and gardens, 120, 128, 132–33
performing arts, 138–40
picnic supplies, 120
pubs, 140–42
recreational activities, 134–35
restaurants, 109–20
  in the center, 109–115
  in Leith, 116–17
  in Preston field, 117
  south of the center, 115–16
  specialty dining, 117–20
Royal Botanic Garden, 128
The Royal Mile, 92, 121, 124–25
Scotch Whisky Heritage Center, 124
shopping, 126, 135–38
sightseeing
  for the architecture enthusiast, 129
  for children, 130
  for the literary enthusiast, 129–30
  for visiting Americans, 130
smart traveler tips, 126
special events, 34–35
sports, 134
temperatures, average monthly, 31
theaters, 138–40
tourist information, 91
tours, organized, 133
transportation, 93–95
walking tour, 130–33
zoo, 130
Edinburgh Castle (Edinburgh), 124–25, 130
Edinburgh Festival. *See* International Arts Festival
Educational/study travel, 39, 41–42
EGILSAY (ORKNEY ISLANDS), 389

EIGG, 347–48
Eilean Donan Castle (Dornie), 338
Eisenhower, Gen. Dwight D., 196
ELGIN, 291–93
ELIE, 233–34
Embassies and consulates, 57
Entry requirements, 28
ERISKAY, 372

FAIR ISLE, 394–95
FALKLAND, 230–31
Falkland Palace and Garden (Falkland), 231
Families, tips for, 38–39
Farmhouse holidays, 41
Fast facts, 56–60
Ferries, 54. *See also individual destinations*
Festivals, 32–35. *See also* Folk music and festivals;
  Highland Gatherings; *and specific festivals*
  International Arts Festival (Edinburgh), 4, 34,
    90–91, 133–34, 139
FIFE, 4, 225–39. *See also specific places*
FINDHORN, 293–94
Fingal's Cave (Staffa), 359–60
FIONNPHORT (ISLE OF MULL), 357
Fishing, 20, 232, 247, 351, 361, 378, 383
Fishing and maritime museums, 232, 269, 281, 333,
  366
Fleming, Sir Alexander, 13
Floors Castle (Kelso), 66
Folk music and festivals, 16–17, 26
  Edinburgh, 140
  Nairn, 323
  Shetland Islands, 395
  Orkney Islands, 378
Foods, 21–22
FORT AUGUSTUS, 315–16
FORTROSE, 326
FORT WILLIAM, 32, 295, 300–303
FOULA (SHETLAND ISLANDS), 403–4
Fyvie Castle (Turriff), 288

Gaelic language, 12, 17, 211, 247, 317, 345, 361, 376
Gardens. *See also* Parks
  Abigland Gardens (Kirkbean), 78
  Achamore House Gardens (Isle of Gigha), 222
  Botanic Garden (Glasgow), 182
  Branklyn Garden (Branklyn), 258
  Carradale House Gardens (Carradale), 216
  Castle Kennedy Gardens (Stranraer), 86–87
  Colonsay House, gardens of (Colonsay), 360
  Crathes Castle and Gardens (Banchory), 278–79
  Cruickshank Botanic Garden (Aberdeen), 282
  Dawyck Botanic Garden (Peebles), 72
  Drummond Castle (Crieff), 264
  Falkland Palace and Garden (Falkland), 231
  Inverewe Gardens (Gairloch), 335
  Kailzie Gardens (Peebles), 72
  Logan Botanic Garden (Port Logan), 88
  Royal Botanic Garden (Edinburgh), 128
  St. Mary's Pleasance (Haddington), 144
  Strone Garden and Pinetum (Cairndow), 213
  Threve Garden (Castle Douglas), 81
  Torosay Castle and Gardens (Isle of Mull), 352
GATEHOUSE-OF-FLEET, 83–84
Genealogy, 40–41
Geography, 1, 4–5
Glamis Castle (Glamis), 273
GLASGOW, 4, 9–10, 33, 149–91
  accommodations, 158–67
    central Glasgow, 158–63

GLASGOW (cont'd)
for children, 164
nearby, 166–67
the west end, 163–66
American Express, 155
arriving in, 151–52
Burrell Collection, 177, 182
car rentals, 154
churches and cathedrals, 179, 183
Cathedral of St. Kentigern, 179
evening entertainment, 188–91
excursion areas, 192–200
Fast facts, 155–58
Frommer's favorite experiences, 182
Glasgow Art Gallery and Museum, 177
Glasgow International Jazz Festival, 186
historic sites, 178–79
itineraries, suggested, 176–77
layout of, 152–53
museums, 177–79, 183
Burrell Collection, 177, 182
Glasgow Art Gallery and Museum, 177
Haggs Castle, 182–83
Hunterian Art Gallery, 178
Hunterian Museum, 178–79
Museum of Transport, 179
People's Palace, 178
Pollok House, 178
The Tenement House, 179
music, 189–91
Necropolis, 182
neighborhoods, 153
parks and gardens, 153, 176
performing arts, 188–90
Provand's Lordship, 179
pubs, 191
recreational activities, 186–87
restaurants, 167–76
central Glasgow, 167–72
for children, 173
nearby, 173
the west end, 172–73
specialty dining, 174–76
shopping, 182, 187–88
sightseeing, 176–83
for children, 182
in Paisley, 183
special events, 186
sports, 186–87
tea rooms, 175
temperatures, average monthly, 31
Theatre Royal, 189–90
theaters, 189–90
tours, organized, 183
transportation, 154–55
walking tour, 183–86
GLENCAPLE, 78
GLENCOE, 299–300
GLENEAGLES, 262–63
GLENLIVET, 289–90
Glossary of terms, 409
Golf, 19–20, 235–36, 289, 361
tours for golfers, 48
Golf courses, 19–20
Balcomie Golf Course (Crail), 234–35
Carrick Knowe Golf Course (Edinburgh), 134
in Glasgow, 187
in Gleneagles, 20, 262
in Port Ellen (Isle of Islay), 223
Port Royal Golf Course (Edinburgh), 134

Prestwick Golf Course, 20, 198
Royal Dornoch Golf Club (Dornoch), 20, 330
Royal Troon Course (Troon), 20, 199
in St. Andrews, 20, 235–36
tours of, 48
in Turnberry, 20, 197
Western Isles Golf Course (Isle of Mull), 351, 353
GOLSPIE, 330–31
GORDON, 66–67
GOUROCK, 151
GRANTOWN-ON-SPEY, 312–13
Grant clan, 314
Graves of the Kings (Iona), 358
GREENOCK, 150
GULLANE, 147–48

HADDINGTON, 144–45
HAMILTON, 32
HARRIS, 365–67
Health concerns and precautions, 35–36
HEBRIDEAN ISLANDS, 5, 12, 336–75. *See also specific places*
traveling to, 336–37
Highland Gatherings, 17–18
Braemar, 18, 33, 274
Carmunnock village, 186
Inverness, 316
Mull, 351
Oban, 205
HIGHLANDS, 5, 200–17, 225–27, 240–54, 295–335. *See also specific places*
HILLSWICK (SHETLAND ISLANDS), 405
Historical and cultural museums
Bannockburn Heritage Centre (Bannockburn), 241
Black Watch Regimental Museum (Perth), 258
Burns Cottage and Museum (Alloway), 195
Castle Gaol (Jedburgh), 64
Clan Donald Centre (Sleat Peninsula), 345
Clan MacPherson House & Museum (Newtonmore), 310
Combined Operations Museum (Inveraray), 212
Doune Motor Museum (Doune), 246
Dumfries Museum (Dumfries), 76
Gordon Highlanders Regimental Museum (Aberdeen), 281
Haggs Castle (Glasgow), 182–83
Highland Folk Museum (Kingussie), 311
Hunterian Museum (Glasgow), 178–79
Inverness Museum and Art Gallery (Inverness), 317
Land o'Burns Centre (Alloway), 195
Loch Ness Monster Exhibition (Drumnadrochit), 314
Mull Museum (Isle of Mull), 353
Museum of Childhood (Edinburgh), 121, 124
Museum of Islay Life (Isle of Islay), 223
Museum of the Argyll and Sutherland Highlanders (Stirling), 240–41
Museum of Transport (Glasgow), 179
Old Byrne Heritage Centre (Isle of Mull), 355
Orkney Wireless Museum (Orkney Islands), 386
People's Palace (Glasgow), 178
People's Story (Edinburgh), 132
Queen's Own Highlanders Regimental Museum (Ardersier), 318
Robert Burns Centre (Dumfries), 76, 78
Royal Museum of Scotland (Edinburgh), 127
Scotch Whisky Heritage Center (Edinburgh), 124
Scottish Horse Museum (Dunkeld), 267

Historical and cultural museums (cont'd)
Scottish Tartans Museum (Comrie), 265
Scottish United Service Museum (Edinburgh), 127–28
Shawbost School Museum (Lewis), 362
Shetland Croft House Museum (Shetland Islands), 406
Shetland Library and Museum (Shetland Islands), 398
Stewarty Museum (Kirkcudbright), 83
Stromness Museum (Orkney Islands), 385
Tam o'Shanter Inn (Ayr), 192
Tenement House, The (Glasgow), 179
Tingwall Agricultural Museum (Shetland Islands), 401
Unicorn, The (Dundee), 271
West Highland Museum (Fort William), 301
Historic sites. See also Monuments and memorials
Abbotsford (Melrose), 68
Abertarff House (Inverness), 317
Andrew Carnegie Birthplace Museum (Dunfermline), 227–28
Auchindrain Township Open Air Museum (Inveraray), 212
Bachelors' Club (Tarbolton village), 193
Barpa Langass (North Uist), 369
Birnam House (Dunkeld), 267
Bishop's Palace (Orkney Islands), 380–81
Blackhammer Cairn (Orkney Islands), 388
Bowhill (Selkirk), 69–70
Broch of Mousa (Shetland Islands), 406
Brough of Birsay (Orkney Islands), 384
Burns Cottage and Museum (Alloway), 195
Burns House (Dumfries), 76
Cambeltown Cross (Campbeltown), 216
Canongate Tolbooth (Edinburgh), 124
Carnish Stone Circle and the Barpa Carnish (North Uist), 369
Carrick House (Eday), 390
Clach an Trushal (Lewis), 363
Clickhimin Broch (Shetland Islands), 398
Culloden Battlefield (Culloden Moor), 317–18
Culross Palace (Culross), 228
Cuween Hill Cairn (Orkney Islands), 383
Dunaverty Rock (Southend), 217
Dun Carloway Broch (Lewis), 363
Dun Telve and Dun Troddan (Gleann Beag), 338
Dwarfie Stane (Orkney Islands), 387
Earl Patrick's Palace (Orkney Islands), 381
Ellisland Farm (Dumfries), 78
Falkland Palace and Garden (Falkland), 231
Fort Charlotte (Shetland Islands), 398
Fort George (Ardersier), 318
Gentleman's Cave (Westray), 392
Georgian House (Edinburgh), 129
Gladstone's Land (Edinburgh), 129–30, 132
Globe Inn (Dumfries), 80
Graves of the Kings (Iona), 358
Hermitage (Dunkeld), 267
Hopetoun House (South Queensferry), 142–43
Hugh Miller's Cottage (Cromarty), 326
Huntly House (Edinburgh), 124, 132
James Dun's House (Aberdeen), 282
Jane Welsh Carlyle Museum (Haddington), 144
Jarlshof (Shetland Islands), 406
John Knox's House (Edinburgh), 124, 132
Kildalton Crosses (Isle of Islay), 223
Kirkmadrine (Stoneykirk), 88
Klipheder Wheelhouse (South Uist), 371

Lady Stair's House (Edinburgh), 121, 129
Lewis Black House (Lewis), 362
Linlithgow Palace (Linlithgow), 142
Loudoun Hall (Ayr), 192
MacLeod's Stone (Harris), 366
McCullochs, tower of (Creetown), 84
Maes Howe (Orkney Islands), 383
Mary Queen of Scots house (Jedburgh), 63–64
Mellerstain (Gordon), 66–67
Mercat Cross (Castlegate), 282
Mercat Cross (Glasgow), 184
Midhowe Broch and Tombs (Orkney Islands), 388
Monkstadt House (Uig), 343
Mote of Urr (Castle Douglas), 81
Necropolis (Glasgow), 182, 184
Ness of Burgi (Shetland Islands), 406
Ogham Stone (Isle of Gigha), 222
Old Bridge House (Dumfries), 76
Old Mercat Cross (Inverness), 317
Orchardton Tower (Castle Douglas), 81
Palace of Holyroodhouse (Edinburgh), 125, 132
Pass of Killiecrankie (Pitlochry), 270
Provand's Lordship (Glasgow), 179, 184
Provost Skene House (Aberdeen), 282
Quoyness Chambered Tomb (Sanday), 391
Rabbie's Bar (Ayr), 195
Ring of Brodgar (Orkney Islands), 383
St. Andrew's-by-the-Green (Glasgow), 186
St. Boniface Church (Papa Westray), 393
St. Magnus Church (Orkney Islands), 389
St. Treadwell's Chapel (Papa Westray), 393
Scarista Standing Stone (Taransay), 366
Scone Palace (Scone), 261
Skara Brae (Orkney Islands), 383–84
Souter Johnnie's Cottage (Turnberry), 197
Standing Stones of Callandish (Lewis), 362
Staneydale Temple (Shetland Islands), 402
Steinacleit Cairn and Stone Circle (Lewis), 362–63
Stones of Clava (Nairn), 318
Tankerness House (Orkney Islands), 381
Teampull Clann A'Phlocair (North Uist), 369
Tolbooth (Kirkcudbright), 82
Tongue House (Tongue), 331
Traprain Law (Dunbar), 145
Traquair House (Innerleithen), 70–71
Unstan Chambered Tomb (Orkney Islands), 383
History of Scotland, 5–10, 24–25
Holidays, 31
Holy Island (Arran), 218
HOLY LOCH, 150
Homestays and exchanges, 40
Hopetoun House (South Queensferry), 142–43
Horse racing (Ayr), 192
HOY (ORKNEY ISLANDS), 387
Hunterian Art Gallery (Glasgow), 178

Information sources, 27–28
INNERLEITHEN, 70–71
Insurance, 35–36, 53
International Arts Festival (Edinburgh), 4, 34, 133–34, 139
INVERARAY, 211–13
Inveraray Castle (Inveraray), 212
INVERBEG, 253–54
INVERGARRY, 305
INVERMORISTON, 315
INVERNESS, 5, 316–23
IONA, 357–58
ISLE OF ARRAN, 217–21
ISLE OF COLONSAY, 360–61

ISLE OF GIGHA, 221–22
ISLE OF INISHAIL, 209
ISLE OF ISLAY, 222–24
ISLE OF JURA, 224
ISLE OF SKYE, 12, 341–46
ISLE OF TARANSAY, 366
ISLE OF WHITHORN, 85
Itineraries, suggested, 54–56

Jacobites, 9, 81, 213, 270, 301, 314, 317, 329, 338
James VI (James I of England), 8, 142, 231, 240, 252
Jarlshof (Shetland Islands), 406
Jazz Festival, Glasgow International, 186
JEDBURGH, 63–64
JOHN O' GROATS, 333–34
Johnson, Dr. Samuel, 16, 296, 336, 349, 351, 355
Jones, John Paul, 13, 78, 82

KEITH, 290–91
KELSO, 64, 66–67
KERRERA, 205
KILDONAN (ISLE OF ARRAN), 220
KILDRUMMY, 285, 288
KILKENNETH (ISLE OF TYREE), 350
KILLUNAIG (ISLE OF COLL), 349
KILMUIR, 343
Kilts, 19, 188. *See also* Tartans
KINCRAIG, 312
KINGUSSIE, 310–12
KINTYRE PENINSULA, 4–5, 214–17
KIRKBEAN, 78
KIRKCUDBRIGHT, 82–83
KIRKWALL (ORKNEY ISLANDS), 380–83
Knitwear, shopping for, 137, 330, 386, 391–92, 394
Knox, John, 7–8, 11–13, 15–16, 124, 132, 144, 178, 182, 184, 240, 257–58, 392
KYLEAKIN (ISLE OF SKYE), 341–42
KYLE OF LOCHALSH, 338, 340

LAGG (ISLE OF ARRAN), 220–21
LAMASH (ISLE OF ARRAN), 219
LANARK, 32–33
LAUDER, 71
Lauder, Sir Harry, 13, 26
LERWICK (SHETLAND ISLANDS), 397–98
LEVERBURGH (ISLE OF HARRIS), 366
LEWIS, 361–65
Lighthouses, 233, 334, 389, 391, 396, 406
Links courses. *See* Golf courses
LINLITHGOW, 142–43
Linlithgow Palace (Linlithgow), 142
Liquor, 22–23. *See also* Whisky
Literature, 15–16, 23–24. *See also specific authors*
Livingstone, David, 13–14
LOCH-A-BHRAOLN, 335
LOCH AWE, 209–10
LOCHBOISDALE (SOUTH UIST), 371
LOCH LEVEN, 230, 298–300
LOCH LINNHE, 298–303
LOCH LOMOND, 225, 251–54
LOCH LONG, 150
LOCHMADDY (NORTH UIST), 367, 369
LOCH NESS, 313–16
Loch Ness monster, 1, 295, 313–14, 352
LOCHRANZA (ISLE OF ARRAN), 218, 221
LOCH VOIL, 248
LOWLANDS, 4, 32, 33, 75–89. *See also specific places*
LUSS, 253
Lutyens, Sir Edward, 147

McAlpine, Kenneth, 6, 205
Macbeth, 6, 233, 279, 324, 351, 356, 357
MacDonald, Flora, 9, 341, 343, 371
MacDonald clan, 6, 18, 217, 224, 299, 344–45, 346, 351, 353, 369–70
MacDonnell clan, 305
MacDougall clan, 210
MacGregor, Rob Roy, 247–48, 251, 310
Mackays clan, 331
Mackenzie, Compton, 361, 372, 374
Mackenzie clan, 363
Mackintosh, Charles Rennie, 14–15, 175, 178, 184, 364, 381
MacLachlan clan, 213
Maclean clan, 351, 352
MacLeod clan, 343–44, 363, 369
MacNeil clan, 373, 374
MacPherson clan, 310
MacRae clan, 338
Magnus, Saint, 380, 389
Malcolm II, 6, 273
MALLAIG, 304
Margaret, Saint, 12, 14, 227
Mary, Queen of Scots, 7–8, 12, 63–64, 124–25, 142, 144–45, 178–79, 214, 230–31, 235, 240, 250, 381, 392
MAYBOLE, 196
Measurements, converting, 410
MELROSE, 68–69
Mendelssohn, Felix, 359
Midhowe Broch and Tombs (Orkney Islands), 388
Military history museums, 127–28, 212, 240–41, 258, 271, 281–82, 318, 386
Miller, Hugh, 326
MOFFAT, 73–75
Money, 28–30
Monuments and memorials. *See also* Historic sites
  Burns Monument and Gardens (Alloway), 195
  Flora MacDonald memorial (South Uist), 371
  Glenfinnan Monument (Glenfinnan), 301
  Lincoln Monument (Edinburgh), 124, 130
  McCaig's Tower (Oban), 205
  Monument to the Massacre of Glencoe (Carnoch), 299
  Nelson Monument (Edinburgh), 129
  Scott Monument (Edinburgh), 125
  Well of the Heads (Invergarry), 305
MOUSA (SHETLAND ISLANDS), 406
MUCK, 348
MUIR OF ORD, 328
MULL, 350–57
MULL OF KINTYRE, 217
Mungo, Saint, 6, 178–79
Museums. *See* Fishing and maritime museums; Historical and cultural museums; Military history museums; Transportation museums
Music, 16–17, 24. *See also* Folk music and festivals; Highland gatherings

NAIRN, 323–25
National Gallery of Scotland (Edinburgh), 125–26, 132
Natural history museum, 177
Natural spectacles
  Bracklinn Gorge (Bracklinn), 247
  Carsaig Arches (Isle of Mull), 355
  Devil's Beef Tub (Moffat), 74
  Dukes Pass (Aberfoyle), 251
  Esha Ness (Shetland Islands), 404
  Falls of Cruachan (Loch Awe), 210

Natural spectacles (*cont'd*)
  Fingal's Cave (Staffa), 359–60
  Glen Orchy (Glencoe), 299
  Grey Mare's Tail (White Coomb), 74
  Kirstan's Hole (Shetland Islands), 403
  Leny Falls (Callander), 247
  Linn of Dee (Braemar), 275
  MacCulloch's Tree (Isle of Mull), 355
  MacKinnon's Cave (Isle of Mull), 355
  Old Man of Hoy (Orkney Islands), 387
  Pass of Brander (Loch Awe), 210
Nature reserves
  Caerlaverock National Nature Reserve (Glen-
    caple), 78
  Corrieshalloch Gorge (Ullapool), 335
  Hermaness Bird Reserve (Shetland Islands), 407
  Highland Wildlife Park (Kincraig), 312
  Isle of May (Anstruther), 232
  Loch Druidibeg National Nature Reserve (South
    Uist), 371
  Loch Gruinart Nature Reserve (Isle of Islay), 223
  Treshnish Isles, 355
NEW ABBEY, 78
NEWHAVEN, 93
NEWTONMORE, 310
Ninian, Saint, 6, 85
Norsemen. See Vikings
NORTHBAY (ISLE OF BARRA), 374–75
NORTH BERWICK, 146–47
**NORTH MAINLAND (SHETLAND IS-
  LANDS),** 404–5
NORTH MIDDLETON, 109
NORTH UIST, 367–70

OBAN, 201–2, 204–8
ONICH, 298
Opera, Scottish, 189–90
ORANSAY, 360
Orkneyinga Saga, 376, 378, 385, 388–89
ORKNEY ISLANDS, 5, 376–94. See also spe-
  cific islands
ORPHIR (ORKNEY ISLANDS), 383–84
Orwell, George, 224

Packing for your trip, 36
PAISLEY, 183
Paisley Abbey (Paisley), 183
Palace of Holyroodhouse (Edinburgh), 125, 132
PAPA STOUR (SHETLAND ISLANDS),
  403
PAPA WESTRAY, 393–94
Parks. See also Gardens
  Argyll Forest Park (Argyll), 4, 201–2
  Balloch Castle Country Park (Balloch), 252
  Bellahouston Park (Glasgow), 187
  Culzean Country Park (Maybole), 196–97
  Dalkeith Park (Dalkeith), 143
  Glasgow Green (Glasgow), 178, 186
  Linn Park (Glasgow), 182
  Pittencrieff Park and Glen (Dunfermline), 228
  Queen Elizabeth Forest Park (Aberfoyle), 250
  Strathclyde Regional Park (Strathclyde), 151
PEEBLES, 33, 71–73
PERTH, 257–58, 260–61
  accommodations, 258, 259
  arriving in, 257
  excursions, 261–63
    golf (Gleneagles), 262
    Scone Palace, 261
  restaurants, 260–61

  sightseeing, 257–58
Picts, 5–6, 11, 151, 257, 261, 266, 326, 376, 378,
  393, 396, 406
PITLOCHRY, 32, 268–70
Pitlochry Festival Theatre (Pitlochry), 268–69
PITTENWEEM, 232
Planetarium, Royal Observatory Visitor Centre
  (Edinburgh), 126–27
Planning and preparing for your trip, 27–60
Politics, 10–11
PORT APPIN, 208–9
PORT ELLEN (ISLE OF ISLAY), 223
PORT LOGAN, 88
PORTPATRICK, 87–89
PORTREE (ISLE OF SKYE), 342–43
PRESTWICK, 198–99

Queen Elizabeth Forest Park (Aberfoyle), 250
Quoyness Chambered Tomb (Sanday), 391

Rainfall, average monthly, 31
Ranald clan, 370–71
Recordings, 25–26
Recreational activities, 19–20. See also specific ac-
  tivities
Reformation, the, 7–8, 12, 244, 355
Regions in brief, 4–5
Religion, 6–8, 11–12. See also Knox, John
RHUM (RUM), 346–47
Ring of Brodgar (Orkney Islands), 383
Robert I (Robert the Bruce), 7, 14, 68, 210, 215, 227,
  241, 252, 278
Romans, 5–6, 396, 403
ROSEMARKIE, 326, 328
ROTHES, 291
ROUSAY (ORKNEY ISLANDS), 388–89
RUTHWELL, 78

ST. ANDREWS, 33–34, 235–39
  accommodations, 237–39
  golf courses, 235–36
  restaurants, 239
  sightseeing, 236
  traveling to, 235
ST. BOSWELLS, 67
St. Magnus Cathedral (Orkney Islands), 380
**ST. MARGARET'S HOPE (ORKNEY IS-
  LANDS),** 386–87
ST. NINIAN'S ISLAND, 406–7
Saints. See specific saints
SALEN (ISLE OF MULL), 353
Salmon fishing, 20, 22, 361
SANDAY, 391–92
SCALLOWAY (SHETLAND ISLANDS),
  400–401
SCARINISH (ISLE OF TYREE), 350
SCARISTA (HARRIS), 367
SCARP, 366
SCONE, 261–62
Scone Palace (Scone), 261
Scott, Sir Walter, 16, 67–69, 81, 84, 124, 130, 179,
  184, 251, 258, 279, 381, 390
Scottish National Gallery of Modern Art
  (Edinburgh), 127
Seal watching, 343, 373, 378, 388, 397
SELKIRK, 32–33, 69–70
Selkirk Common Riding (Selkirk), 32–33
Senior citizens, tips for, 37–38
SHAPINSAY (ORKNEY ISLANDS),
  387–88

SHETLAND ISLANDS, 5, 10, 376–77, 395–408. *See also specific islands*
Sinclair clan, 333
Single travelers, tips for, 38
Skara Brae (Orkney Islands), 383–84
SKEABOST BRIDGE (ISLE OF SKYE), 344–45
Skiing, 135, 306, 310
SKIPNESS, 215
SLEAT PENINSULA (ISLE OF SKYE), 345–46
SLIGACHAN (ISLE OF SKYE), 342
Smith, Adam, 14, 16
SORISDALE (ISLE OF COLL), 349
SOUTHEND, 217
SOUTH MAINLAND (SHETLAND ISLANDS), 406–8
SOUTH RONALDSAY (ORKNEY ISLANDS), 386–87
SOUTH UIST, 367–68, 370–72
Special events, 32–35. *See also Highland Gatherings; and specific events*
SPEYSIDE, 309–13
Sports, 19–20. *See also specific sports*
STAFFA, 357, 359–60
Standing Stones of Callandish (Lewis), 362
Stevenson, Robert Louis, 16, 72, 130, 298, 332, 351, 356, 357, 407
Stewart, Earl Patrick, 381, 400–01, 406
STIRLING, 240–44
    accommodations, 241–42
    excursion to Bannockburn, 241
    restaurants, 242–44
    Stirling Castle (Stirling), 240
STRACHUR, 213–14
STRANRAER, 86–87
STRATHCLYDE, 151
STROMNESS (ORKNEY ISLANDS), 384–85
STRONSAY, 389–90
Stuart, Charles Edward ("Bonnie Prince Charlie"), 9, 19, 78, 240, 252, 301, 310, 317–18, 341, 343, 363, 372
Stuart, James. *See* James VI (James I of England)
Stuart, Mary. *See* Mary, Queen of Scots
Student travelers, tips for, 39
SUMMER ISLES, 335
SUTHERLAND, 329–32
Sweetheart Abbey (New Abbey), 78

TALBERT (HARRIS), 365–67
TARBERT, 214–16
TARBET, 254
Tartans, shopping for, 19, 137–38, 188, 265, 301, 329, 330
TAYSIDE, 4
Temperatures, average monthly, 31
Thirlestane Castle (Lauder), 71
THORNHILL, 78
Threve Garden (Castle Douglas), 81
THURSO, 334
TIRORAN (ISLE OF MULL), 356
TOBERMORY (ISLE OF MULL), 32, 351, 353–54
TONGUE, 331–32
Torosay Castle and Gardens (Isle of Mull), 352
Tourist information, 27–28
Tours
    for disabled travelers, 37
    of Edinburgh, 133
    of Glasgow, 183
    for golfers, 48
    of the Hebridean Islands, 336
    of the Highlands, 317
    by rail, 48–49
    by sea, 49–50
    for senior citizens, 37–38
    for single travelers, 38
Train travel
    Mull Railway (Isle of Mull), 352
    in Scotland, 50–51
    to Scotland, 46–47
    Strathspey Railway (Aviemore), 306, 308
    tours, 48–49
Transportation museums, 179, 246
Traquair House (Innerleithen), 70–71
Traveling
    in Scotland, 50–54. *See also individual destinations*
    to Scotland, 42–50
TRESHNISH ISLES, 355
TROON, 199–200
TROSSACHS, THE, 4, 224–25, 251–54. *See also specific places*
TRUMISGARY (NORTH UIST), 368
TRUMPAN, 344
TURNBERRY, 197–98
Tweeds, shopping for, 138, 188, 223, 291, 329, 330
TYREE (TIREE), 348–50

UIG (ISLE OF SKYE), 343
ULLAPOOL, 334–35
Universities, 178–79, 184, 236, 282
Unstan Chambered Tomb (Orkney Islands), 383
UNST (SHETLAND ISLANDS), 407–8

Victoria, Queen, 18, 276, 301, 331, 359
VIDLIN (SHETLAND ISLANDS), 404
Vikings, 5, 7, 12, 15, 186, 214, 222, 326, 331–32, 341, 360, 361, 373, 376, 378, 380, 383–84, 388, 390, 395–96, 398, 403, 406, 407
VOE (SHETLAND ISLANDS), 404

WALLS (SHETLAND ISLANDS), 402
Water sports. *See individual destinations*
Watt, James, 14, 150
Weather, 31
WEST HIGHLANDS, 200–17, 295–335. *See also specific places*
WEST MAINLAND (SHETLAND ISLANDS), 401–4
WESTRAY, 392–93
Whisky, 10, 22–23, 289
    Glenfarclas Distillery (Ballindalloch), 289
    Glenfiddich Distillery (Dufftown), 289, 290
    Glen Grant Distillery (Rothes), 291
    Glenlivet Distillery (Glenlivet), 289
    Glenturret Distillery Ltd. (Glenturret), 264
    John Dewar & Sons (Inveralmond), 258
    Laphroaig Distillery (Isle of Islay), 223
    Scotch Whisky Heritage Center (Edinburgh), 124
    shopping for, 138
    Strathisla Distillery (Keith), 291
    Tamdhu Distillery (near Marypark), 289
    Tobermory Malt Whisky Distillery (Isle of Mull), 351
Whisky Trail, 289, 297, 309
Whistler, James McNeill, 177–78
WHITEHALL, 389

WHITENESS (SHETLAND ISLANDS), 401–2

WHITHORN, 85–86

WHITING BAY (ISLE OF ARRAN), 220

WICK, 332–33

Wildlife. *See* Nature reserves

Wilkie, Sir David, 15

Wilson, James, 286

Wolfe, Lt. Col. James, 318

Woolens, shopping for, 136, 138, 223, 291, 401

Zoo, Edinburgh, 130

Now Save Money on All Your Travels by Joining
FROMMER'S ™ TRAVEL BOOK CLUB
The World's Best Travel Guides at Membership Prices

FROMMER'S TRAVEL BOOK CLUB is your ticket to successful travel! Open up a world of travel information and simplify your travel planning when you join ranks with thousands of value-conscious travelers who are members of the FROMMER'S TRAVEL BOOK CLUB. Join today and you'll be entitled to all the privileges that come from belonging to the club that offers you travel guides for less to more than 100 destinations worldwide. Annual membership is only $25 (U.S.) or $35 (Canada and foreign).

The Advantages of Membership

1. Your choice of *three* free FROMMER'S TRAVEL GUIDES (any *two* FROMMER'S COMPREHENSIVE GUIDES, FROMMER'S $-A-DAY GUIDES, FROMMER'S WALKING TOURS *or* FROMMER'S FAMILY GUIDES—plus *one* FROMMER'S CITY GUIDE, FROMMER'S CITY $-A-DAY GUIDE *or* FROMMER'S TOURING GUIDE).
2. Your own subscription to **TRIPS AND TRAVEL** quarterly newsletter.
3. You're entitled to a **30% discount** on your order of any additional books offered by FROMMER'S TRAVEL BOOK CLUB.
4. You're offered (at a small additional fee) our **Domestic Trip-Routing Kits.**

Our quarterly newsletter **TRIPS AND TRAVEL** offers practical information on the best buys in travel, the "hottest" vacation spots, the latest travel trends, world-class events and much, much more.

Our **Domestic Trip-Routing Kits** are available for any North American destination. We'll send you a detailed map highlighting the best route to take to your destination—you can request direct or scenic routes.

Here's all you have to do to join:

Send in your membership fee of $25 ($35 Canada and foreign) with your name and address on the form below along with your selections as part of your membership package to **FROMMER'S TRAVEL BOOK CLUB, P.O. Box 473, Mt. Morris, IL 61054-0473.** Remember to check off your *three* free books.

If you would like to order additional books, please select the books you would like and send a check for the total amount (please add sales tax in the states noted below), plus $2 per book for shipping and handling ($3 per book for foreign orders) to:

FROMMER'S TRAVEL BOOK CLUB
P.O. Box 473
Mt. Morris, IL 61054-0473
(815) 734-1104

[ ] **YES.** I want to take advantage of this opportunity to join FROMMER'S TRAVEL BOOK CLUB.
[ ] **My check is enclosed.** Dollar amount enclosed_____*
(all payments in U.S. funds only)

Name_____
Address_____
City_____ State_____ Zip_____
All orders must be prepaid.

To ensure that all orders are processed efficiently, please apply sales tax in the following areas: CA, CT, FL, IL, NJ, NY, TN, WA and CANADA.

*With membership, shipping and handling will be paid by FROMMER'S TRAVEL BOOK CLUB for the three free books you select as part of your membership. Please add $2 per book for shipping and handling for any additional books purchased ($3 per book for foreign orders).

Allow 4–6 weeks for delivery. Prices of books, membership fee, and publication dates are subject to change without notice. Prices are subject to acceptance and availability.

Please Send Me the Books Checked Below:

FROMMER'S COMPREHENSIVE GUIDES
(Guides listing facilities from budget to deluxe,
with emphasis on the medium-priced)

	Retail Price	Code		Retail Price	Code
☐ Acapulco/Ixtapa/Taxco 1993–94	$15.00	C120	☐ Japan 1994–95 (Avail. 3/94)	$19.00	C144
☐ Alaska 1994–95	$17.00	C131	☐ Morocco 1992–93	$18.00	C021
☐ Arizona 1993–94	$18.00	C101	☐ Nepal 1994–95	$18.00	C126
☐ Australia 1992–93	$18.00	C002	☐ New England 1994 (Avail. 1/94)	$16.00	C137
☐ Austria 1993–94	$19.00	C119	☐ New Mexico 1993–94	$15.00	C117
☐ Bahamas 1994–95	$17.00	C121	☐ New York State 1994–95	$19.00	C133
☐ Belgium/Holland/ Luxembourg 1993–94	$18.00	C106	☐ Northwest 1994–95 (Avail. 2/94)	$17.00	C140
☐ Bermuda 1994–95	$15.00	C122	☐ Portugal 1994–95 (Avail. 2/94)	$17.00	C141
☐ Brazil 1993–94	$20.00	C111	☐ Puerto Rico 1993–94	$15.00	C103
☐ California 1994	$15.00	C134	☐ Puerto Vallarta/Manzanillo/ Guadalajara 1994–95 (Avail. 1/94)	$14.00	C028
☐ Canada 1994–95 (Avail. 4/94)	$19.00	C145	☐ Scandinavia 1993–94	$19.00	C135
☐ Caribbean 1994	$18.00	C123	☐ Scotland 1994–95 (Avail. 4/94)	$17.00	C146
☐ Carolinas/Georgia 1994–95	$17.00	C128	☐ South Pacific 1994–95 (Avail. 1/94)	$20.00	C138
☐ Colorado 1994–95 (Avail. 3/94)	$16.00	C143	☐ Spain 1993–94	$19.00	C115
☐ Cruises 1993–94	$19.00	C107	☐ Switzerland/Liechtenstein 1994–95 (Avail. 1/94)	$19.00	C139
☐ Delaware/Maryland 1994–95 (Avail. 1/94)	$15.00	C136	☐ Thailand 1992–93	$20.00	C033
☐ England 1994	$18.00	C129	☐ U.S.A. 1993–94	$19.00	C116
☐ Florida 1994	$18.00	C124	☐ Virgin Islands 1994–95	$13.00	C127
☐ France 1994–95	$20.00	C132	☐ Virginia 1994–95 (Avail. 2/94)	$14.00	C142
☐ Germany 1994	$19.00	C125	☐ Yucatán 1993–94	$18.00	C110
☐ Italy 1994	$19.00	C130			
☐ Jamaica/Barbados 1993–94	$15.00	C105			

FROMMER'S $-A-DAY GUIDES
(Guides to low-cost tourist accommodations and facilities)

	Retail Price	Code		Retail Price	Code
☐ Australia on $45 1993–94	$18.00	D102	☐ Israel on $45 1993–94	$18.00	D101
☐ Costa Rica/Guatemala/ Belize on $35 1993–94	$17.00	D108	☐ Mexico on $45 1994	$19.00	D116
☐ Eastern Europe on $30 1993–94	$18.00	D110	☐ New York on $70 1994–95 (Avail. 4/94)	$16.00	D120
☐ England on $60 1994	$18.00	D112	☐ New Zealand on $45 1993–94	$18.00	D103
☐ Europe on $50 1994	$19.00	D115	☐ Scotland/Wales on $50 1992–93	$18.00	D019
☐ Greece on $45 1993–94	$19.00	D100	☐ South America on $40 1993–94	$19.00	D109
☐ Hawaii on $75 1994	$19.00	D113	☐ Turkey on $40 1992–93	$22.00	D023
☐ India on $40 1992–93	$20.00	D010	☐ Washington, D.C. on $40 1994–95 (Avail. 2/94)	$17.00	D119
☐ Ireland on $45 1994–95 (Avail. 1/94)	$17.00	D117			

FROMMER'S CITY $-A-DAY GUIDES
(Pocket-size guides to low-cost tourist accommodations
and facilities)

	Retail Price	Code		Retail Price	Code
☐ Berlin on $40 1994–95	$12.00	D111	☐ Madrid on $50 1994–95 (Avail. 1/94)	$13.00	D118
☐ Copenhagen on $50 1992–93	$12.00	D003	☐ Paris on $50 1994–95	$12.00	D117
☐ London on $45 1994–95	$12.00	D114	☐ Stockholm on $50 1992–93	$13.00	D022

FROMMER'S WALKING TOURS

(With routes and detailed maps, these companion guides point out
the places and pleasures that make a city unique)

	Retail Price	Code		Retail Price	Code
☐ Berlin	$12.00	W100	☐ Paris	$12.00	W103
☐ London	$12.00	W101	☐ San Francisco	$12.00	W104
☐ New York	$12.00	W102	☐ Washington, D.C.	$12.00	W105

FROMMER'S TOURING GUIDES

(Color-illustrated guides that include walking tours, cultural and historic
sights, and practical information)

	Retail Price	Code		Retail Price	Code
☐ Amsterdam	$11.00	T001	☐ New York	$11.00	T008
☐ Barcelona	$14.00	T015	☐ Rome	$11.00	T010
☐ Brazil	$11.00	T003	☐ Scotland	$10.00	T011
☐ Florence	$ 9.00	T005	☐ Sicily	$15.00	T017
☐ Hong Kong/Singapore/			☐ Tokyo	$15.00	T016
Macau	$11.00	T006	☐ Turkey	$11.00	T013
☐ Kenya	$14.00	T018	☐ Venice	$ 9.00	T014
☐ London	$13.00	T007			

FROMMER'S FAMILY GUIDES

	Retail Price	Code		Retail Price	Code
☐ California with Kids	$18.00	F100	☐ San Francisco with Kids		
☐ Los Angeles with Kids			(Avail. 4/94)	$17.00	F104
(Avail. 4/94)	$17.00	F103	☐ Washington, D.C. with Kids		
☐ New York City with Kids			(Avail. 2/94)	$17.00	F102
(Avail. 2/94)	$18.00	F101			

FROMMER'S CITY GUIDES

(Pocket-size guides to sightseeing and tourist accommodations and
facilities in all price ranges)

	Retail Price	Code		Retail Price	Code
☐ Amsterdam 1993–94	$13.00	S110	☐ Montréal/Québec		
☐ Athens 1993–94	$13.00	S114	City 1993–94	$13.00	S125
☐ Atlanta 1993–94	$13.00	S112	☐ Nashville/Memphis		
☐ Atlantic City/Cape			1994–95 (Avail. 4/94)	$13.00	S141
May 1993–94	$13.00	S130	☐ New Orleans 1993–94	$13.00	S103
☐ Bangkok 1992–93	$13.00	S005	☐ New York 1994 (Avail.		
☐ Barcelona/Majorca/Minorca/			1/94)	$13.00	S138
Ibiza 1993–94	$13.00	S115	☐ Orlando 1994	$13.00	S135
☐ Berlin 1993–94	$13.00	S116	☐ Paris 1993–94	$13.00	S109
☐ Boston 1993–94	$13.00	S117	☐ Philadelphia 1993–94	$13.00	S113
☐ Budapest 1994–95 (Avail.			☐ San Diego 1993–94	$13.00	S107
2/94)	$13.00	S139	☐ San Francisco 1994	$13.00	S133
☐ Chicago 1993–94	$13.00	S122	☐ Santa Fe/Taos/		
☐ Denver/Boulder/Colorado			Albuquerque 1993–94	$13.00	S108
Springs 1993–94	$13.00	S131	☐ Seattle/Portland 1994–95	$13.00	S137
☐ Dublin 1993–94	$13.00	S128	☐ St. Louis/Kansas		
☐ Hong Kong 1994–95			City 1993–94	$13.00	S127
(Avail. 4/94)	$13.00	S140	☐ Sydney 1993–94	$13.00	S129
☐ Honolulu/Oahu 1994	$13.00	S134	☐ Tampa/St.		
☐ Las Vegas 1993–94	$13.00	S121	Petersburg 1993–94	$13.00	S105
☐ London 1994	$13.00	S132	☐ Tokyo 1992–93	$13.00	S039
☐ Los Angeles 1993–94	$13.00	S123	☐ Toronto 1993–94	$13.00	S126
☐ Madrid/Costa del			☐ Vancouver/Victoria 1994–		
Sol 1993–94	$13.00	S124	95 (Avail. 1/94)	$13.00	S142
☐ Miami 1993–94	$13.00	S118	☐ Washington, D.C. 1994		
☐ Minneapolis/St.			(Avail. 1/94)	$13.00	S136
Paul 1993–94	$13.00	S119			

SPECIAL EDITIONS

	Retail Price	Code		Retail Price	Code
☐ Bed & Breakfast Southwest	$16.00	P100	☐ Caribbean Hideaways	$16.00	P103
☐ Bed & Breakfast Great American Cities (Avail. 1/94)	$16.00	P104	☐ National Park Guide 1994 (avail. 3/94)	$16.00	P105
			☐ Where to Stay U.S.A.	$15.00	P102

Please note: if the availability of a book is several months away, we may have back issues of guides to that particular destination. Call customer service at (815) 734-1104.